Curzon

'Exemplary biography . . . meticulously researched and elegantly written.'
C. A. BAYLEY, *Times Literary Supplement*

'A superb new biography . . . a tragic story, brilliantly told.'
ANDREW ROBERTS, *Literary Review*

'A fine biography . . . a consummate and skilful attempt to capture
the elusive personality of one of the most talented of modern British
statesmen.'
SIR ROBERT RHODES JAMES, *The Times*

'David Gilmour has brought to this study qualities which few
biographers attain . . . Curzon's story, sometimes portrayed as a study
in failure, is here restored to the high ground . . . David Gilmour
has given the whole life its due.'
MARTIN GILBERT, *Guardian*

'Well researched, soundly constructed, sometimes witty, sometimes
eloquent, always admirably fair. Curzon needed and deserved a significant
new biography; Gilmour has done him proud.'
PHILIP ZEIGLER, *Daily Telegraph*

'*Curzon* is a magisterial piece of work, worthy of the best traditions of
British biography.'
JULIAN CRITCHLEY, *Country Life*

DAVID GILMOUR is the author of *The Last Leopard: A Life of Giuseppe di Lampedusa*, which won the Scottish Arts Council Spring Book Award and the Nelson, Hurst and Marsh Biography Award for 1989. He has also written several highly acclaimed works of political history, including *The Transformation of Spain* and *Lebanon: The Fractured Country*, and *Cities of Spain*. He is a contributor to the *London Review of Books*, the *Spectator* and the *Times Literary Supplement*. A Fellow of the Royal Society of Literature, he lives in Edinburgh with his wife and four children.

Curzon

DAVID GILMOUR

PAPERMAC

To my father Ian Gilmour

First published 1994 by John Murray (Publishers) Ltd

This edition published 1995 by Papermac
an imprint of Macmillan General Books
25 Eccleston Place, London SW1W 9NF
and Basingstoke

Associated companies throughout the world

ISBN 0 333 64406 9

1 3 5 7 9 8 6 4 2

A CIP catalogue record for this book is available from
the British Library

Printed and bound in Great Britain by
Mackays of Chatham plc, Chatham, Kent

Contents

Contents

Illustrations

(between pages 300 and 301)

The author and publishers would like to thank the following for their kind permission to reproduce photographs: Plates 1, 2, 4, 5, 13, 15, 16, 27, 28 and 34, Lady Alexandra Metcalfe; 6, 7, 20, 21, 25, 35, 38, 39 and 41, Hulton Deutsch Collection Limited; 8, 9, 14, 17, 18, 19, 26 and 31, India Office Library; 10, the Duke of Westminster; 12, 22, 23, 24, 32, 33, 36 and 37, Mansell Collection; 29, Jane Lady Abdy and Mr Christopher Davson.

Preface

GEORGE CURZON WAS obsessively anxious about the judgement of posterity; according to Walter Lawrence, his Private Secretary in India, he was 'always thinking of the verdicts' which history would pronounce on his career. Although he believed those verdicts would be more favourable than the assessments of his contemporaries, Curzon was too accustomed to criticism to be complacent. Shortly before his death he tried therefore to pre-empt posterity by inviting his former secretary to write his biography. Lawrence declined with regret. As his association with Curzon had been the great event of his life, he was sure 'the world' would consider any book by him to be 'distorted by blind devotion and admiration'. His old chief reluctantly accepted the excuse but grumbled that he would be 'pulled to pieces' after his death.[1]

Within weeks of his funeral, Curzon's literary executors began the search for a biographer. One of their first decisions was to reject the claims of Lord Birkenhead, who considered himself a suitable candidate and threatened to write a book even if his application was rejected. It was a curious ambition for a man who had persistently attacked his intended subject after the fall of the Lloyd George Government and who had tried unscrupulously to bring about his resignation. Had Curzon drawn up his own list of potential biographers, Birkenhead would have been very near the bottom, just above Lord Beaverbrook.

After several writers, including John Buchan, had been approached, the executors chose Lord Ronaldshay, a former Governor of Bengal and, as Marquess of Zetland, a future Secretary of State for India.

Written with remarkable speed, three stately volumes soon appeared, imposing and somewhat sombre monuments of industry, diplomacy and tact towards those of Curzon's opponents who were still living. Had the official biography been written by another candidate, Harold Nicolson, who had worked under Curzon at the Foreign Office, it would have gained in flair but lost in diligence. Yet although he decided not to write the Life, 'the problem of Lord Curzon's personality' remained 'almost an obsession' with Nicolson, and later he wrote not only *Curzon: The Last Phase* but also the incomparable portrait in *Some People* and the article in the *Dictionary of National Biography*. Lady Curzon's refusal to let him use the private letters she had promised – on the grounds that she herself was going to write a book – helped turn *The Last Phase* into a study of diplomacy rather than a portrait. Flawed though the book is by its author's intrusive views on foreign policy and his reliance on Ronaldshay's research, it is acute, jaunty, readable and sympathetic. Why Grace Curzon thought it a caricature of her husband remains a mystery.

Curzon's reputation thus survived the first two verdicts of history. In the early 1930s, however, Lord Beaverbrook launched an assault on it that lasted for nearly thirty years and ensured its virtual destruction. In a series of racy and tendentious books the newspaper tycoon directed a crescendo of abuse culminating in the allegation that his victim had been 'inconsistent, unreliable, untruthful and treacherous'. His principal charges were that Curzon had 'changed sides on almost every issue during his long career' and that he had given Asquith 'an absolute pledge' that he would not serve under Lloyd George in 1916.[2]

Beaverbrook's judgements were accepted with a strange lack of inquiry by some distinguished historians, who repeated his statements and in some cases developed them so that it soon became almost obligatory to describe Curzon as a 'turncoat' or 'deserter' always joining the winning side. Pre-eminent among them was A.J.P. Taylor, who portrayed him as 'one of nature's rats', a weak and irresolute figure who in 1922 'deserted Lloyd George as successfully as he had deserted Asquith'.[3] Another highly respected scholar, A.M. Gollin, took up the theme of Curzon's 'political somersaults', claiming that before the First World War 'he often advocated certain definite policies, only to change his mind at the last moment and reverse his course'.[4]

These and other allegations will be examined in their right place. But it may be stated here that no impartial survey of the evidence could conclude that Curzon had been any more of a 'deserter' than the other

Unionist ministers in 1916 or that he was guilty of disloyalty to Lloyd George six years later. Such a survey would find it equally difficult to sustain Professor Gollin's charge against a man who at the time was often accused of the opposite vice, of being too inflexible in his views. Far from being a performer of somersaults before 1914, Curzon's one substantial change of mind occurred in 1911 when, at the age of 52, he advocated the passing of the Parliament Bill.

In his campaign of denigration Beaverbrook acquired an unexpected and presumably unsuspecting ally in 1956. The year before, Grace Curzon had damaged her husband's reputation by publishing her *Reminiscences*, the sort of book that makes people wonder why Britain never experienced a revolution: it describes inspections of the wrists of aspirant footmen to appraise their elegance when holding plates, and recounts how in her widowhood she canvassed for her Conservative son in East London accoutred with fur coat, French maid, Rolls-Royce and hampers from Fortnum and Mason. Then, a quarter of a century *after* Beaverbrook began his assault on her husband's memory, she granted him – in return for £2,000 – exclusive rights over Curzon's papers for five years and non-exclusive rights thereafter.[5] That the documents were left after Grace's death to the Kedleston trustees, who eventually recovered them thanks to Mr Kenneth Rose, did not affect Beaverbrook. Long before losing control he commissioned Leonard Mosley, a Canadian journalist, to carry out the biographical assassination which for obscure reasons he desired. The result, published in 1960, was *Curzon: The End of an Epoch*, a book that contains scarcely a page free of error, misquotation or bogus psychoanalysis.

From depths that not even Curzon could have anticipated, his reputation was partly salvaged by the publication of two excellent books in 1969. Kenneth Rose's *Superior Person* is a justly celebrated portrait of Curzon and the society he grew up in, a work which elegantly and precisely captures the ambience of late Victorian privilege. Simultaneously, David Dilks produced *Curzon in India*, an original and authoritative study of the viceroyalty in two volumes.

Lady Alexandra Metcalfe, Curzon's youngest daughter, was concurrently searching for a biographer to supersede Ronaldshay, who was by then out of date as well as out of print, and to produce a scholarly reassessment after the distortions of Mosley. Sir Philip Magnus, who had already written lives of Gladstone, Kitchener and Edward VII, started work in 1969 but abandoned the task three years later for reasons of ill health and lack of enthusiasm. Subsequently, Nigel

Nicolson was tempted to write the book his father had turned down nearly half a century before, but preferred in the end to write an engaging and sympathetic life of Curzon's first wife Mary.

When, almost a generation later, I suggested writing a biography, Lady Alexandra responded with inexplicable enthusiasm to an author whose earlier studies of politics had dealt with Spain and the Middle East, and whose previous excursion into biography had been the life of an indolent Sicilian prince who had achieved nothing before writing a great novel in old age. Despite these unpromising credentials, she gave me continuous help and frequent hospitality for five years, the benefit of a remarkable memory, and unrestricted access to the papers in her possession, notably the private correspondence between her parents. It is impossible to express adequately my gratitude for such assistance so selflessly given with never a suggestion that criticisms of her father might be modified or removed. No biographer could have had a less complicated task in this respect.

I have been fortunate besides to have received much useful information from several other relations of Lord Curzon, including his step-daughter Mrs Marcella Rice, his niece Mrs Noreen Wright, his great-niece Lady Aldington, his great-nephew Sir Roger Cary, his nephew Lord Scarsdale and his grandson Lord Ravensdale. I am most grateful to all of them.

Many other people over the years have been generous with their time and knowledge. I would particularly like to thank Mr Kenneth Rose both for his advice and for kindly giving me access to his archives, Charles Sebag-Montefiore for allowing me to study the unsorted papers of Sir Philip Magnus, Dr Margaret Maison for material on Pearl Craigie, Mr David Yates Mason for information about the Paraman family, Mr Patrick French for advice on the expedition to Tibet, and Mr Christopher Davson as well as Sir Anthony and Lady Glyn for answering enquiries about their grandmother, Elinor Glyn. I have also received information and assistance in other ways from Jane Lady Abdy, the late Lady Arthur, Dr Ben Benedikz, Professor Edmund Bosworth, Mr Roy Davids, Professor David Dilks, Mr Robin Harcourt-Williams, Mr Colin Harris, Mr Michael Meredith, Lord Rees-Mogg, Sir Steven Runciman, Dr Kathryn Tidrick, and a great number of archivists all over the country. Lord Crawford, Mr Nigel Nicolson, Lord Salisbury and Lord Shelburne combined generosity with ancestral papers with hospitality at their dining-tables. And at the India Office Library, where I have been happily studying for several years, Dr Richard Bingle and

Mr David Blake have been unfailingly helpful. My heartfelt thanks to them all.

I am especially grateful to Mr John Grigg, to my father Ian Gilmour and to my brother Andrew, each of whom kindly read the entire manuscript and made a large number of invaluable suggestions. So did my editors, Gail Pirkis and Grant McIntyre, from whose patience, skills and encouragement the book has greatly benefited.

Lastly, I have to thank my wife Sarah for her continuous support and at the same time apologize to my children who have – understandably – derived less enjoyment than their father from the late Lord Curzon's excellent but somewhat overwhelming company.

Edinburgh, June 1994

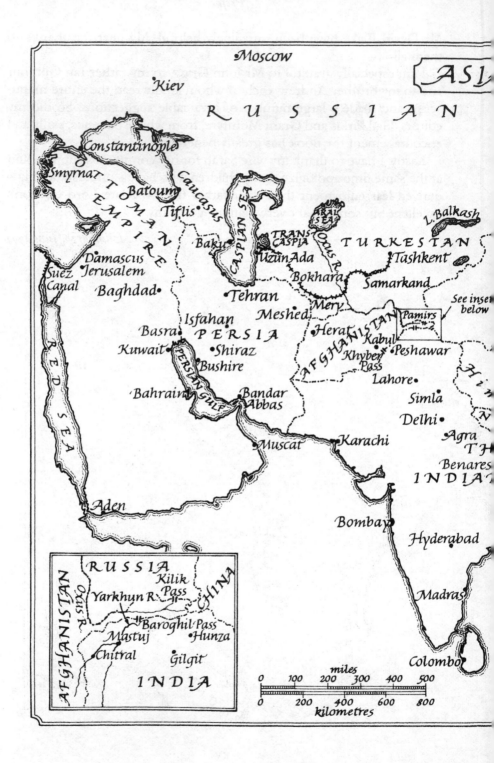

Moscow

Kiev

RUSSIAN

ASI

Constantinople

Smyrna

Batoum

Caucasus

Tiflis

OTTOMAN EMPIRE

Baku

CASPIAN SEA

ARAL SEA

TRANS CASPIA

Uzun Ada

Oxus R.

TURKESTAN

Tashkent

Damascus

Jerusalem

Baghdad

Suez Canal

Bokhara

Samarkand

Tehran

L. Balkash

See inset below

Meshed

Merv

Isfahan

PERSIA

Basra

Kuwait

Shiraz

Bushire

PERSIAN GULF

Herat

AFGHANISTAN

Pamirs

Kabul

Khyber Pass

Peshawar

Lahore

Hi

N

RED SEA

Bahrain

Bandar Abbas

Simla

Delhi

Agra

TH

Muscat

Karachi

Benares

INDIA

Aden

Bombay

Hyderabad

Madras

RUSSIA

Kilik Pass

CHINA

Yarkhun R.

AFGHANISTAN

Oxus R.

Baroghil Pass

Mastuj

Hunza

Chitral

Gilgit

Colombo

INDIA

miles

0   100   200   300   400   500

0   200   400   600   800

kilometres

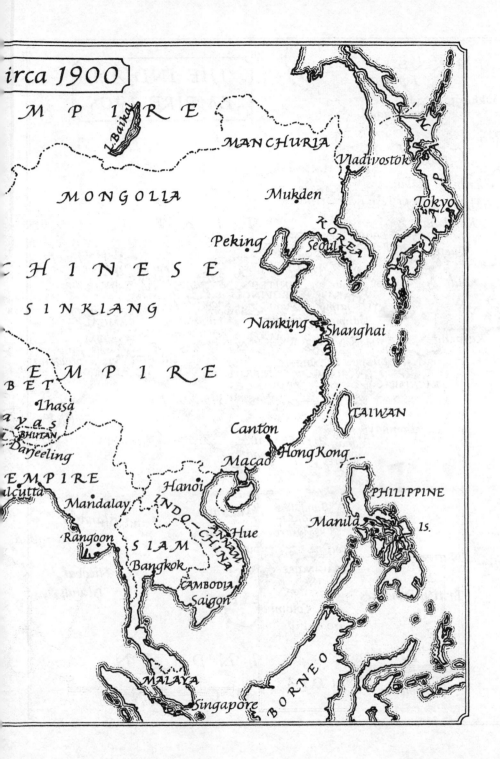

irca 1900

M P I R E

MONGOLIA

MANCHURIA

L. Baikal

Vladivostok

Mukden

Tokyo

CHINESE

KOREA

Peking

Seoul

SINKIANG

Nanking

Shanghai

EMPIRE

Lhasa

TAIWAN

BET

Canton

YA·S

BHUTAN

Macao

Hong Kong

Darjeeling

EMPIRE

Hanoi

PHILIPPINE

alcutta

Mandalay

INDO-CHINA

ANNAM

Manila

15.

Rangoon

SIAM

Hue

Bangkok

CAMBODIA

Saigon

MALAYA

Singapore

BORNEO

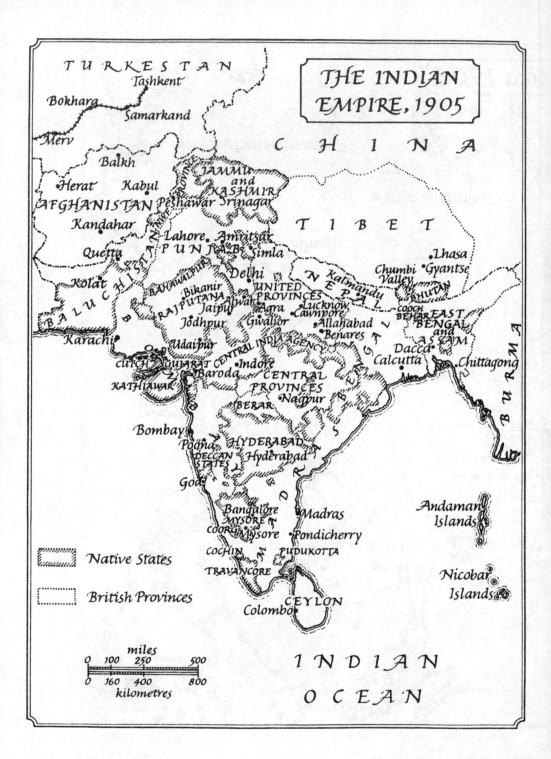

THE INDIAN EMPIRE, 1905

TURKESTAN
Tashkent
Bokhara
Samarkand
Merv
Balkh
Herat   Kabul
AFGHANISTAN Peshawar Srinagar
Kandahar
JAMMU and KASHMIR
CHINA
TIBET
Quetta
Kolat
BALUCHISTAN
Lahore Amritsar
PUNJAB Simla
Delhi
Karachi
BAHAWALPUR
Bikanir
RAJPUTANA
Jaipur
Jodhpur
Alwar
Agra
Gwalior
Cawnpore
UNITED PROVINCES
Lucknow
NEPAL
Katmandu
Lhasa
Chumbi Gyantse
Valley
BHUTAN
COOCH BEHAR
EAST BENGAL and ASSAM
Udaipur
CUTCH GUJRAT CENTRAL INDIA AGENCY
Baroda
KATHIAWAR
Indore
CENTRAL PROVINCES
BERAR
Nagpur
Allahabad
Benares
Dacca
Calcutta
Chittagong
BURMA
Bombay
Poona
DECCAN STATES
HYDERABAD
Hyderabad
Goa
Bangalore
MYSORE
COORG Mysore
COCHIN
TRAVANCORE
Madras
Pondicherry
PUDUKOTTA
CEYLON
Colombo
Andaman Islands
Nicobar Islands

INDIAN OCEAN

Native States
British Provinces

miles
0 100 250 500
0 160 400 800
kilometres

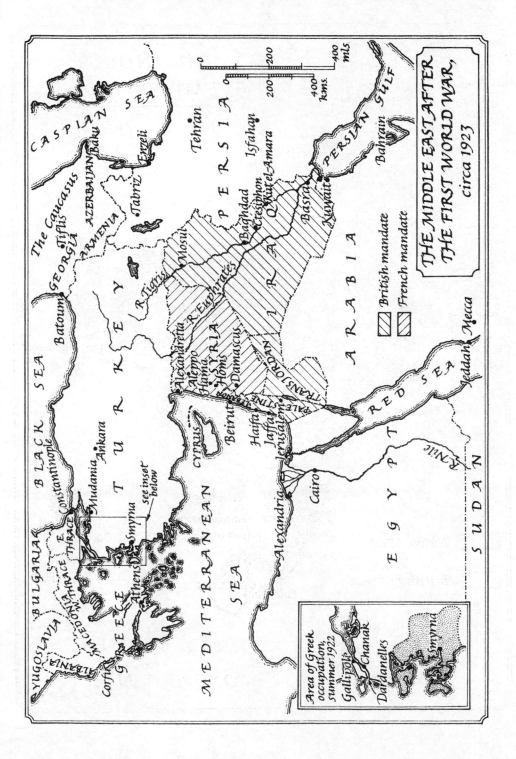

THE MIDDLE EAST AFTER
THE FIRST WORLD WAR,
circa 1923

British mandate

French mandate

Area of Greek
occupation,
summer 1922

0   200   400
mls

200   400
kms.

CASPIAN SEA

Tehran

PERSIA

Baku

Enzeli

AZERBAIJAN

Tabriz

Isfahan

ARMENIA

Tiflis

GEORGIA

The Caucasus

Batoum

Mosul

Baghdad

Ctesiphon

Q. Kut-el-Amara

Basra

I R A Q

Kuwait

PERSIAN GULF

Bahrain

BLACK SEA

R. Tigris

R. Euphrates

ARABIA

TURKEY

Alexandretta

Aleppo

Hama

SYRIA

Homs

Damascus

TRANSJORDAN

RED SEA

Jeddah

Mecca

Ankara

Mudania

Constantinople

E. THRACE

BULGARIA

Smyrna

see inset
below

CYPRUS

Beirut

LEBANON

Haifa

Jaffa

PALESTINE

Jerusalem

YUGOSLAVIA

ALBANIA

W. THRACE

MACEDONIA

GREECE

Athens

Corfu

MEDITERRANEAN

SEA

Cairo

Alexandria

EGYPT

R. Nile

SUDAN

Gallipoli

Chanak

Dardanelles

Smyrna

I

Ancestral Silence

———————— ◆ ————————

GEORGE NATHANIEL CURZON was born on 11 January 1859 at
Kedleston, the Derbyshire estate his family had owned for more
than seven hundred years. Proud of his birthplace, one of the finest
country houses in England, and of his birthright, he once admonished
an historian who had failed to trace the Curzons back beyond the
fifteenth century. The family's descent, he wrote, went 'straight back to
a Norman who came over with the Conqueror', while Kedleston had
belonged to the Curzons, most of whom were buried in its church,
since the twelfth century. 'I think there are only two or three families in
England', he added, 'who can prove a similar descent. Each stage of
ours was verified some years ago at the College of Heralds.'[1]

While George Curzon was proud of his family's longevity, he was less
impressed by its achievements. 'My ancestors', he used to say, 'were a
feeble lot. No family could have remained in possession of the same
estate since the twelfth century had they manifested the very slightest
energy or courage.'[2] In the hundred years before his birth, however,
some junior members had led active lives outside Derbyshire. One illegitimate great-uncle was killed at Waterloo, another joined the navy and
was decorated for his services at Navarino. An uncle of these fought in
turn against the fleets of Bourbon, revolutionary and Napoleonic
France, and supervised the evacuation of the British army at Corunna.
He was eventually made a full admiral, although not until he was too old
to command a fleet.[3]

Military careers had little appeal to those Curzons who were neither illegitimate nor younger sons. They remained on their estates except for brief appearances at Westminster, their immobility and lack of adventure symbolized by the family's strikingly unambitious motto, 'Let Curzon holde what Curzon helde'. Serving as sheriffs and justices of the peace in the later Middle Ages, they also provided some of Derbyshire's knights in Parliament. By the early eighteenth century the county was represented in the House of Commons by the head of the family, while a son or younger brother usually sat for Clitheroe in Lancashire. The Tory Curzons were nearly always unopposed in their own county, even when their party was out of office. Until the general election of 1734, Derbyshire returned two Tory members; afterwards the Curzons and their Whig rivals, the Cavendishes of Chatsworth, each nominated a family representative.[4]

The official parliamentary histories of the eighteenth and early nineteenth centuries almost invariably describe an MP of the Curzon family as 'an inactive member' who seldom made a speech and often did not vote. Sir John Curzon, who was killed out hunting in 1727, was an exception, at any rate in his voting habits: after George I had been placed on the throne in 1714, he voted against the government in every recorded division. Compared to his younger brother William, regarded by Horace Walpole as 'a nasty wretch and very covetous', this was a fairly positive record. MP for Clitheroe for thirteen years, William 'never paid the compliment of attending at his own election' and appears never to have voted in the House of Commons.[5] Until George Curzon was elected in 1886, the family's performance scarcely improved. Robert Curzon, an elderly cousin who died when George was a child, made only one parliamentary speech in his first twenty-four years as a member.[6]

In spite of their dislike of the Hanoverians, the Curzons were too prudent to become Jacobites. During the rising of 1745 Sir Nathaniel Curzon joined the Duke of Devonshire and other Derbyshire gentlemen in contributing to a fund established to 'defend our excellent Constitution in Church and State'. Yet his opposition to the government seems to have led Jacobites to believe that he was a potential supporter of the Stuarts, because in 1743 one of their agents had informed the King of France that Sir Nathaniel had an annual income of £12,000 and employed 10,000 miners.[7] Although both figures are exaggerated, the Curzons' wealth had increased over the previous century, and the family had acquired property in neighbouring counties as well as in London. By 1759 Sir Nathaniel's son, another Nathaniel, believed his family's status had reached a point where it would be adequately reflected only by a peerage and a great country palace. Both were attained. Although regarded with some scorn for the persistency of his application, Curzon received the title of Baron Scarsdale in 1761. The new peer was disappointed, however, by his failure to become Lord-Lieutenant of Derbyshire and mortified by the achievement of his brother Assheton, whose zealous self-advancement gained him a barony from William Pitt and a viscountcy from Henry Addington. Yet Assheton, the least inactive Curzon in Parliament until the arrival of George Nathaniel, felt that even a viscountcy was insufficient and asked Spencer Perceval for an earldom.[8] Despite his failure to obtain it, his grandson and heir (descended through his mother from Admiral Howe) was made Earl Howe in 1821. Jealousy between the branches and confusion over their titles re-emerged in a later generation and complicated relations between George Curzon and his Howe cousins.

The building of Kedleston was the first Lord Scarsdale's main achievement. His architect, Robert Adam, thought him the ideal patron, 'a man resolved to spare no Expence, with £10,000 a Year, Good Temper'd & having taste himself for the Arts and little for Game'. Unlike many of his aristocratic contemporaries, Scarsdale did not undertake the Grand Tour and rarely travelled, one of several family traditions to be emphatically broken by his great-great-grandson. Yet his taste was similar to that of those connoisseurs of Palladian architecture, Lord Burlington and Lord Leicester, and the plan for Kedleston, like Holkham in Norfolk, is based on the illustrations of Palladio's unbuilt Villa Mocenigo.[9]

Demolition of the existing house, a red-brick mansion constructed sixty years previously on the site of a medieval manor and an Elizabethan hall, began in 1759. A few months later, Adam was placed in charge of building the main block, and in the subsequent fifteen years most of his designs for the house and park were carried out. The great north front, elegantly adapted from the plans of two previous architects, was constructed as Adam intended. Lack of funds, however, curtailed his schemes for the south front, and the powerful façade with its projecting rotunda was built without the pavilions he had designed to flank it. Inside the house few economies were made, however, and the Corinthian grandeur of the façades is continued in the saloon, based on the Pantheon in Rome, and in the pillars of the great marble hall. Considerable expenditure also went on paintings, bought by an agent in Italy, although these were not always what they were claimed to be. Two of Lord Scarsdale's

Rembrandts were subsequently demoted, a fate they shared with a purchase of his most prominent descendant; convinced that he had picked up a painting by the Dutch master for £10 in 1893, George Curzon was forced to concede a few weeks later that he had been deluded.[10]

The building of Kedleston was accompanied by major alterations to its surroundings. As a traveller to the county noted in 1783, 'the village is removed (not destroyed, as is too often done), the road is thrown to a considerable distance, out of sight of the house, the scanty stream is encreased into a large piece of water, and the ground disposed in the finest order'.[11] By then the park contained a bridge and a cascade built by Adam, an hexagonal summer house, and a delightful fishing pavilion from which ladies could cast their lines without becoming sunburnt. Apart from the Gothic church, made sacrosanct by so many interred Curzons, little was left undisturbed. The changes were almost uniformly praised, one writer declaring it to be 'the glory of Derbyshire, eclipsing Chatsworth, the ancient boast of the county'.[12] Dr Johnson was not impressed, foolishly saying 'it would do excellently for a town-hall', but Boswell was 'struck with the magnificence of the building' and the 'verdure' of the park, which 'agitated and distended [his] mind in a most agreeable manner'.[13]

The architectural extravagance of the first Lord Scarsdale, followed by the gambling debts of the second and the intestacy of the third, considerably reduced the family's wealth. The new circumstances preserved Kedleston from nineteenth-century 'improvements' but also imposed a comparatively frugal existence on its occupants. The Curzons therefore relinquished their rivalry with the Cavendishes and opted for even more sedentary lives as squires and rectors of their own parish: between 1795 and 1916 they held the living of Kedleston without interruption. The family's genealogical descent as well as its fortunes were complicated by the second Lord Scarsdale, but with no lasting detriment to the lineage. After the death of his first wife, with whom he had a son and a daughter, he fled abroad to escape his debts and lived with a Flemish lady who produced ten children – six of them before the wedding took place. After his death in 1837 Scarsdale was thus succeeded by the son of his first marriage, who had no children, and then by the son of the seventh (but first legitimate) child of his Flemish alliance. Although two survivors of the illegitimate six may have been tempted to query the date and validity of their parents' marriage, they declined to do so, and the fourth Lord Scarsdale, George Curzon's father, took possession of Kedleston in 1856.[14]

The younger son of a younger son (his elder brother had been killed in a riding accident the year before), the new Lord Scarsdale had not expected to inherit Kedleston and refused to change his way of life when he did. He had become the village rector in 1855 and retained the post until his death sixty-one years later. Although a curate usually officiated at church services, Scarsdale carried out the combined duties of 'squarson' for the rest of his life, visiting parishioners, restoring the church and looking after his land. He cared more about the estate than the house where his zeal for economy was such that he used to wander around the rooms removing pieces of coal from the fires.[15]

An austere, uncouth figure sporting large fluffy whiskers and often a billycock hat, Lord Scarsdale believed in the long-held family tradition that landowners should stay on their land. 'Why don't you stay at home and be quiet,' he asked his son George, 'look after the estate, and take an interest in the tenants as I have done, instead of roaming about all over the world?'[16] When writing to congratulate Mary Leiter on her engagement to George, he informed her that the Curzons were 'a quiet, home-loving family'. Her reactions on staying with him at Kedleston a few months later were unfavourable: he was despotic, unattractively eccentric ('very fond of examining his tongue in a mirror') and disagreeable to his daughters, whom he criticized for being unmarried while giving them little opportunity to meet young men. A few years later, however, she admitted that he had become 'tender and affectionate' to herself and good with his grandchildren.[17]

Scarsdale was the most unindulgent of fathers, obsessed by punctuality and intolerant of luxury and pretensions. He did little to encourage ambition in his children and was grudging in his praise for their achievements. George complained that he took such little interest in his career that he never read one of his books or speeches. When he won a French prize at Eton, his father told him not to celebrate his success by growing his hair over his ears. 'Your talents are given to you by Almighty God and I fervently pray you will ever use them rightly, and be a comfort and blessing to your parents.' Above all, Lord Scarsdale exhorted, 'do not, dear boy, be unduly puffed up at your comparatively early victory'. The potentially baneful effects of the French prize also exercised his mother who hoped 'great shiverings and ailings' would not 'proceed from overtaxing [his] brain' and bring 'depression and bodily languor'.[18] Contemporary photographs indicate that George obeyed his father's demand for short hair, but his career is proof that he paid little attention to his mother's warning about the effects of overwork.

Lord Scarsdale married Blanche Senhouse, from Netherhall in Cumberland, in 1856. The next year they had their first daughter, Sophy, followed in 1859 by their eldest son. In all George's enormous correspondence there is virtually no mention of the Senhouses beyond a description of his uncle as an 'amiable country gentleman'. Yet his mother's genes seem to have influenced his character and interests more profoundly than those of his father. The Curzon family had shown no concern for archaeology, cheerfully obliterating their ancestors' works, until George came along and restored a number of monuments in Britain and a great many more in India. An ancestor on his mother's side, by contrast, has been called 'the father of British antiquarianism'. John Senhouse began the excavation of an ancient fort in Cumberland in the sixteenth century and assembled a remarkable collection of Roman and Celtic items which was preserved and enlarged by his family for four hundred years.

Contemporary descendants of the Senhouses recognize that some of them share certain character traits with George Curzon: precision, persistence, meticulousness over details, and a tendency to point out other people's mistakes. Every evening in old age his sister Sophy kept her *Burke's Peerage* up to date by adding information from the births and deaths columns of *The Times*.[19] Judging from the few relics of their mother, precise accounting was also a characteristic of Blanche Scarsdale, who recorded details of the most insignificant purchases down to the last farthing. Yet it is difficult to form an overall idea of her personality. George's references to her in his letters are affectionate, but the meagre existing evidence suggests that his love for her may not have been strongly reciprocated. Probably they managed to see even less of each other than most Victorian families of the same class. Until he went to his boarding preparatory school, George was under the close and domineering supervision of his governess, while his mother spent most of her time in pregnancy. Before he was 7 she had had five more children.

'One of the delights of childhood', Curzon recalled many years later, 'is the eternal gullibility of children about the birth of a new brother or sister.' Led to believe that the family babies appeared among the nettles in the Hay Wood at Kedleston, he used to command expeditions across Adam's triple-arched bridge and up the opposite slope in search of 'fresh ones. We always thought it an extraordinary place for them to be found. But it never occurred to us to doubt it.'[20]

Blanche Scarsdale had eleven children in all, one of whom did not survive, before she died in 1875 at the age of 37. Most of them belonged to that unambitious family strain so dramatically challenged by their eldest brother. 'Alfred does nothing but is an excellent fellow,' George remarked when his brother was 34.[21] Sophy, his eldest sister, was married to an 'excellent clergyman', while young Blanche kept house for Lord Scarsdale. Curzon was fond of his siblings, particularly Blanche and his youngest sister Margaret, but he was not very close to any of them except Frank, who enjoyed a successful career on the Stock Exchange. He and George were several times forced to bail out their other brothers, especially the youngest one, Assheton, who earned himself a reputation as the family's 'black sheep'. In 1914, after various other transgressions, Assheton was caught stealing securities from his office in order to raise money which he subsequently lost in speculation on the Stock Exchange. George and Frank, with the help of their father, saved him from prison by replacing the stolen securities but demanded disciplinary action. The only solution for Assheton, declared his eldest brother, was the classic remedy for black sheep: exile to the colonies.[22]

George was more talented than his brothers and sisters and also better-looking. None of them much resembled him except Frank. Apart from Margaret, his sisters were generally plain, most of the family having inherited their father's long narrow head as well as a slightly pro-truding lower lip. George's head, by contrast, was abnormally large and spherical, with a normal lip, while his pink cheeks, high forehead and fine hazel eyes gave him an almost cherubic appearance.

A diary George kept at the age of 7 suggests a happy and conventional childhood. There were drives with his mother and his governess ('darling Parrie') in a pony cart, walks to the farm and the village, excursions to Derby to see the dentist, a first ride on a new pony, an initiatory fishing expedition which landed four perch. And in the summer the family went to the seaside, usually to the Channel resorts of Brighton, St Leonards or Broadstairs. But the idyllic primrose-gathering existence at Kedleston was marred by the Scarsdales' governess, who disapproved of toys and permanently infected the Curzon girls with her view that theatres and dancing were sinful.[23] No doubt she superintended the children's diaries. 'Darling Parrie' was an unlikely phrase for George to have used volun-tarily at that time to describe the terrifying Ellen Mary Paraman.

In later years Curzon recognized that Miss Paraman had been a fine teacher who had impressed upon him 'good habits, economy, neatness, method, and a dislike of anything vulgar or fast'. Yet she was also 'a brutal and vindictive tyrant [who] persecuted and beat us in the most cruel way and established over us a system of terrorism so complete that not one of us ever mustered up the courage to walk upstairs and tell our father or mother'. At mealtimes she kept all the 'dainties' for herself and made her charges eat tapioca and rice pudding which they loathed. 'She forced us to confess to lies which we had never told, to sins which we had never committed, and then punished us savagely, as being self-condemned.' Her punishments were a combination of the convention-ally physical (beating the children and locking them up in darkness) and the bizarrely psychological, designed to humiliate. George was made to write and ask the butler to make a birch for him to be beaten with. He also had to make a calico petticoat which he was forced to wear with a large conical cap. After attaching words such as 'liar', 'sneak', or 'coward' to this costume, he was then made to display himself to the gardeners and the village. 'I suppose no children well-born and well-placed', he later reflected, 'ever cried so much or so justly.'[24]

Lord Scarsdale was evidently a believer in tough governesses, for after Miss Paraman's retirement he employed a formidable German Lutheran to administer a strict religious upbringing to his youngest daughters.[25] Yet Miss Paraman was plainly exceptional even in that age, and her behaviour suggests that neither of the Scarsdales took much trouble to examine her methods or to see what was happening beyond the nursery door. Nor do they seem to have informed themselves about her dis-agreeable family. They probably knew that two of Miss Paraman's sisters were governesses to well-known landowning families in Norfolk, that a third taught at a school in Norwich, and that their father was governor of Norwich gaol. But they cannot have known anything about the notori-ously sadistic regime at the school, where Eliza Paraman* inflicted pun-ishments on her pupils similar to those carried out by her sister at Kedleston. And they must have been ignorant of the fact that the Paraman parents forced their children to witness executions over which their father presided in Norwich gaol.[26] An upbringing which included such spectacles may explain much of Miss Paraman's behaviour as an adult and adds weight to Curzon's view that she was virtually insane.

While there is no reason to doubt the accuracy of his adult recollec-tions, it is interesting to learn that George's childhood attitude towards his governess was not one of truculent rebelliousness. Her reign of terror seems to have compelled a respect for her methods, and by the

---

*Re-named but undisguised as Eliza Pergamon, she is the villainess in Mary E. Mann's novel, *The Memories of Ronald Love*, published in 1907.

age of 10 he was collaborating in her efforts to instil discipline in her other charges. Before going to his preparatory school for the first time, he wrote a letter to his eldest sister solemnly urging her to please Miss Paraman, to leave off all her 'idle habits' and to set an example to the others. For his part he would try 'with God's help' to remember all their governess had told him and to be a good boy at school. Three weeks later he repeated the exhortation and told Sophy that his longing for the 'dear old holidays' was marred by the thought that Miss Paraman would be away on her own leave by the time he returned. His schoolfellows laughed at him, he added, because he took both his prayer book and Bible to church, but he liked to do so in remembrance of his sister and his governess.[27] By such methods do tyrants win followers. In Curzon's case, moreover, the loyalty lessened only slowly with the years. Even after her authority had vanished, he wrote to her from Eton and in 1892 attended her funeral, dressed strangely, according to Miss Paraman's nephew, in a red tie.[28]

George was removed from the daily influence of his governess at the age of 10 and sent to Wixenford, a preparatory school in Hampshire. In the curiously mature letter he left for Sophy to read after his departure, he admitted how much he would miss his family and think of the happy days spent together; he also wanted her to know how much he loved her because he realized he had not been able to make this clear before.[29] On arriving at Wixenford, he was more miserable than he had expected. 'I remember to this hour', he wrote much later, 'the horrible moment when I saw the fly and white horse drive away carrying my mother who was dearer to me than anyone in the world.' 'Innocent and sensitive', he spent the first night in a room with two other small boys, both 'endeavouring to reassure and fraternise' with him. He was worried about being homesick but believed that this was a physical illness and was relieved that he experienced no actual desire to be sick.[30]

Although he had to adapt to a regime of cold beef for breakfast and classroom work at seven in the morning, George did not take long to adjust to boarding school. He liked the headmaster, the Revd R. Cowley Powles, in spite of thinking him weak and querulous. After his initial misery the first term was successful. 'He has been uniformly industrious,' Cowley Powles told Lord Scarsdale, 'obedient and well-mannered.' The next term's report was even better, George coming first in all subjects except classics, in which he was second, and geography, where he came third. 'I continue to believe', wrote Cowley Powles, 'that in character, in ability, and general disposition, your son is a very unusual boy.'

If he carried on like this, prophesied the headmaster, he would 'certainly be a distinguished man in the best sense of the term'.[31]

By an unlucky coincidence Wixenford contained a male equivalent of Miss Paraman in the shape of the assistant master, Archibald J.C. Dunbar. Like the governess, he was both a good teacher and a savage disciplinarian. 'He was a master of spanking,' recalled Curzon, and, although 'he used to say that it hurt him nearly as much as it did us', he plainly took an unnatural pleasure in the endless 'swishing on the posterior'. George was one of his favourites and, although this position gave him no immunity from the beatings, he was genuinely fond of the schoolmaster, who shared the boys' enthusiasm for climbing and other pursuits. Under Dunbar's supervision he acted as the private banker of the boys in the school, keeping their accounts and employing specially printed cheque-books. Proudly recalling that the accounts were always correct down to the last penny, he later declared that the activity 'was a wise one as inculcating both business habits and economy'.[32] Other habits inculcated at Wixenford were hard work, a desire to compete – in his last term he won five prizes – and an investigative curiosity about the eccentricities of nature: he was greatly excited at witnessing a spectacular aurora borealis and sent Sophy a diagram of the bands of red light. From this period one can also date that love of sonorous and elaborate language which he never lost. As a 12-year-old he wrote to tell his mother that 'a hamper is undoubtedly requisite under the present circumstances' and must include 'several pots of superior jam' and 'one of those very jolly cakes . . . which Mrs Halliday fully knows how to fabricate'; potted meat was also 'indispensable'.[33]

It is tempting to ascribe almost all the qualities and defects of Curzon's adult character to the influences of Miss Paraman and Mr Dunbar. In one interpretation he is alleged to have spent the rest of his life looking for similar figures against whom he could bruise himself.[34] But such speculation, based only on evidence written many years later by Curzon himself, fastens on a psychological explanation and ignores all others. Dunbar and Miss Paraman no doubt encouraged the obsessional side of his nature and stimulated his ambition, yet hereditary and other factors were also important influences on his character. Curzon's brothers and sisters suffered Miss Paraman without aspiring to become bruised viceroys. Alfred, a year younger than George, received an almost identical education and yet remained 'an excellent fellow' who did little until taking over the administration of the Kedleston estate from his father. It is not unusual for families to throw up a single talented figure from a large flock of unremarkable relations: many noble lines base their nobility on a founder whom his descendants have seldom been able to emulate. In Curzon's case the immemorial mediocrity of his ancestors undoubtedly inspired him to achievement. 'They were just ordinary country gentlemen,' he later remarked; 'I made up my mind I would try to get out of the groove.'[35] Conscious that his family had been unworthy of its great house and long lineage, he wanted to be a fitting master for Kedleston. In the closing words of the epitaph he composed for himself, 'he sought to serve his country and add honour to an ancient name'.

2

'Passionate Resolves': Eton, 1872–1878

THE YEARS GEORGE CURZON spent at Eton were a period of transition for the school. According to his friend Edward Lyttelton, who later became headmaster of Eton, 1875 was the moment when 'open barbarism gave place to something like decorum'.[1] In some ways barbarism was receding even before then. By the 1860s floggings had been greatly reduced from the days of the notorious Dr Keate and were no longer administered before an audience.[2] Bullying had also declined. Twenty years earlier Robert Cecil, the future Lord Salisbury and Prime Minister, had been 'bullied from morning to night' and kicked so hard every time he appeared in the dining-room that he was 'obliged to go out of dinner without eating anything'.[3] J.E.C. Welldon, a later friend of Curzon who became headmaster of Harrow, experienced 'the tail-end of bullying in College' (the scholars' house) in the 1860s: it was disagreeable, he remembered, but no longer 'dangerous or even serious'.[4] With its 900 boys, Eton was still the largest and freest of the public schools, but by the 1870s the virtual anarchy of earlier decades had mostly disappeared.

Lyttelton blamed the indiscipline on the boring curriculum and the defects of the housemasters. 'The intellectual training', he recalled, 'was concentrated almost entirely on Latin composition,' a situation equally deplored by Welldon who criticized the school for clinging with 'unreasoning tenacity to the practice of compelling boys, who would not be thought capable of writing two verses in their own language', to write week after week poetical exercises in a language they could not speak.[5]

The predominance of the classics, however, had been criticized by the recent Clarendon Commission and, by the time of Curzon's arrival at Eton in 1872, languages and mathematics were being treated as serious subjects. Another development, of doubtful use in the reduction of violence but allegedly crucial to the elimination of vice, was the cult of sport promoted by the new headmaster, the Revd J. Hornby. The boys responded with an eagerness that seemed to preclude a simultaneous enthusiasm for the cult of the intellect. The cricket match between Eton and Harrow at Lord's, which had excited negligible interest in the 1850s, was described by Lyttelton a generation later as an occasion that 'seemed to us to be the annual climax of the history of mankind'.[6] It ended, however, with an exhibition of upper-class hooliganism. 'As soon as the last hit had been made,' recalled Curzon, 'there was a simultaneous rush from all parts of the ground to the front of the pavilion, and a regular scuffle with a plentiful shower of blows on tophats from umbrellas . . .'[7]

It was of course possible to combine an interest in sport with a desire to learn. Etonians of the 1870s could receive a reasonable education if, like George Curzon, they wanted one and found a teacher to inspire them. Edward Lyttelton praised the 'zeal and pastoral sympathy' of younger masters appointed after 1870, who managed to 'drive vice into holes and corners, instead of letting it flaunt its hideous face in public'.[8] In fact Eton's most inspiring teachers of the period, William Johnson and Oscar Browning, were forced to leave the school at least partly because of their own inclinations towards one particular vice. Johnson, a great classical scholar who was said to write the best Horatian lyrics since Horace himself, retired after an 'indiscretion' in 1872 and later wrote a defence of pederasty to one of his sympathizers.*[9] His view that boys derived more benefit from intellectual conversations than from Latin construes was shared by Browning.

Oscar Browning was the third of the major educational influences on George Curzon's life. He was also the most harmless, for his homosexuality, unlike the perversions of Miss Paraman and Mr Dunbar, did not affect his relationship with his pupil. Oscar Browning, known affectionately as O.B., was a snob and an egoist who boasted that his 'chosen work' was 'educating statesmen'. He was also one of those rare teachers capable of identifying and stimulating a boy's latent interests. In return, his favourite pupils were devoted to him. Curzon remained a friend for

---

*He changed his name to Cory and is mainly remembered as the author of 'Heraclitus' and the 'Eton Boating Song'.

fifty years and introduced him to his first wife with the words, 'Whatever I am, my dear, I owe it all to Mr Browning.'[10]

Uninterested in any form of sport, the portly Browning was the most ostentatious member of a small, beleaguered group of intellectual masters. Crusading against the school's pervading philistinism, he encouraged interest in music and language and founded the Literary Society. Talented boys were invited to his house on Sunday evenings to listen to music or browse in his library. 'You would wander about,' his pupil A.C. Benson recalled later, 'take down a volume, ensconce yourself in a corner, perhaps overhear an animated discussion proceeding between boys like J.K. Stephen, Lord Curzon, and Cecil Spring Rice, and lose yourself in admiration at the depth of erudition and the readiness of argument and rejoinder that were manifested.'* Browning bustled fussily among them, throwing in provocative and critical remarks. If construes and duller boys were rather neglected, many brighter pupils owed their first experience of intellectual life to O.B.[11]

After three years at Wixenford, George had no difficulty in adjusting to Eton. He liked the school from the beginning, enjoying the football he played four times a week while deploring the theory of compulsory sport. His desire to learn and his need to compete were soon evident. 'I longed to be equipped with a furniture of universal information', he wrote later, 'and to know as much as possible about a great variety of subjects.'[12] He was invariably among the leaders in school examinations and won the major prizes in Latin, French, Italian, history and declamation. Twenty-three times he was 'sent up for good' – a distinction awarded for an outstanding piece of work – a record he shared with his friend Welldon. The young Curzon was motivated by a 'passionate resolve to be at the head of the class' and by the need to prove himself to teachers who did not take him seriously enough. They 'never could realise', he complained, 'that I was bent on being first in what I undertook, [and] that I meant to do it in my way and not theirs'.[13]

Doing it his way inevitably caused resentment among the school masters. In later years Curzon listed his 'passionate desire to win' as one of three flaws in his character which had annoyed them. The others were the concealment of such virtues as he might have possessed and an

---

* Browning's library would thus have contained the authors of two famous patriotic anthems. Spring Rice wrote 'I vow to thee my country' shortly before he died in 1918, while Benson penned the much less memorable words of 'Land of Hope and Glory'. Stephen, who died in his early thirties, was the author of some delightful light verse.

'innate rebelliousness' demonstrated by keeping wine in his room, although he did not like drinking, going to Ascot races, although he did not care for racing, and once playing tennis in the statue-lined Upper School, 'the tennis balls cannoning off the heads of Chatham and Canning and other heroes of the past'.[14] What his teachers most resented, however, was his arrogance. In his first term, at the age of 13, he was already complaining to his mother about 'silly' tradesmen and 'idiotic' tailors. Not long afterwards he was treating his tutors with similar haughtiness. The Italian master Volpe, he told Browning, was 'such a fool' that it was impossible to learn anything from him: 'his English is utterly unintelligible, the Italian as a consequence much more so'. After a quarrel Curzon gave up attending his class, studied the set texts in private and then infuriated Volpe by winning the Italian prize. In almost identical circumstances he carried off prizes for French and history.[15]

Curzon's disdain, from which only Browning and a few other masters were exempt, was openly displayed towards his housemaster, the Revd C. Wolley Dod. They annoyed each other from the beginning. During his first year Wolley Dod called him an 'impertinent brat' and complained to Lord Scarsdale about his 'tendency to say silly things and to make silly remarks about the lesson'. Two years later a protest from his mathematics master, whom Curzon considered 'a huge joke', prompted another letter to Kedleston. 'He is often childishly and pertinaciously naughty,' wrote Wolley Dod, exasperated that the boy was now too old to receive 'the best punishment, a whipping'. He was 'far too ready with his tongue and however he may be in the wrong he always argues that he is quite right and is very difficult to silence . . . he is apt to be impertinently loud in his self-justification.' After remonstrations from his parents, George complained to them about the time-wasting punishments for trivial offences and accused Wolley Dod of being bitter and spiteful towards him. By the summer of 1875 there was a truce, and the housemaster was able to inform Scarsdale that his son was not 'so wilful, or so importunately persistent if he could not do as he liked'. Within months, however, it collapsed, and relations deteriorated until a climactic confrontation took place in June 1877. The 18-year-old Curzon, who was by then captain of the house and a member of Sixth Form, had played cricket with a sprained ankle and then, having exacerbated the injury, asked permission to miss a class. Wolley Dod's furious reaction to one of the hardest-working and most senior members of the school is curious and may have been provoked by Curzon's assumption of 'a most haughty dictatorial tone of insolence'. In any case he angrily refused the request, called the youth 'a rank shuffler', and regretted he was not in another house. In the same week Curzon had rows with two other masters, one of whom told him he was grossly insolent and without gentlemanly feelings; afterwards he began to think there was a conspiracy to turn him out of Eton.[16]

Much of Wolley Dod's animosity was aroused by his pupil's clear preference for the company of a rival housemaster. Oscar Browning regarded Curzon at the age of 15 as 'one of the most brilliantly gifted boys' he had ever come across, invited him frequently to his house and sent him editions of Dante and Tennyson as presents. Although he himself was undoubtedly attracted to the precocious schoolboy, Browning helped preserve him from the attentions of others. Curzon's fresh good looks aroused both interest and comment. According to a contemporary, he was 'the brightest, cheeriest little being imaginable, round of face with pink and white complexion, big, serious eyes, an exceptionally determined mouth, and a high square forehead'.[17] The captain of his house warned Browning that the boy was in moral danger from associating with dubious companions. Another senior boy wrote asking for advice because 'the most hideous construction' had been placed on a chance encounter between the two of them.[18] Even the Scarsdales suggested that their son should approach Browning for guidance. Despite the jealousy and insinuations of others, O.B.'s influence, both educational and moral, was beneficial to the young Curzon.

The advantages of their association were not, however, recognized by Wolley Dod. Disagreeing with Browning's positive assessment of Curzon's character, he also disapproved of the interest O.B. showed in his pupil. On learning that they had gone together for a drive in a carriage, Wolley Dod lost his temper and complained to Hornby, the headmaster. He presumably anticipated a congenial reaction. A pioneer of Alpine climbing and a skating enthusiast, Hornby had never liked Browning, who was a difficult and argumentative colleague frequently proposing reforms and trying to change the curriculum. Upon receiving the protest from Wolley Dod, Hornby summoned O.B., hinted that his interest in Curzon was physical and demanded a pledge that he would stop meeting him. The outraged Browning argued, appealed to the Provost and wrote to Curzon's father, who supported him. 'I exceedingly regret this very unpleasant complaint of Mr Wolley Dod's,' Lord Scarsdale assured him in July 1874, adding that he gave O.B. 'full credit for acting from the purest motives' and thanking him for 'rescuing George from companions of more than doubtful repute'.[19]

All attempts at changing Hornby's mind failed. When one of O.B.'s few supporters among the masters remonstrated, arguing that if Browning was unfit to see Curzon he was unfit to be a master, Hornby agreed with the deduction.[20] But he needed a pretext to get rid of him altogether and found one a year later when Browning exceeded the maximum number of boys permitted in a house. Dismissed for the infringement, O.B. retired to King's College, Cambridge, where he divided his time between improving the minds of favourite pupils and writing bad history books for 'grocers and cheesemongers'.[21]

Neither the prohibition on their meeting nor Browning's subsequent dismissal ended the friendship with Curzon. In his sympathetic letter Scarsdale had told the schoolmaster he did not wish 'the kindly relations between you and my boy to fall through', and thus they continued to correspond and see each other in the holidays. Curzon blamed the whole problem on 'the unkind, ungentlemanly and obstinate conduct' of his tutor whom he increasingly detested, and in a subsequent letter referred to Wolley Dod as a 'postdiluvian monster'.[22] His letters to O.B. also described the 'rural amusements' that occupied his holidays at Kedleston: sporadic hunting and shooting, and cricket both as a modest participator with a local club and as an enthusiastic spectator at Derby, especially when W.G. Grace was playing. In the hard December of 1874 he reported that the rabbits and hares were too thin to be worth shooting, but in compensation the skating was glorious, and Kedleston had a magnificent Christmas tree.

It was the last Christmas the family enjoyed together, for Lady Scarsdale died of blood poisoning in London in the spring. When her condition became hopeless, her younger children were sent out of the way to Brighton, but George remained and thus saw her dead, her 'dear face' as 'it used to be, with a happy smile on, but of course very grey and calm, like marble'. He ordered black trousers for his brothers and told Alfred they must try to bear the loss and comfort their distraught father, who for many years afterwards used to take the face of his youngest daughter in his hands and say despairingly, 'So like your blessed mother'.[23] Lord Scarsdale's grief was intensified by the guilty feeling that he had been responsible for his wife's death by forcing upon her so many pregnancies. Writing to his elder sons at Eton, he exhorted them to uphold the memory of their mother: 'May her example be *deeply* graven in your heart and keep you from evil ways and bad influence.'[24] Unable to bear living at Kedleston as a widower, he shut up the great house and moved his children to a smaller family property nearby. In the autumn George returned to them to nurse a broken collar bone and described the melancholy of his ancestral home in a poem called 'Kedleston':

> Still as ever, proud thou standest,
> Green thy meadows as of yore,
> But a chill of desolation
> Mid the sunbeams clouds thee o'er.
>
> Many voices that but lately
> Laughing echoed through thy halls
> Sound no longer there, and silence
> Reigns instead within thy walls.*

In January 1878, the last Christmas holidays of his Eton career, Curzon accompanied Oscar Browning on a journey to the South of France. 'We were very great friends before our tour,' he wrote afterwards, 'but if I may say so, we are still greater now.'[25] Browning agreed and sent his mother a eulogy of Curzon's virtues: 'A purer, brighter, or more simple spirit does not exist, and his cleverness, vivacity, and good temper make him the most charming of companions.[26] O.B. recognized, however, that his 'great qualities' were not 'fully appreciated by either boys or masters at Eton'. Then, as later, it was difficult for anyone to be neutral about Curzon. 'It is strange to remember', reflected Benson in his diary on the day of Curzon's death, 'how *entirely* we disliked and mistrusted him at Eton.' Three years his junior, Benson believed Curzon had been guilty of sexual immorality and cheating in one of the prizes, but the accusations seem to have been based less on testimony than on personal dislike. The diary does not elaborate on the second charge, an obscure incident from which Curzon was officially cleared at the time, but its evidence for the first – that he had invited 'a very handsome, incredibly tiresome and priggish boy' called Macnaghten to breakfast – is hardly damning and suggests that Benson, himself a homosexual, found solace in trying to identify other homosexuals.[27]

Among older boys the young Curzon often enjoyed remarkable popularity. One of them told Browning he wanted to meet him, 'knowing of what a superior quality he really is and how often he has been in a dangerous position here,' but dared not do so because 'a big fellow cannot even come across a little fellow in the most casual way

---

*Verses three and four.

without its being remarked'.[28] No doubt George's good looks accounted for some of his popularity with the 'big fellows', but his character must have been the main attraction, because several of them were close friends in adult life. On his last day at Eton, Edward Lyttelton, who had hesitated about writing to Curzon, finally asked him for his photograph and thus initiated a long friendship. Alfred, another of the boisterous, intelligent, cricket-mad Lyttelton brothers, dated his lasting affection from the moment he heard George's 'charming treble voice and cameo cut elocution' in Keate's Lane at Eton. St John Brodrick's friendship, which survived for thirty years before ending in political acrimony, began at Slough Station when Curzon, 'tall, breathless, pink-cheeked and well-groomed', burst into his railway carriage.[29]

In his last years at Eton and afterwards at Oxford, Curzon received much epistolary advice from his older friends. He answered politely, sometimes with humility. When Regy Brett, the future Lord Esher, warned him against the evil effects of flattery, Curzon expressed gratitude towards his friends for pointing out his faults and admitted they had achieved 'many little improvements' in him. But he did not think flattery was dangerous in his case as he was aware that it was unmerited.[30]

By his last year George Curzon had achieved almost as much at Eton as a non-athlete is capable of achieving. Apart from being captain of his house, a position in which even Wolley Dod recognized his efficiency, he was Captain of the Oppidans (the boys outside College), and a senior figure in 'Pop', the élite society granted sartorial and other privileges in return for acting as an amateur police force. He was also a conspicuous literary figure, editing a school journal as well as a book of poems and miscellaneous articles called *Out of School at Eton*. Published in the summer of 1877, the *Spectator* welcomed the book as 'a frolicsome little miscellany' although the *Athenaeum*'s reviewer severely criticized it for containing 'little but feeble imitation, a straining after the facetious which is not comic, and an occasional grandiloquence which is anything but impressive'.[31] Curzon's personal contribution to the anthology included a rather arch description of his 'maiden essay as a climber' on Scafell Pike, a poem about a Cumberland lake which the *Spectator* thought showed a 'real feeling for nature', and a 'Song of Liberty', written in imitation of Swinburne ('Come forth from the gloom of the gloaming / In which you have passionless run, / And quit the dull paths of your roaming / For the light of the life-giving sun.').[32] Parodying contemporary poets was a hobby Curzon shared with two of his collaborators, Stephen and Spring Rice. Girls he loved in the years to come were frequent recipients of his parodies.

In 1877 Curzon became president of the Literary Society, which had been founded by Oscar Browning, and delivered various papers including one on the French Revolution that was written, he admitted later, in 'bad, boyish Carlylese'. The society was also addressed by such distinguished figures as W.E. Gladstone and John Ruskin, whose rapt face the president later recalled 'as with eyes closed he stood at the desk and poured forth a flood of golden English'.[33] Curzon was an ambitious and undoubting Tory from an early age, but his partisanship was not extreme. Commenting on the 1874 election to his mother, he had welcomed the victory of her brother-in-law, Sir Wilfrid Lawson,* even though he was a Radical, while deploring that of the 'awful cad' who represented Eton as a Conservative.[35] In the spring of 1878 he wrote to Gladstone, the school's most distinguished old boy, to say that a visit from him would add a special distinction to his last term as president of the Literary Society. He also visited him in London, sending in his card during a large breakfast party, and persuaded him to come and lecture on Homer. After a successful talk some weeks later, the elderly statesman went to the 'Pop' rooms and laughed at the reports of the debates he had once taken part in. He also visited Curzon's room and was appalled by the pictures, flowers and armchairs he found there. Such luxury at Eton, he declared, was bound to have an enervating influence.[36]

In his final year Curzon became Captain of the Oppidans and thus enjoyed his first experience of administrative responsibility. He was dismayed, however, to discover that the powers and privileges of the position had been much diminished, and endeavoured to restore them. In a long report at the end of his year's office, he set out his views on school issues for the benefit of his successors. He did not attempt to be radical because he was aware that 'antiquated absurdities' were 'infinitely more tenacious of life at Eton than anywhere else under the sun'. But he did lay down moderating rules for caning and for fagging, a custom he regarded as 'one of the grandest institutions of which Eton can boast'.

---

*Two years earlier Sir Wilfrid Lawson had been one of only two MPs to vote for a republican motion of Sir Charles Dilke aiming to set up a select committee to enquire into the Civil List. An eccentric figure, he was a leading spokesman of the temperance movement and a teetotaller so fanatical that he had smashed the contents of a magnificent cellar he had inherited in Cumberland; the silver teapots he invariably gave as wedding presents had an obvious symbolic purpose.[34]

He also tried to end the practice of nude bathing in the Thames. Various letters to *The Field* had alleged that Etonians exposed themselves indecently when ladies passed by in pleasure-boats. While the Captain of the Oppidans denied that any such thing had taken place, he admitted that nude bathing might 'be reproached with indecency' and therefore 'advocated the institution of bathing drawers, as worn at almost every other bathing place, certainly on every river, in England'. He convinced the headmaster and the leading members of Pop, but the scheme collapsed through the opposition of the powerful Dr Warre, Hornby's deputy and successor, and other masters, who 'objected on the sole and valueless ground that it had never been found necessary before'.[37]

The climax of Curzon's Eton career was the Fourth of June, the school's principal festival, in his final year. As Captain of the Oppidans, the organization of the event was largely in his hands and gave him an opportunity to display that zeal for economy he had learnt at Wixenford. By refusing to patronize the wine merchant at Eton, as other 'credulous' captains had done, he reduced the cost of the boat crews' supper; and by providing ample supplies of soda water, he avoided drunkenness.[38] His great moment, which he described later as the most triumphant of his boyhood, was 'Speeches', the occasion at which members of Sixth Form declaim memorized passages from classical and other authors.* Curzon's performance the previous year had been much praised for its 'dramatic intensity', although the *Daily News* noted that his French accent had 'the true British ring about it'. In 1878, however, the same paper declared that his voice was 'as melodious, as clear, and as flexible as it is possible to conceive', and predicted that its possessor would make a name for himself in the world. Afterwards Curzon found himself almost overwhelmed by the congratulations of unknown people and the complimentary remarks made at a banquet given by the Provost and Fellows. Even Lord Scarsdale was moved to felicitation, sending his son £5 as 'proof of satisfaction'.[39]

Yet when term ended a few weeks later, Curzon was glad to leave Eton. He had been there too long, over six years, and still felt bitter at the treatment he had received from many of the masters, that 'carping flock led by Hornby'. The atmosphere of Eton, he told a friend, was

---

*Since his death Curzon has featured both as author and subject at Speeches: in 1950 James Bruxner delivered the speech Curzon made to the Byculla Club at Bombay, and four years later another boy recited his conversation as described by Harold Nicolson in his book *Some People*.

'either highly rarified or exceedingly clogged with noxious elements'. Yet he recognized that his feelings were ambivalent, products both of turbulence and of success, and he was sufficiently attached to the school to write an embarrassing elegy on his reluctance to bid it farewell.[40] There had been many difficulties in his life there – the 'moral dangers', the Browning episode, the hostility of masters he had antagonized – but his performance as an academic and a senior boy had been outstanding. Looking back after an adult career overladen by far greater difficulties, the bitterness of his Eton past dissolved, and he remembered it as 'a happy and glorious time, perhaps the happiest and most glorious that it will ever be given me to enjoy'.[41]

3

'Laying the Foundations':
Oxford, 1878–1883

IN RETROSPECT IT seems wholly appropriate, indeed almost inevitable, that George Curzon should have gone to Balliol, the most stimulating Oxford college of the time and a kindergarten for aspiring politicians and diplomats. But at one stage he looked certain to go elsewhere. In the summer of 1876 a friend advised Lord Scarsdale to send his son to Magdalen rather than Balliol, which was full of ambitious 'hard readers', or Christ Church, where George would 'be surrounded by a lot of "fast" young men such as there always are there'. Scarsdale, who considered Balliol a 'free-thinking place', agreed with him, and so, surprisingly, did his son. Although he would not necessarily be infected by its spirit, George told Browning, it would be 'best to keep clear' of the place. He was willing to go to Magdalen, he added uncharacteristically, because of the attraction of its music, chapel and grounds. The reasons for the ultimate rejection of both Magdalen and Merton, Scarsdale's old college, are unclear. All that is known is that in his last year at Eton he failed the scholarship examination to Balliol but decided to go there as a commoner to read for a classical degree. After advice from Browning to guard against the prevailing scepticism and a warning from his father to steer clear of wine and women, he went up to the 'free-thinking place' in October 1878.[1]

Between school and university Curzon had a brief holiday in France. It was his second visit. At the beginning of the year he had travelled with Browning from Calais to Cannes and on into northern Italy where they had managed to gatecrash a memorial service to

King Victor Emmanuel at Milan cathedral. Unfamiliar food and language prompted a very English response: the soup at Calais was 'infernally salty' and the snails 'absolutely blackguard'; he would not 'try them again in a hurry'. As for the French, they 'jabbered' their language so much that he could not understand a word of it; the strong accent and fast delivery of a troupe of Parisian actors made their play virtually incomprehensible. On his second visit, to see the Paris Exhibition, he was determined to learn the language thoroughly. Supplied with advice on French literature by Brett, and accompanied by Welldon, he stayed with a chemist and, according to Edward Lyttelton, displayed 'the most unruffled serenity through various little trials which attend on life in a French family'. He visited the city's major sights, 'looked down upon the crowd of madmen yelling and gesticulating in the Bourse', saw Sarah Bernhardt in *Hernani*, the first time he believed he had seen top-class acting, and gazed at Napoleon's tomb at the Invalides; it was 'something' that the French had 'duly appreciated the genius' of 'that marvellous man'. Curzon saw Lyttelton in Paris and went to stay with him in Fontainebleau before going on to Dinard. 'He grows a more delightful companion every year he lives,' reported Lyttelton. The holiday improved the fluency of his French (though not apparently his accent), but did nothing to increase his enthusiasm for the cooking. One had to be inured to it, he decided, before French dishes could be appreciated. Yet he never was. For the rest of his life he complained about 'greasy French cooking' and English attempts to emulate it.[2]

After his return from France, Curzon felt acute pains in one hip and noticed it had become unusually prominent. He went to London to be examined and received the shattering advice that he should postpone his plans for Oxford and lie flat on his back for six months: he was suffering from a curvature of the spine which had been further weakened by overwork. Asked for a second opinion, Sir James Paget decided that Curzon could go up to Balliol so long as he wore a steel appliance to support his spine, spent much time lying down in a specially constructed chair, and took no violent exercise. Grateful for the reprieve, even though it condemned him to the existence of a semi-invalid, the patient was soon enjoying the university. Life at Oxford lacked the restrictions which he had found irksome during his last terms at Eton. People there treated each other more charitably, he thought, and there was 'every opportunity for sensible conversation or discussion'.[3] A month after his arrival he was visited by Browning, who found him 'admirably started, simple, bright, modest, popular, everything that his friends would like to see him'.[4] As usual Curzon teased his old teacher about the need to improve his handwriting, begin his *magnum opus*, and diminish his paunch by taking dancing lessons.

In February of the following year Curzon was ill with neuralgia and toothache, which caused him sleeplessness and exhaustion, and brought on his back trouble again. Several rear teeth were extracted, and the doctors, blaming the Oxford climate, twice sent him away for a few days. Illness throughout much of his second term made him languid and desultory, nullifying his resolve to work. The least languid of people by nature, however, he was soon disobeying Paget's orders to rest and alarming his friends by his habits of hard work and late hours. Alfred Lyttelton felt obliged to harangue him about going to bed earlier.[5]

A good deal of other advice came from the group of older Etonian friends. Regy Brett, whose future wife at the age of 13 remarked on his desire 'to improve himself and everybody',[6] wrote a series of priggish letters about changing people's perception of Curzon's character, which he said was widely but unfairly regarded as superficial. The only way to refute the accusation, he maintained, was for Curzon to allow himself 'to feel strongly and deeply, even passionately', about his friends. More solid advice came from Brodrick, the most interfering of Curzon's companions, who told him what cutlery to bring and on what occasions he should serve sherry. Alfred Lyttelton, by contrast, took a moralizing line, advocating an examination of his young friend's aims and opinions before going to Oxford and comparing them with his actual achievements later on.[7]

Lord Scarsdale's view of Balliol was no doubt largely determined by the remarkable personality of Benjamin Jowett, whose reforming influence on the college had long preceded his appointment as Master in 1870. Jowett had offended traditional churchmen by his contribution to the notorious *Essays and Reviews*, published in 1860, a book which tried to reconcile Anglicanism with both the theories of Darwin and the largely German school of scientific biblical criticism; in his own essay he had emphasized the importance of the use of reason in the interpretation of scripture. At Balliol he abolished compulsory attendance at chapel and reduced the length of services, but his reforms affected most secular aspects of college life as well. A proponent of music, sport and amateur dramatics, he improved the standard of cooking and did away with the lengthy 'grace-duet' that traditionally took place in the middle of each meal. His enlargement of the college brought an increase in the number of undergraduates, whose social backgrounds Jowett was able to vary by the foundation of more scholarships and exhibitions. While the college still contained a number of landed elder sons, whom he inspired to take an active interest in public affairs, it also attracted poorer students from Glasgow and other parts of Britain, as well as a number from Asia: there were more Indian undergraduates at Balliol than at all the other colleges put together. The engaging Nasr-al-Mulk, who became Prime Minister and Regent of Persia, was an eloquent opponent of Curzon in the debating society.[8]

By the time Curzon came up, Jowett was in his sixties and a less active reformer than before. But he was far from being the 'extinct volcano, and even [a] bit of a reactionary' of Asquith's unkind phrase.[9] He remained particularly interested in his pupils' careers and in the Indian Civil Service, whose probationers he sometimes poached from other colleges. Perhaps Jowett's most useful skill was his ability to identify a talent and encourage its possessor to use it. An enemy of enthusiasm, he had no desire to create disciples eager to spread his ideas. Instead he aimed to persuade his undergraduates to prepare for their futures by working hard for their degrees, thinking about their careers and sometimes studying subjects other than classics. His success was remarkable. Had it not been for Jowett, Lord Lansdowne once remarked, he would have done little with his life.[10] The Master set him on a course that led him to become Governor-General of Canada, Viceroy of India, Secretary of State for War and Foreign Secretary. Other future Cabinet ministers who preceded Curzon to Balliol included H.H. Asquith, Alfred Milner and St John Brodrick, while Edward Grey followed him there soon afterwards.* Besides impressive groups of academics and journalists, the college also produced large numbers of MPs and, from a single year, four senior ambassadors. A farewell dinner for Milner before his fateful journey to South Africa in 1897 included no less than eleven Balliol men who had been presidents of the Oxford Union.[12] No more appropriate place for Curzon could have been envisaged. It is impossible to imagine him enjoying the

---

* The extent of Jowett's personal influence is often difficult to judge, particularly with regard to Grey. The future Foreign Secretary did no work at Balliol and was sent down from the university. Exhorted by Jowett to be less indolent, he was allowed back to take his examination in the summer of 1884 but achieved only a Third in jurisprudence. Yet a latent political ambition must have been stirred during this period because the following year Grey became the youngest member of the House of Commons.[11]

music and grounds of Magdalen while such a vibrant intellectual atmosphere existed nearby.

Balliol's success inevitably provoked envious detractors, who saw the college as a combination of crammer and masonic lodge for careerists. The Liberal leader Sir Henry Campbell-Bannerman, who went to Cambridge, was intensely irritated by what he called the *religio milneriana*, the loyalty of Balliol Liberals to Milner in the Boer War: according to one of his biographers, he regarded 'this blind belief in a Balliol hero . . . as a psychological infirmity of the Oxford mind'.[13] Writing some years later of Asquith, the Liberal journalist A.G. Gardiner claimed that 'no Balliol man of the Jowett tradition' could 'utter great thoughts' because 'the Balliol mind distrusts "great thoughts" even if it thinks them'. While conceding that the college had produced the 'finest mental machines of this generation', he insisted that they were 'cold and heartless', worthy of admiration and respect, but not of love. Balliol, he declared, was 'atrophy of the heart . . . exhaustion of the emotions'.[14]

Such criticism seems wide of the mark if aimed at Asquith, Milner or Grey. It is certainly nonsense in the case of Curzon who combined one of the 'finest mental machines' with inexhaustible emotions. Jowett's effect on him is not easy to assess because, as at other times in his life, Curzon seemed to play the part before he filled it. He was like an undergraduate of Jowett's Balliol before he met Jowett or went to Balliol. While still at school Curzon's immediate future had been described by Brodrick as 'that brief interval which must intervene between Eton and the cabinet',[15] a joke based on the widespread view of his contemporaries that he was marked out for a successful political career: in his last days at school a friend had extracted a promise that Curzon would appoint him Chancellor of the Exchequer when he became Prime Minister.[16] He thus went to Balliol in a confident mood, seeing his time there not as a tiresome interlude or an end in itself but as a period of preparation from which he would later launch his career. Work was important, and the challenge of prizes continued to lure him, but the main task was to be 'laying the foundations' of his future. As he wrote to Brett,

I go to Oxford with a certain amount of reliance on myself and belief in present convictions but perfectly prepared to find many of them modified, some perhaps eradicated, after three years' time. I do not know that I build many castles in the air for Oxford specially. My castles come later in life and perhaps have dim chance of realisation: but I recognize at any rate that they *cannot* have any unless this Oxford time is spent in laying the foundations and preparing for the superstructure. My main desire is to leave Oxford very much wiser than I entered it: to be able to give an opinion and state an argument: to see the right and wrong of things and to look at everything from a temperate and manly point-of-view.[17]

Oxford gave him plenty of practice at stating an argument, at the Union, the Canning Club and the college debating society. In these diverse forums he soon established himself as the leading Conservative undergraduate of his day and filled one American student's 'ideal of what a young representative of the Conservative and especially the aristocratic party should be'.[18] The convictions he had mentioned to Brett were only slightly modified during his Oxford years. He read and was impressed by radical authors such as J.S. Mill, but they barely influenced his ideas. His conservatism was hereditary and temperamental, a feudal view from Kedleston which merged at Eton with an enthusiastic acceptance of the imperial mission after listening to Sir James Stephen lecture on Britain's dominion in India. At Oxford his views became more sophisticated and more attractive, reflecting Disraeli's creed of paternalism with social reform, national honour with the mandatory vision of empire. But the essentials remained, and remained always. To his contemporaries Curzon seemed both more mature and more rigid than themselves, a man untroubled by the natural doubts and changing ideas of young men. In the opinion of one of them, his mind was 'fixed and completed' at the age of 21.[19] A similar remark was made by Alfred Lyttelton about Brodrick, and perhaps it was true of others of their self-confident generation. But with Curzon it was particularly striking; few people can have experienced so much in their lives while changing so little.

Curzon was never a political intellectual. He cared for the display and workings of politics, for oratory, statesmanship, the practice of government. He was not much interested in the ideas of Tory philosophers. Hume and Burke interested him far less than Pitt or Canning. Principles were more important than ideas, and efficient administration more important than either. At Oxford he reformed the Canning Club, changing it from a slothful gambling society into the 'centre and crown of Conservatism' at the university. Week after week earnest papers on political issues were read and debated by a small group of members; their contributions, recorded by Curzon in the minutes, were later printed privately as a memorial to the efficiency of his two years as secretary. In a paper of his own, 'The Decadence of Parliament', he maintained that the 'legacy of statesmanship', handed down from one generation to another, was in danger of perishing when Disraeli and Gladstone had both gone. Disraeli's death two years later, he said, 'deprived the Conservative Party of the greatest leader it had ever had' and left the Liberals in a position of intellectual superiority. A more surprising position was his support for a tunnel under the English Channel, which he predicted would be completed a hundred years earlier than has proved to be the case. He saw 'no danger, but only good, from an increased contact with continental manners and feeling'.[20] Alarmingly serious though the club may often have seemed, it was capable of lighter moments. Only six members turned up to a meeting that took place during examination time and, as a quorum required seven, they transformed themselves into a claret-drinking whist club. At the end of the evening Curzon rose and 'proposed in an informal manner the health of the inventor of the noble game of whist'.[21]

At first he found the Oxford Union unappealing and had little inclination to speak in its debates. The degraded audience there, he priggishly remarked in his second term, combined vulgarity, bad taste, shocking ignorance and rowdyism.[22] But he grew to like the Union and was soon debating there like a practised parliamentarian; one of his friends recalled that even then he spoke like a prime minister.[23] His early speeches included defences of the government's policy on Afghanistan and of a proposal favouring the restriction of vivisection, as well as incomprehensible opposition to a plan to allow undergraduates from the two newly established women's colleges to use the Union library. In April 1880 he spoke long and well on a motion regretting the Liberal election victory, and a few weeks later he was elected president by a large majority. The following year he defended Oscar Wilde in a farcical incident. The Union library had requested and received an inscribed copy of Wilde's *Poems*, but then had to hand it back to the author when the Union ruled that the poems were plagiarisms. Curzon spoke scornfully against the motion to return the book but failed to save Wilde's sympathizers from a narrow defeat. The aggrieved poet was grateful for his 'chivalrous defence'. 'You are a brick,' he told Curzon. 'Our sweet city with its dreaming towers must not be given entirely over to the Philistines.'[24]

Everyone agreed that Curzon was an eloquent and impressive speaker. Lord Lytton, the former Viceroy of India, told him he had remarkable oratorical ability and predicted a brilliant and probably great career ahead of him. Some people, however, thought his accomplishments rather absurd in someone so young, and one critic noted that he 'exhibited a lamentable tendency to become prolix'. B.H. Sumner, a Balliol colleague, recalled that he had a powerful voice, excellent elocution and an ornate and elaborate style that seemed artificial for a man of his age. 'He spoke copiously, even long, was more inclined to overpower than to persuade, and in repartee or sarcasm was apt to be too heavy-handed.'[25] Concerned about the effect of verbosity on Curzon's future career, Jowett warned him about it a few months before he became a parliamentary candidate for the first time. Having too much to say, said the Master of Balliol, was a most serious fault 'if left uncorrected, because it destroys the impression of weight and of thought and gives the impression, probably very undeserved, of conceit and self-sufficiency'. In Jowett's eyes the fault was evidently left uncorrected, for a few years later he wrote again, urging Curzon to be 'shorter, in speaking, writing, conversation'. Too many words, he maintained, were 'probably the only bar which stands in the way of your rising to eminence'.[26]

Curzon's appearance contrasted awkwardly with his manner. In group photographs at Oxford, among rows of bewhiskered adult heads, the round, clean-shaven face seems by far the youngest. His complexion, later compared to a milkmaid's, was said to be 'so brilliant as to suggest artifice in an older man'. His self-confidence was equally transparent. 'He appeared to be incapable of shyness,' wrote Sumner, and 'his self-possession seemed to near the boundary of self-esteem'.[27] Curzon's expression, memorably described later by Margot Asquith as one of 'enamelled self-assurance', combined with his manner and bearing to give him the reputation of superiority which inspired the famous lines believed to have been written by two Balliol contemporaries, J.D. Mackail and Cecil Spring Rice:

> My name is George Nathaniel Curzon,
> I am a most superior person,
> My cheek is pink, my hair is sleek,
> I dine at Blenheim once a week.

During the years of his ascent Curzon could laugh at the jibe and even use it in his own light verse; in political adversity the 'accursed doggerel', and the boring frequency with which it was quoted, infuriated him. In one particular the accusation of superiority was unfair: unknown to his critics, his stiff bearing was a consequence of the brace he nearly always wore for his spine and not a practical demonstration of pre-eminence. But in other respects Curzon did little to deflect the criticism. 'As far as his demeanour in speech and mode of address went,' thought Sumner, 'it was a fair hit and he brought it on himself.' The impression of arrogance caused resentment even among those who saw behind the haughtiness. G.A. Bliss, his college servant, disliked Curzon's 'very standoffish manner' which he did not experience from other undergraduates. Yet he admitted that the pride was not as bad as it seemed; Curzon was not too standoffish to attend college servants' parties, where he recited verses and danced with the wives.[28]

Had he been as insufferable as the rhyme – and the later reputation – suggest, Curzon would not have been tolerated by a large number of companions whose friendship he retained for thirty or forty years. Had there been nothing to him but pride and politics, he would not have been found so attractive by the women he met in London society and at country-house parties. Nor would he have appealed to Oscar Wilde or his disciple and fellow aesthete, Rennell Rodd. 'I have not got tired yet of hearing Rennell Rodd call you perfect,' Wilde told Curzon in 1881; a few years later he addressed him as 'you brilliant young Coningsby!'[29] Rodd broke with Wilde, whose flouting of conventions was embarrassing for someone starting a diplomatic career, but he remained close to Curzon and later described him as 'always the most loyal and truest of friends'.[30] The frequency with which similar phrases appear in his correspondence testifies to Curzon's attachment to his friends. Another recipient of that loyalty was Dick Farrer, who died of tuberculosis in 1883. Curzon's 'affectionate thoughtfulness', wrote Farrer in a letter opened after his death, had been 'so conspicuous during [his] long illness' that it had greatly helped him in his final months.[31]

Curzon did not acquire his taste for travel until after he left Balliol. Apart from one summer trip with O.B. to see the Passion Play at Oberammergau, the university vacations were spent between London, the country houses of friends and relations, and Kedleston, which his family returned to in 1879 four years after Lady Scarsdale's death. At his old and beloved home he performed in ceremonies such as his coming-of-age, when the tenants and estate workers presented him with a candelabrum and a silver inkstand, and his sister Sophy's marriage, at which she recalled him proposing the bridesmaids' health in 'a little flowery speech'. After the visit to Oberammergau in 1880 he stayed at Blenheim, where he was impressed by the audacity of Lord Randolph Churchill but pronounced Sir Michael Hicks Beach to be 'the most incompetent cabinet minister [he] had ever set eyes on', a ridiculous view which he soon reversed.[32] He then returned to Kedleston where he divided his time between writing a paper for the Canning, learning a part for an amateur theatrical, and 'reducing an abundant crop of hares'. As with others in his circle such as Brodrick, who set out to 'demolish' his partridges which had 'enjoyed too long immunity', there is a rather callous facetiousness in Curzon's descriptions of shooting. This was probably because he did not take the sport very seriously. As one of his closest companions noted a generation later, he had no 'ingrained desire to go out and kill something'.[33] He shot as much from custom as for pleasure and was less enthusiastic than most of his contemporaries. The only protracted excitement he obtained from any form of hunting was tiger shooting in India.

Visits to London, where the family had a house in Wimpole Street, were always convivial. As a child he had been taken on expeditions to the zoo, where he had been shocked by the living conditions of many animals, and to the National Gallery, where his relations had tried to interest him in the dogs and stags of that Victorian hero of the senti- mental, Edwin Landseer. He much preferred, however, 'the gorgeous colours and the tempestuous imagination of Turner'.[34] Painting appealed to Curzon more than any other art except architecture, and he once said his knowledge had been formed by endless visits to Christie's.

In 1879 he took his 'first drink of the cup of society's allurements', a new kind of life which he found 'somewhat hollow, but very attractive, wasteful of time but productive of good' in the shape of interesting friends and acquaintances. He was a frequent attender of dances and went to one fancy dress ball as a Spanish gypsy with a 'rather becoming' costume.[35] By the end of his time at Oxford he had acquired so pro- digious a social life that in the 'season' of 1882 he dined at home only once in the course of a month and went to dances five nights a week.[36] At other times of the year he allowed himself less formal evenings with Balliol friends such as Rodd and Spring Rice. Fortified by a good deal of whisky, the three of them once visited a debating club near Temple Bar with the intention of each making 'a violent speech in a sense diametri- cally opposite to his natural political convictions'. Curzon's subversive eloquence, recalled Rodd, 'so roused the indignation of a medical student that he invited "this pink-cheeked Oxonian" to come out behind the bar and have his head punched'.[37]

At the end of his second year at Balliol, Curzon had gained a First in 'Mods', the first half of the Oxford classical degree, and hoped to repeat the achievement in 'Greats' at the end of his fourth year. Much of his time in the interim had been occupied by politics and other things, but for a man of his intelligence he had worked hard enough to get a First in Greats. In the final examinations he felt he did not do himself justice, writing a certain amount of 'bosh' in his papers on logic and philosophy, but thought his history and translations should have compensated. The news that he had in the end only got a Second was thus 'a reverse of a serious nature', and it was little comfort to learn that the decision had been extremely close. Letters of consolation poured in as if he had suffered a bereavement. Lord Eskdaill sent a message to say he was 'frightfully disgusted with your filthy examiners', while Edward Lyttelton admitted the result was 'a mouldy bore'. More encouraging commiseration came from Alfred Lyttelton who pointed out that Curzon would certainly have got a First if he had denied himself the Union, the Canning and the other enterprises that had earned him 'the name of the most famous Oxonian' of the age. Jowett was also complimentary, advising him to regard the result as an accident, for his industry and ability had merited a First.[38]

The letters from friends had some effect. Curzon had previously thought a Second would be so humiliating and make his life so insupportable that he would have to retire somewhere and hide his face from the world. That so many friends had written to say the result was not important and that their opinion of him had not changed, restored some confidence. But he still felt that in the public eye he was 'stamped with the brand of respectable mediocrity' and allegedly threatened to devote the rest of his life 'to showing the examiners that they had made a mistake'.[39] His reactions were similar to those earlier feelings he had experienced after clashing with masters at Eton. Then he had sought to demonstrate that his teachers were wrong by winning prizes without attending their classes. Now he determined to efface the memory of the Second by winning two of the hardest Oxford prizes and by gaining a fellowship to the college of All Souls. In 1881 he had come second in the Lothian History Prize with an essay on the Polish king, John Sobieski, and, after leaving Oxford in the autumn of the following year, he decided to make another attempt. This time, however, it was to be a secret because, in the event of failure, he could not bear to publish 'to the world another rebuff'.[40]

The subject for the 1883 prize was the Byzantine Emperor Justinian, a more congenial subject for a classical student. The main problems were time and suitable conditions in which to write. Curzon had long before arranged to go on a winter tour of the eastern Mediterranean with Welldon, Edward Lyttelton and the Eton master F.W. Cornish. He also had various social obligations to attend, such as Lord Cranborne's coming-of-age at Hatfield and a visit to Eaton Hall, the Duke of Westminster's house in Cheshire, which he thought vulgar and tawdry, 'a most regal but most disappointing pile'.[41] He had thus barely a fortnight in London to read about Justinian before setting out for Italy in December. Armed with his notes, a volume of Gibbon and a French edition of the anecdotes of Procopius, he then composed the essay in various trains, inns and steamers between Italy and Egypt.

Apart from writing his essay, Curzon kept a diary, the first of many enormously long and detailed journals of his travels over the next twelve years. As with its successors, this one reveals a remarkable knowledge of the places visited and an insatiable desire to see anything of historic or artistic interest. It also contains grandiloquent descriptions of landscapes and rather less resounding reports of their inhabitants. Northern Italy was majestic, 'every fresh sweep discloses to the foreigner, however fastidious, some spot where it would be no penalty to dwell'. Rome was not so much appreciated, for the museums were closed and Michelangelo's buildings on the Capitoline prevented him from picturing the hill in its imperial era. As for Naples, he wrote to his friend Lord Wolmer, it was 'a town of divine situation, unutterable blackguardism . . . and inconceivable stinks'. It also provided another sightseeing disappointment. Although the party spent the greater part of a day in Naples, such was 'the cursed rascality of its inhabitants and their fiendish proficiency in the arts of deception', that, by the time they had been prevented from stealing the luggage, the museum had closed.[42]

The four of them sailed from Naples to Athens, 'being horribly tossed the whole way'. Cornish, the only one who remained upright, flitted between the cabins of his suffering friends. 'What do you think George Curzon is doing?' he asked Lyttelton. 'He is sitting up in his bunk writing an Oxford prize essay on Justinian, in between his paroxysms.' Welldon groaned and said, 'A man who can do that can do anything.'[43]

Lyttelton, whose aunt was married to Gladstone, emerged for that reason as the protagonist of the Greek tour. Since becoming Prime Minister for the second time in 1880, Gladstone had renounced Disraeli's pro-Turkish policy and secured the cession of Thessaly to Greece. His nephew's visit was thus very welcome to the Greek Prime Minister, who telegraphed the news to each place on the itinerary:

whole villages duly turned out to cheer him, and frequent deputations arrived to pay homage to a relative of '*le grand* Gladstone'. Curzon described the ludicrous scene with Lyttelton in 'knickerbockers and fives shoes . . . bowing and making politic speeches in mediocre and metallic French', and the other three in the background 'trying to look honoured and suppressing convulsions of laughter'.[44]

In Athens Curzon made a prolonged inspection of the monuments of the Acropolis and found it difficult to decide whether Lord Elgin was right to have removed the Marbles from the Parthenon frieze. In the end he conceded that, while technically they should not have been taken, especially with such 'extreme and unpardonable carelessness', Elgin had been justified by the Greeks' disregard for their monuments and by the likelihood of the Acropolis becoming a military target in a future war. Although Curzon's main interest was in the Greeks' classical past, he also made notes on the country's present inhabitants. Before the trip, he admitted, no one had been less of a Philhellene than himself, but the character of the people had changed his views. They were 'a fine stalwart lot' who demonstrated 'great enthusiasm for Greece as their country and for England as their benefactress', but he found the rural population more masculine and attractive than the 'keen, versatile and as a rule unscrupulous' citizens of the towns. The Greeks struck him as a democratic people, with many of the qualities necessary for national development, but he believed they had been too recently released from Turkish oppression to be ready for representative government. In addition, the women still occupied far too low a position in society: their status, he thought, should have improved somewhat since 440 BC.

Christmas lunch was eaten at Marathon and New Year's Day spent at Delphi. Shortly afterwards Curzon left his companions, who had to return to England, and sailed to Egypt. After a tiresome and uncomfortable voyage, he arrived at Alexandria and found little to impress him. The only interesting thing about the city was the state of its fortifications after their bombardment by the British fleet the year before: the place was 'worth visiting to observe the effect of modern artillery', but two or three hours were ample to see the rest of the town. Upper Egypt was more rewarding. Taking a Cook's steamer up the Nile, he filled his diary with notes on the excavations of temples. As always he was fascinated not only by the buildings but also by their construction; at Abu Simbel he recorded his amazement at the elevation of the Colossus of Rameses II. Edfou alone was 'worth a visit to Egypt', and the temple of Karnak was 'the most wonderful block of ruins in the world'. But his strongest impression of the Nile was 'the sense of the unchanged and as it seems unchangeable life and character of the people'. He thought they were the same as in the times of the Pharaohs and doubted whether they would ever be civilized. Yet at Luxor he entered a school where the children were studying the Old Testament in English and offered to examine them. Their answers 'of tolerable correctness in tolerable English' appeared to him 'a remarkable instance of what civilisation can do'.[45]

After his return cruise down the Nile he stopped at Cairo to visit mosques and meet senior British officials. He took a puritanical view of the ambience, telling a friend that people seemed 'to carry on in rather an open fashion, but perhaps the warmth of the climate is reflected in that of the affections'.[46] He was also unimpressed by a minister plenipotentiary who liked the company of rowdy young soldiers and amused ladies by standing on his head in his drawing-room. A few days in the city softened his disapproval, and he was soon leading such a full social life that at times he even found sightseeing an effort. Every moment was occupied, he told a friend, hinting that some of the occupation was sexual rather than social. As usual with matters concerning Curzon's private life, the evidence is oblique, but he appears to have visited a brothel and to have described the experience to Rennell Rodd. The letter has disappeared, but in his reply Rodd expressed surprise that 'oriental vice [was] so unattractive' and suggested it may have been 'better managed in private establishments'.[47] A more satisfying encounter took place with the Baroness de Malortie, a beautiful Englishwoman called Lilia. He told Dick Farrer that he 'had got to know her most intimately (this for your *private* ear only)' and counted her as one of his dearest friends. To his diary he admitted that the Baron was 'far from being a dull companion: and in addition to, or fortunately often instead of his own society, gave me that of his beautiful and charming wife'.[48]

It was typical of Curzon that he could not enjoy the seductiveness of Cairo without feeling that his life there had become aimless and unprofitable. 'I experienced a sense of disorganisation,' he wrote, 'almost of disintegration which after a while began to be painful.'[49] It was frustrating also to work on his essay on Justinian, because he could not find the right books in Cairo and had to write to Oxford for important references. At the end of March he escaped to Jaffa and travelled through Palestine into Syria. He did not care for the landscape of the Holy Land and spent most of his time comparing the sites he visited with the events associated with them in the Bible. This led to disappointment and sometimes disgust. The River Jordan turned out to be 'a dirty twisted stream – so beastly we positively could not take a dip'. In Jerusalem he was appalled by both the impostures of the native guides and the superstitious credulity of visiting Christians who swallowed every fictitious site they were shown. 'At Bethlehem of course one is shewn the precise spot where our Lord was born and where the manger stood – also where the shepherds watched their flocks etc.' Similar irritations awaited him in Damascus. On being pointed out the house where Paul was supposed to have lodged after his conversion, he confessed he was unable to take the smallest interest in it or any other allegedly holy spots since he could not for a moment believe in their authenticity.[50]

The temples of Baalbek were the best things he saw after Egypt. As with the Parthenon and Karnak, he had the luck to see them 'under the light of a splendid moon' and later could say, like Shelley's Alastor, that he had seen 'Athens and Tyre and Baalbec, and the waste / Where stood Jerusalem.' After four months of intensive sightseeing it was rather a relief to find that Damascus had comparatively few ancient monuments. He found it exciting, nevertheless, to be 'among the people of the Arabian nights' in the most oriental place he had seen, 'a city of flowing water, green gardens and howling fanatics'. They were 'the best-looking set of townsfolk' he had ever seen. Like most Englishmen of his era who wandered in Arab lands, he preferred the desert to the cultivated areas, the oasis towns to the Levantine 'fleshpots', the unfettered Bedouin to the haggling merchants of the bazaars. The Syrian women were 'not dirty and squalid as at Cairo' but displayed 'big laughing eyes and clear complexions from behind their veils'; their sons did not have 'a regiment of flies camping in each eye' but were handsome enough to 'have satisfied even the ancient Greeks'. As for the men, they were 'fine stalwart bronzed figures' without 'the hangdog look of an experienced Asiatic scoundrel'.[51]

Curzon enjoyed his first taste of camp life in spite of various discomforts: insects in his bed, animals tethered outside his tent, and 'the irrepressible loquacity' of the muleteers who seemed to do all their talking at night, combined to hinder his sleep. Yet the overall experience of the Holy Land disappointed him. He had expected to find some spiritual benefit but was unable to shut out the present, to forget his wretched surroundings and find the solitude to ponder the truths of Christianity. 'It was always an effort calling up the past and remembering that the ground one stood upon was holy because it had been trodden by God himself.' Indeed, the effort required even to imagine 'the fusion of Godhead and Manhead' in that place was almost too much for him.[52] In one of his rare references to his own religious beliefs, he admitted he felt

> no sense of being a better Christian on leaving Palestine than on entering it. One has a kind of vague floating idea beforehand that a tour of the Holy Land, to the birthplace, the home, the scene of the death of Christ will bring with it a spiritual reawakening, a stirring of torpid pulses, a kindling of dormant fires . . . I can detect no moral influence as resulting from my tour of Palestine . . . I do not find it any easier after visiting the country and dwelling place of Christ to live more like Christ.[53]

Curzon travelled home through Turkey, visiting Smyrna, where he had to deal with 'offensive and insolent' officials, Troy, where he spent much time contemplating the authenticity of different sites, and Constantinople, which he thought 'a unique and noble picture, a Queen among the capitals of the world'. In spite of 'all the villainy of its people', he felt he was once again 'within the pale of civilisation'. By the middle of May he had reached Budapest to find a copy of *The Times* containing a satisfying announcement. The essay on Justinian, completed and despatched to Oxford some weeks earlier, had won the Lothian prize. Considering the circumstances in which it had been written, he concluded that his competitors must have been 'a set of duffers'.[54]

Curzon regarded the success as insufficient to redeem the failure in Greats and looked around for new conquests. Returning to England in June, he soon began to prepare for the examination to All Souls, the Oxford college which elects Fellows but not undergraduates. After six months abroad it must have been tempting to enjoy a leisurely social life in London and the country; Oscar Wilde wanted to visit him, smoke cigarettes and hear about the East.[55] But Curzon, dissuaded by Jowett and Farrer from taking the All Souls examination in 1882, was determined to become one of the two Prize Fellows of 1883. He allowed himself a short London holiday in June and then retired to Kedleston where he attempted to read a volume of Gibbon every two days. Apart from a weekend in Cheshire, he refused all other invitations, including the St Leger meeting at Doncaster and Lord Weymouth's coming-of-age at Longleat. By October he was in London again, still working hard but increasingly discouraged by his prospects of success. It seemed absurd, he reflected, to try to attain a knowledge of the entire range of history in three months and to compete with people who had been studying the subject for years. Although he had read a lot, he told Brodrick, many of the necessary books remained untouched on his shelves, and he doubted whether it was worthwhile even going to Oxford to take the exam. Doubtless he was underplaying his chances so as to dampen his friends' expectations. But in the event he did go and at the beginning of November was elected, together with the future historian, Charles Oman.

There were good reasons for becoming a Fellow of All Souls, for the college offered him a comfortable base and a stimulating environment from which he could pursue the next steps in his career. But there was no point in subjecting himself to the equally arduous labour needed to win the Arnold, a prize awarded annually for an essay of book length. He entered in a spirit of pure competitiveness after seeing another Balliol man, Anthony Hope Hawkins, hard at work in the Bodleian Library. Assuming, wrongly as it turned out, that Hawkins, the future author of *The Prisoner of Zenda*, was studying for the Arnold, Curzon was determined to thwart him; he had defeated him in the Lothian and would do so again. At the beginning of 1884 he thus retired to his father's London house in Wimpole Street and began research on the life of Sir Thomas More. Each day he went to the British Museum and studied in the Reading Room from 11.15 a.m. until 8 in the evening; it was, he recalled , 'a perfect haven of Elysian study and delight'. He then relaxed over a half-crown dinner at the Horse Shoe Tavern in Tottenham Court Road, spent half an hour at the Oxford Music Hall, and was at his desk in Wimpole Street by ten o'clock. For the next six or seven hours he wrote, to the great inconvenience of the old housemaid who complained to Lord Scarsdale about having to make him so many cups of tea. Curzon eventually completed his essay on the day of the deadline, travelled up to Oxford and delivered it to Old Schools as midnight struck. By his own account, he apologized to the janitor for waking him up and informed him it was the winning essay. How the janitor reacted to such self-confident brinkmanship is not recorded, but the arrogance turned out to be justified by the result.[56]

4

Twin Passions: 'Women and Work',
1882–1885

———❖———

POLITICS WERE GEORGE CURZON's only full-time professional ambition. There is no evidence that he ever considered some other career, no trace of schoolboy fantasies that he might become an engine-driver or a policeman or a great general. Even if Brodrick's description of Curzon's post-Eton period as a 'brief interval' before the Cabinet was a jocular exaggeration, the Oxford years were planned as a preparation for government and their successors as an advance to the House of Commons and high office. His reputation as the outstanding Conservative at the university was such that he was already wanted on the Opposition backbenches. 'We are a very motley lot,' wrote Brodrick, who had been elected for West Surrey in 1880, dismissing his colleagues as 'far too many eldest sons and dunderheads'. And a few months later, in Curzon's final year at Balliol, he told him it was ' a wonderful feat to achieve – to be wished for in the House before you have left Oxford'.[1]

As a youth Curzon often visited the House of Commons to listen to debates from the gallery. Although he disagreed with Gladstone on almost every issue, in later life he regarded him as the greatest statesman of the age and 'the foremost orator of the last half-century'. Disraeli, whom he heard in the House of Lords as well as in the Commons, was also a compelling speaker, but a rhetorician and an actor rather than an orator. After their deaths, Curzon later remarked, the traditions of parliamentary speaking had been maintained by Lord Salisbury, Lord Rosebery and Lord Hugh Cecil, but the art of oratory had declined. Various factors, such as the pressure of legislation and the increase in party discipline, had circumscribed the field of the orator. 'We see this decline of oratorical furniture in the rapid diminution of quotation and literary allusion in the speeches of the day': during his years in the House of Commons he heard only two Greek quotations – both from Balliol men. He lamented also that the use of imagery and alliteration was disappearing along with 'phrase-making' and 'the faculty of repartee'.[2] If Curzon felt nostalgia for the parliamentary eloquence of mid-Victorian Britain, it was not surprising, for his own brand of oratory belonged to it.

The student of Parliament was also an assiduous cultivator of influential contacts and from Oxford visited several of the great political country houses of England. Just before taking the All Souls examination he went to Knowsley, the home of Lord Derby, Disraeli's former Foreign Secretary who had changed sides and was about to serve as Gladstone's Secretary of State for the Colonies. He was several times at Hatfield as a guest of Lord Cranborne, whose father, the Marquess of Salisbury, led the Conservatives in the House of Lords. And if he did not, as the rhyme suggests, dine at Blenheim every week, he went there quite often to see Lord Randolph Churchill, the mordant and unpredictable MP for Woodstock. Curzon admired Churchill, in spite of his rudeness and inconsistency, and spoke on his behalf at a political meeting. When Lord Randolph first contemplated leaving Woodstock to fight a Birmingham constituency, he advised the local committee to invite Curzon to stand in his place.[3]

George Curzon's progress to Parliament, however, was not a single-minded advance in which he devoted all his time to politics. He realized that if he wanted to become an expert on foreign affairs he needed to travel, and that both as a traveller and as a Member of Parliament he would have to earn some money. MPs were still unpaid – he believed they should remain so – and Lord Scarsdale's allowance of £1,000 a year was inadequate to fund either his journeys abroad or a life at Westminster. Journalism was the most obvious profession that could be combined with travel and politics, and was more suited to Curzon's talents than any form of business would have been. As early as 1881 he was writing articles in the Oxford vacations on the topography of Derbyshire for the *Derby Mercury*. A few years later he graduated to the national quarterlies, and for his travels in Asia he arranged to write articles for *The Times* and other newspapers.

The pursuit of politics did not entail the neglect of his social and private lives. No one, recalled Margot Asquith many years later, 'could turn with more elasticity from work to play than George Curzon'. Some of those who saw him at play found it difficult to believe he did any work at all. One of four Tennant sisters romantically attracted to Curzon in the 1880s, Margot told him he was 'born to be bright and gay and make others the same' – a view distinctly at odds with the traditional image of its subject.[4] Her elder sister Charty, the wife of Lord Ribblesdale, had an even more extraordinary picture of her friend. Writing to him in February 1883, when Curzon was labouring over his Justinian essay on a steamer in the Nile, she confessed that with an effort she could imagine him reading a book. Nevertheless, it was 'of course difficult to realise that the gilded butterfly one sees fluttering about London' could in any way be serious.[5]

The man they described was a popular guest at house parties. He talked brilliantly, wrote playful limericks about the other guests, and excelled at after-dinner word games; afterwards he sent poems or parodies as thank-you letters. His summers in London were crowded with social engagements. 'A tolerably full evening' in June 1883 consisted of dinner with Lord and Lady Wimborne, a play at Drury Lane, a visit to the Salisburys' house in Arlington Street, and a supper party at the Bachelors' Club afterwards. Next day, in spite of his dislike of racing, he accompanied the Salisburys to Ascot. A glance at his engagement book a couple of years later reveals that he went to a dinner party almost every day of the week except Sunday and received three or four other invitations each evening which he had to refuse.[6] His ability to endure such a programme and still work during the day owed much to his self-control. He was 'never self-indulgent', Margot Asquith recalled. 'He neither ate, drank nor smoked too much.'[7] Curzon was indeed fortunate in his relationship with alcohol. He did not need it as a stimulant, it did not affect him when he drank it, and he did not suffer from hangovers afterwards.

Social life was not, however, all flirtation and parties. He dined also at his clubs, White's and the Beefsteak, and, although he rated acting 'low among the artistic faculties', he enjoyed the best plays. He saw Henry Irving and Ellen Terry in their principal roles and declared that Sarah Bernhardt was 'by far the most gifted actress' he ever saw.[8] Despite his own mediocre skills at cricket, the game was a passion for him. He became a member of the Marylebone Cricket Club in 1879 and claimed there was no greater pleasure in the sphere of recreation than watching a good match from the Lord's pavilion on a summer's afternoon: it was vital, he asserted, to watch from behind the bowler's arm, where he could 'follow every turn or thrust of the ball' rather than to sit at right angles where it was impossible 'to see anything of the science of the game'.[9] Until he became Viceroy of India, he accompanied Brodrick almost every year to the Eton and Harrow match, and he also made an effort to go to Lord's when W.G. Grace was playing there. Writing to the *Daily Telegraph* in 1895, he admitted that for twenty years he had invariably turned to the cricket columns of the papers before reading any other news, and that the first item that interested him was the score Dr Grace had made on the previous day.[10]

Curzon's closest friend and confidant during these years was St John Brodrick, who preceded him by three years to Eton and Balliol and by six to the House of Commons. It is difficult now to understand how the solid and heavy-featured Brodrick, in many ways a prototype of Anthony Powell's Widmerpool, managed to be such a friend not only of Curzon but also of Arthur Balfour, the Tennant sisters and many of those who later made up the group known as the Souls. He was sometimes boorish, often tactless, and the possessor of a coarse and plodding sense of humour – characteristics quite alien to the other members of the group. Perhaps he was valued for his loyalty to friends which sometimes took the form of self-abasement before them: in a typical letter to Curzon in 1898 he claimed that it had been 'one of the brightest elements in my life, to work with you and see you gaily flying the fences which I have laboriously climbed'.[11] But even that loyalty was not always welcome because it tended to exhibit itself in frank analyses of his friends' defects. As Balfour once remarked, 'St John pursues us with his malignant fidelity'.[12] Alfred Lyttelton, a close friend who referred to him as 'the Brodder', noticed that this trait became more pronounced as he grew older: his 'sense of the infirmities of character of his friends', he once told Curzon, 'their want of judgment, wisdom – morals – deepens, though his loyalty and kindness of heart repairs some (not all) of the breaches which he makes in our reputations'.[13] As Curzon himself discovered in 1905, the Brodder's loyalty and kindness of heart did not always win through.

In spite of his censorious nature and undoubted respectability, Brodrick was Curzon's curious choice as the man to whom he confided the details of his erratic love life. From his first problems as an undergraduate in 1879 to his marriage in 1895, Curzon requested and received advice about the complications of love from a man who had married very young and appeared to have no similar experiences himself. The women in the correspondence are usually anonymous and not always identifiable, but they probably include most of the upper-class women he was involved with at least until 1887. Perhaps Curzon was aware of the limits of Brodrick's sympathy, for neither his escapades with women from less privileged backgrounds nor his problems with mistresses in the four years before his marriage feature in the letters.

Since his years at Oxford Curzon had been passionate and often reckless in his advances to women. Brodrick told him he realized 'Wilde's ideal of a man bound by many anchors and every shred of them a woman's hair', but also cautioned him for the way in which he subjected women to his fascination.[14] Rapidly becoming a focus for gossip, Curzon was warned by other friends that he was too obviously familiar with women in public. Charty Ribblesdale once playfully accused him of trifling with women's affections, but she was eager to know about his affairs, asking him to write her 'a slight sketch of [his] conquests and repulses with loss' before remembering that he had once told her he had had no experience of rebuffs.[15]

Although he remained a bachelor until the age of 36, Curzon very nearly married while he was still at Oxford. A letter from Brodrick in November 1879 expressed relief that George, who was still only 20, had decided against an engagement which would have fettered his life and caused pain to his father.[16] Whether the girl was the same one he tried to marry the following year is uncertain. In any event, during the Christmas holidays of 1880 he went to stay with Harriet Vernon-Wentworth at her parents' house in Yorkshire and asked her to marry him. The engagement lasted only so long as the information took to reach her parents, who considered the couple far too young and persuaded Harriet to break it off. The girl then seems to have disappeared from Curzon's life, leaving little trace in his papers apart from a long and serious letter, written a few weeks before the engagement, in which she criticized his interpretation of the Passion Play he had seen with Oscar Browning at Oberammergau.[17] An even more shadowy figure of this period was a girl called Selina Beresford who died in November 1880 at the age of 19. The extent of Curzon's attachment to her is unknown, the only evidence for it contained in a poem he wrote somewhat in the manner of 'Heraclitus', which ended with the lines,

> I weep because, till you were dead I feel I did not know,
> Sweet girl that though I loved you, I ever loved you so.[18]

By the time he left Balliol, Curzon had transferred his attentions to married ladies. The woman who consoled him after his exertions in 'Greats' was Alma, daughter of the Duke of Montrose and wife of the Earl of Breadalbane. During July 1882 Curzon was lunching or dining at her house at least twice a week and causing suspicion among his friends about the nature of their relationship. Alma confessed to Brodrick that she preferred Curzon's company to that of anyone in the world. But the confidant was not impressed by his friend's taste. Meeting her at a country-house party, she struck him as very odd, walking and dressing like a man and flirting outrageously with one of the other guests. Chaffing Curzon for being 'an Endymion in real life', Brodrick regarded Lady Breadalbane as 'fresh proof of [his] extraordinary Catholicism in the matter of friends'. In the opinion of a rival, Lady Ribblesdale, Alma was a 'siren' and an 'enchantress' who had stolen his heart.[19]

Although Charty believed he was still worshipping at 'the shrine' of Lady Breadalbane as late as August 1884, by then Curzon had been for some time deeply in love with the recently widowed Lady Grosvenor. Gentle, kind and beautiful, Sibell Grosvenor had appeared in his life towards the end of 1882. Brodrick was informed that they had had a tête-à-tête, had then gone to the theatre and had later begun an affair with the permission of her husband, a fragile epileptic whose chief passion was steam engines. By December a number of people had become suspicious. Curzon was anxious and pleaded with Brodrick never to mention Sibell's name in connection with his own, to 'throw cold water on the idea if anyone else suggests it', and 'to do the part of a true friend in *checking* (even at the cost of perfect accuracy) any rumours which gossip may chance to circulate . . .'[20] A few days later Curzon set off on his trip to Greece with Welldon and Edward Lyttelton and did not see her again until the following summer. As Brodrick predicted, the rumours appear not to have circulated. Visiting the Grosvenors' house at Saighton in Cheshire, Alfred Lyttelton noticed a photograph of Curzon on Sibell's table and wrote to tell him about it with the air of someone imparting unexpected information.[21] In spite of his Egyptian dalliance with the Baroness de Malortie, whose existence was kept from Brodrick, Sibell remained constantly in his thoughts. 'That sweet creature', he informed his confidant from Constantinople, 'has written to me since I left England more regularly than anyone else, home letters included. The fidelity of women is something touching, something amazing.'[22] For Curzon, whose own capacity for fidelity was rather limited, it must have seemed strange indeed.

When he retired to Kedleston in August 1883, the Grosvenors were the only friends permitted to disturb his work for All Souls. 'Our trio met again for a short but delicious spell' at Saighton, he reported, 'one husband being discarded pro tem, the other making himself particularly agreeable'. After bringing them back to stay at Kedleston, he informed Brodrick that bigamy was 'quite an honourable vocation' which had been 'undeservedly looked down upon by the world!'[23] In October he told Sibell he was 'altogether taken up with love of' her,[24] and the following week 'the trio' were together again in London, happily consuming time Curzon had allotted for his final burst of research in the British Museum. Brodrick was by now worried that his friend's whole life was being absorbed by 'the trio' and suggested they had a talk.[25] But Curzon was in too romantic a mood to listen to advice. He gave Sibell a volume of Rossetti's poems inscribed with his personal touch – a parody of the poet's style – and told her he liked to recite '*our* Blessed Damozel' while thinking of her. The following year he presented her with a book of Browning's poems and in 1886 a work of Pater's, each complete with a parody of its author.[26]

By the end of 1883 Curzon was more intensely in love than at any other time in his life. His letters to Sibell are more anguished, gushing, passionate and poetical than those he wrote later to his future wives. He longed for a glance from her, 'a look with those eyes of deepest violet with their pupils dilating like a young fawn – and one touch of that soft cheek, that soft delicious flushing cheek'.[27] Even short separations were unbearable. 'All this week', he told her three days before Christmas, 'I have done nothing but dream of you the whole night long and then when I wake up so great is the disappointment that my morning is one of unhappiness.' His despair was increased by the suspicion that she did not love him as much as he loved her.

> Angel love me in a letter do. You can make me happy by loving me and you would not surely make a human creature, a fellow creature, unhappy. You take all I have, you know you do: you must give me a little in return. Other people ask me to love them and I cannot because you have taken it.

On Christmas Eve he was more cheerful after receiving a present and a letter which seemed to bring her before him in all her 'surpassing charm and loveliness'. But his reflections on her goodness and his love still depressed him.

Sweet woman I pray for you this night that no thorns or briars may hinder
your path through this thorny world but that your simple pure and Godlike
nature may fill all that it meets or touches with its own sweetness and purity
– as it does me – aye and fills me too with a longing that grows weary and that
is beyond the power of words.

As Curzon's passion became more intense, Lord Grosvenor's health
rapidly deteriorated. Sibell wrote daily reports from Saighton, and
Curzon replied with violets and letters of love and sympathy.

I think of him lying there by the fireside in the very bed I was. I cannot bear
to fancy that room a room of death. No Sibell, he shall live. He shall laugh
and play with us again as before . . .[28]

But all of them, including the patient, knew that he would not live, and
by late January he was dead.

A logical consequence of Lord Grosvenor's death would have been
the marriage of his widow to her lover. It was undoubtedly what
Curzon wished and Brodrick expected. But according to the custom of
the times, it was easier to have an affair with a married woman whose
husband was complaisant than with a wealthy widow who found herself
suddenly surrounded by dozens of suitors. Sibell could inspire passion
in others but seems to have experienced little of it herself. Placid by
nature, she had accepted Curzon as a lover yet now hesitated about
sharing her whole life with such a tempestuous and energetic figure. In
the event she prevaricated for nearly three years after her husband's
death, alternately raising and dampening his hopes, before finally
turning him down.

In 1885, at the nadir of the relationship with Sibell Grosvenor, a
rather coded letter from Brodrick welcomed the arrival of something
'so beautiful and elevating' entering Curzon's life just 'when it was
needed – and when it will worthily replace what is gone'.[29] If there was
a new passion at this time she has remained anonymous since, and in
any case she cannot have been very serious because the following year
Curzon made a final effort to change Sibell's mind. Flirtation and
consolation in this difficult period, however, were offered by the
Tennant sisters, the bright, merry and attractive daughters of the
Glaswegian industrialist, Sir Charles Tennant.

Curzon's early advances to Charty Ribblesdale were made almost
simultaneously with those to Alma Breadalbane and Sibell Grosvenor,
but received a cooler response. He sent her flattering letters to which

she replied with unrequested advice and a prohibition on the use of Christian names between them. 'You say you have two passions,' she wrote to him in Egypt, 'and I notice that with your usual gallantry you put "women" before "work".' But the priority was wrong, she declared, and she urged him to change it. After two rather unpromising years, however, she softened and confessed to feelings of jealousy when she heard he was visiting her sisters in Scotland while she was in South Africa. Eventually, in the summer of 1885, she succumbed for a single afternoon, and her husband found out. To Curzon she wrote,

> Though I was miserable at the time at having vexed Tommy with my 'clumsy indiscretion', as he called it, I do not and cannot regret it now, for how should I ever have got to know you as I do now ? I look upon them as three precious hours well spent in which I have gained a blessing, for what greater blessing can there be on this weary earth than a friend who loves one? . . . You love several but I feel proud to be amongst them.[30]

It seems unlikely that the three hours were added to. They remained close friends for many years, but within three months of her 'clumsy indiscretion' she felt 'a horrid conviction' that two women she referred to as 'the white daisy and the fair goddess' had supplanted her in his affections.[31]

Curzon obeyed the social convention that while discreet adultery was permissible, affairs with unmarried girls from the upper classes were not. With each of Charty's unmarried sisters, Laura and Margot – and indeed with the unhappily married Lucy as well – his relationship took the form of *une amitié amoureuse*. In the autumn of 1884 he visited them at Glen, the enormous house Sir Charles had built in the Border hills a few miles from Peebles. Curzon was evidently at his most flirtatious and on the journey south he composed a poem, a parody of Edgar Allan Poe, to the two sisters. Laura lamented his departure. 'Oh George! The sun smiles, the purple is triumphant and the whole glen calls for you, and you are wasting your wit and wisdom on ecclesiastics.'[32] With the vivacious and unconventional Margot the relationship seems to have been uncomplicated: she told him he was much nicer to her than anyone else and often referred to him as the 'dearest and best of friends'. But for the gentler and more charming Laura – whom he later compared to 'one of those ethereal emanations that sometimes flash for a moment from the unseen and disappear again into it, leaving a sense of wonder and enchantment'[33] – his feelings were stronger. Perhaps, following a rebuff from Sibell, he thought of marrying her: an enigmatic letter written after she had married Alfred Lyttelton expressed the hope that nothing she did in the future would ever hurt him again.[34] Whatever she had done to him, Curzon's reaction to her engagement was characteristically generous. He congratulated Alfred on having secured 'the dearest little girl in the United Kingdom', while to Laura he wrote of his sadness that she was lost to him and his joy that 'one of my dearest men friends in the world marries without exception the dearest girl friend I have ever had'.[35]

Curzon's search for a parliamentary constituency began, with no great urgency, soon after he left Balliol. Within a year he had been approached by Conservative committees in several seats in London and the Midlands. He was handicapped, however, by inexperience and lack of money. As early as November 1882 Lord Salisbury recommended him to Preston as a candidate for a by-election, but the local committee, Curzon grumbled to Brodrick, was not interested in 'unknown fledglings'.[36] A greater obstacle was his relative poverty, for the constituency parties expected their candidates not only to pay their election expenses but also to make a large annual contribution to the associations. Still living on Lord Scarsdale's allowance, Curzon was in no position to finance an election campaign.

A solution was eventually found in South Derbyshire, part of the county his ancestors had represented so ineffectually over the centuries. In March 1884 one of the sitting members, Sir Henry Wilmot, announced his retirement at the next election, and Curzon was selected to replace him. Wilmot generously agreed to pay the bulk of the election expenses, contributing £740 while his successor scraped together £305. But in spite of the family connection, which had been allowed to lapse over the previous hundred years, South Derbyshire was a far from ideal constituency. It had been a marginal since the First Reform Bill, and in 1859 the second seat had been won by a single vote. In subsequent years the winning margins had been almost as narrow, and in 1880 the parties had come to an agreement, each providing an unopposed candidate for the two-member constituency. Assured of a contest at the next election, however, Curzon knew it would be a difficult one. The Third Reform Bill, passed after his selection, and the creation of single-member seats, made it more difficult still.

Curzon's adoption took place just after he had completed the eight months of intensive labour required for his successes at All Souls and in the Arnold essay competition. For the first time in many years he had neither an examination to take nor a prize to compete for. So in March 1884 he set out on a long tour of Spain, staying with his Balliol contemporary, Arthur Hardinge, in Madrid, and travelling with him to Toledo and Seville. Continuing alone through Andalusia, he crossed over to Tangier from Gibraltar and returned in a steamer up the east coast of the peninsula to Barcelona. Later he recorded his impressions of Seville, where he saw Lagartijo, one of the greatest of Cordoban bullfighters, perform in Holy Week. Courage, cruelty and skill combined in a spectacle which filled him 'with alternate admiration and disgust'. He was particularly struck by the behaviour of the crowd which heaped frenzied admiration and passionate abuse on both the bulls and the matadors. It all seemed 'very foreign to British ideas of sport'. An English crowd, he reflected, might occasionally barrack a particularly defensive batsman, but it would never hiss a footballer for missing a goal or insult a racehorse for coming last in a race.[37]

In the course of the following twelve months, while he waited impatiently for the general election, Curzon turned to journalism. A perennial collector of heroes, he wrote eulogistic pieces for the *Oxford Review* on two whom he had actually met. He had come across General Gordon in 1883 and considered him to be one of England's most heroic figures. Outraged by Gladstone's subsequent failure to rescue him from Khartoum, Curzon wrote a panegyric comparing him to the Roman soldier-consul, Germanicus. A different type of hero was Tennyson, his favourite poet, from whose 'Tears, idle tears' he used to quote at melancholic or nostalgic moments; he could even do an impersonation of the poet himself reciting the verses. In the summer of 1884 he accompanied Laura Tennant on a visit to Tennyson and stayed the night at his house near Haslemere. Both of them were slightly disappointed by the laureate's appearance. Laura thought him rather dirty and untidy, while Curzon found that his face, 'though noble and striking, had not quite the majesty with which photographs endow it'. He was delighted, however, by Tennyson's reading of his poems, 'a guttural solemn chant in a rolling resonant monotone'.

> Myriads of rivulets hurrying thro' the lawn,
> The moan of doves in immemorial elms,
> And murmuring of innumerable bees.

After intoning these lines from 'The Princess', the poet said they were the most beautiful he had ever written and hoped that one day they would be accepted as some of the most beautiful in the language.[38] Shortly afterwards Curzon described Tennyson in print as

the poet of modern Conservatism, the sweet singer who, with no uncertain sound, and with unrivalled felicity of diction, has proclaimed the articles of that faith, an ordered Progress, a regard for Tradition, a love for Constitutional Freedom, and a defence of the unity and prestige of the Empire.[39]

In the spring of 1885 Curzon embarked upon another European journey, this time to Italy and Tunis. He crossed the Channel with Laura, who was travelling with her mother to buy her wedding dress in Paris, and carried on to Venice where he happily indulged his love of pictures. He was delighted by the works of Carpaccio and Giovanni Bellini, felt an increased respect for Titian, and was struck by the originality and inventiveness of Tintoretto. An assiduous tourist in Padua and Ravenna, he decided he could be 'conscientiously lazy' in Bologna because there was not much to see. 'A relentless tyrant' lurked within him, he noted in his diary, forever forcing him out to climb towers, visit churches and tramp around innumerable galleries, but in Bologna, which he considered to be almost bereft of sights, he allowed himself to relax. On Easter Sunday he lunched in Florence with Ouida, the romantic novelist who later became a friend. While admitting that she was 'courteous and affable to the last degree', his first impression of her was uncharitable. She was 'particularly ugly', he noted, 'the upper part of the head that of a well to do Padre, the lower that of a professional pugilist'. He continued with a priggish denunciation of her character, believing her to be blind to virtue and destitute of moral sense.[40]

From Tuscany he hurried south via Perugia, which he thought the most romantic town he had ever seen, to Rome and Naples, which he had visited two years earlier. Both cities continued to irritate him. He admired the Forum and the Colosseum as representatives of republican and imperial Rome, and he retained 'a most permanent veneration' for the works of Michelangelo. But he was tired of 'all the tawdry fripperies of Papal pomp' and convinced himself that St Peter's was a very inferior building to St Paul's in London. He did not linger in Naples, where he was sure he would be cajoled and swindled by its inhabitants, but crossed to eastern Sicily where he found Etna much more impressive than Vesuvius. He then enjoyed four days in Palermo, which he described with an optimism unshared by other travellers. 'It seems so happy, everything and everyone appear to fare so well', is a curious impression to have received from a city plagued by poverty, harrowed by violence and embittered by the failure of united Italy to address the problems of the south.[41]

Always eager to cross the Mediterranean when he found himself on its northern shore, Curzon sailed over to Tunis. He did not care much for the capital, which he thought had lost its character since the French occupation, but eagerly visited the religious city of Kairouan, where he stayed in a hotel so awful that his two nights there 'might have been spent in one of the subordinate sections of the Ark'. The most interesting aspect of the visit to Tunis was his opinion of the French officials. Considering the contempt he later showed for French colonialism in Asia, it is worth recording his positive view of it in North Africa. 'Coming as conquerors', he noted in his diary, the French 'posed as custodians and friends. They appear to have the knack . . . of conciliating and establishing friendly relations with the natives.'[42]

Some months after his return to England in May, Curzon was reminded of a Sicilian train journey in which he had spent several hours enthusiastically telling his fellow passengers about the history, geography and mythology of the landscape they were passing through. A few days before the general election in the autumn his agent received a telegram inquiring whether the Mr Curzon who was standing for South Derbyshire was the gentleman who had travelled in a first-class railway carriage from Catania to Girgenti on 1 May 1885; if so, the sender would come and vote for him. Canvassing among the Derbyshire miners, Curzon could recall little of that journey until, on entering his agent's office on polling day, he recognized the traveller who had been inspired by his companionship to support him.[43]

5

The Journey to Westminster,
1885–1887

❦

GEORGE CURZON FINALLY had his chance to fight an election in November 1885. Gladstone's government, embarrassed by African setbacks and internal divisions over Ireland, had been defeated over the budget in June and had resigned the following day. But the new electoral registers, required by the recent extension of the franchise, had not been completed, and a general election could not be held before November. Much against his will, Lord Salisbury therefore agreed to form a minority government until the dissolution of Parliament could take place.

The Third Reform Bill, which increased the electorate by about eighty per cent and gave the vote to some two-thirds of the adult male population, was accompanied by a redistribution bill altering the nature of constituencies and redrawing their boundaries. The principle of single-member seats was adopted, and boundary commissions were established to draw up new constituencies of roughly similar size. Overall the reforms gave no particular advantage to either of the main parties. But the enfranchisement bill added several thousand mainly radical workers to the electorate of South Derbyshire and thus effectively ruined the chances of the Conservative candidate.

In his electoral address Curzon condemned 'the melancholy experience of the past five years – with its terrible record of national humiliation, of squandered treasure and of wasted blood'. The Conservatives, he claimed, would 'defend the Constitution of the Realm', 'maintain the integrity of the Empire' and 'undertake the noble and never-ending work of Social Reform'. With a Disraelian flourish he grandly declared that 'the material and moral elevation of the masses as the end of all politics, is an object which I shall ever strive to promote'. Derbyshire's masses, however, proved disappointingly unresponsive. A month before polling day he believed he was ahead in the agricultural districts but would be outvoted by three to one in the more populated area around Burton where his opponent lived. As for the colliers and manufacturers who formed over a third of the electorate, they refused to listen and would vote solidly against him. So certain was he of defeat that he was already planning a journey around the world in the spring.[1]

Nevertheless, he worked tirelessly at his campaign, speaking at no less than sixty-three public meetings but receiving little help from his supporters. Canvassing in the collieries and potteries was a sinister and dispiriting experience. 'You have no conception of the tyranny that prevails,' he told Brodrick. No shopkeeper dared admit he was a Conservative for fear of losing his customers, and even the publicans had to pretend they were Radicals. 'A man who stood up for me the other day at a tavern was knocked down and put on the fire!'[2] The result justified his pessimism. In a poll of just over 10,000 he lost decisively by 2,092, receiving a lower percentage of votes than any Tory candidate for the seat until Labour captured it in 1929. Curzon reacted to his defeat with a defiant gesture, offering to wager that he would address the House of Commons before his opponent, a challenge which the victor, wisely as it turned out, refused.

The national result was more confusing. Gladstone's appeal for a mandate to govern independently of the Irish MPs provoked Parnell to instruct his followers in Britain to vote Conservative, an intervention that probably cost the Liberals some twenty-five seats. Nevertheless, they performed well to return 335 MPs, only a dozen fewer than in their comfortable victory in 1880. The Conservatives won 249 seats, a mere gain of 10, and, together with the 86 Irish MPs, equalled the strength of the Gladstonian forces. Salisbury was thus forced to continue in office until the more logical partnership between Liberals and Irish reasserted itself and voted his Government out.

In the New Year Curzon went to stay at Hatfield, a house he loved and which he regarded as the most quintessentially English in the country. He also had a high opinion of its inhabitants and once remarked that he wished 'there were more Cecils in the world'.[3] For Lord Salisbury, the bowed, bearded, patriarchal figure who presided over a family of talented and argumentative children, his respect had grown since his undergraduate days. Then he had feared that the succession of great statesmen stemming from Pitt was at an end, but personal contact with the Prime Minister changed his view. Salisbury was no longer the 'great master of jibes and flouts and jeers' who had savaged Disraeli, even though he was still capable – especially when discussing the Irish – of oratorical indiscretions. A pessimist, a believer in scientific but not human progress, he remained aloof, religious and highly conservative. But the prematurely venerable figure who mistrusted democracy had revealed himself to be an astute and very practical politician. He had become, in Curzon's view, a 'mellowed and majestic statesman, cautious in his policy, imposing in his reserve'. Moreover, he was an impressive speaker, appearing 'to suggest embodied wisdom . . . the philosopher meditating aloud'. Curzon had been with him at Newport during the election when he had delivered a major speech, lasting one and three-quarter hours, without a single note except a quotation from Joseph Chamberlain.[4]

Among Lord Salisbury's guests that January was Lord Randolph Churchill, the Secretary of State for India. Curzon had long admired the brilliance of his speeches and described him as 'the Rupert of the young Tory bloods from John O'Groats to Land's End', a cavalier who had 'pricked the portentous bubble of Gladstonianism at the moment of its *maximum* and most intolerable inflation'. It was natural that Curzon, who believed in social reform but had no experience of the worlds of commerce or industry, should have been attracted by Churchill's so-called Fourth Party. Aristocratic championship of the working class fitted both his politics and his romantic temperament. But he was not a demagogue and he doubted whether Churchill had a real programme behind his sneering, anti-bourgeois mockery. Lord Randolph's career had prospered, he thought, in spite of 'the most colossal errors of taste and judgment ever perpetrated by a public man'.[5] He was, moreover, an extremely tiresome colleague, judged by Salisbury to be half-mad. At Hatfield in January 1886 Curzon found him 'in rather a distant and haughty mood'. The cordiality of earlier years had vanished. 'Since he has become a great swell, he will scarcely look at his subordinates, and the barest civility is all that one can expect.' His intolerance, Curzon noted, made it impossible to arrange a dinner for him in London because 'four out of five of those who may be asked to the party he describes as asses or bores'.[6]

Another Hatfield guest, destined to influence Curzon's career even more dramatically than Lord Salisbury, was the Prime Minister's nephew, Arthur Balfour. Ten years older than Curzon, this sceptical and amusing intellectual had as yet made little impact on the House of Commons: indeed, his languid pose and lack of robustness had gained him various feminine nicknames at Westminster such as 'Clara', 'Tiger Lily', and 'lisping Hawthorn bird'. But his chief characteristics, his charm, his intellect and his indolence, had been evident since his days at Cambridge, where a contemporary recalled that he was 'not reputed to be a great reader, but to have a wonderful capacity for picking the brains of other people'.[7] At Hatfield Curzon found him 'cynical and charming', describing him in his diary as 'one of the most attractive men in society', and they became close friends. Many years later, when the friendship had soured and each of them seldom saw beyond the faults of the other, Curzon was still able to describe Balfour as 'the acutest mind that has been dedicated to politics during the past century'.[8]

While he had been regarded as a member, although a rather detached one, of the Fourth Party, Balfour had calculated that his career would prosper better with his uncle than with the mercurial and unreliable Churchill. Curzon made the same calculation and offered to work as an unpaid private secretary to the Prime Minister. Lord Salisbury was almost embarrassing in his gratitude, behaving as if he was the recipient of an enormous favour. Curzon was requested to do some research for various speeches and was soon at work in one of his favourite places, the Reading Room of the British Museum. The co-operation, however, was short-lived, because within a few weeks the Government was defeated in Parliament and the party returned to opposition.

In December, after the election, Gladstone had suggested to Salisbury through Balfour that the Conservative Government, with Liberal support, might care to solve the Irish problem by enacting a bill that would satisfy Irish political aspirations. This invitation to break the Conservative Party in order to avoid a Liberal split on the issue was naturally spurned by the Prime Minister. Almost simultaneously Gladstone's son Herbert flew the celebrated 'Hawarden kite', suggesting that his father had been converted to Home Rule – a suggestion the Liberal leader neither refuted nor confirmed – and the Irish MPs abandoned their tactical alliance with the Tories. On 27 January 1886, after a curious display of Conservative incompetence in the Commons, an amendment criticizing the absence of proposals to benefit agricultural workers in the Queen's speech provided the moment for Liberals and Irish to unite and defeat the Government.[9]

'I am sorry we are out,' Curzon noted in his diary, 'for there is an end of my work for Lord Salisbury for the present. He wants very little help when in opposition, being peculiarly self-dependent and personally industrious.'[10] Gladstone's parliamentary victory was equally regretted by Queen Victoria, who told her secretary she wanted it known that she had 'the greatest possible disinclination to take this half-crazy and in many ways ridiculous old man' as prime minister.[11]

In his youth and middle age Gladstone had been able to adapt his views, if not his principles, to the changing circumstances of the century, but old age produced the dogmatism and inflexibility that provoked the Liberal schism over Ireland. He decided to fight for Home Rule in August 1885 during a cruise in the Norwegian fiords and came to see the cause as the principal justification for his return to power. Liberal anxieties were plainly visible: over seventy Members of Parliament had abstained on the amendment that drove out Salisbury, and eighteen, including the principal Whig magnate, Lord Hartington, had voted with the Government. But Gladstone persevered, regardless of the opposition in his party, and formed a cabinet intent on setting up an Irish legislative body. Although Hartington refused to join it, Joseph Chamberlain, the Radical leader whom Gladstone persistently mishandled and misunderstood, became President of the Local Government Board. Only when he had seen the Home Rule proposals a few weeks later did he resign, precipitating the Whig-Radical secession from the Liberals. The bill was introduced in April, and at the end of May fifty followers of Chamberlain and Hartington voted against its Second Reading.

Gladstone had made Ireland the central issue of British politics at a time when a majority of the electorate was strongly opposed to Home Rule. During a decade which saw British control extended to Egypt, Burma and much of Africa, its voluntary surrender in Ireland seemed to many people illogical. Salisbury saw the opportunity and used it to bring about a realignment of British politics which gave the Conservatives, for long the natural party of opposition, a predominance that lasted twenty years. In May he made a speech reminiscent of earlier times in which he declared that the Irish were as incapable of self-government as the Hottentots and suggested they should emigrate to Manitoba. In the House of Commons, where the bill's chief opponent was Churchill, the Liberal rebellion expanded during the spring, and at the beginning of June ninety MPs joined the Conservatives to defeat the Government by 341 votes to 311. Two days later Gladstone decided to appeal to the country.[12]

Since his defeat at South Derbyshire the year before, George Curzon had been searching for another constituency. After approaches from a number of associations, he selected Southport, which the Liberals had won by a narrow majority in 1885. Although the town may have seemed almost as unpromising as Derbyshire, he knew there was a Tory majority among the Lancashire working classes, above all in nearby Liverpool, where the year before Conservatives had won eight of the nine seats; it was the one place in England where Tory democracy, based not on a mystical alliance between the upper and lower classes but on the anti-Irish, anti-temperance Protestant community, actually worked. Once again, however, Curzon had a financial problem. The Southport Conservatives asked him to pay three-quarters of the election expenses as well as make a sizeable annual contribution to the association. Curzon's plea that he could not afford either sum led to a lengthy correspondence with the chairman and a reduction in the requests. In admiration for the style of his campaign, the association later decided to pay his entire election expenses although it still expected a donation and an annual payment of £50.[13]

In his election address Curzon concentrated on the issue of Home Rule, urging the people of Southport to repudiate a policy which 'shatters the authority of Parliament and the Crown, intensifies friction, where it affects to create harmony, between England and Ireland; and if carried, would be a source of danger to the one, and of disaster, social and economic, to the other'. The experience of campaigning was more enjoyable than in the previous year. 'This is a most gentlemanly constituency,' he told Brodrick after the first meetings, 'and so far I have only seen one elector drunk.'[14] The contest was nevertheless a robust one, and he was forced to apologize for an unguarded remark about 'the dregs and refuse of the Liberal Party'. The town's press was divided, the *Southport Visiter* supporting him with enthusiasm, the *Southport Guardian* mocking the presumption of 'this juvenile apprentice' who knew nothing about real life, had no experience of running even a village, and yet considered himself fit 'to manage the affairs of an empire upon whose dominions the sun never sets'. On polling day the Liberal newspaper claimed that even the Tories regarded it as 'absolutely certain' that Curzon would lose.[15] But the swing was going the other way and, in a poll of just under 7,000, he won comfortably with a majority of 461.

Home Rule was rejected by most of the country. The Conservatives made major gains, winning 316 seats, and with the Liberal Unionists of Chamberlain and Hartington they had a majority of 120 over the

Gladstonian Liberals and their Irish allies. A significant aspect of the election was the difference in voting patterns between England and the Celtic fringe: Gladstone lost heavily in England, but his supporters won a majority of seats in Scotland, Wales and Ireland. Nevertheless, the English predominance gave victory to Salisbury and enabled him to set about the composition of his second ministry. As Hartington refused to join him, he formed a purely Conservative cabinet in which Churchill became Chancellor of the Exchequer and Leader of the House of Commons.

At the end of the nineteenth century the full parliamentary session usually began in January, and Lord Salisbury had no desire to bring the date forward. The new Parliament therefore met in August 1886 to complete unfinished business and was prorogued before the end of September. George Curzon, whose contribution to the Southport association had left him without funds to travel abroad, found that for once in his life he had little to do. He went to Bradford for the meeting of the National Union of Conservative Associations and was much praised for a speech on Imperial Federation; he also made speeches at Preston and other towns. But his principal preoccupation at the end of 1886 was the ending of his relationship with Sibell Grosvenor.

It was the second personal blow of the year. In the spring Laura Tennant had died in childbirth eleven months after her marriage to Alfred Lyttelton. Shattered by the loss of one of his greatest friends, Curzon went up to Peeblesshire for the funeral and was moved by the widower's fortitude and the way he talked about his dead wife. Later he wrote him a long letter of condolence in which he quoted the last lines of Tennyson's 'Tears, idle tears', and said that 'among the reasons why we worshipped her was because we knew her to be better and purer than ourselves'. He also wrote of the importance of memory.

> To me, Alf, the surest solace in all affliction, indeed the most stable enjoyment in life, is memory. The present may interest, and the future stimulate, but the one is a worry and the other a dream. On the other hand the past is a great fact which neither trouble nor anxiety can affect – a rock in the wilderness from which, if you invite it, there gushes a never failing stream of healing water.[16]

Alfred Lyttelton replied in the same vein, agreeing that the object of a life like his should be 'not to obliterate memory, but continually to revive it'.[17]

Curzon's untypical moments of depression during this period were usually brought on by his now unrequited love for Sibell Grosvenor. At the end of 1886 he made a last attempt to persuade her to marry him. By then, however, he had acquired a serious rival in George Wyndham, a handsome former Guards officer and future Member of Parliament, a sportsman and literary critic memorably described by T.S. Eliot as an example of a 'peculiar English type, the aristocrat, the Imperialist, the Romantic, riding to hounds across his prose, looking with wonder upon the world as upon a fairyland'.[18] But Curzon still had hopes and, after a visit with Sibell to Oxford in September 1886, he described 'these tranquil interludes amid the shocks of life [as] possibly foretastes of what is to come'. After some function a fortnight later, however, he complained that 'other and newer Georges made such a victim of you that I could scarcely get in a word or a look edgeways, and at times it made me quite mortified and sad'. By October he was desperate, sending an epistle – now lost – which Sibell mentioned to his rival and which Wyndham considered 'the most selfish letter' he had ever heard of.[19]

In early November Sibell agreed to marry George Wyndham, but because of the opposition of her former father-in-law, the Duke of Westminster, the engagement was not announced until the following month. Devastated by the news, Curzon wrote miserably to his former mistress,

And so the end has come, and you have done what I always felt and said you would some day do, *viz*, take the happiness out of my life. You have a right to do this of course: you gave and you can take away . . . I cannot write this without emotion: my tears are falling now on the blotting paper as I write. The taking out of a man's life of that which he has grown to regard as a treasure and core of his being is not accomplished without a pang. And yet I would not make you sad in what I hope and presume is your gladness. I do not want my last letter to you to be one of bitterness or reproach. Let me therefore say on this last time that I bless you for all the marvellous and most beautiful happiness which you have given me. For nearly eight years you have been more to me than anyone else. You have given me thoughts and feelings and emotions – aye – and hours and hours of life which I can never forget till I die.[20]

Generally magnanimous in personal relationships, Curzon felt no resentment towards his opponent. 'I must say I like George Wyndham immensely,' he told Brodrick; 'however much I may mourn for her I can bear no tinge of animosity against him.'[21] A few days after the announcement, the two men met at a dance and, according to Wyndham, got on 'capitally well'. The successful suitor hoped Curzon realized how he liked and admired him for his 'perfect manners and good fellowship to me'.[22] But self-pity was as much a characteristic of Curzon's as magnanimity, and on Christmas Eve, as he lay ill in bed, he wrote asking Sibell to think of him during his 'miserable and solitary Christmas with no thoughts but memories and no relief but tears. I think of you blessed and happy and all my heart is full of joy that others are not suffering as I do, and that there are angels among the living as well as among the dead.'[23] Writing on the same day to Brodrick, however, he was more philosophical and admitted he had made mistakes with which his correspondent was familiar. He felt 'great sorrow' but confessed that if the cards had gone wrong, it was 'as you know entirely my own fault. I played my own hand, ran the risks and have lost with my eyes open.' He would now settle down to celibacy, he added unconvincingly, and end up like Arthur Balfour.[24]

There was fortunately enough political excitement to keep him from brooding too long. Lord Randolph Churchill had spent the first five months of the Conservative Government quarrelling with his colleagues, and the week before Christmas he resigned on the issue of military expenditure. As Chamberlain put it, he had resigned once too often and on the wrong subject, and in any case had not meant his resignation to be taken seriously.[25] His mind unhinged by sickness, Churchill believed himself to be indispensable. But Salisbury was delighted to let him go and appointed a more tractable chancellor in George Goschen. Curzon was staying at Hatfield when the resignation became public and witnessed 'the thanksgivings and hosannahs' that accompanied it. He realized that Churchill had acted in a fit of selfish temper and that the Prime Minister would not forgive him. Lady Salisbury was outspoken in her relief, declaring that 'an open enemy is better than a false friend'.[26]

Curzon spent Christmas at Panshanger, the Hertfordshire home of Lord and Lady Cowper, and then went to Southport where he delivered five speeches in a week. He found his supporters there 'more exacting than words can describe' but was gratified by their enthusiasm and by the diamond pin a working-men's association gave him for his birthday. Since his election the seat had cost him nearly £200 in subscriptions and railway journeys, and he now felt 'a veritable pauper' seeking London lodgings in 'some unambitious quarter near Piccadilly'.[27] Eventually he rented rooms in St James's Place – not exactly a pauper's haunt – and furnished them with chairs borrowed from his father. While he waited to make his parliamentary début, he was elected to the Carlton, the Tory politicians' club. Balfour commiserated with him. It was 'a beastly club, infested by the worst of the species *viz* the bore political', but he thought Curzon was right to join. 'It must be accepted, like late hours and constituents, as a necessary, though disagreeable, accompaniment of a political career.'[28]

George Curzon made his maiden speech in the debate on the Address on the last day of January 1887. It was an impressive performance, although perhaps too presumptuous for a début, for on these occasions the House of Commons is more indulgent of nervous novices than of self-assured and precocious eloquence. He devoted the first part of his speech to ticking off previous speakers and the second to ticking off the Irish. The Radical MP Charles Bradlaugh was berated for 'precipitancy and ignorance', Lord Randolph Churchill was admonished for the 'undesirable metaphor' he had used in describing the Liberal Unionists as 'a political crutch' for the Tories, and Mr Gladstone, who had once held three posts at the same time, was accused of hypocrisy for having criticized Lord Salisbury's simultaneous tenure of the Foreign Office and the premiership. A fourth speaker, an unfortunate MP from Cornwall, was then disparaged for making a speech which reminded Curzon of the Commination Service read on the first day of Lent. The crescendo came with an attack on Home Rule and the Irish nationalists' 'Plan of Campaign'. Why, he wondered, did Parnell's men speak so forcefully about the misery of Irish tenants when they had remained silent about the greater miseries suffered under Gladstone's rule? And why did they protest about only one side's violence, remaining 'as silent as stones' about the Fenian terror, 'the loaded gun, the mutilated animals, and the murdered men and women'?[29]

Henry Labouchere, the veteran Radical MP who, in spite of differences on almost every issue, later acquired respect and a certain liking for Curzon, rose next and congratulated the new member. 'We have seldom heard a more clever and, certainly, seldom a more lively, maiden speech,' he said before observing that the young Tory had 'spoken more in dispraise than in praise . . .' The press reaction was mainly favourable. *The Times* called it 'brilliant', other newspapers described it as 'capital' and a 'decided success', and the *St James' Gazette* deemed it 'very successful' though 'unnecessarily flippant in tone'.[30] Various journalists believed the newcomer would be a second Randolph Churchill, a prediction which would once have delighted him.

But even after this first effort there were reservations about Curzon's approach to the House of Commons, about his tone, his manner, his transparent 'sense of his own great destiny'. In a harsh but understandable verdict a commentator in the *Observer* noted there was something 'almost smug' about the young man whose mission seemed to be 'to save his country and immortalise himself'.

> It was at once amazing and amusing to witness a very young man who looks even younger than his years calmly haranguing the House with a coolness, an assurance, and a fluency which would have done credit to the most experienced and impassive cabinet minister of twenty years' standing . . . Seldom, indeed, if ever, has a young man addressed the House with such consummate ease – with such unconquerable 'cheek'.[31]

Many years later Curzon told the young Winston Churchill he knew his speech had been 'execrable',[32] but that was probably not his view at the time. Certainly, he made little effort to modify the haranguing. In his other speech of the session, delivered in support of Balfour's Irish Crimes Bill in March, he had a second go at the nationalist politicians. For Curzon, Irish MPs were as unworthy of respect as mathematics masters at Eton, and he decided to amuse himself at their expense. After denying John Morley's charge that Conservative MPs despised the Irish people, Curzon conceded that his colleagues were likely to form unfavourable impressions of the Irish character from the exhibitions of it displayed in the House of Commons. Were they 'compelled to form a diagnosis solely from the symptoms seen below the gangway opposite, it might not be a very flattering one'; but fortunately he could 'assure hon. Members from Ireland that a far higher opinion was entertained of their constituents than of themselves . . .' In the serious part of his speech he admitted that wrongs had been inflicted on Ireland by England in the past, but brazenly claimed 'they had been expiated by honest repentance on the part of the present generation, and by an ample atonement on the part of the British Parliament'. In any case, the injuries of the past would be minor compared with those 'which would be inflicted on Ireland by England at the present moment if the British Government allowed all law, Statute law and the moral law, to be trampled underfoot'.[33]

Once again the congratulations of the press were tempered by irritation with his manner, with what the *Daily News* called his 'air of ineffable superiority'. The content of his speech was applauded by the *Whitehall*

Review, but the paper hoped it would be pardoned 'if we tell him there are moments when he is a trifle too priggish, a thought too petulant for the position at which he aims'.[34] Everyone agreed that Curzon's early performances were polished and eloquent, but some found them curiously anaemic. 'He's quite a success,' Sir Edward Grey told a cousin: 'perfect delivery, wonderful command of language, and never dull, added to which the "appearance" so well known to all his friends attracts favourable attention . . .Yet he never makes his opponents feel uncomfortable.'[35] Grey was a good judge, regarded by Gladstone as the best speaker of the younger generation and 'the man with the real parliamentary manner'.[36] For all his skills, Curzon showed early on that he did not have a good parliamentary manner. In spite of his oratorical talents, he lacked both the tact and the judgement to understand the temper of the House of Commons. Nature had made him an administrator but had withheld the parliamentary accompaniment.

6

'Travel with a purpose',
1887–1890

————————◆————————

UNTIL 1887 GEORGE CURZON had travelled only in Europe and in some regions of Africa and Asia along the Mediterranean seaboard. In that year, however, he embarked on a series of much longer journeys which ended only with his marriage in 1895. The nature and purpose of his expeditions changed with their destination. The 'youthful rover' turned into a more earnest observer, the tourist became, in his own words, a traveller with a purpose. Of course he retained a zest for seeing everything, a perennial curiosity which made him study and write about subjects as diverse as waterfalls, Japanese wrestling and the kow-tow. He remained captivated by the charms of the Orient: 'Do we ever escape from the fascination of a turban, or the mystery of the shrouded apparitions that pass for women in the dusty alleys?'[1] But the journeys to the countries of the East were not made primarily to experience that fascination. He visited them in order to study and report on those areas where the future of the British Empire would be decided. He had what he called a 'scheme of Asiatic travel' that would make him the most knowledgeable politician of the age on India and the wide regions which bordered the Subcontinent. The first journey, a hurried circumnavigation of the globe, was something of a reconnaissance. The subsequent expeditions, which took him to Asia in each of the next seven years except 1891, concentrated on specific areas and resulted in a crop of long and authoritative volumes.

Curzon felt mildly guilty about setting off on his first world tour while Parliament was still sitting, but there was little for a backbench supporter of the Government to do in the House of Commons. He had not made another speech since the Irish debate and his last utterance in the Chamber had been in June when he enquired about the 'distressing condition' of unemployed chain-makers in Staffordshire. Accompanied by two friends, he thus embarked on 4 August with an immense amount of baggage including an air cushion donated by Alfred Lyttelton which established itself as an essential item in his luggage for future travels. His companions were Stuart Donaldson, an Eton housemaster, and his old friend J.E.C. Welldon, who had gone with him to Greece and was now Headmaster of Harrow. Their journey was planned and executed with meticulous precision. 'Every item of our tour as mapped out beforehand', Curzon reported from San Francisco, 'has been successfully accomplished.'[2]

They crossed the Atlantic in a slow, uncomfortable, evil-smelling boat, their welfare in the hands of an even more evil-smelling steward. The food was greasy, the service slovenly, and on the 12th Curzon experienced a 'spasm of regret' that he was not spending the day shooting grouse in Scotland. The Canadian cities were also slovenly and disappointing, making it hard for him to appreciate that he was on British soil amid British subjects. But the natural sights were impressive, and his diary of the journey, which runs to 600 pages, contains immensely long descriptions of landscapes. After seeing eastern Canada they crossed the border and travelled via Chicago and Salt Lake City to San Francisco. From there the schoolmasters returned to their schools, Welldon leaving behind a touching poem about the strength of their friendship. Curzon expressed similar feelings. 'It is a privilege to travel with such a man,' he told Brodrick; 'a more unselfish and tonic-like fellow traveller I cannot conceive.'[3]

The Pacific voyage was even more of a trial than the Atlantic crossing. It began in vile weather, which made Curzon, who considered himself an 'excellent and seasoned sailor', very sea-sick. Then it became monotonous, with nothing to see – not even an albatross – and no one to talk to, for there was 'no one on board with a parallel taste or interest'. He conceived a strong dislike for a group of American missionaries who contributed 'about as much excitement to the voyage as would a company of tortoises'. Nor did he sympathize with their purpose. They were not 'self-sacrificing martyrs going out to danger and perhaps death in a distant country' but 'commonplace middle class folk' engaged in a worthless enterprise. Missionary activity, he thought, was usually harmful both to the natives themselves and to the interests of the imperial powers. In China, moreover, there was little chance of success: 'You might as well try to convert a Chinaman as a cocoanut.'[4]

Reading was the principal occupation of both voyages. He had read a good deal of history, particularly for his Oxford prizes, but he was not a great reader of fiction and at the age of 40 confessed that *The Count of Monte Cristo* was the only very long novel he had read from beginning to end.[5] On board ship, however, he devoured a fair amount of literature, alternating between a serious book and a more frivolous one because he found the contrast relieved his brain and brought him 'back fresh to the interrupted repast'. Shortly after sailing from Liverpool, he had begun with Horace, finding him a 'delicious reprobate' and regretting that he had been made to treat him at Eton as a 'solemn business' when in truth he was 'the veriest relaxation'. The first novels he read were less satisfactory, especially *Pendennis*: 'Thackeray's dialogues with the "gentle reader" and soliloquies with himself about the foibles and frailties of mankind' were 'decidedly tedious'. A selection of novelists from Cervantes to George Eliot were sampled during the Pacific crossing, as well as several works on China and India. Thackeray was then given a second chance, which resulted in some bitter-sweet reflections for his reader. After perusing *Esmond*, Curzon wrote to tell Sibell Grosvenor* how closely the character of Lady Castlewood resembled her, 'more closely indeed than any other I remember to have come across in fiction'. The success of his reading programme may have mellowed his disdain for the missionaries and other passengers. At any rate he agreed to participate in an entertainment at the end of the voyage, reciting a poem by Longfellow and giving his imitation of Tennyson's 'deep chested' rendering of 'Tears, idle tears'.[6]

Despite Japanese officials, who appeared to take pleasure in keeping him waiting, Curzon was 'positively charmed' by Tokyo. It was 'a paradise of gardens', and a journey through the streets was like a 'magic lantern with an unending series of slides'. Furthermore, he reported to Sibell, it contained 'such alluring Delilahs that even St Francis might have consented to become a Samson'.[7] Sumo wrestling occupied much of his interest in Japan, and after his return to England he turned his lengthy notes on the subject into an article for the *New Review*. On leaving the country, he told Brodrick he was 'already flushed with the fever of desire to come again', for Japan was a place he could not see too

---

*After her marriage to George Wyndham she preferred to keep her first husband's name.

often. If he found China less attractive, his visit there nevertheless left him with 'a far more favourable opinion of the Chinese' than he had held beforehand. He visited Shanghai, Canton and the Portuguese enclave of Macao, a place of 'dingy dilapidation . . . illustrating so eloquently the decline and fall of a once conquering race'. From Hong Kong he boarded an unpleasant Austrian steamer bound for Colombo in which he spent thirteen days with a single companion, an 'American cad of the first water', whom he felt inclined to push overboard whenever he saw him.[8]

Curzon's first sight of Britain's Asian empire prompted strong feelings of patriotism. 'No Englishman', he noted, 'can land in Hong Kong without feeling a thrill of pride for his nationality. Here is the furthermost Eastern link in that chain of fortresses which from Spain to China girdles half the globe.' Visits to other links were equally gratifying. In Singapore he was 'very much struck by the stamp of men who represent the British Government'. Rome had depended on the calibre of its consuls and proconsuls, and so did Britain. Her officials abroad were 'as able and enlightened a body of men as ever carried or sustained a conquering flag in foreign lands', a view which was somewhat modified during his later command of a good many of them. By contrast with the French who, with their 'tortuous' diplomacy and 'irksome' rule, were not popular in the East, Britain's subject peoples displayed a 'satisfied and grateful acquiescence in our domination'. The Chinese, for example, poured into places where they could live and trade under the British flag, confirming his view not that his countrymen were a superior race but that they had a special genius for government. Their civilizing mission, he convinced himself, was a noble one.[9]

After an enjoyable ten days in Ceylon, travelling at night by bullock cart to remote ruins, he crossed to the mainland and took another boat from Madras to Calcutta. The viceregal city impressed him as 'a fine town, a worthy capital of an Empire that is not far short of the entire size of Europe'. Staying at the Bengal Club overlooking the Maidan, he visited Government House and had lunch with the Viceroy, Lord Dufferin, of whom he formed a rather higher opinion than historians have done since. An enthusiast for colossal scenery, he then went to Darjeeling because he had been told that its view of Kanchenjunga was the finest in the world. It was certainly the most majestic he had seen until then. But elation at Darjeeling was followed by disgust at Benares, especially with the monkey temple and its evidence of animal sacrifice, and he hurried westwards to Agra, Delhi and the North West Frontier.

At Amritsar he succumbed to the traditional British prejudice in favour of the Sikhs, whom he found 'a splendid looking set' of warriors, just as earlier he had conformed to the view that the Bengalis were 'not an inspiring or manly race'. He thought the red sandstone forts of Delhi and Agra 'the two grandest specimens of the architecture of fortification' he had ever beheld, and considered Bombay the most beautiful city in India.[10]

The most poignant and rewarding moment of the entire tour was his visit to 'the pearl of fabrics, the gem of man's handiwork', the Taj Mahal. Of all the buildings he had ever seen, this alone was 'without flaw or blemish, exquisite, irresistible', impossible to criticize, incapable of improvement, 'the most perfect structure in the world'. The mausoleum had a powerful aesthetic and emotional impact on him, and he went three times to gaze at it. The Alhambra in Granada, which he thought the most beautiful Saracenic building in Europe, could not in his view compare with the Taj, and he scoffed at those who tried to disparage it 'by talking of wedding cake smartness'.[11] As he put it to Brodrick,

> The Taj is incomparable, designed like a palace and finished like a jewel – a snow-white emanation starting from a bed of cypresses and backed by a turquoise sky, pure, perfect and unutterably lovely. One feels the same sensation as in gazing at a beautiful woman, one who has that mixture of loveliness and sadness which is essential to the highest beauty.[12]

He always retained this sensual and melancholic love for the building, revisiting it several times as Viceroy and devoting many hours to its restoration. In the miserable aftermath of his resignation, he was able to find some tranquillity and consolation in returning to see it for the last time. 'I have learned', he said eighteen years after his first visit, 'to love this place more than any other spot in India. Here it is always peaceful and always beautiful.'[13]

After half a year's absence, Curzon returned to England in February 1888 at the beginning of the parliamentary session. The following months were dominated by a local government bill providing for the establishment of elected county councils. Curzon disagreed with certain clauses in the bill but played little part in its long passage through Parliament. He was frustrated by the lack of opportunities for a government backbencher and described himself as a member of 'the great silent brigade in the House of Commons that [sits] mute amid a universal babble'.[14] Hoping to establish a name for himself as an expert on Asia, he spent two evenings in the House trying to make a speech in a debate on India. But the Speaker never called him. His principal contribution to the session was a speech in March in favour of reforming the House of Lords. To Labouchere's motion proposing to abolish hereditary membership of the Upper House, Curzon moved an amendment calling for reform and modification of the hereditary principle. It was not true, he declared, that the House of Lords was completely unrepresentative, for it included bishops, law lords, former judges and colonial governors, as well as nearly two hundred men who had once sat in the House of Commons. Nevertheless, he conceded that various interests were barely represented in the Chamber and that the House would benefit from a broadening of its membership.

The speech received acclaim from the press. The *Scotsman* described him as 'by far the most dashing of the young Ministerialists' with 'remarkable aptitude in debate', while the *Observer* declared that no more promising speech had been made by a young member since the early days of Randolph Churchill.[15] After a promise from Lord Salisbury that he would consider a scheme for House of Lords reform, Curzon developed the theme in two articles for the *National Review*. In the first he contrasted the Upper House's debates, performed on a 'lofty plane of courtesy, dignity and decorum', with the unseemly brawls, the 'rancour and vulgarity' of certain speeches, and the 'weeks of aimless and arid palaver' which the House of Commons might devote to a single clause. In his somewhat eccentric view the House of Commons was 'the playground of jesters and the paradise of bores', while the House of Lords extinguished 'the jester by a chilling silence and exterminates the bore by a buzz of sound'. Nevertheless, the composition of the Lords was weighted in favour of property and wealth to the detriment of learning and administrative experience, and the hereditary system should be mitigated so that 'the men of culture, the men of public service, and the men from the colonies' could be brought in. As the eldest son of a peer, Curzon's continued membership of the House of Commons depended on the health of his father, and in the second article he argued that peers should be allowed to choose as well as be chosen. Membership of the House of Lords should be limited to those who had distinguished themselves in some form of public life, yet it should not be made obligatory. If a qualified peer preferred to sit in the Commons, he should be entitled to do so.[16]

The session was punctuated by brief excursions out of London. He spent Easter at Wilton, Lord Pembroke's great house at Salisbury, where he impressed Matthew Arnold, who told him he would 'succeed'.[17] At Whitsun he visited Brittany and the Channel Islands. And at the end of the session he rushed north for the beginning of the grouse season in Perthshire. But he had decided to deny himself a lengthy Scottish season of sport and society. Refusing invitations to several country houses, including the Tennants' home in Peebleshire and Arthur Balfour's mansion at Whittingehame, he arrived at the beginning of September in Southport to give four speeches in two days to enthusiastic audiences. The visit was a diplomatic one for he was about to desert his constituents and his friends for a second purposeful visit to the East.

The new expedition was more serious and intensive than its predecessor. It also had to be considerably shorter because the opening of Parliament had inconveniently been brought forward to the beginning of November. Curzon's objective was to penetrate the khanates of central Asia, to observe the strength of the Russians, and to assess the threat that their galloping expansion posed to the British position in India. He thus became a participant in the 'Great Game', that bizarre and often heroic contest that seemed destined to end in an epic struggle between the world's two largest empires.

He left England on 6 September 1888, accompanied by Rodd and another friend as far as Berlin, and then made his way to St Petersburg in order to acquire introductions for his journey to central Asia. Despite problems with bureaucrats over a permit to visit Transcaspia, he formed a favourable view of the Russians. They were civil and amiable, and he believed their hostility to be directed at Germany rather than Britain. Moreover, their sympathy with France was largely artificial, a necessary corollary to hatred of the Germans. No country in Europe, he decided, had a more healthy contempt for France's 'epicene civilisation' and her 'music hall statesmanship'.[18]

Travelling via Moscow and Georgia, he arrived at Baku in the Caucasus and took a boat across the Caspian Sea. At Uzun Ada on its eastern shore, he boarded a train and sped eastwards to Bokhara along the recently opened Transcaspian Railway. But from Samarkand, then the railway's terminus, he travelled in a horse-drawn tarantass, 'a sorrowful and springless vehicle', to Tashkent, where the Russian Governor of Turkestan had invited him to stay. Throughout the journey he indulged his appetite for detail and his taste for grandiloquent description. The population statistics, the rolling stock, the vegetation of oases, the numbers of camels in Transcaspia, all were meticulously noted. Eastern sunsets, 'incomparable in their tranquil glory', were contrasted with 'the troubled grandeur of our Western skies'; the desert beyond Merv had 'the appearance of a sea of troubled waves, billow succeeding billow in melancholy succession, with the sand driving like spray from their summits, and great smooth-swept troughs lying between, on which the winds leave the imprint of their fingers in wavy indentations just like an ebb-tide on the sea-shore'.[19]

Bokhara made a colourful impression on a traveller perennially fascinated by the Orient. Its men, turbaned and bearded, dressed in long robes which reflected 'the instinctive good taste of the East', were fine-looking and industrious, 'a far less extortionate and rascally lot than their fellows in the marts of Cairo and Stamboul'. As for the town, a Russian protectorate still ruled by its Emir, Curzon considered it 'the most interesting and intact city of the East'. Samarkand may have had 'the noblest public square in the world', but it had declined after twenty years of Russian rule, its bazaars straightened out and its streets 'generally squalid and uninteresting'. Bokhara, however, could still be called 'the Noble', and he rejoiced that he had seen it in 'the twilight epoch of its glory'. In a few years' time, he calculated, there would be electric light along the highways and window-panes in the houses, tea would have been supplanted by Russian beer, and opium supplemented by vodka. Yet he was far from condemning all aspects of Russian influence in central Asia. The conquest had been brutal, the subsequent administration had lacked any moral or enlightened impulse, but order had been imposed on a barbarous region, and the resolute though tolerant government was not unpopular. The Russians were an energetic people destined to greatness, and the British, he thought, should regard their presence in Asia with equanimity and wish them God-speed in their undertaking.[20]

Curzon later acquired a reputation as an alarmist, a confrontationist, an exponent of the 'forward' school of British strategists eager to extend the frontier into Afghanistan and challenge the Russians. This is a distortion. In a typically Curzonian dedication, at once orotund and facetious, he offered the book of the journey 'to the great army of Russophobes who mislead others, and Russophiles whom others mislead': it would be found, he predicted, 'equally disrespectful to the ignoble terrors of the one and the perverse complacency of the others'. In the course of his travels he had been able to interview many

Russians, including generals and senior officers. He knew that the Transcaspian Railway made them 'prodigiously strong' and greatly increased the threat to Persia and Afghanistan. But he did not think they had a clear, single-minded policy which impelled them remorselessly towards India. Despite the many successful invasions from the north which had shaped India's history, he believed that a Russian conquest of the Subcontinent was impossible and would not be attempted. Nevertheless, Britain had to be prepared for the possibility of a diversionary attack launched to dissuade her from interfering with Russia's schemes for Constantinople. British policy should thus be guided by neither jingoist hysteria nor smug complacency but by a determined resolve to 'render any hostile intentions futile, to see that our own position is secure, and our frontier impregnable, and so to guard what is without doubt the noblest trophy of British genius, and the most splendid appanage of the Imperial Crown'.[21] The key to that position, as everyone knew, was Afghanistan.

Nowhere in the world had Victorian foreign policy been less successful than in Afghanistan. Since 1838 it had led to diplomatic disaster and military humiliation on a scale unparalleled elsewhere. As Curzon put it, there had been no 'Afghan Amir whom we have not alternately fought against and caressed, now repudiating and now recognising his sovereignty, now appealing to his subjects as their saviours, now slaughtering them as our foes'.[22] After forty years of blundering, however, the British had produced a master move in the 'Great Game' when in 1880 they offered the empty throne to Abdur Rahman, the legitimate heir who had been living in exile under Russian protection in Samarkand. In February of that year he had returned to his country with Russian rifles, raised the northern tribes in revolt and moved southwards to claim his rights. The rapid offer of the throne, coupled with a promise to withdraw troops from Kabul, and followed by defeat of a rival claimant, gained Britain what she had needed all along, a buffer state run by a strong, subsidized and friendly ruler.[23] There were advocates of the 'forward' policy who, despite the lessons of the past half century, wanted to keep garrisons in Afghanistan; some even wanted to invade central Asia and turn Russia out of her recent conquests. Curzon disparaged such 'infatuated nonsense'. Britain was pledged to defend the Emir against a Russian invasion, but he thought it folly to commit British troops to a defence of the rather nebulous frontier between Afghanistan and the Russians. If Russia seized Herat, he argued in an article in the *National Review*, Britain should retort with an extended movement along the frontier and occupy Kandahar. She should neither embark upon a 'wild goose chase into the Khanates of Asia' nor 'sit twiddling her thumbs upon her Indian threshold'.[24]

It had been the most unleisurely of journeys. By 25 October, seven weeks after leaving London, he was on the Black sea, 'working like a Trojan' during the return journey on a series of sixteen articles he had agreed to write for a syndicate of provincial newspapers. Over the following months they were expanded into a 400-page book. As with Curzon's subsequent works, *Russia in Central Asia in 1889* only appeared after lengthy disputes with the publisher over royalties and matters such as the cost of the illustrations. But when it did reach the bookshops in the autumn of 1889, the reviewers regarded it as a solid and valuable contribution. In *The Times* it was hailed as 'a volume of great and varied interest' and its author congratulated for demonstrating 'how a weighty and instructive volume may be written without detracting in the least degree from its interest'. Applause also came from anti-Conservative papers: the *Star* speculated that if the author had spent as much time studying the social problems of Britain as he had devoted to those of the East, he would undoubtedly have become a member of 'the party of progress'.[25]

Curzon's parliamentary duties remained far from onerous. The Temperance Movement tried to recruit him to the cause of total abstinence, one of its supporters in the Commons assuring him that 'the little personal self-denial that is needed to give up stimulants is far more than made up for in the power of good so gained'.[26] Others put pressure on him to vote for a bill that would close public houses on Sundays. Although illness prevented him from voting on the bill, he would have abstained, he told its supporters, because he believed that local people should decide the matter in their own areas. He also felt that closing the pubs on the day of rest would lead to 'home drinking, the foulest form of alcoholic excess', and added, in more liberal vein, that he was 'anxious where possible to restrict the arbitrary interference of the State' with what he held to be the 'legitimate liberties of English citizens'.[27]

Labouchere's almost annual attempt to abolish hereditary peers prompted Curzon to make another speech on the House of Lords in May 1889. He was more forceful in his criticism of that assembly than in the previous year, confessing that he could not look at the future of an unreformed House without apprehension. Denying that there were many 'black sheep' among the peerage, he admitted that the number of 'piebald sheep' – 'the idler, the spendthrift, and the habitual absentee' – was too large, and argued that their places should be taken by worthier folk. By means of life peerages, he suggested, the House of Lords could be made to represent the middle classes, the labouring classes, the dissenting denominations and every branch of industry and business.[28]

In the same month he clashed with Gladstone over Ireland and shortly afterwards included a mildly disrespectful remark about Mrs Gladstone and her white umbrella in a speech at Hatfield. After Herbert Gladstone had admonished him for the allusion to his mother, Curzon apologized for the discourtesy, explaining that 'in addressing summer afternoon crowds one is apt to fall into thoughtless and ill-advised expressions'.[29] The tone of his speeches had also begun to irritate journalists who made disparaging references to his belief in 'his superiority over the rest of mankind'. 'Another young man of his age', declared the *Political World*, 'would feel some compunction at speaking of Mr Gladstone in the sneering contemptuous way which Mr Curzon affects: in any other youth it would have seemed somewhat bad taste to scoff and jeer at a man almost three times his age.'[30] A further, still uncorrected fault, as Jowett reminded him in the autumn, was his long-windedness.[31]

In addition to politics and authorship, Curzon had embarked on a third career as a part-time businessman. Members of Parliament were then, as now, invited to become directors of companies dealing with subjects with which they were not closely acquainted. Curzon's offers, for instance, included a seat on the board of a company building London's Bakerloo line and a directorship of the Clerical, Medical and General Life Assurance Society. In these cases it is not clear what contribution was expected from the MP for Southport, who made a condition in accepting such jobs that the work would not interfere with his foreign travels. Yet following his appointment to the board of Hadfield's munitions factory in Sheffield, he certainly worked for his emolument. After rapidly becoming an expert on munitions, he wrote a series of letters to Brodrick, now Financial Secretary at the War Office, extolling the merits of its armour-piercing shells. When the military preferred to deal with the Woolwich Arsenal, he implored his friend to support private firms and warned that his company would have to make many workers redundant unless it received fresh orders. But the only one of these directorships for which Curzon was in any way qualified proved a failure. In the spring of 1890, after his journey to Persia, he became a director and shareholder of the Persian Bank Mining Rights Corporation which spent three years trying to develop oil in the Shah's dominions. The company's failure was so complete, however, that for many years afterwards Curzon scoffed at the idea that large quantities of oil could be found in Persia.[32]

The spring and summer of 1889 gave Curzon his usual opportunities for short jaunts to Europe. He spent Easter with Rennell Rodd in Berlin and later stayed in Paris with the Prince de Wagram, a grandson of Napoleon's Chief of Staff, Marshal Berthier. In August he sailed up the Rhine and went on to Bayreuth where, although he had little ear for music, he sat through three of Wagner's operas. But the main objective of his year was another, longer visit to the East, this time to Persia, where Britain and Russia competed for influence over an ancient and decadent country of vital strategic importance. 'I am grieved but not surprised at your preference of Persia to Scotland,' wrote Arthur Balfour, whose ideal holiday consisted of renting rooms in North Berwick and playing one round of golf in the morning and another in the afternoon. 'Travelling is worse than drinking,' he added. 'Take my blessing with you, and come back full of beans, and without another book in embryo. Authorship is killing work.'[33] Curzon did feel a tinge of guilt about abandoning his constituents for the third year running. He had hoped to spend the winter in England, he told his association chairman, and devote himself to Southport, but felt compelled to take the opportunity to visit Persia and continue his study of the central Asian question.[34]

There was no thought of heeding Balfour's advice. Curzon, who did not find authorship as 'killing' as his friend, planned to write an immense work on every aspect of Persia: two volumes in small print totalling 1,300 pages were the result. As before, the book would be preceded by articles written on the spot. But they would no longer appear in papers such as the *Manchester Courier* or the *Sheffield Independent*: this time the editor of *The Times* was prepared to pay £12 10s. for each of the dozen articles. Because the journey was to be longer and more arduous, there also had to be more comprehensive preparations. In central Asia he had spent most of the time in trains, but as Persia had no railway and only two carriageable roads, he would be obliged to travel everywhere on the back of a horse or a mule. Following this experience, he therefore advised later travellers to take, among many other things, two Gladstone bags, an English military saddle, a snaffle and a two-reined bridle, a Norfolk jacket, towels and a folding indiarubber bath ('Persians do not wash in our sense of the term'), a revolver, a Cardigan waistcoat, and tins of Crosse & Blackwell's 'quite excellent' soup. The most important items, however, were a suit of dress clothes and a large flask which he kept in one of his holsters. Commiserating with the teetotaller who had to ride through Persia, he warned that a traveller would be tempting providence if he did not have some restorative at hand.

The most irritating incident of the journey took place in Constantinople on his way out in September 1889. Taking no notice of his parliamentary rank or his courier's red passport from the Foreign Office, Turkish customs officials searched every piece of his baggage, made him pay duty on the watches he had bought as presents for Persian khans, and quickly caused him to lose his temper. Further annoyance awaited him at Tiflis, where he was relieved of his purse, and at Uzun Ada, where the train was delayed because its passengers refused to form queues and tried to bargain over the cost of the tickets. It was with some relief that he left the nineteenth century behind at Ashkhabad and began his experience of 'the peculiar and doleful idiosyncrasies of Persian travel'. His first goal was the holy city of Meshed, where, since he was forbidden to visit the holy sites, he found nothing to interest him except the system of temporary marriages which pilgrims could arrange for their stay there. 'There is probably not a more immoral city in Asia,' he declared. From Meshed he rode to Tehran, a journey of 560 miles without scenic attractions. Almost the only sight worth seeing was the tomb of Omar Khayyám at Nishapur, but even that stood without inscription in a wasteland of weeds.[35]

Curzon was a good traveller, resourceful and resilient. His youthful good humour helped him survive discomfort, cold, squalor and officials, and enabled him to write cheerful accounts of his travails to his friends. Riding seventy-five miles a day, he told them, was tiring and uncomfortable, but his heart was in the thing and he was happy. On his long solitary rides through the northern desert he recited 'The Blessed Damozel' and thought without too much misery of Sibell Grosvenor.[36] The horses on the road to Tehran were 'at a low level of equine mediocrity', emaciated and broken-down, but better mounts transported him further south. The best moment of the day, if travelling by caravan rather than post-horse, was the arrival at the place he had chosen to camp when he could stretch out on a carpet and relax while the samovar was put into action; at such a time a cup of tea seemed the finest drink in the world. He usually cooked his own meals but enjoyed Persian hospitality when it was offered. The food was better, he thought, than in any other oriental country and, although the wine was extremely nasty, sherbet proved a refreshing beverage. Other Persian products were appreciated, especially old ceramics and carpets with their 'imperishable colours, mellowed but uneffaced by time', and he succumbed to the 'exquisite solace' of the Persian water-pipe. Although in England he smoked only one cigarette a day, after dinner, he much enjoyed the tobacco of Shiraz, 'a few perfumed inhalations' sufficing 'to fill the remotest cells of the brain with an Olympian detachment'. And despite his obsession with facts, the calculations of the Nestorian population of Azerbaijan or the leasehold value of the slaughter-houses of Tehran, he was still under the spell of the East. Among the strangest and most powerful memories of the journey were the nocturnal encounters with camel caravans, the sound of the bells, the animals looming out of the darkness, and the procession stalking by before being swallowed up in the night.[37]

The central part of Curzon's journey was his stay in Tehran, where he arrived parched and exhausted, grateful for the glass of champagne proffered by the British Minister. He stayed for two weeks and had audiences with the Shah and numerous officials. The Persian monarch and his entourage emerge from the subsequent book in a slightly better light than its author had intended, because on the eve of its publication Curzon joined the Government. British relations with Persia were difficult in any case and would not have been improved by a minister's description of the Shah's wife as a woman who looked like a melon and wandered about her home in a ballet dress with naked legs. Lord Salisbury therefore requested the censorship of offensive passages. When Curzon replied that what he had written was true and that by oriental standards it was no insult to call a woman melon-shaped, the Prime Minister explained that it would not be 'safe to handle the Shah with the truth and freedom which is permissible and salutary in the case of Mr Gladstone'. Personal references to the lady, known as 'the Glory of the Empire', were thus reduced or removed. So were Curzon's opinions of the Shah as a man 'entirely destitute of military knowledge and ability' who enjoyed a military parade 'much as a child enjoys a Punch and Judy show'.[38] Less damning proclivities, such as a passion for cats and a sense of humour based on puns and practical jokes, were allowed into print.[39]

Curzon recognized that there was a good side to the Shah. He was diligent, patriotic, 'fairly just' and, in spite of occasional instances of cruelty, 'a man of humane disposition'. The Government was secure and respected, commerce had expanded, and the telegraph had been extended to the principal towns. Public works, however, were almost entirely neglected, and administration was still regulated by bribery. Corruption seemed to exist in every corner of the country, allowing all jobs in government and the armed forces to be bought or inherited. Any policy of reform, Curzon believed, would be thwarted by the prevailing national apathy. 'Persia knows well enough that she is weak,' he wrote, 'but at the bottom of her heart she would prefer to be left alone in her weakness.'[40] And in a wise but uncharacteristic reflection at the end of his book, he recognized that this attitude might have merits.

> Above all we must remember that the ways of Orientals are not our ways, nor their thoughts our thoughts. Often when we think them backward and stupid, they think us meddlesome and absurd. The loom of time moves slowly with them, and they care not for high pressure and the roaring of the wheels. Our system may be good for us; but it is neither equally, nor altogether good for them. Satan found it better to reign in hell than to serve in heaven; and the normal Asiatic would sooner be misgoverned by Asiatics than well governed by Europeans.[41]

The 800-mile ride from Tehran to the Gulf gave Curzon the chance to immerse himself in historical and archaeological controversies. He stayed in Isfahan, which possessed 'one of the most imposing piazzas in the world', and enjoyed the spectacle of its bazaars, that 'ever-changing kaleidoscope of the unchanged Orient'. On his journey south he halted to deal with a disputed point about the site of the tomb of Cyrus the Great, upon which he delivered a twenty-page judgement in his subsequent book. Equally detailed treatment was awarded the sculptured tablets of Shapur, but the most astonishing section of the entire work was the eighty-page chapter he devoted to the history and ruins of Persepolis, a subject on which in his opinion almost every previous author had written with unbelievable inaccuracy. No wonder his despairing publisher implored him to curtail some of the 'retrospective details'; and no wonder he refused Curzon's request to publish a third volume consisting entirely of appendices.[42]

The principal objective of the long ride south was the shore of the Persian Gulf, where he wanted to examine the strength of the British position and assess the likelihood of a Russian advance to a warm-water port. From Bushire he visited the head of the Gulf, saw the pearl fishers of Bahrain, and on a visit to Muscat predicted that the Union Jack would one day fly from its towers. Reflecting on the British protectorate over the Gulf, he felt pleased that the pacification of the area and the growth in commerce had been the result of Britain's determination to stamp out piracy. His country had invested so much in the region, he concluded, that its position must not be jeopardized by the challenge of another power. Although he later became aware of the threat from Germany, the most likely danger at that moment came from Russia, whose influence in northern Persia matched Britain's in the south. But whereas the British had little interest in their rival's area of influence, the Russians would clearly benefit from the use of naval facilities in the Persian Gulf. Curzon, obsessed by the need for buffer states between the Tsarist empire and India, thought that any Russian move southward must be countered, partly through closer relations with Persia but ultimately by the threat of military action. Looking back at the history of Anglo-Persian relations, he saw that British policy had been vitiated by what he termed 'the criminal reign of masterly inactivity',[43] and that unless a tougher approach was quickly adopted, Russian influence would soon predominate. The failings of Britain's Persian policy remained to frustrate and infuriate him for many years to come.

7

'The Coming Man',
1890–1895

C<small>URZON DID NOT</small> return from his travels so 'full of beans' as Arthur Balfour had hoped. Indeed he was so exhausted after Persia that his health gave way twice within the next twelve months. Both Westminster and his constituency thus had to resign themselves to sporadic glimpses of the Member for Southport. He made a brief parliamentary appearance in March 1890 to answer another of Labouchere's attacks on the House of Lords, declaring it to be impertinent and preposterous to sit in annual judgement upon a more distinguished chamber; and he made a short speech on the same day appealing for tax relief for lodging-house keepers.[1] But his doctors were worried about his condition and, fearing he might be in the early stages of tuberculosis, ordered him to the Mediterranean.

Early April found him in Cannes, staying with his friends the Wagrams in the Villa Rothschild. The explorer Stanley came to lunch, told Curzon of his meeting with Livingstone, and denounced Gladstone as 'the most dangerous and incompetent of statesmen', quite unfit to rule an empire he had never visited.[2] Sailing from Marseille to Greece, Curzon then stayed with Rennell Rodd in Athens before embarking on a cruise which took him to Thermopylae, Meteora and Constantinople. He returned to London for the season and in September set off on a long tour of the country houses of his Scottish friends. Not until the autumn did he begin serious work on his Persian volumes.

Shunning the distractions of central London, Curzon decided to rent rooms in the southern suburb of Norwood. There he worked all day and for much of the night, stopping only to row on the Crystal Palace lake in the afternoons and to read *The Times* or *The Count of Monte Cristo* during dinner. He was in good health and high spirits, enjoying the isolation and the 'furious exhilaration' of his own society.[3] He also enjoyed the work, although it was arduous, requiring an examination of almost every book written on Persia in any European language over the last five centuries. The most complicated part of his task was the compilation of facts and figures ('in their very essence, an insult to Oriental imagination'): certain lines of the book, he claimed, cost him hours of work and pages of correspondence. Characteristically, he overdid it and prompted his doctors to order him abroad again, this time to Switzerland for two months to 'freeze out any lingering germs'. In advance it seemed 'a dismal prospect' to be stuck 'all alone in a great caravanserai of middle class consumptives, who skate all day and tea and tattle all night'.[4]

The reality was less dismal. Arriving in St Moritz in January 1891, he found the place 'not merely tolerable but in many respects comic and in some exhilarating'. He divided the caravanserai into three groups: a band of 'old grey virgins, comatose matrons and hectic yellow-haired girls' whom he did not get to know, a smaller number of people he became 'reasonably familiar' with, and a few whom he liked so much that he danced with them and asked for their addresses when they left. He took some exercise, tobogganing down the hill from the hotel on to the lake ice, and skating, which he did very badly, admitting he could do 'nothing more than run about on the ice'. Within a month his health had improved, enabling him to report that he was 'rapidly establishing an ascendancy of luck over lung' which would bring him back in April.[5] In the meantime he worked hard on his book but still had time to write parodies of Tennyson and some excruciating doggerel which were published in the *St Moritz Post*. He also wrote to the *Fortnightly Review* about a matter which had exercised him since his visit to Greece the previous May. Horrified by the 'hideous replicas in terracotta' which now defaced the Parthenon as a result of Lord Elgin's removal of the originals, he had suggested to Gladstone that some of the sculptures from the British Museum should be returned to the Acropolis. Discouraged by the old statesman's reply that this would create a precedent for the return of all the Elgin marbles, Curzon now publicly advocated the restitution of some Parthenon relics to their original places on the sacred rock.[6]

The seclusion of Norwood and St Moritz enabled him to make such progress with the Persian book that by early February the first volume was nearly finished. He estimated he had written the equivalent of five hundred pages of print in four months. Work slowed down over the summer but by the beginning of September he was installed once again in Norwood, grinding at 'old Persia, with his panorama of mingled splendour and squalor, the superb ornamental medley of dignity and decay'.[7] Distracted by little more than a Beethoven concert at the Crystal Palace, he galloped through the second volume and reached the final chapter in November. By then, however, the strain had again become too much. On his doctor's advice he cancelled a number of political meetings and went to France for a month's rest which included a breakfast with Oscar Wilde and Wilfrid Blunt in Paris. Wilde told them he was writing a play in French for the Théâtre-Français, and they promised to go and see it when Curzon was Prime Minister.

While in France a laconic letter arrived from Lord Salisbury asking his former secretary whether he was 'disposed to undertake' the under-secretaryship for India which Sir John Gorst's 'migration to the Treasury' had left vacant.[8] Curzon had no hesitation in accepting the offer even though it obliged him to censor his Persian book. The required alterations, however, were much less drastic than the Prime Minister had at first demanded. Instead of omitting or rewriting the long chapter on the Shah and submitting the result to Lord Cross, the Secretary of State for India, the original text was sent to Sir Alfred Lyall, the author of some delightful Anglo-Indian verse and a distinguished veteran of the Indian Civil Service. Lyall's censorship turned out to be extremely mild, requiring the substitution of certain adjectives and sentences rather than the rewriting of long passages. The suggested changes, Curzon told Lord Salisbury, were 'at once considerate to H.M. the Shah, and agreeable' to himself, and he could assure the Prime Minister that 'no feeling of resentment lingers in the bosom of the shorn lamb'.[9] Disputes with the publisher, however, were less harmoniously resolved. T. Norton Longman was horrified by the length of the first volume and asked the author, unsuccessfully, to prune it. On receiving the first instalment of the second, his despair increased, and he begged him to make the remaining chapters as short as possible because the book was already costing far more than he had anticipated. Curzon ignored the request and countered with allegations that the printers were unreasonably slow and that Longman refused to see his point of view. The acrimony continued long after the book had been published, Curzon complaining about Longman's failure to provide detailed information of sales on his royalty statements. The work was not a financial success for either author or publisher. Ten years after its publication, *Persia and the Persian Question* had earned Curzon £406, a sum he dismissed as 'a miserable return'.[10]

Published in May 1892, the book had a generally favourable reception. Some reviewers grumbled that it was too long or too self-important or too fatiguing to read, and a rogue polemic in the *Sunday Sun* declared that with 'uncompromising egotism' and 'detestable prose' Curzon had achieved the remarkable feat of writing a dull book on a most interesting subject. But the detractors were far outnumbered by the volume and quality of the praise. *The Times* applauded 'the enormous amount of patient, accurate, well-directed research', while the *Standard* commended the earnestness of Curzon's study of the East and asserted that his ponderous and elaborate volumes embodied 'all that is known, and nearly everything that is knowable, about modern Persia'. In the *St James' Gazette* the author was congratulated not only for his learning, industry and faculty of exposition, but also for the 'statesman-like impartiality and breadth of view'. It was a book that would 'greatly add to a high and growing reputation'.[11] Curzon was pleased to learn that so many people were reading the book and already regarding it as a classic: Lucy Graham Smith, one of the Tennant sisters, told him she was reading it aloud to her mother while taking the sulphur baths in Harrogate. He was still more delighted by the reviews published later in the year in the journals, although not until he was in the Far East in the winter did he come across *Blackwoods'* verdict that his work was 'incomparably the best book on any Asiatic state in the English language'.[12]

Since his election to Parliament in 1886, Curzon had been only a part-time politician, attending the House of Commons for most of the sessions but speaking seldom. He remained conscientious, however, about his constituency and visited it regularly whenever he was well and in England. Even his solitude in Norwood was interrupted several times by journeys to Southport to make speeches. These were formal party occasions in which he berated the Liberals in a conventional way, especially over Home Rule, and accused them of trying to destroy a constitution which the English had been building for nine hundred years. At Westminster he took a more independent line and in his rare contributions was prepared to criticize the Government over its policies on Asia. While he admired Lord Salisbury's mastery of the House of Lords, he was highly critical of the party leadership in the Commons. In spite of various qualities, W.H. Smith had proved a failure as Leader of the House, unable to inspire his supporters or push legislation smoothly through the Chamber. As early as 1888 Curzon had hoped for Smith's replacement before he gave the entire party 'creeping paralysis'.[13] He even wished for the return of Lord Randolph Churchill and believed the Tories would forgive his 'pranks and peccadilloes' if he reformed himself and studied 'the rudimentary canons of fair play'.[14] In the event Smith remained at his post until his death in October 1891, when he was substituted by Balfour. Although the new Leader of the House claimed he never read the papers and once shirked a function with the Kaiser in order to watch Eton and Harrow play cricket,[15] Balfour had developed into a serious politician in the course of Salisbury's second government. As Chief Secretary for Ireland, he had confounded the Irish nationalists, who had greeted his appointment with derision, and his firm policies after the passing of the Irish Crimes Act prompted his opponents to replace the effeminate nicknames with 'Bloody Balfour'. Curzon was delighted by his colleague's success and by his performances on the front bench after Smith's death. 'Balfour is getting better every day,' he told a friend, 'debates admirably, and is always the gentleman, polished, courteous, magnanimous, statesmanlike'.[16]

In spite of Curzon's frequent absenteeism, he and his friends thought that by 1891 the time had come for him to join the Government. The post he most coveted, the under-secretaryship for Foreign Affairs, fell vacant two months before the job at the India Office when Sir James Fergusson was appointed Postmaster-General. The press assumed the position would go to Curzon, and so did his friends. In fact Lord Salisbury gave the job to J.B. Lowther, explaining to Balfour that he had done so because the Queen had refused to agree to Fergusson's transfer unless she knew the name of his successor. Forced to make a decision on the spot, Salisbury had opted for Lowther because he was a diplomat's son and a good linguist and had been recommended by the dying Smith.[17] Unaware of the circumstances, Curzon was despondent. 'It is a bore', he wrote, 'to lose one of the few things for which I have combined taste and qualification as the chance may not recur.'[18] But his friends expressed greater disappointment than he did. Alfred Lyttelton was incensed by the omission, declaring it to be 'perfectly loathsome that the best men who have studied and become authorities on these subjects should be left out'.[19]

The Indian under-secretaryship, however, was equally congenial and, for a 32-year-old specialist in Asian affairs, a more appropriate position. It was certainly the right place for a man who had decided to dedicate his current book to 'the officials, civil and military, in India, whose hands uphold the noblest fabric yet reared by the genius of a conquering nation'. Curzon's months at the India Office were some of the happiest of his life. He found the routine there absorbing and the work entertaining. Claiming to treat the officials with untypical deference, he was surprised by the 'amazing affability' of 'the old boys there who were authorities and swells' before he had been born.[20] The evidence suggests that he too was appreciated both by the Office and by British officials in India. One frontier officer considered him better informed on Indian subjects than anyone he had ever met.[21] The Permanent Under-Secretary was equally impressed: writing many years later, after he had become an ungenerous critic of Curzon, Sir Arthur Godley recalled that the young Under-Secretary had been excellent, a most efficient representative of the Office in the House of Commons, and 'in every way agreeable and amusing to work with'.[22]

Curzon's first performance at the despatch box was polished, confident, entirely in character. He 'leaned on its lid', reported the *St James' Gazette*, 'as carelessly as if he had been accustomed to stand there all his life; he even slapped the box with the familiarity of an old friend.'[23] In his first major speech a few weeks later, 'he stood at the table, looking like the great Sir Robert Peel, or some statesman of forty years' experience, instead of a young Under-Secretary in his first innings'. If his diction was 'rather Johnsonian', the onlooker noted, the performance was nevertheless clear and convincing.[24] Much of Curzon's time during the session was occupied by answering questions on a range of subjects from famine in Madras to regimental band funds, and replying to the accusations of J.G. Swift MacNeill, the MP for South Donegal, who claimed it was as difficult for natives to get appointments in India as it was for Catholics to gain them in Ireland.[25] His principal responsibility, however, was to steer an amendment bill to the India Councils Act (1861) through the House of Commons.

From the day of his appointment in November 1891, Curzon had been showered with advice about native appointments in India. The sick and elderly Jowett urged him to settle 'the burning question of admitting the Natives to the Governor's Council', but others, including Lord Harris, the Governor of Bombay, recommended caution. Harris, who had once captained the English cricket team against Australia and did much to popularize the sport among Indians, exhorted Curzon to offer 'a bold face' against appointments which the vast majority of Indians did not want.[26] The bill itself was a fairly mild measure, enlarging the legislative councils in India by adding some elected members

and giving them wider powers to criticize and question the governments. Gladstone accepted it in spite of its limitations, but it was too
advanced for Harris who argued that the introduction of the elective
principle would promote divisions among the Indians and make it
impossible to keep them united.[27] Curzon himself, who certainly did
not view the measure as a prelude to parliamentary government, agreed
in principle more with Harris than with Jowett. For the Indians in their
present stage of development, he told the Commons, a representative
system would be 'in the highest degree, premature and unwise'. Lord
Cross, the Secretary of State for India, regarded the bill as 'a safe and
truly conservative measure' and some years afterwards, when his deputy
had become Viceroy, enquired how it had turned out in practice. The
experiment, Curzon replied, had been an 'immense success' which had
transformed the Imperial Legislative Council into a thoroughly representative body. The provincial councils, however, had flourished less
well, because in Bombay and Madras the native members sometimes
tried to emulate the Irish at Westminster by making foolish speeches
and theatrical exits.[28]

Curzon's performance as Under-Secretary added to his reputation at
the same time as it widened the divide between his admirers and his
detractors. While *The Times* and other newspapers predicted a great
career, some publications could see nothing admirable in him at all.
One journal, which scoffed at his speeches for exhibiting 'well-bred
signs of interior pleasure', was repelled by his 'air of perfectly infuriating and absolutely imperturbable conceit'.[29] The *Evening News*
attempted a balanced view, admitting the 'ability and brilliancy' of his
speech on the Second Reading of the India Councils Bill while lamenting the fact that he irritated the House 'by the redundancy of his verbal
ornament and his blissful innocence of anything approaching to
modesty of statement': his arrogance and dogmatism made ordinary
mortals experience a compulsive urge 'to kick him out of sheer envy
and resentment'.[30] It is hard to find reports at this period which do not
stress Curzon's awareness of his own talents or which fail to quote versions of the 'superior person' rhyme, most of them demonstrably inaccurate ('My hair is black, and smooth, and sleek') or pointlessly
exaggerated ('I dine at Blenheim twice a week'). On his appointment to
the India Office, his old antagonist Labouchere advised him to eschew
his current mode of speaking. Employing an image which the *Illustrated
London News* had used to describe John Morley's view of George III, he
urged Curzon to realize he was not 'a divinity addressing black beetles'

when explaining the Indian policy of the Government.[31] In the opinion of his enemies – and some of his friends – the advice was comprehensively neglected.

After Curzon had spent barely half a year as Under-Secretary, the country went to the polls in July 1892 in an election that was not expected to return an enervated Tory Government. Although Salisbury himself had an ambiguous attitude towards the predicted result, his nephew Balfour unequivocally wanted to lose. Remaining in power after the election was something he could neither 'desire nor anticipate', and he looked forward to a long holiday in which to prepare a new edition of his book, *In Defence of Philosophic Doubt* – a publishing event that did not in fact take place for another twenty-eight years.[32] Curzon, however, naturally wanted to win and managed to increase his own majority at Southport. To his electors he once more denounced the iniquities of Home Rule, condemning Liberal policy as one of cowardice, reckless folly and 'certain and culpable failure', because it was bound to lead to civil war. He also stressed his commitment to progressive Conservatism, listing his party's achievements in education, local government and allotments for working men. The one departure from previous manifestos was his acceptance of temperance reform, a change sufficiently pronounced for the Bishop of London to invite him to take charge of the Church of England's temperance bill in the Commons in 1894.[33]

Gladstone, who fought the election on a radical programme he did not really believe in, gained a modest victory. His Liberals won 270 seats, two more than the Conservatives, but his Irish supporters outnumbered Salisbury's Liberal Unionist allies and gave him a majority of about forty. No one was more distressed about the result than Queen Victoria, who considered it 'a defect in our much famed constitution to have to part with an admirable Government like Lord Salisbury's for no question of any importance, or any particular reason, merely on account of the number of votes'. Salisbury's Government resigned in August and, after a doleful meeting between the monarch and the Liberal leader during which each decided the other had become senile, she was obliged to entrust the Empire 'to the shaking hand of an old, wild, incomprehensible man of eighty-two and a half'; on inspecting his Cabinet at Osborne, the Queen found them 'a motley crew to behold' captained by a 'half crazy, half silly' old chieftain. Her opinion of her remarkable Prime Minister never changed: a year later she still regarded him as 'a deluded old fanatic'.[34]

Curzon was also dismayed by the change of government. He had found his Indian work 'entrancing' and had regarded the possibility of defeat as 'heart-rending'. 'I hate leaving my office', he confessed in August, 'just as much as I have loved occupying it.' Electoral defeat did, however, leave him free once more to travel, to make 'one great and final and remote wander'.[35] Two and a half years' confinement to Europe had been too much for him, and within days of leaving office he had embarked from Southampton for another voyage around the world. He was pursued by a letter from Balfour chiding him for his 'inveterate restlessness' and complaining that for six months of the year Curzon was 'quite lost to all the finer feelings of either love or friendship'. To the obsessive golfer of North Berwick, it was incomprehensible that his friend should voluntarily transform himself into an explorer of wildernesses and a 'student of effete civilisations'.[36]

The first half of the journey, westwards to Japan, was tiresome but fast. Offered cheap but luxurious tickets by a German shipping line, Curzon soon regretted his acceptance of the bargain. As usual, he disliked and despised his fellow passengers, most of whom were 'commercial Germans' and middle-class Americans: it was an 'aesthetic distress', he noted in his diary, to be surrounded by so many hideous people. Arriving in the United States, he spent a few days with some friends in Washington before crossing the continent on the Canadian Pacific Railway. By the end of August he was in Vancouver and a fortnight later, one month after leaving England, he reached Japan, the first of the countries he had chosen to study on this journey. His previous travels had resulted in volumes on central Asia and Persia. This expedition was intended to produce two more on the Far East, and a further couple were planned for what he called the Central East, regions bordering India to the north and north-west. They all belonged to his vast and comprehensive project to study the problems of Asia and their implications for British India, which he saw as the true fulcrum of Asian dominion. Although one book did not materialize, a second was aborted by events, and a third emerged much shorter than he had intended, the final achievement – five authoritative volumes totalling over 2,300 pages – established him as the country's leading expert on Asian affairs.

Curzon again enjoyed his stay in Japan, finding the country beautiful and its people attractive and hospitable. His visit was enhanced by the presence of his friend Cecil Spring Rice at the embassy, and by the hospitality of Montague Kirkwood, a legal adviser to the Japanese

Government, whom he had met with his wife Ethel on the Pacific voyage. He accepted Kirkwood's invitation to stay and then began a flirtation with his wife, whom he persuaded to act as his guide among the Shogun's shrines and as his interpreter while hunting for curios in Tokyo markets; on an excursion to some temples he arranged matters so that he would drive alone with Ethel, whom he referred to as 'the Kirkina', while her husband and Spring Rice went by train. Curzon's behaviour on these expeditions can be guessed from the tone of a letter (part of which he destroyed) written six months later by Ethel. Thanking him for a virtually unrecognizable photograph he had sent her, she declared it must have been taken when he had 'been feeling very very good, angelic in fact, and you know you never gave me a chance of seeing you act the goody goody role, did you?' Writing to Spring Rice, Curzon declared that the Far East would always be endeared to him by the memories of his companionship as well as the smiles of 'the Kirkina'. Letters from Spring Rice, written a year after the visit, give the impression that she was pining for him.[37]

Curzon also worked in Japan, interviewing the Prime Minister and other officials, and seeing enough of the country to realize it had a brilliant future: it would soon, he predicted, achieve a technical equality with the Western powers and become 'on a smaller scale, the Britain of the Far East'. His impression of Korea, which he visited in October with Spring Rice, could hardly have been more different. Its capital he found malodorous, its people supine and spiritless, and its military 'not a standing army but a standing joke'.[38] The tour began with a row over transport as soon as they landed. Arguing with an extortionate horse-dealer in front of the local council and a large crowd of onlookers, Curzon's tactics were high- and heavy-handed. He 'got very angry,' Spring Rice noted in his journal, 'explained that he was one of the most important people in England, and that it was a matter of vital importance that he should see the king that week.' When they finally reached Seoul he became diplomatic, taking photographs of the ministers and inviting the Home Secretary to Britain. Encouraged by the King to agree that England was a fine and large country while Korea was a very dirty one, he managed to avoid giving a direct reply.[39]

Although Peking was also extremely dirty, Curzon was mesmerized by its street life, 'a phantasmagoria of excruciating incident, too bewildering to grasp, too aggressive to acquiesce in, too absorbing to escape'. He was fascinated by China, 'a country stupefied with the pride of the past', a nation in need of that modernizing impulse to which Japan, by contrast, had too incontinently yielded. Despite China's present weakness, he believed that she and Britain, sharing a common enemy in Russia, were natural allies, and he regretted that Chinese suspicion of foreigners provided such an obstacle to an alliance. He admitted, however, that the principal cause of that suspicion was the activities of Christian missionaries which he wished to have curtailed. Missionaries everywhere continued to irritate him. Their work was sometimes merely ridiculous, as in the case of American women trying to convert the Japanese to temperance, yet often also dangerous, as in the case of China, where they excited native hostility without achieving any compensatory advantage.[40]

In China, after almost two months in each other's company, Spring Rice parted from Curzon and returned to Japan. 'Springy', noted Curzon in his diary, had been the most amusing and unselfish of travelling companions, and during their time together they had not exchanged a jarring word. The trip had evidently had its entertainments as well as its serious side, for Curzon described his friend as 'equally provided with philosophic reflection and bawdy anecdote', and congratulated him on his sexual as well as his mental agility.[41] Spring Rice was unable to describe his companion as equally unselfish, for Curzon had been demanding throughout, treating the Consular Service as if its principal purpose was to arrange journeys and provide information for people like him. He admitted, however, that Curzon was 'a really splendid man', an excellent traveller and a prodigious worker. A fellow pupil of Oscar Browning, a fellow undergraduate at Balliol, and at one stage a rival for the same girl, Spring Rice felt an admiration for Curzon tinged by envy of his success. After returning to Tokyo, he admitted that Curzon had 'mentally' overtaken him and his contemporaries. Wondering whether his friend was destined for greatness, Spring Rice noted that the quality of mind and the energy that accompanied it were reminiscent of Joseph Chamberlain.[42]

The next stage of the journey, tramping through Annam and Cambodia, was the most arduous. Curzon was delighted by his visits to fading oriental courts and his audiences with dragon-robed monarchs, but there was no one who spoke English, and the French officials were unhelpful and unimpressive. French imperialism in Asia annoyed him because he was sure it stemmed merely from 'schoolboy patriotism' and jealousy of the British position in India.[43] Its representatives in Indo-China, moreover, were like 'hair cutters', lazy, ill-educated and uninterested in foreign affairs. In addition, while they were civil to him personally, they did all in their power to prevent him obtaining useful information and even tried to stop him reading the newspapers. The only consolation, he later recalled, was the knowledge that at the end of each day's journey he could look forward to a bottle of Moët champagne. Such luxury was not to be found on the P & O steamer he boarded after a tour of Siam. The ship had a brand of champagne so second-rate that he had to make do with Chablis and soda water instead.[44]

On returning to England in March 1893, Curzon settled into his routine of parliamentary attendance during the session, followed by a retreat from society to expand his latest *Times* articles into a book, in turn succeeded by interminable quarrels with his publishers about payment and production. As with Persia, he planned to write two volumes but on this occasion to publish the first one as soon as it was completed. In the event only the book dealing with Japan, Korea and China ever appeared; marriage, another journey and his return to office prevented a sequel on Indo-China and Siam from being written. Publication of the first edition of *Problems of the Far East* in the summer of 1894 went reasonably smoothly: Curzon even accepted Longman's recommendation to omit a chapter on Japanese wrestling. But he rejected advice not to employ an agent to bargain with Longman, with the result that this intermediary, Mr Colles, soon embroiled his client in a row which led him to publish a cheaper and revised edition with Constable. Curzon quickly fell out with his new publisher as well, accusing him of dawdling and failing to advertise the book properly. By 1896 he was regretting having taken his agent's advice, and a few years later even Colles realized he had made a mistake and suggested returning to Longman for a new edition.[45]

Problems of the Far East had the good fortune to be published shortly after two of the countries it dealt with had gone to war over the third. This led to increased sales – the book earned him fifty per cent more than *Persia and the Persian Question* – and greater public appreciation of his knowledge and judgement. It also enjoyed considerable success in the United States where one reviewer extolled its author as a 'philosophical scholar, thoughtful traveller, sympathetic man of the world' and the possessor of a 'mind of singular penetration'.[46] In Britain the critics sometimes seemed to be reviewing Curzon's politics and personality rather than his book, but as on previous occasions applause was louder and more widespread than denigration. *Problems of the Far East* is probably the best of his early works. The unmistakable Curzonian resonance, what the *Westminster Gazette* called 'the touch of the Corinthian in his style', pervades a book appropriately dedicated 'to those who believe that the British Empire is, under Providence, the greatest instrument for good that the world has seen and who hold, with the writer, that its work in the Far East is not yet accomplished'. It contains faults common to the age rather than to Curzon, such as superficial judgement of national characteristics, especially when French, but it is well argued, well structured and less crammed with detail than its predecessor. In addition, the Japanese victory over China showed that he had been perceptive in his estimate of the respective strengths of the warring powers.

After his return from the Far East, Curzon spoke more often in the House of Commons. His books and his spell at the India Office had enhanced his reputation, and he was often referred to as 'the coming man' on the Conservative benches, a worthy antagonist of H.H. Asquith and Sir Edward Grey. Although the early 1890s were a particularly turbulent period in his private life,* he worked hard to maintain his reputation as an Asian expert, keeping up an enormous correspondence with consuls and other British officials stationed in the countries he had visited. He gave lectures, published articles, wrote letters to *The Times* and made speeches on all issues affecting Britain's position in Asia. His constant theme was the defence of the empire. Indeed he became so obsessed by his country's Asian dominion that he often seemed to underestimate her other strengths. Seldom referring to Britain's contribution to constitutional or industrial development, he argued that India was the strength and greatness of England, and that only by maintaining that strength would she survive. History would judge Britain by her treatment of India, that great and sacred responsibility which 'for some peculiar and inscrutable reason' had been entrusted to her by Providence. It was only when this fact was understood that people would realize that 'every nerve a man may strain, every energy he may put forward, cannot be devoted to a nobler purpose than keeping tight the cords that hold India to ourselves.'[47]

In his books and speeches of previous years he had concentrated on the Russian menace to India from the north-west. But during his recent journey he had identified another threat, the insidious expansion of French territory to the south-east, which, if unchecked by Britain and pursued in a combined move with the Russians, might present a real

*See next chapter.

danger to India. Between 1893 and 1895 the majority of Curzon's parliamentary interventions dealt with French encroachments in Siam and the feeble response of the British Government. As Siam fell within the orbit of the Indian system, he argued that Britain could not be indifferent to her destiny nor acquiesce in her extinction. Through the weakness of the Liberal Government, the French had been allowed to grab far more of Siam than they had ever expected, and they must now be told that no future encroachments would be tolerated. Regularly in the course of three parliamentary sessions he stood up and asked Grey, the Under-Secretary for Foreign Affairs, for information on Siam, and regularly he received courteous and largely uninformative replies. 'France has behaved criminally,' Curzon told a friend, 'England weakly, Siam foolishly, and when folly, weakness and crime are in competition, it is the last named that as a rule wins'. There was some consolation, however, in the thought that, in the event of war with France, the British would be able – so long as they held the Suez Canal – to pick up the French colonies in Asia.[48]

On domestic issues Curzon's views were less original, less independent and more prejudiced by instinct than his positions on foreign affairs. He spoke twice in the House of Commons against the payment of MPs, arguing that such a move would encourage 'needy, impecunious adventurers' attracted by the salary and prestige of Parliament.[49] He was also opposed to female emancipation, which he regarded as 'the fashionable tomfoolery of the day', and campaigned against the acceptance of women members by the Royal Geographical Society. Claiming that ladies were out of place in a scientific body and that their presence in the Anthropological Society had destroyed its scientific character and value, he succeeded in persuading the RGS to vote narrowly against the admission of women.[50] Less reactionary, however, was his stance on the House of Lords. He continued to advocate the reform of the Upper Chamber and he supported the unsuccessful attempt of Lord Wolmer to remain in the Commons after the death of his father, the Earl of Selborne.

Ireland dominated the session of 1893 from Gladstone's remarkable introduction of his second Home Rule Bill in February until its massive and predictable rejection by the House of Lords in September. The old man's resignation the following spring, pleasing though it was to Queen Victoria, did little to energize a labouring and divided Government. It was said that Henry Campbell-Bannerman was the only member of Lord Rosebery's Cabinet who was on speaking terms with all his colleagues,[51] and the hostility between ministers, particularly between the

Prime Minister and his Chancellor of the Exchequer, Sir William Harcourt, was so intense that the Government was not expected to survive long. Observing the Liberal decline and realizing that he might soon be back in office, Curzon decided on a 'last wild cry of freedom' and embarked on his final, most dramatic and most perilous expedition to the East.

Two regions remained unfilled in the jigsaw puzzle of his Asian adventures: Afghanistan and the mountains of the Pamirs, that area on the north-west frontier through which an invading force could conceivably descend upon India. Curzon had long wanted to go to Afghanistan and had asked both the present Viceroy and his predecessor for permission to visit what was in effect a client state of the Government of India. As Britain's relations with the Emir were delicate and could easily be blighted by a diplomatic mistake, the governments in London and Calcutta had, after some prevarication, refused the request. Privately cursing the Secretary of State for his obstinacy and 'mulish ignorance',[52] Curzon then wrote with creaseless self-confidence to the Emir himself for an invitation. In a brilliant epistle oozing with flattery and oriental devices, he wrote of his admiration for the Afghan ruler and his desire to see 'the person of Your Highness which is in your dominions like unto the sparkle in the heart of the diamond'.[53]

Without waiting for a reply, Curzon sailed to India at the beginning of August 1894. At Bombay he found a letter from the Viceroy, Lord Elgin, confirming the Indian Government's refusal to allow him to travel in the Pamirs or to enter Afghanistan. But Curzon, armed with the support of Rosebery and Lord Roberts, who had commanded the Indian Army until the previous year, travelled straight to the viceregal summer quarters in Simla and persuaded Elgin and his Council to change their minds. Permission was given both for the journey to the Pamirs and, provided he received an invitation from the Emir in the meantime, for him to go on into Afghanistan afterwards. The only conditions he had to accept were the avoidance of a certain district in the Pamirs and an assurance that he would not cause problems with his projected articles for *The Times*. He paid more attention to the first restriction than to the second. Elgin was irritated by the pieces that later appeared and would have been even angrier had an official in Kashmir not persuaded Curzon to tear up an article he had drafted on the timidity of the Viceroy's Government.[54]

Always a bold and usually a lucky traveller, Curzon was exhilarated by his success with Elgin and even more by the arrival a few days later of the Emir's invitation. While still in Simla, he also had time to reflect on his more distant future. On entering Viceregal Lodge, he wondered whether he would one day be its master and to his diary he consigned the ambition to succeed Elgin in 1899.[55]

As a connoisseur of majestic scenery, Curzon appreciated the great crests of the Pamirs, the vast and shining glaciers, the beauty of the Hunza Valley where Nature had exerted her supreme energy and showed 'herself in the same moment tender and savage, radiant and appalling, the relentless spirit that hovers above the ice-towers and the gentle patroness of the field and orchard, the tutelary deity of the haunts of men'.[56] As he travelled north from Gilgit, he took careful notes of the topography of the region and, after crossing the Kilik Pass beyond Hunza, became the first Western traveller to see the source of the River Oxus. He also pursued the *ovis poli*, a wild ram with extravagant horns named after Marco Polo, and shot two of the beasts, one of them at the height of 17,000 feet. A comparison between this animal and its cousin, the *ovis karelini*, was included in one of three papers written after his return which the Royal Geographical Society later published together in a short book called *The Pamirs and the Source of the Oxus*. The RGS also awarded Curzon its gold medal for his exploration of the area.

After travelling for some eighty miles alongside the Oxus, he turned south-west, crossing the Baroghil Pass and coming down on the upper waters of the Yarkhun River. Opposite him 'gleamed the frozen cataract of the Great Chatiboi glacier, just as though some vast Niagara, pouring down from the skies, had suddenly been congealed in its descent, and converted into pinnacles and towers of ice'. Thanks to the help of local chiefs and British frontier officers, he managed a daily average march of twenty-one miles. But the hardships of the journey were enormous: in one day he and his pony had to ford mountain torrents twelve times. By then he had run out of liquor and was desperate, not as in Indo-China for a bottle of Moët, but for a simple glass of beer. Luck or telepathy was at work. When he finally reached grassier country at Mastuj, he was met by the native servant of a friend, Captain Younghusband, who greeted him with a bottle of Bass. Another discomfort could not, alas, be remedied by Younghusband's servant. For the entire journey, he told Spring Rice, he had suffered from such a painful dearth of female society that he could almost feel desire for a telegraph pole surrounded by a petticoat.[57]

One of the finest of frontier officers, Francis Younghusband had the year before been appointed Political Agent in Chitral, a small, unstable state further down the Yarkhun Valley. He had known Curzon for some time and shared the fear, based on his own experiences in the region, that the Russians were preparing to create trouble along the frontier. He also shared the view that Chitral, described by Curzon as 'this small chink in the mountain palisade', must not be occupied by the Tsarist army. Meeting in Mastuj, the two travelled together to Chitral, crossing the river by means of hazardous rope bridges, made of birch or willow twigs twisted together into a cable, which, as Curzon complained, had 'a detestable habit of swinging'. In the town itself, which they reached in October, they were entertained by the Mehtar, or ruler, who, fearful for his security, pleaded for the British officer attached to his court to be stationed with his Indian Army escort at Chitral instead of Mastuj. When the time came for the Englishmen to entertain the Mehtar, they were asked to invite the ruler's half-brother, Amir-ul-Mulk, whom Curzon described as 'a sullen and repulsive figure, with long black locks and a look of gloom'.[58] Two months later, when Younghusband was on leave and Curzon was on his way home, the Mehtar was murdered by this sinister half-brother.

As with Spring Rice, Younghusband's admiration for Curzon was qualified by feelings of irritation and resentment. Recalling their days together many years later, he remembered his companion as both a pleasure and a trial. He and his fellow officers were pleased that a prominent politician took such an interest in their work on the frontier but were annoyed by the endless arguments he pursued in order to discover their real opinions. Curzon's debating manner, allied with his self-assurance, grated on the young men living solitary lives in responsible positions among the mountains. Younghusband believed it would have been toned down, to the benefit of his career, if he had served with a regiment instead of going to Oxford. Yet he realized that Curzon's manner, however tiresome, was allied to a 'remarkable tenderness of heart' and a gift for warm and loyal friendship. Later he admitted he felt a deeper affection for Curzon than for any man outside his own family.[59]

From Chitral Curzon returned to Gilgit by a more southerly route, and then made his way to Peshawar before entering Afghanistan through the Khyber Pass in mid-November. He had made elaborate preparations for his reception by the Emir. Remembering the mediocre impression his drab Under-Secretary's uniform had created at the Korean court, he had gone to a theatrical costumier in London and had hired an enormous pair of gold epaulettes together with several glittering foreign decorations. He had then bought a pair of patent leather boots in Bombay and borrowed a gigantic curved sword from the Commander-in-Chief in India. Thus attired he duly presented himself at Kabul where a large escort of Afghan cavalry accompanied him through cheering crowds to meet his host. The Emir asked him some difficult questions about the medals but did not appear to doubt their authenticity. He was impressed by his guest, the first Englishman who had visited him as a private individual, and loaded him with money, which Curzon tactfully returned through gifts to the Emir and tips to his servants. In his autobiography the Emir recalled that he had found Curzon so genial, witty and well-informed that he had been determined to meet other members of the British aristocracy as often as possible.[60]

The visitor was no less enchanted with his host. The fancy dress, the oriental pomp, the ambience both savage and sensual, appealed strongly to him. Curzon always had a soft spot for rogues so long as they were open about their roguery, and he was delighted to be the guest of a man described by a British official as 'a sort of Afghan Henry VIII'. He recognized him as a tyrant and a man of blood. Yet he appreciated the man's 'shrewd but untutored intellect' and applauded his skill in welding the Afghan tribes into a unity which they had never previously enjoyed. The Emir, 'at once a patriot and a monster, a great man and almost a fiend', attracted the strong romantic side of Curzon's nature. Had he lived in an earlier age, unrestricted by the rival empires of Britain and Russia, the Englishman thought he 'might have founded an Empire, and swept in a tornado of blood over Asia and even beyond it'.[61]

Curzon remained his guest for over a fortnight and was summoned for daily audiences often lasting for several hours. Speaking in Persian through an interpreter, the Emir discoursed on subjects as diverse as the lost tribes of Israel and the efficacy of cruelty as a deterrent. In light-hearted moods he fantasized to Curzon about his expertise as a dentist, a painter and a clock-mender. On more serious days he discussed the Russian threat to their frontiers and the possibility that he might visit England. Both subjects required diplomatic handling. If Afghanistan and Britain were allies, he liked to ask, why did he not receive more weapons to defend his people against the common enemy? And disregarding the experiences of sixty years, he wondered why the British should want to strengthen their frontier with Afghanistan rather than fortify their common 'wall' against the Russians.

Some time earlier the British Government had invited the Emir to London. He had not yet replied, partly because he was unsure about the reception he would receive in England and partly because he was justifiably nervous of what might happen in Afghanistan during his absence. But after long discussions with Curzon, he decided to go to Britain and composed a letter of acceptance for his new friend to take to Queen Victoria.[62] As a sequel to the fairy-tale character of his visit, Curzon hoped to deliver the message personally to the Queen and was much annoyed when her Private Secretary told him it could only be done through the Secretary of State. In the end the Emir, increasingly worried by the thought of a coup while he was away, decided not to go. No doubt it was just as well, for he would have been bewildered by London and disappointed when he did not receive quite the welcome – the Queen, the royal family and both Houses of Parliament waiting for him in Westminster Hall – which he envisaged.

8

Hearts and Souls

───────◆───────

THE HOSTILITY GEORGE CURZON often aroused in public life puzzled many who only knew him socially. Since leaving Oxford he had been one of the most sought-after men both in London and in country-house society. He was welcomed for his sense of fun, for what one friend called 'the Rabelaisian humour and the inventive spirit which he displayed',[1] and for the quality of his talk. 'Through all his conversation,' recalled Lady Warwick, 'like sunlight dappling a wooded stream, gleamed the constant flash of his wit, and the ripple of laughter that seemed the more wonderful to me because I knew of his constant pain.'[2] The most frequent and appreciative beneficiaries of this wit were members of that élite and enigmatic group known as the 'Souls'.

Judging that its members spent an exorbitant amount of time discussing their souls, Lord Charles Beresford is supposed to have given the group its name in the late 1880s. Among each other, however, they usually referred to themselves as 'the gang'. Its membership consisted largely of friends of Laura Lyttelton who, disconsolate at her death and unwilling for a time to resume an elaborate social life, preferred each other's company. Laura herself, with her charm, her fantasies and her rather fey sensibility, would have been a typical Soul. Her sister Margot, although more intellectual, self-centred and unconventional than most of the other women in the group, was one of its leading members. So were Mary Elcho and Ettie Grenfell, who entertained the Souls at their respective country houses, Stanway and Taplow. Beauty, wit, flirtatiousness and an emphasis on sentiment – qualities required of the group's women – were matched by similar characteristics in the men. Several of them were politicians, but they were also writers and wits and were usually good-looking. Within the circle there was much speculation as to which of the young Tory Souls – Curzon, Wyndham or Harry Cust – would have the most successful career.[3]

The Souls' notoriety owed much to Curzon who, unable to entertain at home, gave two large dinners for them at the Bachelors' Club, introducing each of his guests with a verse of what he himself called 'doggerel appalling'. These functions, which took place in 1889 and 1890, caused some resentment in the rest of London society and gave the impression that the group was more cohesive and homogeneous than it was. What really bound the Souls, apart from friendship, was what they liked and disliked doing at weekend parties in the country. Saturday was not spent racing, gambling and drinking oneself under the table. Cards were shunned in favour of literary and acting games. If shooting sometimes took place, it was not a more integral part of life than tennis or long walks, and it was a good deal less important than the incessant talking.

'No history of our time', Balfour told Margot Asquith, 'will be complete unless the influence of the Souls upon society is dispassionately and accurately recorded,' a remark which may have been taken more seriously than its author intended.[4] Balfour suggested it was under the influence of the Souls that leading politicians from opposing parties began to meet each other. Yet the fact that Balfour could drink Asquith's champagne before attacking him in the House of Commons owed as much to the temperaments of the two men as it did to their connection through Margot. The bias of the Souls was heavily Tory – apart from those mentioned they included Balfour himself and Brodrick – and even Alfred Lyttelton, who was a nephew of Gladstone, entered the House of Commons as a Liberal Unionist and later joined Balfour's Cabinet. As a group the Souls were no doubt rather frivolous and self-regarding, exposed, as one journalist put it, to 'the insidious dry rot of mutual admiration'.[5] But they were more attractive than the Prince of Wales's Marlborough House Set and, through their civilized and mildly unconventional activities, set a better example of upper-class behaviour. Keynes's description of his Bloomsbury circle – 'water spiders, gracefully skimming, as light and as reasonable as air, the surface of the stream without any contact at all with the eddies and currents beneath'[6] – is perhaps more appropriate for its precursors among the Souls.

The society columns of the press regarded Balfour, who was considerably older than the others, as the chief luminary of the group and

Curzon as the number two. Lady Paget, however, identified Curzon as the 'Captain of the Souls' and Frances Horner as the 'High Priestess'. At first sight Curzon seems an improbable member. The traveller in the Persian deserts hibernating in Norwood to produce long, scholarly volumes does not fit easily with the image of charades in the drawing-room at Stanway. The fact that he was so completely at home at Stanway illustrates the range of his personality and the way he could lead different, almost unconnected lives. As one Soul put it rather cryptically, those of his 'emotions which are not consistent with the harmless associations of the Souls he reserves for situations in which no Soul is involved'.[7]

Curzon's conversation was regarded by 'the gang' as the most brilliant and also as the most reckless: one member remarked that there was a '*diablerie*' about his dialogue which sometimes went too far and led to rebukes from the others.[8] But despite this trait, he was much in demand as an adviser and confidant. Margot Tennant, whose mind was made up on almost every other issue, could not decide whom to marry and eventually turned to Curzon for advice. Several years earlier she had been engaged to a man so unsuitable that her mother had exclaimed, 'You might as well marry your groom!'[9] Persuaded to break off the relationship, she was still unmarried in 1893 when, at the age of 29, she had two suitors, H.H. Asquith, the Liberal Home Secretary whose first wife had died in 1891, and the much younger Evan Charteris, a brother-in-law of Mary Elcho. Although she was not in love with either of them, she thought she ought to marry one and asked Curzon which he recommended. For someone as emotional and impulsive as Curzon, his advice was surprisingly judicious. While Charteris would give her youth, looks and physical charm, he told her, the combination would last a maximum of ten years, while Asquith would bring 'devotion, strength, influence, a great position – things that last and grow'. Take the older man, he said, and 'though you will miss the fugitive you will gain the permanent'.[10] Margot accepted the advice and married Asquith, to the despair of his Liberal colleagues who were soon complaining that he neglected his department in order to stay in smart houses and learn how to ride.[11]

Social life for the Souls naturally extended outside their circle, especially for the men who had their club lives and various male functions to attend. Political dinners, like that given in 1893 for all Balliol men in Parliament (forty-nine of them in the House of Commons alone), were almost as agreeable to Curzon as the badinage of an evening at Taplow. He liked clubs too, and was much pleased to be the youngest member elected to Grillion's, a dining club whose small and very select membership included Gladstone, Morley and Chamberlain. His other clubs included White's, the Athenaeum and, in an eccentric and hedonistic league of its own, the Crabbet Club.

The Crabbet was founded by Wilfrid Scawen Blunt, the satyric traveller, poet and campaigner for Irish and Egyptian nationalism. Although he modelled himself on Byron (whose granddaughter he married) he was, like his cousin George Wyndham, a man whose talents were too diffuse for him to achieve a great deal in any field, and the principal triumphs of his life were philanderous. While he despised the Souls as a group, he liked them enough as individuals to attempt, with varying degrees of success, the seduction of their women, and to invite some of their men to the annual weekend of the Crabbet Club at his Sussex home. The club's purpose, as defined by Wyndham, was 'to play lawn tennis, the piano, the fool and other instruments of gaiety', but the chief event of the weekend was the yearly poetry competition.[12]

Although he was nearly twenty years younger than Blunt and disagreed with most of his political views, Curzon was an enthusiastic member of the Crabbet Club. He liked his host but regarded him as an 'incorrigible charlatan' and once, after encountering him in Egypt, wrote in his diary: 'My dear Wilfrid, your poetry is delightful and your morals, though deplorable, enchanting. But why are you a traitor to your country?'[13] Curzon was elected to the club in 1891 at the same time as Oscar Wilde, and his *'diablerie'* immediately got the better of him. Appointed to the role of 'devil's advocate' to oppose Wilde's candidature, Curzon embarked on a clever, amusing and unkind speech about sodomy and the treatment of the subject in *The Picture of Dorian Gray*. 'Poor Oscar', noted Blunt, 'sat helplessly smiling, a fat mass, in his chair,' but pulled himself together to make a witty reply. To the mingled amusement and embarrassment of the other members, the duel continued long into the night, brilliant and ferocious, recalled Blunt, who doubted 'if anything better was ever heard, even from Disraeli in his best days'.[14] Several years later, when Wilde was in exile and Curzon was Viceroy, the playwright described his antagonist's speech as the height of bad taste and claimed that everyone had roared with laughter at his own. But at the end, he said, Curzon had been charming and apologetic, and the talking had continued until dawn. Then the younger men, including Curzon and Wyndham, had gone for a swim in the lake and afterwards, in Wilde's words, they had begun 'playing lawn tennis, just as they were, stark naked, the future rulers of England'. Blunt's daughter remembered Wilde also playing tennis, 'a great wobbly blancmange trying to serve underhand'.[15] He never went to Crabbet again.

Curzon, however, returned the following year and again in 1893, when Blunt recorded that he was 'as usual, the most brilliant, he never flags for an instant either in speech or repartee'.[16] His verses at the meetings, which even Wilde praised as sharp and well-tuned, were better than his usual efforts, and in 1893 he won the Crabbet 'laureate's' award for a poem in praise of 'sin'. For its final stanzas he wrote:

> And so when some historian
> Of the period Victorian
> Shall crown the greatest exploit of this wonder-working age,
> His eye shall light on Crabbet
> And, if truth shall be his habit
> The name of every one of us will shine upon that page.
>
> To us will be the glory,
> That shall never fade in story,
> Of reviving the old axiom that all the world's akin,
> That the true link of union
> Which holds men in communion
> Is frank and systematic and premeditated Sin![17]

The most interesting feature of Curzon's Crabbet verses is their self-mockery, the jibes about his appearance and 'superior person' image which conflict with traditional perceptions of their author. In one poem, long predating Max Beerbohm's description of him as 'Britannia's butler', he confessed:

> My looks are of that useful type – I say it with elation –
> That qualify me well for almost any situation –
> I've sometimes been mistaken for a parson, and at others
> Have recognised in butlers and in waiters long lost brothers.

With Balfour as a non-runner, George Curzon had some claim to be the most eligible bachelor in England. A few weeks before dying in 1893, Jowett asked him when he was going to exchange 'All Souls for one body'.[18] As at that stage Curzon had only just made up his mind, he decided to keep the date and the choice a secret. He was then 34, still a faithful observer of the convention that unmarried girls from his own class could not be subjected to more than flirtation and that physical relationships must be restricted to married friends or girls from other backgrounds. His habit of flirtatious chaffing is well illustrated by his behaviour on a visit to Stanway in January 1889 when the chief entertainment was a fancy-dress concert. The object of his attentions was 24-year-old Edith (known as Didi) Balfour, who afterwards on paper tried to reproduce Curzon's 'swelling eighteenth century manner and phraseology'. He had heard of her, he said, 'as a great addition to our circle, clever, brilliant; a good talker, and I had imagined to myself a woman of a certain age, without any other charms but those of intellect. What do I find? A buxom creature, charming . . .' He continued in this vein for the rest of his visit and one morning, finding themselves alone in the breakfast room, shut the door and kissed her fervently. Didi was bewildered but not displeased, she recalled, even though she was not physically attracted to him.[19]

Curzon's recollections were rather different. Afterwards he wrote her a series of letters about his 'memory of her voice, particularly in that song upon the moonlit steps', her talk, her eyes and above all her lips. He called her the 'most original and subversive of girls' because she wanted 'her mind and imagination taken captive *as well as* her *heart*!' After Didi had expressed remorse about letting herself be kissed, Curzon told her not to be ashamed or nervous about the memory. 'Seals cannot be put upon the door of lips or of anything else that have been voluntarily opened.' Declaring himself the last person, however, 'to misinterpret or exaggerate or hug' to himself 'conceited illusions', he realized he was not going to win her, and they soon reached the stage of uncomplicated friendship.[20] Didi became Alfred Lyttelton's second wife in 1892, and the couple invited Curzon to be the godfather of their second son, who died in infancy. Their eldest boy, the future Lord Chandos, recalled many years later that Curzon treated him 'like a nephew, almost like a son', and hoped he would marry one of his daughters.[21]

Outside the ranks of the Souls, Curzon found a more passionate response from the American Mary Leiter, who will be discussed later on, and the American-born Pearl Craigie, who wrote novels under the pseudonym John Oliver Hobbes. Married at the age of 19, Pearl Craigie had soon separated from a husband who infected her with venereal disease, an experience which persuaded her to take a vow of chastity and to join the Catholic Church. Yet in about 1892, almost immediately after she had committed herself to her new life, she conceived a great passion for Curzon, admitting years later to her confessor that she had loved him 'to an extraordinary and fatal degree' and had placed her soul at his disposal. This passion greatly upset another suitor, the novelist George Moore, who became extremely jealous of Curzon and, after obtaining some of his letters to Pearl after her early death, apparently planned to publish them.[22] As with Curzon's other affairs, all evidence of the relationship in his possession was destroyed, and her letters which survive among his papers were written later, after she had become a friend of his wife. Her own evidence, while no doubt sincere, is unreliable and sometime contradictory; her love for Curzon, combined with her religious fervour and her revulsion for her husband, had clearly left her in a tormented and near hysterical frame of mind. In her letters to her confessor, a Father Brown, she at times gave the impression that Curzon had proposed to her and had been turned down, and at others that she would have accepted him had he asked her. In 1900 she told the priest she had made a great sacrifice when she rejected him, but three years later admitted she 'would have married [him] beyond question', and in 1904 confessed she had been 'madly devoted' and 'would have sacrificed everything' for him. Later still she claimed to have refused persistent invitations to become his mistress after his marriage.[23]

The period of Mrs Craigie's real distress was in 1895 when, as she later revealed, she 'went through agonies over the Curzon story [which] weakened my heart and prostrated me again and again'. The date she referred to strongly suggests that he never in fact proposed to her. Deeply upset by the announcement of his engagement in the spring of that year, she later claimed that the event had equally depressed him, that he had become ill as a result and had told her he wished he was dead. As Curzon had by then been secretly engaged for two years, it is an implausible story, and no evidence from his friends or anyone else supports it. Moreover, the fact of the secret engagement, which Pearl Craigie was unaware of, seems to dispose of the theory that he proposed to her during this period. Her other claim, that Curzon tried to seduce her and that she, though tempted, refused to surrender, sounds more plausible. So does his alleged complaint that she was unresponsive and like an 'iceberg'.[24]

Until his unpremeditated engagement in March 1893, Curzon appears to have had no strong marital ambitions since his failure to secure Sibell Grosvenor seven years earlier. It had taken him a long time to recover from losing her to George Wyndham. As late as 1891, when Wyndham was already bored with her and Sibell was engaged in an inconclusive flirtation with Wilfrid Blunt, Curzon told her he would always regard her 'as my nearest dearest truest friend. I loved you earliest and I have loved you longest; and the joy and treasure you have been to me, although we have never been married, has been as great as most wives can give their husbands.'[25] It was a love he did not hide even from his future wife. In a letter describing various friends and relations just before their marriage, he admitted that Sibell Grosvenor was 'the sweetest woman (bar one!)' that he had ever known.[26]

A more difficult letter he had to compose in the same period was a reply to a lecture from Brodrick about his treatment of women.

> I will say nothing about the past save this, that (with one exception – due to special causes of which you heard something from me the other day) I believe I have never caused any woman sorrow or bitterness or regret, and also that I have never left any woman morally worse than I found her. To some maybe I have even done good. And those who may have heard hints or caught glimpses of this or that surrender, do not know but should not therefore ignore that there may have been (and in far greater number) acts of self-denial and renunciation.[27]

This justification must have been broadly true because otherwise Curzon would not have dared send it to such a forthright critic who was aware of many of the circumstances. But Brodrick had become less of a confidant in recent years, and the defensive plea probably does not cover the cases he knew nothing about. It may have been true, as Pearl Craigie believed, that Curzon was 'always kind to all women – young, or middle-aged, or old', that he, 'alone among libertines', always spoke well of his mistresses, and that he had that 'rare gift: *il sait aimer*'.[28] But one woman whom he certainly caused both bitterness and sorrow was an anonymous mistress living in London's Westbourne Terrace. As usual the details have been obscured by Curzon's order that all evidence should be burnt, and the affair has only come to light because George Wyndham failed to destroy the letters in his possession.

Wyndham was a natural intermediary whose charm and negotiating skills were successfully used to overcome frictions within the Souls and employed, with less success, by his cousin Lord Alfred Douglas in an attempt to prevent the trial of Oscar Wilde.[29] In the course of 1891 Wyndham acted as Curzon's intermediary with the woman from Westbourne Terrace. Evidently refusing to accept that their affair had ended, she began to blackmail Curzon, set a detective to watch his movements, and tried to send telegrams denouncing him to the Cabinet, which were stopped. In November Wyndham went on a long and exasperating mission on Curzon's behalf, and by the end of the month a final meeting between the former lovers in front of witnesses seems to have ended the matter. At the interview, according to Curzon, the woman produced her normal display of tears, hysterics and play-acting but accepted that there would be no more meetings and promised to go to St Moritz with a nurse. He then told her he would not breathe a word of forgiveness until by leaving the country she had made some reparation for the injury she had tried to inflict on him. Presumably realizing that she now had nothing left to lose, the dis-traught woman ended the meeting by telling him that on the night of one of his departures from England she had picked up a man off the street and gone to bed with him. Her taunt provoked the desired reac-tion. 'Tingling with black anger and shame' and nearly beside himself 'with horror and loathing', Curzon worked himself into a state of hypo-critical hysteria and said he never wanted to set eyes on her again. 'Treachery, betrayal, anger, abuse, revenge – all I have forgiven but coarse and vulgar sin never – no, not till I die.'[30]

It was not the only escapade of its kind. 'Curzon was madly reckless with women,' recalled Pearl Craigie, whose evidence seems more reli-able when she was not personally involved. He had had a dozen mis-tresses, she said, not casual acquaintances such as 'actresses or street-nymphs' but women of whom he was 'exceedingly fond'. On one occasion, however, his recklessness landed him in an adventure in which he was 'cornered by a terror with six children and a past'; the affair ended in 'much woe and shattered nerves *and* a considerable pension to the aggrieved female'.[31] Considering the damage which divorce or sexual impropriety could inflict on a political career, Curzon's foolhardiness is surprising. Before him loomed the fate of Parnell and the example of Sir Charles Dilke, who had seemed Gladstone's probable successor until a murky divorce case precluded his future participation in government. He knew that W.T. Stead, the puritanical editor of the *Pall Mall Gazette*, would crucify him in print if his activities became known.* And there were limits to tolerance even

---

*Curzon lightly mocked Stead in his prize-winning poem at the Crabbet Club.
> In an epoch so degenerate
> That no one dares to venerate
> The ruffian and the libertine, the criminal and rogue,
> When all our old criteria
> Have been shattered by hysteria,
> And the moral standard set by Stead is the new and patent vogue . . .

among the Souls, where marital infidelity might be forgiven but bad behaviour was not. Harry Cust, a notorious philanderer, was called a cur for his treatment of a girl he had seduced and was later forced to marry. And Curzon himself had been censorious of Cust's conduct towards a previous lover, agreeing with Brodrick that if the miscreant continued 'to play the blackguard with her', he could not retain their friendship.[32]

Affairs among the Souls were unlikely to land the lovers in the divorce courts. Mary Elcho could give birth to a daughter of Blunt's and Violet Granby to a daughter of Cust's without Lord Elcho or Lord Granby threatening legal action. Curzon could seduce Charty Ribblesdale or pay elaborate if unrewarded court to Ettie Grenfell without unduly annoying their husbands. But straying outside that circle, even while remaining within the same social class, could be hazardous. Only months after settling the Westbourne Terrace problem, Curzon found himself in another potentially disastrous situation. On discovering a batch of compromising letters, a nephew of Lord Middleton called Machell decided to instigate divorce proceedings against his wife and to name Curzon as co-respondent. The lovers' reaction is unrecorded, but they were doubtless relieved when Machell's own solicitors persuaded him to abandon the action on the grounds that he himself might be thought to have condoned the affair and that in any case he would not be coming into court with entirely 'clean hands'. In 1920, twenty-eight years later, the firm discovered it still possessed thirty of Curzon's letters to Mrs Machell and invited their author to pay £100 for the privilege of watching them being burnt. Curzon, who was then Foreign Secretary, claimed he had paid for their destruction many years earlier and refused to do so again. The letters were burnt without payment.[33]

Most of the episodes related in these last pages occurred during Curzon's long and idiosyncratic courtship of Mary Leiter, an attractive and musical American girl of much charm and beauty. Tall and graceful, her large grey eyes set in an oval face framed by fine auburn hair, Mary's 'presence' invariably drew attention. To one Englishman in India, she was 'a vision of loveliness' that made him realize why 'the Greeks had besieged Troy for so many years'.[34] Her father was Levi Zeigler Leiter, a Chicago millionaire and philanthropist widely but wrongly assumed to be of either Jewish or Dutch Calvinist origin; he was in fact descended from a Swiss Mennonite who had emigrated to Pennsylvania early in the eighteenth century and whose family had later founded the village of Leitersburg in Maryland.[35] Her mother, Mary Teresa Carver, was a warm-hearted but somewhat foolish woman, 'a dear, kind soul', noted an American friend, notorious for 'using the wrong word at the wrong time or place'.[36] Socially ambitious, in 1881 she persuaded her husband to move their young family of four children from Chicago to Washington, a city where he had few friends and little to do. Although the Leiters rented an enormous and very expensive house in Dupont Circle, the couple enjoyed little social success until Mary, their eldest daughter, 'came out' and established herself as the débutante of the year in 1888. Her ability to further her mother's ambitions must have been very gratifying; even before her eighteenth birthday Mary had become one of the closest friends of President Cleveland's young wife.[37]

Cultural as well as social reasons took the Leiters so often to Europe that Mary later feared they would become 'a family of wandering and Europeanised Americans'. In London as in Washington it was Mary, at the age of 20, who achieved the social *entrée*. Arriving in England with her mother and sister Nancy in the summer of 1890, she was reduced to reading about the London season in the newspapers until a letter of introduction led to luncheon at the Admiralty followed rapidly by invitations to numerous smart functions including the Duchess of Westminster's ball at which she danced the opening quadrille with the Prince of Wales. George Curzon was much struck by her appearance that evening, but they did not meet properly until a few days later when they were guests together at a country-house party. He found her very attractive and later confessed that only with great difficulty had he restrained himself from kissing her in the rose garden. Mary fell in love almost on sight and was thrilled by a little amulet he gave her. On her return to London she had a pearl set from her necklace which she sent to him as emblematic of the tear she shed on leaving him. Curzon thanked her for the 'blessed keepsake', promised to wear it frequently in his tie, and called her 'the dearest girl' – not one of his most exclusive designations – that he had met for a long time.[38]

At the beginning of August the Leiter party renounced England and various invitations to Scotland in favour of a Continental tour. Bored and unhappy, Mary sent Curzon a small Bavarian Madonna and looked forward to seeing him on their return to London. But by then the temptations of the rose garden had largely evaporated, and he told her he was looking for a quiet spot near London to write his book and enjoy the isolation which such work required. He would be engaged upon the task for the rest of the year, he added discouragingly, a labour that would take him 'every minute of every hour of every day'. By early

October he had shut himself up in Norwood with his Persian manuscript and refused to be distracted. While Mary was bewailing the fact that she would have to spend three days in London without seeing him, he was describing by post the 'furious exhilaration' he experienced living and working by himself. On the day before the Leiters sailed for America, he finally dragged himself to central London to say goodbye. Mary sang for him, and they spent a 'sad and happy' evening together, but the next day she departed 'at the zero of despair' and at the end of her voyage the sight of the Statue of Liberty for once filled her with sadness rather than delight. Soon after her return she received a photograph of Curzon wrapped in three of his speeches which she read imagining herself as a loyal constituent 'in the front row of enthusiastic listeners'. A photograph sent the other way produced a disappointing response, its recipient condemning it as a caricature and criticizing the hairstyle for spoiling 'one of a woman's fairest gifts, the outline of the head'. He also found fault with the sitter's expression. It made her seem stern, contemplative and severe, whereas a woman ought to look tender, yielding and gentle.[39]

Curzon was more forthcoming when she returned to England with her mother the following spring. He gave a dinner on their arrival and saw her frequently in London during the parliamentary session. In the middle of May Mary went to Paris, where his friend, the Princesse de Wagram, planned to marry her off to a French nobleman, but she returned to England before an introduction could be made; like Curzon, she found the French rather foppish and insincere. The rest of the season was spent at social events in London or at the country houses of various Souls who liked her enough to tolerate the chaperoning of her embarrassing mother. Curzon was attentive and charming, she noted, and on her twenty-first birthday he gave her an enamelled silver box from Canton accompanied by a pompous note congratulating her on having achieved 'complete and sensible womanhood'. She was even allowed to visit him at Norwood, where he rowed her around the Crystal Palace lake while Mrs Leiter sat on the bank. But his amiability never indicated passion, and he sometimes appeared indifferent. When her father came over in late July and made them stay in a Brighton hotel, far from the attractions of the Souls, Mary mentioned Curzon's coldness and indicated the nature of her feelings for him. At Christmas the following year in Rome she crawled up the Scala Santa on her knees and prayed that he would marry her.[40]

The problem was that Curzon's gallantry could be directed at several women at the same time. While Mary was rejecting French, Italian, British and American suitors, she remained only one of a group of women at whom he deployed his charm. In the early years of their friendship he enjoyed similar relationships with Ettie Grenfell and Pearl Craigie, he had a mistress in Westbourne Terrace and he was having, or had recently concluded, an affair with Mrs Machell. During Mary's visits to London he showed her the sort of affection he had once felt for Laura Tennant and Didi Balfour, but it was far less than the passion he had given Sibell Grosvenor. There was no question of his being in love with her. She intruded little into his bachelor's existence either at Norwood or at Westminster. He wrote to her from time to time but, unless they happened to be in central London simultaneously, he made little effort to see her. In August 1892 he went to America and stayed a night in Washington without attempting to make contact or even find out if she was there.

Curzon's indifference would not have been comprehensible to those who observed his later love for his wife and assumed it must have been preceded by an ardent courtship. Yet he probably thought less about Mary in the months before their engagement than of several other women. When he left England in August 1892 for his second round-the-world trip, his dreams were of Ettie Grenfell, whose 'little clinging hand' he had held under a table and upon whose 'willowy form' he had briefly pounced on his last evening.[41] In America her place was taken by Amélie Rives, whose family he had stayed with in Virginia. 'Upon me Amy shone with the undivided insistence of her starlike eyes. Oh God!' he exclaimed to his diary, 'the nights on the still lawn under the soft sky with my sweetheart!'[42] Whether the thought of Amy kept him going till he reached Japan is uncertain, but there it was clearly supplanted by the charms of Ethel Kirkwood, whose presence remained vivid over the return leg. While he was steaming through the Suez Canal in February 1893, he learnt that Mary, whom he had not seen for eighteen months, was in Cairo, and he therefore wrote a friendly but far from passionate letter regretting he could not get off the ship to meet her. The tone of this missive was not surprising because on the same day he wrote to Spring Rice telling him he 'still thrilled' at the thought of 'the Kirkina'.[43] What is extraordinary is that a few days later he proposed to Mary in a Paris hotel.

Mary and her mother had sailed to France immediately after Curzon and, on finding him in the French capital, invited him to dine at the Hôtel Vendôme. Many years later he described what ensued:

I had entered the hotel without the slightest anticipation that this would be the issue. After dinner, when we were alone, this beautiful, sweet and faithful woman told me her story. How she had waited for nearly three years since the time when we first met, rejecting countless suitors and always waiting for me. I told her that, while I felt from the beginning that we were destined for each other, I had not dared to speak, and had even run the risk of losing her because there was certain work in my scheme of Asiatic travel which I had resolved to do, and which I could not ask any married woman to allow her husband to carry out. Some of it, notably the journey to the Pamirs and Afghanistan, still remained undone: and even now when we became secretly engaged, it was on the understanding that I should be at liberty to complete my task before we took the final step. This did not happen for 2 years, during which we remained engaged to each other, unknown to a single human being . . . Was there not something wonderful in this long trial, in the uncomplaining and faithful devotion of this darling girl? I think it was the foundation of the great happiness that she gave me . . . Could there be a greater glory than to be the one and only love of such a woman? Eleven years of married life left us both unchanged.[44]

On the anniversary of that evening Mary recalled the 'after dinner talk which began so timidly and ended so lovingly', her fiancé 'slipping away in a half-startled way' at midnight, beseeching her to keep the engagement a secret.[45] But if Curzon's description of the event is accurate, his explanation of the background and his feeling of 'destiny' should be accorded due scepticism. He wanted the world to consider their romance as a fairy tale and so he burnt evidence which threatened this interpretation. But although he could destroy love letters from others, he could not invent ones to Mary he had not written or infuse those he had with a passion he had not possessed. His marriage turned out to be a good one and, although he still dreamed of other women, only Pearl Craigie's evidence suggests he went beyond dreaming. But his courtship was far from romantic. His letters to Mary, infrequent and unpassionate, his occasional coldness, his attachments to others, above all his failure to see her very often, all ridicule that claim to a common destiny. He did not propose, as he wished people later to believe, because he was in love. Nor did he propose, as people have often assumed, because he wanted Mary's money; had that been his objective, he could have secured a hefty marriage settlement in the autumn of 1890 instead of waiting and risking its loss later. The only credible explanation is that put forward by Mary's own biographer – that he acted out of impulse.[46] An emotional man, weary after a long and exhausting journey in the East, he arrived in Paris and after a good dinner learnt that this beautiful young woman had been waiting for him, uncomplainingly, for nearly three years. Prompted by long-standing affection, by sudden emotion, perhaps also by a sense of guilt, he proposed and was accepted. His offer was unpremeditated, made spontaneously in the magic of a moment, and from it years afterwards he conjured a romantic aura over a pre-marital relationship which on his part had been decidedly unromantic.

Curzon's behaviour during his engagement shows him at his most unsympathetic. The conditions he imposed at the Vendôme dinner were difficult enough: their wedding would not take place for two years, their engagement must remain a secret, and he should be allowed to make an extremely perilous journey to an unknown part of Asia in the meantime. The following day he added a fourth – that he would not write too often 'for fear of exciting suspicions' – while a fifth – that they would scarcely meet during the next two years – was made implicit. The situation suited Curzon very well. 'I am spared all the anxiety of what is called courtship,' he told Mary complacently, 'and I have merely when the hour strikes to enter into possession of my own.' He also spared himself the trouble of writing love letters; his correspondence during the engagement resembles that between a guardian and his ward. Asking her if she hated the idea of a critical husband, he conceded it might be 'rather maddening' before launching himself prematurely into the role. He wrote to her about her complexion, about eating enough, about practising different ways of doing her hair in a coil or knot: he did not want it 'brushed up from the ears, but waving along longitudinally in deep rich undulations'. He also gave advice about music, a subject Mary knew very much more about than her fiancé. 'Learn some sweet simple songs for me,' she was instructed, 'things that touch and move and tell of quiet love and pathos and peace'. She should not, however, concentrate entirely on singing. There was 'much sweet solace in the pianoforte', she was reminded, for a woman's fingers were 'given her as ministering angels to heart as well as head'. Still more intolerably, she was told to polish up her spelling and given examples of her mistakes. Spring Rice's nickname, for instance, should have been spelt Springy not Springie, for 'the latter [was] a termination suitable only to small women and pug dogs'. When she declared that several of the words he had corrected were spelt differently in America, back came the insufferable reply: 'You must learn how to think and spell as an Englishwoman, my child.' After eighteen months of this, she was driven to suggest that he might tell her that he loved her, for it was 'a good long time since you have thought something loving of your devoted Mary'.[47]

Curzon occasionally recognized that the advice and education should not be entirely unilateral. After their marriage he hoped Mary would teach him French and German because if he ever became Foreign Secretary he would need to be more fluent 'in order to score off those ambassadors'. He was also capable of feeling mild remorse for his behaviour and hoped she would not think him a unique 'phenomenon of preconnubial selfishness'. But he did not appreciate Mary's feelings of unhappiness and insecurity. During their long engagement they met only twice, for two days in London (which he promised to cram with 'a century of emotion') and for a few hours in France (where he was able to 'pardon the French for being able at least to make beautiful dresses for beautiful women'). Mary was forced to spend over seven hundred days alone with her secret, badgered by other suitors and anxious about George's safety. He could write of his tranquillity and of his serene trust in the future quite unaware that these feelings could not be shared by his fiancée.[48]

Mary acquiesced in his journey to the Pamirs but she did not pretend to like it. Her letters of this time, natural, loving and sincere, reveal anxiety and sometimes desperation. Her hair would be white, she told him, and the long practice of patience would have crushed her spirit by the time he came back – if he came back. In response to a letter referring to the possibility of him dying on his travels, Mary declared that if that happened she would devote the rest of her life to charity and never marry. She would renounce her inheritance except for a fraction for her work and, as a final gesture to George, whatever sum was needed to pay off various debts of the Kedleston estate. Curzon acknowledged the nobility and generosity of this offer but assured her that neither he nor his father could possibly accept it. He also told her that in the event of his death he wanted her to marry someone else because otherwise she would always resent him for ruining not only her youth but the rest of her life as well. In a subsequent letter he calmed her fears that he would abandon her for more travels soon after their marriage. It would not be fair on her, he proclaimed, for a 'disconsolate and dejected bride' was in a worse position than 'a forlorn fiancée'.[49]

Mary's anxiety was increased by the gloomy predictions of Curzon's friends. Spring Rice told her that the dangers of his journey were almost insurmountable, while a Tory colleague remarked that he had one chance in ten of getting safely out of Kabul. From London Mary wrote in desperation to India, imploring him not to travel from the Pamirs to Afghanistan. She had learnt that the Emir was ill and might die, and feared his successor would be a 'monstrous fellow with a death and destruction policy to all foreigners'. To pay him a congratulatory visit on his succession, she asserted, would be mad, 'inhuman', and 'a kind of out and out desertion' of herself. Only when she heard that he had returned safely could she admit that the ordeal had been of any personal benefit. Tests and patience improved a woman, she was now able to conclude, adding that they would be happier together for the experience. From his ship off Aden, Curzon conceded that she had been 'a Niobe of patience without the tears', and wrote a long letter about the wedding arrangements.[50] His last great journey, the boldest and most hazardous of all, had been successfully completed without injury and probably without infidelity to Mary. Ettie Grenfell had received a letter from Kabul in which he had sighed for a kiss on a blood-red sofa in front of a fire, but he does not seem to have gone further than that.[51] There had been no Amy Rives or Ethel Kirkwood on this trip. Even the Baroness de Malortie, whom he met in Cairo on his way home, offered no temptations this time. The 'darling' and 'goddess' of his Egyptian sojourn twelve years before now bulged 'with thickened neck and fattened limb, crowned by the artificial glory of saffron-dyed hair. Oh Lilia!' he expostulated to his diary. 'How any more can I kiss you?'[52]

Curzon was curiously anxious about breaking the news of the engagement to his father and went to the interview armed with various apologetic defences and explanations. In the event they were not needed. 'So long as you love her and she loves you,' Lord Scarsdale said, 'that is all. You are not likely at your age to make a mistake. She is old enough to know her mind.'[53] Another problem which worried him was how they could explain the logistics of their engagement. He did not want anyone – except Mary's parents who had been told the previous summer – to know of the two-year wait for fear that 'it might not be understood'. Yet it was difficult to explain how he had managed to propose either from Asia when she was in Europe or after his return when she was in America. 'It was clever of you', wrote the invalid Lord Pembroke, 'and extremely characteristic to get engaged to Miss Leiter at Washington from the top of the Pamirs – you must tell me how it was done.' Close to death from tuberculosis at the age of 49, he added with admirable nonchalance, 'The way I go on trying to die without doing it is intolerable and a bore to everyone. I apologise.'[54]

Among the many letters of congratulation, Curzon particularly treasured that of the Emir of Afghanistan, to whom he had sent a photograph of Mary. Abdur Rahman congratulated his 'very wise friend' on his choice, told him he could see from the picture that she would be faithful, wise and honest, and added, 'If she should at any time thrash you I am certain you will have done something to deserve it.'[55] Less welcome was some advice from Brodrick who, like others of his friends, was worried by Curzon's growing indifference to religion. Love and mutual admiration were important, he told him, but a successful marriage required the help of religion to sustain it.[56] To Brodrick's further admonition to be faithful to Mary, Curzon replied spiritedly that he had always been very loyal to those he had loved and that he would be even more loyal to the girl who had consented to link her fate with his. 'I do not enter upon matrimony except with the idea and intention of being faithful to its highest and deepest as well as to its external and superficial obligations.'[57]

The weeks between Curzon's return from Afghanistan at the end of January 1895 and his departure for the wedding in America in early April were a more than usually hectic time for him. His brother Assheton nearly died of pleuro-pneumonia in February, and his own back gave way in March, forcing him to spend over a week in bed. Yet he insisted on playing an active part in Parliament, asking questions about Siam and making speeches about MPs' pay and the right of peers to remain in the House of Commons; he also became embroiled in the issue of Chitral, whose ruler had been murdered on New Year's Day. Yet even Curzon could not fulfil all his commitments on time and he was forced to take work with him on his voyage to New York. He had agreed with the publisher Macmillan to write an introduction to a new edition of James Morier's *The Adventures of Hajji Baba of Ispahan*, a satire on the Persian people which he admired for its 'good-humoured flagellation of Persian peccadilloes' and its masterly portrait of 'the salient and unchanging characteristics of a singularly unchanging Oriental people'. Apologizing to Macmillan with a white lie, he blamed his failure to meet the deadline on his impending marriage, a contingency he could not have contemplated when he accepted the offer.[58] Three days before the wedding, he sent the piece from Washington.

Curzon was not the sort of man to allow the preparations for his wedding to be monopolized by his bride and her family. Mary was not even permitted to choose her wedding dress without an injunction about the way it should hang from the waist. The most important and time-consuming issue, however, was financial. Mary's wealth did not seem to Curzon a good reason for renouncing his claim to the much more limited Scarsdale funds. He even intimated to his father, on whom he wasted little tact or charm in business matters, that a generous settlement from him would stimulate still greater generosity from Levi Leiter. Asking for a covenant of £1,000 per year, he also suggested that Scarsdale might wish to avoid death duties by settling the Kedleston estate on him or a future son with £10,000 income for its upkeep. He pointed out that, had he been marrying a penniless English girl, his father would have been compelled to pay her a jointure if his son predeceased him as well as provide for the children. Lord Scarsdale's good fortune in escaping this dual obligation was advanced as an argument in favour of treating his heir more liberally.

While father and son were thus negotiating, Mr Leiter behaved with what Curzon recognized as 'really princely generosity'. Mary and her descendants were offered immediately the annual income from $700,000 (£140,000) worth of bonds which totalled $33,500 (£6,700), while on her father's death her marriage settlement would receive a further sum of at least one million dollars. In the event of Mary predeceasing him, her husband was to be allowed for his lifetime whatever portion of the £6,700 that he and Lord Scarsdale desired. Astonished at such munificence, Curzon suggested to his father that 'it would be only gentlemanly as well as wise not to appear to be too grasping' and that they should therefore ask for only £4,000 of the income. Nevertheless, the Indenture eventually stated that he could have the entire income if Mary died childless and retain one-third for himself if they had children. This liberality did not, understandably, produce an improved offer from the other side. Lord Scarsdale agreed to pay his son an annuity of £1,000 but he did not make over Kedleston or commit himself to do so after his death. He did state, however, that it was his intention to leave the estate to his eldest son.[59]

Curzon's closing letters to his fiancée were dominated by the curious behaviour of one of his closest friends. Cecil Spring Rice and Lord Lamington were almost the last unmarried friends of Curzon's generation, and were thus both candidates for the role of 'best man'. When he heard of the engagement in Washington, Spring Rice turned 'summer-saults of joy', told Curzon it was the best news he had heard for a long time, and promised as a wedding present a cabinet he had bought on their trip in the Far East; he also expressed his relief that Mary had not been 'lost' to an American. But soon afterwards he told her that Curzon's family and friends would disapprove of the match and followed this up by observing that her fiancé had been very fond of a Miss Morton whom 'everyone' had assumed he would marry. Mary began by feeling 'rather blue' about these revelations but soon became deeply upset, telling Curzon that Springy's one pleasure consisted in giving her pain.[60]

From the other side of the Atlantic her fiancé tried to calm her down, claiming that the Miss Morton story was 'simply grotesque' because he had only met her twice and had paid her not the slightest attention. Springy's disloyalty was merely 'jealous trash', a consequence of his love for Mary, and should be ignored. Some years earlier Spring Rice had indeed proposed to Mary and had been rejected. He had then gone to Japan and during their travels had advised Curzon himself to marry her. As his companion seemed unwilling to make a commitment, Spring Rice thought that he might still have a chance when he was again posted to Washington in 1894. Although Mary was by then secretly engaged, Springy refused to give up hope until he knew for certain that she loved someone else. On eventually learning of the engagement and realizing there must have been some understanding of which he was kept ignorant, he reacted with understandable emotion, alternately jealous and delighted by the news. Curzon, who claimed not to understand jealousy himself, recommended leniency to her old admirer. But Mary needed constant reassurance that the rumours were not true, and in his last letter before the wedding Curzon was still imploring her not to believe Springy's nonsense. He was in fact remarkably lenient towards his old friend and did not remonstrate about his behaviour. Recognizing, however, that Spring Rice had disqualified himself as a potential best man, he relegated him to the role of usher.[61]

Accompanied by Lamington and his brother Frank, Curzon arrived in New York on 17 April, reached Washington the next day and quickly sat down with lawyers to draw up the legal settlements. On the 23rd the wedding took place at the fashionable Episcopalian church of St John's, Mary wearing a dress from Worth and a diamond coronet from Kedleston. George at her side was suffering from acute backache but managed to disguise it from the guests. The ceremony was followed by a reception and a banquet in the Leiter mansion, after which the couple left for a short honeymoon in a country house in Virginia. Prodigious numbers of wedding presents had been accumulating in both Washington and England. A dozen of Curzon's closest friends had clubbed together to buy an immense silver-gilt centre-piece, suitable for grand dinners in future mansions. More personal and no doubt more poignant gifts were a case of Japanese silver spoons from Ethel Kirkwood and a morocco-bound copy of Rossetti's poems from Sibell Grosvenor. But Mary was now his 'Blessed Damozel' and remained so for the rest of her life. A verse from that poem is engraved on her tomb at Kedleston.

9

Number Two at the FO

L ORD ROSEBERY'S GOVERNMENT hobbled on until June 1895 when, to the relief of its leading members, it more or less voluntarily expired. On the 21st of that month the War Secretary, Henry Campbell-Bannerman, was censured by the Conservatives, at the instigation of Brodrick, for his alleged failure to supply the army with sufficient cordite. Although he was an outstandingly idle man, Campbell-Bannerman was an able as well as a popular minister, and Brodrick's allegation seems to have been largely spurious. But it was a Friday night, the Liberal Whips were unprepared and, before they could rally their followers, the Government had been defeated by seven votes. Had he wished, Rosebery could have reversed the vote and continued in power, but he was too thin-skinned to carry on with his cantankerous and demoralized Cabinet, and on the following day he resigned. Dismayed though she was by the Tories' treatment of Campbell-Bannerman, the Queen was relieved to be rid of the Liberals. Without pressing Rosebery for a dissolution of Parliament, she accepted his resignation and invited Lord Salisbury to form a government.

The Conservative leader realized it was time to transform his alliance with the Liberal Unionists into a coalition government. Admiration for Joseph Chamberlain among Tory MPs was still qualified by distrust, but it was widely felt that he should now be tamed by responsibility inside a cabinet. The ambivalent Conservative attitude towards the leader of the Radical Unionists was typified by George Curzon, who admired him as an orator while deploring him as a demagogue.[1] Two of Chamberlain's biographers have suggested that Curzon was the anonymous author of an unpleasant article in the *New Review* which called for an end to the situation whereby the Member for Birmingham enjoyed influence without drudgery or responsibility. Chamberlain, it had argued, should be made a minister as soon as the Conservatives were next in power, for nobody was 'capable of better and more useful work so long as he is driven and is not on any account allowed to drive'.[2] Whether or not Curzon wrote the article – there is no evidence for it among his papers or in the letters of his friends – Salisbury agreed with its argument if not with its tone. A day after receiving the Queen's invitation to form a government, he and Balfour met the leaders of their Liberal allies, Chamberlain and the Duke of Devonshire (formerly Lord Hartington). Reserving the leadership of the Commons for Balfour, Salisbury gave Devonshire a choice between the Foreign Office and the Lord Presidency (a post which included the chairmanship of a defence committee to co-ordinate the armed forces) while Chamberlain was offered the Exchequer, the Home Office or any other post he cared for. Considering Salisbury's prestige in foreign affairs, the Duke made the logical decision to become Lord President, but Chamberlain, whose favourite issues hitherto had been Ireland and social reform, surprised everyone by eschewing the domestic departments in favour of the Colonial Office. Upon this nucleus Salisbury built a strong Government with Goschen at the Admiralty, Hicks Beach at the Exchequer and the Marquess of Lansdowne at the War Office.

Although several of Curzon's friends thought he should have had a seat in the Cabinet, there was no obvious position for him. The only post for which he was really qualified was the India Office, which went to Lord George Hamilton, the former Under-Secretary in Disraeli's Government. Many years later, Winston Churchill argued that Curzon's failure to enter the Cabinet in 1895 indicated that the House of Commons considered him a lightweight: a first-rate parliamentarian, he argued, would have managed to establish a claim to Cabinet rank during the three years in opposition since his spell as a junior minister.[3] If Churchill was comparing Curzon's rate of advancement with his own, he was being unfair because each had plotted a very different parliamentary course. Unlike his critic, Curzon had decided to make a political name outside the Commons by becoming his country's leading authority on Asiatic affairs. His books and journeys were an admirable preparation for much of his later work, but they did not make him an indispensable candidate for the Cabinet at the age of 36. In addition, the demands of coalition politics forced Lord Salisbury to restrict the number of Tory Cabinet ministers to fourteen.

While Curzon himself had hopes of a place, he expected to be appointed Under-Secretary at the Foreign Office, a job he welcomed if it meant serving under Lansdowne but not if Devonshire became his chief.[4] In the event Salisbury kept the Foreign Office for himself, somewhat disingenuously telling Curzon he had done so against his will and wished the Duke had taken it instead.[5] Invited to act as his Under-Secretary in the Commons, Curzon replied with an acceptance of the job and a request for a privy councillorship, explaining that the honour would offset his constituents' disappointment that he had not achieved promotion to the Cabinet. Salisbury had anticipated the request and, barely a week after Rosebery's resignation, Curzon became the youngest man in living memory to be 'sworn of Her Majesty's Most Honourable Privy Council'. Rennell Rodd wrote from Cairo to congratulate him on his new post, suggesting it was the right job for him at that juncture and would prepare the way for control of the Foreign Office in the future. Congratulations were also offered by Churchill, then a subaltern at Aldershot, who went to a party at Devonshire House and found the new ministers dressed in their official blue and gold uniforms. Looking 'very splendid and prosperous', Curzon received his congratulations 'with much affability' and told the young cavalryman he hoped to have a share in making foreign policy instead of merely defending and explaining it in the House of Commons. A good deal more impressed by this parliamentary 'lightweight' than he recalled forty years later, Churchill studied Curzon and the ministerial uniforms and 'felt free to give rein to jealousy'.[6]

Salisbury had made it clear that Parliament must be dissolved as soon as the House of Commons had voted the new Government an interim financial supply. The election campaign thus began in July, the Liberal leaders traversing the country to deliver conflicting messages while Salisbury kept his party united with a moderate programme that included a few concessions to Chamberlain on social reform. The disarray in the Liberal Party, stemming from personal antagonisms as well as ideological differences, virtually assured its defeat. But the scale of Salisbury's victory took almost everyone by surprise. The Conservatives alone won 340 seats which, allied to 71 Liberal Unionists, gave them an enormous majority over 177 Liberals and 82 Irish nationalists.

To the electors of Southport, Curzon offered his usual blend of hostility to Home Rule, ambiguous endorsement of temperance, and sympathy for social reform, in particular for 'some provision for the old age of the thrifty and deserving poor'. In other respects 1895 was different from previous campaigns. Levi Leiter had removed any financial anxiety by giving him £1,000 for the election and later offering to increase his gift to whatever his son-in-law required. Mary was also there to help canvass and was such a success with the electors, always smiling and graceful, that her husband assumed she must be very happy. In fact she was miserable. Southport was 'a 4th-rate Brighton', she told her father, and its inhabitants were 'an idle, ignorant, impossible lot of ruffians', quite unworthy of George. Desperately homesick for America and her family, she could find nothing attractive about the place and regretted that victory would oblige her to visit it each year.[7]

Success at the polls was not made any less likely by the Liberals' choice of candidate. Until the beginning of 1895 Herbert Naylor-Leyland had been a Conservative MP and so great an admirer of Curzon that he had not only invited him to speak in his constituency but had also plagiarized his speeches. A sudden conversion to Home Rule had then induced him to change parties, an action for which Rosebery awarded him a baronetcy, and he was now challenging his erstwhile hero in a seat in which his uncle was a prominent Tory. It may not have been a particularly happy campaign for Sir Herbert – each morning he looked out of the window to see the word 'Rat' freshly painted on the wall opposite – but he did well to restrict Curzon's majority to 764.[8] Three years later, after his opponent had resigned to take up the viceroyalty, Naylor-Leyland captured the seat for the Liberals. Following his early death in 1899, Southport was held briefly by Curzon's first opponent there, Dr (later Sir) G.A. Pilkington, before returning to the Conservatives in the 'Khaki Election' of 1900.

The new Under-Secretary recognized that the closing years of the nineteenth century were a critical period for British foreign policy. He understood how rapidly international relations were changing and knew there was room neither for complacency about his country's position nor for delusions about a world happy to bask in a sunny Pax Britannica. Soon after the election he warned at Derby that the lull in foreign affairs was over. 'The world is unquiet. Uneasy symptoms are abroad. We hear the moaning of sick nations on their couches, and we listen to and witness the struggles of dying men.'[9] While Turkey and Persia slithered into apparently irreversible decadence, Russia continued her expansion into Asia while a new predator in Berlin, only a generation old, had appeared upon the scene. As Britain's industrial supremacy was now under challenge from both Germany and the United States, he saw that her international position could be maintained only by a combination of naval strength and astute diplomacy.

The presence of Salisbury at the Foreign Office and Chamberlain at the Colonial Office indicated that international affairs would not be neglected by the new Government. The venerable Prime Minister, who in appearance resembled both the cricketer W.G. Grace and 'one of Michelangelo's versions of God',[10] knew as much about diplomacy as any man in Britain. He had already been Foreign Secretary three times and Secretary of State for India twice. With experience and wisdom he combined patience, realism, a knowledge of the requisites of imperial power and an understanding of what could be achieved by diplomacy. He also appreciated the interaction of policies in distant continents. When one of his daughters wondered why he had reacted so mildly to a piece of Russian aggression in China, he replied that in six months' time he would be on the verge of war with France in Africa and could not afford to antagonize Russia beforehand.[11] While he was prepared to use force if necessary, he saw the futility of a small island, which refused to accept conscription, threatening to fight simultaneous wars in different parts of the globe. It was more sensible to concentrate on a few strategic points, such as the Upper Nile and the Indian frontier, and stay flexible on the rest. Above all it was important not to gloat over victories, because the concealment of diplomatic triumphs made it easier to repeat them. It was necessary, Curzon was told before one parliamentary appearance, to avoid 'all observations at all wounding to France' – unwelcome advice for someone who thought the best way of handling the French was to say frankly what he thought of them. On another occasion the Prime Minister observed that gratuitous hostility to Russia, with no object but the expression of indignation and patriotic temper, could only be counter-productive.[12] Diplomacy was a persuasive not a triumphalist profession. To be successful, it had to persuade the Cabinet, then the foreign powers and in the last resort the British people.

Salisbury was not a secret diplomatist but he was, as his Under-Secretary soon discovered, a secretive operator. He generally communicated with his deputy through minutes, Curzon sending a lengthy query about policy and receiving in reply a pithy couple of sentences in red ink. When asked whether the Court should go into mourning for the Empress Dowager of Japan, the Prime Minister replied, 'Better not make a new precedent. If there are several wives, are we to mourn for all?'[13] On more important issues Curzon often found it impossible to discover either from Salisbury or from the Foreign Office what the Government's policy was. In March 1896 he asked his chief if he might be allowed to see the private telegrams and despatches between the FO and its representatives abroad: it would be easier to defend the Government in the House of Commons, he pointed out, if he knew what was going on. Salisbury's acquiescence did not satisfy his deputy's thirst for information, and a few weeks later Curzon asked if he might be present when the Prime Minister received deputations. Although other parliamentary under-secretaries invariably attended deputations in their departments, he never even learnt of their existence until they had already left the Foreign Office. He would have liked, for instance, to have been present at a deputation about Indo-Chinese railways, a subject which particularly interested him, but the first he heard of it was from a report of one of Salisbury's speeches in *The Times*.[14]

Curzon's problems were sometimes simply the result of timing and communication. As he later told Lord George Hamilton, the Foreign Secretary and his deputy should have met every day to discuss policy before the Under-Secretary had to explain it in the House of Commons. But in his case this was impossible because Lord Salisbury spent the morning working in his house in Arlington Street and did not reach the Foreign Office until half-past three, at which hour Curzon was already answering questions on the Government front bench.[15] But the Under-Secretary's troubles often stemmed from the Cabinet's unwillingness to discuss an issue or from its inability to make up its mind. When dealing with a complicated matter in West Africa, Curzon felt miserable at the prospect of defending a policy 'without the slightest idea what the Cabinet really think or by what steps they arrive at their mysterious conclusions'.[16] For someone who always knew his own mind, indecisiveness was inevitably frustrating. It also placed him in an awkward position for, by remaining the Government's spokesman, he laid himself open to accusations that he defended from loyalty policies of which he disapproved from conviction.[17]

In spite of these problems, Curzon was an undoubted success as Under-Secretary. Efficient and self-assured, he had to make statements or answer questions from the front bench on subjects as diverse as the Uganda railway line, trawling in the Moray Firth, and the abolition of slavery in Zanzibar, a territory recently acquired from Germany in exchange for the island of Heligoland. Members from both sides of the House tried to trip him up, but he was invariably reliable: almost his only recorded mistake occurred when he turned over two pages of notes together and left out a passage on Madagascar. If he felt he had been badly misrepresented, he sometimes followed up a debate with furious letters and demands for an apology.[18] More often he treated his opponents with a disdain in which he taunted them with ignorance while refusing to supply them with information. The 'succinct discreetness' of his parliamentary replies prompted the Conservative MP T. Gibson Bowles to quip that 'just as words were given to conceal our thoughts, so under-secretaries were given to conceal' foreign affairs.[19] If, noted a parliamentary sketch-writer, the questioner pointed out that his query had not been answered, Curzon assumed a look of pained surprise and then repeated his reply with a slight variation of words but without satisfying the supplicant with more information.[20] Occasionally he employed blandness in place of dissimulation. When Bowles, a persistent tormentor, enquired whether the military operations in the Sudan were being carried out under a British or a Turkish flag, he replied that he did not know because he hadn't been there.[21]

The growth in Curzon's reputation during his period as Under-Secretary can be measured by the reaction to his major parliamentary speeches. Opponents might still deplore the tone and the partisanship, but they increasingly admitted that Curzon had become one of the most formidable debaters on the Treasury bench. His speech on Crete in May 1897, declared the Irish nationalist T.P. O'Connor, was one of the strongest and most masterful defences of a policy he had ever heard. 'Deliberate, certain of his facts, strong in his opinions, with a fine voice, even, well controlled, but resonant with passion, scorn, and self-will,' Curzon had dominated the debate and rattled his opponents.[22] Scoffing at MPs who protested with their 'mouths full of denunciation and [their] brains empty of suggestion', he had provoked another Irish member to accuse him of being 'very superior'; but his opponents were incapable of contesting his interpretation of the Christian-Muslim antagonism on the island.

By the following year commentators were even agreeing that Curzon's chief flaw – the arrogance of manner, that 'superior person' tone that had marred his earlier speeches – was much less evident.[23] In a debate on the Indian frontier in February, Labouchere admitted he had made by far the best speech, overshadowing both Balfour and Asquith, while the Liberal Unionist peer Lord Grey found himself wholly converted to Curzon's viewpoint.[24] It was not surprising that a politician who had travelled all over the ground should overwhelm opponents who had only vague notions about the nature of the frontier and its inhabitants. Nonetheless, Curzon's parliamentary successes now marked him out as the Tories' most likely champion in the coming years against Asquith and Edward Grey. As one supporter observed, there was no one else on their side who could match him: Curzon and Grey, he believed, were destined to be the Pitt and Fox of the future.[25]

The Under-Secretary found Lord Salisbury a good chief to serve under, admiring his wisdom at the same time that he regretted his intrinsic distaste for strong measures. Yet by temperament and viewpoint they were ill-suited to work together, and in a moment of exasperation Curzon later referred to him as 'that strange, powerful, inscrutable, brilliant, obstructive deadweight at the top'.[26] Lansdowne observed that the Prime Minister might 'intimidate his [foreign] visitors and curtail their stay by waggling his foot at them',[27] but he refused to employ intimidating tactics against foreign governments. When the French annexed Madagascar after promising not to, Salisbury shrugged his shoulders and told Curzon the action would merely be carried to France's debit in her account with Britain. He reacted similarly to their behaviour at Tunis which was not as bad as in Madagascar and 'well within the French code of honour as habitually practised'.[28] Curzon was exasperated by this attitude. On the Prime Minister's advice he told the House of Commons that the 'Concert of Europe' was a beneficent organization which occasionally did some good, but he did not believe that in practice European co-operation benefited his country. A better approach, he thought, would be to accept the individual hostility of all the great powers and use diplomacy to prevent them from uniting against Britain. There was no point relying on American sympathy, which was limited to the upper classes, or German friendship, which was confined to the Kaiser, just as it was futile to try to come to terms with Russia or France in Asia, because neither country was prepared to surrender her territorial ambitions. After he had left the Foreign Office, he repeatedly compared Salisbury's diplomacy to throwing bones to different dogs to keep them quiet. All that happened, however, was that the dogs, particularly France and Russia, devoured the bones and snarled for more. Britain had not gained anything from allowing the French into Djibouti and Madagascar or from surrendering her treaty rights to them at Tunis without exacting a similar concession with regard to Egypt. Nor had Germany become any friendlier after receiving Heligoland or installing herself at Dar-es-Salaam. Britain's good-natured and timorous policy of 'ceaseless, gratuitous, uncalled for and unrewarded concessions to everybody all over the world' had not even earned her the gratitude of her rivals.[29]

Curzon compared his position as Under-Secretary to that of 'Tommy Atkins' in Kipling's poem. He was like the 'thin red line of 'eroes' during the parliamentary session but found himself 'elbowed out of the show altogether' in the autumn.[30] Over some areas of foreign relations he had no influence whatever. Wisely, perhaps, he was largely excluded from formulating policy on contentious issues with France. For several years he had been obsessed with the threat to Siam and believed the French would absorb that country as well as the vassal territories to the east of the Mekong River. Although he hailed the Anglo-French Agreement of 1896 – which recognized the neutrality and independence of Siam – as one of the triumphs of the Government, he privately feared that France would eventually gobble up the rest of the kingdom. As Viceroy of India a few years later, he was reluctant to give a Buddhist relic to the King of Siam because he thought the treasures of the royal palace in Bangkok would one day end up in the Louvre.[31]

Africa was another area over which he was largely sidelined. He was not, he complained, 'allowed an innings' with the Germans and the Portuguese over Delagoa Bay but was required to labour at length over schemes for the abolition of slavery in Zanzibar. He defended with verve the Anglo-Egyptian advance to the Sudan, but he seems to have had little influence on Salisbury's long waiting game with the French in East Africa. By the time his chief, after years of patience, had finally excluded them from the area and turned the Nile Valley into an axis of British power, Curzon was in India.

The Under-Secretary did, however, have the satisfaction of seeing his policy prevail in two Asian matters he considered of crucial importance. Curzon's visit to Chitral during his exploration of the Pamirs at the end of 1894 had been quickly followed by the murder of its pro-British ruler, the Mehtar, the deposition of his assassin by a small British force from Gilgit, the encirclement of that force in Chitral by a large army of Pathans and Chitralis, and a desperate siege that was finally broken by the arrival of a British relief column. Following this classic set-piece of Victorian valour, Rosebery's Government decided to withdraw from Chitral, a policy powerfully opposed by Curzon in a series of letters to *The Times*. To those who argued that Chitral's inaccessibility guaranteed it from Russian invasion, he pointed out that, while none of the advocates for retreat had been within 150 miles of the place, their opponents included the Viceroy and the Government of India, the previous

Viceroy, the previous Commander-in-Chief and every British official in Kashmir. The placing at Chitral of a political officer with an escort, he maintained, was essential both for the security of the frontier and for the maintenance of internal order in a volatile region.[32]

The fall of Rosebery's Government before the withdrawal had been carried out forced Curzon to turn his powers of persuasion on his colleagues. The nature of the country was such, he argued whenever a retreat was being considered, that even a small British force would be able to repel, or at the very least greatly to retard, any Russian advance. If, however, Chitral was evacuated, the tribes of the Hindu Kush and the Indus Valley would rise against the British while the Russians would move in and obtain an easy line of descent upon Jalalabad, turning the British flank and threatening any forward movement to Kabul. Salisbury was soon convinced, a garrison was sent, and in the frontier uprisings of 1897 there were no disturbances in Chitral. Liberal attempts to blame the troubles on the Government's determination to stay in Chitral and build access roads were unconvincing, especially when accompanied by geographical ignorance. An unfortunate reference by Asquith to the 'half-naked tribesmen' of Swat, one of the highest habitable regions in the world, prompted Curzon to speculate in public on whether the Liberal politician was as knowledgeable about their feelings as he was about their appearance.[33] The Under-Secretary knew the area better than any other politician and could afford to be derisive. Events, moreover, supported him, for the retention of Chitral proved to be cheap and successful, while evidence from Russian officers later revealed that their army had been ready to seize the place as soon as the British withdrew.[34] No one was more responsible than Curzon for their failure to do so.

The Under-Secretary also induced his colleagues to counter a Russian move in the Far East. As government ministers often repeated, British interests in China were commercial rather than territorial and favoured the preservation of that country's independence. The survival of such a policy, however, depended on the willingness of other powers to show similar forbearance over a nation trying to recover from its recent defeat at the hands of the Japanese. When in November 1897 the Germans seized the port of Kiaochow, and shortly afterwards a Russian naval squadron arrived in Port Arthur 'to spend the winter' – a stay that predictably outlasted the season – Curzon decided that some action must be taken to preserve British interests in northern China. In February 1898 the Chinese Government offered Britain a third port in the Gulf of

Chihli, Weihaiwei, but Salisbury thought that an acceptance would be contrary to British policy. Suffering from a bad attack of influenza, the Prime Minister then went to the South of France for a rest, and the matter was set aside. Curzon, however, had prepared a memorandum arguing that Britain, which had greater commercial interests in China than any other nation, should not allow herself to be squeezed out of the northern part of the country by Russia and Germany. In March he distributed it to the six leading members of the Cabinet and remained undeterred by their unfavourable reactions. Despite the continued opposition of Hicks Beach and Chamberlain, he managed to persuade Balfour to bring the matter before the whole Cabinet and was invited to several meetings to argue the case in favour of accepting the lease for Weihaiwei. After his standpoint had eventually prevailed, Balfour telegraphed the Prime Minister for his approval. As with Chitral, Salisbury came to see the merits of his deputy's firmness and thanked him for persuading the Cabinet to accept his point of view.[35]

The strain of Weihaiwei, the working weekends and the late nights spent editing draft papers to be sent to Lord Salisbury in France, finally laid him out. For nearly three years, the longest period in his adult life, Curzon had survived incessant work without his health breaking down. But by Easter 1898 he was flat on his back with his old complaint, spinal weakness. Unable to bend or stoop without acute pain, he took to his bed, attended by a doctor and a masseur, and lay editing and re-editing the papers on China. After a month he returned to the House of Commons, but the recovery did not last, and before the end of the session he had collapsed once again. At the same time his insomnia, which had hitherto been sporadic, became chronic. The slightest light through a window prevented him sleeping, so his wife had darkened curtains made which they could take on their travels.

Mary also suffered from the strain and absorption of George's work. Her arrival in England after their marriage had been a triumph, thousands of people lining the streets of Derby to cheer while a crowd of tenants and estate workers waited to welcome them at Kedleston. Lord Scarsdale and his children were kind and charming, and George was in high spirits, joking with the gamekeepers' wives. Her second visit to the ancestral home, which took place after the disillusioning experience of Southport, was much less enjoyable. Her father-in-law now struck her as an ogre, 'an old despot of the 13th century' who made 'fiendish grimaces' and refused to allow his eldest son to make improvements, even at his own expense, to the dilapidated and uncomfortable mansion.[36]

London, a city where she had enjoyed such social success a few years earlier, was also a disappointment. Shortly before their marriage her husband had taken 5 Carlton House Terrace, in Nash's imposing row overlooking St James's Park, where he had organized the decoration and hired the staff. He always had great confidence in his own taste and seldom trusted anybody else's. When Mary gave him a ring, he declared that a ring on a man's finger was no less absurd than a hoop through a woman's nose, and put it on his watch chain.[37] During his bachelor years he had prided himself on the way he had arranged his various lodgings and told Mary he thought he could have made a career as a decorator. He was 'mad on furnishing', he wrote during their engagement, and looked forward to doing it together after their marriage.[38] But poor Mary was never given the chance. By the time she reached her enormous new home, the house was already decorated and inhabited by a large number of surly and incompetent servants. After an unhappy few months there, George decided the rent was too high, and they moved to a slightly smaller house at the end of the row, 4 Carlton Gardens, a former residence of Lord Palmerston which now belonged to Arthur Balfour. The staff problem, however, did not improve and drove Mary to complain that English servants were so stupid and disagreeable that they made life almost unbearable.[39] The persistency of such complaints at these and other residences suggests that she was inept at handling people who worked for her.

The Curzons' first daughter, Irene, was born in January 1896 at the house in Carlton Gardens. The pregnancy had been a difficult one, threatening a miscarriage and later a premature birth, and even causing Mary to fear for her own survival. Four days before the birth she made a new will leaving much of her jewellery, if she did not survive her confinement, to George's next wife.[40] Irene was followed two and a half years later by Cynthia, an event which drew commiseration from some who realized how much Curzon wanted an heir and who encouraged him with examples of couples who had bred sons after a succession of daughters.

Irene's birth did little to reduce the feelings of loneliness and homesickness which had afflicted Mary since arriving in England. Married life in the capital turned out to be entirely different from those seasons of balls and country-house parties at which she had once shone. She was no longer an exotic and temporary novelty on the social stage but a settled woman who suddenly found it difficult to make new friends. She pined for Washington and longed to see members of her family, but their visits left her feeling even more homesick afterwards. She was still in love with her husband but she rarely saw him except when he was working at home. 'He sits and sits at those Foreign Office boxes', she wrote, 'until I could scream.' Curzon did indeed work harder than most ministers, virtually abandoning his social life and never taking any exercise beyond the short walk home from the House of Commons at night. But Mary did not object or try to alter him. She had heard complaints that Asquith's second marriage had led him to pay less attention to politics than to his social life, and she did not want to be responsible for a similar change in George.

While Mary was pregnant and feeling miserable, her husband was telling Spring Rice that matrimony was a success so overwhelming that celibacy, which had once been a delight, had now become a puzzle.[41] Curzon was a loyal and affectionate husband but not a considerate one. He loved to be with Mary and the babies, to tease them and use baby talk and nicknames: he always called her 'Kinkie', a name then without connotations, while she called him 'Pappy', which may have been a derivation of 'Bab', a name his brothers and sisters knew him by before he went to Wixenford. But he did not concern himself very much with Mary's happiness when he was not with her. In London they hardly ever entertained or went to dinner in other people's houses. Nor did they pay many country-house visits, although once they went to Chatsworth, Kedleston's Derbyshire rival, and took a strong aversion to the Duke of Devonshire's guests. 'That fashionable card-playing, race-going lot are an idle set,' Curzon observed, 'and their life is very empty and vapid.'[42] Only at weekends at The Priory, a Georgian house which they rented near Reigate, did Mary have a chance to entertain people.

Throughout his adult life as a bachelor, Curzon had lived uncomplainingly in small flats in the middle of London or in rooms in the suburbs. After his marriage he never lived in anything other than a large and very grand mansion. Apart from Carlton Gardens and The Priory, he also rented Scottish castles for grouse-shooting. Mary did not see much more of her husband on holiday than she did in London. On one visit he spent six days in bed with an injured foot while she, confined indoors by incessant rain, entertained members of his family and dealt with a fresh set of servants. In good health or bad, Curzon began the day working in bed with his Foreign Office papers and then summoned the head keeper at half-past seven to plan the day's sport. He and the other guns set off at nine and walked all day with only a break for lunch.

Proud of the fact that he could tramp for eighteen miles a day over the moors without having taken any exercise since the previous September, he sometimes insisted on walking home afterwards as well. Sending his guests back to the castle in a carriage, he liked to return with the keepers on foot, asking them numerous questions about the district and its inhabitants and telling them stories about his travels abroad.[43]

I O

Sailing to Bombay

———————◆———————

GEORGE CURZON HAD made little secret of his desire to become Viceroy and Governor-General of India. As early as 1890 he had admitted at a dinner in the House of Commons that it was the greatest of his various ambitions.[1] The British presence in India had inspired him since hearing Sir James Stephen describe in a lecture at Eton how their country held on 'the Asian continent an empire more populous, more amazing and more beneficent than that of Rome'.[2] He came to believe that British rule in India was the greatest thing his countrymen had achieved and he dedicated his Persian volumes to the officials who carried it out. The preservation of British dominion had been the chief object of his work both as a writer and as a politician, and thus it was logical that he should aspire and petition to direct it. As Brodrick observed on his appointment, 'never was a goal sought with so much resolution and won by such merit and perseverance'.[3]

Curzon once described the East as 'a university in which the scholar never takes his degree' because he was doomed to remain a learner.[4] But few people had worked harder for that elusive degree than himself. No previous Viceroy had been so well qualified to govern the Sub-continent. No one else since Lord William Bentinck had had any particular interest in India except for Sir John Lawrence, the Mutiny hero who had been sent back as Viceroy in 1864; and Lawrence unfortunately lacked that experience of the home Government which the highest post required. No other Viceroy, besides, had anything approaching Curzon's knowledge of India's frontier and its neighbours.

His qualifications were widely recognized by contemporaries. In 1895 Colonel Neville Chamberlain, the inventor of the game of snooker, had written from Kashmir observing that he would be retiring at about the time Curzon became Prime Minister and suggesting his correspondent might bridge part of the interval by ruling India as Viceroy. The Liberal Unionist peer, Lord Grey, was more forthright. The Indian empire, he told the Under-Secretary, required the best man available, and if he were Prime Minister he would insist on Curzon going out to govern it.[5]

If Lord Elgin retired as expected in January 1899, Curzon would then be a few days short of his fortieth birthday. That was much younger than the average age of previous Viceroys and Governors-General, but only two years less than the one he most admired, Warren Hastings, and in fact slightly older than the two he most resembled, the Marquess Wellesley and the Marquess of Dalhousie. He wanted to succeed Elgin partly because he had other ambitions for later decades but also because he believed that the Indian climate and conditions of work required a youthful and vigorous Viceroy. In the spring of 1897 he therefore wrote to Lord Salisbury a long epistle, composed in a style alternately self-deprecating and egotistical, requesting the post. The Prime Minister replied that Curzon would be fully worthy of the appointment, that India would be richer and the Foreign Office poorer for the transaction, but that a decision did not have to be made for a year and a half, and he could not at that stage commit himself. Exactly a year later, nothing having been said or written in the interval, Curzon wrote another lengthy letter in the same tone as before, pointing out that he had spent the last twelve years striving to make himself fit for the position. His chief was once again noncommittal, although by then he had in fact advised Queen Victoria that his Under-Secretary would make a good Viceroy. Curzon had great ability, he told her, as well as extraordinary industry and knowledge; he had developed a good deal at his present post, and his only fault was occasional rashness of speech in the House of Commons.[6]

Lord George Hamilton, the competent and mild-mannered Secretary of State for India, was alarmed at the prospect of such a replacement for the docile Elgin. Curzon, he was misinformed at the India Office, was 'a regular Jingo, with Russia on the brain', and he feared the appointment would lead to trouble with India's neighbours.[7] Hamilton was also worried about his health and persuaded Salisbury to insist on a medical examination. Curzon had fortunately just recovered from a breakdown that had kept him from the House of Commons for several weeks and was able to procure a surprisingly unambiguous health certificate. Had he been making a report for a life assurance office, wrote the surgeon Sir Thomas Smith, he would have recommended insurance at the ordinary rate.[8] Less than two months later, after the Queen had formally accepted Salisbury's advice to appoint him, Curzon's back gave way again.

On receiving Smith's report, the Prime Minister forwarded a letter which the Queen wanted her next Viceroy to see. Her Majesty's pungent views on Indian policy had not mellowed as she approached her eightieth birthday. Ten years earlier she had rebuked Salisbury himself for referring to Indians as black men, and to the end of her life she exhorted Englishmen to treat her Indian subjects fairly. Her instructions to Curzon, based though they were on an unfair assessment of the Indian Civil Service and influenced by the universal dislike of her Indian servant 'the Munshi', were uncompromising in their zeal. The future Viceroy, she declared, must shake himself free from his 'red tapist, narrow minded Council and entourage' and not be 'guided by the *snobbish* and vulgar, overbearing and offensive behaviour' of British officials. He should become more independent, '*hear for himself* what the feelings of the Natives really are' and be careful not 'to trample on' the Indians or 'make them *feel* that they are a conquered people'. Of course they must feel that the British were their masters, but this 'should be done kindly and not offensively' as had often been the case in the past.[9]

The appointment, announced on 11 August 1898, excited a certain amount of private envy among Curzon's acquaintances. Rennell Rodd reflected sadly that he was falling behind his contemporaries, while Spring Rice railed against their friend's ambition: one could accept the self-interest of people like Pitt or Wellington, but it was galling when the successful self-seeker was of the same age and had been to the same school and university as oneself.[10] Public comment, however, was generally very favourable. There was a little carping in the press, particularly from the *Daily Chronicle*, but almost unanimous approval from Parliament. Such disparate leaders of the Opposition as Morley, Labouchere, Edward Grey and O'Connor united in welcoming the appointment. All of them also regretted Curzon's departure from the House of Commons both because of the loss of his skills and the loss of his comradeship. O'Connor, who disagreed with him on nearly every issue, thought he had 'a real genius' for Parliament, while Grey, who had been his principal opponent for six years, declared that no Tory was more admired on the Liberal benches.[11] A less solemn note of congratulation was struck by the anti-imperialist Blunt, who wrote to terminate Curzon's membership of the Crabbet Club and to express the hope that his fellow rhymester would prove to be the best, the last and the most frivolous of Viceroys.[12]

The recurrence of back trouble in August made both Salisbury and Balfour doubt whether Curzon would in the end be fit enough to take up his new post. Another specialist was consulted who once again produced an over-optimistic forecast. There was no organic disease, reported Howard Marsh, all the muscles and nerves were perfectly healthy, and the curvature of the spine could be corrected in favourable conditions. His patient's state was merely the result of over-work and would be much improved by horizontal rest and the avoidance of fatigue. No treatment was prescribed beyond douching of the spine with very hot water which could be done at the spa of Strathpeffer in Scotland.[13]

Curzon went north at the beginning of September, a few days after Mary had given birth to their second daughter Cynthia. While in Scotland he was summoned to Balmoral where he heard from the Queen her views on 'red-tapism' and other Indian problems. The two of them also discussed his viceregal title. Although Curzon did not particularly like the House of Commons and spent little time in the lobbies or the smoking room, he was reluctant to be forced into the House of Lords before his father's death; he still hoped one day to head a government from the front bench of the Lower House. Lord Salisbury suggested the problem could be overcome by giving him an Irish peerage which did not confer automatic membership of the House of Lords.* Although several Governors-General, including Wellesley and Lord Moira, had held Irish titles, they had also had some connection with Ireland, while Curzon was linked to the island neither by blood nor interest nor even holidays; in fact it was one of the few places in Europe he had never visited. There appeared, however, to be no other solution, and at the end of September he was made Baron Curzon of Kedleston in the peerage of Ireland.

His illness and Mary's pregnancy were not allowed to delay their preparations for departure. They did not need to hire servants for their official residences in India but they had to engage some senior staff. Lord Cromer, Britain's powerful Consul-General in Egypt and a man

---

*The Act of Union with Ireland, like that with Scotland, gave the country's peers the right to elect a certain number of their representatives to the House of Lords. The remainder, like Lord Palmerston, could become members of the House of Commons.

Curzon greatly admired, sent excellent advice on policy but some curious suggestions about personnel: the Viceroy-designate, he believed, should choose a Military Secretary with no opinions and a Private Secretary who knew nothing about India.[14] Colonel Sandbach was a fine soldier without many opinions but turned out to be a complete failure as a Military Secretary, whose principal duties were social; Curzon soon realized that he was more deficient in social tact than anyone he had ever come across. For Private Secretary he decided to ignore Cromer's advice and chose Walter Lawrence, a Balliol graduate and former member of the Indian Civil Service who had recently become the Duke of Bedford's agent in England and never expected to see India again. His tact, competence and knowledge of the Subcontinent proved invaluable to his new chief. Curzon also trusted to his own instincts when selecting a nanny for his children. The candidates were rigorously interviewed by him, and a long report on the most prepossessing applicant was then submitted to Mary.

A certain amount of financial anxiety clouded the Curzons' departure. They discovered that an immediate outlay of nearly £10,000 was needed to transport themselves out to India and to buy most of Lord Elgin's possessions there, including his horses and carriages. An appeal was made to Mary's father, but he was unable to help much because he had just lost nearly ten million dollars in his son's attempt to corner the American wheat market. Curzon also suffered some financial loss when Lord Salisbury decided it would be inappropriate for a Viceroy to publish a book on India; he therefore had to return a publisher's advance of £1,500 as well as pay the printing costs of his latest work, *On the Indian Frontier*, a book which never subsequently appeared. In the middle of these problems Curzon suddenly decided to buy the lease of 1 Carlton House Terrace, one of the great pavilions flanking Nash's row next to the lesser house they had been renting from Balfour. Admitting it was a curious time to buy property, he told his father it was the only house that they really liked and that he considered £25,000 for a 25-year lease to be a bargain. Although Levi Leiter's offer to buy the house for them had reluctantly been withdrawn, Curzon borrowed the money from a bank and went ahead with the purchase. The annual interest of nearly £1,000 on the loan was offset by the rent paid by the American Ambassador, Mr Joseph Choate, but the arrangement was to cause the Viceroy persistent irritation. From India he wrote Scarsdale a series of letters complaining about the offensive rudeness and extortionate demands of his tenant.[15]

The leave-taking was appropriately both formal and festive. The couple spent two nights at Windsor Castle where the Queen talked to Mary about Indian life and congratulated George on his wise and beautiful wife. They were now being treated like grandees, Mary informed her parents: station masters always met them, carriages were reserved, crowds gathered and people bowed. At the end of October over two hundred Old Etonians assembled at the Monico in Piccadilly Circus to eat a twelve-course meal in honour of three of their number: Lord Minto, who had been appointed Governor-General of Canada, J.E.C. Welldon, who had abandoned the headmastership of Harrow to become Bishop of Calcutta, and Curzon. Lord Salisbury refused to attend on the grounds that he had been miserable at Eton and would have been out of place at a glorification of the school.[16] Lord Rosebery therefore took the chair and proposed a toast, along with Lord Roberts, Lord Lansdowne and the Provost of Eton. The occasion was indeed a self-congratulatory glorification of a school which since Queen Victoria's accession had produced a majority of the Viceroys of India and the Governors-General of Canada. In his speech Curzon described how his interest in India had begun at Eton and spoke of his determination to emulate his Etonian predecessors and to remain 'true to the honour and the credit of that ancient foundation'.

A less grandiose but equally self-regarding function was held in December, when the Curzons' friends gave them a farewell party at the Hotel Cecil. The event was similar to the 'Souls' dinners George had given before his marriage, but this time Wyndham wrote the ballads and Lord Elcho delivered the speech. In his reply Curzon compared Wyndham to Sir Philip Sidney, hoped he would enjoy a similar fame but escape a similar fate, and invited all his friends to India where they would soon discover that 'behind the starch of a purely superficial solemnity' there lurked the same incorrigible characteristics which they had alternately bewailed and pardoned in Britain.[17] Mary rushed from the dinner to catch the night train to Plymouth, where her children were already in their bunks on the SS *Arabia*. Her husband joined them three days later at Marseille but was not permitted to escape without a last warning from Brodrick. It would be folly, he was told, to jeopardize a potentially great career by the disease of overwork. Yet if he carried on as he had done over the previous ten years, he would return from India as broken as his mid-century predecessors, Dalhousie and Canning. To the people who gave him his exalted post, to the friends who had championed his career, and to the wife whose life was wrapped up in his, he had a duty not to gamble with his health and risk the loss of everything.[18]

On the voyage out Curzon demonstrated his limited respect for Brodrick's advice. He toiled day and night, recalled Walter Lawrence, writing, reading and extracting information from any expert on India who happened to be on board. His Private Secretary, who regarded voyages as intervals of forced rest, did not think the pace could last, but in fact it quickened in the heat of the Red Sea and never slackened during nearly five years spent with the Viceroy in India.[19]

The journey had become much shorter since the eighteenth century when it took five or six months to sail around the Cape to Madras and Calcutta. By the time of Curzon's birth a different route had been adopted – sailing to Alexandria, travelling overland to Suez and then boarding another ship – which cut the voyage by more than half. And by the time of his appointment it had been reduced to three weeks. The passenger steamer left Plymouth on 10 December, reached Aden on Christmas Day and dropped anchor at Bombay on the 30th. On dis-embarking, the Curzons received an address of welcome from the municipality and then drove with a guard of honour through cheering crowds to the Governor's house at Malabar Point. In the evening the viceregal couple were given a dinner by Lord Sandhurst, an old friend of George's who was now Governor of Bombay, followed by a reception at which 1,400 representatives from the city's various communities filed past them as they stood on a golden rug. The next day they were escorted to the station, which was swathed in red carpet, while troops presented arms and a band played 'God save the Queen'. Guards of honour were present at all the principal stations between Bombay and Calcutta, and at their destination they were welcomed by the Lieutenant-Governor of Bengal and conducted through large crowds to the viceregal residence.

The reception at Calcutta was not so well organized as that at Bombay. The train drew up at the wrong place, complained Curzon, the red carpet was 'the size of a postage stamp', and the band forgot to play the national anthem. Elgin's Military Secretary failed to remember the names of most of the people he introduced to the new Viceroy, no bands played in the streets, and the ADCs were huddled into a chara-banc so that they looked like a party going to the Derby.[20] Curzon was delighted, however, by the hearty welcome of the Elgins. The old prac-tice, whereby the departing Viceroy handed over to his successor as soon as they met and then stayed on for a while as his guest, had been abolished. He now entertained the incoming Viceroy for a few days of advice-giving and was superseded only half an hour before his departure. On 6 January 1899, therefore, Curzon marched in procession to the throne room of Government House, listened to the warrant proclaiming him Viceroy and then escorted the Elgin family to the landing-stage on the River Hooghly.

Few moments in Curzon's life gave him as much satisfaction as taking charge of the Viceroy's palace. He regarded it as the finest government house in the empire and superior to anything occupied by a representative of any sovereign anywhere in the world. It was a source of additional pleasure that the building, erected a century earlier by Wellesley, had been based on the plan of Kedleston. Although it is often said that the two palaces are very alike, Curzon himself recognized that the differences exceed the similarities. The idea of a central pile containing the state rooms with four pavilions radiating outwards is common to both, although at Kedleston only two of the wings were ultimately built. They both also possess a great marble hall supported by columns and a dome above the southern façade. But the materials used – sandstone in Derbyshire, brick and plaster in Bengal – the heights of the corridors leading to the pavilions, and the arrangement of the interiors are quite different. Curzon thought the external aspect of Government House more imposing but that of Kedleston more harmonious. In the quality of the furnishings there was no comparison between the two, because Calcutta lacked the Adam fittings of his ancestral home; besides, its rather low marbled hall could not be 'mentioned in the same breath' as its magnificent forerunner of alabaster columns in Derbyshire.[21]

Airy and ventilated, Government House was well designed for the climate but not for ease of living. To visit her children, who lived in a different wing, Mary had to walk along her own corridor, cross two large drawing-rooms and a ballroom, and then go down a further corridor before reaching the nursery. The position of the kitchens was even more inconvenient. These were located two hundred yards from the house, and all the food had to be carried across the garden in wooden boxes slung on poles. The organization of viceregal life in these conditions tended to be trying. On Monday mornings Mary arranged the details of the week's entertainments with Colonel Sandbach, then worked out the various menus with one ADC, organized the invitations with a second, and discussed the house arrangements with a third. After lunch she went on a house tour and decided where her guests were going to sleep. As the enormous house was barely half-furnished, ornaments and furniture had continually to be carted around the house to make the selected rooms habitable.[22]

The new Viceroy was exhilarated by Calcutta and found the work, the climate and the people equally delightful. Everything was rose-coloured, he reported home, the natives enthusiastic, the press jubilant, and British society full of praise and encouragement. He realized there would be storms ahead but expected them to be mild in comparison with parliamentary life at home. It was a glorious thing, he confessed, to have the power to do good without being thwarted by colleagues or checked by the House of Commons. He was impatient to tackle everything, particularly the bureaucracy which was in need of a radical overhaul: the filing system, for example, was so clumsy and unscientific that he had to ask Selborne at the Colonial Office to send him information about how it was arranged in Whitehall. But he realized he should take his 'fences' slowly and not reform everything in sight straightaway. Later he claimed, not quite accurately, that his first six months had been a period of 'conciliation and deference to official susceptibilities'.[23]

The Curzons participated with enthusiasm in Calcutta's social season that spring. Excluding lesser entertainments, they gave a State Ball, a State Dinner and a State Garden Party for 1,800 people, an Evening Party for Indian gentlemen, two Levees, and weekly dinners with dancing afterwards for sixty or seventy people. The protocol to be observed at the ball was formidable. They were escorted by their ADCs through the marble hall, up the staircase and along the ballroom while the guests bowed and the band played 'God save the Queen'. Mary then danced 'the State Lancers' with Sir John Woodburn, the Lieutenant-Governor of Bengal, while George danced with Lady Woodburn. Afterwards they sat on a dais covered with a golden carpet and sent their ADCs to bring them people to talk to. Next they were required to do a tour of the room, preceded by the Military Secretary and one of the ADCs, before Mary danced a second 'State Lancers' with the Commander-in-Chief. They then had to march in procession to the marble hall for dinner before returning to the ballroom for another session afterwards.

Mary preferred the dinner-dances which were less formal and where, instead of a conspicuous dais, there was an arrangement of chairs at the end of the ballroom. She liked Calcutta society and was interested by her visits to hospitals and schools, but she found it a great strain, especially as she was often unwell, to have to entertain and make polite conversation day after day. Her husband also enjoyed Calcutta and felt obliged to assure Queen Victoria that its society was not second-rate nor frivolous nor particularly dull: it was unfortunate, he thought, that the 'malevolent impressions' bandied in Britain should have been reinforced by the over-cynical stories of Mr Kipling.[24] Yet both Curzons soon realized that the enjoyment of their social life was blunted by repetition. Precedence was observed so rigidly in British India that they were always obliged to sit next to the second and third most important couples at any function. Mary thus found herself almost invariably beside the Commander-in-Chief, the Bishop of Calcutta, the Chief Justice, or the Lieutenant-Governor of Bengal. In the opinion of Bishop Welldon, who found the etiquette insufferable, any senior official in Calcutta during the season would be 'pretty well bored to death' by the necessity of taking the same lady into dinner night after night.[25]

Social variety was provided by the mass of visitors who descended on Government House during the winter months. But personal guests could also be trying. Having taken the trouble to go all the way to India, they settled down to enjoy themselves at the Viceroy's expense and often showed little inclination to move on. Lord and Lady Lonsdale, who arrived in Calcutta soon after the Curzons themselves, stayed for over seven weeks. A different type of hazard was exemplified by Winston Churchill who talked so incessantly for a week that Curzon gave him a lecture on the dangers of garrulity.[26] Fortunately the incident did not affect the young guest's enthusiasm for the Viceroy. Two years earlier he had told his mother that Curzon was 'the spoiled darling of politics . . . the typification of the superior Oxford prig', but he now confessed he had misunderstood him completely. The Viceroy, he reported to his grandmother, was a remarkable man with great charm of manner, and the two of them had enjoyed several long and delightful conversations.[27]

Curzon grew fond of Calcutta and used to take Mary for afternoon drives in his barouche, accompanied by postilions, outriders and body-guards, to different corners of the city. He loved the Maidan, the great park to the south of Government House, and he was fond of the River Hooghly, although he lamented the gradual disappearance of the high-masted sailing ships and their substitution by steamers. Immersed in the history of the city, he eagerly explored its streets to find the places where Macaulay wrote, where Thackeray was born or where Rose Aylmer, the subject of Landor's exquisite lines, was buried. He used to ruminate on the lives of past Governors and imagine himself in the position of Warren Hastings or Dalhousie or 'Clemency' Canning. He also came to know the native city and recalled with pleasure how their carriage was once stopped at Kalikut by an Indian crowd which insisted on showing them 'the reeking shrine of the sanguinary Goddess' Kali, the terrifying black deity with her garland of skulls and her earrings of little children.

Yet he was well aware that the capital of British India needed a massive programme of improvements. Conditions in 'the huge and palpitating slums', he declared, were a standing disgrace to the corporation which administered them. He longed to take control himself and once astonished the Bengal Chamber of Commerce by remarking that he felt tempted to become Chairman of the Calcutta Corporation after concluding his term as Viceroy. But there was a limit to the extent to which he could overrule the inactive, non-interventionist policies of the Bengal Government or interfere with the cumbersome municipal administration shared by British and Bengalis. On arriving in India he was forced to deal with a Calcutta Municipal Bill providing for a new executive committee with a British majority while leaving in position the old, overmanned corporation with its Bengali predominance. Curzon quickly decided it was an unworkable measure and set about redrafting it. By reducing the corporation to 'more manageable and less garrulous proportions', he made it more efficient, but by removing the native majority he provoked an early display of Bengali hostility and a mass of resignations.

In municipal administration as in many other things, Curzon's reforming zeal was hindered by cautious bureaucracy. Improvements in urban sanitation could not be accelerated because of Sir John Woodburn's fear of annoying the business community by increased taxation, while the Viceroy's attempt to combat industrial smog – a phenomenon which besmirched 'the midday sky with its vulgar tar-brush and turns our sunsets into a murky gloom'[28] – was retarded by the India Office's delay in sending out a smoke expert. Curzon refused, however, to postpone his plans to repair the city's monuments, and within weeks of his arrival he had informed Woodburn of his intention to restore the Old Fort and to rebuild at his own expense the monument to the victims of the Black Hole, which had been demolished in 1821. He thus had the satisfaction of seeing most of his work completed while he was still in office. The monument, to which he devoted much energy in trying to verify the location of the atrocity and the names of the people who died in it, was re-erected at the end of 1902. At the same time he was able to open the new Imperial Library as well as Hastings House, a residence of the former Governor-General which Curzon bought and restored as a guest-house for the Indian princes. He was also well satisfied by improvements he had made to the environs of Government House, which by then were well paved and properly lit, and by his work on the residence itself. During his time large classical urns were placed on the roof to break the monotonous line of the parapet, and a large coat of arms was inserted into the northern pediment. The house, which for climatic reasons needed repainting every autumn, also changed colour, becoming white instead of a 'dirty umber or yellow'.[29] Inside the building the Viceroy ordered a number of changes to make life easier for Mary and the children, and he renovated the pillars in the marble hall and the hangings in the throne room. Uncharacteristically, however, he neither reformed the absurd kitchen arrangements nor, until his final year, installed a bathroom with running water.

Winston Churchill had seen Mary with fever and feared her bad health might destroy the viceroyalty. Since her arrival she had suffered from colds, headaches and stomach ailments, and at the end of February a high fever caused her temperature to reach 106°. Realizing that she would not recover quickly in the Calcutta climate, her husband arranged for his family to embark on the annual migration to Simla a month in advance of himself. At the beginning of March Mary therefore left the plains of Bengal and found herself transported to an English village of tin-roofed houses in the foothills of the Himalayas. She loved the views of the hills, the slopes covered with pines and deodars, but she was not impressed by Simla. She would never be able to understand, she told her husband, why the Government had chosen it as India's summer capital.

The choice had in fact been made more by custom than by decision. Bentinck had established Simla as a popular hill-station by visits in 1831 and 1832, and Dalhousie had spent three successive summers there from 1849 during the annexation of the Punjab. Despite the immense trouble involved in transporting the files and personnel of the Government each year to a remote hill village some twelve hundred miles from Calcutta, John Lawrence was convinced that Simla should become the permanent summer headquarters of the empire. If the distance between the places was too great, he argued, the winter capital should be transferred to Delhi or Agra. But the British Government refused to abandon Calcutta and eventually agreed to a system of two capitals very far apart and each possessing obvious geographical drawbacks. The Radical MP, Sir Charles Dilke, defended Simla on the grounds that it gave 'vigour to the Government, and a hearty English tone to the State papers issued in the hot months'.[30] Yet while the benefits of a mountain climate may have been obvious, the alleged advantages of Simla were less evident. It was not, for example, as beautiful as Naini Tal, the summer capital of the North-Western Provinces, or Ootacamund, where the Madras Government retired during the hot weather. One civil servant found it so English and unpicturesque that he felt he might almost be in Margate.[31] Nor was the climate the best that the mountains could offer. April was often cold, May could be dusty, and the monsoons had usually begun by the end of June. In spite of Simla's altitude of some 7,000 feet, Curzon thought the climate enervating and monotonous and only found the air bracing when he went up another thousand feet. Mary was also disappointed by her new environment, for the fevers and headaches which had blighted her first months in Calcutta continued to assail her in Simla.

All Viceroys had complained about the town's accommodation. Until the 1880s the Government rented buildings for its offices, and the Viceroy himself lived in an unimpressive rented house called Peterhoff. But in 1885 the Civil Secretariat and the Army Headquarters moved into two large new offices, buildings ugly enough to remind people of warehouses in Liverpool.[32] Earlier, Lord Lytton had tried to build an appropriate house for the Viceroy, but his architect produced a grandiose and impractical design which had to be abandoned. It was not until Lord Dufferin's arrival in 1885 that revised plans for Viceregal Lodge were finally accepted and construction begun. The result, a neo-Elizabethan jumble of turrets and cupolas, was widely regarded as lacking in taste. Mary Curzon was dismayed by the first sight of her new home. It was 'hydropathic and American combined', she wailed to her husband, the sort of building a Minneapolis millionaire would revel in. Parts of the interior were even worse. She found the vulgarity of the dining-room beyond belief and felt like crying at so much 'needless hideousness'.[33] How, she wondered, could Lady Dufferin have selected a 'sultry brown yellow' for the walls when there were so many noble colours to choose from?

Curzon, who had made a detour into the Punjab and inspected the mosques of Lahore, arrived at Simla in early April. He shared Mary's views about Viceregal Lodge and in due course made substantial changes to the décor and even to the structure of the building. He also agreed that it was a strange summer home for the Government. Feeling cut off not only from the world but even from India, he told one official it was like being in a German spa. Yet he was in good health, suffering neither from backache nor from insomnia, and although he worked all day and took no exercise, Mary was relieved that he went to bed at midnight. He never cared for Simla but in that first spring he was glad to be away from the bustle of Calcutta so that he could settle down to a prolonged study of India's problems and plan his programme of reforms.

II

The Governance of India

———————— ◆ ————————

'As you and I know,' Curzon wrote to Lord George Hamilton, 'though perhaps it is desirable that the world should not, India is really governed by confidential correspondence between the Secretary of State and the Viceroy.'[1] To Hamilton's successor at the India Office, Curzon defined the relationship between the two positions. The Secretary of State, he declared, was the constitutional ally of the Viceroy, and the two of them were the joint heads of the Indian administration.[2] This may often have seemed to be the case, but in theory and sometimes in practice it was not. The Secretary of State for India was in fact the Viceroy's constitutional superior, responsible for the actions of the Indian Government to the Cabinet and to Parliament.

Both titles dated from the Government of India Act of 1858 when the British Government completed its slow absorption of the East India Company's role and took formal responsibility for the administration of India. The Secretary of State and the India Office were created to oversee the work of the Government of India, to approve legislation and changes of taxation, and to formulate policy, in conjunction with the Cabinet and Parliament, towards the Subcontinent. Since 1773 the chief executive in India had been the Governor-General, and he remained so until independence in 1947. In 1858, however, he was given the additional title of Viceroy to symbolize the fact that he was now the representative of the sovereign. Lord Canning, the first Viceroy, preferred it to the older, less resonant designation, and his successors were usually referred to as Viceroys, although 'Governor-General' remained their only statutory title. As the direct representative of the Queen, who assumed the title Empress of India in 1876, the Viceroy gained additional prestige and thereby confirmed popular perceptions of his relationship with the Secretary of State. When a Viceroy like Curzon coincided with a minister like Hamilton, a wise and gentle Freemason wrongly regarded as a nonentity by people who barely knew him, the Secretary of State might seem to be merely the Viceroy's agent in Britain who once a year told an exiguous audience in the House of Commons that all was well in India.[3] But when the Secretary of State was an autocrat like Morley and the Viceroy was the mild Lord Minto, the true constitutional position tended to reassert itself.

If the long weekly letters between Curzon and Hamilton arranged much of the governance of India, the shorter fortnightly correspondence which the Viceroy exchanged with Sir Arthur Godley, the Permanent Under-Secretary at the India Office, decided many details of administration. A pupil of Jowett, whom he revered, and a former secretary to Gladstone, whom he also revered, Godley had been appointed to his post at the age of 35. Although the India Office had to deal with every matter on the Subcontinent from irrigation to frontier policy, he had never been to India and had no particular knowledge of its problems. By the time of his retirement twenty-six years later, he had become immensely knowledgeable but he still had never visited, or expressed much desire to visit, the vast region to which he had dedicated his career. Shrewd, self-effacing and unflappable, he was valued by Curzon for his competence and good sense. Godley admired the talents, though not the character, of his fellow Balliol graduate, and once declared in an unctuous and disingenuous sentence that he never forgot he was 'a small man writing to a great man'.[4]

While the Secretary of State could overrule the Viceroy, he himself could be overruled by the Council of India, a body consisting mainly of retired officials who met regularly under Hamilton's chairmanship at the India Office. The councillors had often enjoyed distinguished careers in India, but by the time they reached Whitehall they were usually old and out of touch with the Subcontinent; Sir Alfred Lyall, who longed to resign his place and return to India as Governor of Bombay, complained that his work on the Council had the savour of chewed hay.[5] Yet the Act of 1858 invested this body with the power of veto on financial matters and legislation. Godley admitted the absurdity of giving the councillors final and absolute control over the policy of the Viceroy and the Secretary of State, but observed that they seldom used their authority on important matters. Curzon found even their interference in minor things a constant irritant and tried to convince Godley that the Act should be amended by Parliament. It was ridiculous to be obstructed by a group of carping old men, with little work and no responsibility, who wanted to preserve India as they remembered it. Godley agreed that 'the tendency of the ex-official to turn and rend his successor [was] a defect inherent in the nature of our Council', but shied away from the prospect of legislation.[6]

Improved communications in the course of the nineteenth century further reduced the Viceroy's independence. News of the Battle of Waterloo, fought in June, had not reached Calcutta until just before Christmas. A Governor-General of that period could thus act on his own accord in the knowledge that he would not learn of his employers' views for another year, and that in any case, even if they disapproved of his behaviour, they could hardly reverse his action. Electric telegraph and the Suez Canal, however, had greatly diminished the Viceroy's scope. It was only after nearly five years at his post that Curzon, while walking in the Himalayas, spent a few days beyond the range of the home Government's wires. Yet within India the Viceroy's powers remained unweakened. His Government was a personal one, observed Curzon, in which he could formulate his policy and draft his despatches on foreign affairs without consulting or even informing anyone else.[7] In India the telegraph had even enhanced the impression of omnipotence, for it was now widely believed that the Viceroy, in touch with his entire dominion, was the fount of all decisions.

The supreme authority in India lay with the 'Governor-General in Council', that is to say the Viceroy and his 'cabinet' of councillors. The Council consisted of four ordinary 'members' in charge of the Financial, Legal, Public Works and Military departments, a fifth who ran both the Home and the Revenue and Agriculture departments, and, if nominated by the Secretary of State, one 'extraordinary member', the Commander-in-Chief. The Foreign Department had no member and came directly under the control of the Viceroy himself, who had almost exclusive responsibility not only for foreign affairs but also for relations between the Government and the Indian native states. The Council, which usually met once a week, was thus much like the Cabinet in England except that the Viceroy could not choose its members – a feature Curzon found anomalous and unsatisfactory – and it had no responsibility to a parliament. The Legislative Council, which operated in Calcutta for the first three months of the year, had been enlarged during Curzon's time as Under-Secretary and had become marginally more representative. Now it consisted of the Viceroy's Council, various officials nominated by the provincial governments and by Curzon himself, a member of the Calcutta Chamber of Commerce, and a handful of Indians elected by the provincial legislatures of Bengal, Madras, Bombay and the North-Western Provinces. Although the councillors had more power than their predecessors, it was difficult for them to obstruct the Viceroy's legislative programme.

The Government of India may have been, as its defenders claimed, benevolent and beneficent, but no one could deny that it was an autocracy. Curzon was surprised that such a form of rule was permitted by the British Constitution and believed it could only have happened in Asia whose inhabitants were by nature followers. In the course of his viceroyalty people came to discern Asiatic features in his own rule. Friends jokingly called him Akbar, but Indian nationalists later compared him to Aurangzeb, the most intolerant of the Moguls, and one thought he had so far forgotten English methods as to embrace Asiatic ways of government.[8]

The Viceroy's duty, in Curzon's view, was to be head not only of the Government but of every department as well. Scrutinizing the workings of the secretariats, he soon recognized that, although the administration was conscientious and permeated by a strong sense of discipline, it had become clogged by bureaucratic procedures and was incapable of initiating policy. Lord Elgin, he discovered, had written admirable minutes about details but had scarcely framed a policy or made an innovation. Day after day he came across matters that had been either shelved or lost from sight in a maze of departmental argument.[9] Examination of files revealed an astonishing system in which proposals were sent around the departments and returned to their starting point after a year or so garnished with an array of minutes from innumerable clerks and assistant secretaries. 'All these gentlemen state their worthless views at equal length,' he complained to Godley, 'and the result is a sort of literary Bedlam.'[10] A matter that could have been settled by the relevant officials in a couple of discussions went unresolved while its file proceeded in a leisurely way around Calcutta or Simla. Curzon, himself a profuse writer of minutes, was determined to reform the system. 'I do not want', he informed the Secretary of the Foreign Department, 'the personal impression or the opinion of everyone in the Department on everything that comes up.'[11] The officials of this department exasperated him too by their inability to write properly, a defect which obliged him to draft all despatches or letters of importance himself. This offence was characteristic of the rest of the administration, above all the army secretariat; by Curzon's exacting standards, there was only one Secretary of a department who could write decent English. Indeed, the Viceroy spent so much time correcting the 'positively villainous' despatches of his officials that he often thought it would be quicker to write them from scratch himself.[12] In some cases he did.

The running of the departments was not assisted either by the members' habit of doing much of their work in their homes or by their fondness for government by correspondence. The location of the Foreign Department, which Curzon ran, was also a hindrance. As it was a quarter of a mile from his office in Government House, he had no way of making references, getting papers or issuing instructions except through messengers running between the two places. It was, he told Hamilton, like conducting the affairs of the India Office without emerging from the Carlton Club.[13] Another anomaly, he soon noticed, was the division of labour in his Council. The Law Member had only two or three hours' work a day outside the short legislative session, while the Home Member, if conscientious, found himself as overburdened as the Viceroy. The Home Department dealt with educational, medical, sanitary, ecclesiastical and judicial affairs, as well as with local government and the police, while its Member was also in charge of the Department responsible for forests, land revenue and the agricultural development of the country. For much of Curzon's time the Home Member was Sir Denzil Ibbetson, one of the most distinguished civil servants of his generation; but as he was also the frailest, much of his work had to be done by a colleague to prevent him breaking down.[14]

'Curzon will hustle you secretaries,' an army officer had warned the senior official of the Foreign Department. 'Oh no!' was the reply, 'he will be paper-logged in three months.'[15] The Secretary's complacency vanished as the Viceroy swept through the departments, shaking up officials and putting an end to what he described as the era of 'tranquil procrastination'. 'Efficiency of administration', proclaimed Curzon, was 'a synonym for the contentment of the governed', and officials soon realized what he intended to do. His whole viceroyalty, remarked the editor of *The Times of India,* was 'one long protest against the laggards and the languid'.[16] So many areas of administration needed fresh ideas that he brought out experts from Britain to examine and report, and in some cases direct, his various projects. The laggards and the languid were in the end largely defeated, and so too were the wafflers. Curzon's note on the system of minuting was distributed to the provincial governments and resulted in a significant decrease in the number of official papers. The only person exempted from its edicts was himself.

Surveying his task that first spring at Simla, the Viceroy felt it would take him ten years to achieve half of what needed to be done. Nothing, he told Pearl Craigie, had been accomplished hitherto under six months. 'When I suggest six weeks, the attitude is one of pained surprise, if six days one of pathetic protest, if six hours of stupefied resignation.'[17] After he had been in India for six months, he claimed he had not had a day off work or one in which he had laboured for less than eight hours. He believed that the foundations of a successful administration must be laid in the first year when the Viceroy was still fresh, because otherwise a man's energies would become dulled by the prodigious routine, the resistance to reform, and the overwhelming weight of tradition and precedent.[18] His capacity for work astonished everyone. Officials from the Foreign Department who sent him a stack of files each evening and observed how meticulously they had been dealt with by nine o'clock the next morning, thought it a 'standing miracle' that he had found time between dinner and breakfast to dispose of them.[19]

The members of Curzon's Council were on the whole a mediocre group, far less able than Lord Dufferin's colleagues eleven years earlier. Of the twenty-two members Curzon had to deal with during his viceroyalty, only Ibbetson, Clinton Dawkins and later J.P. Hewett were first-rate officials. Dawkins, a Balliol contemporary, was Finance Member and much appreciated by the Viceroy for his intelligence and intolerance of humbug, but he left after only a year to work for Pierpoint Morgan's interests in London. At about the same time Ibbetson, whose health had not recovered from his labours as Chief Commissioner in the famine-ridden Central Provinces, was sent to England to recuperate and did not return as Home Member until 1902. The Viceroy was dismayed at losing his two best men so quickly. Ibbetson was replaced by Sir Charles Rivaz, whom Curzon regarded as loyal and sensible but 'totally deficient in initiative' and incapable of relieving him of any work.[20] The successor to Dawkins was Sir Edward Law, who had no experience of India and believed he could settle its problems with solutions that had been successfully applied in Finland and Greece; he was so wrong-headed about so many things that several of his colleagues regarded him as 'slightly cracked'.[21] After Law had designed a tiger for the reverse side of the new rupee, Hamilton questioned the wisdom of choosing the creature which most frightened the natives. Law then opted for a lion, until Curzon observed that, as there were only a handful of these beasts still living in India, it could hardly be regarded as a suitably symbolic animal.[22]

Among his other colleagues, the Viceroy considered only the Legal Member, Sir Thomas Raleigh, to be of any real use. Whereas Dufferin had had Roberts as Commander-in-Chief and Sir George Chesney in the Military Department, Curzon found their places occupied by General Sir William Lockhart, who was a poor administrator, and General Sir Edwin Collen, whom he regarded as 'an obsolete amiable old footler, the concentrated quintessence of a quarter of a century of departmental life'.*[23] Entertaining such views of his Council, it was hardly surprising that Curzon refused to delegate to its members and insisted on doing much of their work himself. Accused by friends, colleagues and relations of working too hard, Curzon derived some consolation from the lessons taught by a biography of Wellington he was then reading. 'That great man', he told Hamilton, 'laid down the axiom that if you wanted a thing done in a particular way the only plan was to do it yourself; and the whole secret of his mastery of the art of war was his supreme attention to detail.'[25]

Curzon had no qualms about instructing his older colleagues even on matters not directly concerned with their work. At Levées and State Balls, he declared, members of Council must wear the white breeches and stockings as ministers did in England and not 'take refuge in the less dangerous but irregular trouser'.[26] He also tended to be a martinet about their living arrangements. Unmarried members could save a good deal of money if they lived in a club in Simla and Calcutta instead of renting a house. But it was Curzon's view that they received large salaries in order to enable them to live in a certain style and to fulfil their social duties by entertaining. Current offenders were thus chivvied until they changed their arrangements, while new members were told bluntly that they were expected to live and entertain in a house and do the bulk of their work in their office.[27] Curbs were also placed on their habit of disappearing on tour just when their chief needed them. They were frequently rushing off, he complained, allegedly to inspect a new barracks or some other building in a distant

---

*Collen was either unaware of the Viceroy's view or else he did not resent it. Ten years later he wrote privately of his 'intense admiration' for Curzon and described himself as one of his 'staunchest friends';[24] he also supported him during and after the controversy with Kitchener.

province, but in reality to have a good holiday. Law was the worst transgressor in this respect because he always disappeared without leaving an address and was next heard of examining a sewage farm in Poona and opening a file on the subject.[28]

Curzon's idea of the Indian administration, a hostile Governor wrote during the rule of his successor, was that of 'a stupendous organ with a multiplicity of stops and key-boards on which he could play at will, and from which he could produce any quality and quantity of sound that he desired'. His colleagues could work the bellows or pull out the stops which he indicated, but they were allowed to do nothing else.[29] The caricature is not greatly exaggerated. Curzon admitted he was a tyrant in his Council, but claimed that his tyranny was accepted and his 'truculent denunciations of departmental imbecility' were overlooked because of the increased efficiency of administration.[30] He also claimed, in most cases accurately, that he was on friendly terms with his colleagues and that their combats did not affect personal relations.[31] Cowed though they may have been by his manner and his personality, the members usually accepted his arguments and agreed with his policies. The unanimity was such that during Curzon's long viceroyalty only three dissenting minutes were sent back to the Secretary of State. The statistic could not have been achieved by bullying alone.

British India was divided into eleven provincial governments headed by the Governors of Madras and Bombay, the Lieutenant-Governors of Bengal, Burma, the North-Western Provinces and the Punjab, and five Chief Commissioners.* Reviewing these officials for the benefit of Queen Victoria, Curzon admitted that, with the exception of Sir Antony MacDonnell, they were not a particularly able group. In the junior ranks of the civil service, he assured her, there were good men coming up, but the standard at the top was temporarily low.[32] Bureaucratic routine had robbed senior officials of energy and initiative. Sir Frederic Fryer, he told Hamilton, was 'an easy-going, lethargic, played-out sort of man' at the head of an incompetent government in Burma. None of the others were much better except MacDonnell, a harsh and antipathetic Irishman who governed the North-Western Provinces and Oudh. Curzon found his character 'unaccompanied by a tinge of sympathy or a drop of generosity' but forgave these defects

---

*The administration of the native states will be discussed in Chapter 13.

because of his ability. 'It is such a God-send in this pigmy-ridden country', he reported, 'to find a man who at least has mental stature.'[33]

The provincial rulers who caused Curzon most trouble during his first year were the Governors of Madras and Bombay, who administered two of the three 'presidencies' (the other was Bengal) of the old East India Company. Like the viceroyalty itself, these were political appointments made in London, and for reasons of tradition were regarded as more prestigious than the lieutenant-governorships. Among the privileges which only the two Governors enjoyed was the right to correspond in person with the Secretary of State. A consequence of the role the two presidencies had played in the building of the empire, the privilege tended to give Governors feelings of self-importance as well as a desire to assert their independence.

Curzon believed that the system of political appointments was justified only if talented politicians could be persuaded to accept the posts. If they were to be used merely as billets for well-connected nonentities, then the system should be abolished and the jobs given to members of the Indian Civil Service (ICS). Two of his friends had become Governors without any apparent qualification for their office. Lord Wenlock, a member of the Souls and a nephew of the Duke of Westminster, had recently returned from Madras, while Lord Sandhurst, a brother-in-law of Earl Spencer, had defeated the superior claims of Sir Alfred Lyall to become Governor of Bombay. The case of Sandhurst was particularly scandalous. Having been regarded by his brother officers in the Coldstream Guards as 'incurably dense', he was considered by his officials in Bombay to be almost illiterate.[34] Curzon declared that a man who could not write a letter without errors of syntax and spelling was not fit to run a province administering nineteen million people.[35] Sandhurst's main defect, however, was his reluctance to communicate at all. Soon after his arrival in Calcutta, Curzon asked the Governor for a statement on the detention of two Indian brothers suspected of conspiracy. Sandhurst replied evasively, assuring the Viceroy he would keep him informed of his views on the matter, until Curzon exploded at the end of May. He had been in India for five months, he pointed out, and he remained in complete ignorance as to why the brothers were still under surveillance, of what they were now suspected, and of how Sandhurst thought they might behave if they were fully released.[36] After meeting him at the end of the year during a tour of areas affected by famine, Curzon found the Governor 'a curious mixture of almost childish simplicity, charming manners, anxiety to do the right thing, and complete administrative incompetence.' About many of the questions affecting his Government he was entirely ignorant.[37]

Even more uncommunicative than Sandhurst was Sir Arthur Havelock, the Governor of Madras, who had succeeded Wenlock. Informed by the Viceroy that he would occasionally like to hear news from the southernmost presidency, Havelock paid not the slightest attention. Madras had long enjoyed a tradition of leisurely self-sufficiency, but it was not one with which Curzon could be expected to sympathize. After five months without a word, the Viceroy complained to Hamilton that he knew more of what was happening in France and Egypt than he did about events in southern India. At that moment Havelock broke silence to inform him that someone had tarred the Queen's statue in Madras.[38] The Governor's abilities, unlike Sandhurst's, were defended by Hamilton, but Curzon was irritated by his pretensions both to grandeur and to autonomy. He found Havelock insufferably pompous and told Hamilton he had excited much ridicule by insisting that 'God save the Queen' was played wherever he appeared in the presidency.[39] The Governor's efforts to extend his autonomy and the Viceroy's determination to curb it ended in a row in which Havelock sent his chief an intemperate remonstrance. Curzon regarded the letter as highly impertinent and refused to correspond further with his subordinate. Lawrence was then deputed to despatch a crushing note about the Viceroy's feelings to Havelock's secretary, a missive which persuaded the Governor to send an apology accompanied by a further grumble that the Government of India was interfering too much in his sphere.[40]

Although Hamilton had encouraged Curzon to correct Sandhurst's waywardness, he was alarmed by the Viceroy's intention of bringing the presidencies of Bombay and Madras under closer control. In August 1900 he received simultaneous letters from Havelock and Lord Northcote, the successor to Sandhurst, each displaying 'the same aggrieved state of feeling', and both complaining of the transfer of powers to the central government and of the reduction of their authority to below the level enjoyed by Lieutenant-Governors. Hamilton felt it appropriate not only to pass on these protests to Curzon but also to warn him about the dangers of humiliating people. If he wanted loyalty and service, the Secretary of State stressed with uncharacteristic firmness, the Viceroy should not make them look small in the eyes of their subordinates.[41]

Reducing the Governors to the level of Lieutenant-Governors was indeed what Curzon had in mind. The expansion of British India and the improvements in communication had made them an anachronism, he thought, removing any justification for their retention of greater powers than the heads of the Government in Bengal and the Punjab. It did not matter if the last two were raised to the status of Governors or if Madras and Bombay were lowered to Lieutenant-Governors. The important thing was to have these 'small deities in petty temples' on the same footing in relation to the Viceroy, to end the Governors' right of appeal to the Secretary of State, and to open their posts to members of the ICS.[42] Hamilton, like Godley, was always eager to avoid action which required a parliamentary bill, and refused to sanction the change. The idiosyncrasies of local life in India, he thought, should be allowed full play, while nothing should be done to increase the Viceroy's workload or the concentration of power.[43] Curzon always maintained that he was pursuing not a policy of centralization but a programme to raise the standard of administration all round. As local governments, he argued with some justice, never initiated reforms of their own accord, they needed the directing hand of the Viceroy. The Bengal Government, for instance, had done nothing about smoke pollution in Calcutta for fear of annoying the factory owners, and legislation to control it would not have been passed without Curzon's insistence.[44] But his arguments were of no avail. The governorships were neither reformed nor opened to the ICS, and the practice of making political appointments continued. When yet another unsuitable candidate was chosen for Bombay in 1903, Curzon longed for the day when a British Government would put the interests of administrative efficiency before those of social rank and prestige and 'sweep away these picturesque excrescences on the surface of the most specialised service in the world'.[45] The fact that this particular 'excrescence' had been the best man at his wedding is an indication of his unsentimental commitment to good government.

India, Curzon once remarked, may have been governed from Simla and Calcutta, but it was administered from the plains by a few hundred men from the Indian Civil Service. Dedicated and incorruptible, the ICS was the most admirable component of the British presence in India. Fresh from Balliol or Haileybury, the young official spent his early career in the district subdivisions, riding for half the year from village to village, his day starting in the saddle at dawn and progressing through visits, inspections and disputes settled from his office-tent under the trees, before ending in the evening stroll, the camp fire and the mosquito net. Promoted after a few years to the post of Collector or Deputy Commissioner, he would then control one of India's 250 districts, an area of perhaps 4,000 square miles where he was responsible for the welfare of some half a million people scattered among about a thousand villages. Several hundred people worked under him, but only the Assistant Commissioner, the civil engineer, the doctor and the police chief were British. Few others of his fellow countrymen would be seen until and unless he was transferred in the course of his career to the secretariat of one of the local governments. If he survived plague and the climate, he might reach the top of the service and end up as a Chief Commissioner or Lieutenant-Governor. It was by any standards an exacting and sometimes dangerous existence that can only have been rewarding for a man who believed that the British held India for the benefit of her inhabitants.

Curzon considered the ICS to be 'the proudest and most honourable' service in the world, yet his standards of efficiency were so high that he was bound to find fault with its performance. His complaints about the mediocrity of the senior officials were acknowledged to be fair by the India Office, but Godley insisted that the calibre of the younger men had improved in recent years. Hamilton believed the ICS had become too bureaucratic, its officials spending too much time in their offices and not enough in the open air talking to natives.[46] He subscribed to the view, impressed upon him many years before by a retired civil servant, Sir George Clark, that the spread of the telegraph and improvements in communications had had a detrimental effect on the performance of officials. In his day, said Clark, the young civilian was sent straight from his ship at Bombay to a district where there was not another European within forty miles and where he had to maintain order by getting to know the local Indian leaders and working with them. Nowadays, by contrast, he had little opportunity to use his brains, for he was given a code in one hand and a telegraph wire in the other and told to carry out the instructions of the local government.[47] Curzon maintained that better steam and postal communications had also reduced the Englishman's attachment to India, bringing the attractions of home life and home associations closer and encouraging him to regard himself as an unfortunate exile. It seemed to the Viceroy a most dangerous trend, for only if his countrymen retained the same sense of duty and affection for Indians as their predecessors would Britain's position remain secure.[48]

By 1901, Walter Lawrence noted in his diary, Curzon had acquired a reputation for trampling on the feelings of his officials.[49] As a great deal of evidence has been published to reinforce this view, and as an almost equivalent amount of testimony exists which disputes it, the point is a difficult one to judge. Far from suffering fools gladly, Francis Younghusband recalled, Curzon 'left them in no doubt that they were fools'. But the Viceroy's behaviour, he maintained, stemmed from a hatred of incompetence rather than from any desire to overbear an individual.[50] Curzon examined a subordinate's work and told him frankly what he thought of it. But if his criticisms were often justified, they were sometimes a disproportionate reaction to a minor misdemeanour. He was equally blunt to an official who had mismanaged an important project as he was to one who had used split infinitives in a note. Yet his exasperation was seldom personal. A natural debater, he used his parliamentary skills to counter arguments he disagreed with and to show them up as shallow and illogical. But whereas politicians accepted such treatment as part of their profession, officials in India merely fumed with resentment. Their complaints eventually reached Hamilton who felt obliged to inform the Viceroy of the bitterness he had caused with his rebukes. As fools constituted the majority of mankind, he remarked, they should be tolerated a little more.[51] Curzon admitted that his manner could be wounding but thought frankness was needed if he was to overcome the inertia and hostility threatening to obstruct his reforms. He therefore used Lawrence 'to pour in the daily oil' to the 'infinitude of persons to be pacified and smoothed'.[52]

Much of the resentment that was aired in London came from officials who had not achieved the promotion they felt was their due. Curzon may not have been good at choosing domestic servants but he was perceptive about selecting people in India. He took a lot of trouble to find out about the candidates for a particular post, to weigh up their abilities, and then to appoint the best one irrespective of age or connections. A man who could oppose the appointment of Lord Lamington, one of his oldest friends, as Governor of Bombay, was unlikely to be lax about other choices. No one was ever given a job simply because he was the next in line. When choosing a Commissioner for the new North-West Frontier Province, Curzon appointed an officer over the heads of older Punjab officials who expected the post. In Burma he found the senior members of the local ICS inadequate to replace Fryer and chose the Secretary of the Foreign Department. In both cases it was recognized that he had done the right thing[53] – although not very tactfully – and in both cases the disappointed officials thoroughly ventilated their disappointments. Mrs Smeaton, whose husband had hoped to become Lieutenant-Governor of Burma, brought her vendetta back to London and made the absurd allegation in the *Daily News* that Curzon had forced the Maharaja of Benares to give him some expensive furniture.[54]

Some enemies were made by the Viceroy's refusal to recommend unmerited honours, and the hostility of the supplicants was increased by his indifference to their flattery. Others were victims of viceregal irritability and impatience. Lawrence observed that officials in a province visited by Curzon were in such an advanced state of nervousness that their minds were not normal and they often said the reverse of what they meant.[55] But while the Viceroy had little sympathy with shyness, a characteristic he had never personally experienced, he valued pluck and plain speaking even when they bordered on impertinence. Evan Maconochie, an ICS official, recalled a visit to the Kolar gold field where Curzon much enjoyed the company of an old Cornish miner who opened their acquaintance by smacking him on the knee in the carriage and addressing him as 'Sonny'. He then told the Viceroy that he knew he would 'ask a lot of damfool questions' and handed him a typewritten paper containing the answers.[56]

The popular image of an aloof and inconsiderate despot was disputed by many who knew him well. Maconochie remembered his 'simple and never-failing humanity' and claimed that no Viceroy had been so accessible or so eager to communicate with men of all classes.[57] Visiting Simla after wrestling with famine and plague in Rajputana, Younghusband found no viceregal pomp but a 'warm-hearted English host doing a kindness to friends who had had a hard time'.[58] After working at his side for over three years, Lawrence noted in his diary that his chief had never spoken a rude word to him, and after a further year he recalled that hardly a day had passed without some striking act of generosity or of practical sympathy for those in trouble.[59]

Such conflicting evidence about Curzon's treatment of officials can only be reconciled by Lord George Hamilton's explanation to Godley: 'the strong, self-reliant men' recognized in him a 'master mind', but the mediocrities feared and disliked him.[60] Those capable of achieving things, said Younghusband, were devoted to him because they knew he was a strong chief who would see them through and stand up for them if things went wrong. 'All the frontier people', an army officer told Gertrude Bell in 1903, 'are fire and flame for him.'[61] Like Wellington, he did not praise easily, but he encouraged and went to great lengths to ensure that those who served well would be rewarded. Percy Cox was one of several young administrators who recognized that the Viceroy's faith in their abilities at a critical moment had been the making of their careers.[62] The autocrat's temptation to surround himself with the second-rate was wholly absent from Curzon's nature. He invariably picked the best men for the job, for the provincial governments, for the frontier, for the secretariats, and he regretted that the constitution did not allow him to choose his own Council. Maconochie spoke for many of them when he called Curzon 'the greatest viceroy of our times – possibly of all time – fearless, creative, ardent, human'.[63] A more impartial though not substantially different testimonial came from a man who owed Curzon nothing. During a four-month stay in India in 1904–5 the future Prime Minister, Neville Chamberlain, sent the following judgement home to his father.

> I have been collecting opinions about Curzon during my travels, and I am gradually coming to the conclusion that he *is* a great Viceroy. The majority of people perhaps dislike him intensely, almost always giving as their reason some childish gossip about his bad manners; but the best I have met have been without exception his devoted admirers. They say he is a man full of courage and strenuousness, no respecter of persons, and not to be bowed by red tape, but ready to take advice if there is common sense in it, and always bent on going to the root of every matter that comes before him.[64]

I 2

'Let India Be My Judge'

GEORGE CURZON HAD a strong and palpable sense of history. He studied it, he wrote it, he sensed, felt and lived it. H.A.L. Fisher regarded him as more of a *savant* and an historian than a political man of action.[1] But Fisher knew him at a later period when they were together in Lloyd George's Cabinet. In India Curzon was as much a man of action as any ruler can be, yet at the same time he was obsessively aware of the past and of the imprint he would leave on it. As Lawrence said in his memoirs, his chief 'was always thinking of the verdicts of history'.[2] Sometimes he consoled himself with the thought that the misjudgements of the present would be corrected by the arbitration of the future. The British might be indifferent to his labour, he once sighed to Mary, as they had been to the work of Hastings and Dalhousie, but it would be 'a different tale in history'.[3]

Unveiling his monument to the victims of the Black Hole, Curzon described Calcutta as a 'great graveyard of memories'. Of nowhere did he feel this more than Government House 'where shades of departed Governors-General hover[ed] about the marble halls and corridors'. He sat at the same desk as his predecessors, imagining their features, their triumphs, their frustrations and their sorrows. Self-pity was a close attendant of his reveries. When thwarted by the British Government and abused by the British in India, he thought of Lord Canning, who had suffered similar treatment without complaint and whose conscientious labour ensured an early death, 'the usual fate of the man doing his duty for the Empire in foreign parts'. When he decided to carry on his work for a second term, he recalled Lord Dalhousie's 'exalted conception of public duty' which had led him to accept an extension 'even though he knew that he was signing his own death warrant by remaining on'.[4] And when he was alone, separated from Mary, whose ill health once nearly resulted in her own death, he thought of both Canning and Dalhousie, who had lost their wives during their terms of office. Three Governors-General had died in India, three more had returned, worn out, to die in England, and others had had to suffer the bereavements so sudden and frequent in the Subcontinent. Most of them, like Curzon, came to view the pomp as empty and transient. All of them knew they could not have the palm without the pain.

In more positive moods Curzon reflected on those achievements of his predecessors which he hoped to emulate. He wanted to appropriate their most conspicuous strengths and synthesize them in his own leadership. He aspired to be the heir of Warren Hastings and Dalhousie but also to add the finer attributes of the others: the energy and vision of Wellesley, who had 'reared the central edifice, lofty and strong, of British dominion in the East'; the architectonic skills of Lord Moira, who had done much to embellish Calcutta; the administrative ability of Lord Mayo, whose viceroyalty had been cut short by an assassin; the evenhandedness of Lord Lytton, who had campaigned for equal justice between Englishmen and Indians. Curzon identified with them so closely that, in a book written shortly before his death, he described some of his predecessors in terms that might almost have been auto-biographical. His catalogue of Dalhousie's characteristics – the rectitude, the administrative capacity, the devotion to duty, the magnanimity and the intolerance which existed side by side – were all attributes that he himself possessed. As for Wellesley, whose faults were magnified versions of his own, the words sound as if they might have come from a hostile critic of himself: 'a man of noble conceptions and petty conceits, a prescient builder of Empire and a rather laughable person'.[5] Curzon endorsed Edmund Burke's theory of imperial trusteeship and believed his country had a mission to rule the Subcontinent for the benefit of its people. He confessed to being 'an imperialist heart and soul' but he was 'very far indeed from being a Jingo' and cared not 'a snap of the fingers for the tawdry lust of conquest'.[6] Like Lord Mayo, who revelled in 'the magnificent work of governing an inferior race',[7] he believed the empire was justified by the benefits it conferred. Writing to the Liberal politician John Morley in the summer of 1900, Curzon set out his vindication of British India.

I do not see how any Englishman, contrasting India as it now is with what it was, and would certainly have been under any other conditions than British rule, can fail to see that we came and have stayed here under no blind or capricious impulse, but in obedience to what some (of whom I am one) would call the decree of Providence, others the law of destiny – in any case for the lasting benefit of millions of the human race. We often make great mistakes here: we are sometimes hard, and insolent, and overbearing: we are a good deal strangled with red tape. But none the less, I do firmly believe that there is no Government in the world (and I have seen most) that rests on so secure a moral basis, or that is more freely animated by duty.[8]

For him India was 'the land not only of romance but of obligation', and, if the obligations were shirked, Britain had no right to remain. As he told members of the Bengal Chamber of Commerce at a dinner in 1903,

If I thought it were all for nothing, and that you and I . . . were simply writing inscriptions on the sand to be washed out by the next tide, if I felt that we were not working here for the good of India in obedience to a higher law and to a nobler aim, then I would see the link that holds England and India together severed without a sigh. But it is because I believe in the future of this country, and in the capacity of our own race to guide it to goals that it has never hitherto attained, that I keep courage and press forward.[9]

Such sentiments no doubt sound quaint today, but they were sincere and widely held then. Later and more self-conscious generations might snigger at the opinion that 'the British empire existed for the welfare of the world', unaware that such views were not confined to Englishmen or that this particular remark was made by Gandhi.[10] Belief in the emergence of a new patriotism, common to both British and natives in India, was not then an absurd ideal, and the survival of British Indian institutions at the end of the twentieth century suggests that the ideal was not entirely destroyed in 1947. The two races, Curzon believed, were tillers in the same field, jointly concerned with the harvest and ordained to walk along the same path for many years to come.[11] The binding of India to England may have been an impossible dream but it was not an ignoble one, nor was it ignobly pursued. A previous Viceroy, Lord Northbrook, had declared during the tariff controversy a generation earlier that the Indian Government's duty was to govern 'for the best interests of the people of India, and not for the interests of the Manchester manufacturers'.[12] Curzon fully endorsed the view and zealously advanced it. His first duty, he told Godley, was to the people of

India, and he would resign rather than sacrifice their interests.[13] He stood up for Indian rights even on minor matters, such as the bill sent to India for a lighthouse in the Red Sea, a waterway hardly confined to Indian shipping. When Lord Cranborne observed that India barely contributed to imperial expenses, the Viceroy sent him a reproachful list of the money and troops she had supplied in recent years.[14]

The British Liberal Party subscribed to the idea of imperial trusteeship but had no clear ideas about its eventual goal in India. Gladstone had declared that Britain had no interest there except the wellbeing of the inhabitants. Believing that Indians should be granted certain freedoms and privileges, he sent Lord Ripon out as Viceroy to implement this policy. But he did not think democracy could be transplanted to a non-Christian society and he insisted that Indians should not be given 'unbounded freedom'.[15] Gladstonian liberalism, doubtfully successful even in Italy, had no answer for India. Unwilling either to rule the Subcontinent as an autocracy or to relinquish it altogether, the Liberals were forced to muddle along, unconvinced about what they were doing or where they were going.

No such doubts had troubled the nineteenth-century Conservatives. Lord Mayo, appointed by Disraeli, had been determined to hold India 'as long as the sun shines in heaven',[16] to do everything in his power for the good of the people, and to make no concessions whatever to the idea of self-rule. Curzon's views, thirty years later, were identical. In his Persian book he had acknowledged that 'the normal Asiatic would sooner be misgoverned by Asiatics than well governed by Europeans', and in the House of Commons he had declared, on behalf of the Government, that the British task in Egypt was not to rule Egyptians but to teach them to rule themselves.[17] He refused to accept, however, that these points should apply to India. While realizing that Britain's international position required the retention of India, he genuinely believed that both countries would suffer from a separation. Egypt and Persia were after all two of the oldest nations of the world, whereas India, despite her ancient civilization, was only a collection of diverse peoples with different religions which from time to time over the centuries had been united under a powerful empire. The removal of the current imperial presence, believed Curzon, would lead – as it had led in the past – to internal dissolution. For that reason he refused to discuss the day when India would be self-governing. A prominent Indian once told Lawrence that his people did not ask for home rule then, or in ten or twenty years; all they wanted was for the Viceroy to keep open the door of hope, to say that perhaps in fifty years India would be self-governing. Lawrence went to see his chief and urged him to agree, but Curzon refused on the grounds that it might embarrass his successor if he raised hopes or expressed an opinion as to when self-government would come. When his secretary pointed out that it must come one day, Curzon replied, 'It will not come in my time, and I cannot say what may happen in the future.'[18]

Educated Indians, the Viceroy uncharitably assumed, cared little for justice, equity or good government. What they wanted was a greater share of executive power, for which he thought them 'as yet profoundly unfitted' and which he insisted he would never let them have.[19] He consulted Indians about subjects such as agriculture, commerce and industry, but he did not want their advice on politics. Asked why he did not appoint a native to his Council, he replied, absurdly, that in the entire country there was not an Indian fit for the post.[20] His attitude to the provincial administrations was similar. Delighted though he was by the appointment of natives to bodies such as the Indian Educational Service, he did not want to see them in high executive positions in the ICS. Answering Sir William Wedderburn, an MP and former President of the Indian National Congress who had urged him to employ more Indians in the senior ranks of the ICS, Curzon said that in his experience, whenever there was an emergency, 'the highly placed native is apt to be unequal to it, does not attract the respect of his subordinates, European or even Native, and is rather inclined to abdicate, or to run away'. He could give, he added, a dozen illustrations of such behaviour during his first year or so in India.[21]

Curzon's view of educated Indians was heavily influenced by his personal experience of Bengalis in Calcutta. In public he complimented them on their eloquence in the English language but warned them not to let their fluency run away with their powers of thought. In private he complained that the 'incurable vice' of the Bengali was his 'faculty of rolling out yards and yards of frothy declamation about subjects which he has imperfectly considered, or which he does not fully understand'.[22] The traditional British view of the Bengali 'babu'* was that he was cunning, perverse, garrulous and muddleheaded, in short among the least attractive of Her Majesty's subjects. Viceroys and Secretaries of State had long been worried that the encouragement of native ambitions would lead to 'the supremacy of Baboodom', and Lord Salisbury

---

*A term, often used disparagingly, to denote a Hindu with some English education.

had admitted in 1877 that he could imagine no more terrible picture for India than that of being governed by babus.[23] Like two of his predecessors, Lord Lytton and Lord Dufferin, Curzon believed that the educated Bengalis were a tiny and unrepresentative minority which should not be allowed to exercise undue influence over the 'real' India. The interests of the peasant millions, they maintained, were far better served by their traditional rulers, the native princes and the British.

Curzon's opinion of the Indian National Congress was coloured by its Bengali predominance, and it is perhaps significant that the only leader of the movement he admired was the Maratha brahmin, G.K. Gokhale. Founded in 1885, Congress had proclaimed its 'unswerving loyalty' to the British Crown and declared that the continued affiliation of India to Great Britain was 'absolutely essential' to the interests of national development; in the view of some of its leaders, British rule was a 'divine dispensation' for the wellbeing of India.[24] Yet at the same time it was a nationalist movement determined to dilute the exclusive Britishness of that dispensation. Although Congress soon divided into a moderate, liberal, pro-Western faction around Gokhale and an extremist faction led by B.G. Tilak, which looked back to a romanticized Hindu past, it was united in pressing for greater Indian representation on the Councils and for the progressive 'Indianization' of the higher services.

During his viceroyalty Lord Lansdowne had realized that freedom of the press and freedom of assembly were bound to produce a body such as Congress, and he had recommended that it should be treated in a friendly manner.[25] Lord Curzon disagreed entirely. Failing to see that Congress was producing a new nationalist élite, he dismissed it as a small, noisy, middle-class movement, and refused to consider it as a future partner in the administration of India. Although the organization seemed harmless, and its leaders applauded his early reforms, he believed it was a movement which 'in the last resort [was] animated by hostile feeling' towards the Government.[26] Aware of the growth of nationalist feeling, he argued that nothing should be done to encourage it. If Congress was innocent, he told Lord Ampthill, Havelock's successor as Governor of Madras, then it was superfluous; and if it was hostile or seditious, it was a national danger. His policy was thus to reduce the organization to impotence by making no concessions or even talking to its leaders, by carrying out reforms so as to deprive it of reasonable ground for complaint, and by showing such sympathy to the natives that the racial issue could not be revived.[27] As he did not trouble to conceal these opinions, it was scarcely surprising that Congress should eventually, after years of rebuffs, convert itself into what he called a 'gramophone of abuse' against himself.[28]

Curzon has been much vilified for his alleged contempt for Indians, particularly for a speech he made at Calcutta University in 1905 when he unwisely remarked that 'the highest ideal of truth is to a large extent a Western conception'.[29] But the resulting outcry ignored both his qualifications and the context of the remark; his point that the great Hindu epics contain maxims such as 'it is better to speak what is beneficial than to speak the truth' went unregarded. He did not think Indians were congenitally corrupt and dishonest but regarded them as the heirs of a great civilization sunk in a decadence from which they must be rescued. He found them childlike and often aggravating, but there can be no doubt that he liked them: they were 'very gentle and sympathetic', he told Ampthill, and should be treated with kindness.[30] The view of Surendranath Banerjea, a hostile Congress leader – Curzon 'loved the people of India after a fashion that they did not appreciate [and] which excited their resentment'[31] – was perhaps true and regrettable, but it does not dispute that the affection was genuine.

Earlier nineteenth-century administrators – most notoriously Macaulay – had dismissed the entire range of Indian culture after no more than a slender acquaintance with it. Curzon admitted only that it was going through a bad stage. To think that the West had a monopoly of wisdom, he declared, was arrogant and foolish; the quality of Indian civilization could be deduced from the country's architectural heritage, which he regarded as 'the most wonderful and varied collection of ancient monuments in the world'.[32] He did not want Indians to become brown Englishmen but encouraged them to assimilate Western thought into their own culture. 'Adhere to your own religion,' he exhorted Muslim students, 'which has in it the ingredients of great nobility and of profound truth': from its foundations they should 'pluck the fruit of the tree of knowledge, which once grew best in Eastern gardens, but has now shifted its habitat to the West'.[33] He was less sure about the noble ingredients of Hinduism: news of a child sacrifice to the Goddess Kali so horrified him that he was once tempted to share Kipling's view that 'never the twain shall meet'.[34] But he resolutely opposed attempts to convert Indians to Christianity. His old friend Welldon, now Bishop of Calcutta, hoped that one day a native prince would declare himself a Christian and, in the manner of Constantine or Clovis, convert the Subcontinent to his creed.[35] Curzon entertained no such hopes and

bluntly told the Bishop that he did not want India flooded with missionaries; he did not believe the country would become Christian or that its
loyalty would be increased if it did.[36] Welldon criticized the
Government's unsympathetic attitude to the missions, which the
Viceroy regarded, in spite of their low rate of success, as dangerous and
troublesome. When the Church of England Missionary Society urged
an alteration in the laws of the southern states of Travancore and
Cochin so as to enable converts to inherit property from their Hindu
relations, Curzon argued that ancient laws should not be dismantled
merely to provide an incentive to Christian conversion.[37]

The chief objects of his rule, declared the Viceroy, were to make
Britain's administration equitable and her dominion permanent,[38] and
the keys to his success would be 'a genuine but never exaggerated sympathy with native thought and ideas [and] a bold lead in everything
else'.[39] He had come to India, he announced on arrival at Bombay, 'to
hold the scales even' between the different races and religions of the
country, and his first commitment was to 'righteousness in administration'. He would not connive at scandals, he told Alfred Lyttelton, or
wink at fraud or hush up ill-doing in high places, because the British
were in India to set an example, and all their actions should be open to
inspection. Only by demonstrating 'superior standards of honour and
virtue' could they continue to hold the country.[40]

No issue caused Curzon greater anguish than British maltreatment
of natives. 'The racial pride and the undisciplined passions of the inferior class of Englishmen' were, he believed, a danger to the survival of
British rule.[41] The difficulty of administering equal justice between
Indians and Europeans had vexed earlier Viceroys, but with Curzon it
became an obsession. When natives were beaten up or occasionally
killed by drunken soldiers, the guilty men were almost invariably lightly
fined or even acquitted. Godley agreed that the failures of justice were
a scandal. 'You may as well', he told the Viceroy, 'expect fair treatment
for an Englishman from a jury of Boers as for a native of India from a
jury of Englishmen.'[42]

The worst offenders were the soldiers and the planters. Curzon soon
understood the wisdom of Lord Cromer's warning that 'uncontrolled
militarism and commercial egotism' were the two main enemies of
imperial rule.[43] The most selfish and rapacious members of the community, he found, were the tea planters who maltreated their coolies in
the knowledge that the local magistrates were on their side. A coolie
who threatened or committed a technical assault upon an Englishman

would be given a year's rigorous imprisonment, but the planter who thrashed a coolie almost to death might be fined a few rupees.[44] The army's behaviour was often worse. A few months after taking office, Curzon was outraged to learn that at least twenty men from the West Kent regiment in Rangoon had raped an elderly Burmese woman who subsequently went out of her mind and died in the following year. The discovery that the local military authorities had tried to hush the matter up increased his fury, and he vowed to expose the whole story and dismiss those responsible. As the West Kent's officers had tried to protect the culprits, he proposed to punish the entire regiment. After Hamilton and the Commander-in-Chief had agreed, it was duly dispatched to Aden and condemned to stay in that inhospitable spot for two years without leave.

Whenever he heard of an incident involving violence or an injustice in the courts, the Viceroy did what he could to rectify the matter. 'I have never wavered in a strict and inflexible justice between the two races,' he told Hamilton. 'It is the sole justification and the only stable foundation for our rule.'[45] Nationalist leaders and the native press applauded him for his efforts to maintain British character in India, while at home the Secretary of State and the Prime Minister strongly endorsed his stance. Yet he was widely abused by his countrymen around him, especially those in the military and the commercial community; whenever he denounced British violence, he recounted, he was accused of injuring the prestige of his race.[46] The reactions of his compatriots often bemused him. The Calcutta businessman was in his opinion normally 'a good fellow', but as soon as any question arose that he thought affected his standing as a member of the superior race, he became 'an excitable fanatic, destitute of reason, fairness or even common sense'.[47] Officials sometimes thought Curzon was too harsh. When he complained about the leniency of jail sentences of three and four years for two Travancore planters who had beaten a native to death, Ampthill countered that imprisonment in south Indian jails was a 'terrible severity' because their high walls and hot bare stones made them like ovens. Ampthill also objected to Curzon's insistence that the captain in charge of the Madras camp at the Delhi Durbar should resign for his involvement in the accidental death of a coolie from a 'push'. The inflexible Viceroy replied that a kick by a European resulting in the death of a native was always described as a push and that in his experience 'angry Englishmen do not push with their feet when in a rage'.[48] The officer resigned.

Curzon's first year and a half in India was overshadowed by famine and plague. The drought which followed the monsoon failure of 1899 led to the worst famine of the century; by the end of the year three and a half million people were receiving famine relief, a far higher figure than the Government had ever had to cope with before. The Viceroy had planned to spend his first autumn tour visiting native states in Rajputana and central India, where many of the most important princes lived. But as the famine spread and intensified, he decided to go to Bombay and other parts of western India suffering from hunger and pestilence. Ignoring Mary's anxieties, he had himself inoculated with Haffkine's serum and set off eagerly to visit hospitals and relief works. After months of inactivity at Simla, he was delighted to investigate the problems on the spot, and he was soon in a position to tell Queen Victoria that he had not only visited every plague hospital in Bombay and Poona but had personally seen almost every infected patient.[49] The visit had an excellent effect, noted Lawrence, despite the Viceroy's habit of upsetting people by complaining about trifling defects.[50] A few weeks later, however, Curzon paid public tribute to officials of the ICS and other services who had risked their lives to relieve the suffering. He was less appreciative of native efforts. On a similar tour during the following summer he observed to Hamilton that responsible Indians were apathetic and indifferent, leaving all the work to British officials. It was a curious thing, he reflected, that the Hindu could be tender-hearted about saving peacocks and monkeys but was quite callous about the lives of his fellow humans.[51]

The energy and thoroughness with which Curzon handled the famine crisis considerably reduced the degree of suffering: by the spring of 1900 five million people were receiving relief estimated to have cost the Government £8,500,000, but the mortality rate had only marginally increased. Although he had channelled the budget surplus away from intended reforms to famine relief, he was determined to find extra funds to invest in irrigation works that would reduce the danger of future droughts. A visit in 1899 to the Chenab irrigation scheme, where 200,000 people were then settled on reclaimed soil, inspired him to expand the work of transforming the semi-desert wastelands of the Punjab. He wanted to concentrate more on canals than railways, he told Hamilton, although he characteristically did both, and indeed ended up building more railways than any other Viceroy. After increasing the annual grant for irrigation projects, he appointed a commission to travel through the country and report on the viability of future works.

When the commission's recommendations were accepted in 1903, an immense twenty-year programme, designed to irrigate six and a half million acres and employ 280,000 men, was begun. Two years later Curzon was able to report that, since his first visit to the Chenab Canal, the area watered by it had doubled while the settled population had multiplied by five.

An American millionaire, Mr H. Phipps, was so impressed by what he saw of the Viceroy's work in India that he offered him £20,000 to spend on any project he fancied. When Curzon replied that he wanted to set up an agricultural research institute, Phipps immediately donated another £10,000. Agricultural projects were accompanied by agrarian legislation to safeguard the interests of the peasants. The Co-operative Credit Societies Act (1904) was the first attempt to solve the problem of peasant indebtedness, while the Punjab Land Alienation Act (1905) prevented moneylenders from taking a holding in settlement of debt. Curzon recognized that moneylenders were essential to agrarian life as it then existed, but he was determined to prevent them from becoming land-grabbers at the expense of the hereditary occupants of the soil. Politically active Hindus opposed the legislation on the grounds of free-market liberalism, while Muslims, who formed the majority of the Punjabi peasantry and whose religion proscribed usury, generally supported it. In spite of Hamilton's fears that the Act might have damaging economic consequences – he was an ardent free-trader himself – it proved a success, and its principles were later extended to the settled areas of the North-West Frontier Province and to Bundelkund in central India. Twenty years later Sir Michael O'Dwyer, who had recently retired as Lieutenant-Governor of the Punjab, saluted Curzon for legislation which had prevented 'the finest body of peasantry in the East' from becoming a 'landless discontented proletariat'.[52]

Not everyone was convinced by Curzon's pronouncements on agriculture. Romesh Chandar Dutt, a former ICS officer who during the viceroyalty became successively President of Congress, lecturer at London University and Revenue Minister for Baroda, wrote a series of open letters in the course of 1901 arguing that a major cause of famine was the high assessment of land revenues. The Viceroy decided that the Government of India would publish a resolution refuting Dutt's points and asked an official to draft a reply. As the resulting draft was deemed inadequate, he decided personally to tackle the subject. Land assessment, he told Mary, was the most abstruse subject in the world, but because his experts were such bad writers, he had to compose the pronouncement himself. In fact it was the kind of dialectical exercise he relished. Shutting himself up in Viceregal Lodge in August, he mastered the question with the help of Lawrence and produced a magisterial, convincing and rather brutal rebuttal of Dutt's arguments. Yet although he denied that the land assessment system was a cause of famine, Curzon himself was in favour of reducing the rate of assessment. In the early years of his viceroyalty the remission of land revenue had averaged £1,200,000, and in 1905 he issued a resolution providing for a reduction in times of bad harvests. Surveying the Government's agrarian policy, Congress leaders not unfairly deduced that it was designed to win the goodwill of the peasants and prevent an alliance between them and the nationalist middle classes. 'Remissions of land revenue,' declared one of their publications, 'institution of agricultural banks, revision of the famine code, inauguration of a new irrigation policy – all these are clearly meant to ingratiate the present rule and the present regime into the favour of the immense agricultural population of this country.'[53] Curzon regarded such accusations as the best kind of compliment; the contentment of the governed remained his overriding aim.

Anyone who studies Curzon's outpourings over a particular period – the despatches, the resolutions, the letters to Hamilton and Godley, the minutes, the telegrams, the epistles to friends, the speeches, the admonitions, the communications to all parts of India – is likely to feel that they took less time for the Viceroy to produce than they do for the reader to study. Although he told Hamilton he had worked at least ten hours each day during August and September 1901, it is difficult to understand how the quantity of work could have been accomplished in less than twenty. Immediately after seeing off Dutt, he decided, single-handedly, to run an educational conference. Sir Charles Rivaz, the Home Member, was technically in charge of both land revenue and education. But he had been of no assistance in the refutation of Dutt, and he now asked to be excused from attending the education conference. Curzon, who complained that Rivaz's knowledge of education was as paltry as his own about motor cars, decided to do all the work himself.[54] He spent two weeks drafting each of the 150 resolutions and then presided over the conference for sixteen days, talking most of the time and guiding the business so that all his resolutions were carried unanimously. By the end he was exhausted and ill, his right leg so painful he was unable to stand for more than two minutes at a stretch. A month later he was still an invalid, working from his bed with a pencil, incapable of walking more than a few yards without intense pain.[55]

In pursuit of his reforms Curzon successfully begged Hamilton to send out various experts to advise his jaded officials. Some came merely to investigate and report, others stayed to take up posts in fields of particular interest to the Viceroy. The experts were not always a great success and in some cases merely caused extra work for Curzon. He had recognized early on that the system of railway management was inefficient and indefensible, but he was so absorbed by reforms of the army, the frontier, the police, the currency, the land laws and education, that he felt he had neither the heart nor the time to sit down and puzzle out a scheme of reconstruction.[56] Yet it was alien for him to tolerate an anomaly, and in 1901 he requested a railway manager from Britain to come out and make a thorough report on the state of the Indian railways. Following an extensive and expensive investigation, the manager duly produced a short, imprecise and very poorly drafted report which the Viceroy refused to accept. After spending several hours going through it and explaining its defects to the author, Curzon assigned the job of redrafting to an official of the Public Works Department.

An even more unsatisfactory expert was Mr Ransome, the government architect sent out at the Viceroy's request by the India Office. Curzon had the traditional nabob's taste for classical buildings and thought Gothic churches tended to look ridiculous in tropical lands.[57] He also deplored the creeping vulgarity he observed both in Indian palaces and in recent government buildings with their flaming carpets, cut-glass chandeliers and 'appalling Tottenham Court Road furniture' reminiscent of Tooting or Sydenham.[58] In India he wanted simple, functional and attractive buildings suitable for the climate. Ransome's early declaration that he aspired to create a new Indian style, a sort of jumble of everything that had preceded it, understandably alarmed him.[59] But the jumble style, as it turned out, was not the principal problem. Ransome had been appointed on the strength of a cottage he had built in Wimbledon for the Political Secretary at the India Office. The cottage no doubt looked very charming in its London suburb, but unfortunately its architect insisted on enlarging and adapting its forms for whatever he was building in India. He also attempted to put Saracenic features on a railway office in Lahore and on the High Court at Rangoon, which Curzon thought absurd in view of the fact that the Moguls had never reached Burma. Ransome continued to submit designs for public buildings in Peshawar and Dehra Dun, and the Viceroy's Council continued to reject them as ugly and unsuited to Indian conditions. At the end of 1903 Curzon minuted his pleasure that he and his Council had hitherto prevented the architect from inflicting any of his schemes on India and added the hope that they would continue to do so. Ransome, who refused to be dismissed without an enormous redundancy payment, made little effort to understand his chief antagonist. On presenting his designs for Mr Phipps's agricultural college at Pusa, the architect explained that his curvilinear pediments at the end of each wing were inspired by Wren, 'an architect responsible for much renaissance work in England'. Curzon minuted tersely that he had studied architecture for twenty years, long enough to learn not only who Wren was 'but also that he never produced anything remotely resembling the two wings of Mr R's building'.[60] A version of Ransome's plan was eventually built at Pusa but was ruined by an earthquake in 1934.

Curzon's instincts to conserve and restore were as strong as his need to reform and instigate. Although unsentimental about animals and responsible for shooting a fair number himself, he did not want to see them suffer unnecessarily and insisted they were not cruelly treated in captivity. Ampthill was asked to explain the clubbing to death of mad dogs in Madras and urged to stop local landowners catching elephants in pits. MacDonnell was instructed to release some wild animals from a cage near Huseinabad. And Woodburn received a letter telling him Calcutta Zoo was a discredit to the city.[61] The Viceroy approved of zoos so long as they were well-kept and humane, and he corresponded with Lord Cromer in Egypt about exchanging Indian and African animals for the zoos in their respective capitals. But the Calcutta Zoo, he asserted, was inferior to that of Karachi, and Lawrence was deputed to make a list of defects for the benefit of its president. He also conveyed Curzon's view that a warmer house should be built for the lions to prevent them dying of rheumatism and arthritis.

Curzon was sensitive to the danger of extinction and refused to accept the argument that wild animals were destined to disappear in India as wolves had in England. Lions had existed in central parts until the time of the Mutiny but were now confined to the Gir Forest in Junagadh. Attempting to reverse the trend, the Viceroy obtained some of these beasts from Africa and persuaded the Maharaja of Gwalior to reintroduce them to his state. He also intervened successfully to save the Gir lions despite a warning from the Nawab of Junagadh that 'their truancy from their ordinary haunts and falling upon domestic animals' might induce villagers to shoot them.[62] Although Curzon wished he could have done more for conservation, his Government did pass an Act for the protection of wild birds which prohibited the export of feathers torn from living birds to adorn ladies' hats in Europe. He supervised the preparation of legislation for a game bill, which was emasculated under his successor, and he also intervened to prevent the spoliation of fine landscapes. Hearing of a scheme for taking water from the Gershoppa Falls, he refused to allow the Bombay Government to 'sacrifice, for the sake of some miserable cotton mill, one of the great glories of the Eastern world'.[63]

Buildings were a higher priority for Curzon than animals, and his travels during his first year convinced him that urgent action was needed to preserve Indian monuments. The British were not so rich in originality themselves, he declared, that they could afford 'to allow the memorials of an earlier and superior art or architecture to fall into ruin'; for him the conservation of India's monuments was 'an elementary obligation of government'.[64] The poor condition of many buildings may have been caused by Indian neglect or by the depredations of Sikh and Muslim conquerors, but that did not excuse either contemporary indifference or the horrors erected by British engineers in the forts of Agra, Gwalior and elsewhere. Curzon believed his country had 'purged itself of the spirit of stupid and unlettered vandalism' which had in earlier days led it to turn disused palaces into barracks,[65] but he was determined to atone for past crimes by a strenuous programme of restoration.

Inertia rather than barbarism was his chief foe. No Viceroy since Lord Northbrook, he observed, had been much interested in the subject, and few of his subordinates troubled themselves about it even now. Responsibility for monuments lay with the provincial governments which, without a central policy and a directing hand, did little to prevent their decay. Only MacDonnell in the North-Western Provinces spent appreciable sums on restoration. Ampthill had never heard of the official archaeologist of Madras, and no one on his Council was even aware of his existence – an ignorance, Curzon told the Governor, which illustrated the disrepute and obscurity into which archaeology had fallen in India.[66] Adamant that such attitudes must be changed, he adopted an intractable policy that permitted no dissent. As he told the Asiatic Society of Bengal,

If there be any one who says to me that there is no duty devolving upon a Christian Government to preserve the monuments of a pagan art, or the sanctuaries of an alien faith, I cannot pause to argue with such a man. Art and beauty, and the reverence that is owing to all that has evoked human genius or has inspired human faith, are independent of creeds, and, in so far as they touch the sphere of religion, are embraced by the common religion of all mankind . . . There is no principle of artistic discrimination between the mausoleum of the despot and the sepulchre of the saint. What is beautiful, what is historic, what tears the mask off the face of the past, and helps us to read its riddles, and to look it in the eyes – these, and not the dogmas of a combative theology, are the principal criteria to which we must look.[67]

Curzon's first step was to find a Director-General of Archaeology who would co-ordinate the Viceroy's policy, his next to give grants to the provincial governments for the purpose of restoration, and his third to exhort them by letter or in person to carry out the duties he had pre-scribed for them. The practice whereby provinces occasionally appointed badly paid archaeological surveyors was in his view chaotic and futile. He wanted to revive the post of Curator of Ancient Monuments, which had existed for a few years until 1889, and relaunch it as the Directorate-General of Archaeology. Hamilton accepted his argument that the conservation of Indian monuments was an 'imperial responsibility' but, in sanctioning the appointment of Mr J.H. Marshall to the position in 1901, stipulated that large sums of money should not be spent on buildings which were in an advanced state of ruin, those which were of no more than local importance and those which had been desecrated by natives generations earlier.[68] Paying little attention to these restrictions, Curzon happily multiplied the grants to local governments by a factor of eight. Marshall was the best of the experts sent out by the India Office, and he and the Viceroy co-operated enthu-siastically on their ambitious programme. The new official, however, fell far below his chief's standards of penmanship and sometimes had to be reproved with preceptorial frankness. Curzon found part of one draft report was so long, contained so many unimportant details and was written in such an uninteresting official style that it should be entirely redone. The Director-General encountered an equally unsym-pathetic response to his claim that a bibliography of Indian archaeology would take up an exorbitant amount of his time. The Viceroy himself had once compiled a bibliography, Marshall was informed, and although it was a task requiring much patience and concentration, it was perfectly easy to do.[69]

The preservationist mission was carried out with biblical fervour. The Viceroy ordered the royal palace in Mandalay to be cleansed of the English club, which was occupying the Queen's chambers, and of a memorial chapel that had been erected in the King's throne room. On finding a squalid post office built into a beautiful Islamic building, he ordered the entire staff to get up and leave.[70] Hot, dusty hours climbing among ruins were followed by long nocturnal stretches listing his demands. Detailed instructions were left on his departure extending to such items as cracked plaster and cobwebs on a staircase; at Ajunta he ordered the bats to be driven out of the caves and the insect nests scraped away. Much trouble was taken to ensure that restoration was carried out with due skill and sensitivity, for he hated the practice of covering faded originals with brash modern colours. On discovering that the ancient skill of *pietra dura* inlay had virtually died out, he went to great lengths to acquire a Florentine mosaicist to repair the Red Fort's marble panels that had been damaged in the Mutiny.

The Viceroy's sightseeing was both tiring and trying for his entourage, because nothing was more guaranteed to make him lose his temper than a visit to a neglected or maltreated building on which he had earlier ordered repairs. Local ignorance and obstructiveness also upset him. He was horrified to find the Jain temples of Mount Abu whitewashed in honour of his visit, and was irritated by the refusal of the Hindu authorities at Bhubaneshwar to allow a Government engineer into the enclosure of the principal temple to see what repairs needed to be done; nor was he mollified by the temple committee's subsequent offer to admit the engineer in exchange for a bribe.[71] Most infuriating of all was the discovery that his own gifts had been neglected. Like his donations to Indian charities, these were often munificent and included a lamp for the Taj Mahal, a clock for the Golden Temple of Amritsar, and the Holwell Monument at Calcutta, where he was once disgusted to find his black marble covered in dust. Visiting Lahore in the spring of 1899, he was prompted to offer a pulpit to one mosque and a lamp to another, after which he discussed their designs with the head of the local art school. Three years later the unexpectedly early arrival of his train at Lahore gave him the opportunity to inspect his gifts in position. To his extreme vexation he found the pulpit covered with pigeon droppings while the lamp was so dirty it appeared never to have been cleaned.[72]

No site received more of Curzon's attention than Agra, his favourite place in India. Believing the town to possess the most beautiful body of architectural remains in the world, he was determined to make them the best preserved as well. A skilled body of craftsmen was therefore trained to reproduce the original seventeenth-century work in marble, sandstone and, eventually, *pietra dura*. The Mogul mausoleums were repaired, the nearby town of Fatehpur Sikri was restored, the minarets of the gateway to Akbar's tomb at Sikandra were rebuilt with white Makrana marble. Alterations that had been carried out to make Akbar's fort more defensible were reversed, and the original battlements were reinstated; from the interior an unsightly army canteen was hurriedly banished. In the precincts of the Taj no work escaped the Viceroy's supervision. He ordered the removal of scraggy trees and garish flowerbeds from the gardens. He rebuilt watercourses and fountains, planted cypresses, and advised MacDonnell to put up screens to protect them from gales and dust storms; he even objected to the dingy garments worn by the custodians of the Taj tombs and asked MacDonnell's successor to change them. By the end of the viceroyalty he had spent nearly £50,000 on the Agra monuments alone, 'an offering of reverence to the past and a gift of recovered beauty to the future'.[73]

The Viceroy's speech in the Legislative Council on the Ancient Monuments Bill of 1904 gave him a chance to describe his work on Indian antiquities with the magniloquence he relished. 'As a pilgrim at the shrine of beauty I have visited them, but as a priest in the temple of duty have I charged myself with their reverent custody and their studious repair.'[74] The egotism was justified, and the achievement, though battered, survives. In November 1905 Curzon ended his last official speech in the Subcontinent with the words, 'Let India be my judge'. Much of his policy over the previous seven years had been controversial, some of it had been mistaken, but of the value of his work of conservation there can be no two opinions. 'After every other viceroy has been forgotten,' Nehru remarked many years later, 'Curzon will be remembered because he restored all that was beautiful in India.'[75]

13

Partners and Colleagues: The Problem of the Princes

A THIRD OF INDIA and about a quarter of its population of almost three hundred millions were administered not by the provincial governments but by the native states. There were nearly seven hundred of these, more than half of them in the west under the tutelage of the Bombay Government, most of the others dealing directly with the Government of India. They came in every kind of scale, wealth and custom. Jammu and Kashmir was the size of England and Scotland combined, and Hyderabad was slightly larger. Akdia in Kathiawar, however, had a population of 216 living in two square miles, while the inhabitants of Jalia Manaji occupied an even smaller territory. The history and ancestry of the ruling families were equally varied. Many of the Rajputs, an ancient warrior caste, claimed to belong to 'the race of the sun'. The Maharaja of Jaipur was supposed to be the 139th direct descendant of Kusha, second son of the god Rama, hero of the *Ramayana*, while the Maharana of Udaipur, the 'sacred man' of the Hindu pantheon, was the living representative of Rama through the Sassanian Kings of Persia and the Caesars of Rome; he was invariably portrayed with an aureole around his head. The Maratha chiefs, by contrast, were proud of their inferior lineage. The Gaekwar of Baroda and the Maharajas of Holkar and Gwalior enjoyed wealth comparable to that of the ruler of Jaipur, but they did not deny that their ancestors had been shepherds and peasants who had risen through the Maratha armies to carve out their states in the eighteenth century. Intermarriage between Maratha and Rajput seldom took place.

The annexation of much of British India had been carried out during the administrations of Wellesley and Dalhousie, who had eagerly sought excuses to acquire more land. Dalhousie was responsible for the policy which prevented native rulers from adopting an heir and led to the annexation of their states if they died without leaving a son to succeed them. Had this system, which provoked much discontent in the years before the Mutiny, continued, there would have been few princes left for Curzon to deal with. Following the rebellion, however, the policy changed. The native chiefs, most of whom had not joined the insurgents, were informed that they could adopt heirs and that the Crown had no intention of extending its territorial possessions. As a result, many of the rulers during Curzon's viceroyalty had no blood relationship with the princes who had preceded them. Five of the six Hindu chiefs in Kathiawar were not legitimate Rajputs; most of them in fact were purchased changelings.[1]

The British view of the chiefs changed after the Mutiny. No longer considered feudal anachronisms waiting to be dispossessed, they came to be regarded as important allies of British rule. The zealotry of Macaulay and Mill, the contempt for native culture and the impatience with antique traditions gave way to a view that the princes, not now considered a threat to the supreme power, added to the gaiety of life as well as the stability of the country. Lord Lytton, the most romantic of Viceroys, encouraged the use of pageantry and hoped to create a sort of Gothic feudalism around the mystical figure of the Queen-Empress. Why not make the Maharaja of Kashmir, he wondered, a Warden of the Marches?[2] This trend in policy was followed, less whimsically, by Dufferin, who restored the great fort at Gwalior to its Maharaja, even though the state's army had joined the rebels in 1858 and had defied the paramount power from the battlements. Lord George Hamilton also extolled the merits of the princes, especially the Rajputs, whom he regarded as 'such gentlemen, and persons with whom it is very pleasant to have personal dealings'.[3]

Guaranteed against annexation or external threat, the native chiefs in return had to tolerate a British political officer charged to guide them along the path of responsible rule. Recruited from both the ICS and the Indian army, the officers were known as 'residents' in the most important states and as 'political agents' in the others. Controlled by the Foreign Department and thus directly supervised by the Viceroy himself, they had to play a complicated dual role as representative of the Government and adviser of the native state. Even if incompatibility of temperament did not hinder relations between ruler and agent, the latter's mere presence often acted as an irritant to the pride and pretensions of the chief. To many people the constitutional position of the princes seemed to be an irreconcilable mixture of oriental autocrat and British vassal. To Curzon, who agreed with Lytton's opinions of their value without sharing his sentimental views of their role, their position was quite straightforward. As he informed King Edward VII,

> The native Chiefs are not sovereigns. They have been deprived of the essential rights and attributes of sovereignty. They cannot make treaties, they cannot keep armies or import arms, they cannot have any relations with each other, beyond those of friendship, they cannot even build railways without the consent of the Government of India. In the event of aggravated oppression or misrule, they are liable to deposition.[4]

The closer post-Mutiny relationship with Britain inevitably led to the Anglicization of many of the chiefs. They went to English public schools or to Indian colleges with British teachers, they travelled in Europe, they learnt to play cricket, they had British tutors and advisers with whom they were in daily contact. People from both nations were apprehensive of the effect of this influence. Alfred Lyall had foreseen as early as 1874 that the next generation of princes would be found 'squandering their revenues in the great hotels of Paris and London . . . demoralising England rather than improving India'.[5] Some years later an elderly Sikh raja predicted that the practice of marrying sophisticated, Westernized sons to wholly uneducated, untravelled girls would result in a breed of mules.[6] A real danger, as Curzon soon discovered, was that the princes became so enamoured of European ways that they lost interest in the mules' mothers and even in their hereditary states. The Raja of Pudukotta, he informed Hamilton, spent most of his time either in Europe with his mistress or in the hill station of Kodai Kanal where he played tennis, danced with English ladies and hoped to be taken for an English gentleman rather than an Indian chief; he even asked the Viceroy for permission to appear at a garden party in English dress instead of native costume.[7]

A Viceroy's relationship with the chiefs was complicated by Queen Victoria's prejudice in their favour. Curzon complained that they were all invested with a sort of halo in her eyes – she liked the unpleasant and half-mad Maharaja of Holkar because he sent her a telegram on her birthday – and were treated, indiscriminately, as if they were important royalty.[8] The Maharaja of Cooch Behar, a third-rank chief from Bengal, was a favoured guest at Windsor and Sandringham and a particular friend of the Prince of Wales; but in Calcutta, where he returned pursued by the unpaid bills of Windsor tradesmen, he regarded it as a compliment to be invited to dine at Government House.[9] Curzon grumbled that almost anyone with a turban and jewels was regarded in Europe as a prince and treated as if he were a descendant of Nebuchadnezzar. One insignificant Raja, who spent almost all his inheritance on women and gambling in Paris, was a guest of the French President at Longchamps and was given an audience by the Queen at Balmoral.[10]

So anxious was Curzon about the harm done to India by the more dissolute chiefs that he felt obliged to inform Queen Victoria of their misdemeanours. Some princes were capable and patriotic, he assured her, but a larger number were 'frivolous and sometimes vicious spend-thrifts and idlers'. Scindia, the Maharaja of Gwalior, was the most intel-ligent and promising of the younger ones, while the Maharaja of Jaipur, an 'enlightened and munificent chief' loyal to the customs and tradi-tions of his people, was a fine representative of the older generation; the southern princes of Cochin and Travancore were also humane and sagacious rulers who happily combined the most conservative instincts with the most liberal views. But the list of failures was much longer. The Rana of Dholpur was 'fast sinking into an inebriate and a sot', the Maharaja of Patiala was 'little better than a jockey', the Maharaja of Bharatpur was a weak and unstable character who had just killed his servant. The Viceroy did not shrink from defining the nature of their misdeeds to his sovereign – the Raja of Kapurthala was only happy phi-landering in Paris, while Holkar, the sender of her telegram, was 'addicted to horrible vices' – but neither did he deny British responsibil-ity for the problem. The rulers had allowed young chiefs to fall into bad hands and had condoned their extravagances and winked at their vices. They had let them learn enough about European ways to become dis-satisfied with their own country and their own people, and to be despised by their subjects in return.[11]

After his famine tour of 1899, Curzon stayed at Gwalior as the guest of Scindia, and delivered a speech at the state banquet on the rights and duties of the princes. Scindia was Curzon's model of a native chief. He rushed about his state, notebook in hand, receiving appeals, examining accounts, chiding or encouraging officials; although only 23 years of age, he had already thoroughly reformed his administration. So remorseless was his determination to run everything on his own – to the extent of checking the sentries in the garden at night and supervising the making of Curzon's bed – that his guest noticed a strong resemblance to himself.[12] Gwalior was thus an appropriate place to define the position of the native chief. 'I claim him as my colleague and partner,' proclaimed the Viceroy, as a fellow administrator who must be 'the servant as well as the master of his people', who must learn that his revenues were 'not secured to him for his own selfish gratification, but for the good of his subjects', and whose figure should not be known merely on the polo-ground, on the race-course, or in the European hotel, because his real work, his princely duty, lay with his own people.[13]

Conscientious chiefs such as Jaipur were delighted by the speech, especially by their classification as colleagues and partners, a phrase the Viceroy believed had done more good in the native states and among the 'better class' of princes than any action of the Government in recent times.[14] Through his long, twice-yearly tours of different regions, Curzon came into closer contact with the chiefs than any other Viceroy. The 'better class' welcomed his strong personal interest, just as they appreciated his entertainment of them at Hastings House in Calcutta, which he restored for them and their followers. Others, who hankered after Europe or merely wished to run their affairs without interference, were less enthusiastic about the new relationship. The Nizam of Hyderabad, ruler of the largest and most populous state in India, cannot have enjoyed an interview in which the Viceroy berated him over his son's education, his attitude towards his chief minister, and his ignorance of famine conditions in his own dominions. Regarded by Curzon as 'an insignificant little creature ... wrapped up in the sloth of the seraglio', the Nizam probably wanted to be anything but his tormentor's colleague.[15]

The Viceroy struggled to persuade the princes and their leading nobles to send their sons to the chiefs' colleges he had reformed at Ajmer, Indore and Rajkot, where they received a sort of English public school education. But the main problem was what to do with them afterwards. Every year, observed Curzon, scores of young men were graduating from the colleges, trained in English habits and ways, taught to ride and love sport, and indoctrinated as far as possible with a sense of patriotism. Yet no suitable employment awaited them. For centuries the duty of the Rajputs had been to wage wars under a stern code of chivalry that had on occasion required fighting to the last man followed by the collective suicide of their families. They still had their castles, their courts, their minstrels and their dancing girls – Walter Lawrence

called it 'the Middle Ages in sepia'[16] – but they were no longer allowed
to practise their immemorial profession. 'I am afraid we do not altogether improve the nobles by keeping them from fighting,' Alfred Lyall
had once remarked,[17] and Curzon agreed that a military career should
be reopened for them. Asked his opinion about the formation of a
cadet corps for Indian nobles, the senior political officer in Rajputana
replied that the typical Rajput was neither brilliant nor a bookworm and
would probably fail any examination required for promotion. He was,
however, a born horseman with a good eye, a keen military spirit, a
strong sense of honour and so thoroughly loyal to the Government that
he would make a fine staff officer.[18]

Curzon felt that a scheme for native commissions was also important
for political reasons: by removing a source of disappointment and gratifying legitimate ambitions, it would help strengthen ties between the
princes and the Government. He was much impressed by a plea from
Cooch Behar, a Maharaja he normally regarded as the 'spoilt child' of
the British royal family, who hoped that his sons, educated at Eton and
Oxford, might acquire commissions in British regiments or, failing that,
in the native cavalry. Otherwise, the chief lamented, their prospects
were hopeless and disheartening, with nothing for them to do but lead
purposeless and indolent lives.[19] The Viceroy's views had the approval
of Queen Victoria but found little backing in Britain. Only Hamilton
and Salisbury supported his idea of setting up a cadet corps that would
in due course provide officers for the Indian army. After a force of
Indian troops had helped rescue the European legations in Peking in
1900, Curzon tried again, this time proposing that the Indians would
become staff officers not attached to regiments. Such a scheme would
overcome the objections of Edward VII, newly arrived on the throne,
whose views on the relationship between the races were different from
his mother's and who was deeply perturbed by the idea of Indians commanding white men.[20] Hamilton and Salisbury persuaded a reluctant
Cabinet to agree to the amended plan, and the Secretary of State
managed to get it through his equally reluctant Council. By Christmas
1901 Curzon was happily drawing up plans for the winter and summer
accommodation of his new corps.

Encouraging the princes to fall into line was supplemented by a
certain amount of goading. In the words of Curzon's native orderly, one
wretched Nawab of doubtful loyalty 'left the presence of the Great
Lord Sahib a wiser and perspired man'.[21] Another troublesome figure
was the Khan of Kolat, an idle and miserly individual who arrived at the

Residency at Quetta with 'two weedy camels and two miserable hacks' for the Viceroy. Curzon refused to accept them or anything else from the Khan, a rebuke which quickly persuaded the ruler to start spending large sums on municipal works. Rebukes also had to be administered to those chiefs, usually Europeanized and not of the first rank, who cultivated delusions of royal grandeur. Pudukotta's extreme Anglophilia led him to sport an imperial crown on his writing paper and a ducal coronet on his seal; when paying an official visit to the Viceroy, his private band played 'God save the Queen'.[22] The Raja of Kapurthala, whom Curzon regarded as a 'third class chief of fifth rate character', always apparently gloating over pornography, had become so spoiled by his chats with the Tsar, the Kaiser and Queen Victoria that he started to style himself Maharaja.[23] Others fed their pretensions by constantly referring to 'the throne' and 'the royal family'. All had to be admonished. There was nothing royal about the chiefs, Curzon asserted, and none of them was in possession of the sovereignty of his state. Their future, he thought, would be safe only if they were transformed into an hereditary aristocracy, a view that horrified Godley who did not want to see the princes reduced to the status of 'glorified noblemen'.[24]

The Viceroy's aim of preserving the 'idiosyncrasies of native thought and custom' was seldom furthered by princes who had been educated in Britain. Curzon was sorry to hear that the Rao of Kutch's eldest son was being sent to university in England, because he did not believe that Oxford graduates should rule native states. There could hardly be 'a worse education', he wrote, 'for a future Indian chief than that of an English university [where] he learns to despise his people, their ways and their ignorance'.[25] Even a single visit to Britain could have a disastrous effect on an impressionable young prince. The Maharaja of Rampur, recorded Curzon, had been a promising and intelligent youth until a journey to Europe transformed him into 'a sensual and extravagant debauchee'; there had been no finer horseman in India than the Rana of Dholpur, but European influence had left him 'a prey to every variety of pimp and shark', turned him into 'a nerveless inebriate' and brought about an early death.[26] Supported by Jaipur, Curzon was determined to curtail these damaging excursions, and in August 1900 he sent local governments a circular defining the chiefs' duties and laying down conditions for their travels abroad: the provincial administrations were to permit a journey only when they were satisfied that it would benefit both the chief and his people, and they were then to monitor the effects of the trip on the character and habits of the traveller.

The Viceroy's decision to issue his circular to the Government *Gazette* distressed Hamilton, who thought the publication of his 'pedagogic lectures' was 'most ill-judged' and bound to cause resentment.[27] Those chiefs with children or mistresses in Europe were dismayed and tried various ruses to induce the Viceroy to let them go: the Rajas of Pudukotta and Kapurthala, two of the principal targets of the circular, attempted to convince him they needed to see European specialists about their increasing weight problems.[28] One senior prince, the Gaekwar of Baroda, took great exception to the circular and announced his intention to travel frequently to England and, when in India, to spend his summers at Naini Tal, a hill station far from the disagreeable heat of Baroda. When the Viceroy remonstrated, pointing out that permission was needed to travel abroad, the Gaekwar replied that he refused to be treated like a cowherd and declined to apply for it.[29] Curzon was furious. Baroda was in fact a cowherd's son who had been adopted to head one of the only three Indian states with the privilege of a twenty-one gun salute. Curzon found him vain and cantankerous, and suspected him, rightly, of pro-Congress sympathies. But he could do nothing about his insubordination. The Gaekwar was intelligent and able, ran an enlightened administration, and took the trouble to find allies during his visits to England. Hamilton, who liked and admired him, was pleased that he set such an excellent example to his fellow chiefs by sticking to one wife.[30]

The Viceroy did not shrink from upbraiding the princes on family matters and their private lives, although he confessed it was an unpleasant duty. He went to great lengths to reconcile the Maharaja of Orchha with his son, who had been banished for making an unarranged marriage, and after bullying the obstinate father he was successful. Sexual matters were naturally difficult to discuss with noble foreigners he scarcely knew. Sometimes they could be dealt with by a stern note to the relevant agent expressing displeasure at so-and-so's 'lewd and immoral conduct', but on other occasions a more personal approach was necessary. In 1903 Curzon had to urge the Raja of Jind 'to resume conjugal relations' with his two Sikh wives whom he had ignored since marrying the daughter of a European aeronaut; it was his duty, the Raja was told, to produce a son and heir for his state.[31] An even more embarrassing task loomed when he summoned the Maharaja of Mysore, one of the premier Indian princes, to try to persuade him to consummate his marriage. British officials in the state had warned the Viceroy that the neglected Maharani was so badly treated by her husband's family that she might commit suicide unless he intervened.[32] In the end Curzon was spared the interview because the Maharaja, who had agreed to listen to the Viceroy's strictures even on so delicate a subject, developed chronic laryngitis.

Homosexuality, however, was hardly a subject that could be discussed in an interview, although attempts to suppress it were made from afar. Curzon was dismayed to find it much more prevalent than he had expected, and he soon learnt why Bharatpur had killed his servant. On discovering that his son was the Maharaja's catamite, the victim had removed him from the palace and had subsequently been murdered by his enraged master, whose plea that both barrels of his shotgun had gone off by mistake was not believed.[33] Bharatpur's immediate neighbour, the Maharaja of Alwar, also had the same 'horrible taint' – 'best suggested', Curzon told Brodrick, 'by the name of Oscar Wilde' – and so did another chief nearby, the Maharaja of Jodhpur, who had, moreover, been encouraged to drink by his wife, 'a consistent toper'. The Viceroy knew about the predilections of the half-crazy Holkar but was horrified to discover that three Rajput princes had the same tastes. For once he had no solutions beyond separating couples and placing young miscreants in the hands of a British officer under a strict regime of discipline and control. In a letter to Hamilton he attributed the problem, eccentrically, to early marriage. 'A boy gets tired of his wife, or of women, at a relatively early age, and wants some more novel or exciting sensation'.[34] The Secretary of State had a more prosaic explanation and a more traditional remedy. What the British called unnatural vice, he declared, was for the Indian 'upper orders, a natural pleasure', and he had no doubt that further revelations would soon follow. But the harder the boys were worked, he suggested, 'and the more they are kept out of doors in manly and military pursuits, the less inclination they will have for this form of vice'.[35]

14

Guarding the Frontiers

———————————❖———————————

VICEROYS, CURZON BELIEVED, tended to be puppets in the hands of their military advisers. Initially ignorant both of India and of military matters, they were confronted on arrival by an array of generals and made to dance to the bombastic tunes of the army. The new Viceroy quickly broke this tradition. On finding the Government of India committed to an expensive programme of fortifying the Khyber and other passes, he promptly cancelled it. As he told Selborne, he had the advantage of knowing the frontier from his earlier travels and he understood what he was talking about.[1] Rather than allow the army to follow its own agenda, he was determined that from the beginning it would be controlled by himself and his Council.

India's armed strength was numerically unimpressive. She had less than 200,000 troops to defend and preserve order in an empire of some three hundred million people stretching from the borders of Persia to the frontiers of Siam. Only a third of them belonged to British regiments, which meant that the ratio of the native population to white soldiers was thus about 5,000 to 1. The remainder comprised the Indian army, a recent amalgamation of the armies of Bengal, Bombay and Madras, which consisted of native regiments commanded by British officers. Before the Mutiny the proportion of Indian soldiers to white troops had been much higher. Most of the victories that had made Britain's empire in India, the battles of Clive, Arthur Wellesley and others against Indian or Franco-Indian troops, had been won by small, outnumbered forces consisting mainly of native soldiers with British officers.

The calibre of Britain's armies at the end of the nineteenth century was not high at home or abroad. Lord Salisbury was puzzled by the poor performance of officers in the Boer War and wondered whether Britain might not have done better with an army of Red Indians.[2] Curzon thought the military suffered from lack of brains and lack of discipline: the navy was better, he told Selborne, who became First Lord of the Admiralty in 1900, because some sailors were intelligent and nearly all of them understood discipline.[3] In action, the Viceroy admitted, British soldiers in India knew their business and acted like men; their fighting capacity and speed of mobilization compared with the best anywhere. But placed in an office and required to work out a reform or plan a strategy, they seemed to be 'incurable bunglers'.[4] Two of the Lieutenant-Generals struck him as 'very second-rate performers' while most of the other senior officers appeared to be very worthy, very brave and very stupid. They treated battles, he told Brodrick, like a game of football. Few of them read or studied or knew anything about military science, and their undoubted courage would be of little use when they were being picked off by an enemy three miles away.[5]

The army was administered by the Commander-in-Chief at Army Headquarters, who was the executive head, and the Military Department, which was under a Major-General on the Viceroy's Council. Curzon accepted the need for the department, which was responsible for transport, supplies and other administrative matters, but initially thought it the most incompetent of those in the Government. It was so overawed by the generals at Army Headquarters that it acquiesced in almost all their suggestions and authorized large sums of expenditure which Curzon considered unjustifiable. One of the functions of the Military Member – to be a second adviser to the Viceroy on army matters – was thus inoperable. General Collen, who held the post from 1896 to 1901, was in Curzon's eyes an officer 'mentally composed of India-rubber' who had learned the lesson of subordination so well that he seldom questioned a proposal from the Commander-in-Chief. This abrogation of responsibility was accompanied by administrative chaos, so that a file sent to the Military Department was apt to remain there for weeks. Not that much happened to it in the meantime because the officers wrote so badly that Curzon refused to allow them to compose their department's despatches. The entire official correspondence on the defence of India, he told Hamilton in 1902, had been written by himself, because it was quicker to produce his own drafts than to correct theirs.[6]

Wherever he looked, he found jobbery, waste and mismanagement, officers putting their own men in billets, engineers building expensive forts in pointless places, a wheat-eating regiment stationed in a rice-growing area where the wheat had to be imported at great cost. 'Oh, these soldiers!' he complained. 'Badly indeed would they fare if I were counsel against them at the Day of Judgment.'[7] As in other fields, he quickly encouraged a series of reforms, rearming the regiments, improving the transport system, providing for a greater degree of self-sufficiency in weapons and ammunition.[8] But he understood that the army was one area where he could not do everything himself and where he needed a vigorous Commander-in-Chief to co-operate with him in the task of reform. There was in his eyes only one suitable candidate. The army required new blood, he told Hamilton at the beginning of 1900, and when the present chief died or was invalided out, it needed Lord Kitchener to pull things together. Three years later, after the hero of Omdurman had been diverted to South Africa, it got him.

Enforcement of discipline in the army was one of Curzon's fixations. He and Collen agreed that British soldiers were overpaid in a country where the cost of living was much cheaper than in England. As most of them were unmarried, they could afford both prostitutes and liquor. Evening excursions into the bazaar after an idle and sweltering day in the barracks frequently led to trouble. In the vast majority of clashes with natives, Curzon declared, 'the cause of the mischief is that the English soldiers are either after a woman or are drunk'.[9] Even the most distinguished Commanders-in-Chief were unable to deal with the problem intelligently. Lord Roberts urged soldiers to join the Army Temperance Association and, under the influence of his wife, ordered the closure of the cantonment brothels where Indian women, subjected to medical inspection, were reserved for white soldiers. Lady Roberts's purity campaign led directly, in the words of Lord Elgin, to 'even more deplorable evils . . . an increase in unnatural crimes' and, for those tempted to the bazaars, a lot more venereal disease. In 1895, two years after Roberts left India, more than a quarter of the British army there was being treated for syphilis.[10] Although the number dropped steadily during Curzon's years, largely because the military brothels had been discreetly reopened, Kitchener was sufficiently alarmed to warn soldiers that those infected in India would suffer 'cantankerous and stinking ulcerations' and that their noses would rot and fall off. The general, who does not appear to have been much troubled by sexual desires himself, could think of nothing better than to exhort his men to use self-control, to take a lot of outside exercise and to imagine the reactions of their mothers on learning that they had the disease.[11]

Curzon did at least have one practical idea. Realizing that army barracks in hot weather were stifling and unbearable places which encouraged soldiers to spend as much time as possible outside them, he insisted on the installation of electric fans. But he was unyielding on the question of indiscipline. General Sir Power Palmer, the second of the three army commanders to serve under him, admitted that the British soldier was 'a rough specimen of humanity', but he felt senior officials in the cool of Simla should remember how terrible life was in the scorching plains when everything was an irritant; indeed, the C-in-C was surprised there was not more 'violence to the irritating native, who becomes more irritating the more he thinks he can score off the soldier'.[12] Curzon was not impressed by this defence. Four or five Indians were killed on average each year by soldiers, sometimes by accident during shooting expeditions, more often in brawls. It was not by any standards a high number, but each death infuriated the Viceroy. In one incident, he told Hamilton, four soldiers had gone shooting 'as usual without passes, without an interpreter' and in violation of the rules. They then 'shot, as usual, a peacock, had the usual row with the villagers, in the course of which their guns went off, as usual by accident, and as usual killed two natives'; at the subsequent trial 'the prisoners were, as usual, acquitted and released'. A case like this ate into his 'very soul'. 'That such gross outrages should occur in the first place in a country under British rule; and then that everybody . . . should conspire to screen the guilty is, in my judgment, a black and permanent blot upon the British name.' He vowed 'to efface the stain' during his time.[13]

Arguing that the British soldier should be regarded as a source of protection rather than alarm by Indians, Curzon concluded that the issue of shooting passes must be limited. The decision immediately reduced the number of collisions between soldiers and natives by more than three-quarters.[14] The Viceroy's inflexibility on matters of justice also led to a reduction in drunken brawling and at the same time increased his unpopularity among the military. Soldiers complained that 'the scum of the bazaars' could now insult them with impunity. They were being 'cheeked', reported Ampthill to Godley, by 'the lowest class of Natives in an intolerable way', and, when they threatened 'to chastise an insolent native, the latter frequently threatens to "tell the Lord Sahib"'.[15]

Curbing the army's natural inclination to fight battles was another problem. The Viceroy was frequently requested to sanction expeditions or punitive raids against allegedly marauding tribes across the border. Sometimes these were necessary, he found, particularly on the north-west frontier, but more often they were an excuse for a 'scrap', a relief from boredom, a chance for soldiers to win medals and promotion. Curzon regarded these as futile, costly and often unjust. During his first year he was persuaded to allow an expedition on the north-eastern frontier against the Bebejiya Mishmis, described as a 'fierce race of cannibals, a very savage, blood-thirsty and dangerous race' which deserved punishment for killing three people, kidnapping three children and stealing three guns earlier in the year, as well as for killing three policemen as far back as 1893. Although the political officer on the spot thought adequate chastisement could be achieved with a force of sixty military policemen, Curzon was induced to authorize a mixed force of 400 soldiers and police which the army subsequently multiplied to 1,200. The cold (it was midwinter), the problems of the terrain, and the need to climb quickly over a high pass forced the commander to reduce the numbers to 127. These eventually arrived at their destination to find that the Mishmis were not cannibals at all but 'on the whole a well behaved and inoffensive tribe, very desirous of being on friendly terms with us'. The children were recovered with one of the guns, but no one responsible for the murders was arrested, and two innocent captives were soon released. The military authorities claimed the expedition had been a success. Curzon minuted drily that the results did not appear to justify the loss of thirty-four coolies, who had died from exposure on the pass, or the enormous expense of the expedition, most of it wasted on assembling a force ten times larger than that actually employed.[16] The 'almost criminal blundering' of the affair persuaded him to veto a number of similar expeditions, particularly those suggested in Burma by Fryer, a man Curzon described as combining administrative apathy with 'the most daring and martial opinions with regard to frontier politics and warfare'.[17]

In the spring of 1900 the Viceroy was travelling up the frontier in Baluchistan, 'inspecting, examining, questioning, interviewing everywhere'. He held a durbar for local chiefs at Quetta ('an old haunt of mine') where he had been five years earlier, after his journey to Kabul, and which he had visited for the first time seven years before that on his journey round the world. He was never so happy, he told Brodrick, as when he was on the frontier, because he knew the tribesmen and how to handle them. 'They are brave as lions, wild as cats, docile as children. You have to be very frank, very conciliatory, very firm, very generous, very fearless'. It was with delight as well as pride that he received the homage of these 'magnificent Samsons, gigantic, bearded, instinct with loyalty, often stained with crime'.[18]

His tour convinced him that India's defence policy on the frontier was seriously flawed. Thousands of troops were cantoned in forts in the protected tribal areas lying between the frontier with Afghanistan (the 'Durand Line') and the administrative border of British India. Lacking communications and easily isolated, they were at the same time a provocation to the tribes and a liability to India. Curzon had 'a strong *a priori* distrust of military schemes for great defensive posts and forts on and across the border', which often required garrisons of half a regiment to defend them.[19] Refusing therefore to sanction further proposals for costly fortifications in tribal territory, he adopted the novel policy of withdrawing regular troops from advanced positions and concentrating them in the rear, while employing tribal forces recruited by British officers to police the tribal country themselves. His way of managing the Pathan tribesman, he told General Chamberlain, was one of

> getting to understand him, and getting him to understand you; to leave him alone where his country is not wanted for purposes of Indian defence; where it is, to enlist and employ him in looking after his own country, and after the roads and passes which it is necessary for us to keep open; to pay him and humour him when he behaves, but to lay him out flat when he does not.[20]

Curzon realized that the frontier needed not only a new policy but also a new administration. The mountainous area between Baluchistan and Kashmir was under the control of the Punjab Government, celebrated in mid-century for its outstanding administrators but by 1900 widely regarded as an unimpressive ruling body. On frontier matters Curzon considered it an instrument of obstruction and procrastination, its officials largely ignorant of the tribes and ill-equipped to handle them. The five previous Lieutenant-Governors, he pointed out, had spent an average of only four months on the frontier in careers which at the time of their appointments had totalled 151 years. Such inexperience, shared by their chief secretaries and other officials, led to indecisiveness and delays in an area which above all others required prompt action.[21]

Lord George Hamilton, who agreed that the Punjab officers carried out their border duties in a wooden and unintelligent manner, had once suggested placing frontier commissioners directly under the

Government of India. But Curzon pressed for a new province to be created by detaching the frontier districts of the Punjab and uniting them with adjoining tribal areas between the administrative border and the Durand Line. The severance was logical not merely for political and geographical reasons. The trans-Indus tracts had little in common with the Punjab, ethnic and linguistic differences separating the Pathan tribesmen from the inhabitants of the plains.[22] Curzon's proposals were supported without dissent by his Council and were accepted by Hamilton and the India Office. In November 1901, on the King's birthday, the North-West Frontier Province came into being.*

As so often in Curzon's life, the right thing had been done in a tactless manner. No one outside the Punjab Government seriously disputed the merits of the reform, but it was easy to take exception to the way it was achieved. The officials naturally resented the publication of their failings in a viceregal minute, especially the Lieutenant-Governor, Sir Mackworth Young, who protested that he had not been consulted about the formation of a new administration in territory which he had 'received a commission from Her Majesty to administer'.[23] Curzon pointed out that Young's views on the subject were on record and argued that no one engaged in framing a scheme needs to ask advice from those known to oppose it.[24] Hamilton agreed with the Viceroy, but the aggrieved Young, encouraged by his wife, decided to publicize the controversy at Simla.

The town was the summer capital of both the Punjab and the Government of India, an arrangement which had facilitated the formulation of frontier policy. But the creation of a new province made continued co-existence unnecessary, and Curzon planned to relieve Simla's congestion by removing the provincial Government to another hill station in the Punjab. After hearing a rumour of the scheme, Young made the mistake of mentioning it during a speech at a masonic dinner, adding that, as his Government was no longer required to give advice on the frontier, 'a hill station where the full glare of the Supreme Government might be softened by distance would possess some fascinations' for himself and his officials.[25] After that relations between the

---

*Curzon's creation survives today, with the same name, as a province of Pakistan. Its birth required a change of title for MacDonnell's province which encompassed Agra, Lucknow and Benares. Originally called the North-Western Provinces because they were north-west of Bengal, their name had long been irrational (they lie to the south-east of the Punjab) and was now changed to the United Provinces of Agra and Oudh.

Viceroy and his subordinate deteriorated so much that the Bishop of Lahore was prevailed upon to mediate, and the Lieutenant-Governor was eventually persuaded to apologize. Unwilling to humiliate Young in public, Curzon refused to publish the apology, a magnanimous gesture which inspired no corresponding response. The situation was exacerbated by Lady Young, who Curzon believed had converted her husband, a 'pious and rather narrow-minded missionary', into a 'vindictive partisan' who plagued him day after day with letters of mingled protest and menace.[26] She slandered the Viceroy in Simla society and then took umbrage when he refused invitations to her house. The affair rumbled on until the following year, with continual reiterations of Young's grievance and rumours that on retirement he planned to sue Curzon for libel. The Viceroy was upset by the long and disagreeable dispute, but it does not seem to have occurred to him that it could have been avoided by an act of elementary courtesy at the outset.

Curzon's policy led to a reduction both in the number of British troops on the frontier and in the amount of actions they were required to fight. Regular garrisons on the Khyber, the Samana and the Kurram were withdrawn and replaced by tribal levies known as the Khyber Rifles, the Samana Rifles and the Kurram Militia; 11,000 British troops were brought back behind the administrative border, and the 4,000 who remained in the tribal areas experienced little trouble. Apart from a few military sallies connected with a blockade of the intractable Mahsud Waziris, the once-turbulent frontier remained largely at peace during Curzon's rule. The tribal levies were not quite so well behaved as the Viceroy claimed, and occasional disturbances, as his successor discovered, sometimes went unreported. But the degree of tranquillity was unprecedented and was reflected in the huge financial saving: whereas over £4½ million had been spent on military manoeuvres on the frontier between 1894 and 1898, the total expenditure during Curzon's longer rule amounted to £¼ million. Lord Salisbury's prediction – that the Viceroy's frontier policy would give Britain an extra fifty years in India – proved inaccurate, but the new province, ably administered by two of Curzon's protégés, Colonel Deane and later Colonel Roos-Keppel, remained largely at peace until after the First World War.[27]

On hearing of Curzon's appointment to India, the Liberal politician Sir William Harcourt had begged him as 'a personal favour' not to make war on Russia during his lifetime.[28] The joke encased the fear, widespread in England, that the Viceroy was an advocate of a 'forward' policy in Asia which might lead to a military confrontation with Tsarist forces. This was both a simplification and an exaggeration. Curzon had acquired the reputation mainly on account of his strenuous opposition to the evacuation of Chitral in 1895, but on no part of the frontier did he advocate an extension of Britain's existing responsibilities. He wanted to stay put, being as opposed to a retreat to the line of the Indus as he was to a conquest of the tribes and the planting of garrisons among them. Anxious at all times to deter the army from embroilments, he waged no wars and sanctioned only one major expedition – the mission to Tibet – during his viceroyalty. The only real campaigns the army was required to fight were on imperial battlegrounds at the request of the British Government. During the Boxer rebellion nearly 20,000 native troops were sent to Peking, where they were the first force to enter the besieged Legations and where they rescued among others the British Minister, Sir Claude MacDonald, whose obituary had already appeared in *The Times* and for whom a memorial service had been arranged in St Paul's Cathedral.[29]

The role of more than 13,000 British troops, sent from India to South Africa in September 1899, was still more critical. Curzon, who predicted that a war against the Boers would entail 'a hideous carnage' and hoped it could be averted, had offered to send a force even earlier, but George Wyndham, the Under-Secretary at the War Office, had assured him it would not be necessary. Soon afterwards the British Government became conscious of its military deficiencies and accepted the offer after all, although a further proposal to send native troops was rejected by Whitehall on the grounds that it would incite the entire Dutch population to rebellion. The British regiments embarked from Calcutta and Bombay with an efficiency which surprised the Viceroy and arrived in Natal in time to prevent its capture by General Joubert. Had it not been for Curzon, Milner wrote later, Boer flags would have been floating over Durban and Maritzburg by the end of October 1899.[30] To the Viceroy the conflict seemed a doleful repetition of the American Civil War in which the North had been consistently defeated until it had 'weeded out all the rotten generals who had made their way, in the long era of peace, to the top'.[31] But he could at least derive some satisfaction from the performance of the troops from India, who outshone those from England. Sir George White, the defender of Ladysmith, sent a telegram to thank the Indian contingent for saving Natal. Arguably the rest of South Africa was saved as well, for it is doubtful whether Britain could have recovered if Natal had been added to the other disasters.

In Asia Curzon's aim was not to extend the frontiers of empire in any direction but to strengthen Britain's political position in all areas which bordered on India. He was happy to be surrounded by buffer states provided they remained genuinely independent of Russia and other European powers. 'We don't want [Kuwait],' Godley told him, 'but we don't want anyone else to have it. That sounds rather bad, when it is baldly stated; but it is the true explanation of a good deal of our diplomacy.'[32] Curzon agreed with the objective but believed that the policy, however negative it sounded, required more vigorous diplomacy than either the India Office or the Foreign Office were usually prepared to pursue. Year after year his letters home railed against the weakness, fatalism, inertia and, above all, non-existence of British policy. He believed that Asiatic rulers, like native chiefs, needed pressure as well as blandishment, and he was eager to exert it on the Shah of Persia, the Sultan of Muscat and the Emir of Afghanistan. Anxious to avoid alienating the Emir, Hamilton annoyed Curzon by refusing to let him send a strong letter to Kabul in 1899. Although the Viceroy admitted that correspondence with his old friend was 'about as fruitless an occupation as throwing pebbles in the ocean', he felt it was necessary to answer 'an Oriental's casuistry' because otherwise 'he thinks he has reduced you to silence'.[33] His belief that he could handle the Emir was not shared, however, by the Government in London, and the firm policy he advocated towards Afghanistan did not prevail.*

By means of trade and the reduction of piracy, Britain had managed in the course of the nineteenth century to establish herself as the paramount power in the Persian Gulf. As no other power had any interests there, Curzon saw no need for concessions in the area, which came within the orbit of the Government of India. He wanted to make a British protectorate of Kuwait, as its ruler had requested, and was outraged when Salisbury desisted for fear of offending Germany. The Sermon on the Mount, he declared, was not relevant to international politics, and 'turning the other cheek' was the wrong way to deal with an ambitious power that had no connection with the Gulf.[34] Similarly, he saw no necessity for placating the French at Muscat just because they were feeling sore about Fashoda. Salisbury's fear of provoking the unpredictable 'Krugers' in the French Chamber should not be removed by agreeing to France's demands for a coaling station in the Gulf. The French had no bona fide interests there, argued Curzon, and no more needed a station in Muscat than the British required one in

---

*See below, pp. 286–7.

Madagascar.[35] Their only purpose, he told Salisbury, was to be able to assist Russian designs in the Gulf in return for Russian support at Bangkok and Tangier.[36] Curzon's approach was eventually adopted by Lord Lansdowne, who succeeded Salisbury as Foreign Secretary in 1900, with the result that the Germans did not gain a protectorate over Kuwait and the French did not acquire a coaling station.

Curzon's views on foreign policy were remarkably consistent and he was fond of saying that there was hardly a word in his *Russia and Central Asia* with which he disagreed fifteen years later. No greater fallacy existed in politics, he believed – wrongly as it turned out – than the idea that Britain could come to an agreement with Russia over Asia. Leaving aside 'the ingrained duplicity' of Russian diplomacy, an agreement was impossible because no government, aware of its country's geographical and strategic advantages over Britain, would ever set a limit on its expansion.[37] As the Russians aimed one day to take the whole of Persia, there seemed little chance of persuading them to divide that country into spheres of interest. Their natural desire was to expand, which they would do unless thwarted – until they had taken Persia, reached the Gulf and established another point of pressure on India.[38] Yet although Curzon believed these to be their objectives, he did not accept that their achievement was ordained, because a Russian army in southern Persia would be separated by nearly a thousand miles, much of it desert, from a Russian railway, while the Gulf ports could be defended and provisioned by the Royal Navy. He therefore rejected Godley's view that a Russian advance to the Gulf was inevitable. If the Russians got there, he argued, it would be a result of British weakness rather than as a fulfilment of national destiny.[39]

In Curzon's view Britain had not had a Persian policy for a hundred years. Successive governments had lived from hand to mouth, changing their minds, alternately cuddling and cuffing the Shah of the day, but never deciding the nature of British and Indian interests, the extent of imperial obligations, or the limit to which a Russian advance might be allowed to go.[40] In September 1899 the Viceroy sent home a long and penetrating despatch containing a comprehensive analysis of Britain's position in Persia. If, as he believed, the contending powers were unable to agree on the future of that country, he urged the Government to state unequivocally that further Russian encroachments in the north of Persia would lead to corresponding moves in the south. Britain, he later told Selborne, should not fear a conflict with Russia on land or sea in any part of the globe.[41] As for the Persians, there was no point competing in oriental diplomacy with them, because the occasional 'show of the boot' was likely to be more effective. He urged, however, the offer of a generous financial loan to Tehran, and was dismayed when Russia was allowed to outbid the richest country in the world.

The despatch on Persian policy arrived in London in the early weeks of the Boer War and was ignored. Six months later Curzon sent a reminder which again went unanswered. After ten months the Government replied that, in view of Russia's capacity to annex northern Persia, it would be futile for Britain to commit herself to the country's independence. Britain was equally powerless, it was claimed, to prevent other countries establishing their influence in the Gulf. In August 1900 Salisbury warned Curzon that Britain's fighting power in Persia must be confined to the coast because any war in the rest of the country would swallow up two or three times as much income tax as the fighting in the Transvaal. In a subsequent letter the Prime Minister admitted that sooner or later Tehran would become a virtual protectorate of Russia and that there was nothing Britain could do about it.[42] Reading these and similarly pessimistic views invariably depressed the Viceroy. Sometimes, he confessed to Hamilton, 'the heart goes out of me as regards the future of our dominions in Asia, and I . . . say to myself, "Is it worthwhile struggling on when our own people and their leaders are themselves engaged in tracing the handwriting on the wall?"'[43]

In 1902 Curzon's perennial complaint that Britain had 'no glimmering of a policy' in Persia paid off. Riled by the Viceroy's 'rather querulous language' employed when commenting on Persian affairs, Lansdowne decided to write a despatch bringing together the various strands of the Government's position.[44] The Foreign Secretary claimed that these had always been part of British policy towards Persia. But Curzon was delighted to find that the despatch was 'almost the transcript of a private letter' he had sent Lansdowne after being invited to state the policy he himself would pursue.[45] The British Minister in Tehran was instructed to tell the Grand Vizier that Britain supported the independence and integrity of Persia but held such interests in the south of the country that she could not accept the rivalry of another power there. Russia's 'superior interest' in the north was accepted, but the Persian Government had to understand that Britain would not allow her to penetrate the south. A military or naval station in the Persian Gulf would be regarded as a threat to India and would not be tolerated. Although the despatch did not put an end to Anglo-Russian rivalry in Persia, the Tsarist Government at last now knew how far it could go without risking a war.

In the summer of 1903 Lansdowne accepted another of Curzon's urgings by proclaiming in the House of Lords a sort of Monroe Doctrine for the Persian Gulf. If any other power, he declared, established a naval base or fortified port in that sea, Britain would regard it as a very grave menace to her interests and would resist with all the means at her disposal.[46] Again the Viceroy was delighted by this unusually bold assertion of British dominance. Apart from anything else, it opened the way for his most celebrated imperial progress, a long-cherished, majestic, flag-waving tour of the Gulf.

15

The Viceroy's Routine

———◆———

EACH OF CURZON's Indian years followed the same pattern except for 1904 when he went to England. A winter season of three or four months in Calcutta was followed by a spring tour of about six weeks, a five- or six-month summer in Simla, and an autumn tour which brought him back to Government House shortly before Christmas. The Simla sojourn was the least enjoyable as well as the longest part of the year. The Curzons redecorated Viceregal Lodge, replacing the Lincrusta and paper ornamentations with damask of less dingy colours, corrected and restored the ancestral shields of the Governors-General, and designed a rose pergola for the garden. But they still disliked the house. They loved the scenery, the crimson rhododendrons, the snows on the mountain tops, the wooded hills all around, but they never loved the town set in the midst of it. Curzon claimed to love everything and every place in India except Simla. Each year he felt more afflicted by its 'garish setting of inane frivolity' and 'its atmosphere of petty gossip and pettier scandal'.[1]

The Simla season, which peaked in June, was the high point of the year for many people, especially for district officers and their families who after ten months in the plains needed a cool respite in the hills. Isolated in their work and suffering from the climate, they grasped the chance of relaxing in the company of their fellow countrymen, playing tennis and polo, going on picnics, organizing dances and amateur theatricals, 'taking the air' in the evenings along Simla's fashionable Mall. It may have been 'inane frivolity', but it was the frivolity of people under strain, the frenzied gaiety of aliens often unsure why they were in India and desperate to enjoy themselves while they could. If, as Bishop Welldon suggested, they were like 'people dancing under the shadow of a volcanic mountain',[2] one should not be too hard on them, or on Simla.

Senior officials of the army or the civil service, cooped up in the place for half the year, felt differently. Clinton Dawkins, who spent a single summer there on Curzon's Council, declared himself amazed by the vulgarity and silliness of English people trying to amuse themselves.[3] As a young Punjab official in 1884, Walter Lawrence had enjoyed Simla: it was bright and cheerful, full of clever and interesting people. But when he returned fifteen years later as the Viceroy's Private Secretary, Simla seemed rowdier and more frivolous. Feeling old and disinclined to take part in society's 'high jinks', he preferred to spend his free evenings advancing through a shelf of Dickens.[4]

Curzon found Simla's social life small, narrow and monotonous. Taste, imagination, interest in art and literature either did not exist or else had been 'sterilised by the arid breath of a semi-court and purely official existence'.[5] He kept his social life to a minimum: the Polo Final, the Old Etonian Dinner, a meeting of the Simla Temperance Association, an occasional visit to amateur theatricals in which his ADCs acted so badly that he felt obliged to offer 'a lot of hints and tips' about the art of the stage.[6] He attended the unavoidable functions but spurned events such as the Horse and Dog Show and seldom found time to go to gymkhanas. Such aloofness annoyed and unnerved people. It was said that in Simla you could not hear your own voice for 'the grinding of axes', and the grinders and gossips were often conflated. One of the town's worst features, Curzon thought, was the 'sinister novelty' of having to begin each season with a new set of gossips and idlers. His unguarded talk at meals was distorted and repeated by his listeners to the rest of Simla, which chuckled about it and referred to him as 'Imperial George'. Little jests were misinterpreted, and remarks such as 'no self-respecting woman would allow cold tapioca pudding to be served at luncheon' were taken seriously and resented. Curzon made no effort to change his image. 'The world saw him in caricature,' wrote Lawrence, 'and unfortunately he was apt to play up to the caricature'.[7]

Although he disliked Simla, the Viceroy could work well there, undisturbed except for the weekly meeting of his Council and the visits of the departmental secretaries. He often wished that discontented people in the plains, who thought government officials spent their time in picnics, balls and gymkhanas, could observe his routine. Sometimes, he told MacDonnell, he did not leave the house for two or three days in succession, and he was seldom in bed before two in the morning.[8] But the whole *raison d'être* of Simla – to rejuvenate officials and restore their health – passed him by. As soon as he arrived there, he was seized by 'the usual Simla reaction', backache and 'utter lassitude', and during his stay was afflicted frequently by fever and sometimes by dysentery.

Weekends were spent at a house called the Retreat, a thousand feet higher in the village of Mashobra six miles from Simla. Curzon did not care for it either, mainly because he was kept awake by the noise of the 'coppersmith' and 'brain-fever' birds, but he admitted the climate was more bracing. He much preferred living in tents at Naldera, a favourite camping ground of Lytton and Dufferin, where he could communicate with Simla, sixteen miles away, by signalling and heliograph during the day and by lamp-flashes at night. The place was 'unutterably peaceful' with no sounds but 'the faint whisper of the wind through the deodars' and the distant humming of the River Sutlej through a deep gorge over 3,000 feet below. The family camped there for two or three weeks each June and loved it, the children rolling about among the pine needles and trying to catch butterflies. Their father arranged the plan of the tents and marked out a golf course where he played daily in the evenings. It was almost his only exercise of the year, for in Calcutta it was too hot to walk, and at Simla he limited himself to an afternoon stroll and, when his back permitted, an occasional game of tennis. Naldera was also the closest he came to a relaxing holiday. When Mary was in England in 1901, he claimed he did little more than six hours work a day, that he was in bed by midnight and that he did not start writing, at his table under the deodars, until just before noon.[9] The open-air life was good for him; both his back pains and his insomnia diminished in the idyllic surroundings.

The chief drawback of the Simla months was the monotony. People at home, he wrote, might think the Viceroy lived in sumptuous palaces surrounded by oriental pomp, but in fact he spent half the year on a single hilltop chained to a sort of middle-class suburb where there was no culture or conversation and where he had to lunch day after day with his ADCs, a set of youths interested only in polo and dancing. Presumably they thought it wise not to discuss such topics with their chief, for Lawrence, who frequently lunched at Viceregal Lodge, observed that they dared not open their mouths. It was perhaps understandable that Curzon should describe Simla life in one of his most celebrated snobbisms as 'like dining every day in the housekeeper's room with the butler and the lady's maid'.[10]

As the Viceroy himself recognized, his official position made it difficult for him to attract the solace, the advice or even the friendly conversation which he craved. He could not see anyone except by sending for him, an action which in itself gave the subsequent meeting a certain formality. Furthermore, the interviewee, whose entire future probably depended on the Viceroy, would feel constrained from telling him unwelcome facts. All India, Curzon realized, was talking about his plans, his caprices, his sayings and his actions, but he knew nothing about what was being said except what he read in the newspapers; even Lawrence dared not repeat gossip.

He did enjoy the company of some of his entourage, notably Captain Wigram ('so dependable a fellow'), the most efficient and intelligent of his ADCs. And he was very fond of Lawrence, who made use of the privilege, open to others though availed of few, of making frank and unresented criticisms. Yet Lawrence and Wigram were both employees who could not treat him as his old friends among the Souls or in the House of Commons had done. 'The great want', he sighed to Brodrick, 'is that of human fellowship.' He had always liked to chaff his friends about their alleged deficiencies: when Ian Malcolm, an MP who had assisted him at the Foreign Office, accompanied the Viceroy on his Burmese tour, he was teased remorselessly about his equestrian defects and his fear of crossing a rope bridge. But Curzon could not behave like that with subordinates. The one man in India he regarded as a close friend left the Subcontinent after only a brief spell as Bishop of Calcutta. Welldon was the Viceroy's intellectual equal and the only person with whom he could have a natural and uninhibited conversation. Yet their friendship had its drawbacks because, as Lawrence observed, it led people to associate the Bishop's unpopular views with Curzon. Tact was not among Welldon's gifts, and in his first few weeks in India he had antagonized almost all classes and sects by his missionary zeal: he even managed to alienate his natural supporters in Calcutta society by closing the cathedral doors to prevent them leaving for dinner before the sermon.[11] Welldon was so out of touch with Indian feeling that he was unable to understand why Queen Victoria appealed more to the natives than Jesus Christ.[12] While they valued his friendship, the Curzons knew Welldon was unsuited to India, and they advised him not to return after a visit to England in 1901.

Life in Calcutta was much less dull than in Simla. There was a wider

British society, annually reinforced by friends and visitors from home, which at any rate ensured an energetic social life. There was the consolation of a fine palace in an imperial city instead of a gloomy villa in a cramped hilltop town. And there was the stimulus of the legislative session, during which the Viceroy's reforms became law, and the budget debate which gave him the opportunity to make an annual 'state of the nation' address. While there was less time to ponder new policies, he still had the midnight hours for the perusal of files and the redrafting of despatches. Besides, Christmas was a good time for serious projects because, as he put it, everyone was 'so engaged in hilarity' that the departments scarcely disturbed him with their day-to-day affairs.

In Calcutta the Viceroy could enjoy the company which the Simla months denied him. Sven Hedin, whom he regarded as the greatest scientific explorer of the age, was entertained at Government House, and later dedicated one of his books to Curzon. Pierre Loti, the exotic French novelist, also received hospitality despite Havelock's warning that he had come to India as a spy for both the Russians and the French. Dismissing the theory as 'absolute moonshine', the Viceroy welcomed Loti who, although he curled his hair and painted his cheeks, seemed 'otherwise to be a very clever and cultured little man'.[13]

Other visitors sometimes proved tiresome, particularly European princes who needed a lot of entertaining and were regarded by Curzon as an 'unmitigated nuisance'. Pearl Craigie came out and wrote some flattering but 'peculiarly rotten' articles. Oscar Browning was egotistical and irritating, noted Lawrence, always telling everyone how things were done at Cambridge; having listened to O.B.'s 'most grotesque' rendering of '*funiculi funicula*' after dinner, the Private Secretary recorded his ambition not to become like him when he grew older.[14] There was also the problem of relations. Coming out for the Delhi Durbar with his sister Evie, Alfred Curzon expected his brother to arrange free shooting and accommodation for their subsequent tour of India; but the Viceroy refused to inflict his guests on native chiefs, and 'Affie', to his disgust, even had to hire a rifle for a tiger shoot. Mary's sisters, Daisy and Nancy, amused Curzon with their boisterous humour, but they were even more troublesome, flirting with the ADCs, mocking the viceregal etiquette and gossiping about their sister and brother-in-law. Mrs Leiter, by contrast, acquired so much respect for court manners in India that ever afterwards she addressed the American President as 'Excellency'.[15]

The cost of entertaining at Government House and Viceregal Lodge was prodigious. Both residences, Curzon complained, were treated like hotels and department stores. People borrowed his tents, his carpets and even his band for their own parties; one total stranger asked for the loan of a horse to ride in a steeplechase. He had to provide good champagne because his guests scrutinized the labels on the bottles, as well as fine cigars which tended to disappear in the pockets of departing gentlemen. The Viceroy soon realized he was being 'colossally swindled' by his French chef, who was sacked after engaging in some 'peculations of a character that excites admiration even in the East'.[16]

Governors-General had received such munificent salaries from the East India Company that they were able to accumulate large fortunes during their period of office. But by Curzon's time it was difficult for a Viceroy to save much of his income without reducing the scale of his entertaining. Initial expenses, including the purchase of Elgin's horses and carriages, cost Curzon £7,200 more than he received as an 'outfit allowance', and during the seventeen months following his arrival his expenditure exceeded his income by over £8,000. Neither of the Curzons had been personally extravagant, and Mary claimed that no Vicereine had been so economical with her wardrobe. Lawrence suggested some economies could be made in the kitchen, which was costing £2,500 more than in the equivalent period in Elgin's time, and in the stables, which were costing £5,700 more. Curzon was so astonished by these figures that he examined the accounts and discovered that, at a time when the average annual income per head in Britain was £40, the Viceroy of India was spending the same amount each year on his guests' chocolates, rather more on their tennis balls, and £307 on their cigars and cigarettes.[17] The Curzons' initial debt was paid off with help from Mary's father, and thereafter they managed to balance their budget. In 1902 he asked the India Office to raise his successor's salary so that no future Viceroy should have to leave India 'without one penny to his credit after five years of the most laborious service in the world'.[18] Hamilton refused.

The Viceroys had a rural retreat at Barrackpore, a plain classical house set in a large park on the River Hooghly fifteen miles from Calcutta. The family used to go there by river launch on Saturday evenings and return early on Monday. Curzon naturally took his files and worked on them for most of Sunday, but he enjoyed the twilight journeys, and years later he recalled sitting on deck to watch the changing panoramas of the river banks, the thick vegetation and the feathery palm-tops, the smoke of native villages, the rows of Hindu shrines at the water's edge, and the white-clad figures moving up and down the dilapidated ghats. Work on Sunday was interrupted by an inspection of the rose garden, which he developed as a nursery for plants needed for state occasions at Government House, and by lunch under a large banyan tree in the garden, a hazardous meal during which native servants with sticks tried to prevent huge kites swooping down and carrying off pieces of meat. After lunch Curzon returned to his papers, while his ADCs lounged about under the banyan tree, eventually rousing themselves to play croquet until the light faded when they retired indoors to play billiards. Late one night Lawrence heard the Viceroy bellowing at them because the click of the balls kept him awake.[19]

A natural prey to gossip all his life, Curzon soon inspired a collection of stories about viceregal pomp and etiquette which travelled to England and were there repeated, magnified and believed. Even Edward VII enjoyed recounting how Colonel Sandbach had resigned as Military Secretary because Curzon had forced him to stand behind his chair during meals.[20] Other circulating fictions included Mary curtseying to him when she woke up in the morning, ladies having to retire backwards after talking to him at balls, people being forbidden to speak to either of them without permission, and lunches at which the Curzons were seated before any guests were allowed into the dining-room. Such stories, expanding with age, continued long after the couple had left India. At Simla in 1919 a member of the current Viceroy's staff was recounting how Curzon 'always went to bed preceded by two ADCs walking backwards and carrying silver candlesticks'. One of them, allegedly, had to wait outside the bedroom door until he was dismissed.[21]

Curzon was exasperated by these stories. Sandbach, who never had to stand behind his chair, resigned because he was more fitted to be a regimental officer than a Military Secretary. Nobody had to walk backwards. The ballrooms at Simla and Calcutta did have a dais where the Curzons stood while people filed by and shook hands, but this was 'a curious Indian custom', he pointed out, not one introduced by them. The social etiquette which they observed, he told Hamilton, was exactly the same as that of the Dufferins and the Lansdownes without any modification except that he did not take 'pretty widows into corners as Lord Dufferin did or slip [his] arm round their waists and call them pretty dears . . .'[22] The Secretary of State was convinced by Curzon's denials, but the King preferred the apocryphal version. '*Qui s'excuse s'accuse*', he scrawled on a letter of explanation sent him by Hamilton.[23]

Other exaggerations continually appeared in the British press. The *Saturday Review* and the *Manchester Guardian* complained that he was always making speeches, but other newspapers, eager to stress the oriental pomp of his life, claimed he was always on top of elephants. A.C. Benson heard that he used them like cabs to meet him at railway stations.[24] In fact he was the first Viceroy who did not possess an elephant and was forced to borrow one from a maharaja for the state entry at the Delhi Durbar. He never otherwise rode the animals except to go tiger shooting – where they were essential – and described the experience as 'one of the most horrible forms of locomotion', especially for someone with a bad back. Criticism of the formality of the viceregal court may have been more justified, because Curzon did nothing to reduce the rituals and indeed restored them to their pre-Elgin level. He certainly enjoyed pageantry and ceremonial, which reached their apogee at the Delhi Durbar, and he correctly estimated their value and importance in the East. But although he loved the splendour of such spectacles, he seldom enjoyed state occasions which were a stress on his physique and a strain on his spirits. Informing Godley in a letter that he was about to put on white breeches and silk stockings, he described the process as 'the prelude to an evening of incomparable tedium – I allude to a function known as the State Ball'.[25]

Curzon's favourite seasons were the spring and autumn tours. These were sometimes long journeys, lasting six weeks or more, to distant places in the south or along the frontier. Others were short excursions in different directions, a tiger shoot or a visit to a famine area, a trip to install a maharaja or simply a roundabout way of travelling between Simla and Calcutta. Curzon spent more time on tour than any other Viceroy and enjoyed visiting places unknown to his predecessors. In one year he went on five separate tours and in another spent sixteen weeks on his journeys; his southern tour of 1900, covering 6,000 miles and including more than forty speeches, lasted eight weeks. Most of the travelling was done in a special train which carried, apart from the Curzons and their personal servants, the Viceroy's Military Secretary, Private Secretary and Assistant Private Secretary, his surgeon and dispensary, four ADCs, nine clerks and about eighty-five native servants; various officials such as the Secretary of the Foreign Department and an Under-Secretary were also included.

The train's chief occupants were treated with due respect during their travels, receiving a thirty-one-gun salute on arrival and departure at any station with a battery or a fort; if they arrived after sunset or on a Sunday, the salute was fired the following morning. Lawrence was sceptical about the usefulness of these progresses: they were too formal and too rapid, officials were so nervous about meeting the Viceroy that they said silly things, too much time was wasted shooting and sightseeing, and little was achieved by the formal banalities exchanged between Viceroy and native chiefs at the state banquets.[26] Other officials took a different view, considering it advantageous for the Viceroy to be seen by so many people and good for the princes to feel that a personal interest was being taken in their affairs. Even Lawrence, whose views had been coloured by a surfeit of dusty clambering over ruins in the footsteps of his chief, later admitted that the sightseeing – and the restoration work that was its fruit – had been worthwhile.[27]

The tours were also good for the Curzons. Although he slept even worse in trains than elsewhere, the Viceroy was still a traveller at heart, eager to see fresh scenery and buildings, still able to enjoy long cart rides over bumpy terrain. His endurance astonished and often dismayed officials who found him impervious to the sun and incapable of fatigue. Lawrence thought him at his best in a camp in the countryside, where he relaxed and told amusing anecdotes of his early journeys. Mary accompanied him on several tours and, in spite of headaches and the heat, also enjoyed them, especially a trip on hill ponies in the Himalayas and a visit to Burma, drifting down the Irrawaddy and admiring the pagodas. They were both exhilarated by the landscape of the south, which reminded Curzon of the India of his nursery books, 'made up of black-skinned, idle, grinning people, and peaceful land-locked lagoons, and groves of feathery palms'. He was similarly aroused by the towns with their 'teeming populations, gross superstitions, and their barbaric and monstrous temples'.[28]

Official visits in British India consisted mainly of speeches, inspections and social functions which included what the Viceroy regarded as 'that grimmest of terrors, a garden party'. Factories and hospitals were seen, statues unveiled, interviews given and monuments closely examined. Much amusement was derived from the decorated triumphal arches which welcomed them to Indian towns with inscriptions such as 'Welcome, our future Emperor' (in Trichinopoli), 'Hail Overworked Viceroy, Karachi wants more Curzons', and 'A Gala Day' converted unintentionally in Jaipur to 'A Gal a Day'. The duration of journeys was much extended by the appeal of history: no place connected with the Moguls or the Mutiny – and few from earlier periods – was overlooked. Instructions for the restoration of ancient buildings and commemorative tablets for even minor Mutiny sites were drawn up before departure. Brigadier John Nicholson's last hours on earth were traced from the breach in the walls of Delhi to the lane in which he was shot and from there to the place of his burial. A memorial tablet for Sir Henry Lawrence was found in the wrong room of the Residency at Lucknow and was removed and put up on the true spot where he had died. Curzon 'never ceased to be amazed' that for over forty years visitors had gazed at the inaccurate tablet without detecting or correcting the error.[29]

The appeal of history reverberated also in the native states. Much as he appreciated Scindia's efficient and progressive state of Gwalior, his imagination preferred the unchanging rituals of Udaipur and the feudal flavour of Kathiawar, which he was delighted to find had retained its archaic and aristocratic features under British protection. Portuguese Goa, still run by a colonial power he had never admired, provided a different type of historical interest. The beauty of the churches impressed the Curzons, but the organization of the visit was so feeble and a military parade was such a farce that the viceregal party found it difficult to control their giggles. At the state dinner the British guests, who spoke no Portuguese, were sandwiched between local officials who spoke no English, and conversation was replaced by the sound of two bands, one in the next room and the other in the street, playing different tunes simultaneously. Fortunately one of the Viceroy's neighbours was a Portuguese lady who had been educated in an English-speaking convent in Macao. After persuading her to translate the last part of his speech and teach him the pronunciation, Curzon was then able to stand up, reply to the Governor's toast in English and deliver an impassioned finale in fluent Portuguese. His hosts applauded wildly, the State Secretary proposing the Viceroy's health with the cheer, 'Heep Heep Hah'.[30]

Most tours included a few days' shooting of 'game' as varied as quail and rhinoceros. Curzon was a good shot who enjoyed the challenge of difficult targets, but he got no satisfaction from massacres or easy hits. After killing one rhino he declined to fire at any others. Nor did he want to shoot at a herd of wild buffalo which, instead of charging on sight, 'shambled about like a herd of tame cattle in a farmyard': there was 'no more sport in the thing than in killing flies on a window pane'.[31] In the Gir Forest he cancelled a lion shoot on discovering that the beasts there were close to extinction, and he displayed genuine sorrow on finding three unborn cubs in a tigress he had just killed. The remorse was insufficient to deter him from future hunting, but few of his contemporaries would have shown any at all.

Nothing was more exciting, Curzon admitted to his father, than tiger shooting. 'You can hear your heart beat as he comes, unseen, with the leaves crackling under his feet, and suddenly emerges, sometimes at a walk, sometimes at full gallop, sometimes with an angry roar.'[32] To another correspondent he described the almost inconceivable 'majesty of the tiger when in a rage'. He had the admiration for his quarry that the best matadors have for brave bulls. One 'most splendid and courageous brute' crouched in the dense Nepalese jungle until the hunters' ring of elephants closed in on him, when suddenly he sprang out and mauled one of them before retreating, growling or roaring, until the next attack. The elephants became so frightened that they 'curtsied and waltzed about' and would not go near the tiger. Curzon eventually got him, but it took four bullets, an unusual number for a hunter who seldom required more than one. On another expedition he needed only seven shots to kill a bear, a black leopard, a sambar and three tigers.[33]

Not all shoots were as successful. In their eagerness to please, Curzon's princely hosts sometimes tried to provide him with easy tigers, fat and possibly drugged, at which to aim. More often they encouraged the Viceroy with reports of large numbers of the species which turned out either to be non-existent or to have moved away. In Hyderabad and Rajputana, where the tigers were hunted not from the backs of a concentring circle of elephants but from a stationary position, Curzon spent entire days on a platform or on top of a boulder with no animal in sight. On one occasion he and Mary sat together in a tree and saw nothing bigger than a frog, while on an eight-day expedition to Rewa he had only one opportunity of firing his rifle. The absence of tigers was usually known, however, before he left camp in the morning and gave him the opportunity to catch up with his work.

The most irritating thing about the hunting expeditions was the behaviour of his staff, whose company was even more intrusive in camp than at Simla. His Indian servants were often annoying, losing his papers or misplacing his shirts, but the ADCs, who had 'not two ideas between them', were even more tiresome. They blazed away at anything that moved but rarely managed to hit it. Curzon thought they shot worse than any body of men in India. Captain Baker Carr, for example, was a 'colossal fraud' who 'gassed' on and on about his sporting exploits in bygone days but was incapable of either catching a fish or shooting a bird. Colonel Baring, who was Sandbach's successor as Military Secretary, was a better marksman but a less agreeable character who showed insufficient respect for his chief and indicated disagreement by curling his lip at him. After the Viceroy had shot his first tiger in Nepal, Baring suggested he should retire until the ten members of the staff had each bagged one too – a proposal which infuriated both Curzon and the Nepalese, who protested that the shoot had not been arranged for the benefit of the ADCs. Curzon's exasperation with his Military Secretary intensified during a lunch on a Himalayan hillside when Baring so annoyed some hornets by flapping at them that they rushed at the Viceroy and stung him all over his neck and scalp. That evening Curzon wrote to Mary, lying in bed with his 'head all swollen up and a thousand aches in every part of it', to complain that Baring had neither uttered a word of regret nor enquired how he was feeling.[34]

Wherever he was, in camp, on a train or in a maharaja's palace, Curzon still worked at his papers and correspondence, writing in the dust and heat of a jolting carriage or late at night in his tent after the staff had retired. A day without tigers enabled him to write thirty or forty letters, while an extended period of blank days, as at Rewa, encouraged him to telegraph to Simla for more files. Asked by Ampthill how he managed to get through his work, Curzon replied 'by never doing anything else', by sitting up into the night and finding another two and a half or three hours after dinner, by rapid writing – 'the result of long practice' – by familiarity with Indian subjects, and by invariably devoting Sundays to some special project. Drafts of his letters, he added, were written 'in bed, or on a boat, or when dressing, or anywhere, whenever the thing comes into my mind'.[35]

Work in Simla and Calcutta included meetings, for which he was notoriously unpunctual, interviews, which he tended to regard as a waste of time, and speeches, which he wrote out beforehand, rapidly memorized and then delivered without notes. But the bulk of the work was in the papers and correspondence which Lawrence brought him throughout the mornings and afternoons. His secretary handed him everything from the Foreign Department but tried to make summaries of cases sent from the other secretariats. If the matter seemed complex, however, the Viceroy insisted on seeing all the papers. He was a voracious reader, observed Lawrence, with a wonderful memory, his brain like 'a splendid and perfect index' which only failed him when discussing Dickens. His secretary, who had made himself an expert on the writer, recalled that Curzon invariably misquoted him and muddled up his characters. Reflecting on the quality of his mind and his obsession with logic, Lawrence suggested 'it would have been better for him and for others if he had known more of Dickens and less of logic'.[36] It is hard to disagree.

Drafting and redrafting remained the most time-consuming occupation. Convinced there was almost no one in the Government, apart from Ibbetson, who could write 'a page of either forcible reasoning or of passable English', Curzon insisted on redrafting despatches on even the most mundane subjects. The situation became particularly bad in the Foreign Department when its efficient Secretary, Hugh Barnes, was promoted to the lieutenant-governorship of Burma in 1902 and replaced by Louis Dane, until then the Resident in Kashmir. The new Secretary's literary defects soon turned him into a special object of exasperation for the Viceroy. One despatch on a simple subject, complained Curzon, was so abominably done that it took him nearly three hours to rewrite instead of the hour and a half he would have needed had he undertaken the job in the first place.[37] His obsession with doing everything himself exceeded even his normal limits at a dinner party in Calcutta when, after the ladies had withdrawn, he remained silently at his place, ignoring his male guests for ten minutes until he had corrected the proof of a note on soldiers' pay.[38]

Curzon never tried to delegate. He grumbled to Lawrence of overwork and sometimes told him he felt he was going mad. But he refused to let his secretary help or to trust the departments to do the work themselves.[39] When a subordinate slipped up, he delighted in exploiting the incident as a vindication of his methods. His reaction to the placing of a suitcase in the wrong railway carriage was to scoff at the notion that one should trust other people to get things done: in his view, there was 'no madder philosophy in the world'. After some minor mistake by Lawrence, he told Mary it was 'no good trusting a human being to do a thing for you. Do everything yourself.' Even Hamilton was treated to an exposition of this theory and informed that 'every really great man from Caesar to Napoleon [had] been a master of detail'.[40]

All his life Curzon piled pointless and unimportant burdens on top of his official labours. After travelling to India on a P & O vessel, he felt obliged to tell Selborne, who was a director of the shipping line, that the food on board was atrocious and had made one of Mary's sisters ill. When Selborne disputed the poor quality, the Viceroy replied with a further eight pages on the subject, and a year later was still sending his friend evidence from other passengers who had suffered from the cooking.[41] Curzon's pedagogic nature could seldom resist the temptation to correct inaccuracies or bad English. Officials, the usual victims, expected it, but authors were sometimes astonished to discover that their literacy had come under viceregal scrutiny. Curzon had little time for books in India, read on average only one a year and, explaining that he was 'somewhat fastidious in syntax and language', subsequently sent its author a thorough criticism of his work. Herbert Maxwell, the biographer of Wellington, received a list of grammatical quibbles which included the recommendation that a genitive absolute should be turned into a nominative, while Lionel Cust was sent a long catalogue of the misspellings, wrong tenses, incorrect use of prepositions and confused metaphors which disfigured his book on Eton. Cust thanked Curzon for the letter, which must have given him limited pleasure, and pointedly expressed his surprise at receiving such a missive 'from one who has millions of lives depending perchance, for all we know, on every minute of his time'.[42]

The Viceroy's most prolonged time-wasting exercise concerned his own title. He had been forced to call himself Curzon of Kedleston because his Howe cousin, who was also called George and who was at that time an MP, held the courtesy title of Viscount Curzon. In 1900 this cousin succeeded his father as Earl Howe and, as there was now no other Curzon in public life, the Viceroy decided to drop Kedleston from his title when signing letters and despatches. The Howes, however, objected and brought their case before the King, who sympathized with their point of view. His Majesty was 'very much surprised', Salisbury's Private Secretary told Curzon, to see the abbreviated signature and wanted the matter 'rectified'. Curzon responded with a combative letter to King Edward's Private Secretary, Sir Francis Knollys, explaining that he had curtailed his signature partly because it saved time (he often had to sign fifty or sixty warrants a day) and partly because he had a right to do so. There was no law or custom, he argued, that compelled a peer to sign his full title, even in order to escape possible confusion with someone else. The Duke of Hamilton did not sign himself Hamilton and Brandon in case he was mistaken for the eldest son of the Duke of Abercorn, and Stanley of Alderley signed himself Stanley even though there was another Lord Stanley in the House of Commons. Furthermore, as the Howes were the junior branch and had taken another peerage, it was too much for them to deny the use of the Curzon title to the eldest son of the senior branch.[43]

Even Mary, who was in Europe at the time, found this missive a 'trifle defiant' and advised her husband to send the King a softer letter of 'butter and molasses'. But the cause was hopeless. Knollys engaged an anonymous genealogical expert to consider Curzon's case and sent the commissioned memorandum, which countered his arguments in a needlessly offensive tone, to the exasperated Viceroy. It was a very Curzonian episode: too much logic, too much indignation and too little sense. The delirium of disputation had once again prevailed over the wisdom of Mr Pickwick.

The Viceroy's life in India, he told Pearl Craigie, was 'strenuous, unceasing, exhausting, an endless typhoon of duty'.[44] He reached his desk at about ten o'clock and, with intervals for meals, a drive and perhaps a public function, rarely left it before two in the morning. He worked with enthusiasm and seldom flagged, but as time went on the self-pity burgeoned. He saw himself as a martyr, attacked in India and unappreciated at home, chained to his desk while everyone else was asleep, forced to go on and on because he was surrounded by incompetents who could not do their work properly. The self-pity went on display during his seventh budget speech when he compared himself to a toiling horse that 'staggers and drops beneath the shafts' of a cart. It was a constant feature of his letters to Mary, especially during her long absence in Europe in 1901. Writing from his solitude in Simla that July, he described his life as

> grind, grind, grind with never a word of encouragement, on on on till the collar breaks and the poor beast stumbles and dies. I suppose it is all right and it doesn't matter. But sometimes when I think of myself spending my heart's blood here, and no one caring one little damn, the spirit goes out of me, and I feel like giving in. You don't know, or perhaps you do, what my isolation has been this summer. I am crying now so that I can hardly see the page. But it has always been so. The willing horse is flogged till he drops and the work goes on.[45]

Reflections on the fate of his greatest predecessors consoled him. They too had been calumniated or ignored but had carried on their task with fortitude, impervious to slander and resolute in their convictions. History had proved them right and would surely justify him as well. Long after he was dead the despatches would be disinterred, and people would recognize that he had been right, that things would have turned out better if his strong and courageous policies had not been sacrificed to timorous expediency. He desperately wanted to be considered 'great'.

He thought constantly about great men, not just about Hastings, Dalhousie and Canning, but about Caesar, Napoleon, Wellington and Lincoln, giants whose biographies were almost his sole recreational reading in India. He once told the journalist Valentine Chirol that he always felt himself 'to be living the very life of all the great men' of whom he had read in history.[46] Yet among his contemporaries he really only admired Lord Cromer and Lord Milner, fellow proconsuls who, in his eyes, were also spending thankless years of uncomplaining toil in the interests of their nation. 'I have often felt for you,' he wrote to Milner on his return from South Africa, 'straining at the leash on the outskirts of Empire, knowing the experience so well myself; and knowing also what it is to be thwarted and over-ruled by those who know so little at home.'[47]

Colleagues, friends and relations constantly urged Curzon not to work so hard. Mary forced him to break off for an afternoon drive but unsuccessfully implored him not to sit up into the small hours. When she was in England both Salisbury and Balfour told her he should work less and sleep more. In letter after letter Lord George Hamilton sent a similar message. All exhortations were useless, Mary told her father, because George said he would 'prefer to work and die than to be idle and live. What *can* you do with such a man?'[48]

Curzon's health held up remarkably well for the first year, but his backaches returned in the spring of 1900 accompanied by persistent insomnia. Much of the rest of that year was spent in a horizontal position, but bed gave him little rest since, by saving time on dressing and undressing, he managed to do more work in it than out.[49] Although his back seldom troubled him the following year, he was then afflicted by neuritis, savage pains in his right leg that struck him when he tried to walk and deprived him of sleep. He spent an entire month in the autumn on his back, even having to berate the recalcitrant Mackworth Young from his bed. His surgeon rubbed the leg with liniment, applied fomentations and made him swallow quinine tablets and 'other tomfoolery', but confessed he had not 'the ghost of a notion what to do'.[50] By the end of October the pains had progressed down his leg to the ankle and instep, prompting him to tell Godley he hoped they would soon evaporate through his big toe. But the following summer they were still there, causing him agony if he had to stand for any length of time. From the lesser ailment of headaches, however, he found relief by putting plantain leaves in his topee.

The children remained healthy on the whole, but Mary seldom felt well at either Simla or Calcutta. Plagued by headaches and insomnia, she was also, according to her husband, 'always thin and rather anaemic in India'. In 1901 he persuaded her to spend the summer in Europe in order to recover her health and become strong enough to have another baby. Much as he missed her, he did not want her to come back in August, fall ill during a bad monsoon passage and be unable to conceive the son they both craved. He was prepared to remain without her – 'It does not much matter to a cabbage whether it leads a vegetable existence for five or six months' – if it strengthened her chances of becoming pregnant. Mary did delay her voyage but failed to conceive on her return. Dejected and unhappy, she was certain 'little George' would come one day, though probably not until they went home to 'vegetate in Scotland'. Her husband was philosophical about the disappointment, refusing to blame her for 'the misfortunes of Nature' and admitting that, for all he knew, it may have been his fault. 'We may not be meant to have a son,' he told her, and 'if that is so, it only remains for us to bow our heads. After all we have a great deal and we have two precious children as it is.'[51] Later he told her not to despair because Lady Chelsea had 'produced the necessary boy at the sixth shot', an inappropriate example as it happened because Lord Chelsea was not the child's father.

The best years of the Curzons' marriage were spent in India. They were often apart and, when together, were seldom alone. He admitted he was such a slave to work, living at such high tension, that he was 'not always sufficiently considerate or understanding or fond'.[52] But no one who reads the letters they wrote when apart could question the extent of their devotion. Both of them were made unhappy even by brief separations. Mary described herself as reviving like a sunflower when George was there and drooping like a crushed weed when he had gone. She did not resent seeing so little of him when they were in the same house: the important thing was to know he was close by, working in the next room, and not hundreds of miles away.[53]

The Vicereine performed her duties with grace rather than enthusiasm, attending social functions which her husband eschewed and acting as an intermediary between him and other people. Yet although she provided him with love and support, she did not give him the frank criticism which he of all people needed. After her death Godley said she had exacerbated all Curzon's faults and on all important occasions given him the worst possible advice.[54] It was a spiteful and unfair judgement that encased one overstated truth. Incapable of self-criticism as he was, the last thing Curzon should have had was a wife who backed him up when he was wrong. Yet Mary had always let him make the decisions, from the conditions of their engagement to the decoration of their houses. Meeting her in London soon after their marriage, Consuelo Vanderbilt, then Duchess of Marlborough, observed that Mary was wholly absorbed in her husband's career and had subordinated her personality to his to a degree that was quite unAmerican.[55] Pearl Craigie found her 'too languorous' and 'too yielding',[56] characteristics she had not possessed in her youth and which were perhaps a consequence of the discrepancy in the couple's feelings for each other at the time of their engagement. Mary saw George as a solitary and uncompromising genius, 'the lofty and lonely man who stood out above all the crowd' at the Durbar, a distant 'giant' dwarfing the political pygmies of England.[57] She followed her husband's example of reading biographies of great men and, inevitably, discovered that he resembled them. In Lord Rosebery's account of Napoleon's last years she found that the author had described George exactly, the same memory, the same intellect, the same mastery of detail, the same independence of ineffectual ministers.[58]

In assimilating Curzon's views, Mary acquired some of his intolerance, and her letters sometimes contain the most intemperate opinions. Her view of Lord George Hamilton as a 'hopeless dotard' and 'a small-minded, ferret-faced, roving-eyed mediocrity' went far beyond anything that even her husband at his most combative wrote about that competent and undemonstrative minister.[59] Like Curzon, she was basically a kind person who disguised her sympathetic nature behind a mask of viceregal aloofness. The Reuters correspondent thought no one had a kinder heart than Mary but admitted that few people were aware of it in Simla.[60] As with her husband, Mary provoked contrasting reactions to herself. On first seeing her in India, Pearl Craigie, who in spite of her own passion for Curzon was very fond of her, found Mary pretty, elegant and, she assumed, well-liked. After staying some time, however, she saw that the Vicereine could be 'cold and arrogant' and was surprisingly unpopular.[61] Her view was confirmed by several of the staff who reported to the unhappy Lawrence that Mary's 'sins of omission and commission' were having a bad effect on people in Calcutta society.[62]

In March 1901 Mary sailed to Europe for what she described as 'a blank six months in search of health and progeny'. April and May were spent in England, but in June she travelled to Germany to undergo some kind of fertility 'cure' at Ems and to sit for the portrait painter Franz von Lenbach in Munich. She hated Ems, which she found hotter than India, and where there was nothing to do except take a special bath containing some ingredient designed 'to work the miracle of an *almost* immaculate conception'.[63] The visit to Munich, where the hotel manager tried to swindle her, was not much more successful. Being a portrait painter under Curzon's instructions must have been a testing task: after one artist had been allowed to sketch him at work in India, the Viceroy examined the finished picture minutely, remarking that his mouth should be more curved and his hair should stick up more on one side before pulling up his trouser leg and exclaiming that the painter had flattered his legs. At Munich Mary was instructed not to allow Lenbach to idealize her by turning her into a Spanish saint or a Bavarian Madonna. Her husband wanted a simple, truthful picture of her face and eyes without a hat or the kind of drapery favoured by Sargent and his school. The instructions were obeyed, but the results did not please Curzon. Lenbach never painted the large portrait he intended and, of the twelve sketches the Viceroy was shown in 1904, only one was bought.[64]

In London Mary had virtually resumed her premarital social life of continuous visits and dinner parties. Once more the centre of attention, she charmed and flattered, making such an impression on Balfour that Lady Elcho, with whom he had a lifelong *amitié amoureuse*, threw a jealous tantrum.[65] But her life also had a serious side, for she was acting as her husband's emissary, talking to the King and to politicians and promoting the Viceroy's point of view. In her letters to India she encouraged George by telling him how Salisbury, Chamberlain and other leading figures praised his work, how even the radicals admired him and why he should be jubilant about the widespread appreciation of his rule. But other news, especially of the general indifference to Indian affairs in England, depressed him. One day Lawrence found him extremely dejected by a letter from Mary describing how she had heard people were saying that 'if a man like Lord Elgin – who had returned to what he was eminently fitted to be, a County Councillor in his Scotch town – could govern India successfully, there couldn't be much required to be a success'.[66]

Mary also sent her husband advice about his future career in British politics. Winston Churchill recommended him not to serve a full term in India but to return to lead his party. Others, including Wyndham, Hamilton, George Peel and Labouchere, referred to him variously as the next Foreign Secretary, the next Tory leader and even the next Prime Minister. Curzon was receiving similar messages in India, including a letter of advice from Selborne about what he ought to do as head of the Government in London. Mary was convinced the time would soon be right for her husband to come back and wake everybody up. Unless he stayed too long in India, the future of the Conservative Party was in his hands. 'You must not', she insisted, 'let another Tory Government be formed with you out of the Foreign Office.'[67]

Curzon told Mary he ought to stay in India, where he could 'do permanent good to the Empire', and to others he argued that there was no point returning to take a cabinet post which could equally well be filled by other people. Besides, there was no obvious ministry for him to occupy. Lansdowne was an ideal Foreign Secretary 'in these abdicating days' and in any case showed no inclination to retire, while the War Office would be such an awful undertaking that he would as soon 'build and row a trireme down the Thames'.[68] Thanking Selborne for his advice, he replied that it would not be for him, because he would be worn out long before he had the chance of becoming Prime Minister. Moreover, he rightly doubted whether India, 'where one is almost despotic', was the perfect training for premiers.[69] Yet he confessed that the idea of true leadership, 'which does not always seem to be lying about', had its attractions, and admitted to Dawkins that, if the present ministry fell and the Liberals were unable to form a government, he would like to lead a cross-party administration of Unionists* and Liberal Imperialists. He would insist, he added, on a small cabinet run on different lines in which he would be 'prime minister in reality instead of in name' and where he 'would be just as much behind every department' as he was in India.[70] The fact that he could even think of treating men like Asquith, Grey and Haldane as if they were members of the Viceroy's Council is almost incredible.

Curzon sometimes felt nostalgia for Britain, but it was the grouse moors and the cricket pitches he missed rather than politics or society. Reading about England on his Simla hilltop made him despondent and censorious. He was 'a little struck', he told Alfred Lyttelton, by 'the apparent dying out of high ideals, real nobility of thought and utterance in political life', although he admitted that from a distance he might have lost perspective.[71] The increasing frivolity of society, however, shocked him far more. People in London, reported Mary, 'were just flirting and dining and dawdling', reverence had disappeared from people's lives since the Queen's death, and 'Edward the Caresser' had become an object of ridicule.[72] This moral disintegration was

---

* The Conservative and Liberal Unionist coalition was usually referred to as the Unionist Party for the first two decades of the twentieth century.

epitomized for her by Asquith who, under Margot's influence, was supposed to have lost 'that old strong granite sense of *right* and his abomination of the disreputable' and was now fat, over-amorous and too fond of champagne.[73] The Souls were dead, reported Lyttelton, and the racing set now dominated the fashionable world. The chief agent for this change, apparently, was the passion for Bridge, a great intellectual leveller enjoyed by the hard-headed and the inarticulate as well as by indolent former Souls like Balfour who played a good deal because it saved 'the effort of conversation'.[74] Curzon deplored the advent of Bridge and, like Campbell-Bannerman, made no effort to penetrate its 'dismal mysteries'.[75] On hearing of a Bridge scandal at Chatsworth, he exclaimed, 'Good God, what is society coming to, rotten to the core, neither purpose nor duty nor morality nor even common honesty in it.' When they returned to London, he told Mary, they must stay on the fringe of society, not at its hub.[76]

From someone who for many years had managed to combine hard work and social frivolity, such views sound curious and hypocritical. Curzon had always enjoyed gossip and *risqué* stories, and he still derived amusement from the letters of Sir Schomberg McDonnell, Lord Salisbury's Private Secretary, who recounted the affairs and elopements of their acquaintances in Britain. The newly acquired disapproval seems to have been as much a result of his own change of circumstances as of a sudden moral decadence in Britain. Curzon adored his wife and probably remained faithful to her during their long separations in 1901 and 1904. Infidelity, indeed, would have been impossible without the connivance of his ADCs, and he was too conscious of his position and its prestige to risk a scandal. But if his moral outlook had changed, his nature remained the same. He was still what Pearl Craigie quaintly called 'very uxorious in his mind and oriental in his instincts',[77] and the effort to control his own nature made him deprecate those who indulged theirs. Yet he evidently wished that the uxorious did not always have to take precedence over the oriental. Describing an erotic dream he experienced in September 1901 to its protagonist, Ettie Grenfell, he wrote:

> For a whole night I have dreamed of you – no hope of reciprocity – they were wonderful dreams, lovers' dreams, in which things uncontemplated in life were realized in that glowing fancy haze. Now that I am awake again and am respectable, it is a heavy shock to find that there is no love, no triumph, no embrace; not even the fugitive consolation of a kiss.[78]

16

1902: Proconsular Zenith

MIDWAY THROUGH THE viceregal term of five years, George Curzon could admit to a sense of satisfaction at what he had so far accomplished. He had defeated the anti-reformist forces, he told Balfour, and felt confident he was achieving something worthwhile. Although he sometimes chafed at being so far from 'the heart and pulse of affairs', he was prepared to sacrifice the best of his life to India if he could leave things in a better state than he had found them.[1] Each year produced a solid legislative achievement and witnessed the preparation of its successor. He claimed not to mind if the British press ignored him because he was constructing his 'own edifice' in India and was 'quite content that the outside world should see and judge it when the scaffolding [was] pulled down'.[2] It was thus a little premature, he thought, for Milner to be acclaimed on his return from South Africa as 'the greatest proconsul that the empire has known'.[3] He hoped the opinion would in due course be associated with himself and boasted to his father that no Viceroy had enjoyed 'anything approaching' his position since Lord Dalhousie.[4]

Curzon's continued unpopularity with parts of the British community in India gave him a certain satisfaction, because he felt that popular regard would have implied weakness or inertia. He was proud to be told that a reformer like himself could not expect to be popular with those he was trying to reform. And in the long run the best men in India came round to his views. Sir Denzil Ibbetson spoke for many when he told the Viceroy that he had stirred up things so much at the beginning that he had made himself disliked. But by 1905 the ICS officers appreciated the administrative achievements of his rule and regarded him as the greatest Viceroy since Dalhousie.[5]

Although Curzon frequently complained about Britain's lack of interest in India, he knew that his work was held in high regard by those in high positions. Appreciation of his record reached him from diverse quarters. Milner thought him a 'great viceroy', Haldane and the Liberal Imperialists admired him, Lord Esher told him he had 'no superiors in the mighty roll of viceroys'.[6] Curzon may have discounted the flattery of Esher, a highly agile courtier and intriguer, but in this instance it was sincere. No other Englishman, Esher told his son, possessed Curzon's qualities as an administrator except for Cromer, and possibly none matched him as a statesman: his imagination, capacity for work and gift of expression made him perhaps the greatest of all viceroys.[7]

Admiration for Curzon's talents was also shared by Hamilton and Godley, the two men he had to work through in London. The Secretary of State was astonished by his vigour and versatility, believed his ability 'almost amounted to genius' and predicted he would become Prime Minister. Godley agreed that he was 'undeniably a great man' with 'a touch of genius' but thought that his temperament and his sensitivity to criticism would prevent him from being a successful party leader. Both lamented the fact that these abilities were marred by a talent for antagonism. When he failed to get his own way, Hamilton complained, Curzon exhibited 'the failings of a child', and his sense of proportion was so deficient that he sometimes appeared ridiculous.[8] A further defect was his self-importance, what Northcote called his 'curious personal vanity, "swagger"', which irritated people.[9] Curzon's viceregal letters justify the reproach. Even a man as patient as Hamilton could not have failed to be annoyed by the excessive use of the first person singular, by the endless references to 'my policy', 'my reforms' and people 'following in my footsteps', by the impression conveyed that he was playing the role of Akbar in India while no one in Britain or the rest of the empire, except for Cromer and Milner, was doing anything worthwhile. 'Such blatant language for the glorification of self', declared Hamilton, was 'unworthy of a big man and amongst other drawbacks irritates my colleagues and makes my task of arguing his case before them much more difficult.'[10]

The year 1902 was the apogee and watershed of Curzon's viceroyalty, one of controversial successes during which his petulance and lack of proportion were as brightly displayed as his talent and integrity. A singular achievement was his settlement of the Berar question, a problem which had bedevilled relations between the Government and the Nizam of Hyderabad for fifty years. In the eighteenth century the East India Company had organized and officered a force, later known as the Hyderabad Contingent, to act both as an ally of the British and as a military prop for the Nizam's authority. This arrangement was altered by treaties in the following century when, in exchange for discharging the current ruler's debts, the Company took over the Hyderabad Contingent as well as the Berar area which provided the revenues to pay for it. Since then the land, while remaining under the nominal sovereignty of the Nizam, had been administered by the British Resident in Hyderabad who handed over to the prince certain revenues not required for the upkeep of the Contingent. The present Nizam, however, objected to this arrangement and wanted his territory back.

Curzon saw that the situation was unsatisfactory and that Hyderabad had a legitimate grievance. Since the treaties had been made, revenue from the Berar districts had increased without corresponding benefit to the Nizam. The British could quote parts of the treaties to show they had been legally in the right to withhold the extra sums, but Curzon recognized that the matter had not been dealt with 'in strict accordance with the most scrupulous standards of British honour'.[11] Yet it was now out of the question to solve the problem by acceding to the Nizam's wishes. He refused to transfer to 'a corrupt and inefficient rule' nearly two million people who for fifty years had 'enjoyed the benefits and profited by the standards of British administration'.[12] Reparation should be made instead through a generous and permanent financial settlement. Although the Nizam had refused to consider the alienation of Berar, two years of famine had forced him to borrow heavily from the Government, and Curzon thought he might prove amenable to the force of his reasoning and the strength of his personality.

The India Office was alarmed by the possibility of the Viceroy travelling all the way to Hyderabad to be rebuffed by a native prince. Recent negotiations between the Nizam and the able Resident, Colonel Barr, had ended in failure, and Hamilton warned Curzon it would be a mistake for him either to fail likewise or to succeed through coercion.[13] Retired officials in London also prophesied a reverse and seemed pleased at the prospect.[14] Curzon paid no attention to any of them and decided to settle the matter during a state visit at the end of March. The Nizam provided his guests with a tiger shoot and a 'Sing a Song of Sixpence' banquet during which live birds flew out of pies when the lids were cut open, but he was personally uncommunicative; Mary had prepared an alphabet of conversational topics ('C for curries, D for diamonds, E for elephants') but it did not last the meal, because the Nizam merely said 'yes' or 'exactly' to each remark.[15] He was more responsive the next day when Curzon announced generous financial terms for a permanent lease of Berar. The Viceroy offered him an annual rent of £167,000 – as opposed to the average of £60,000 that Hyderabad had been receiving since 1860 – although for some years this sum would be used to pay off existing debts. Curzon also declared that the contentious area would never be restored to the Nizam and that, if the present offer was rejected, it was highly unlikely he would ever receive another. Confronted by an inflexible Viceroy presenting an intransigent case, the Nizam did not hesitate to accept the conditions. Curzon told Hamilton that the prince had not yielded out of deference, weakness or alarm but because he had been convinced by the arguments and believed the Viceroy to be a friend of his state. The Nizam, who had been the recipient of viceregal lectures in the past, might have given a different explanation. But twenty years later Curzon claimed that the deal had been a 'splendid bargain' for the prince who 'never ceased afterwards to express his contentment'.[16] Lawrence identified the central ingredient of the success as Curzon's personality; he was sure Lord Elgin would not have achieved it.[17]

During the summer following his return from Hyderabad, the Viceroy embarked upon a series of confrontations with the British army in India, the Council of India in London and his Conservative colleagues in the Cabinet. Each time he was almost entirely in the right yet marred his case by the manner in which he pursued it. In April, during the revelry that followed the arrival of a British regiment at Sialkot in the Punjab, a native cook was beaten up and taken to hospital where, after identifying his assailants as cavalrymen, he died shortly afterwards. The military authorities ordered a casual and inadequate investigation, and a court of enquiry, consisting of officers from the regiment in question, reported itself unable to discover the ruffians. News of the affair eventually reached Curzon and enraged him. Such wicked and scandalous incidents, he told Godley, gave him sleepless nights and days of misery: British soldiers, with their violence and their lust, were 'pulling the fabric of our dominion down about our ears'. It made no difference that the perpetrators of the outrage belonged to the 9th Lancers, a fashionable regiment proud of its record in the Mutiny and elsewhere. Curzon refused to sacrifice what he regarded as 'the most solemn obligation imposed upon the British race to the licence of even the finest regiment in the British army'.[18]

As with the Rangoon case, the army made little effort at any stage to discover the truth. Sir Bindon Blood, the Lieutenant-General commanding the Punjab, was surprised that the incident had caused so 'much silly excitement at Simla', and forwarded an army report accompanied by a complacent letter from himself suggesting that 'the cause of the whole business was a fight among the cooks and a "plant" to get the soldiers blamed'. Writing his memoirs at the age of 90, he remained 'fully satisfied' that the regiment had been punished unjustly* and recalled that following the submission of the report, 'something rude was written' to him.[20] That 'something' was a long and devastating minute from the Viceroy which, although the general may not have noticed it, dissected, ridiculed and demolished Blood's case. Curzon described the exculpatory report as 'one of the most disgraceful productions' he had ever read, but his savage and disparaging reply managed to alienate officers who admitted Blood was in the wrong.[21] The collective punishment of the regiment also provoked opposition to Curzon, even though it was proposed by the Acting Commander-in-Chief, Sir Power Palmer, and was not in any case severe: cancellation of winter leave, the main part of the sentence, was no great hardship in India. Nevertheless, the Lancers' sympathizers in England exaggerated the punishment, the details of which were not made public, and accused the Viceroy of vindictively penalizing an entirely innocent regiment. The distortions were spectacular even for a case involving Curzon, with some British papers claiming that his sole object was to curry favour with the native press.[22] The King thought the Viceroy was in the wrong until Hamilton told him the facts. So did Lord Roberts, who like most people in England believed Curzon had ordered the punishment and asked him to remit it at the Delhi Durbar. On learning the truth, the former Commander-in-Chief admitted the regiment had got what it deserved and observed, regretfully, that Sir Bindon Blood was 'a most disappointing man'.[23]

Military questions were one of the few matters that did not produce ructions between the Viceroy and the Council of India. From the beginning Curzon had been irritated by that body of retired veterans who, like judges, could not be dismissed and who could overrule the Viceroy and

---

*In the autumn the commanding officer of the regiment admitted he knew the identity of one of the culprits but said his guilt could not be proved in court.[19]

the Secretary of State on financial matters and on legislation. He did not care initially if they thwarted him on minor issues so long as they did not emasculate his important reforms. But he was soon unable to tolerate even their obstruction on small things. On grounds of economy they regularly turned down his requests for the establishment of posts such as a clerk of the works at Simla, a British librarian for the Imperial Library in Calcutta, or an administrator for Government House and Barrackpore. The Viceroy was then forced to restate his case, pointing out, for example, that it would be cheaper to have an Englishman running the Calcutta houses efficiently than to hand them over to an 'incompetent babu' who looked after them so badly that they had to be restored at great expense before his return from Simla. He usually prevailed in the end but at the cost of a good deal of labour and irritation.

The Secretary of State defended his Council in March 1901, arguing that it controlled expenditure with a lighter rein than any other treasury and that it had not rejected any of Curzon's important schemes. But the Viceroy, who reacted alike to minor checks and major reversals, was not mollified. Privately he blamed Hamilton for being weak, although the Secretary of State's handling of his councillors was in fact diplomatic, astute and largely successful. The Viceroy, however, seems to have been justified in suspecting that retired officials sometimes envied his success. Former Residents of Hyderabad, for example, cannot have been overjoyed to find that the 'insoluble' problem of Berar had had a solution after all. Curzon received support for his view from Richmond Ritchie, the new Political Secretary at the India Office, who attributed the councillors' lack of sympathy to their belief that Viceroys 'should be run by the bigwigs' of the ICS. It was natural, Ritchie told him, for them to feel that Curzon's 'energy and originality [were] an exposure of their own slavery to routine', especially as many of his reforms might have been applied advantageously in their day. But as they did not dare to tackle him on the big questions, they tended to gang up on issues like the clerk of the works at Simla; 'eleven old gentlemen determined to die rather than let you have your own way', until reluctantly persuaded to be reasonable by Godley.[24]

In the summer of 1902, however, the Council questioned the Indian Government's handling of the vital issues of police and educational reforms. Despite Hamilton's assurances that Curzon remained relatively unfettered, one hostile councillor doubted privately if any Viceroy had seen so many of his proposals rejected.[25] Curzon's protests were on the whole justified, but in his exasperation he over-reacted to such an extent that he antagonized his main allies, Hamilton and Godley. At the end of May he sent them a list of twenty-two instances in which he claimed that the Council had defeated or delayed his proposals. He was working the whole day and much of the night, he told Hamilton, in difficult and hostile conditions, 'habitually harassed, constantly weary, and often in physical distress and pain'. If, in addition to his other anxieties, he was to be 'perpetually nagged and impeded and misunderstood' by the Council at home, he would rather give up the task. A week later, without waiting for an answer, he returned to the attack. It was 'really too ridiculous', he declared, that 'a batch of old gentlemen at home should casually stroll into the India Office, and endeavour to upset the whole apple-cart' merely because they found an active and reforming Viceroy distasteful; so long as these absurd ideas prevailed, he added, he was not anxious to continue his work.[26] Never one to soft-pedal a grievance, he broadened his complaint a fortnight later to include the Foreign Office. He had been sent out to India as an expert, he asserted, and yet his advice (on the delimitation of Aden) was treated as if it had come from 'an impertinent schoolboy'. He was 'not disposed . . . to be so treated again' and, if this sort of thing continued, 'some more docile victim' would have to be found.[27]

Reviewing this barrage of complaint, Hamilton wondered whether Curzon was breaking down from ill health or overwork. 'His schedule of the Council's offences', he told a sympathetic Godley, was 'almost childish'. Until that moment Hamilton's letters to the Viceroy had been gentle, appreciative and only on occasion mildly remonstrative. Deciding the time had come to be argumentative, he declared it was essential to examine reforms being applied to 'a country of almost archaic immobility' inhabited by a fifth of the human race. He then surveyed the list of offences, observed that the Council had accepted three-quarters of the propositions it had queried, and concluded that no minister he had ever known had had his way to such an extent as Curzon had in India. Privately he told Mary he was certain her husband would not have written those letters had he not been unwell and overstrained, and he begged her to persuade him to take more rest.[28]

That same summer Hamilton's colleagues in the Cabinet also experienced the acerbity of the viceregal reproach. Had Lord Salisbury still been Prime Minister, they might have been spared because Curzon, in spite of disagreements over foreign policy, retained deep respect for the man to whom he owed every post he had ever held. But the last of the great Victorian premiers had resigned in July shortly before sending the Viceroy a valedictory of apocalyptic pessimism.

> It may be a misconception – but I cannot resist the impression that we are near some great change in public affairs – in which the forces which contend for the mastery among us will be differently ranged and balanced. If so it is certainly expedient that younger men should be employed to shape the policy which will no longer depend upon the judgments formed by the experience of past times. The time will be very difficult. The large aggregations of human forces which lie around our Empire seem to draw more closely together, and to assume almost unconsciously a more and more aggressive aspect. Their junction, in menacing and dangerous masses, may be deferred for many years or may be precipitated with little notice at any moment. It is fortunate for us that the satraps of the Empire were never more conspicuous for intelligence and force than they are now – yourself, Cromer, Milner, Kitchener.[29]

Arthur Balfour feigned reluctance to succeed his uncle,[30] but no one else of comparable stature sat on the Unionist benches apart from Chamberlain, who remained unacceptable to much of the Conservative Party. Curzon believed his old friend from the Souls had the intellect and moral character to become a great Prime Minister if he could purge himself of his intellectual nonchalance and his philosophical indifference to the mundane aspects of political life.[31] Unhappily the purge did not take place. Ministers who served under A.J.B. shared Curzon's exasperation with what he called Balfour's 'cultured ignorance'. Like almost everyone else, H.O. Arnold-Forster found him brilliant and delightful but added that he was 'always far too clever to know the facts'. As Balfour's Secretary of State for War, Arnold-Forster had the painful experience of serving a man who thought himself an expert on strategic affairs but who, according to his minister, knew 'nothing whatever about the army' and who in a Commons debate revealed he was 'not even dimly acquainted' with a military proposal he himself had sanctioned. Balfour treated the army as 'the subject matter of the most charming dialectical exercises' and was so pleased with his 'little logical deductions' that he would defend them doggedly against any argument which was based merely upon facts and experience.[32]

Balfour's tone of well-born, clubbable, intellectual levity permeated his Cabinet. Asquith had identified the principle behind Salisbury's last reshuffle as to promote 'one's incapables and provide for one's family',[33] a formula which Balfour showed no desire to alter. He was linked to many of his Cabinet by ties of kinship, the Souls or the hierarchical mysteries of Etonian ritual. 'Hotel Cecil' was left undisturbed, Balfour's brother remaining at the Board of Trade, a cousin in Curzon's old post at the Foreign Office, and a cousin's husband at the Admiralty, an arrangement which prompted the Viceroy to exercise one of his lesser talents.

> In Trade's keen lists, no alien herald
> His trumpet blows, but Brother Gerald;
> Foreign affairs have Cousin Cranborne
> To hint that ne'er was greater man born;
> While Cousin Selborne rules the fleet,
> Even the sea is 'Arthur's Seat'.[34]

Among the other appointments Lord Lansdowne, who had been Balfour's fagmaster at Eton, remained at the Foreign Office, while Lord Londonderry, who had been the Prime Minister's fag at the same institution, was promoted to the Board of Education. Brodrick, who engaged A.J.B. to be best man at his second wedding, stayed at the War Office, while George Wyndham reached the Cabinet after Lady Elcho, Balfour's confidante and Wyndham's sister, threatened to make the premier's life a misery if he didn't.[35] Not all this nepotism was as bad as it looked. Lansdowne and Selborne were successful ministers, and Wyndham deserved his promotion. But Gerald had been widely regarded as the weakest member of Salisbury's Cabinet, Brodrick was floundering at the War Office, Cranborne had been hesitant and unimpressive at foreign affairs, while Londonderry's appointment was so inexplicable it has been described as 'Caligulan'.[36]

From India Curzon watched with incredulity as Balfour continued his policy of arranging cosy cabinets consisting largely of friends, relations and the sons of past colleagues. By contrast with Salisbury's Government, in which the ministers were addressed by their official designation, cabinet meetings now degenerated, observed Hamilton, into 'cliquey conversations between "Arthur" and "Bob" and "George" – sometimes almost unintelligible in their intimate allusions to the outer circle of the cabinet'.[37] Soon after the departure of the three great figures of the nineties – Salisbury, Chamberlain and Devonshire – Balfour found senior posts for their respective heirs and overrode the King's opposition to the elevation of Cranborne (by then the 4th Marquess of Salisbury) to the Cabinet. He was only just dissuaded from appointing the Duke of Montrose, who had never spoken in the House of Lords, as Secretary of State for Scotland.

Curzon thought it a great error for Balfour to be constantly selecting men such as Lord Bath and Lord Stanley, neither of whom had demonstrated much political talent, and giving the impression, in Brodrick's words, that 'blue blood [was] the only passport to promotion'.*[38] 'I should have thought it wiser', the Viceroy observed, 'to democratise the Conservative Party rather than to emphasise its aristocratic flavour.'[39] Yet, however much he deplored Balfour's appointments in principle, Curzon should have been pleased that the Cabinet he had to deal with contained four of his closest friends (Balfour, Brodrick, Wyndham and Selborne) and was later reinforced by two more (Salisbury and Alfred Lyttelton). Other friends and admirers included Lansdowne and Hamilton (who were brothers-in-law) and Arnold-Forster. Yet Curzon was so unsentimental about politics that he did not value political friendship. Innocent of nepotistic tendencies himself, he preferred to deal with a competent opponent than with a less efficient friend. Loyal to them in personal matters, in politics he treated friends as he did other politicians, to be scolded and argued with until they had accepted the logic of his point of view. This uncommon attitude helps explain why he embarked on two major confrontations with Balfour's Cabinet in the second half of 1902.

Both disputes arose from the accession of King Edward VII and the manner of its celebration by his Indian subjects. Queen Victoria's death in January 1901 had been profoundly mourned throughout India. As Curzon put it, the figure of the Queen-Empress had had an 'overpowering effect on the imagination of the Asiatic':[40] in Calcutta the roadside vendors of sweetstuffs voluntarily closed their booths on the day of the funeral and followed the greater part of the city's population on to the Maidan, where the vast crowd sat mourning all day, without food, their diverse groups identified by banners such as 'We poor Musulmans from Sialdah grieving'.[41] The Queen's interest in India and sympathy for her people had lasted till the end. In her last two years she had written the Viceroy thirty letters in her own hand, imploring him to look after the Indians, to make allowances for the princes, to do everything he could to reduce friction between the races. Her indignation was not confined to India: France was 'utterly disgraced', she once told the Viceroy, by her 'monstrous treatment of poor Dreyfus', to which

---

*The appointment of Victor Cavendish as Financial Secretary to the Treasury was the best example of the hereditary principle in action. He was the nephew and heir of Devonshire and the son-in-law of Lansdowne.

Curzon replied that French acquiescence in such 'a travesty of justice' indicated a 'widespread moral degeneration' in the country.[42] He was impressed that she should have continued to write to him at her age. Yet he found her handwriting almost impossible to decipher and was 'flabbergasted' when she complained to Hamilton that the Viceroy's own calligraphy – clear at most times and especially bold and legible when writing to his sovereign – was difficult to read because the words ran into one another. One of the vagaries of her old age, as her Private Secretary had experienced, was that she blamed her reading problems on the handwriting of her correspondents rather than on her own declining eyesight.

Impressed by the strength of Indian feeling towards her, Curzon accepted Lawrence's suggestion that he should build a memorial so imposing that it would not only commemorate Queen Victoria but also impress upon the Bengali people the strength of her – and the British – connection with Calcutta. It was to be a historical museum and national gallery intended to represent everything that was glorious in the British Indian past. Enemies of Britain would be included if they were honourable and valiant foes like Hyder Ali and Tippoo Sultan, but Curzon would not 'admit so much as the fringe of the *pagri* [turban] of a ruffian like the Nana Sahib', the butcher of Cawnpore.[43] He wanted a building at least as fine as anything in the British empire, 'a magnificent shell, pure and severe in its simplicity', with galleries and corridors radiating around a central space devoted to Queen Victoria. Its architectural style was determined early on. 'A Gothic building in India', the Viceroy told Esher, 'would be like putting the Taj in Hyde Park.' The Mogul and Hindu styles were equally inappropriate because Calcutta was a European city in origin and construction, possessing little indigenous architecture of its own. To Curzon the only sensible solution seemed to be a building in Palladian or Italianate style designed by a European architect. A hundred and twenty years earlier, he remarked, he would have chosen Robert Adam, the architect of Kedleston.[44]

The Viceroy not only determined the style of the building and the range of its contents but characteristically decided to raise the necessary funds and to collect suitable treasures. A vast correspondence was directed at the descendants of past Governors-General asking them to bequeath portraits and other mementoes of their ancestors. 'Curzon's folly' was inevitably derided by his critics who sneered that it was a memorial to himself rather than to Queen Victoria. Nonetheless, he managed to attract the enormous sum of £400,000, to which he himself generously contributed, as well as an impressive collection of exhibits which he put on display in March 1904. His successor's lack of enthusiasm for the project, followed by the First World War, delayed completion of the hall until 1921.

Curzon had a less favourable opinion of the new King than of his mother. Edward VII had tact and *bonhomie*, he admitted, but he was 'perhaps not everything that a king might or ought to be' and he did not set 'an irreproachable example to his subjects'.[45] Besides, he did not appear to share his mother's concern for India and was reluctant to hear from the Viceroy unless there was 'anything of importance or interest to relate'. As he was the King-Emperor, however, Curzon tried to persuade him to come out to India for a special coronation. Although the suggestion apparently caused amusement in royal circles, Curzon saw nothing odd about it. The entire trip, he argued, need take only seven weeks and would be no more unconstitutional than a long visit by the King to Cannes.[46] But in the end it was decided to invite certain Indian princes to the coronation in London and to hold a great proclamation durbar, attended by a member of the royal family, at Delhi.

Curzon was alarmed by the prospect of the princes going to London, because he thought the occasion would be an excuse for 'all the well-known Indian *flâneurs*' to revisit 'the haunts of their pleasure or indulgence'.[47] Invitations were limited, however, to a select and representative group of chiefs and senior officials. The Raja of Pudukotta, one of the most prominent *flâneurs*, pleaded to be allowed to join them but learnt from Lawrence that the King had 'dispensed' him from attending the ceremony in London and provided him instead with the opportunity of going to the Delhi Durbar.[48] Several of the invitations placed their recipients in a dilemma. Some, such as the southern rulers of Cochin and Travancore, were persuaded by their brahmins that the journey would be contrary to the tenets and customs of Hinduism. Even so enlightened a man as Justice Banerjea, one of the ablest Indian judges, was obliged to tell Curzon that, much as he wanted to visit England, and highly as he appreciated the compliment, his position in his own family circle would become impossible if he crossed the sea: his daughters, he added, might even fail to find husbands as a result.[49] Other devout rulers decided they could travel if they made certain arrangements: the Maharaja of Jaipur sailed to England in a chartered ship accompanied by four hundred followers and enough water from the Ganges stored in vast copper vessels to preserve them from the contaminating effects of Europe.

Hamilton was preoccupied by the problem of princely precedence and asked Curzon whether it should be calculated according to the antiquity of lineage or the size of the gun salutes. The Viceroy was more concerned about the behaviour of the chiefs in England. A sharp look-out, he warned, must be kept on Scindia's nocturnal excursions, because the Maharaja was 'a little devil for women' and had apparently developed a taste for white ones. Indian soldiers, whom the King wished to have present, created a similar problem because, 'strange as it may seem, English women of the housemaid class, and even higher', were attracted by their uniforms and physique and offered themselves to these warriors.[50]

The young Maharaja of Bikanir, who had commanded his Imperial Service regiment in China in 1900 and had won Curzon's praise for the way he governed his state, received a viceregal warning not to acquire 'extravagant and undesirable tastes' in Britain or to think 'more of amusement and self-gratification than of duty'. Bikanir responded to this pedagogic homily by saying how proud he was to receive 'such friendly and free advice', but protested his devotion to his work, his state and his family, and said he much preferred his native existence to 'the idle and gay life' in London.[51] In fact both existences seem to have been equally congenial to him. Hamilton was rather disgusted by the sight of 'the smart ladies' making a fuss over him and feared he was being corrupted by 'the gambling, racing, fast set' which was then enjoying 'great favour in the highest circles'.[52] This danger was exacerbated by the King's appendicitis which led to the coronation's post-ponement for six weeks. Bikanir, however, avoided the 'fast set' for at least part of the time by accompanying the Maharaja of Jaipur on a visit to Kedleston, a jaunt Curzon regarded as a sort of pilgrimage, 'a very touching mark of interest and respect'. Afterwards Jaipur told Lawrence he had watched the rabbits playing in the Derbyshire grass and 'wondered how English Sahibs could ever go to India'; had he been one of them, he would have stayed there for ever, playing the flute and watching the animals gambolling in the sun.[53]

Curzon's troubles over the coronation arose not from the behaviour of the princes but from the question of who would pay for them and the other Indian representatives. As a result of the continuing expense of the Boer War, the Government of India had agreed to pay for the voyages of the guests and a thousand soldiers (but not of course for the vessel chartered by Jaipur for himself and his followers). It was thus outraged to be told after the war was over that India would have to pay also for their expenses and entertainment in England, including £7,000 for a reception at the India Office. An official protest was sent on 10 July, followed by a letter from Curzon asking the British Government to pay the bill and telling Hamilton what a miserly impression London's attitude would produce in India. On the same day he wrote to Balfour suggesting that India's services during the war – saving Natal and housing thousands of Boer prisoners – merited 'this simple act of generosity'.[54] The Secretary of State, who unknown to Curzon had already asked the Treasury to pay part of the sum, was irritated by the truculent tone of the viceregal despatch; he assumed it had been written in a temper, but Godley later discovered it had been composed during an illness. Nonetheless, the logic of the case was on Curzon's side. India was organizing her own event to mark the accession and planned to pay for the entertainment of the British guests. To Hamilton's embarrassment she was subsequently asked to pay the entire costs of the Duke of Connaught, the King's brother, who was coming out for the Durbar with his wife and entourage, and who expected a holiday at India's expense afterwards. Learning of this development by telegram, Curzon suggested the Secretary of State should ponder whether it was 'possible or practicable to make us pay for our Royal guests whom we did not invite, but who offered themselves here, at the very moment that you are declining to pay for the Indian guests whom you specially invited to England'.[55]

Scolding Curzon for his Government's protest, Godley let him know that he had annoyed everybody, especially Balfour and Hamilton, who was a 'most loyal supporter' of the Viceroy and who was 'greatly hurt' by his behaviour.[56] The Secretary of State realized, however, that the Government would have to back down because, in the event of a public row, Parliament and public opinion would support India. He and Balfour appealed for the protest to be withdrawn, but Curzon refused unless they agreed to pay for everything including the India Office party. In early August, when he was in Mysore officiating at the coronation of the young Maharaja, Curzon received the news that the Government had capitulated. Jubilant at the outcome, he could not resist crowing about his success to Mary: 'It is a great triumph. No one will know here how it has been obtained, but one day it will come out how by a single strong despatch and by a little courage I defeated them all.' He was not 'in the least disturbed', he told her, by Hamilton's information that the despatch had met with 'an absolutely universal chorus of disapprobation from the cabinet'.[57] As so often, he failed to gauge the effect of his actions on other people's feelings. Godley, who warned him that members of the Government would not forget the incident, was proved right by their behaviour during the next row.

The splendorously staged pageantry of the Delhi Durbar attracted mockery as well as admiration and, like the Victoria Memorial Hall, it was criticized as a glorification of the Viceroy rather than of his sovereign. A wag dubbed it the 'Curzonation' and, as so frequently happened in his life, the tab followed 'superior person' and other phrases into the repertoire of Curzonian anecdote. Yet it would have been extraordinary had a durbar not been held for the proclamation of the King-Emperor. The installation ceremony, Curzon pointed out, was 'a feature of a hallowed system' in India, held not only by native chiefs but by titled noblemen and large landowners as well.[58] It was thus logical to stage a royal durbar in order to impress India with the power and majesty of the Crown. Doubtless it was an exaggeration to claim for the event that 'from the Arab sheikhs of Aden to the west to the Shan chiefs of the Mekong on the borders of China, they felt the thrill of a common loyalty and the inspiration of a single aim'.[59] But few people outside Congress disputed its impact. Curzon understood the importance of oriental pageantry better than most of his countrymen and realized that to be effective the Durbar must be majestic – 'the biggest thing ever seen in India' – and so well executed that he must organize it himself. If the King would not come in person, then according to the constitution the Viceroy had to be the protagonist, a point imperfectly understood in India and by many people in Britain. Curzon thus hoped that the Prince of Wales would not come out and confuse matters, because it would be awkward taking precedence over the heir to the throne. In the event people were confused by the sight of the King's brother taking second place to the Viceroy.

The planning of the Durbar occupied much of 1902. After settling the Berar question at the end of March, Curzon travelled to Agra to check the progress of his restoration programme and to Delhi, where he inspected the Durbar site. From there he journeyed up to Peshawar to inaugurate the new North-West Frontier Province and to hold a durbar for the frontier chiefs and their followers, before returning via Dehra Dun to inspect the new Imperial Cadet Corps. His visit to the Corps, which was to form his bodyguard at the Durbar, delighted him: its tone and spirit seemed admirable, and he believed its well-born apprentices were as enthusiastic about their life there as if they had been English public schoolboys. Unfortunately, it soon transpired that the Corps shared another trait popularly associated with public schoolboys. One of the cadets was found to be having an affair with the Maharaja of Alwar and was expelled from the academy. Another scandal, which provoked the sirdars of Jodhpur to petition for the removal of their Maharaja, luckily did not break until after the Durbar. Jodhpur, who had been regarded by the Viceroy as one of the finest cadets, returned to his state on holiday and was reported to have 'embarked on a carnival of drinking and unnatural vice'. When news of the palace orgies became public, Curzon decided to take action. He removed the Maharaja from the Cadet Corps, arranged for a doctor to treat him for syphilis, and banished him from Jodhpur for two years.[60]

The Viceroy planned the details of the Durbar from the programme of events, which spanned a fortnight, to the architecture of the arena, the layout of the camps, and the movement and accommodation of about 150,000 people. He determined the width of the roads, the placing of the tents, the planting of the flower-beds. He also chose the hymns for the church service. Realizing it was sensible to select hymns which British soldiers could sing with 'hearty vigour', he had opted among others for 'Onward! Christian Soldiers', but cancelled it on remembering the lines – 'Crowns and thrones may perish/Kingdoms rise and wane' – which he deemed inappropriate for the coronation of a monarch. The scale of the entertainment was enormous. Special camps were allotted to native chiefs, heads of provincial governments, senior generals, and the residents and agents of princely states. The Viceroy's camp consisted of no less than 2,774 people, containing among them 138 guests, 266 rickshaw coolies, 283 policemen and 1,190 servants. The guests included a good number of friends and relations as well as royalty, but Curzon was disappointed by one refused invitation. 'I must go down to the Cape this winter,' wrote Rudyard Kipling with regret, 'when instead of seeing India consolidated I shall have the felicity of watching South Africa being slowly but scientifically wrecked . . .'[61]

The Viceroy believed that the Durbar required more than just a pageant and a speech which, after all, could only be enjoyed vicariously by the majority of Indians. People of the East, he told Hamilton a year before the event, associated successions and coronations with the grant of privileges and the removal of disabilities. Something of this nature should therefore be announced at the Durbar. Surveying possible concessions, he thought it imprudent to extend political privileges by expanding representative institutions, adding to the number of legislative councils, or appointing natives to higher places than they then occupied. Tax reductions, which the economy could now afford, would be preferable because they would benefit everyone as well as increase the new King's popularity. After considering the various options, he told Hamilton in September 1902 that he wished to announce at the Durbar a reduction of the salt tax together with a rise in the level of income tax exemption.[62]

The Secretary of State replied that he was in favour of a reduction in the salt tax but feared an awkward precedent might be established if it was associated with the accession of the monarch. Balfour, Godley, the Chancellor of the Exchequer and the India Council agreed with him, and in November he rejected the Viceroy's proposal. Curzon declared himself 'sick at heart' on receiving the telegram and said he would prefer not to hold the Durbar at all. He then telegraphed the King's Private Secretary, Lord Knollys, to enlist royal support for his attempt to save the Durbar from becoming a 'regrettable and gratuitous failure'. The Cabinet was angered by this unconstitutional step, which Lawrence defended on the grounds that the coronation was the King's business and he was therefore entitled to be warned about the consequences of mistaken policy. The Viceroy's secretary was also indignant at the attitude of 'the wretched India Council' which, as he saw, was revenging itself for its 'humiliation over the Coronation guests'.[63]

The Cabinet's attitude suggested that similar considerations may have been affecting the behaviour of some of its members. After a meeting on 19 November, Brodrick telegraphed the Viceroy to report that its opinion had been 'unanimously unfavourable' and to warn him 'not to push the question to extremities' because it would gain him nothing; Wyndham and Selborne, he added, agreed with him.[64] Unperturbed by the implication that his resignation would be accepted, Curzon responded by telling Balfour he did not want to be 'the instrument of this great failure' and suggested that someone else should carry out the Government's policy. The position of the Cabinet remained inflexible until it learnt from the Viceroy's next telegram that he had not planned to reduce the tax in the King's name but simply, as head of the Indian Government, to commemorate the event with the concession. If the ministers remained adamant despite this elucidation, he asked permission to make a general statement indicating the hope that circumstances would shortly permit financial relief. He could not conscientiously do less, he declared, because the people of India had suffered economically in recent years and now deserved their reward. The compromise, weighted as it was against the Indian Government, proved acceptable in London and elicited a kind letter from Balfour, who chided his old friend for regarding himself as injured whenever he failed to get his own way; he added, however, that no difference of opinion would diminish either the warmth of his friendship or the enthusiasm of his admiration.[65]

Curzon was not mollified by either the compliments or the compromise. He was particularly hurt by a letter from Brodrick informing him that the Cabinet had been prepared to throw him over. 'What a light', he sighed to Mary, 'it throws upon human nature and upon friendship.' The best way to deal with this 'eye-opener', he added, would be to take not the slightest notice of it and to treat the matter with 'silent disdain'. He thus refused to write to Brodrick for three months and, when asked for an explanation, replied that he could not forget as long as he lived that the entire Cabinet, including his greatest personal friends, had been willing to break off his Indian work and ruin his career either on a point of 'purely constitutional pedantry' or – Brodrick was given the choice of motive – because he wished to announce at the Durbar the tax reduction he would have been allowed to make eleven weeks later in his budget speech. The episode, he added, would affect him throughout his political career.[66]

Brodrick retorted that for four years the Cabinet had given him loyal support and a free hand on almost every issue except 'questions like Persia', where Lord Salisbury had been immovable. But over the Durbar Curzon had exaggerated the importance of tax remission and had then committed the 'capital crime' of trying to enlist the King on his side. The War Secretary claimed to have intervened to promote the compromise, but Curzon was not impressed. To overrule the Viceroy on such an issue, he declared, and to contemplate breaking his career over it, was 'a cruel injustice'. Mary agreed that the incident would always leave a scar.[67]

The row clouded the build-up to the Durbar. Lawrence thought the Viceroy was at his best during a crisis and praised his actions over the 9th Lancers and the telegram to the King. But as the ceremony approached, he noticed his chief was restless, fretful, abnormally impatient, worrying about little things, complaining about everybody's slowness. Even after all the arrangements had been made, there were still things to be done: composing the King's message, clearing his own speech with the India Office, planning the Connaughts' trip (and asking them not to visit the Maharaja of Alwar because of 'these abominable habits' he still indulged in). All sorts of things, over which he had no control, might go wrong: there was a worry over Lord Kitchener, newly arrived as Commander-in-Chief, who was reported to be such a bad rider that he might fall off his horse in the procession. On the eve of the ceremony the Viceroy was in a dejected mood. People might sneer at the 'Curzonation', he told Hamilton, and scoff at his pleasure at being its central figure, but they were quite mistaken. The Cabinet's behaviour over the salt tax had left him indifferent to the proceedings, and he looked forward with no relish to being the centre of a military society where three-quarters of the audience would be cursing him for having dared to do his duty in the case of the 9th Lancers.[68]

The ceremony opened on 29 December with the state entry into Delhi, an imposing procession of elephants bringing the Curzons, the Connaughts and the leading princes from the railway station by a circuitous route, past the Red Fort, round the Friday Mosque, and out through the Moree Gate to the Durbar site. Mrs Wilson, the wife of an ICS officer, said she would always remember Mary in the royal procession, 'the trailing lilacs which fell from her drooping hat forming a background to her exquisite beauty. She seemed a part of the sunshine and to emanate joy.'[69] She was 'perfectly exquisite', Mrs Thompson, who was also married to a civil servant, noted in her diary. The elephants, surrounded by attendants with spears to prevent them from bolting, were laden with rich trappings. The Curzons themselves sat on a gold howdah underneath a gold umbrella to ward off the winter sun, and gold featured brightly on the elephants of the Maharajas; some had large gilt candelabras fastened to their tusks, Mrs Thompson observed, and looked 'most absurd'.[70]

Subsequent days were taken up by cavalry and gymnastic displays, performances of massed bands, and a good deal of sport, especially polo. On the second day Curzon opened an Indian Art Exhibition designed to display all that was rare, characteristic or beautiful in Indian art from pottery to brocades. The event gave him an opportunity for one of his preceptorial lectures to the princes. If they decided to patronize Indian art, he told them, it might flourish, but if they preferred to fill their palaces with 'flaming Brussels carpets' and 'Tottenham Court Road furniture', then there was not much hope.[71]

The Durbar ceremony was held on New Year's Day in a large horseshoe amphitheatre, specially built in Mogul style with Saracenic arches and cupolas tipped with gold paint. The most moving moment came at the beginning, when the band struck up 'See the Conquering Hero Comes' and over three hundred veterans of the Mutiny, most of them Indians who had fought on the British side forty-five years before, entered the arena. It was a 'most affecting sight', remarked Mrs Thompson, to watch these 'little old creatures tottering and hurrying along to keep up to the time that they once marched without difficulty'. The crowd rose and cheered, but when the march was followed by 'the wailing pathos' of 'Auld Lang Syne', many of the audience broke down in tears. After this the Connaughts were received with rather less emotion, although one woman 'obliged with a loyal tear' because the Duke looked so like his mother. The royal couple were followed by Curzon's carriage, escorted by the surviving members of the Imperial Cadet Corps, who looked suitably dashing on black horses with white uniforms and pale blue turbans. Mrs Thompson thought it 'very cruel and unfair' that the Viceroy, who had run 'the whole thing magnificently', did not receive a really good cheer, but perhaps she was unaware of the state of feeling over the 9th Lancers. Sympathy for the cavalrymen may also have accounted for the outbreak of coughing during Curzon's proclamation.[72]

Other events included a state dinner and a state ball, where Mary appeared in her celebrated dress with its pattern of peacock feathers, a 'Garden Party for Native Gentlemen', a firework display, a church service and on the penultimate day a grand military review. The Viceroy took the salute on an enormous chestnut horse which he later learnt was notorious for bucking off generals; on this occasion, however, the animal merely proved to be obstinate, disliking the experience of standing alone in the open and continually edging backwards to join the horses behind. Curzon thought it ridiculous that he, a civilian unloved by the military, should be taking the salute while just behind him rode a royal and popular Field Marshal. His position became still more uncomfortable with the appearance of the 9th Lancers, whom the previous Commander-in-Chief had actually tried to ban from the ceremony.* As the cavalrymen rode by in their blue and white uniforms, they were greeted by loud cheering from Europeans in the crowd and even by some of the viceregal party. Afterwards Curzon told Hamilton that as he

---

*Although the Lancers were unaware of the fact, they owed their presence in Delhi entirely to an intervention on their behalf by the Viceroy.

sat alone and unmoved on my horse, conscious of the implication of the cheers, I could not help being struck by the irony of the situation. There rode before me a long line of men, in whose ranks were most certainly two murderers. It fell to the Viceroy, who is credited by the public with the sole responsibility for their punishment, to receive their salute. I do not suppose that anybody in that vast crowd was less disturbed by the demonstration than myself. On the contrary, I felt a certain gloomy pride in having dared to do the right. But I also felt that if it could truthfully be claimed for me that 'I have (in these cases) loved righteousness and hated iniquity' – no one could add that in return I have been anointed with the oil of gladness above my fellows.[73]

On the last night of the Durbar seven soldiers from a Welsh regiment beat a native policeman to death on the Ridge outside Delhi. 'It is a pity', the Viceroy remarked laconically to his wife, that 'we cannot have another Review for them to receive a popular ovation.'[74]

A certain amount of carping inevitably accompanied the Durbar. A group of MPs were indignant because they had not been given the best seats, while Lord Ampthill complained because he was not allowed to ride an elephant; Mary found the Ampthills so irritating she suggested they should be treated like anthills and stepped on.[75] Ill-informed criticism from Britain condemned the Viceroy's extravagance. He was compared to Nero and accused by a former Member of Parliament of squeezing £2 million from the Indian taxpayer to aggrandize himself.[76] In fact the total cost of the festivities ran to £213,000 or about one-sixth of a penny for each human being in India.

No one disputed that it had been a magnificent and well-managed spectacle. 'Everything was perfectly organised', Mrs Wilson wrote home, 'with that genius for big ideas and grasp of detail for which our great Viceroy is already renowned in other domains.'[77] Curzon was pleased with the success, which as usual he ascribed to his habit of overseeing everything himself, but he doubted whether the Durbar had enhanced his reputation except as a first-rate organizer, 'a magnificent State Barnum, an imperial Buffalo Bill'.[78] Gertrude Bell came away with the impression that the Viceroy was 'extremely unpopular' and 'yet something of a great man'.[79] Balfour told Mary Elcho that friends returning from the Durbar unanimously agreed that 'the show was the best show ever shewn' and that George was 'the most unpopular viceroy ever seen. Whether this is because his reforms are too good or his manners too bad seems doubtful.'[80] Resentment at the treatment of the 9th Lancers was in fact stronger than either reason suggested by the Prime Minister. Lord Selborne came close to an explanation of the Durbar's success when he complimented Curzon on his invaluable but very un-British gift of being able to take himself seriously at such a pageant.[81]

17

Fatal Appointments,
1902–1903

L ORD SALISBURY HAD referred to Curzon as one of the four satraps of the empire conspicuous for force and intelligence. The three civilian members of this group shared a number of characteristics. Like Curzon, Milner and Cromer were zealous, high-minded, hard-working imperialists, inclined to see themselves as sacrificing their lives in distant corners of the empire without adequate support from an indifferent government at home. Their views of themselves, their work and their compatriots in Britain might be summarized respectively in Kipling's poems, 'The Pro-Consuls' (which was inspired by Milner), 'The White Man's Burden' (although this was directed at the United States) and 'The Islanders' in which the poet berated his countrymen for their sloth and complacency. Like Kipling, all three remained faithful to the Victorian sense of imperial mission and were similarly disquieted by the laxer but less certain currents of the Edwardian age.

The military member of Salisbury's quartet had few of the qualities of the other three, and yet in public estimation he outstripped them all. The first hero of the empire was Lord Kitchener of Khartoum, a warrior of stoked and smouldering energies who enjoyed greater fame and reputation than anyone from his profession since the Duke of Wellington. These had been acquired in the Sudan, where he defeated the Dervishes, and in South Africa, where he was more successful as Chief of Staff to Lord Roberts, a better commander, than he was on his own. Even an admiring member of his staff admitted that Kitchener had 'a very slight knowledge of tactics' and wisely left the details of a battle to his subordinates.[1] He enjoyed a formidable reputation as an organizer, a British Carnot, although this was later tarnished in the First World War and even at the time it puzzled some who worked with him. General Sir Ian Hamilton, his second-in-command against the Boers, believed it was a myth repeated by people who could find no more plausible explanation for his success.[2] Other generals nicknamed the conqueror of Khartoum 'Kitchener of Chaos' or more simply 'K of Chaos' after he and Roberts had mistakenly reformed the regimental transport system in the middle of the South African war.[3] He also had a reputation for brutality and looting, but maltreatment of the Dervishes and digging up the Mahdi's skull for use as a desk ornament were forgiven by a public delirious at the avenging of General Gordon. Kitchener's reaction to revelations of the homosexual activities of Sir Hector MacDonald, a distinguished soldier who had risen from the ranks to command the British forces in Ceylon, illustrates another side of his nature. Whereas Roberts hoped the disgraced general would go to some distant part of the world and be forgotten, Kitchener, who may have been a repressed homosexual himself, wanted him courtmartialled and shot.[4] In the end MacDonald shot himself.

Kitchener was adored by a public which saw him as an incarnation of John Bull with the smoke of patriotism pouring out of his nostrils. He looked hearty, direct and honest, but was in fact artistic, devious and unscrupulous. The craggy, impassive exterior concealed an ambitious intriguer who, as Esher observed, became a combination of Juggernaut and Ignatius Loyola in order to achieve a purpose. Milner, who had been as anxious to get him out of South Africa as Cromer had been to remove him from Egypt, thought Kitchener had never been able to distinguish between fighting the Mahdi and fighting his own colleagues and countrymen.[5] In spite of this weakness, he attracted the adulation of a number of influential people who were aware that he did not 'run straight' but forgave him because they thought he was, or might be, a genuine war hero. Among them was a group of highly intelligent men including Balfour, Esher and Rosebery, as well as Lady Cranborne, the future Marchioness of Salisbury, who worshipped Kitchener and did everything she could to further his career.

Shortly before Curzon left England in 1898, Kitchener told him he wanted to serve on the Subcontinent and even sent a photograph for Mary to 'remind her of the man who means to take her down to dinner some day in India'. A few months later he called unexpectedly at the India Office and announced his desire to be considered for the post of

Military Member of the Viceroy's Council. Curzon thought he would be more suitable as Commander-in-Chief, a job which did not require as much departmental work or co-operation with colleagues as the military membership. But as soon as the idea became known, several of Curzon's friends, including two former Viceroys, advised him not to contemplate Kitchener as C-in-C. Lord Lansdowne endorsed the common view that the general was a great organizer, but then proceeded to distrust his judgement, to rank him as an inept commander who had driven the Egyptian army to the point of mutiny, and to 'shudder at the thought of turning him loose without previous apprenticeship in India, to deal with the native army'.[6] Lord Northbrook was even more forthright. Kitchener was intensely unpopular in the army at home, he told Curzon, and had 'no knowledge whatever of the native army, no tact and no aptitude for civil work'.[7] Naturally unreceptive to advice, the current Viceroy ignored the warnings.

Similar alarm was expressed in India. The entire army, reported Collen, the Military Member, was hostile to the appointment of Kitchener, who knew nothing of either India or the Indian soldier, and would offend everybody and turn everything upside down.[8] It was not the wisest way to appeal to Curzon, who believed the army in India needed to be turned upside down and who hoped that Kitchener would give it the same sort of treatment that he himself had applied to the administration. The Viceroy wanted the best man available and, compared to the other mediocre candidates, the victor of Omdurman stood out. Curzon claimed to know about Kitchener's 'somewhat unlovable temperament' and realized he could be imperious, stubborn and difficult to get on with. But he believed himself to be now 'too firmly seated' to worry about that.[9]

The man who sanctioned the appointment was St John Brodrick, the War Secretary, who had been very critical of Kitchener in Egypt but later claimed to have made an enormous sacrifice in letting him go to India.[10] The Field Marshal's departure, however, was delayed by the Boer War, and Sir Power Palmer became Acting C-in-C while he was in South Africa. Returning to England in the summer of 1902, Kitchener insisted on taking a holiday, which Curzon suggested should be spent looking for a wife, and did not reach India until November. *Punch*'s farewell cartoon reflected Brodrick's feelings by showing Britannia with helmet and trident pointing to Kitchener and saying to the sari-draped India, 'We can ill spare him; but you see we give you of our best.'

Curzon's wife and secretary were apprehensive about the potential for friction between two such autocratic and self-willed characters as the Viceroy and the Commander-in-Chief. Mary wrote the newcomer a welcoming letter telling him of her husband's 'intense satisfaction' that he was there and warning him it was 'the prayer' of the soldiers that 'the two giants would fall out'.[11] Curzon was impressed by his first meeting with Kitchener and relieved that he no longer had to deal with generals who were 'phantoms'. The new C-in-C was highly unconventional, he reported, but it was 'a grand thing to get a man of power, determination and prestige in this country, and when he makes the veteran automatons skip and hop I view the spectacle with sympathetic relish'.[12] Curzon was also delighted by his determination to enforce higher standards of behaviour on the British soldier.

Kitchener enjoyed his life in India, especially when he could set off with a band of ADCs and scour remote parts of the frontier – a habit Curzon deplored because the tribesmen became suspicious and nervous when they found the C-in-C in their districts. But he intensely disliked office work and refused to try to understand how the system of departments worked. While he liked to ruminate on schemes to redistribute the frontier garrisons or renumber the native regiments, he was bored by details and let his adoring staff deal with them. His laziness provoked the amazement and admiration of his Military Secretary. 'It is wonderful', Colonel Hubert Hamilton told Lady Cranborne, ' how he gets through his work – 3 or 4 hours a day does it all, and only 5 days a week . . . He discards all detail on the one hand and, on the other, makes his staff work very hard, and very willingly, at all the bigger questions he takes up.'[13]

Kitchener's leisure was spent in pursuits as out of tune with his popular image as flower arranging, interior decorating, collecting plants and porcelain, and designing his servants' liveries. Aggrieved to find that Snowdon, his house at Simla, was so much smaller than Viceregal Lodge, he grumbled that the Indian Government had 'no proper feelings' about how the C-in-C should be lodged.[14] After bullying the Finance Department into agreeing to pay for his alterations, he added a hall, a drawing-room, a dining-room and a library; one of the papier mâché ceilings, constructed from files of the Military Department, was a replica of the library ceiling at Hatfield. Similar enlargements were made to his house in Calcutta. Proud as he was of his decorative skills, Kitchener was equally vain as a collector of porcelain. Like his plants, which tended to be 'annexed' from neighbouring gardens, the collection demonstrated the acquisitive as well as the artistic side of his nature. Wise hostesses locked up their best pieces because, like royalty, he expected to be given anything he had vocally praised. When this did not happen, he was observed on occasion to pocket it. Mary Curzon was much amused to find herself solicited for her mother's collection of rare bottles.[15]

Mary went to great lengths to befriend Kitchener. In her opening letter she hoped they would meet frequently and that he would drop in to play billiards with her husband. Soon she was sending him notes and giving him presents such as gold mustard pots for his birthday. Kitchener appreciated the efforts they both made towards him. 'Curzon is all one could wish and as kind as possible,' he reported home after his first few weeks in India. Six months later he wrote that both had been very kind to him and that Curzon was 'really a first-rate viceroy'.[16] Mary came to believe that she was a 'great friend' of the C-in-C, a view also held by her husband who afterwards thought that Kitchener had been her devoted admirer and that she had been 'almost the only solace of his rather lonely life in India'.[17] Both of them were misled by the general's friendship and remained deluded until the end. No doubt Kitchener liked the mustard pots and the dinners and perhaps even the billiards; but there are enough snide comments in his letters and those of his subordinates to show that the friendship meant little to him.

Four months before Kitchener's arrival in India, Curzon had been warned about his intentions in a letter from an old friend. Meeting the soldier in London, Clinton Dawkins had found him 'able, energetic, domineering, very little troubled by scruples' and determined to run 'the whole show' in India. Kitchener had told him frankly that he would spend a year looking around, that he would not collide with Curzon, but that he would use 'the whole of his popularity and prestige to dominate the next viceroy'.[18] Lady Edward Cecil reported a similar encounter. 'I don't mean to quarrel with Curzon,' Kitchener had said with an inflexion in his voice 'to suggest what would be the fate of the next viceroy'.[19]

Dawkins correctly identified Kitchener's chief objective as the elimination of the Military Member of the Viceroy's Council and the assumption of his duties by the C-in-C. Curzon, who did not understand why he was so anxious to destroy a system he had no experience of, was unaware that a senior general had gone to England specifically to prejudice Kitchener against the Military Department. The Adjutant-General, Horace Smith-Dorrien, decided to resign his post early in 1902 because he could no longer tolerate the alleged obstructiveness of the department. Asked to withdraw his resignation by Palmer, Smith-Dorrien agreed on condition he was given leave to go to London to warn Kitchener, who had just arrived from the Cape, how his hands would be tied in India. Taking with him a summary of the department's perceived misdemeanours, the Adjutant-General showed it to the South African hero who gasped, 'Is this the sort of thing I have got to compete with?'[20] On arriving at Bombay later in the year, Kitchener found Smith-Dorrien's views reinforced by Palmer himself, who had just quarrelled with the new Military Member, General Sir Edmund Elles, on a trivial matter; embittered by the row, Palmer told his successor that the department had become too powerful. Kitchener's reaction was to tell Curzon at his first meeting that, given this state of affairs, he should have come out as Military Member rather than C-in-C. Adding his opinion that the Viceroy's principal military adviser should be the Commander-in-Chief, he announced his desire to abolish the Military Department. Curzon naturally expressed extreme surprise that a new C-in-C should make such a proposal after having spent three days in India, a point which Kitchener seemed to find reasonable, because he agreed not to raise the matter again until he had gained some experience of the country's administration.[21]

The new Commander-in-Chief arrived in India with an exaggerated view of the power of the Military Department which he intended to exaggerate still more to others until he had obtained its abolition. The department was not in fact acquiring new powers but was recovering under Elles some of those it had lost under the gentle and acquiescent regime of General Collen. What had been the most incompetent of government departments when Curzon arrived had greatly improved in the hands of an officer of administrative ability, and was now performing a useful role. The Viceroy was convinced it had not encroached upon the prerogatives of Army Headquarters, which remained immeasurably more powerful. The Commander-in-Chief in India had greater powers than any other military officer of the empire, certainly more than the C-in-C in England, because he was not merely the executive head of the army, responsible for its organization, training, mobilization and campaigning; he was also, as the second-ranking member of the Viceroy's Council, the equivalent of a senior cabinet minister. The Military Member, whose position was much less prestigious, headed the department which handled the army's finances and administration, and acted as a second military adviser to the Viceroy. It was this latter function, important at any time but essential when – as in this case – the C-in-C had no experience of India, that infuriated Kitchener and led to his campaign against the Military Department. 'When I am Commander-in-Chief,' he had declared in England, 'nobody is going to have a word in criticism of my proposals, and no department which renders this possible shall exist.'[22]

Disregarding his promise to Curzon that he would acquire some experience of Indian affairs before embarking on a crusade, Kitchener immediately started a quest for allies by mail. Lady Cranborne was as always an easy convert and could be relied on to preach about the iniquities of the system to the Prime Minister, her husband's first cousin. Lord Rosebery was also approached and told that the system was just about as bad as it could be, though not quite so bad as at the War Office in London.[23] But Kitchener failed to enlist Britain's most illustrious military figure, Lord Roberts, whose experience of the Indian army had lasted over forty years. It had never been inconvenient, Roberts replied, to have supply and transport run by the Military Department, because they had automatically come under his orders during manoeuvres or when a force took the field. Besides, his inspection tours in the winter and his work at Headquarters and on the Viceroy's Council during the hot weather had given him enough to do without taking over the functions of the Military Member.[24] Kitchener, who was too lazy even to get through the C-in-C's work properly, was annoyed by the reply but undeterred by its arguments; he continued to press for the abolition of a system he insisted on referring to as 'dual control'. The phrase, with its implication of divided command and the suggestion that it would lead to hesitation and inefficiency in time of war, convinced many people in England that Kitchener was right. In fact it was a highly misleading description of a system which divided different duties between two men because they were too onerous for one.

In January 1903 Kitchener was so impressed by an article in the *Contemporary Review*, which advocated the abolition of the Military Department, that he invited its author, Captain Malleson, to India to write the C-in-C's notes and memoranda. The following month he submitted a formal proposal based on Malleson's article and told Curzon he wished to clip the wings of the Military Member and reduce him to a position of impotence. The Viceroy strongly deprecated the idea and urged Kitchener to spend a year in India before pulling the system to pieces.[25] Once again the C-in-C accepted the advice and once again failed to follow it. Yet while he continued to rail against the existence of the Military Department, his own inexperience tended to demonstrate the case for its retention. When asked by the Secretary of State to recommend the size of the force required to escort a political mission into Tibet, Kitchener and Smith-Dorrien, who had no experience of fighting at Himalayan altitudes, suggested sending 6,000 troops. This absurd number might have been despatched had the Military Department not greatly reduced it. In the end a force of 2,000 men proved adequate to carry out the assignment.

Kitchener's 'year' of cogitation lasted three months, although even during this tranquil season he pursued his grudge against the Military Department and tried to emasculate it by tempting its best officers away with offers of promotion. He then went on a tour of the frontier and on his return in May, without having acquired any further administrative experience since his first proposal, produced a new scheme to place the Military Member under his orders, to house the Military Department under the same roof as Army Headquarters, and to take charge of matters of supply, transport and ordinance. He was so delighted with this document that he thought even the Military Member would be convinced by it. Elles, however, disagreed with each point, and so did Curzon. For the third time in five months the Viceroy advised Kitchener not to persevere with the scheme, which he thought the other members would unanimously oppose, but to wait and find out how the administration really worked. 'What is at the bottom of it all?' Curzon asked him during a conversation on the same day, 'what do you object to? You admit you have no case against the military department from your own experience, and yet you want to destroy it; where does the grievance come in?' Kitchener replied that he could not tolerate criticism or rejection of his proposals from a subordinate military authority. 'You may be unable to understand it,' he added, 'for it is all a question of military feeling and military discipline.' Reporting the conversation to Hamilton, Curzon pointed out that Kitchener was aiming at an absolute dictatorship in all military matters for the Commander-in-Chief.[26]

The procedure of making notes on proposals was common to all departments and areas of the Government. Plans put forward by a Lieutenant-General were noted upon at Army Headquarters, those proposed by a Lieutenant-Governor were minuted by the Government in Simla or Calcutta; even the Viceroy's views toured the departments and were commented upon. But Curzon was prepared to go far to accommodate the C-in-C and on 21 May he issued orders that Kitchener's proposals should not be noted upon or criticized by junior officers in the Military Department but should be sent directly to the most senior official, the Secretary. On the same day the C-in-C told Curzon that while a 'vast majority' of officers shared his opinions, he had decided, in view of the Viceroy's opposition, once again to withdraw his proposals. Explaining his decision to Lady Cranborne, he said that on reflection it seemed better to wait a year before inflicting them on the next Viceroy; in the event of Curzon receiving an extension, he would resign his post and return to England. Four days later he changed his mind after hearing from the Viceroy that the Military Department had slightly altered the wording of a confusing and carelessly phrased order while he had been on his frontier tour. Losing his temper, he demanded to know whether Curzon's view on the issuing of orders could be taken as 'a final ruling in the matter'. If it was, he added, he must stick to his principles and resign.[27]

Curzon replied that he had given no ruling but had merely described the existing practice. Kitchener was invited to propose changes to that practice to the Council, which he did, and once again Curzon went far to remove a grievance by creating a new category of Indian army orders to be issued only by the Commander-in-Chief. Writing to Hamilton, the Viceroy could justifiably claim that he had done everything possible to prevent Kitchener's resignation and remain on good terms with him. To his father he admitted that the C-in-C was 'a most difficult customer to manage, very impetuous, quite ignorant of India, and impatient of the least control'. Kitchener possessed rigour and energy, but his foolish behaviour showed that he was deficient in both judgement and ability.[28]

Six weeks later Curzon reported that the atmosphere with Kitchener was much better. Although the C-in-C had 'splashed about a bit at the beginning' and made a number of stupid mistakes, he was now seeing his way and 'acquiring focus'.[29] But if Curzon thought his good humour and improved vision indicated a change of attitude, he was mistaken. Knowing that his views would be communicated to the Prime Minister, Kitchener was still writing to Lady Cranborne about resigning. Although he liked India, he told her, it was 'too heart-breaking to go on seeing inefficiency rampant and fostered in every way'. There was no doubt he should clear out, he went on, and do something else. Could it not be arranged, he asked her, for Lord Cromer to join the Cabinet so that he could have a go at running Egypt?[30]

*

Kitchener's future actions, as he had told Lady Cranborne, depended on whether the Viceroy's rule was extended beyond the normal term of five years. For some time Curzon had been tempted to emulate Dalhousie by remaining longer to oversee the fulfilment of all his reforms. Cromer, who was the *de facto* ruler of Egypt for twenty-four years, had suggested as early as 1898 that Curzon should stay on and make India the main work of his life.[31] In 1901 the Viceroy told his father he preferred to make a great name for himself in India while he still had the strength rather than wait at home for Lansdowne's retirement, when he might be too feeble or crippled to take the Foreign Office.[32] A year later, despite his rows with the India Council and the Cabinet, he felt he should stay on and cement his work in case a weak or ignorant successor allowed it all to collapse.[33] Many reforms were in place and could hardly be undone, but some were in the process of implementation and others were barely started. In the summer of 1902 he began his last major commission of enquiry, yet at the beginning of his fifth year in India he was still waiting for the commission reports on railways, irrigation, the police and the universities that would permit him to initiate legislation he hoped would determine India's future for the first half of the twentieth century. Many people in India wanted him to stay and complete his reforms, and many friends in England wanted him to return and nurture his career. As usual he was impervious to advice. His mind was dominated by the single thought that to leave after five years would be to leave his job half done.

First among the advisers he spurned was Mary. He had made his name in India, she argued, and no extra years could add to his magnificent reputation. Since he was already in danger of being forgotten as a politician and regarded as a permanent proconsul like Cromer, she had a 'burning eagerness' to bring him home in time to fight the next election. If the Conservatives won, he would be given foreign affairs or at the very least the Colonial Office, but in any case his magnetism and personality were such that the young men of the party would want him as their next leader. Desperate to return home herself, Mary used every argument she could find to influence her husband. Her least promising approach was to tell him that he had started all the 'mighty changes' and that he was 'far too brilliant and able' just to stay in India and keep the machine pushing along. She also made more personal appeals, begging him not to stay until either he killed himself or the *joie de vivre* had died in them. Cecil Spring Rice had told her mother, she reported, ' "For God's sake get him home. Can't Lady Curzon make him come?" Poor Lady Curzon,' sighed Mary from Simla, 'she couldn't make him move an inch.'[34]

The Viceroy received his wife's exhortations during an unsuccessful tiger shoot in Gwalior with his friend Scindia. He sympathized with her evident depression and blamed himself for being so absorbed by his work and its problems that he was not sufficiently loving or considerate towards her. Turning to her eagerness to put him in the Cabinet, he pointed out that there was no vacancy and that Lansdowne was not going to retire just to oblige him. Yet he must work somewhere while he was still strong, and if there was 'no thwart unoccupied in the home boat', he should continue 'to pull the stroke' in India. His decision to stay emanated from a sense of duty guided by the self-sacrificing examples of former Viceroys. In camp at Gwalior, he told Mary, he was reading a life of Lord Canning who had been hounded in England and in India and yet had continued to do his duty without a murmur of complaint.[35] Mary must have cursed her husband's habit of self-conflation with his predecessors.

During the early months of 1903 Curzon was repeatedly urged by friends in Britain to go home and prepare himself to lead the party, to become Foreign Secretary or Prime Minister, to save the country from Joe Chamberlain. George Wyndham, whose career had not yet been destroyed by drink and Ireland, was regarded as his only possible rival for the succession to Balfour as Tory leader. Among those who wanted to see him in the forefront of domestic politics was Lord George Hamilton, who sympathized with Mary's efforts to bring him home. Clinton Dawkins believed he would be the next Tory Prime Minister but confessed that people were worried that he had lost interest in home affairs and had developed 'such masterful tendencies' that he would be impossible to work with in Parliament. Curzon himself wondered whether he might have become 'too eager and strenuous' and now lacked the flexibility to lead at home.[36]

Sir Schomberg McDonnell, who for many years had been Salisbury's Private Secretary and was still close to the Court, had no such doubts. The Cabinet, he reported in the spring of 1903, was so unimpressive – Brodrick was hated, Lansdowne stale, Gerald Balfour useless and Stanley 'a standing joke' – that Curzon would have no problems of readjustment on his return; indeed he was already spoken of as the next Prime Minister. In a subsequent letter written after the death of his old chief, McDonnell described Salisbury as 'the last of his race of statesmen' and declared that only Curzon from the present generation could be compared with him. He was glad that the Viceroy had missed the explosion over Tariff Reform and was thus not identified with either the free traders or Chamberlain's supporters. But he believed that a prolongation of his term in India would wreck both his health and his career. Writing at the end of the year 'with the brutality of friendship', McDonnell told Curzon he was 'a street ahead' of all his contemporaries in ability and urged him not 'to sacrifice the certainty of being prime minister to the splendid ambition of being India's greatest viceroy'. 'Every thoughtful man' that he had spoken to looked forward to his return and his leadership and would lose heart if Curzon stayed in the East; his work there had been accomplished, and the time had now come for him to direct other Viceroys. Lapsing into the jargon of the turf, he claimed to have been 'head lad' of the Prime Minister's string for so long that he knew Curzon was the only 'stayer' in the field. 'Writing in deadly earnest', he beseeched the Viceroy to train now for the Prime Minister's Cup so that, after winning that race, he could run the empire from home.[37]

Flattering though it was to receive such appeals, Curzon was not tempted to help 'a somewhat sick and debilitated party' to the extent of filling an undesirable post like the War Office in the present Cabinet. In any case he was convinced that his duty lay in India, and no power on earth could have persuaded him otherwise. Balfour was therefore sent a long letter explaining why the extension should be made and including a request for a four- or five-month holiday in England or, as the Viceroy put it, 'a brief respite from labours longer and more unbroken than any other servant of the Crown in a similar position will have undertaken for nearly half a century'.[38] Six weeks passed, to Curzon's mounting frustration, before a telegram indicating general approval arrived from Balfour. It was followed, to his fury, by a letter containing the King's opinion, shared by the Prime Minister, that it would be dangerous for the Viceroy to spend more than six or eight weeks in Britain. Curzon was hurt and astonished that the Government should offer him so little, especially as Cromer spent three months annually in England and Milner had already been home twice from South Africa. Could the Government not realize, he asked Brodrick, that he was staying on at a positive risk both to his reputation and his health, and that only the strongest feelings of duty towards India had led him to contemplate it? Accusing Balfour of treating him as the recipient of a great favour, he suggested that six or eight weeks at home was a very ungenerous offer to someone who was staying on purely in the public interest. To Mary he disparaged the Prime Minister's arguments as 'utterly academic' and characteristic of his mind, and to his father he complained that his treatment was typical of the levity and ignorance with which Indian affairs were too often dealt with at home. Dalhousie and Canning were the only men who had stayed beyond five years for half a century, and both had killed themselves in the process, coming home as broken men to die shortly afterwards. It was the old story, he told Lord Scarsdale, of the willing horse driven till he drops between the traces.[39]

Ian Malcolm, a backbench MP devoted to Curzon, appealed to Brodrick to press the Viceroy's case in the Cabinet. The War Secretary reacted by banging his fists on the table, declared that nobody was indispensable and refused to stir a finger to disturb the tradition whereby Viceroys remained in India throughout their term of office.[40] In June, however, Balfour accepted Curzon's vacation requests and took advantage of the concession to lodge a justified protest against his friend's 'epistolary style'.

The Viceroy was still popular in India, except in military circles, and his extension was welcomed by both the native and the British press. It was regretted by his supporters at home, by Kitchener's partisans in England and in India, and eventually by a great many other people including educated Bengalis and the British Cabinet. The outstanding reforms were duly completed; one of Curzon's late unsung achievements was the shake-up of the corrupt and inefficient police, the creation of a national force and the establishment of a directorate of Criminal Intelligence. But the personal and political cost was enormous. Balfour later told Morley he had made two mistakes as Prime Minister: the first he had forgotten and the second was to allow George Curzon to return to India.[41] For the Viceroy himself it was the greatest mistake of his life. As Sir Schomberg McDonnell had foretold – yet in a more decisive way than he could possibly have feared – it wrecked Curzon's chance of succeeding Balfour and seriously blighted the rest of his career.

Why the Prime Minister let him go back remains a mystery. Hamilton reported that there had been only two willing candidates for the viceroyalty, Brodrick, who was now regarded as too tactless, and Lord Balfour of Burleigh, who, it was now believed, would succumb to liver disease or an apocalyptic fit after two years' work under a tropical sun.[42] But Selborne had long been regarded as Curzon's successor and, as one of the few successful ministers in the Cabinet, he was a perfectly plausible candidate. Originally believing that the offer of such a meagre holiday had been designed to bring him home at the normal time, Curzon subsequently ascribed his extension to the 'interest and desire of so many to keep' him away. 'Awful stories of my autocracy get home', he told Pearl Craigie, 'and make the flesh of the cabinet creep'.[43] One Indian chief, Sir Pertab Singh, believed that London politicians were envious of Curzon and eager for him not to return, a view Lawrence also encountered after his return to London in the autumn. Godley and McDonnell told him that members of the Cabinet were frightened of Curzon and found him too successful, too strenuous and too unsympathetic to their views and problems. Lawrence observed that it was not a question of fear but of jealousy.[44]

The second half of 1903 saw the ending, to Curzon's regret, of three successful working relationships. Walter Lawrence, his tactful and efficient secretary, acceded to the demands of his wife and her health and left in October. Before a farewell dinner given in his honour, Lawrence begged his chief not to make any jests in his speech. 'Jest!' was the reply, 'I am far nearer to tears.' Although ill on the night, Curzon presided over the dinner but returned to his bedroom afterwards, leaving his secretary to sing 'Auld Lang Syne' with Mary, Kitchener and the other guests. Long after midnight Lawrence went upstairs to wish him a final farewell and found him still at work, writing a long note on education.[45]

Another regretted departure was that of Lord Northcote, the Governor of Bombay, who had been promoted to the governor-generalship of Australia. After an early skirmish over the powers of the Governors, Curzon had co-operated well with Northcote and had come to respect his subordinate's ability. Both Viceroy and Secretary of State recognized that, despite the belief of Bombay officials that they ran an advanced and progressive administration, it was in fact one of the most backward in India and needed an effective replacement at its head. Hamilton hoped that Sir Antony MacDonnell, who had retired from India and was now Under-Secretary in Ireland, could be enticed back, and Curzon, who had always thought the governorship should be opened to the ICS, agreed with him. The most obvious candidate still in India was Ibbetson, but he was an indispensable figure on the Viceroy's Council who hoped eventually to return to his old province, the Punjab, as Lieutenant-Governor. When MacDonnell fell through, Curzon urged the appointment of James Bourdillon, who had revealed unexpected talents after being passed over for the lieutenant-governorship of Bengal. But Hamilton did not think a reject from Bengal would be acceptable to Bombay and decided to appoint his second choice, Lord Lamington, who had been best man at Curzon's wedding. After the rather embarrassing governorships of Lord 'Bingy' Wenlock and Lord Sandhurst, Curzon did not believe that another society appointment could be foisted on India. Lamington, he told the Secretary of State, was one of those 'delightfully irresolute people' who never know which train to travel on. As one of his most intimate friends, he added, it had been his duty to make up his mind for him on almost everything, even to the extent of deciding which girl he should propose to. In India Lamington would presumably do nothing without consulting the Viceroy in advance, but that was of little comfort to Curzon who had no use for yes-men. The appointment, he told Hamilton, meant 'goodbye to administrative reform in Bombay for another five years, and that unhappy presidency, already deep in the mud, will sink lower and lower down'.[46]

An even more unfortunate appointment of an even closer friend followed. In September Balfour attempted to retain a balance in his Cabinet by a discreditable manoeuvre which provoked three free trade ministers to resign at the same time as Joseph Chamberlain. One of the resentful victims was Lord George Hamilton, a close parliamentary colleague of Balfour for twenty-nine years. Unlike the Prime Minister, who parted from him without regret, Curzon was genuinely sad to see Hamilton go. Despite the arguments over the coronation expenses and the salt tax, the Viceroy recognized that Hamilton had been a wise counsellor and an important ally in his programme of reforms. For his part, the Secretary of State, conscious though he was of Curzon's foibles, regarded him as a great Viceroy and remained an admirer of his Indian policy. Neither of them were encouraged at the prospect of Hamilton's replacement by St John Brodrick, a politician who had hitherto displayed little interest in India.

Although he had not seen his old friend for nearly five years, Curzon had heard a good deal about Brodrick's life both from his letters, which exhorted the Viceroy to work less and be more considerate to people, and from those of friends. 'The Brodder' did not seem to have changed much and was still, reported Wyndham, 'the same old ass in the matter of jests, sticking indecent labels on my tonic for the edification of the man who makes up the fire in my room'.[47] Inheriting Curzon's post at the Foreign Office, Brodrick was reported to be 'endeavouring to develop humour which [was] rather an effort and not always quite successful'.[48] His much-dreaded, self-awarded privilege – that of examining his friends' faults and trying to correct them – had been retained. An entire Easter house party, related Alfred Lyttelton, suffered at Stanway because Brodrick 'dealt with horrible faithfulness with the whole company one by one beginning with A.J.B. and finishing with Hilda [his wife] who retired to the breezes of the monument hill in tears and would not be comforted [or] at least would not come to luncheon till her impervious consort had left the meal'.[49]

After the Unionist victory in the 'Khaki election' of 1900, Brodrick had been promoted to the War Office, an appointment which perturbed Balfour's secretary who foresaw the difficulty of convincing people that the best man had been put in what was then the most onerous and important post in the administration.[50] The new Secretary of State immediately launched a scheme to reorganize the army into six corps, half of them consisting of regulars providing a strike force of 120,000 men, the other three of militia and volunteers. Too hasty, too ambitious and insufficiently prepared, the plan proved to be unpopular with the army, the public and the politicians. At the end of a very costly war few people wanted to pay for a force that would be expensive in peacetime yet inadequate to make a significant contribution to a European conflict. As Winston Churchill argued, one corps of regulars was 'quite enough to fight savages, and three not enough even to begin to fight Europeans'.[51] The popularity of the project was not increased by the rancorous deportment of its initiator. Complaining of Brodrick's 'insufferable' manner at the despatch box, Lord Hugh Cecil defined it as 'hectoring pomposity stiffened with pipe clay'.[52]

Sympathetic though he was to his friend's problems at the War Office, Curzon resented Brodrick's efforts to make India contribute to their solution. In an attempt to improve recruitment in 1902, Brodrick chose to increase soldiers' pay, a decision which applied to any part of the empire in which they were serving. India, which paid for those stationed in her territory, would therefore incur an extra annual charge of £780,000. Curzon deprecated the measure on grounds of expense but also because the low cost of living in India meant that British soldiers there were already overpaid. The increase in pay, he warned Godley, would merely 'find its early correlative in increased syphilis and intoxication'. While equally deploring the pay rise, the Permanent Under-Secretary pointed out that the matter had to be settled in Britain and that India had no right to be consulted.[53]

The following year Brodrick put forward a suggestion that a special garrison of 15,000 men should be stationed in South Africa ready to be transported to India in an emergency. A firm proposal, backed by Hamilton, was made in July, with the cost to India reckoned at £400,000 a year. Neither Curzon nor Kitchener were impressed by the plan. India had recently sent troops, without advance payment, to help the empire in China, South Africa and Somaliland, yet now she was asked to contribute to the upkeep of a force she might never need. Before the Indian Government had a chance to discuss the scheme, Brodrick told Hamilton he had to mention the possibility of an Indian contribution in the House of Commons. Although Hamilton stressed that he must not commit the Indian Government, Brodrick in his 'never-ending gaucherie' declared his view that India ought to pay.[54] He was thus very annoyed when the Government in Simla refused. 'Those who love you best in the cabinet,' he told Curzon with asperity, hoped that while 'teaching us the benefit of your vigorous policy' in Persia, Afghanistan and Tibet, 'you would endeavour to teach India the necessity of adequately supporting it'. The Viceroy replied tersely that he had given India five years of peace and could not be reproached for rejecting a proposal to pay for troops he had not asked for and did not want.[55]

Brodrick rapidly became the most unpopular member of the Government. Sympathy over the unexpected death of his wife evaporated when he found a replacement a little over a year later; even his friends, Schomberg McDonnell reported, were shocked by 'the indecent rejoicing over his second marriage'.[56] As he became deafer, remarked Hamilton, Brodrick became more tactless than ever, as self-opinionated as always and now unable even to hear other people's opinions.[57] At the War Office he managed to antagonize any official, military or civilian, he had to deal with, while his continuing 'gaucheries', often unimportant in themselves, laid him open to constant ridicule.[58] In the House of Commons he was baited by Churchill, who called his reorganization scheme 'a humbug and a sham', and made himself so 'phenomenally unpopular' that the survival of the Government was at risk. 'Many good observers', noted Balfour, 'think that feelings against St John so violent that we shall never get through Army Estimates without a fall! He is naturally depressed, poor old boy.'*[59]

---

* A 'whipping' scandal in the Grenadier Guards, after which the commanding officer was suspended on half pay, was an additional – and unfair – reason for Brodrick's unpopularity.

A reshuffle plainly had to be made. The Prime Minister was not renowned for standing by his friends in a crisis – Churchill once observed that, had he lived during the French Revolution, he would have been thoroughly polite about consigning an erring colleague to the guillotine[60] – but Brodrick enjoyed an immunity from discardment that puzzled his associates. When Arnold-Forster went to the War Office, he was constantly subjected to pleas from A.J.B. to save 'St John's face at the expense of everything and everybody', an experience he found 'exceedingly tiresome'.[61] Brodrick, who seems to have been unaware that he was not improving his reputation at the War Office, wanted to become Viceroy of India, an aspiration that was apparently taken seriously by Balfour and even by Selborne, who took modesty beyond extremes by declaring 'the Brodder's' claims to be superior to his own.[62] Curzon was staggered to learn that an exchange of roles was being contemplated and that he might be invited to return to England to clear up the mess left by his friend with the military. It was no comfort to hear that the War Office was so discredited that only three men – Cromer, Chamberlain and himself – were thought capable of reforming it. Nothing, he declared, would induce him to take the post. As for the succession in India, he was determined to convince Hamilton of the obvious fact that Selborne would make a much better Viceroy than Brodrick.[63]

Eventually it dawned upon the Cabinet that it would be 'politically unsafe' to put the beleaguered minister in 'a position of such unique authority . . . where his discretion would be so unfettered'.[64] The problem of where to put him remained unsolved for several months until Balfour decided in September that, instead of succeeding Curzon in India, Brodrick would become his superior in Whitehall. Hamilton warned the Prime Minister that the choice would provoke a 'howl' in India and doubted whether Brodrick would get on with Curzon or manage the India Council with success. One councillor, who thought the change 'a great nuisance', said the new minister was 'not a nice man to work with' and was 'sure to fight' with the Viceroy, while Kitchener, who had worked with Brodrick during the Boer War, described the possibility of his appointment as 'too dreadful to contemplate'.[65] In India the native and British press each raised the predicted howl. One newspaper identified Brodrick as 'the very last person' it wanted to see in the India Office, another believed he would be 'almost as disastrous for India' in his new post as he would have been as Viceroy, while a third confessed that the evolution of a successful Secretary of State for

India out of an unsuccessful Secretary of State for War was a process beyond the grasp of its comprehension. The howl was repeated and amplified in Britain by the *Daily Mail* which attacked Balfour for lacking the courage to save 'three hundred millions of our subjects from affording a fresh field and opportunity for the display of Mr Brodrick's incompetence'.[66]

Curzon did not expect much trouble from the new minister. Brodrick's unpopularity and his unfortunate excursions into Indian politics while at the War Office would, he thought, encourage him to make a quiet beginning, and in all probability the Unionists would be voted out of office before he had a chance to assert himself. The new relationship was initiated by a patronizing viceregal letter about the proper role of the India Office. Pointing out that the Government of India was very much more in touch with the Subcontinent's affairs than the India Council in London, Curzon told Brodrick that the duty of the Secretary of State – as the 'constitutional ally of the Viceroy' – was to ensure that the Council never defeated a proposal on which the two allies were agreed.[67] Sensing that he was taking advantage of the ministerial change to extend his autocracy, Godley wrote to remind the Viceroy that responsibility for his actions lay with the Secretary of State and the Cabinet, and that they enjoyed 'a corresponding right of control, absolute and unshared' over the Indian Government. Curzon, amused by 'so rollicking and whole-hearted a statement of the finest old crusted doctrines of the royal prerogative', paid no attention.[68]

The Viceroy's hopes that the new Secretary of State would be content with a largely passive role at the India Office were quashed by three telegrams at the beginning of November. The first, which will be discussed in the following chapter, was a confusing, unnecessary and ultimately damaging statement of Government policy towards Tibet. The second called upon the Government of India to send 20,000 coolies to work on the railways in the Transvaal and requested a reply within four days; it also warned Curzon that disagreement might not be tolerated by the Cabinet. And the third, again requiring an answer in four days, asked for a detailed statement from the C-in-C and the Viceroy on the number of soldiers Russia might place on the Afghan frontier in case of war, together with the number India would need to counter them.[69]

Since the members of the Indian Government were scattered over the country far from their departments, it was impossible for them either to discuss these vital matters or to refer to their papers. Kitchener thought the military question would require months of study, while from Assam Ibbetson telegraphed his view that the Transvaal scheme was politically inadvisable and morally indefensible. Curzon, who was touring the Punjab, was annoyed by the impossible demands for rapid answers, and angered by Brodrick's threat to order him to send coolies to South Africa. Two years earlier he had refused a Rhodesian request for Indian labour on the grounds that Indians were abominably treated in the Transvaal and Natal. Repeating this view to Brodrick, he asked why India, which had saved South Africa from the Boers, now had the duty to develop it.[70] The wrangle which followed ended with India's refusal to send the coolies and a new grievance for Brodrick. Considering the furore which later broke out over Chinese coolies in the Transvaal, it is not hard to imagine the scale of the scandal – and the damage to British rule in India – if Curzon had agreed to the request.

During his first months at the India Office Brodrick oscillated between contrasting moods. George Wyndham thought his experiences at the War Office rankled so deeply that he had neither heart nor interest in his present job.[71] Certainly a good deal of time was spent trying to prevent his successor, Arnold-Forster, from dumping his army scheme. Curzon noticed this side of him and ascribed the consequent periods of tranquillity to the War Office tribulations of the 'poor old boy' as well as to the 'dire results' of his 'early splashes' into Indian politics.[72] Brodrick sometimes liked to present himself as the humble Polonius of the friend he had always adulated. He told Mary he had practically abdicated his legal function to become 'George's ambassador at the Court of St James', while to Lord Scarsdale he wrote of his 'great joy' at being able to work with his son even though the sphere of action was one of which George knew so much and he so little.[73] Perhaps Brodrick had touches of Uriah Heep as well as Polonius and Widmerpool.

Yet there was another side to the Secretary of State. Understandably seeking to repair in his new office the reputation he had damaged in the old, he realized this could not be achieved by simply serving as a mouthpiece for Curzon. Wary of provoking another quarrel of the dimensions of the Transvaal coolies, he began to display what the Viceroy described as 'the sort of obstinacy that revels in . . . petty manifestations of superior authority'. This trait was most obvious in the matter of appointments, a field in which Curzon and Hamilton had co-operated without tension. On being asked by Brodrick to recommend a judge for the High Court in Calcutta, the Viceroy put forward a barrister from Allahabad only to find that a stranger from England was chosen instead. When he was asked to suggest a new Law Member for his Council, his recommendation was once more disregarded. As an obsessive believer in promotion by merit, Curzon cannot have been consoled by Brodrick's assurance that the new member, H. Erle Richards, 'should be thoroughly agreeable socially' because he had been Alfred Lyttelton's fag at Eton and was married to the Master of Trinity's niece.*[74]

Nevertheless, in the light of his later behaviour, it is impossible to attribute Brodrick's obstructiveness simply to his desire to distinguish himself after the humiliations of the War Office. Harry Cust, a fellow member of the Souls, suggested that his actions at the India Office constituted a revenge for Curzon's constant teasing during their three decades of friendship. While this explanation also seems a little facile, it surely contains an essential truth. Brodrick had once said that 'one of the brightest elements' of his life had been watching Curzon 'gaily flying the fences' which he had 'laboriously climbed'.[76] Yet, as mutual friends were aware, he was also jealous of Curzon's superior talents, and later, when he too had reached the top, he resented the Viceroy's failure to take his views more seriously. Placed suddenly and unexpectedly as his former hero's superior, he took advantage of the position to enforce the missing deference.

---

*After working with him for a year and a half, Curzon declared that Richards was 'a charming fellow' but 'so utterly useless in administration' that he doubted whether he ought to receive an honour customarily bestowed on members of the Viceroy's Council.[75]

18

The Gulf, Bengal and Tibet

IN MAY 1901 the Viceroy had proposed a tour of the Persian Gulf to create a salutary impression of Britain's interests and influence in the area. The plan had been vetoed, however, by Balfour and Lansdowne who feared it might provoke retaliation by other powers at a time when Britain was still tied up in South Africa. Two years later, after the Foreign Secretary had publicly asserted Britain's paramount position in the Gulf, Curzon tried again, suggesting it was an opportune moment to show the flag. Although the Cabinet was apprehensive whenever the Viceroy suggested a course of action outside India's borders, it could find no valid reason to oppose him. In August 1903 Curzon therefore wrote to the admiral commanding the East India Squadron asking him to bring his flagship and as many vessels as he could muster for a visible demonstration of Britain's dominance in the waters of the Gulf.

On 16 November the Curzons embarked on the *Hardinge* at Karachi and steamed towards Muscat, accompanied by two telegraph and despatch boats and a naval escort of four ships supplied by Lord Selborne at the Admiralty. Two days later they entered Muscat to the sound of artillery salutes crashing and echoing against the harbour walls. Percy Cox, later to become a legendary figure in Anglo-Arab history, had been selected four years earlier to carry out Curzon's policy in the Gulf as Resident at Muscat. He had rapidly acquired an ascendancy over the Sultan, who had become fervently pro-British, and France's claims of equal influence now looked ridiculous. Curzon had long thought French colonial officials resembled haircutters, and his meeting with the Consul at Muscat reinforced this opinion.[1] After a series of official visits, including a durbar on the cruiser HMS *Argonaut* at which the Sultan compared Mary to a pearl and Curzon asserted Britain's determination to maintain her paramountcy in the region, the flotilla set off up the Gulf.

The durbar for Arab sheikhs at Sharjah was a hazardous ceremony because both Arabs and British officials in full dress had to be conveyed by boat through a high sea to the *Argonaut*; most people felt sea-sick, but only one of the sheikhs' retainers fell overboard. Seated on a dais under a great awning with his epauletted officers on chairs to his left and the robed Arabs, many of them sitting on the floor, to his right, Curzon told the sheikhs that Britain had come to their waters before any other power in modern times, that she had found strife and had created order, that she had protected the inhabitants of their shores and had opened their seas to the ships of all nations. In the process Britain had neither seized their territory nor destroyed their independence, and she would not now abandon them. 'The peace of these waters must still be maintained; your independence will continue to be upheld; and the influence of the British Government must remain supreme.'[2]

Sharjah was followed by visits to Bandar Abbas, where the Persian Governor dined on board the *Hardinge*, and Bahrain, where the ruling sheikh was lectured on the financial condition of his island. At Kuwait the Viceroy received an impressive reception from tribesmen mounted on camels firing into the air and an almost embarrassing manifestation of loyalty from the Sheikh; in a scene that would no doubt have dismayed the Cabinet, the Arab chieftain accepted Curzon's gift of a sword of honour by announcing his desire to be considered a fighting man of England.[3] The only unfortunate incident of the tour came at Bushire where the Persians altered the protocol governing the Viceroy's landing, and their intended visitor angrily refused to meet them.

It is not easy to measure the political impact of largely ceremonial events. Curzon believed the tour had been a great success and had raised British prestige in the area. The Sultan of Muscat, for example, had behaved more like 'a loyal feudatory than . . . an independent sovereign', while the Sheikh of Kuwait described himself as an ally under the protection of Great Britain. The tour also provided an opportunity for the navy to examine the strategic conditions of the Gulf in case it had to defend parts of it from a Russian attack. Like the Delhi Durbar and other successful pageants involving Curzon, it provoked ambivalent reactions: in government circles, Brodrick informed the Viceroy, the Persian Gulf was now known as the Curzon Lake.[4] Whatever else may be said about the jaunt, the facts remain that no other Viceroy devoted as much time to the Gulf, and no other area of Muslim Asia remained pro-British for so long.

After spending Christmas with her husband in Calcutta, Mary, who was then five months pregnant, sailed for home with the children to have her baby under Mrs Leiter's supervision in London. Curzon stayed behind for the legislative session, 'grinding at this eternal millstone', and hoped to join her soon after the birth. Missing his family, bored by the routine and angered by the increasing hostility of the press, he was consoled by the year's legislative achievement yet resentful that 'all these great measures that [would] leave an indelible mark on Indian history' excited less interest among the people of Calcutta than the circus on the Maidan or the birth of an elephant at the zoo.[5] The Acts included two of his most far-reaching reforms, on agricultural banks and ancient monuments, and one which provided the rare spectacle of the Viceroy being overruled by his Council. This was an Official Secrets Bill which he opposed on principle and took no part in framing. On discovering it had been badly drafted by the Legal Department and carelessly handled by his colleagues, he grumbled that this was the result of 'relaxing one's supervision even for a moment' and insisted on making changes.[6]

At the end of March 1904, after three days' discussion of over one hundred amendments, the Legislative Council passed its most contentious measure of the year, the Universities Act. Educational reform had been one of Curzon's domestic priorities from an early stage. At the long Simla conference in September 1901 he had identified many areas where change was needed, and afterwards he had set up a commission to visit the universities and produce a report that would form the basis of new legislation. At the beginning of the century higher education in India was provided for about 23,000 students in nearly two hundred colleges and controlled by five universities set up in 1857 and afterwards on the model of London University. Nobody, British or Indian, could pretend that the universities had progressed very considerably since their foundation. Governed by bloated senates crammed with Fellows of limited educational attainments, they were little more than examination halls for students who could obtain a degree only through dedicated cramming and learning by memory. None of them had a library, a laboratory or provision for postgraduate study.[7]

Arguing that education of the Indian people was the responsibility of the central Government, Curzon was determined to improve standards even at the cost of infringing the universities' autonomy. His two most controversial measures reduced the size of the senates to a maximum of 100 Fellows – Bombay's had grown to 310 – and empowered the Government to decide which colleges should be affiliated to the universities and to inspect those chosen to ensure they complied with the agreed academic requirements. Curzon claimed the senates would retain much of their independence and described their future position as 'self-governing institutions watched parentally by the Government in the background'.[8] This view was not shared by outraged critics who claimed he had insulted the Bengali nation by attempting to weaken its institutions. The senate of Calcutta University was controlled by nationalist politicians who saw the Universities Act not as an educational improvement but as a blow to their political aspirations. Aware that many Indian leaders agreed with his views, and that two of them had voted for the Bill in the Legislative Council, Curzon dismissed the outcry as 'largely hollow and manufactured'.[9] Yet his refusal to compromise and his disregard for Indian feeling alienated moderate opinion and allowed extremist slogans to attract popular support. 'Efficiency was his watchword,' the nationalist leader Banerjea declared later; 'popular sentiment counted for nothing, and in his mad worship of this fetish Lord Curzon set popular opinion at open defiance.'[10]

Popular opinion in Calcutta was already being defied by the even more controversial measure to partition Bengal. The proposal had evolved from an idea first mooted early in 1901 to transfer a district from the Central Provinces to Orissa, and had drifted on a file between the departments for over a year before the Viceroy eventually heard of it. Curzon minuted his extreme surprise that the secretaries and deputy secretaries should have spent so much time carving up and rearranging India's provinces without acquainting him with their projects. 'Round and round', he noted, 'like the diurnal revolution of the earth went the file, stately, solemn, sure, and slow; and now, in due season, it has completed its orbit, and I am invited to register the concluding stage.'[11] In fact Curzon had already mentioned to Hamilton that the settlement of the Berar question provided a good occasion to examine the boundaries of local governments; he had also observed that Bengal was too large to be run by a single administration.[12] Although the province had not been a prominent candidate for readjustment in the departmental plans, schemes for its partition were soon circulating. In November 1902 Andrew Fraser, later Lieutenant-Governor of Bengal, suggested that the province of Assam should be enlarged by the eastern districts of Bengal, and it was reported that local opinion at Chittagong favoured the idea.[13]

In 1900 Bengal was by far the largest and most populous administrative unit in India. Its Lieutenant-Governor had jurisdiction over an area of 189,000 square miles inhabited by more than seventy-eight million people, a population slightly larger than that of the United States and almost double that of Great Britain. The province's centre of gravity was in the west at Calcutta, and the eastern districts, with poor and difficult communications, tended to be the destination of the less able officials of the ICS. They had few police stations, a high crime rate, and a thinly spread administration which rightly considered itself neglected by the richer and more populated west. Mymesingh, a district the size of traditional Yorkshire with a population of four million people, was administered by a single British official.

Curzon originally thought Bengal might be shorn of Chittagong, inhabited mainly by Bengali Muslims, and Orissa, populated largely by non-Bengali Hindus.[14] At the end of 1903, however, he endorsed Fraser's suggestion, which favoured religious rather than ethnic separation, to place the eastern districts of Bengal under Assam. His plan was published and produced an outcry, one nationalist newspaper pleading, 'O Lord Curzon: O Sir Andrew Fraser: Pray . . . do not drive [the Bengalis] from the bright and radiant land of Bengal into the dark and dire cave of Assam.'[15] The very thought that a Bengali could be turned into an Assamese was regarded by *The Bengalee* as 'little short of maddening', while the *Dacca Prakash* compared the dismay of the Bengalis at contact with the 'naked barbarians of Assam' to the feeling a Londoner would have if transferred to the north of Scotland.[16] Dismissing the criticism as 'rhetoric and declamation', Curzon remarked that he had not discovered a single line of argument amid all the denunciations.[17] In February 1904 he went on tour in eastern Bengal, where he became even more convinced that partition must take place but also realized that Fraser's plan was mistaken. While no one in the area wanted to belong to Assam, the Muslim inhabitants, who formed seventy per cent of the population, would be happy with a new province based at Dacca to which Assam could be united.

While this solution was to please the Muslims of east Bengal, it was no more palatable than the first proposal had been to the Hindus of Calcutta and the western districts. The lawyers, newspapers and nationalist politicians denounced a plan that would reduce their sphere of influence, and condemned Curzon's alleged aim of cleaving the Bengali nation in twain with his sword.[18] Supporters of the Viceroy who dismissed the nationalist clamour on the grounds that Bengal was not a nation but a province created by Britain, missed the point, because nationalism has never needed the antecedents of a nation to be genuine or effective. Congress and its sympathizers were convinced that partition was a deliberate attempt to weaken and divide the forces of political nationalism, and they were partly right. The project's genesis may have been a combination of viceregal musing and departmental daydreams, and its development may have been inspired by the drive for administrative efficiency. But the political benefits soon became apparent. Bengal could have been reduced by removing the Hindi-speaking area of Bihar or the Oriya-speaking region of Orissa. But the division of the Bengali-speaking areas had the advantage of weakening the Bengali-dominated Congress Party. Curzon was convinced by H.H. Risley, the Secretary of the Home Department and a scholar who had written *The Tribes and Castes of Bengal*, that partition would disrupt the Bengali sense of nationhood and weaken the influence of Calcutta. The outcry, Curzon predicted, would be loud and fierce in the capital, where 'the best wirepullers [of Congress] and its most frothy orators' resided, but it would not last. As a 'native gentleman' had told him, Bengalis 'always howl until a thing is settled: then they accept it'.[19]

The partition of Bengal was one of two controversial matters that Curzon left the Indian Government to deal with when he sailed for England in the spring of 1904. The other was the British excursion into Tibet. For some time rumours had been circulating that a Mongolian Buddhist called Dorjiev, believed to be a Russian agent, was plotting to bring Tibet within the orbit of the Tsarist empire. In May 1902 the Chinese Emperor's former tutor announced in Darjeeling that the Dowager Empress had signed a secret treaty ceding China's sovereignty over Tibet to Russia, and a few weeks later the British Minister in Peking reported that some agreement was believed to have been made. Curzon told Hamilton that, if this was the case, he would put a British army into Lhasa 'without the slightest delay'. Russia had no interest in Tibet, he pointed out, no subjects, no trade and no object in going there except one of hostility to Britain. Since a Russian protectorate over Tibet would be a threat to India and even more to Nepal, Britain's ally, it must be prevented at all costs.[20]

Relations with Tibet were supposedly regulated by agreements made by Britain and China in 1890 and 1893, which had been intended to settle questions of trade and boundary demarcation. But the Tibetans, who paid little attention to their Chinese overlords, took no notice whatever of the agreements, and the Viceroy's annual letters to the Dalai Lama were returned unopened. Curzon was determined to quell this defiance. As he later told Mary, an expedition should be sent to prevent Russian intrigues from culminating in a protectorate, to exact some reparation from the Tibetans for their violation of the pacts on trade matters and frontiers, and to negotiate new terms that would provide for trade with India and exclude 'any hostile political influence' in Tibet.[21] In January 1903 the Government of India urged the despatch of a mission to Lhasa, escorted by a military contingent, to negotiate a new agreement that would include the establishment of a British agent in the Tibetan capital. As misleading rumours reached him that some sort of Russian expedition was actually on its way to Lhasa, Curzon pressed Hamilton for prompt acceptance of his plan. Having spent a hundred years successfully keeping the Russians out of Afghanistan, he suggested that Britain would look very foolish if she meekly let them into Tibet and thereby incurred the additional expense of having to make a defensible frontier for Sikkim, Bhutan and Assam.[22]

Despite Hamilton's support, the plan was not appreciated by the Cabinet. Balfour was nervous that a mission would be regarded by other powers as an attack on Chinese integrity, a strange anxiety since that integrity had already been broached in various places by several of the powers in question. Lansdowne asked for Russian assurances that there was no secret treaty with Tibet and no intention to set up an agent at Lhasa. The Russian profession of innocence, which arrived in April, did not impress Curzon who believed that only British threats had prevented both the agreement and the agent from assuming a less tentative existence. Inspired by Hamilton, the Cabinet reacted to the Russian assurances by agreeing to Curzon's alternative proposal to open negotiations with China and Tibet at a place just inside Tibetan territory called Khamba Jong. There the Viceroy hoped to frighten the delegates into accepting a commercial treaty and a British trading agent at Gyantse, about halfway between Lhasa and the Indian border, by threatening to advance on the capital itself.[23]

Curzon appointed Francis Younghusband, his old friend from Chitral days, as the Commissioner in charge of the mission. After a briefing from the Viceroy, Younghusband picked up an escort of Sikh riflemen and in July arrived at Khamba Jong. There he remained, while the Chinese equivocated and the Tibetan delegation refused to negotiate, for five months. Eventually the mission was withdrawn, and

Curzon managed to persuade an extremely reluctant Cabinet to sanction – 'in the event of a complete rupture of negotiations' – a larger expedition to Gyantse. Proud of the 'tremendous' and unanswerable case he had made to the Government, he then summoned Younghusband for another briefing before the new mission disappeared into the interior of Tibet. The Commissioner's account of the visit, recorded in a letter to his father, throws an interesting light on the viceregal conduct of business. For nearly two hours Curzon questioned him on his proposals for an advance, probing his arguments and disputing his reasoning. Realizing that this was his method of examining an idea, Younghusband was unperturbed. The next day he was taken to a meeting of the Council where Curzon used all the arguments and adopted all the proposals he had challenged the day before. The Council seemed cowed, Younghusband noted, except for Kitchener who treated the whole business as rather a bore and seldom opened his mouth.[24]

It was at this stage that Brodrick, newly arrived at the India Office, despatched the series of telegrams which so exasperated Curzon. Influenced by Balfour's distaste for 'permanent entanglements' in Tibet, the Secretary of State plunged in with a telegram reminding the Viceroy that the advance on Gyantse was contingent on a rupture of negotiations that had not taken place, and demanding to know the cost of the expedition and the number of troops needed to maintain communications. As the Tibetans had refused to negotiate at all, only a pedant could claim that there had been no rupture. After Curzon had answered Brodrick's questions and argued against withdrawal or inaction, the Secretary of State telegraphed what came to be regarded as the definitive statement of British policy on 6 November. The mission would be allowed to proceed to Gyantse, it being understood that such a move would not lead to occupation, interference in Tibetan affairs or the establishment of a permanent mission. 'The advance should be made for the sole purpose of obtaining satisfaction, and as soon as reparation is obtained a withdrawal should be effected.' This could hardly be considered a very edifying objective. Younghusband longed for a British protectorate and the liberation of the Tibetans, 'slaves in the power . . . of ignorant and selfish monks', while Curzon wanted a commercial treaty, an agent in Lhasa, and the spiking of Russia's alleged designs. These imperialistic ambitions may have been excessive, but they represented a rather higher aim than the basic punitive expedition now authorized by London.[25]

The mission, consisting of 2,000 fighting men, most of them Gurkhas, set off in mid-December but, owing to the extreme caution of its commander, Brigadier Macdonald, was nowhere near Gyantse by the time freezing weather forced it to hibernate for three months. The force was shadowed by a larger body of very unwarlike Tibetans, who occasionally sent delegates to Younghusband telling him to go back to the border if he wanted to negotiate. One day the Commissioner returned the visits, riding into the Tibetan camp with a couple of companions in an attempt to break the stalemate. It was a reckless thing to do, as Younghusband soon realized when some senior monks attempted to detain him until he had named a date for the mission's withdrawal. On receiving a report of the incident with the dangers diluted, Curzon exhorted his Commissioner not to take personal risks: had he been captured, the Viceroy's standing would have been gravely damaged and the Government would have been forced to march on Lhasa.[26]

At the end of March the mission resumed its progress towards Gyantse. A large force of Tibetans, who did not want to fight, blocked the way. Macdonald and Younghusband declined to attack them but decided they must be disarmed. Scuffles broke out, the Tibetans refused to hand over their matchlocks, and the Lhasa commander lost his head and shot a Sikh soldier, an action that led to general firing and an appalling massacre of his own men. By the middle of April the mission had reached Gyantse, the destination specified in Brodrick's telegram, and Younghusband found himself in the usual position of waiting for negotiators who never appeared. Their absence did not greatly disturb the Commissioner, who wanted an excuse to go on to Lhasa, or the Viceroy, who hoped that Tibetan obstructiveness would force the Cabinet to accept his views on an eventual settlement. But at the end of April Curzon sailed for England, and Tibet was no longer his responsibility. His temporary abdication did not, however, prevent him from trying to influence events, and the Tibetan denouement, played out over the following six months, was the outcome of a four-cornered tussle between Curzon and Brodrick disagreeing in England, Younghusband in Tibet and the Indian Government in Simla. The departing Viceroy hoped foreign affairs would be kept quiet during the interregnum and left 'two golden rules' for his successor: '1) Do nothing. 2) If something must be done, do the reverse of what Dane [the Secretary of the Foreign Department] advises.'[27]

Curzon had been dismayed by Northcote's departure for Australia the year before, declaring he would rather forego his holiday than be succeeded as Viceroy by Ampthill for the duration of his leave. Although impressed by his ability and hard work, Curzon was irritated by those traits in Ampthill which others observed in himself: pomposity, over-sensitivity and an excessive love of ceremonial. The young Governor was a 'fiery hidalgo', he complained, who regarded criticism of a subordinate as a charge of dishonour to himself; furthermore, his self-importance was such that he was invariably accompanied by a band playing 'God Save the King'. Another defect was his priggishness, which had led him to upbraid a lady at dinner during the Durbar because she had no wine left in her glass for the King's toast.[28]

These foibles, which the Viceroy was not perhaps in a strong position to criticize, had coloured Curzon's judgement, and later he admitted that Ampthill had been 'an excellent, loyal and trustworthy substitute'. For his part the Governor was greatly impressed by the Viceroy's 'stupendous talents and industry': after taking over at Simla he told Godley and Brodrick that Curzon's powers and personality were 'most inspiring' and a constant topic of conversation among his colleagues, who regarded him with real affection and admiration. It was both his duty and his desire, he declared, to carry out Curzon's policy in matters great and small. To Brodrick he confessed his ambition was 'to hand over the helm' when Curzon returned in September, 'without having deviated in a single point from the course on which he has set the ship of state'. Such sentiments were extremely unwelcome to the officiating duo at the India Office, who hoped to settle various contentious matters during Curzon's absence. While recognizing his 'very great and very extraordinary qualities', Godley subtly warned Ampthill against Curzon and advised him not to act under the influence of his strong personality.[29]

19

'An Infinitude of Trouble': England, 1904

———————◆———————

AFTER REACHING ENGLAND at the beginning of February, Mary was soon recounting the kind of things that made her husband unanxious to return home: the foolishness of her sister Daisy, the unfriendliness of his sister Evie, the social intrigues of Margot Asquith, the ponderous and wearying humour of St John Brodrick. The Secretary of State for India, who chortled that Mary's return alone gave him the *droit de seigneur* over her, ascribed George's speed in Tibet to a desire to invite the Dalai Lama to be the new baby's godfather. Other 'corkers' followed. The problem with Brodrick's jokes, her husband replied, was that they combined great vulgarity with 'a soupçon of rather offensive indelicacy [but] no real humour or dash to carry them off'. He rather shuddered at the prospect of becoming the victim of his 'bovine pleasantries'.[1]

One apparently trivial incident had a significance that both Curzons missed. The incorrigibly flirtatious Daisy Leiter had just jilted one young officer and taken up with another, Eustace – known in the army as 'Useless' – Crawley. Mary, who thought she might as well marry a coachman or a stud groom, was exasperated by Daisy's inability to 'differentiate between horsey young gentlemen who can pilot her across Leicestershire and youths desirable to marry'. Curzon urged his wife to break up the affair because he believed 'people who fall into the hunting set seem to lose social and moral perspective'; besides, Crawley was enormously in debt and had been searching for an heiress for years.[2] Daisy did end the relationship and eventually married the Earl of Suffolk, one of her brother-in-law's ADCs, an officer equally horsey but socially more presentable. In India he kept a pack of jackal hounds.

While few people seem to have been concerned about Crawley's feelings, much resentment was aroused by Daisy's treatment of her previous suitor. Captain Raymond 'Conk' Marker, who had known Daisy since 1899 when he too had been one of the Viceroy's ADCs, had served in South Africa before returning to India as a member of Kitchener's staff. Meeting her again at the time of the Durbar, he was encouraged to believe that his passion for her was reciprocated and he was thus greatly upset to be told later that she preferred Crawley. Marker was like a character in a P.G. Wodehouse novel who needs to tell everyone he meets about his broken heart, and soon his woes were known all over Calcutta. Kitchener's staff, a closely knit, fiercely loyal group whose members referred to each other as 'the family circle', was outraged by Daisy's behaviour. One of them, Major Frank Maxwell, wrote to Lady Salisbury about 'that pig of a girl', another told her the history of the whole affair, and Kitchener himself complained to Mary.[3] All of them, moreover, blamed Marker's misery on the snobbery of the Curzons who allegedly wished for a much grander brother-in-law. The charge of snobbery, for which no evidence was produced against the Viceroy, did not come well from Maxwell, who told Lady Salisbury he hoped Daisy would 'marry somebody nearer in strain of blood to that of her own family – a butcher for choice. How the hairy heel does thrust out.'[4]

Kitchener encouraged Marker to believe he had been the victim of the snooty Curzons and suggested he took a posting in London. The heartbroken ADC accepted the idea and soon found himself installed at the War Office, acting officially as Private Secretary to Arnold-Forster and unofficially as a spy for Kitchener, sending him coded messages about military matters concerning India. Attempting to see Daisy when she came over to England, he was simultaneously rebuffed and informed about her intended marriage to Lord Suffolk. Unable to revenge himself on the fickle Daisy, Marker decided to work out his grievance on her brother-in-law. No one in Kitchener's camp except Lady Salisbury was more useful in the campaign against the Military Department, and no one worked more effectively for the Viceroy's downfall.

In their letters the Curzons referred to their forthcoming baby as Dorian or Nalder, but Mary feared she was going to have another girl. Her husband assured her the sex did not matter but continued to use masculine pronouns when writing about the baby. Later, in a letter timed to reach Mary just before the birth, he wrote:

> If it is a boy we will bless and thank Almighty God. If it is a girl we shall still bless and thank him. If the child does not live we will then bless and thank him for those we have already. If you are ill you must keep up your heart and soon get well. You can remember that you have never done one thing that has not been true and sweet and loving towards me, and that you have been to me for nine years a strength, a delight and a blessing. We have been very very happy and there are under Providence many happy days in store for us in the future.[5]

Before she received this letter Mary had given premature birth to her third daughter. As the telegram with the news arrived three weeks before schedule, Curzon thought it might be a hoax sent by Mrs Smeaton or some other person with a grudge. When he realized it was true, he wrote a letter of consolation. The baby's gender was unimportant and could easily have been his fault, the only thing that mattered was that Mary was all right, and in any case there was plenty of time for them to follow the example of one of his predecessors, Lord Lytton, and have a son after three daughters. Meanwhile 'Nalder' became Naldera, after the camp near Simla where she was conceived, and subsequently Alexandra Naldera because the Queen, when agreeing to be her godmother, wanted the baby to have her name; from birth, however, she was always known by friends and relations by her Indian nickname 'Baba'. The choice of godfather seems to have been automatic. Curzon, who had just received another selection of Brodrick's 'buckish jokes with just that savour of unwitty impropriety which he so greatly relishes', expected the Secretary of State would think he had 'an absolute right' and so duly appointed him. As Brodrick's personal relations with the Curzons were soon to come to an end, it was not a successful selection. Many years later he confessed he had not been a diligent godfather. Baba agreed with him.[6]

Curzon admitted to his father that a third girl was rather 'a blow' but claimed it was worse for Mary because 'in these matters a man philosophises whereas a woman cannot'.[7] This dubious theory turned out in this instance to be correct. Mary was miserable at the thought that they would leave no name for their descendants and that not only Kedleston but also George's titles would go to 'that dreadful brother Affy'. She hoped her husband would receive a title after India which their eldest daughter could inherit, so that they could at least found their own line. 'I think much of this,' she told her father, 'and bring up Irene with it in view.'[8] Some years later Curzon received the barony of Ravensdale with remainder, in default of male issue, to his eldest surviving daughter. After the death of Irene, who never married, it was inherited by Cynthia's son, the writer Nicholas Mosley.

In June, a few days after receiving Mary's letter about titles, Levi Leiter died in Maine. Wise and generous, he was the member of the family Mary most loved and the one she most resembled. His last gift to his eldest daughter had arrived a few weeks earlier: £1,000 to cover her expenses for returning home and having her baby in London. Over-indulgent to his children, Levi Leiter had managed to keep the family together in spite of the reckless speculations of his son. After his death, however, it fell apart, and wrangling over the inheritance continued for three generations.

In March 1904 Curzon was offered the sinecure of Lord Warden of the Cinque Ports, an ancient title dating from the eleventh century. Its holders had originally been in charge of the coastal defences of the south-east, but by the end of the eighteenth century their post had become a largely honorary one held by leading statesmen. The historical traditions associated with the Lord Warden inevitably attracted Curzon who was delighted to succeed Lord Salisbury as well as earlier incumbents such as Pitt the Younger and the Duke of Wellington. But what most commended the post to Curzon was the fact that Lord Dalhousie had also received it during his fifth year as Governor-General in India. Its only tangible advantage was the official residence, Walmer Castle, a medieval fortress on the Kentish coast which Wellington had loved and where he had died. Curzon was doubtful whether they would enjoy it very much, because it was a long way from London and offered little amusement except boating, for which he had no enthusiasm, and golf, which his back no longer allowed him to play. But he was sure they would like 'the old-world distinction' of the castle, while the sea air would be excellent for the children's health.[9]

Mary travelled down from London and quickly entered into the spirit of the place. She gazed at the Iron Duke's boots and wash basin, found the spot where Pitt had said farewell to Nelson, and from the ramparts watched 'the Channel fleet do foolish manoeuvres in the deep blue sea'. The air was indeed good, she reported to George, but it was all there was to live on, for the castle's drains were so appalling that the building was uninhabitable. Assisted by Frank, the one member of her husband's family to be consistently helpful, she installed herself in a hotel in Deal where the food was inedible and then moved into a villa called Walmer Place. Here she found luxuries she had not previously experienced in England such as electric lights and telephones. Electric bells for summoning the staff were a particularly useful novelty; in London they had sometimes been forced to go outside and ring the front doorbell when they wanted a servant to appear. Even at Walmer Mary was afflicted by domestic problems, by maids who broke plates, by a cook who had to be discharged, and by 'an idiotic old fool of a butler' whose first act had been to drop a full ink-pot on to Mary's desk, damaging the table, ruining her clothes, and splattering the carpet as he carried the dripping wreckage to the pantry.[10]

Curzon spent the voyage home arranging and indexing his departmental files and writing to his secretary about omissions. He also went through the household accounts which turned out to be surprisingly healthy. The food on board was as bad as usual and the wine undrinkable, so he lived largely on lemon squash. He felt no excitement about seeing England, he told Mary, or even about being with his friends, but he was longing to see her again 'and be happy and peaceful, not to be eternally overwrought nor to be a slave to boxes, but to have another little honeymoon ere I pass into middle life'. And of course there was 'the excitement of making the acquaintance of Alexandra Naldera'.[11]

After a four-month separation, they met at Dover in the middle of May, spent the night at Walmer and travelled up to London the next morning. Curzon had not expected anyone to take the slightest notice of his arrival or go to the station to meet him. People in England did not care about India, he moaned; nobody had greeted Dalhousie or Warren Hastings, and there was no reason for him to be more favoured.[12] In the event he was given a terrific reception both by the press and by a large crowd at Charing Cross which included nearly all the members of the India Council with whom he had been feuding for so long. From there he was driven straight to Buckingham Palace for an interview with the King, and later went to see his father. During the following days he was able to see most of his friends. On the 19th Brodrick invited forty-four of them to a dinner in his honour at which, according to Godley, Curzon was 'in great form'. A week later he stayed with the Cowpers at Panshanger, where he much enjoyed a ride in a motor-car; Mary was so terrified, however, that she put a blanket over her head.

In the Red Sea Curzon may well have wished for 'another little honeymoon' away from the slavery of boxes, but within a couple of days of his return he was bored. After being reunited with Mary, meeting the King and catching glimpses of friends he had not seen for over five years, he told Pearl Craigie he felt 'terribly stranded and rather miserable' without his work.[13] Mary was in despair. He seemed lost and wretched, she told her father, wandering about saying 'What *am* I to do? What *am* I to do?' He had begun to go through fifty packing cases he had brought from India, which would keep him busy for a day or two, but she did not know what to do with him afterwards.[14]

A graver problem was her husband's health. His leg gave him a good deal of pain, and his back was so troublesome that she was determined to consult the best spine specialist in Europe. A rest, which was one of the main objects of the holiday, would no doubt have helped, but he refused to rest. Even when flat on his back he insisted on transacting a mass of business and found time to write Brodrick 'twelve heavy pages' about a portrait of Warren Hastings. Ill health dogged him constantly during his six months in England. In June Ampthill was informed that he had spent the last two weeks in bed with neuralgia, in July that he could not walk more than a few yards and was laid up for the greater part of the day, and in September that although he could still eat a grouse he could no longer pursue one. He had not been able to fire a shot or put on country clothes since he had been in England, and his holiday had been 'one of almost continuous pain and depression, relieved only by struggles to push forward' policies about which he felt strongly.[15]

Curzon was able to dispel some of his boredom by making plans for Walmer Castle. The building's insanitary condition seems to have been caused by a labyrinth of clogged drains constructed because the Duke of Wellington insisted on putting a lavatory either in or just beside every bedroom. Mary described the castle as a 'rabbit warren' of these 'horrible little places', and her husband was determined to reduce their number. Yet while Walmer gave him an opportunity to exercise his architectural skills, it also provided the scene for a long and ridiculous dispute with the new Lord Salisbury. Curzon objected to the practice according to which the Lord Warden was expected to buy his predecessor's furniture. Walmer had been low down on the late Prime Minister's list of residences and was furnished with discarded items which Curzon's agents described as 'absolutely unsuitable for a gentleman's house'. Having no other country house, the new occupant wished to decorate the castle properly, but not wanting to quarrel with his old friend, who had become the fourth Marquess, he agreed to buy all the superfluous furniture except for broken chairs, threadbare carpets and a dilapidated stable used by the gardener's chickens.

If the two men had merely appointed a valuer and accepted his decision, the matter could have been solved quite rapidly. But it was dealt with by agents and lawyers who relished the argument and kept it going. Curzon found Salisbury's lawyer particularly offensive and was infuriated by the delays he caused which prevented the family from moving into the castle. In June he complained because he could not move in before his installation and the following month grumbled that he would have to take a seaside house for the children somewhere else. Eventually the question was resolved at the end of August when Curzon paid the arbiter's valuation of £1,557. But he remained resentful about a dispute that had cost him two letters a week and a good deal of annoyance throughout the summer. When Salisbury observed irritably that the affair had been more bother than the settlement of the Entente Cordiale, Curzon answered with an aggrieved twelve-page letter stating that he had not wanted to buy anything at all, that he had only done so because he was dealing with an old friend, and that the discourteous behaviour of the Marquess's agents had caused him 'an infinitude of trouble' that had gone far to embitter his brief holiday in England.[16]

The only moment of pleasure Curzon received as Lord Warden was at his installation in July. Arranged by the town clerk, who as an organizer could compare in efficiency with Curzon himself, the ceremony consisted of a procession through decorated streets, a church service, a carriage drive and the installation at Dover College Close, where the Lord Warden, according to medieval custom, momentarily presided over the Court of Shepway. At the official lunch in the town hall Curzon's health was proposed by George Wyndham, the MP for Dover, and in the evening the public buildings were illuminated. Like Curzon, Wyndham and other participants, *The Times* declared itself in favour of the preservation of such ancient and cherished traditions.[17]

There were further events and ceremonies to mitigate the disappointments of his English holiday. During a speech at Eton on the Fourth of June he joked that the school's recent record should give it a permanent right to appoint India's Viceroys, a remark that was misinterpreted by the Reuters correspondent and then further misunderstood by Indian newspapers which promptly denounced his proposal to appoint permanent Viceroys! On receiving the freedom of the Borough of Derby in July, he made one of several speeches about the

Englishman's duty in India. Godley remonstrated, arguing that it was undesirable to increase British interest in India which would merely lead to interference from Parliament.[18] Curzon thought informed parliamentary interference would be beneficial. At the end of the eighteenth century the House of Commons had filled rapidly to hear Burke or Fox speak on India, but now it no less rapidly emptied as soon as the affairs of the Subcontinent were discussed. Curzon had once complained that an Indian famine excited 'no more attention at home than a squall on the Serpentine', and despaired at the public's indifference to British dominion in India.[19] He now consciously set out to inspire his listeners with a belief in themselves and their destiny, and to a surprising extent he succeeded. In July, presented with the freedom of the City of London at the Guildhall, he told his audience that their rule in India was the greatest thing the British people had done, 'the highest touchstone of national duty'. Their task was to build a bridge between the races, a bridge on which 'justice must stand with unerring scales' if their rule was to last. It should not be imagined, he argued, that Britain's work was drawing to an end because, as the years rolled by, the call became 'more clear, the duty more imperative, the work more majestic, the goal more sublime'. And in phrases worthy of the Authorized Version he proclaimed: 'To me the message is carved in granite, it is hewn out of the rock of doom – that our work is righteous and that it shall endure.'[20]

His eloquence made a strong impression, inducing people to tell him how their hearts and imaginations had been touched by such inspiring words. Lord Selborne said it was the best speech his friend had ever made, 'and devilish few better ones have ever been made'. Even the earnest Arnold-Forster was much moved and told Curzon it was 'the most brilliant and stately piece of English' he had heard or read in 'all the records of modern oratory in our country'. For a nation still unsettled by the Boer War and uncertain of the future, the returning Viceroy had boosted morale. 'Curzon's magnificent speeches', Earl Grey reported to Ampthill, had 'stirred the blood and lumped the throats of the great majority' of people who had read them.[21]

In March Balfour had told Mary that the sight of her husband, 'dear old boy', would settle the points of contention between the governments of Britain and India. But the old friendships of the Souls days had deteriorated, especially that between Curzon and Brodrick, and the problems turned out to be as intractable in the intimacy of a London club as they had been down a 6,000-mile telegraph wire. Although this was partly the result of genuine disagreement, it was exacerbated by altered personal circumstances. Under pressure in his new job and still struggling with the legacy of his old one, Brodrick found it difficult to re-establish a friendship with a man who showed no respect for his views and who, he thought, was trying to run India while ill in bed in England. Curzon, for his part, was contemptuous of a Secretary of State 'who knows little or nothing about India, and does not seem concerned to learn'.[22] To Ampthill he complained that India's interests were suffering because three-quarters of Brodrick's time was being wasted in trying to prevent Arnold-Forster expunging the last traces of his occupancy of the War Office.[23] In April the new Secretary for War had infuriated his predecessor by abandoning his army corps proposals and thereby exposing him to the abuse and sarcasm of the press. 'Mr Brodrick's great achievement', declared the *Daily Mail*, 'is thus condemned by his colleagues within one short year of its accomplishment.' No example occurred to the newspaper of a minister in such a position who had not resigned after his policy had been condemned and reversed.[24] Embarrassed and resentful, Brodrick spent much of 1904 opposing Arnold-Forster's own reforms and attempting to prove he had been a much misjudged War Secretary.[25]

During Curzon's visit to England Balfour and Brodrick tried sporadically to settle their differences with him over Afghanistan, Tibet and the military administration in India. Since the death of Abdur Rahman in 1901, Curzon had been trying to persuade his successor, Habibullah, to come to India to negotiate a new agreement on the arms and subsidy supplied to Afghanistan as the price for keeping her as an ally and conducting her foreign relations. The new Emir had prevaricated about the visit, arguing that the agreements with his father had been made between governments and did not need to be renegotiated. The British, however, considered them to be vague, unsatisfactory and inadequate to deal with the dangers caused by Russia's recent penetration of central Asia. Suspecting Habibullah of wishing to develop relations with the Russians, Curzon was eager to reach a clear settlement committing the Emir to the British and allowing their troops into Afghanistan in the event of a Russian invasion. If Habibullah opted to become Russia's ally, he thought the Indian Government should not hesitate in occupying Kandahar.

Curzon had found negotiations with the Emir particularly difficult because all his important communications with him were sent home and 'gutted' by the India Office and the Cabinet who, he told Mary, did not know 'the ABC of Afghan politics. They will not leave me to handle the Amir as I think he ought to be handled, and then they blame me if the letters are a failure.'[26] The Cabinet was indeed extremely ignorant of Afghanistan, its well-informed membership limited, since the departure of Hamilton, to Lansdowne. Ministers perceived the danger of flooding the country with weapons without having any guarantee how they would be used, but they were terrified of doing anything that might provoke a third Afghan war. Consulted by Brodrick and Balfour during his stay in England, Curzon agreed with Ampthill's view that, as the Emir would not come to India, an envoy should be sent to Kabul to open negotiations. Yet while Ampthill wanted a firm agreement on military co-operation against Russia and a guarantee from Habibullah that he would abstain from political relations with other powers, the British Government recoiled from anything more ambitious than renewal of those agreements made with Abdur Rahman. This divergence of aim, which angered Ampthill, became still more critical when Curzon returned to India.

A more urgent matter was the fate of the expedition to Tibet. At the time of Curzon's hand-over, Brodrick had thought Younghusband too eager to advance and instructed Ampthill to give him 'a hint against undue precipitancy'. The British Commissioner, who had already spent ten months in Tibet, was indignant at the thought of being considered a 'rampant adventurer' and felt it futile to go on waiting for negotiators to turn up at Gyantse. Yet his mission might have been becalmed indefinitely had it not been suddenly attacked, vigorously but ineffectually, by a large Tibetan force at the beginning of May. The home Government could hardly have reacted otherwise than to sanction an advance to Lhasa, although Brodrick insisted on giving the Tibetans another month in which to produce their negotiators before the expedition rolled on. Irritated by the delay and by other restrictions, Younghusband reacted petulantly by refusing to answer one telegram from the Indian Government and by sending an aggressive reply to another. Ampthill responded in the middle of June with what Younghusband described as 'a very God-Almighty to a blackbeetle style of telegram' which provoked the Commissioner to resign.[27]

Somewhat against his inclinations, Ampthill persuaded Younghusband to withdraw his resignation. The Acting Viceroy's views on Tibet had been modified, and he now wondered whether it might be better to sacrifice the objects of the mission than to court the hostility of Russia. These doubts, confided to others, quickly reached Curzon, who was incensed to learn that while he was battling for the success of the mission in London, his understudy was contemplating with equanimity its failure in Simla. All their efforts and sacrifices, he predicted to Ampthill, would now be thrown away, and his only consolation would be that he was devoid of responsibility. The Acting Viceroy ascribed the outburst to ill health, a wise reaction commended by Godley who agreed that Curzon deserved to be 'forgiven for ebullitions which, in a smaller man, might fairly be regarded as unpardonable'.[28]

As the mission was now limbering up for its final push to the Tibetan capital, decisions had to be made about what it should do when it got there. In the telegram that had so annoyed Ampthill, Younghusband had scoffed at the idea of a quick round of negotiations at Lhasa followed by a withdrawal before winter: as he had already spent eleven months in the country unable even to begin negotiations, it was absurd to think that anything could be achieved with such obstructive people as the Tibetans in the two or three months allotted him. Curzon was arguing a similar line to the Cabinet. If the Dalai Lama had fled Lhasa before Younghusband reached it, he thought the British should be prepared to occupy the city until a treaty could be concluded and then leave an agent to see that its provisions were carried out. This case, stated at a Cabinet meeting on 1 July, was contested by what he termed 'the reparation school' of thought that did not care about a treaty and wanted the expedition to be merely retributive. Britain's claims, argued Brodrick to Ampthill, could be established by 'the mere fact of a British force marching on Lhasa and slaughtering a great number of Tibetans on the way . . .' If the mission found neither the Dalai Lama nor anyone else in Lhasa to negotiate with, it should destroy the city's arsenal, wells and fortifications, and withdraw with as large an indemnity as it could obtain.[29]

Laying waste the Buddhists' most holy city before dashing out of the country without making arrangements for future relations between India and Tibet did not seem a sensible or attractive plan to Curzon, Younghusband or the Government of India, but it was the one that for the moment prevailed. In the list of terms telegraphed to Simla for Younghusband to dictate to the Tibetans, the home Government instructed the Commissioner not to demand a resident at Lhasa or elsewhere. The Cabinet may not have known very much about Afghanistan, but its members did recall that the British Agent in Kabul, Sir Louis Cavagnari, had been murdered in 1879 and they did not want to risk a similar incident in Lhasa. They do not seem to have realized that docile Tibetan Buddhists did not resemble fierce Afghan tribesmen: indeed, so unwarlike were the Tibetans that in a surprise night attack on the mission's garrison of 120 men, 800 of them managed to do no more than wound 2 Indians at the cost of 250 losses of their own. On 26 July the Simla Government sent a despatch that argued strongly for an agent, pointing out that India already had one in Nepal and claiming that such an official would be in a position to oversee new arrangements with Tibet and protect Britain's rights. Curzon complimented Ampthill, whose pessimistic views were not shared by the rest of his Council except Kitchener, and regretted his despatch 'produced no more impression in Downing Street than it would have done had it been read in the streets of Lhasa'.[30]

At the beginning of August Younghusband at last rode in full diplomatic uniform in the shadow of the great Potala palace through the gates of Lhasa. The Dalai Lama had indeed fled and was making for Outer Mongolia after leaving his seals of office with an elderly Lama called the Ti Rimproche. Believing there was no one to negotiate with, the 'reparation school' concluded that the mission had no option but to exact retribution and depart. Balfour informed the King that the British force could not 'retire without striking some blow at [the] enemy', and the Cabinet decided it should 'destroy such buildings as the walls and gates of the city, and . . . carry off some of the leading citizens as hostages'. Brodrick hoped Younghusband would reduce the scale of the fiasco by bringing away 'a substantial indemnity' that 'would go a long way to ease off matters'. The Commissioner's unpromising position did not improve when the Amban, the Chinese representative, forwarded the views of a body of notables known as the National Assembly: the Tibetans refused each of his demands and argued that any indemnity should be paid by Britain. Nor was the task made easier by the pusillanimous escort commander, who said his troops could not winter in Lhasa and must leave in the middle of September.[31]

In these extremely unpropitious circumstances, Younghusband managed through force of personality together with Chinese assistance to conclude an extraordinary treaty. The Tibetan leadership that had not fled eventually accepted his demands, agreeing to open new trade marts, to destroy all fortifications between Lhasa and the Indian frontier, to have no dealings with any foreign power without Britain's consent, and to respect the agreements of the 1890s that had hitherto been ignored. The Tibetans also agreed to two articles not included in the terms telegraphed by London. Although the home Government had rejected Ampthill's proposal that an agent stationed at Gyantse should have access to Lhasa, Younghusband discovered that the

Tibetans did not object to the idea and he therefore incorporated it in a separate agreement. As for the indemnity, Brodrick had admitted that the Government's ignorance of Tibet's resources made it impossible to suggest a figure; he merely hoped for a 'substantial' sum to be paid over a period of three years and secured against a British occupation of the Chumbi Valley near the Indian border. When the Commissioner demanded £500,000, the Tibetans first claimed they could not afford the sum but subsequently suggested paying it in seventy-five annual instalments, a remarkable offer that would have given Britain the right to occupy for three-quarters of a century a piece of land regarded by Younghusband as 'the only strategical point of value in the whole north-eastern frontier from Kashmir to Burma'. The Commissioner could not wait the twelve days needed to get a message to Simla and back or the longer period required to receive an opinion from cabinet ministers scattered over the grouse moors and golf courses of Scotland. He had to judge the offer himself, and to a frontier officer it was irresistible. On 7 September in the audience hall of the Potala he signed, together with the representatives of China and Tibet, the convention he had been striving for fourteen months to achieve.[32]

This wholly unexpected outcome, to which the Amban and the Ti Rimproche had contributed a good deal, was naturally welcomed by the British. Ampthill recommended its acceptance, the King sent a laudatory telegram, and Brodrick, telegraphing his hearty congratulations, declared that Younghusband's actions would be supported. Within hours, however, the Secretary of State had changed his mind and decided that the terms were a provocation to Russia and therefore unacceptable. A minister who had hoped to disguise his Government's expected humiliation by extorting a 'substantial indemnity' and sacking parts of Lhasa, was now embarrassed because his representative had secured a favourable treaty and a 'prodigious' indemnity without blowing up a single building. Brodrick, who had refused to give Younghusband any indication of the sum of money he should demand, now suggested that the Commissioner ought to stay in Lhasa to negotiate a reduction of the indemnity in return for trade concessions. Younghusband received the message as he was leaving the capital and ignored it. Had he re-opened negotiations, he told Ampthill, he might have come away without any convention at all, and he would certainly have forfeited Tibetan goodwill. Two weeks later, as he rode to Darjeeling to see his wife and child after a year's absence, he received a telegram from the Secretary of State accusing him of insubordination.[33]

While Brodrick's transformation from admirer of the convention to angry antagonist can partly be ascribed to Russian objections, his vindictiveness towards Younghusband can only be explained by the sudden conviction that his Tibetan policy had been deliberately upset by Curzon. Younghusband, it dawned on him, had been ignoring the Government's instructions in order to carry out the policy of the former Viceroy. But unable to fasten the blame on Curzon, he was determined to make a scapegoat of his protégé. Balfour was converted, a good three weeks after the terms of the convention had become known, to the view that Curzon was culpable and that national honour demanded the public repudiation of Younghusband. The Commissioner's 'indiscretion' – in achieving a settlement so much more favourable than anything the Government had expected – made it impossible, said the Prime Minister, for Britain to clear herself from 'the very unjust imputation of copying the least creditable methods of Russian diplomacy'.[34]

The foreign correspondent of *The Times*, Valentine Chirol, ascribed Brodrick's behaviour to stupidity and jealousy of Curzon, and regarded the 'meanness of the subterfuges' used against Younghusband as 'almost past belief'.[35] The Commissioner was censured, snubbed and awarded the lowest possible decoration, the KCIE. But the Government of India did ratify his convention after attaching a declaration reducing the indemnity by two-thirds and the occupation of the Chumbi Valley to three years. Younghusband, a hero in many people's eyes including the King's, passionately resented his treatment. At Port Said on his way home he met Curzon returning to India and related the whole story. Greatly cheered by the friendship and approval of his former chief, he told Mary that for him or for her he would do anything in the world, but for a whole cabinet of ministers he would not 'feel inclined to stir across the street'.[36] In London he saw the King, who approved of what he had done, and Lansdowne, who was plainly embarrassed by the paltry honour and congratulated him on the expedition. He also had a revealing interview with Brodrick who 'in a kind of galumphing way . . . intended to be cordial' and told Younghusband he was 'the victim of circumstances'. The Secretary of State then managed to give him the impression that his real targets had been Curzon and the Government of India who needed to be shown that they could not behave as they liked.[37]

Relations between Curzon and Brodrick were now almost beyond repair. Curzon had been amused by Edward VII's description of the Secretary of State as 'a most ridiculous personage' about whom he could never think 'without bursting out laughing'.[38] But he himself was no longer moved to laugh at the antics of his old friend. Brodrick declared himself 'hurt and distressed' by the withdrawal of Curzon's friendship,[39] pleaded for a new start and told him he was constantly fighting his battles in the Cabinet and the India Council. Anyone who reads Brodrick's correspondence will marvel at the audacity of the claim, for he was in fact busy misrepresenting Curzon's views to all sorts of people, above all Balfour. The Secretary of State had become obsessed by the idea that the former Viceroy was sabotaging the policy of the Government by trying to run India through his correspondence from home. He regarded it as a great concession to consult Curzon, who had no official capacity in England, on Indian matters instead of considering it a normal way of treating someone who would shortly have to deal with those matters in India.[40] When Curzon complained he had been kept in the dark about various important questions, Brodrick disingenuously replied that he had not wished to worry him during the illness of his wife and his own periods of ill health.

Since Baba's birth Mary had yearned for a baby boy and had told her doctor she wished he could arrange one.[41] She became pregnant again early in the summer but, after moving into Walmer Castle in August, she suffered a miscarriage which was clumsily handled by a second doctor. According to Mary, his failure to remove some of the afterbirth for two days led to an abscess causing peritonitis subsequently exacerbated by phlebitis. She may also have been infected by a poorly repaired drain underneath her bedroom window.

The illness flared up on the night of 20 September, three days before they had planned to return to India, and the following day she seemed to be dying. On the 22nd her husband began to keep notes of every-thing she said while lying on what both believed to be her deathbed. Emerging from a series of comas, she gave him instructions about what to do with the children, what presents she wished to leave her friends and how she wanted to be buried in the vault at Kedleston instead of in the ground. At times when she thought she was close to death she asked him to say the Lord's Prayer, Tennyson's 'Crossing the Bar' or their favourite psalm, 'Lord who shall dwell in thy tabernacle: or who shall rest upon thy holy hill?' He read them through a mist of tears. In the late afternoon she said goodbye to the children but later revived with brandy, milk and hypodermic injections of strychnine. Yet the doctor said there was no hope because she could not survive the anaesthetic for the necessary operation.

Against the odds Mary's condition improved sufficiently for an operation to be performed on the 24th, but three days later perforation of the intestines was discovered. Believing recovery was impossible, she summoned her husband and asked him not to read 'Crossing the Bar' because she did not want to go. Later she became more composed and said it was no good fighting any longer. She told George he should return to India to complete his work but that he must leave the children behind with her mother. Then she sent again for the girls to bid them goodbye and thanked the doctors and nurses.

> I asked whether in another world, if there was one, she would wait for me till I could come. Yes, she said, I will wait. When I said that we had loved each other long and been all in all to each other, she asked that that might be inscribed on her tomb. She asked that we might be buried side by side with a marble effigy of each of us looking towards each other, so that we might one day be reunited . . . She said our love letters have been wonderful and who that read them could doubt that ours had been a wonderful love. We talked of our marriage day, and of her look at me and mine at her as we stood side by side on the steps of the altar and the lovelights shone in her eyes.[42]

Later the doctors returned and encouraged her to keep fighting. She did. For twenty-five days she came and nearly went until pneumonia was overcome in the middle of October, and her recovery became consistent. She had been five times given up, Curzon told a friend, but her tenacity and resilience had brought her through. 'I am convinced', he said, 'that no man could have survived.' The local post office stayed open during the nights to receive anxious messages from India, America and many parts of Britain. Every Indian prince telegraphed. Lord Scarsdale wrote of the great sympathy in Derby and sent two brace of partridges with an apology that they were 'Frenchmen' and not the tastier English variety.

As soon as she was strong enough, Mary was moved from Walmer Castle to the villa nearby where they had stayed earlier. Curzon said that nothing would induce him to spend another night in that 'charnel house', and the King later agreed that it was uninhabitable. As residence at Walmer had been a condition of the lord wardenship, he resigned his office but characteristically remained interested in the castle's history and for many years afterwards collected material for a projected book.*

---

* *Walmer Castle and its Lords Warden* was published two years after his death. Most of the early sections are as he wrote them, but the last part was compiled from his notes by the editor, Stephen Gwynn.

In November, barely a month from the beginning of Mary's recovery, her husband returned alone to India. After failing to find a locket with 'Buck Up' inscribed in diamonds as a parting gift, he went to Charing Cross and, as he admitted, 'broke down rather disgracefully' in front of a large crowd. It was with 'a sad and miserable heart' that he went, leaving all that made life worth living behind him and 'going out to toil and isolation and often worse'. In the train and at sea he repeatedly contrasted his melancholy situation with the optimistic journey they had undertaken together six years earlier. 'Then all was health and high hopes,' he reflected, ' now there is little but duty and great sadness.' He thought of her all the time, he said, of her love, her courage, 'her combat with all the foes of evil and death'. But one consolation, he added, was that they had been drawn very close in this 'furnace of affliction', and he hoped to become less selfish and more considerate in future.[43]

Profound though it was, Curzon's unhappiness was exceeded by his wife's. Her letters from Highcliffe, a Hampshire house they rented for her convalescence, are desperate, heart-rending and hardly rational, evidence both of an all-consuming love – 'it is terrible to love as I do you' – and of extreme generosity of character, for she did not reproach her husband for his extraordinary decision to leave her. She wrote of her efforts to be brave and her inability to control herself: her 'pent up sobbing burst forth and shook the house', and she had to be put to sleep with drugs. Once she tried to kiss his photograph but she did not have the strength to get out of bed to reach it. 'The light of the world has gone out,' she wrote and wondered, without self-pity, if she could live through the winter by herself.[44] Looking at the broken handwriting distorted by love and despair and sickness, it is hard to understand how anyone could have read those letters without returning home.

Nothing but a feeling of obligation persuaded Curzon to go back to India. Every other argument was in favour of him staying: personal health and happiness, consideration for his wife, the interests of his career, the certainty of disputes with the home Government and Kitchener. Only the sense of mission, the need to complete his task and settle outstanding questions, drove him on. He called it destiny, a convenient and not unreasonable euphemism for the actions of stubborn people who insist on doing what they believe to be their duty.

At an official banquet following the landing at Bombay, his friend Lord Lamington proposed his health in 'such charming terms and with such apposite and touching references' to Mary that, as Curzon recounted, he 'broke down most discreditably' in his reply. Describing the incident to his wife, he explained that he had been

> stretched nearly to breaking point, and any reference to you destroys my balance at once. I also feel so keenly the shameful way in which I have been treated by the native press and by so many of the Europeans in this country, and now my coming back to this rack of duty all alone with you still ill at home, excites such poignant contrasts and emotions in my mind that I feel at times quite unhinged, and it will be some time before I recover complete command.[45]

According to Lamington's account of this 'most touching scene', his guest managed to recover his self-control and went on to talk passionately about his devotion to his work in India.[46]

Anxious to avoid a repetition in Calcutta, Curzon implored Ampthill not to talk much about Mary's illness at the large banquet the Acting Viceroy had organized for his arrival. 'He looked sad, worn and sombre,' Ampthill reported to Brodrick, 'and shook hands with everybody with the air of a dying man.' At the slightest allusion to his wife, he broke down at once. Ampthill had been apprehensive at the thought of spending twenty-four hours with Curzon before handing over his office, but in the event there was no problem. The returning proconsul 'could not have been more considerate and deferential,' Brodrick was informed, if he had been a newcomer and Ampthill the Viceroy with five years' experience.[47]

20

Kitchener's Conspiracy

———◆———

ON THE EVE of his departure for England in April 1904, Curzon had received yet another note from Lord Kitchener advocating a reduction in the powers of the Military Department. As the document contained proposals similar to those put forward the year before, and as he thought the issue would not be raised in his absence, Curzon paid little attention to the note. A month after his arrival in England, however, he was amazed to find that it had been circulated to the Imperial Defence Committee. Protesting to Balfour, he pointed out that proposals for constitutional change should not bypass the Secretary of State and the Government of India, and that in any case the internal administration of the country was not a matter in which the Imperial Defence Committee had any business to interfere. The Prime Minister agreed with him, and the note was not discussed. Curzon heard no more of Kitchener's views until August.

The incident should have shown him that the Commander-in-Chief was prepared to go beyond constitutional limits to gain his objectives. But, straightforward himself, Curzon was strangely naïve about the deviousness of others. Although frequently presented with evidence that Kitchener was an incorrigible intriguer, both he and Mary either failed to take it seriously or else believed he was directing his energies at other targets. Yet Kitchener's appetite for plotting was such that he even exhorted his victims to spy on his behalf. Before she left for England in January 1904, he thanked Mary for the unfailing kindness she had shown him in India and gave her a turquoise he had acquired at Mount

Sinai. As soon as she had gone, he pursued her with letters disparaging Brodrick ('I wish you would tell him to shut up and let us do what we can out here') and asking her to intrigue on his behalf. His request at the end of January for her to write 'with the utmost indiscretion as you know it goes no further' must have had some success because seven weeks later he expressed the hope that she would *continue* to write indiscreetly about what was going on.[1] The ingenuous Vicereine was entirely deceived and believed they were the closest of friends; when she thought she was dying at Walmer a few months later, Mary asked her husband to give Kitchener a parting present. She had no inkling that he was simultaneously disparaging them to other people and blaming them for the break-up of Marker's romance.

Curzon had no idea how Kitchener's note had reached the Imperial Defence Committee and made little effort to find out. In fact it had been provided by Colonel Herbert Mullaly, a member of the C-in-C's staff who had been sent to London to represent his superior on the committee, where he worked hard to convince people, including its chairman, Sir George Clarke, of the iniquities of the Military Department. A more vital agent in Kitchener's network was Marker himself who had brought his broken heart and his grievance back to England and now operated from the private office of the Secretary of State for War. His new posting was 'a godsend', Kitchener told him, and 'just in time to be of use to me'. As the C-in-C explained to Lady Salisbury (formerly Lady Cranborne), Marker was in the perfect position to pass on confidential information through private coded telegrams. Although Kitchener and his staff believed this route to be secure, they later became nervous and in July 1905 sent him a safer Indian Army 'Y' cypher which no one else possessed. The precautions were in fact too late and, if they had been dealing with a less honourable man than Curzon, they would have been exposed. 'A native gentleman of good position', the Viceroy later recalled, had offered him copies of Kitchener's cypher telegrams to the War Office, but he had been too high-minded to look at them. Had he perused their contents, it is unlikely that Lady Salisbury would have been such a regular and welcome guest at his house over the next twenty years. More importantly, he would have realized what was happening while there was still time to do something about it.[2]

Marker's unofficial duties ranged from the rapid dissemination of material to influential people to the more subtle handling of a propaganda campaign. At moments of crisis Kitchener telegraphed, ordering him to mobilize supporters such as Lady Salisbury or General Stedman, the Military Secretary at the India Office, so that they might intercede on his behalf.[3] At less urgent times Marker received instructions by letter, often written by Colonel Hubert Hamilton, Kitchener's Military Secretary, who relieved his chief of much of the tedium of using a pen. In October 1904 Hamilton told him to be prepared to enlist the press on their side. It might not be necessary, he thought, because the Government probably realized it 'would lose more votes by K's resignation than over all their other bungling put together', but it was as well to be ready.[4] By the beginning of 1905, however, Kitchener's team had decided not to take any chances but to begin educating the public through the press. H.A. Gwynne, the editor of the *Standard*, was duly enlisted, and so was Colonel A'Court Repington, the military correspondent of *The Times*.

A clever and unscrupulous character who had been on Kitchener's staff in Egypt, Repington had been forced to leave the army after a scandal involving a brother officer's wife. Curzon later believed he had campaigned for Kitchener in an effort to be reinstated. Whatever the truth of the theory, Repington proved to be an enthusiastic conspirator, proposing as early as August 1904 that he should go to India 'ostensibly for manoeuvres' but in reality to write a series of articles for *The Times* 'setting out the present situation from K's point of view . . .' Although the journey itself did not take place, he still sent an article on the subject to Marker for his comments and boasted with justification that he had persuaded G.E. Buckle, the editor of his paper, to back Kitchener. He also told Marker to arrange for a series of supporting letters to appear in the papers after his articles had been published. 'You can manufacture a public opinion if you go the right way to work.' The most revealing thing about Repington's correspondence, one which suggests Curzon's explanation of his conduct may have been on the right lines, is that it shows he did not really believe in Kitchener's case. In words that could have been employed by someone on the other side, he warned Marker of the need to explain to the public why 'we desire concentration of power in the hands of the c-in-c in India and the reverse at home', declared that the 'weak point in Lord K's armour' was the question of who would run the army if he took the field, and frankly doubted whether any successor could carry out the combined duties of Military Member and Commander-in-Chief.[5]

No such doubts disturbed Kitchener's most ardent and influential agent. To Lady Salisbury the grizzled soldier was a hero who could do no wrong. She sent him an inkstand, a carriage clock and other presents as well as regular letters of admiration; he replied with animal skins, X-ray photographs of his broken leg, and warnings of disaster if the Indian Army had to fight Russia under its present system of administration. The several drafts of her letters reveal a woman revelling in the delights of boudoir conspiracy, eagerly discussing recondite matters of military organization and exhorting her fellow plotters to burn their incriminating letters. They are gushing and rather skittish, addressed to 'my dear Sirdar'* and telling him how wonderfully he had done and how excellent and admirable his arguments were. She shared vicariously his hopes and disappointments, communicating her 'overwhelming regret' on hearing of the extension of Curzon's viceroyalty and agreeing it was 'very very despairing' for Kitchener's plans to be thus thwarted. She accepted no criticism of the Sirdar. Even Balfour, himself a partisan of Kitchener, found her so biased that he committed 'a breach of all propriety' by sending her a private letter from Ampthill to Brodrick with evidence of the C-in-C's ignorance and carelessness of details. Lady Salisbury bridled furiously at the suggestion and declared that she was neither convinced nor converted by Ampthill's evidence.[6]

Kitchener's correspondence at Hatfield contains only one line of argument reiterated over and over again: that the Russian danger was increasing, that the system of army administration in India was 'effete' and 'a source of the utmost danger if we went to war', and that he was determined to resign if it was not altered. It is difficult to understand why he was taken seriously when he declared, for example, that the Military Department 'do not believe in being ready and think that time-wasting is really what they are paid for'.[7] But that credulity which blinded the British public until long after his death now afflicted figures as intelligent as Balfour, Godley and Esher.

Kitchener's letters to Alice Salisbury, which were passed on to Balfour, were supplemented by those of his adoring staff. 'The family circle' of officers such as 'Hammy' Hamilton, 'Brat' Maxwell, 'Conk' Marker and 'Birdie' Birdwood, merely parroted their chief's message. Lady Salisbury entered into correspondence with the first three of them and duly received testimonies of her hero's genius and warnings of his impending resignation. 'It is painful', observed Hamilton, 'to watch this genius perched on the Himalayas like a caged tiger while less able minds' were trying to solve the army question.[8] The staff's views

---

*Kitchener's title as Commander-in-Chief of the Egyptian army.

were invariably the same as their chief's, and sometimes 'the Boys' simply copied his expressions. Hamilton's silly claim that Curzon's motto was 'Perish the empire sooner than that [he] should be thought in the wrong' was merely a badly worded variation of Kitchener's favourite slander.[9]

The Kitchener-Balfour axis that pivoted on Lady Salisbury was the most important but not the only lever for the Commander-in-Chief's intrigues. Another fulcrum was General Stedman at the India Office who passed on Kitchener's private communications to Brodrick and arranged for the C-in-C to telegraph him by secret code. Stedman reported that the chief's messages 'have had very great effect in pushing business on', but he realized they were highly dangerous and should be burnt afterwards.[10] Although the direct approach appealed to him less, Kitchener did not neglect it: he therefore personally sent his case to Clarke at the Imperial Defence Committee and even to Brodrick, who admitted that their correspondence would be unconstitutional but decided to 'break the rule for once on the principle that "when the cat's away the mice will play"'.*[11]

Another correspondent was Lord Roberts who was kept regularly informed of the situation and of Kitchener's intention of resigning his post and leaving the army altogether rather than go to the War Office or 'become one of the old officers in London clubs'.[12] He was also told that the Military Member was 'almost de facto and certainly de jure c-in-c', an assertion that Roberts, who had had far more experience of the system than Kitchener, knew to be untrue. The elderly Field Marshal was finally badgered, however, into agreeing to a note drafted by Kitchener's acolyte Mullaly recommending an increase in the powers of the C-in-C by giving him control of supply and transport. When Kitchener took this to mean that he favoured the abolition of the Military Member, Roberts apologized for having given that impression because in fact he considered it vital to retain the post: firstly, he declared, nobody could satisfactorily carry out the duties of both officials, and secondly, the Government of India needed – particularly when the C-in-C had no experience of the Subcontinent – the advice of an official with an intimate knowledge of India and its army. Annoyed by Roberts's attitude, Kitchener told him the army had changed since his day and tried to recruit another former C-in-C, Sir George White, to use his influence with the victor of Kandahar. After it transpired that White

---

*Brodrick wrote this when Curzon was on his way back to England.

1. Lady Scarsdale

2. Lord Scarsdale

3. Kedleston Hall

4. George Nathaniel at the age of 6

5. The competitive schoolboy, aged 12, in his last year at Wixenford

Oscar Browning (in retirement),
who regarded Curzon as 'one of the
most brilliantly gifted boys' of his
generation

7. Benjamin Jowett, creator of the
Balliol mystique, who warned his pupil
of the dangers of verbosity

8. Oxford insouciance: Curzon (*left*) and William Palmer (later Viscount Wolmer, later still Earl of Selborne)

9. Straight bats: Alfred and Edward Lyttelton

o. Curzon's 'Blessed Damozel': Sibell Grosvenor painted by Edward Clifford in 1887

11. 'A divinity addressing black beetles': Curzon as Under-Secretary portrayed by 'Spy' in 1892

12. Curzon soon after his appointment as Viceroy in 1898

13. Family group at Kedleston after Curzon's wedding. Behind the married couple are (*left to right*), Geraldine, Frank, Margaret, Lillian Okeover (who married Assheton), Lord Scarsdale, Assheton, Sophy, Elinor, Sir James Miller, Evie (married to Miller), and Affie. All Curzon's brothers and sisters are present except Blanche.

14. Curzon with his daughters, Irene (*left*) and Cynthia (Cimmie)

15. Government House, Calcutta

16. Viceregal tour of the ruins of the Lucknow Residency

17. The Vicereine at the Durbar: Mary in her celebrated Peacock dress

18. The Viceroy's family and staff at Simla, 1899. Behind Curzon stands Walter Lawrence between Captain Baker Carr (*left*) and Colonel Sandbach. Captain Wigram is standing wearing a pale waistcoat on the left. Seated at the far right is Daisy Leiter with Captain Marker (whom she jilted) at her feet and Lord Suffolk (whom she married) sitting cross-legged in front of Wigram

19. The Curzons' visit to Hyderabad, 1902. The Nizam is sandwiched between his guests.

20. St John Brodrick (later Lord Midleton),
Secretary of State for India, 1903–5

21. Lord George Hamilton, Secretary of
State for India, 1895–1903

22. Lord Ampthill, Governor of Madras,
1900–6, Acting Viceroy, 1904

23. Earl of Minto, Viceroy, 1905–10

24. Lord Kitchener, Commander-in-Chief
in India, 1902–9

25. John Morley, Secretary of State for
India, 1905–10

26. Tiger shooting at Hyderabad, 1902

27. Tennis at Hackwood

28. Lord Lansdowne (*right*) with Curzon, who followed in his footsteps from Eton and Balliol to the Indian viceroyalty, the Foreign Office and the chairmanship of the trustees of the National Gallery

29. Elinor Glyn in mourning at
Montacute

30. Grace Curzon in her boudoir at Hackwood

31. Curzon making a speech at Tattershall in 1912. On the right is Mr Weir, the architect who helped him restore the castle

32. Lord Cromer

33. Lord Milner

34. Lord Curzon as Foreign Secretary

35. Lord Salisbury

36. Arthur Balfour

37. H. H. Asquith

38. David Lloyd George   39. Andrew Bonar Law

40. Stanley Baldwin at the Imperial Conference, 1923:
(*left to right*), Curzon, Mackenzie King (Canada), Baldwin
and Bruce (Australia)

41. Premature old age: Lord Curzon at the age of 66, a few weeks before his death

also had doubts about the abolition of the post, Kitchener's Adjutant-General, Sir Beauchamp Duff, sent him a thoroughly tendentious letter about 'the full tyranny' of the Military Department which under Elles had become 'even more completely masters of the situation'.[13]

While it is difficult to judge how far the correspondence between Kitchener and Lady Salisbury influenced the Prime Minister, its effect appears to have been considerable. Balfour was highly intelligent and a man of independent mind, but he was also an armchair strategist who combined a reputation for military thinking with a rather meagre knowledge of military matters. Enraptured by great ideas, he was bored by the details needed to put them into practice and in this case simply thought 'the Hercules of the Himalayas' should be allowed to exercise his genius unencumbered by the red tape of the Military Department. By 1901 he had discovered – as Curzon could have told him a dozen years earlier – that the most vulnerable point of the entire British empire was the north-west frontier of India.[14] Shortly after this revelation he began to receive Lady Salisbury's enclosures warning that the Indian army faced disaster on that frontier unless its organization was changed in accordance with the scheme devised by the empire's principal war hero. The Prime Minister's conversion to Kitchener's point of view was soon complete. By the end of 1903 he had decided that the existing system was indefensible and in October of the following year he could assure Lady Salisbury that he was 'entirely' with Kitchener. He greatly regretted, moreover, that he had not made a renewal of Curzon's viceroyalty conditional on his making a genuine attempt to reform the system.[15] The returning Viceroy would take no action on the matter, he thought, because he disliked carrying out reforms he had not thought up himself. It did not occur to Balfour that Curzon might reject this one because he had studied the system and concluded that it was not in need of reform.

According to Lord Esher's indiscreet correspondence with his son, the Prime Minister was hoping as early as June that Curzon would not return to India and had already secured Selborne's agreement to succeed him.[16] Balfour's differences with his old friend over Tibet and Afghanistan no doubt contributed to this desire, but the motivating factor was his determination to prevent Kitchener's resignation. At the beginning of August Curzon was summoned to the Prime Minister's room in the House of Commons where Balfour and Brodrick, backed by Godley, urged the abolition of the Military Department and asked him to set up a commission to propose a new scheme of administration.

Curzon refused and suggested his successor should be invited to undertake the task. Supported on the whole by Roberts, he said he was not aware of any general dissatisfaction with the existing system in India, that he did not know when or where it had broken down, and that he saw no reason to destroy it simply to please Lord Kitchener. The result of the meeting, he predicted complacently to Ampthill, was that nothing would be done.[17]

The Commander-in-Chief in India was meanwhile engaged in a slicing operation designed to emasculate the Military Department by removing its control of supply and transport. To Elles and Ampthill this was a transparent prelude to the destruction of the department altogether, but when the Military Member put his doubts on record, Kitchener responded with a warning of 'the nemesis of fate' that 'assuredly' awaited him unless these 'illogical excrescences' were lopped off.[18] Brodrick was delighted by the opportunity of pleasing Kitchener while Curzon was away, Roberts, who really thought the excrescences should stay where they were, was persuaded to change his mind, and Curzon himself conceded that if the alteration was made in his absence he would not reverse it on his return.[19] Under heavy pressure from Brodrick, Ampthill then reluctantly agreed to do the lopping. Nevertheless, he told the Secretary of State it was a retrograde move and said he could see no reason for accepting Kitchener's 'system of combining executive and administrative functions under one head, a system which no longer exists in any other army in the world, which India abolished fifty years ago and which has at last been finally and emphatically condemned in England'.[20]

The Acting Viceroy was altogether disappointed by the behaviour of his Commander-in-Chief. Not knowing Kitchener beforehand, he had assumed him to be 'far too loyal to think of taking advantage of Lord Curzon's absence', and was shocked to discover his deviousness. It was 'indisputably wrong', he told the Secretary of State, to propose a great constitutional change behind Curzon's back, and he invited Brodrick to imagine what would happen if the Financial Member made proposals to the Chancellor of the Exchequer without the knowledge of his colleagues and the India Office.[21] Ampthill was also disillusioned by 'the perfunctory character' of Kitchener's work, for he was 'ignorant and careless of details', and his staff were far from thorough.[22] As an example of 'the difficulties of working with the great Kitchener of Khartoum', Ampthill sent Brodrick a description of a Council meeting at which the C-in-C had behaved like 'a great spoilt schoolboy'. When

Kitchener complained it was 'perfectly monstrous' for the Military Department to take so long to deal with a matter of vital importance, Elles answered that it could not act until it had received the C-in-C's opinion of certain documents he had been sent; thereupon Kitchener blustered that he agreed with their contents, that it was 'red-tape' to insist on written assent and that he had not received the documents anyway; it immediately transpired, however, that they had been sitting in his office for six weeks.[23] A few days later, reported Ampthill, Kitchener insisted that the creation of racially homogeneous brigades was vital to his scheme of military reorganization; yet in Council he was 'not able to argue the case at all' or remember why the step, which was likely to cause resentment among Indians, was so vital. Although Kitchener wanted to be 'invested with papal infallibility' on army matters, it was clear to Ampthill that he was quite ignorant of his own scheme.[24]

During that same week in September 1904 Kitchener tried to regain the initiative by sending in his resignation. After ordering disciplinary action against a junior officer of the Nilgiri Volunteers, he had been asked by the Indian Government to cancel it because it was *ultra vires* under the existing regulations. Claiming that this request had impaired his authority with the army, he promptly informed the War Office that he had placed his resignation in the hands of the Viceroy and wished to retire from the army. Ampthill was furious that Kitchener should attempt to resign for a reason so 'paltry and contemptible' and indignant that he should have done so on the day that the postponement of Curzon's return had been announced and when he himself had just set off for his first free weekend since April. In a combative reply he asked the C-in-C whether it was dignified and worthy of his reputation to resign over a petty matter concerning a volunteer adjutant and declined to accept his resignation on such grounds. Realizing that the punishment of Captain Swan was perhaps an inadequate excuse, Kitchener then told the Acting Viceroy that the real problem was the power of the Military Department which made his position 'impossible'. Ampthill, whose weekend in camp was by now irrevocably ruined, responded by pointing out that no problem between the department and Army Headquarters had materialized during the months of his viceroyalty and that on the one substantial issue that had arisen – the control of supply and transport – the Military Member had yielded to his wishes. Kitchener was also reminded that during their discussions on that matter he had expressly disclaimed any desire to reduce the remaining powers of the Military Department. At a long and tiresome interview two days later, Ampthill tried to persuade his colleague to withdraw his resignation. To begin with, Kitchener argued that such a course would be 'puerile' without appearing to recognize that the adjective might more appropriately have been applied to his earlier conduct. When eventually he withdrew his immediate threat, he expressed the hope that the Government would allow him to retire later if nothing was done to improve the situation.[25]

This ludicrous incident turned out to be a victory for Kitchener because it convinced the British Government that it must work fast to avert another attempted resignation. The Commander-in-Chief's behaviour had not impressed his supporters. Godley admitted there was 'little or nothing to be said' for his methods, while Balfour could see he was trying to 'force everyone's hand by an absurd resignation'.[26] Yet instead of calling Kitchener's bluff, they reacted by trying to accommodate his demands. Their sense of urgency was heightened in late October when Britain nearly found herself at war after a bizarre incident in the North Sea when the Russian Baltic Fleet, on its ill-fated voyage to the Far East to engage the Japanese navy, mistook some English trawlers for Japanese torpedo-boats and opened fire. Brodrick and Balfour increased the pressure on Curzon, the Secretary of State warning him a few days later that Kitchener's resignation, which had been only provisionally withdrawn, 'would be regarded more anxiously at this moment than any other', and that the Prime Minister judged the position serious enough to be considered by the Cabinet.[27] From Walmer, where Mary was still very weak, Curzon replied with a long note restating his views on the matter, pointing out that no one could combine the executive and administrative functions of such a large army, that the Military Member was a crucial source of advice for the Viceroy, and that in the six years since he had set out for India calls for change had come from only one quarter. A day later he told Balfour that, if it would be easier to carry out the Government's wishes with a new Viceroy, he would resign. The Prime Minister, who had been longing for this to happen for at least five months, felt unable to accept an offer so unenthusiastically made.[28]

Balfour's case concentrated less on the merits of the proposed change than on the threats variously posed to his Government by Russia, Kitchener and the British public. No one could deny, he said, that the extension of her railways to the Afghan border made Russia a more serious menace to India than ever before. To meet it, Britain had sent out her most renowned active soldier who had declared the 'dual system' to be unworkable and who would certainly resign if it was not modified. As 'the vast weight of opinion' in the country would support Kitchener if he resigned, it was essential, he argued, not to let the subject drift but to 'make up our minds to modify, or, at all events, thoroughly to re-examine' the relations between the Military Member and the Commander-in-Chief.[29]

On 9 November Curzon saw Balfour for the last time before returning to India. The Prime Minister, according to his own account, gladly accepted the suggestion that his Government should send a despatch asking India to examine the issue, even though Curzon warned that no member of his Council would take Kitchener's side. Sketching the procedure for Brodrick's benefit, Balfour said that if the home Government was dissatisfied with India's reply, it could then appoint a commission of investigation to judge the matter. He believed his plan could not be much bettered, because it would be 'impossible for us from here to make a revolutionary change in the Indian government against its wishes and without consulting it; and even after consulting it we could not force our views upon it without making independent enquiry'.[30]

Curzon returned to India with an advance copy of the despatch which he immediately sent to Kitchener for his opinions. While the C-in-C was still formulating them, the Viceroy received a telegram from Brodrick urging him to hurry the matter on because Kitchener was apparently becoming very restless. This and subsequent communications surprised Curzon who had been assured by Kitchener that he saw no reason for great haste and was content for the ordinary official procedure to be followed; it still had not occurred to Curzon that the Commander-in-Chief might write in one sense to the Viceroy and in quite an opposite one to his allies in England. By the New Year Brodrick had decided that the matter should be dealt with by a commission headed by Lord George Hamilton. On 12 January he therefore urged Curzon to forward his Government's reply as soon as possible so that the commission's members could be appointed and sent out to India. Although he was pleased that Hamilton had been chosen, the Viceroy unwisely insisted on pointing out the constitutional problems raised by Brodrick's procedure. How could the Government of India, he asked, request an inquiry when only one of its members had had a chance to examine the despatch and write an answer? Brodrick then suggested that Curzon should telegraph him privately if, as was expected, Elles's minute disagreed with Kitchener's. The Viceroy again said it would be unconstitutional for him to do so before his other colleagues had considered the matter, and asked why the home

Government did not send out a commission on its own responsibility. Before this fruitless exchange could go any further, the scheme collapsed. Hamilton had been prepared to go and had already bought his tropical clothes. But on realizing that – if Curzon's timetable was followed – he would not arrive until March, when the Calcutta heat would be dangerous for his wife, he changed his mind. Of course, he could still have been sent out in the autumn. But Balfour and Brodrick were not prepared to spend the summer waiting for Kitchener's next resignation, and the idea of a commission was scrapped.[31]

If Curzon's return had not been delayed by Mary's illness, the whole matter would have been settled during the cold weather. The delay of two months made Brodrick's scheme impracticable – for the commission could have achieved little in a sweltering fortnight when all the departments were busy with the budget – unless Curzon was prepared to break the procedure. Had he been a better politician and a less obstinate constitutionalist, he would have done so instead of telling Brodrick it was an 'indefensible step' to send out a commission 'to investigate, and possibly revolutionise, our constitution simply upon a threat of resignation put forward by the c-in-c in a fit of which you know to be personal temper and for a cause which was absolutely childish'. Yet a three-man commission which included, as the Secretary of State had intended, both Hamilton and Roberts, could not have failed to support Curzon's position and would have been authoritative enough to reduce the impact of Kitchener's resignation. The Commander-in-Chief was in no doubt that such a commission would have been disastrous for himself. On learning that it was being contemplated, he had frantically telegraphed London to urge Stedman and Lady Salisbury to arrange for three of his supporters to conduct the inquiry. When the news came that it had been abandoned, he was vastly relieved. 'As long as I am backed at home,' he reflected to Marker, 'I have no fear of the ultimate result.'[32]

It is difficult to be charitable about Kitchener's personal behaviour during this period. Neither his attempted resignation in September nor the death of Lady Elles* the following month had deflected his vendetta

---

*Lady Elles was one of the most remarkable Englishwomen in India. Gentle, charitable and compassionate, her death achieved the almost impossible feat of subduing Simla. '"She was a saint," said men who had never spoken to [Mrs Wilson] about "saints" before, but who were as white and drawn as if she had been "their own mother" too . . . Women who never showed anything but smiles to the world were silently weeping now; and when talkative Simla returned to the Mall, not a voice broke the silence of the long drive to our homes.'[33]

against the Military Member, and on his return Curzon found him 'pursuing [it] with relentless animosity – sticking at absolutely nothing' and losing 'no opportunity of showing his personal antagonism and spite'.[34] To the Viceroy Kitchener remained affable, inviting him to look at the improvements he had made to his house, offering to drive or talk with him whenever he wanted, and accompanying him on an excursion to the battlefield of Plassey which Curzon intended to commemorate. But emollition to his face was matched by continuous misrepresentation behind his back. Kitchener spread it about that Curzon supported the Military Department because its abolition would reduce his powers of interference in military matters. 'Perish the Empire sooner than any such sacrilege is his motto', the C-in-C was fond of declaring.[35] Such childish assertions were unlikely to impress any but his most narrow-minded supporters. As Lord Milner told Dawkins, 'the whole world would not persuade me that George Curzon would oppose or omit anything in the interest of the army and of the military organisation in India.'[36]

In the New Year the Commander-in-Chief asked the leading generals of India if they agreed with his views on 'dual control'.* As they depended on him for their future careers, it was not surprising that obsequious messages of support for Kitchener's position came rolling in. It was later suggested, however, that some of these had been sent under compulsion, and even Repington admitted that such had been the case with General Gaselee.[37] On learning of the survey, Curzon told Kitchener that the issue of the Military Department was a constitutional question which had nothing to do with the generals; outside authorities, he added, should not in any case be consulted except by permission of the Government of India. In his reply the C-in-C admitted the force of Curzon's reasoning, promised to confer with him in future before acting, and claimed he had wanted the generals' opinions in order to convince Lord Roberts that the Military Department should be abolished. The Viceroy answered that it was unconstitutional to use the generals to influence Roberts to put pressure on the home Government to back Kitchener, and asked to see their opinions when they had been received. Alarmed by the request, the C-in-C then contradicted what he had written twenty-four hours earlier and declared that they had been collected not for Roberts but for his own use and

---

*He did not ask General Sir Edmund Barrow, the commander of the Peshawar Division, or of course Elles, both of whom would have disagreed with him.

were not intended for anyone else.[38] In fact he had already despatched them to Lady Salisbury and thus set them on an odyssey during which they disembarked in due course at the India Office, Downing Street, the Imperial Defence Committee and the offices of *The Times*.

Kitchener complained to Hatfield about Curzon's 'rather nasty letters' on the subject and said the Viceroy should have been a lawyer for he was 'a past master at turning things into unpleasant meanings'.[39] He was very anxious that this particular intrigue, about which he had lied so brazenly to Curzon, should not be discovered, and he begged Lady Salisbury to ensure secrecy, especially with the tactless Brodrick. A similar anxiety guided the destination of his minute replying to the despatch on the Military Department, which should have been sent to London with the rest of the Indian Government's reply in March. In fact it was sent by itself to Lady Salisbury at the beginning of January with instructions to show it to the Prime Minister, who found it unanswerable, and anyone else she thought suitable except Brodrick. Proud of the composition, which he thought would give the Military Department the '*coup de grâce*', he also arranged for it to be shown to H.A. Gwynne, the editor of the *Standard*.[40]

The document, which was ably drafted, contained Kitchener's familiar complaints about the alleged omnipotence, interference and dilatory behaviour of the Military Department. Elles's reply was less well framed but successfully countered many of Kitchener's mistatements. The Viceroy then drafted his own rather mild note in which he listed various measures his Government had taken to strengthen the position of the Commander-in-Chief, and tried to correct a misconception of Kitchener's – evidently shared by ministers at home – by pointing out that the Military Member did not criticize the C-in-C's proposals as an independent military authority but as the constitutional representative of the Government of India. The matter then went to Ibbetson and the other members of the Council who all opposed the C-in-C's scheme. Kitchener was dismissive of their behaviour, telling Birdwood they had followed Curzon like sheep because they wanted lieutenant-governorships; he did not admit that the generals might have followed him because they too aspired to higher commands.[41]

On 10 March 1905 the Council met to discuss the question before sending its reply to England. Kitchener briefly expressed his regret that all his colleagues disagreed with him and said he did not want to discuss the matter further. Elles felt, however, that he had been so criticized in the C-in-C's minute that he wanted to know if the other members, who supported the constitutional position of the Military Department, also supported him personally against Kitchener's accusations. They emphatically did so, beginning with Curzon who told Brodrick it must have been a painful moment for Kitchener

> who was practically told to his face that he had hurled a number of reckless and unsupported charges against a colleague which he had wholly failed to sustain, and who learned, not only that he had failed to convince the minds of his colleagues, but that he had not attracted even one ray of sympathy.[42]

In rather less adult language Kitchener told Lady Salisbury how Curzon had made

> a somewhat impassioned speech describing Elles as a poor abused angel and poor me in very dark colours as unwarrantably attacking the immaculate creature. He was so eloquent that he made us all see a sort of halo appear around Elles's head through which his few remaining hairs protruded. The viceroy was in his best parliamentary form and rallied his speechless council to support their much abused colleague.[43]

That evening Curzon drafted a tactful despatch which his colleagues wished had been less restrained. Kitchener appreciated the consideration with which it was framed and admitted he took no exception to the language.[44] The usual practice for dissenting members was to sign the despatch and append a minute of dissent. The C-in-C's minute contained two statements, however, which Curzon thought so unjust and exaggerated that unless modified they would provoke a further reply from the Council. Kitchener therefore withdrew them, leaving a brief statement in which he claimed, astonishingly, that his facts had been disputed but without success, his assertions contradicted but not disproved, and that his arguments remained uncontroverted because they were incontrovertible.

Referring to this statement a few months later in the House of Lords, the former Viceroy Lord Ripon said that a man who makes that sort of declaration in that kind of tone 'does so because he cannot reply, because he has no answer to what his opponent has said'.[45] That may be a good general rule, but in this case it was not true. Kitchener had in fact already drafted – or overseen the drafting of – an immense reply which he decided, characteristically, to distribute behind the Viceroy's back, presumably to avoid its refutation, to his influential supporters in England. Two days before the humiliating Council meeting, he had sent a typed letter of forty pages to General Stedman at the India Office in which he once again claimed that the Military Member was 'the supreme authority in military matters' and the C-in-C his subordinate, and included, for the benefit of those who had not already seen them, the opinions of the generals. Although it was a private letter, Kitchener told Stedman he hoped Brodrick would use some of its points 'so as to ensure the cabinet not coming to a decision without a correct appreciation of the case from all points of view'.[46]

The letter was more successful than Kitchener could possibly have hoped. Brodrick had it printed and circulated to the committee he had set up to investigate the question in London. One copy was naturally sent to Lady Salisbury, and another to Sir George Clarke who showed it to Lord Esher who in turn passed it on to the Prime Minister. Esher was so struck by the document that he pressed Balfour to 'bring the full force of his personality to bear upon the right side'. A.J.B. may not have needed much pressing because, as Clarke was able to assure Kitchener, he read every word of the letter himself and was 'very much impressed'. Kitchener's timing had been excellent. By writing home before the Government of India had sent its despatch, he was able to convince people of his case before they had even seen the arguments on the other side. A few weeks later parts of it were published by Repington in *The Times*, but Curzon and Elles, whose case he was meant to be answering, remained unaware that it had even been written. The Viceroy himself knew nothing about it until the end of the year when he was handed a copy by the assistant manager of *The Times*.[47]

Kitchener's press campaign opened in the *Standard*, a newspaper whose owner, Mr A.Pearson, and whose editor, Gwynne, were among the C-in-C's strongest partisans. Encouraged by Marker and an advance copy of Kitchener's minute, Gwynne published a leading article at the beginning of February asserting that the hero of Omdurman, whom the nation wanted 'as a kind of military dictator' in India, was being thwarted in his efforts to reform the army and improve the empire's defences. Later in the month two articles and another leader reinforced the message with more details and more exaggerated language. Curzon, who was in camp when he heard about them, wired both the C-in-C and the Secretary of State about issuing a contradiction of these charges. Kitchener replied that he was 'very much annoyed' by the articles and thought them 'most unfortunate', while Brodrick advised against action on the grounds that they had attracted no attention. He added that no one in England knew where the *Standard*'s inspiration had come from. As Gwynne later admitted to Curzon, it came of course from Kitchener.[48]

Much more important was the backing of *The Times*, which the C-in-C managed to obtain despite the fact that the paper's assistant manager, Moberly Bell, and its leading expert on Indian affairs, Chirol, took Curzon's side. Leo Amery, who was then on the editorial staff, recalled in his memoirs that Kitchener 'worked hard to secure my support, both through Marker and in personal correspondence',[49] but the crucial influence was Repington, the military correspondent, who had converted the editor. Having plied Marker with advice during the second half of 1904, Repington wrote to Kitchener in the New Year suggesting that Hamilton or Birdwood should send him a weekly letter to keep him in touch. Although Kitchener wanted to have no dealings with the journalist after his 'disgraceful' behaviour with a brother officer's wife, he recognized a useful ally and replied that Birdwood would answer any questions he might care to ask.[50] As he explained to Chirol a year later, he could not afford to be 'too squeamish' about the instruments he used.[51]

At the end of May Repington followed an earlier article on military administration with a sensationalist piece called 'The Crisis in India', which was largely a summary of Kitchener's letter to Stedman and included the sycophantic opinions of the generals. He began by denying that anything in 'the article had been received by him from Lord Kitchener or from any officers or others under his lordship's command',* and after thus exhibiting the extent of his integrity, launched into an attack on 'the curse of dual control' which was 'a public danger and an administrative scandal' that would 'infallibly condemn our arms to disaster at the first touch of serious war'.[52] Seeing the generals' views for the first time, Curzon was naturally interested to find out how they had got into print. Pointing out that the officers should not have been quoted to the public in England while the head of the Indian Government remained ignorant of what they had said, he reminded Kitchener of his assurance that the opinions had been for his private use and asked him whether the version given in *The Times* had been correct. Kitchener replied brazenly that he really did not think he could be held responsible for what the papers published and, when

---

*The disingenuousness of the disclaimer is breathtaking. Repington had received the information from Marker who was working harder for Kitchener than anyone but was no longer formally under his command.

Curzon requested an answer to his question, declared that none of the generals had used the words stated in the telegraphed version of the article.[53] If all the copies of his letter to Stedman had been destroyed, he might have got away with this particular lie. In the event he was fortunate that Curzon did not discover it until after his return to England.

In his memoirs Lord George Hamilton recalled that Kitchener 'so manipulated public opinion and the press that Curzon's case was almost unknown and certainly not seriously studied, though it had behind it a phalanx of the best military and administrative opinion'.[54] The Viceroy's refusal to use the press was considered a great mistake by Chirol, who told General Barrow, one of Curzon's few supporters in the Indian army, that it had given Kitchener's partisans a virgin field to exploit on a subject which no one in England really understood. Barrow remarked that the Viceroy relied on the strength of his case rather than on press agitation, to which Chirol replied that such a rationale would not sway a Government influenced by popular opinion shaped by the press.[55]

Barrow correctly stated Curzon's position, and Chirol correctly explained why he lost. The Viceroy believed his case was unanswerable and tried to persuade Balfour and Brodrick of its justice. But he did not try to convince his other friends in the Cabinet, or Members of Parliament, or journalists in either England or India. The English newspapers in India backed him not because he talked to their editors or sent them confidential documents – he did not even know his supporters by sight – but because they believed he was right. Roberts warned him that public opinion at home was ignorant of the issue and strongly inclined to support Kitchener, but he paid no attention.[56] After sending the despatch, he did nothing to enlist support in England beyond writing a long letter to the Prime Minister restating his position, a document which Balfour either did not read or else quickly forgot about.[57] The Viceroy never understood the size of the forces ranged against him or realized the extent of the intrigue which galvanized them. Nor did he appreciate how the balance in London had changed. Three years earlier the conspiracy could never have succeeded: Lord Salisbury, a former Secretary of State for India, was Prime Minister, Hamilton was at the India Office, Lyall and Crosthwaite, the ablest of former ICS officers, were still on the India Council. In 1905 the last three supported Curzon but were no longer in positions of power. At his most critical time the Viceroy had to face a hostile Premier and Secretary of State, an India Council in which his only real supporter was Barnes, the former Lieutenant-Governor of Burma, and a Cabinet whose knowledge of the

Subcontinent was epitomized not by Lansdowne's experience but by George Wyndham's cheerful public admission that he was 'colossally ignorant of Indian affairs'.[58]

Curzon undoubtedly played his cards badly at times, especially with the Secretary of State. Despite Brodrick's claim to have an open mind on the issue, neither Curzon nor anyone else believed him. In October 1904 Balfour had told Lady Salisbury that his colleague was 'entirely with [him] on this point', and a month later he informed the Viceroy that Brodrick was 'strongly in favour of abolishing the present dual system'. In December the Secretary of State even promised Kitchener support for his cause.[59] Yet for reasons that remain unintelligible, Brodrick subsequently offered Curzon a way out through a commission of inquiry dominated by Hamilton and Roberts who would certainly not have recommended abolition. But the Viceroy's rigid constitutionalism, and the arrogance with which he expressed it, destroyed the scheme and in the process irrevocably alienated Brodrick. Although he still professed to have an open mind, from that moment the Secretary of State was committed to Kitchener's triumph.

Brodrick's fervent partisanship was not accompanied by any closer understanding of the question of military administration in India. In his correspondence with Ampthill during the spring of 1905 he revealed an ignorance that is barely credible in someone who had been at the India Office for over eighteen months and who had earlier aspired to become Viceroy. In one letter the Governor of Madras reported that Kitchener with his 'narrow comprehension' had been unable to understand the constitutional practice and principle involved, only to discover a fortnight later that they had similarly eluded his correspondent. 'You will never induce people here to believe', Brodrick asserted, 'that a dual system, in which the junior gives orders to the senior, is a correct one.' Ampthill despaired at such a 'lamentable misconception of the constitutional principles underlying the question'. It was not a case of Elles giving orders to Kitchener, he pointed out, because the Military Member's orders were not his own but those of the Indian Government, and the question was whether that Government 'should retain the power of giving orders to the c-in-c or whether the c-in-c should be largely emancipated from that control'. As Ampthill had pointed out earlier, Kitchener's position in India was analogous to that of senior generals in England who had obeyed orders from Brodrick when he was Secretary of State for War although he was only a major in the yeomanry.[60]

The Governor wrote with a similar blend of patience and exasperation on other points which Brodrick had not quite grasped. He also vol-
unteered the suggestion that the Government should let Kitchener
resign. The C-in-C's name might have been useful, he conceded, but he
was no Napoleon or Wellington, had never shown any sign of military
genius, and was besides so lazy and inconsiderate that it would be better
for him to go before he was discredited. As Ampthill was then reading
a life of Lord Dalhousie, he drew Brodrick's attention to the resemblance between Curzon and his predecessor, remarking also on the sim-
ilarity between the present situation and the struggle between
Dalhousie and his Commander-in-Chief, Sir Charles Napier, whose
attitude had been so like that adopted by Kitchener now. 'How history
repeats itself,' he observed, 'and I hope that the repetition in this case
will include a cordial support of the viceroy by the home government.'[61]

But Brodrick's mind was no longer open to history lessons from
Ampthill. In January he had proposed a commission for India
favourable to Curzon, but in April he appointed a committee to settle
the matter from London which could not fail to back Kitchener.
Brodrick installed himself as chairman although it was, as Curzon later
remarked, 'a somewhat unusual proceeding for the secretary of state to
preside over a committee appointed to advise himself'.[62] The composition of this body was as remarkable for its omissions as it was for those
included. There were no former Viceroys, Secretaries of State or
Military Members, all of whom might have been expected to understand the constitutional position, but two former Commanders-in-
Chief, two members of the India Council, the Cabinet Minister most
likely – after Balfour and Brodrick – to back Kitchener, and the only
former member of the Viceroy's Council who really opposed Curzon.
Kitchener grumbled about the unfairness of putting Roberts on the
committee, but he must have realized that all the other members had
been picked because they were known to favour his views.[63]

Roberts regarded the committee as packed against Curzon but was
doubtless unaware of the weight of the packing. The appointment of
Lady Salisbury's husband was in the circumstances outrageous, while
Brodrick's justification of it can only be described as malicious: he told
Curzon that the Marquess had been chosen because of his 'good
general acquaintance with the whole subject', while to Lord Cromer,
who was not in a position to appreciate the black humour of the
remark, he explained that Lord Salisbury had 'had some special opportunities of learning the ins and outs of this particular subject'.*[64] The

inclusion of Sir Edward Law, who had supported Kitchener against Ampthill the previous year, was no less bad. As Ampthill belatedly told Brodrick, everything Law said should be discounted because he was 'a hopeless crank' with 'a morbid and distorted mental outlook' and 'animated by a strong personal dislike of Lord Curzon which prejudices all his opinions'.[65] In addition to the pro-Kitchener members, the committee's two secretaries could also be relied on to expedite things in the C-in-C's favour. One was Stedman, the recipient of the famous letter, and the other was Godley who, like Brodrick, professed to be neutral but was in reality completely on Kitchener's side. Although he told Curzon he had acted as an 'honest broker' on a sub-committee set up by the Secretary of State to advise the committee, he had in fact used it to try to abolish the Military Member. And while the committee itself deliberated, supposedly in secret, he kept Lady Salisbury fully apprised of its proceedings.[66]

Considering how unrepresentative the committee was, Brodrick could hardly avoid inviting various authoritative figures to give evidence or send in their opinions. These included two former Viceroys, Lansdowne and Elgin, two former Finance Members, including Lord Cromer, and two former holders of the threatened post. Lansdowne, who regarded the abolition of the Military Member as an 'insensate proposal',[67] wrote a minute for the Cabinet which Brodrick asked him to tone down. The latter did not try to disguise his efforts to influence the committee or the experts and expressed his disappointment when the second former C-in-C, Sir George White, changed his earlier views and backed Roberts.[68] But the worst instance was his attempt to produce a favourable reaction from Lord Cromer in Cairo. Prejudging the issue by informing him that the entire committee except for Roberts wanted to remove the Military Member, Brodrick then contradicted Kitchener's claim that Curzon interfered too much in military matters by describing him as 'a viceroy who takes little interest in the army, and has apparently allowed matters to drift, although, to use [the previous] Lord Salisbury's words about him, "he always asks us to negotiate as if we had 200,000 men at our back".'**[69] Cromer was not impressed. Recalling the fright given by the Mutiny in 1857, he warned that it would be 'a grave error'

---

*In the event Lord Salisbury was too ill to attend the committee and did not sign its report.

**Brodrick frequently repeated this anecdote, which no one else seems to have heard, and later expanded the figure to 500,000.[70]

to abolish the Military Member and thereby give sole control of the army to a general without Indian experience.[71]

The unanimity of the experts put Brodrick in a quandary. Having solicited their opinions, he could hardly disregard them completely and carry on with the abolition of the Military Department. Yet if he published their views in the committee's report, the case against Kitchener's proposals would look invincible. He and Godley therefore reluctantly accepted the need for a compromise in Kitchener's favour. Against the opposition of three Viceroys and two Commanders-in-Chief, it was impossible to abolish the Military Member altogether, but the post could be transformed and shorn of most of its powers. Moreover, the problem of the experts' views could be solved simply by not mentioning them in the report. The shamelessly tendentious document that emerged highlighted any evidence that could be found to criticize the existing military system while suppressing all testimony that defended it. The names of the experts, moreover, were given without a hint of the views they had expressed. The following year Godley admitted that this proceeding had been somewhat questionable. Commenting on the charge that Brodrick had pocketed the opinions of the experts and taken them away with him because they were unfavourable to the new scheme, he confessed to the new Viceroy with laconic understatement, 'Between ourselves, there is some truth in this.'[72]

Brodrick's proposals and Curzon's reaction will be discussed in the next chapter. Roberts believed they represented a genuine compromise and that the new official, to be known as the Military Supply Member, would have a worthwhile position. But few others agreed with him. Godley read and re-read the contents of the report and told Lady Salisbury he was 'lost in amazement' every time he saw Roberts's signature attached to a document that everyone else on the committee regarded as 'a real victory for Kitchener'.[73] Coded telegrams were soon on their way to tell the C-in-C of his success. The Viceroy had to wait another eighteen days, however, before receiving the news in the ordinary way by mail.

The chronology of these events provides a revealing commentary on the levity with which Balfour's Cabinet could deal with an important matter. As the committee reported on a Friday, 26 May, Brodrick's consequent despatch could not have been circulated to ministers before Monday night. Yet on Tuesday morning the Cabinet met to discuss and approve it, and the following day it was on its way to Simla. As Lord

George Hamilton later told Curzon, several ministers had not read it, and even Lansdowne had misunderstood its purport, as he afterwards demonstrated in a speech in the House of Lords.[74] Many years later, when writing his memoirs, the still indignant Hamilton encapsulated the issue.

Balfour was not prepared to face Kitchener's resignation, so to retain his services the cabinet forced on India that very system of administration they had abolished in Great Britain as inefficient and ineffective. The weight of administrative authority, both past and present, was strongly against the change, but it was engineered through with skill at the very end of the life of the existing Parliament. It was never discussed in either House, nor by the Council of India. It was sent from this country as a mandate of the British Government.[75]

2 1

The Breaking of the Viceroy

━━━━━◆━━━━━

GEORGE CURZON'S CHIEF anxiety at the beginning of 1905 was not Kitchener but Mary. Alone in Calcutta and unsure of the extent of her recovery, he had found no pleasure in the resumption of his work. People were very kind, he reported home, and even Kitchener 'seemed to sympathise with [him] very sincerely'. The Proctor of St Xavier's College prayed every day for Mary's recovery, made all his Fathers do the same and 'asked the good nuns to join in' his supplications. But almost everything else managed to depress him. The chef had 'gone all to pieces' in his absence and now 'served up the dirtiest and most ancient of meals', while the band had dwindled in numbers and efficiency and seemed to have learned no new tunes. He felt 'utterly miserable and desolate' in his solitude with no one to talk to or turn to, surrounded by memories and not daring to enter Mary's bedroom in case he burst into tears. When deprived of news of her, he felt 'almost all the anguish of Dalhousie and Canning when they were left alone'.[1]

At the beginning of January he told Mary he was ready 'to chuck India tomorrow' if she wished; he hoped, however, that she would be willing and well enough to come out with the children in April so that he could complete his work before returning home early in 1906, two years after his first term had expired. Two code words had been left for her doctors to telegraph their decision on her fitness to travel. Had they used the negative one, he remarked some years later, he would have gone home at once and been succeeded by Selborne, there would have been no row with Kitchener, Mary would still be alive, and he would be 'first favourite for any appointment under a Conservative prime minister'.[2] But the other codeword was sent, and at the time he was overjoyed. As Mary, however, wanted to be reunited with her husband in England rather than in India, a series of unconvincing arguments had to be deployed to persuade her to come out. Life in London was depicted as likely to be bleak, unhealthy and marred by servant problems, while her existence in India would be extraordinarily rosy and quite unlike her previous experience. He could not deny that Simla would be tedious, but the climate was divine – 'how wonderful one only realises after six months at home' – she would have an absolute rest without household worries, and before going up to the hills they could take the Circuit House at Agra for a fortnight 'and lounge about in the garden of the Taj'. Still more implausible than this Omar Khayyám image of himself was Curzon's prediction that his workload would be so much reduced now that his task was nearly over that he would have leisure to win Mary back to health and happiness. A more reasonable argument was that his wife's recovery had robbed him of an excuse to resign before the military question had been resolved and at a moment of crisis in India's relations with Afghanistan.[3]

In spite of her reluctance to return to the Subcontinent, Mary was glad to leave Highcliffe where her bedroom fire smoked and dead rats were found under the floorboards. It had been a terrible year, her father's death so nearly followed by her own, redeemed only by her sister's marriage and by the birth of Baba. On board with the children she felt better, her cough had nearly gone by the time they reached the Red Sea, and the cow they had brought with them provided excellent milk. The most accurate of her husband's predictions about her new life in India was the enthusiasm that greeted her return in March. 'People treat me', she told her mother, 'as though I were a miracle returned from the dead, and the affection is affecting. No one has ever had such a welcome to India . . .' At a crowded thanksgiving service in Calcutta Cathedral the Bishop preached a sermon on God's answer to prayer with the preservation of Mary's life as an example.[4] Both Curzons were so moved by the overwhelming reception that, as a gift to the city, they decided to erect on the Maidan a marble reproduction of the canopied stone fountain at Trinity College, Cambridge.* George's own tribute to his wife was an unexpected and endearing love poem.

---

*Detailed drawings were made, and Curzon intended to go ahead with the plan even after Mary's death. He later abandoned it because, in his own words, 'the violent outbreak of

I would have torn the stars from the heavens for your necklace,
I would have stripped the rose-leaves for your couch from all the trees,
I would have spoiled the East of its spices for your perfume,
The West of all its wonders to endower you with these.

I would have drained the ocean, to find its rarest pearldrops,
And melt them for your lightest thirst in ruby draughts of wine:
I would have dug for gold till the earth was void of treasure,
That, since you had no riches, you might freely take of mine.

I would have drilled the sunbeams to guard you through the daytime,
I would have caged the nightingales to lull you to your rest;
But love was all you asked for, in waking or in sleeping,
And love I give you, sweetheart, at my side and on my breast.

Mary felt well in Calcutta apart from pain in one leg; she did not have to entertain and she hardly moved except to go for a drive with her husband each afternoon. But things began to go wrong when she reached 'dreadful' Simla at the end of March, and a few days later she was nearly killed in an earthquake. She moved the children out of the badly damaged Viceregal Lodge to a staff bungalow and donated $3,000 to charity as a thanks-offering for another providential escape. Shortly afterwards she took the family to the cottage at Mashobra and soon fell ill with racking headaches and swollen eyes. Her husband, who had been at Agra at the time of the earthquake, quickly rejoined them but also became an invalid. Towards the end of May Mary reported that he had barely been out of bed for six weeks.

Earlier in the spring the Viceroy had told Ampthill that his reforms were nearly all in place and there was little left to do before 'the exhausted reactionary' could leave. Both as statement and as prophecy his '*Nunc Dimittis*' was far from accurate. Even leaving aside the problems of Bengal and military administration, there was still much for him to do in India. Predictably, the visit to Agra did not become a lotus-eating fortnight lounging about the Taj garden with Mary but a dash without her to make sure his restoration work was being carried out properly. He had already received dispiriting news of Delhi from

---

(*cont.*) sedition in Bengal in 1908–9, accompanied by a good deal of rancorous abuse against myself, led me to fear that any monument erected by me in Calcutta would be liable to desecration at the hands of Bengali agitators. Such a fate for the memorial of my darling I could not contemplate.'[5]

Marshall, who reported that soldiers from the Royal Irish Rifles had been amusing themselves by picking out the *pietra dura* inlay in the Red Fort, while the newly restored gardens of Humayun's tomb had been leased to an Indian who had broken the water channels with his cows and planted the new lawns with turnips. The Viceroy's secretary sent the report to the Lieutenant-Governor of the Punjab with the ominous preface that it had just been read 'with considerable annoyance' by his chief; to Mary, Curzon announced that he would drive out to the tomb 'and woe betide the deputy commissioner who [had] been responsible'.[6] But he was happy to be in the United Provinces, which he regarded as 'the ideal place in India: no disloyal class, no offensive press, no Bengalis, but an atmosphere of general courtesy and contentment.' He was relieved too that his restoration of Agra had gone so well. 'If I had never done anything else in India,' he told Mary, 'I have written my name here, and the letters are a living joy.'[7] In his final year he continued writing it, reinstating the flame-shaped battlements on the fort and rebuilding the marble minarets of the gateway to Akbar's tomb; in his last week in India he was still giving orders at Agra. The Saracenic hanging lamp, his personal gift to the Taj Mahal, was made in Cairo and hung above the tombs of Shah Jehan and his Queen after he had left.

Military administration was not the only contentious issue between Viceroy and Secretary of State. They disagreed on most things, small matters as well as large. Nearly every day, Curzon grumbled, a telegram arrived with some inept criticism or futile suggestion which made him and his Council 'howl with despair'. Brodrick seemed to take particular pleasure in rejecting the Viceroy's recommendations for new appointments. On two occasions, after Curzon had suggested names for his Council, Brodrick turned them down, searched for alternative candidates and, having failed to find them, finally accepted the Viceroy's nominees with the claim that he had done so in deference to his friend's wishes. He also objected to the appointment of Ibbetson as Acting Lieutenant-Governor of the Punjab when Rivaz went on leave because he believed the post would be too onerous for him. If Brodrick had only consulted someone at the India Office, lamented Curzon, he would have been told that the Lieutenant-Governor's workload was only a fraction of what Ibbetson had to do in his departments.[8]

Curzon remained at odds with the home Government over Afghanistan and Tibet. He had no confidence in Louis Dane, who had been sent to negotiate in Kabul, and watched with exasperation as the Emir outwitted him. Realizing, he noted, that they had 'a duffer' on

their hands, the Afghans were 'advancing the most preposterous pretensions' that were beyond the capacity of Dane to handle.[9] Britain's
long policy of timidity, he said, had made the Emir insolent, and he
believed Dane should leave without signing a treaty rather than surrender to the Afghan's demands. Frightened that a rupture might lead to
closer ties between Kabul and Russia, the London Government disagreed. In March 1905 Dane therefore signed a treaty which, by renewing the agreements made a generation earlier with Abdur Rahman,
negated the Afghan policy Curzon had pursued for six years.

If Afghanistan was an issue relatively unaffected by the personal hostility between Curzon and Brodrick, the same could not be said of the
final episode of the Tibetan saga. In January the Secretary of State took
the curious step of publishing a parliamentary Blue Book on the
Tibetan campaign. Thinking that his colleague had become 'really very
odd', Balfour could not understand why he wanted to wash 'all our and
Younghusband's dirty linen in public by giving the whole correspondence to the world'.[10] In fact Brodrick had not published the 'whole'
correspondence but only an edited version designed to show Younghusband and the Indian Government in an unfavourable light: by
removing almost all references to Russia, for instance, he managed to
give the impression that the expedition had been virtually motiveless.
Even more extraordinary was his decision to send copies to certain
newspaper editors accompanied by a letter drawing their attention to
passages indicating the soundness of his own policy and the disobedience of Younghusband. Brodrick was severely criticized by several
newspapers for this clumsy manoeuvre and also received a disgusted
letter from Curzon. It was astonishing, wrote his estranged friend, that
a Secretary of State, who was forever claiming to fight Curzon's battles
in England, should invite the London press to join him in censuring the
Government of India and the Viceroy.[11]

The partition of Bengal was the one issue on which Brodrick really
did fight Curzon's battle, but his motives for doing so do not appear to
have included agreement with the scheme. Ever since the end of 1903,
when partition was mooted in the press, Curzon had been advancing
towards legendary status in the demonology of Bengali nationalism, a
position he soon reached and which, nearly a century later, he has not
lost. On taking over in 1904, Ampthill had expressed outrage at the
'monstrously unfair' manner in which the newspapers assailed him with
'the pettiest sarcasm and vilest abuse'.[12] For nearly five years they had
praised Curzon for his reforms and for his stance on equal justice

between natives and Englishmen. Like his work on Indian monuments, his reforms continued into his last year – the Department of Commerce and Industry was set up in March 1905 – but they were nullified in the eyes of the politically vocal by the Viceroy's attempts to rectify the deficiencies of the universities and to alter the administration of Bengal. Embittered by the persistent vilification, Curzon reacted with increasing contempt for educated Indian opinion. Without the newspaper attacks, it is unlikely that he would have gone to Calcutta University in February 1905 and told his audience that the highest ideal of truth was largely a Western conception; with all the attendant qualifications, it was a highly provocative remark. Later in the year he seems to have concluded that it was useless trying to reason with Bengalis over partition and he even looked forward to their hostility with a certain relish. 'Conceive the howls!' he exclaimed to Ampthill. 'They will almost slay me in Bengal.'[13]

The borders of the new province were decided during Ampthill's term and accepted by Curzon on his return. Called East Bengal and Assam, its population of thirty-one million divided in a Muslim-Hindu ratio of three to two, while the rest of Bengal, consisting of some fifty million people, remained overwhelmingly Hindu. Historians have argued that Bengal should have been shorn of Bihar instead of its eastern districts, but the nationalists of the time opposed such a plan and only suggested it as an alternative afterwards; any reduction in the size of the province would probably have been resented by Congress. Partition has also been blamed for the agitation which continued intermittently until the British left India and for the sectarian rivalry between Hindus and Muslims which resulted in the carnage of 1947. These theories, condemned by one Bengali historian as displaying 'a very narrow view of history',[14] are clearly oversimplified. Many other things contributed to India's nationalist 'awakening'. As another historian from the Subcontinent has argued, partition may have been a factor, but the most significant event of the period was the victory of an Asian power, Japan, over Russia in the war of 1904–5.[15] In any case, the development of national consciousness is a complicated process, and its causes and stimulants have a multitude of founts.

In 1912 Godley referred to the partition of Bengal as 'a complete blunder' but at the time he told Curzon it was a 'great scheme' with which he was 'in complete sympathy'.[16] The man with reservations in 1905 was Brodrick, who realized the Bengalis were bound to object. Why the Secretary of State, who consistently disputed insignificant matters with the Viceroy, should have let him have his way on a major issue for which he himself had no enthusiasm, would be a mystery without the evidence of Godley, who recounted how his chief instructed him to bring the India Council into line. The Council was not enthusiastic and wished to modify the plan, but Brodrick appealed to the members and 'made no secret of the fact that he was very anxious not to veto the proposal or refer it back, for the simple reason that he was already having a deadly struggle with Curzon over the military member question, and intended to over-rule him on that'.[17] The Council played up admirably, and at the beginning of June Godley was able to report that the 'great scheme' had been passed without a dissentient voice. At the end of August, however, Brodrick gave the game away by the publication of a telegram implying that partition had gone through to humour Curzon rather than because the India Office appreciated its merits. After that it was widely believed by Bengalis that they had been sacrificed as 'a sop to Cerberus' in an attempt to appease the Viceroy after his defeat on military administration.[18]

During the spring of 1905 Lord Kitchener's confidence had fluctuated. Knowing that Roberts and Lansdowne were working against him, he realized he was unlikely to win an outright victory. But so long as he gained 'fundamentals', he said in the middle of May, he was prepared to come to an arrangement to save Curzon's face. Four days later he thought the issue 'an even toss up' and shortly afterwards had a presentiment that it would turn out badly. On learning the result by telegram the following week, he told Lady Salisbury he was so happy he did not know what to write; he remembered, however, to ask her to relay his gratitude to Balfour and to thank Brodrick for all the hard work he had done on his behalf. After commenting to Marker on the '$2\frac{1}{2}$ years well spent in getting such a satisfactory result', he told him to ensure that Stedman burnt his private letters and left nothing that had been received privately on record.[19]

Curzon's confidence had also been unsteady. Still believing his case to be unassailable, he had told his father in March that Kitchener was 'sure to be beaten', but the composition of the committee and the array of hostile forces later convinced him the matter would end in a compromise.[20] The Viceroy had the disadvantage of being without informers and of therefore not knowing what was going on in London. On 14 June, two weeks after Kitchener had learnt the result, Curzon still had no idea what the despatch was going to propose. Although the King thought he should be given some intimation of its contents, the suggestion was rejected by Brodrick.[21] Curzon remained in ignorance until the despatch reached him on the night of 18 June at his camp at Naldera. There under the shamiana, on the ninetieth anniversary of his old hero's defeat at Waterloo, he read of his own defeat at the hands of his oldest friend.

Various efforts were made to persuade Curzon that there were no winners or losers. The King hoped the decision would 'prove satisfactory' to both parties, while Godley, who had just told Lady Salisbury that the result was 'a real victory' for Kitchener, now pretended to the Viceroy that it was a fair compromise.[22] For his part, Brodrick represented his decision 'not as a compromise designed simply to avoid giving a rebuff to either party in the controversy, and therefore perhaps pleasing to neither, but as a genuine solution, which will stand any amount of hammering'.[23] Curzon, who saw that the Government had accepted Kitchener's case – 'although a disembowelled military member has been left to prevent me from resigning'[24] – was unimpressed by such sophistry. In any case he was able to learn the truth from other correspondents such as Roberts, who soon regretted his signature on the committee's report, and Lansdowne, who regretted that he had not opposed the despatch in Cabinet. From the account of Roberts, it emerged that Brodrick's 'genuine solution' had not been the one favoured by the Secretary of State himself. Influenced by public opinion and the press, Brodrick and Godley had tried to do away with the Military Member altogether and had only been deterred by 'the strong opinion expressed by everyone personally acquainted with the working of the Government in India as to the supreme importance of retaining' him.[25]

The despatch bore the brusque, tactless and somewhat muddled hallmark of Brodrick's style instead of the feline clarity with which Godley generally drafted such communications. It is thus not always easy to follow. The Military Member was to be abolished and his duties to be distributed between a new official, the Military Supply Member (MSM), and the Commander-in-Chief, whose powers were considerably increased and who now became 'the sole expert of the government on purely military questions'. The duties of the MSM, who was to head what Curzon referred to as 'a store-keeping department', were not entirely clear. If, as in the present case, the C-in-C came from the British service, the MSM had to be 'an officer of considerable Indian experience and of administrative capacity, and intimately acquainted with the characteristics of the native army'. With all his experience, however, he was not allowed to 'give expert opinions on military questions', and his 'functions were to be limited to supply'. Although he was a soldier, he was to advise the Viceroy 'on questions of general policy as distinct from purely military questions', a restriction which would give him less say in army affairs than the civilian members who were allowed to give advice and opinions on any matter that came up in Council. To Curzon such distinctions were anyway meaningless, for 'who would determine when a military question became a question of general policy, or when the storekeeper was to blossom into the adviser? or again, when his advice would be regarded as expert and when non-expert?'[26]

If the details of the despatch were confusing, no such accusation could be made of its tone or its method of argument. The tendentiousness that had characterized the report reappeared in the despatch. Brodrick quoted one criticism of the system made by Roberts as Commander-in-Chief in 1889 but ignored other occasions when the veteran general had defended it; besides, he even omitted the concluding paragraph of that criticism in which Roberts had recommended not a sweeping change in the duties and positions of officials but merely a simplification and unification of office procedure.[27] A more unexpected feature of the despatch was the sarcastic tone adopted by its author, who taunted the Viceroy about not knowing 'what was in Your Excellency's mind' and about constitutional 'processes which though familiar to Your Excellency do not appear to have been fully weighed in the [Indian Government's] despatch'. Curzon wrote to Alfred Lyttelton, who had joined the Cabinet in 1903, to ask why the home Government had wanted to treat him to a 'long series of rebuffs delivered in the most humiliating way'. He had not been invariably wrong, and even if he had, 'even supposing that all of us here have been wrong, was it wise or just of the cabinet to expose us to the slur of the Tibetan Blue Book and to the despatch about military administration?'[28] To the King he bluntly declared that the instruments of His Majesty's rule in India could not be openly humiliated without weakening the foundations of that rule itself.[29]

Brodrick later claimed that his despatch 'was certainly conceived in no invidious or discourteous spirit'.[30] Even now it is difficult to find anyone outside the Cabinet or the India Office who agreed with him. The former Viceroy, Lord Ripon, declared in the House of Lords that not since Lord Ellenborough's notorious despatch to Lord Canning about the affairs of Oudh in 1858 had the Indian Government 'received such a rebuff in the face of India and in the face of the world'.[31] Other Liberal peers with Indian experience thought the despatch disgraceful in tone and dangerous in content, for it meant that the Viceroy was no longer supreme in military matters.[32] Even Kitchener's supporters agreed with *The Times* verdict that Brodrick had been 'unnecessarily harsh' in his treatment of the Viceroy. Colonel Hamilton in Simla thought the despatch 'unsuited to the occasion unless indeed it was intended to provoke the V's resignation', and General Stedman at the India Office took a similar view. Regretting that Godley, 'a recognised master of the English language', had not written it, he told Kitchener that Curzon had been 'handled with rather unnecessary roughness'. The following January the new Viceroy, Lord Minto, admitted he had not met anyone who approved of the despatch and that even Kitchener thought it a disastrous document which had put everybody's back up.[33]

On reading the Government's decision, Curzon immediately felt he should resign. 'I am quite willing to go', he told Mary, who was ill at Mashobra, 'if you would like to. India has long ceased to give me any pleasure, and if the cabinet at home want someone to lie down and lick the hand that chastises him, I have no doubt plenty of suitable animals will be forthcoming.' Mary would have welcomed any excuse to leave but felt her husband should only resign if the whole of his Government went as well.[34] All the civilian members of the Council agreed with him on the issue, as of course did Elles, but they were not all prepared to sacrifice their careers. The two men of real weight, Sir Denzil Ibbetson and J.P. Hewett, offered to throw up the certainty of lieutenant-governorships and resign with Curzon. At the same time Ibbetson argued that it was the Viceroy's duty to stay in order to preserve the Indian constitution from destruction and to try to mould Brodrick's unwise plan into a more practicable shape. Influenced by the appeal, which he described as the strongest he had ever received, Curzon also saw the difficulty of resigning on a question of principle when most people did not understand what the principle was and would think he had resigned out of pique.[35]

After consulting his colleagues, he decided not to make a decision until he had seen Kitchener and told him of his intention to resign unless the C-in-C agreed to join in recommending various modifications to Brodrick's scheme. Curzon began their meeting at Mashobra on the 25th by stating his position, whereupon Kitchener insisted that he was the one who ought to resign. As it was the C-in-C who had triumphed, Curzon said that was out of the question, and the only matters to discuss were the conditions on which he would agree to stay. Among these he stipulated that the Military Member should retain his former designation and still be available for consultation by the Viceroy upon any military proposal emanating from the Commander-in-Chief. These modifications, which went far to restore the position of the Military Member, were accepted, astonishingly, by Kitchener, welcomed by the Council and then submitted to Balfour with a harsh preamble from Curzon asserting the Indian Government's belief that Brodrick's scheme, 'if unmodified in important particulars', would be 'mischievous, if not unworkable, in operation' and would impose an 'intolerable burden upon the viceroy while depriving him of indispensable advice'. The telegram also made it clear that the Viceroy would resign rather than accept the decision – 'conveyed in so invidious and derogatory a form' – without modifications.[36]

This communication naturally caused consternation in London. It was a ridiculous situation for Balfour and Brodrick, who had invested so much effort in Kitchener's cause, to watch their champion throwing away the victory they had so unsqueamishly won for him. The Prime Minister wired back his extreme surprise at learning of such an alteration in the C-in-C's views and asked for a full statement of his reasons for the change. Warned by Marker that his friends thought he had given away points they had gained with the greatest trouble, Kitchener became extremely unhappy and requested a second interview with the Viceroy on the 30th. Never at his best in situations which required logical argument, he soon regretted this discussion as much as he had the previous one. According to Curzon's version, Kitchener said that the one modification which caused him anxiety was the proposal that the Military Member should retain his current designation, thereby giving the impression that nothing had changed. After a long discussion Curzon conceded the point, whereupon Kitchener 'showed as much relief and pleasure as a schoolboy' and declared that in return he would join the Viceroy in resignation unless the Government quickly agreed to the other modifications.[37]

Afterwards Kitchener felt obliged to make excuses for these performances to his London allies. Explaining his original acceptance of the modifications to Edward Stanley, who had been asked by Brodrick to telegraph him in code, he said the only 'tip' he had had for dealing with Curzon was Stanley's advice 'to let him down easy', and he wanted to avoid a resignation that would have made the Viceroy seem 'a martyr to the maintenance of constitutional government'. He also claimed, quite implausibly, that he had 'never contemplated for a moment that, having got his modifications, Curzon would or could turn round and ask for them officially in the way he did'. Kitchener's second acceptance of all but one of the modifications five days later needed a more dramatic explanation. Reporting to Marker on the day of the interview, he admitted that he had been so pleased by Curzon's agreement to the department's title that he had rashly associated himself with the Viceroy's position. A week later he was sending home spicier versions of the episode. Lady Salisbury was informed of a stormy meeting in which Curzon had collapsed, an incident so distressing to the sentimental soldier that he had immediately accepted his 'puerile requests'. 'I could have bitten my tongue out', he added, 'for making such a stupid remark but really I was rather excited with the discussion. I was prancing up and down his room talking to him very straight.' The Viceroy's collapse was not mentioned in Kitchener's first report to Marker, nor in his reply to Stanley, nor in anything written by Curzon, a man not normally reticent about recording breakdowns. In all probability the incident is merely another illustration of Kitchener's chronic mendacity. It is hardly likely that two distraught men, one of them sobbing on a sofa and the other 'prancing up and down', could draft a sober and lucid telegram to the Prime Minister expressing 'absolute agreement' between themselves and concluding with words added purposely by Kitchener: 'Above proposals are so cordially agreed to by both of us that if H.M.G. are not able to accept them, Lord K. desires to associate himself with any action that [the Viceroy] may take in the matter.'[38]

Although Balfour privately regarded Kitchener as a traitor,[39] he realized there was little to be gained by further investigation of his mysterious change of mind. On 1 July he therefore telegraphed his delight at the satisfactory new arrangement and conceded it would be 'most improper to limit right of viceroy to consult whom he pleases'. Believing there was still room for misunderstanding about the rights of the new MSM, Curzon replied that he and Kitchener wanted the official to be available for consultation by the Viceroy on all matters, in place of the despatch's limitation that he should advise on 'questions of general policy as distinct from purely military questions'. Balfour rather curiously denied there was anything in the despatch which prevented the MSM from being consulted on any subject and accepted the Viceroy's view of the matter. 'After one or two more ineffectual wriggles,' Curzon reported to Kitchener, the home Government had 'given in and our proposals are all accepted.'[40] It seemed that the crisis was over.

The principal loser from these developments had turned out, unexpectedly, to be Brodrick. Within a month of claiming that his scheme could stand 'any amount of hammering', it had been hammered out of shape with the consent of the man it had been designed to help. Brodrick had already been made to look ridiculous at the War Office and he was determined to avoid a repetition. Yet he realized he could only salvage his position over the despatch by minimizing the significance of the modifications and pretending that the Indian Government had accepted it with merely minor alterations. Unfortunately, this view could not be squared with the official telegram sent to London on 6 July which submitted the modifications and in its preamble repeated the view that Brodrick's unaltered scheme would be 'mischievous if not unworkable in operation'. On being asked by the Secretary of State to delete the preamble, Curzon offered to omit the words 'mischievous if not' and to soften a couple of other phrases, but insisted on retaining the rest because it explained why his Government considered the modifications to be necessary.[41] His own interests and those of the Government of India compelled them to take the opposite course from Brodrick and to emphasize that the scheme was a bad one which could only be ameliorated by serious changes.

Denied the co-operation of the Simla Government, the Secretary of State went ahead with his plan. In the official reply of 14 July Curzon was informed that he had 'misapprehended' the Government's orders and that some of the modifications, far from contravening the provisions of the despatch, were 'in exact fulfilment of the wishes and intentions which it conveyed'. Although this was an odd way of describing a set of conditions which had caused Balfour such surprise and which Stanley, writing on Brodrick's behalf, had described as 'great and most serious alterations', he repeated this view three days later in the House of Commons, adding that the modifications were 'entirely in accord' with the despatch.[42] Curzon, who had made it clear he would only stay in his post if the scheme was substantially altered, was disgusted by this attempt to put the concessions in a light which, he believed, rendered both them and him ridiculous. Suffering from dysentery and acute diarrhoea, he rose from his sickbed on the 18th to inform the Legislative Council at Simla of the arrangement the Governments of Britain and India had reached with regard to military administration. As his own views, expressed in the minute sent home in March, had already been published, it would have been absurd for him to welcome Brodrick's scheme, but he gave a fair account of the negotiations, explained why his Government had insisted on the changes, and left it to the future to judge whether the new system would be superior to the old. The speech contained nothing more provocative than a reference to 'the manner in which it was thought necessary' to convey Brodrick's orders and the comment that the Indian Government had been 'very glad to make [the] discovery' that some of its modifications were 'in exact fulfilment of the wishes and intentions' of the despatch.[43]

A highly misleading summary of this speech was cabled by Reuters to London where it caused an uproar. Without waiting for a transcript of the full text, the 'deeply grieved' Prime Minister immediately informed the King that the speech was 'deplorable in taste and temper' and that 'no such public exhibition of disloyalty had ever yet been made by an Indian viceroy'.[44] On the same day Sir Henry Fowler, who had been Rosebery's Indian Secretary, asked Brodrick in the Commons what he intended to do about the 'extraordinary speech' that had so 'severely, if not offensively' criticized the Government. The minister replied that he had telegraphed for the text and would make a statement the following week. In the meantime he studied the speech, let the Viceroy know that several passages had created a painful impression, and evidently concluded that it did not merit the censure that would have caused Curzon's resignation.[45]

During the second half of July Viceroy and Secretary of State were also in dispute over two other issues, alleged disclosures to the press and the nomination of the Military Supply Member. Suspicious of the unanimity of the Indian newspapers, both English and native, in their support for Curzon, Brodrick deduced that they had been manipulated. On this issue he had been anticipated by Mr Pearson's newspapers in London which claimed, quite falsely, that the Simla Government 'blacklisted' correspondents who disagreed with it and suggested that the Viceroy was responsible for the one-sided utterances of the Indian press. Remembering how the *Standard* had printed Kitchener's views almost verbatim in February, its performance in July was shameless in its hypocrisy: after expressing surprise that Curzon should have condescended to use such methods, the newspaper brazenly denied that the C-in-C had committed a similar indiscretion.[46]

Although Brodrick had no evidence beyond these assertions, the allegations of Kitchener's entourage, and the hostility of the Indian papers to himself, he spread it around that Curzon was blatantly 'tampering with the press'. To the Viceroy he despatched a telegram listing examples of recently leaked documents and asking whether the person or persons responsible for disclosing them could be dealt with under the Official Secrets Act. Reading between the lines and seeing what Brodrick was driving at, Curzon asked Ampthill if he could conceive of anything in an official telegram 'more spiteful or yet more puerile' than the suggestion that he should apply the Official Secrets Act to himself. To the Secretary of State he observed that the information allegedly leaked, such as his intention of resigning over the despatch, had not been confined to official documents but was well known in Simla: he also countered with examples of more serious disclosures, mainly concerning Kitchener, that had appeared in the London press.[47] Curzon's innocence in the matter of the press may have seemed unbelievable to those familiar with the tactics of his opponent, but Brodrick's obsessive and unsuccessful attempt to prove it false suggests that he was motivated by vindictiveness rather than by mere disbelief. As Ampthill complained, the C-in-C's 'mean intrigues fostered by low unscrupulous agents . . . made the cabinet suspect conspiracy on the side on which it does not exist'.[48]

Curzon was unable to account for Brodrick's behaviour towards him, which he found all the more intolerable because it was accompanied by 'unctuous protestations of friendship'. Ever since he had returned to India, he believed the Secretary of State had pursued him with 'a tortuous malevolence rare in the annals of politics and unprecedented in those of friendship'. Sometimes, he said, he had to rub his eyes to make sure that it really was himself who was being thus treated, 'and treated by a man who has failed in every office that he has filled' and who 'would never have had the chance of being a failure as Secretary for India if he had not already been a failure as Secretary for War'.[49] Further astonishment was caused by Brodrick's treatment of Younghusband and Elles, whose principal crimes seemed to be that they were allies of the Viceroy. Elles, whose life had been made miserable in recent months by the death of his wife and the vendetta of Kitchener, suffered a third blow in June in the form of a despatch from Brodrick demanding his resignation by 1 October. As he had already offered his resignation twice, he did not require such humiliation to force him out. 'Poor Elles', Curzon remarked to Mary, 'only had to be told by me that he must go and he would have done it without a murmur. But St John must needs go and rub it in – literally kicking him out. I think this is almost the worst of all.'[50] Supported by Curzon, Elles offered to resign on condition that the demand was cancelled, but for obscure reasons – which do not become clearer after an examination of the relevant telegram – Brodrick refused the condition.[51]

At least until August the Viceroy's hostility was directed far more strongly against his superior at home than against his opponent in India. This was largely a result of Kitchener's ability to disguise his second face. Despite evidence from the British press and elsewhere, both Curzons were astonishingly slow at comprehending his conspiracy. Earlier in the year Mary had referred to Kitchener as 'so great a friend' that she deplored his inability to compromise with Elles, and at the end of March she had told her husband that his resignation would be 'a kind of debacle in a fine strenuous stubborn career of good'. She once declared that his 'utter dependence' on her was very appealing especially because he talked to her as if she was a man.[52] That this 'dependence' was illusory, however, seems to be confirmed by a sentence from a letter to Lady Salisbury in which Kitchener, presumably referring to Mary, wrote: 'I almost imagine she must have deluded herself into thinking she had some influence over me.'[53]

In late June, during the turmoil of the despatch, Mary sent a note to Kitchener about his next birthday present; she also wrote to his former ADC, 'Brat' Maxwell, who was working for the C-in-C's cause in London, to say how much she missed him - a feeling which 'the Brat' did not reciprocate.[54] But her innocence is displayed at its most pathetic in two letters to Lady Salisbury in July. Admitting 'great qualms over boring you with our crisis out here', which at home 'must seem so flat', she told her correspondent that Kitchener, who had been 'splendid' and in 'complete accord' with George, blamed everything on Brodrick. 'Neither G nor Lord K had any idea what shape the scheme would take as neither had had a word on the subject'.[55] Lady Salisbury's replies, if she attempted the tricky task of writing them, do not appear to have survived.

Mary still believed at the end of July that no one was 'more indignant' about Brodrick's behaviour than Kitchener,[56] but by then new developments were changing her husband's view of his military colleague. Curzon wished to recommend General Sir Edmund Barrow, then stationed on the North-West Frontier, as the new Military Supply Member. As a former Secretary of the Military Department, he had the administrative experience for the post and was regarded as one of the ablest officers in the army. Curzon saw him in Simla on 8 July, told him he was 'incomparably the finest soldier in India' and said he wished to recommend him to the Secretary of State. Barrow admitted he was doubtful of the merits of Brodrick's scheme but said he would join the Viceroy in attempting to construct a workable organization. He also mentioned that he had just seen Kitchener, who knew he might be selected for the post, and had spent an hour discussing the matter with him. According to Barrow, the C-in-C was satisfied to have him as MSM and told him to urge Curzon to make the appointment at once because he could not get along with Elles.[57]

As so often happened in the aftermath of his interviews, Kitchener soon regretted what he had said. Presumably he remembered that Barrow had been opposed to the abolition of the Military Department, and for that reason his views on the subject had not appeared with those of his colleagues in *The Times*. Realizing that the general might therefore display an unwelcome independence at the new department, the C-in-C hurried to stop the appointment by telegraphing the War Office to say Barrow was unacceptable.* After acquiescing in Curzon's suggestion on 8 July, Kitchener could hardly admit his change of mind during an interview with the Viceroy on the 9th. But he did say, after wishing that Barrow could substitute for Elles at once, that he thought him almost too good an officer for the post and that he would prefer to have him as his Chief of Staff. This was another piece of confusion Kitchener created for himself. Strong evidence that he wanted Barrow as Chief of Staff – and that he actually offered him the post – co-exists with the testimony of his telegrams deprecating the idea to Marker. And to obscure matters further, he declared at the beginning of August that he would 'far sooner see Barrow military supply member *outside* my office than *C of S* inside'.[60]

The confusion was resolved by Brodrick, who declined to accept the Viceroy's recommendation for the head of the Military Supply Department. Asked for an explanation by Curzon, who told him he needed an officer of the highest calibre to set up the new organization, the minister replied by saying that Barrow's former employment in the Military Department made it unlikely that he would inaugurate the system with an open mind. He went on to remind Curzon that the

---

*Winston Churchill believed Curzon had seen this telegram and thought he should have 'called on K to explain himself, accused him of being the liar and intriguer he was, and reported the whole thing to the War Office, when it would have been Kitchener who would have had to resign'.[58] But Curzon had declined to look at the C-in-C's telegrams (see above p.297) and did not learn of this episode until it was too late.[59]

Secretary of State was responsible for the selection of Council members and told him to ask Kitchener who was the man best qualified for the post. Brodrick evidently did not regard it as invidious to reject the Viceroy's nominee and then to invite a nomination from his subordinate. Nevertheless, Curzon agreed to see Kitchener, and an 'extremely painful' meeting took place on 5 August. Doubtless remembering the results of the interviews in June, Kitchener worked himself into a temper beforehand and, 'trembling violently' according to Curzon, denied that he had ever accepted Barrow as MSM or suggested him as Chief of Staff. After mentioning that his ideal MSM would be General Sir C.H. Scott, an officer described by Curzon as 'a placid old dummy' who would never dare to criticize his chief, Kitchener 'lost all command of himself, raged and blustered and eventually stalked out of the room'. Disregarding the Vicereine's efforts to persuade him to stay for lunch, he returned to his house but left after a few minutes in case he was followed by what his staff called a 'Mary to the rescue' letter. Curzon commented later that he had learnt more about Kitchener's character and intentions from that interview than he had from the previous two years of working with him. But not until it was too late did he become aware of 'the unblushing lying and intrigue' with which the C-in-C had played his game. 'Like a fool,' he told the Liberal politician, Lord Crewe, 'I brought him to India believing as so many do in his reputation.' Now he understood the defects that Cromer and Milner had warned him of beforehand.[61]

At the beginning of August Curzon told Dawkins that for five years his post in India had been a source of 'honourable pride and pleasure', but that in a year and a half Brodrick had 'converted it into almost daily misery and persecution'.[62] The Barrow affair was the last straw not because he had failed to get his own way over an appointment but because it was a further indication that Brodrick regarded the agreed modifications to the despatch as nominal. If he was to inaugurate the new system, he said, he required the confidence of the home Government; if it denied him the officer he needed for the task, then it was clear to him that he did not have that confidence. On 5 August he therefore repeated his request for the Government's support and for Barrow's assistance, informing Brodrick that without them he would resign. Realizing that he could hardly back down now on the appointment, Godley urged the Secretary of State to accept the resignation in order to save his scheme from 'a fatal blow'. But at that moment the Prime Minister intervened with a conciliatory telegram that loftily missed the point. Balfour, who told his secretary it was 'a wretched world' and he really could not get to 'the bottom of the Kitchener-Curzon squabble', stated that the choice of Council members rested solely with the Secretary of State – a prerogative the Viceroy had never questioned – and asserted that Barrow would prefer an active post to that of MSM. The second point, which originated from Brodrick's misrepresentation of an interview with Barrow, now on leave in London, was untrue.[63]

A strong appeal for Curzon to stay was sent by the Foreign Secretary on 7 August. Lord Lansdowne, who felt ashamed that he had only recently begun to appreciate what 'a really commanding intellect and character' Curzon possessed,[64] had opposed the abolition of the Military Member but accepted Brodrick's scheme in Cabinet. An intelligent and natural moderate, he supported Curzon's interpretation of the modifications and was placed in a ridiculous position when forced to defend the despatch against Lord Ripon in the Lords on 1 August. Yet his speech showed either that he did not fully understand the despatch or that he was not prepared to champion Brodrick's version of it, for he asserted that the new member of Council would 'remain very much in the position which he has always occupied'. Of the scheme in general, which Brodrick had thought so enduring it would stand 'any amount of hammering', Lansdowne remarked that there was 'no finality in these things' and the details might need to be reconsidered.[65] When he advised Curzon to accept the terms on which the issue had been settled, it was not clear, therefore, which terms he was referring to. Curzon replied that he could only work the scheme if he received continuous support from home and was not given a 'dummy' as MSM. Otherwise the task was hopeless.[66]

In his reply to Balfour's telegram on the 10th, Curzon included a summary of Kitchener's proposals, which had just reached him, about the duties and functions of the Military Supply Department. To the Viceroy it was clear that Kitchener, stiffened by his staff officers, had reverted to his original scheme of reducing the Department to insignificance: under the conditions proposed by the C-in-C, the MSM would not have two hours work a day, and his job and his Department would be an unpardonable waste of public money. If Kitchener's point of view prevailed, he told the Government, it was useless for him to remain in India, and he repeated the conditions under which he would consent to stay. Answering the following day, Brodrick refused to back down on Barrow and did not refer to Kitchener's proposals. Having received this missive with 'much regret', the Viceroy replied on the 12th that the lack of support from home had forced him to conclude that the differences in policy between the two Governments were too wide to be bridged and that he therefore wished to place his resignation in the Prime Minister's hands. As the Curzons waited in suspense for four days, Mary prayed that her husband would at last be allowed to go. Balfour told Brodrick there was 'no use in fighting him further. If he will go, he must go.' On the 16th the Prime Minister wired to say he knew not how to combat the Viceroy's apparently fixed resolve and he had therefore, with the profoundest regrets, communicated his wishes to the King.[67]

Curzon met defeat with a pose of cheerful defiance. After everything he had endured, he told friends, his resignation was one of the happiest and proudest moments of his public life; he would leave India a happy man with his 'work for the most part done, and most of the harvest in the barn'.[68] His three mistakes, he told Ampthill, were that he had not resigned after receiving the despatch, that he had believed the Government to be sincere whereas it was now clear it had merely been 'bamboozling' him, and that he had trusted Kitchener, whom he now realized was 'without truth or honour'.[69] His tardy resignation robbed him of much of the support he would have received earlier and gave rise to various misinterpretations about why he had gone. His departure was – and still is – attributed to personal antagonism between Curzon and Kitchener, 'two masterful men . . . in conflict', 'two strong and self-willed men [who] could not work together', 'two tigers in the same jungle', 'two kings of Brentford' with a single throne.[70] The theory is obviously mistaken because Curzon only learnt of Kitchener's antagonism on 5 August, long after he had first considered resignation. Besides, his desire to have him as his C-in-C in the first place shows he was not the sort of tiger who minded having other tigers in his jungle.

Kitchener's most eminent and most critical biographer, Sir Philip Magnus, wrote that Curzon showed 'he was prepared to compromise on the question of principle, and then, characteristically, resign[ed] on a personal issue'.[71] As Curzon did not resign on any other occasion from any political post, it is difficult to see how this could be regarded as characteristic. In any case the observation is untrue. The question of principle may in the end have been narrowed down to the question of General Barrow, but it was the same principle that had been at issue since June. For nearly eight weeks Curzon had made it clear that he would stay under certain conditions, and only when he concluded, rightly or wrongly, that those conditions would not be met, did he insist on resignation. He went not because of Barrow but because he was the victim of a prolonged intrigue, which by deceitful methods had drawn in the two crucial figures in the Cabinet and turned them into fellow conspirators. It is hard to disagree with Ibbetson's explanation to Curzon that he had been sacrificed by a tottering Government frightened of 'the personal popularity of an unscrupulous intriguer; and you are going because you are honest, and he is not.'[72]

British India's reaction outside the army was almost unanimous, and even among the military there were officers who dreaded Kitchener's predominance and wished that the C-in-C rather than the Viceroy had resigned.[73] The Governor of Madras wrote to the Governor of Bombay of his 'indignation and regret at this lamentable ending to Lord Curzon's magnificent administration', and told him he would be 'horrified at the part which K has played'.[74] Lamington reflected what a 'tragic farce' it was that a decrepit and moribund Government 'should expel from the most responsible office the most able and expert occupier of it'.[75] The press took a similar view, the three leading newspapers commenting variously on Brodrick's untruthfulness, subservience to Kitchener, unsuitability for office and 'nauseating' efforts to excuse himself. *The Times of India* expressed some trenchant views on 'the sardonic and sinister figure' of Kitchener, the brutality of Brodrick, and a Prime Minister who had never been nearer to Asia than the Franco-Italian border.*[76] Brodrick informed the King, without the smallest attempt at substantiation, that the attack was 'specially inspired' by the Viceroy.[77] There remains no evidence for the claim.

From England Walter Lawrence told Curzon that the Secretary of State was 'a poor creature and not worth your powder and shot. No one has a good word for him, and he goes about bleating about his sorrow and his friendship for you'.[78] The sorrow may have been genuine but it did not hinder Brodrick from organizing, in concert with Godley and to a lesser extent Balfour, a propaganda campaign to discredit his friend. Even before Curzon knew that his resignation had been accepted, Balfour was being urged both by his secretary and by Brodrick to square Buckle in order 'to prevent a silly line being taken by *The Times*'; and on the 17th Godley duly trotted round to the editor with a selection of documents.[79] Attempts were also made to convince people that Curzon's

---

* The last charge was unfair. Balfour had seen several Asian coastlines during his voyage round the world in 1875.

real reason for resigning was the unrest in Bengal which would have embarrassed him had he stayed to entertain the Prince of Wales during the proposed royal visit in the winter.[80] Other ploys of Brodrick's included the claim that Curzon had returned to India pledged to abolish the Military Department, that he had misinterpreted Kitchener's views on several occasions, and that his alleged untruthfulness was due to the fact that he was ill and hardly sane. 'I wish I felt any real confidence in his fairness and uprightness,' he wrote to Lord Salisbury. 'One must try and think these aberrations are due to ill-health.' To Lord Scarsdale he ascribed the crisis to the unceasing strain of work since his son's return from Afghanistan ten years before.[81]

Later in the year strenuous efforts were made to suborn Lord Cromer, who had supported the Viceroy on the issue of the Military Department. Knowing that Curzon would break his journey in Egypt to see the surviving member of the proconsular trio, Brodrick asked Cromer to persuade him not to continue the controversy in England. In his letter he enclosed a catalogue of viceregal misdeeds including various allegations which Cromer had already received in the spring together with the news that 'Curzon is posing as a man who has been deeply wronged', that 'despotism has got into his brain', and that 'from first to last [he] has dealt with the question in the way most to embarrass us'. Disconcerted both by Cromer's refusal to co-operate and by his view that the Viceroy's office had been dealt a very severe blow, Brodrick subsequently repeated the falsehood that Curzon had neglected the army and told his correspondent how much he disapproved of the Viceroy's 'sort of sham imperialism which takes up a very bold position without an adequate force to support it'.[82]

Brodrick's official telegram acknowledging the resignation was described by Curzon as 'a resurrection dish of all the stale and oft-refuted charges of the previous two months, dressed up again so as to impose upon the public and discredit me in the hour of my fall'. Plainly drafted for journalistic consumption, it even spoke of Brodrick's 'constant support' for the Viceroy. Curzon was too weary to answer the points all over again and contented himself with contesting two examples of distortion and observing what little justification there was for the claim that he had been given constant support. Subsequent communications dealt with the publication of telegrams to explain the resignation to the public. Kitchener objected to the summary of his proposals sent home on the 10th, which he said severely misrepresented his views, and demanded the publication of a lengthy rejoinder.

Curzon studied all the documents again, found there had been no misrepresentation, and drafted a reply which he sent to London together with the C-in-C's protest. The debate degenerated into an angry squabble after the Viceroy pointed out in his minute that Kitchener had actually made a note on a document he claimed not to have seen. Subsequently admitting that he had seen it, the C-in-C then declared it had not contained the information on ordnance officers which Curzon had referred to; he therefore asked him to make a correction to the press. Sending for the papers in question, the Viceroy found that the information was not only included but actually highlighted by a green slip on the very page on which the C-in-C had written. A correction was therefore not issued. Continuing angrily to deny that he had seen the information, Kitchener told Lady Salisbury that in the old days he would have called Curzon out and shot him 'like a dog for his grossly insulting letter'.[83]

Although confident of his case, Curzon advised against publication of the notes written by Kitchener and himself on the grounds that a printed wrangle between the two of them was not in the public interest. Brodrick deferred once more, however, to the C-in-C's views, the papers were released to the Indian press and, on the basis of a telegraphic summary, *The Times* published an article blaming the Viceroy for their publication. On asking the Secretary of State to correct this impression, Curzon was told that the truth was becoming known and that the Government deprecated further public discussion of recent events. It was a pity Brodrick had not deprecated it before sanctioning the publication of the notes, an action Lord Ripon considered to be 'utterly indefensible' and proof that he was quite unfit to be Secretary of State.[84]

Curzon had long wished to be succeeded by either Selborne or Milner, who had also been Balfour's first choices. But Selborne had got bored of waiting and had gone off as High Commissioner to South Africa, while Milner was not prepared to shoulder another proconsulship. The King favoured Ampthill, but the Madras Governor had supported Curzon so articulately in his letters to Brodrick that he was ruled out of contention. In the end the Prime Minister and the Secretary of State could come up with only two candidates, the Earl of Jersey and the Earl of Minto. Balfour admitted that neither was ideal but thought Minto had more 'go'. Brodrick suggested that the 'mass of business' would 'puzzle Minto considerably', and preferred Jersey. Minto was chosen, however, because he was regarded as energetic and tactful, although Balfour regretted he was not 'cleverer'. The King was unimpressed by the choice, believing that Curzon and Minto were as comparable as Pitt and Perceval. Winston Churchill, who thought Curzon's viceroyalty was almost the only thing that had enhanced the Government's prestige in recent years, took a similar view. 'For cynical disdain of public interests and contempt of public opinion', he told his mother, the elevation of Minto exactly matched Brodrick's appointment to the India Office.[85] But it turned out to be a good deal less disastrous.

On hearing of the appointment, Curzon is alleged to have said, 'Imagine sending to succeed *me* a gentleman who only jumps hedges',[86] a remark which has subsequently been used as proof of his arrogance and superiority. Lord Minto was indeed a celebrated amateur rider, an unsuccessful veteran of the Grand National, and a man whose recreations were limited, according to *Who's Who*, to hunting, shooting and fishing. But it is highly improbable that Curzon made the remark. The two were old friends, had shot rabbits together on Ben Nevis in 1896, and had been the principal guests of honour at the Old Etonian dinner before Curzon went to India and Minto sailed to Canada as Governor-General. Indeed, Curzon had recommended Minto for that post, telling Salisbury he was a capable man who knew Canada and its Government well, and six years later he congratulated him for his 'splendid service to the Empire' across the Atlantic. As soon as he learnt the identity of his successor, he sent him advice about household appointments. For his part, Minto wrote of his feeling that he was succeeding a very old friend.[87]

Brodrick and Godley were both eager to avoid the possibility of the new Viceroy's indoctrination by his predecessor. They therefore suggested that Curzon should be brought home at once and the luckless Ampthill appointed to direct another interregnum until Minto could come out; the best solution would be to arrange for the Viceroys to pass each other on the high seas.[88] Balfour, who pointed out that Viceroys normally overlapped, did not agree with this scheme, and neither did the King. There was also the problem of the Prince of Wales's visit, scheduled for November, which Curzon had taken a great deal of trouble to organize. 'I own I shall feel rather bitterly', he told the Prince after his resignation, 'when I think of someone else doing the honours at Government House at Calcutta.'[89] Brodrick's plan to remove the Viceroy before the visit was wrecked by Edward VII, who had generally supported Curzon during the struggle, and who thought the retiring Viceroy should stay on both to receive his son and to meet his successor. Minto was anxious not to run 'the risk of being belittled' by being in India while Curzon was conducting the ceremonies with the Prince of Wales. But he was quite prepared to wait until these had been completed. He considered the reception of the Prince would be a fitting close for Curzon's Indian career and was saddened by the Secretary of State's inability to grasp this point.[90]

The disruption of Brodrick's plans caused a hiatus at Simla during which little business was accomplished. Aware that he was not popular in the summer capital, Kitchener took himself off on a prolonged excursion. Mary, who had only accepted the truth about her 'dependent' friend after her husband's resignation, liked to think of him 'wandering about in the heat of the plains', 'abhorred by everyone' for his lies and intrigues, and afraid to show his face at Simla.[91] Letters of condolence and support arrived in their hundreds, banquets were given, and a ball was thrown in their honour by the town's residents. In Bombay the editor of *The Times of India* was struck by the depth, sincerity and 'extraordinary unanimity of feeling amid which the viceroyalty closes'.[92] An emotional farewell took place at Simla on 25 October. Kitchener returned reluctantly for the occasion, grumbling that it was not very pleasant to shake hands with a man who had called him a liar.[93]

Curzon's final Indian journey was ruined by illness which kept him in bed for a week at Lahore. But he managed to get down to Bombay in order to greet the Prince and Princess of Wales and to deliver a speech at the city's Chamber of Commerce before retiring to Agra until the arrival of the Mintos a week later. A friend who accompanied him to the place he loved more than any other in India, a place where it was 'always peaceful and always beautiful', described the fallen Viceroy still absorbed by his restoration work, exploring every corner of the fort, measuring the growth of the cypresses he had planted in the gardens of the Taj, knowing every stone and legend of Fatehpur Sikri.[94] By the middle of November Curzon was back in Bombay to deliver his farewell oration at the Byculla Club, an immense speech which, if slightly marred by egotism and self-vindication, was still an inspiriting justification of the British dominion in India. His closing sentences reached the summit of his particular brand of oratory.

A hundred times in India have I said to myself, Oh that to every Englishman in this country, as he ends his work, might be truthfully applied the phrase, 'Thou hast loved righteousness and hated iniquity.' No man has, I believe, ever served India faithfully of whom that could not be said. All other triumphs are tinsel and sham. Perhaps there are few of us who make anything but a poor approximation to that ideal. But let it be our ideal all the same. To fight for the right, to abhor the imperfect, the unjust, or the mean, to swerve neither to the right hand nor to the left, to care nothing for flattery or applause or odium or abuse – it is so easy to have any of them in India – never to let your enthusiasm be soured or your courage grow dim, but to remember that the Almighty has placed your hand on the greatest of His ploughs, in whose furrow the nations of the future are germinating and taking shape, to drive the blade a little forward in your time, and to feel that somewhere among these millions you have left a little justice or happiness or prosperity, a sense of manliness or moral dignity, a spring of patriotism, a dawn of intellectual enlightenment, or a stirring of duty, where it did not before exist – that is enough, that is the Englishman's justification in India. It is good enough for his watchword while he is here, for his epitaph when he is gone. I have worked for no other aim. Let India be my judge.*[95]

The Byculla Club was Curzon's real farewell to India. An altogether more unfortunate event was the reception of Minto followed by his own departure. Curzon had been busy preparing notes on important matters for his successor and looking forward to discussing them with him at Bombay. The Mintos' ship, however, was delayed by adverse currents after leaving Aden and arrived half a day late. When it finally reached the port, a pilot came on board to say that Curzon was so eager to have enough time with the incoming Viceroy that the official reception had been postponed until the following morning. Puzzled and disappointed by the news, the Mintos disembarked privately and were driven to Government House where they were even more surprised to find that Curzon was not waiting to greet them. Mary, Lamington and the Ampthills, who had come to say goodbye,

---

* The most farcical episode of the Curzon-Kitchener saga took place four years later on the eve of the C-in-C's departure from India. Too lazy to compose his farewell speech at Simla, Kitchener entrusted the task to his Chief of Staff, Sir Beauchamp Duff, who, also finding it rather an effort, imagined he could plagiarize Curzon's Byculla Club speech without anyone noticing. A correspondent in *The Times* took much pleasure in printing extracts from the two speeches and showing readers how Kitchener had borrowed whole passages from his rival unaltered but for the occasional use of a synonym. Lord Minto, an admirer of the C-in-C, thought the episode particularly absurd because Kitchener had little else to do, hardly ever wrote his own notes and, according to various people, never did any work after midday.[96] Appointed C-in-C in 1913, General Duff was the first person to have to plan a major campaign under Kitchener's system. The new organization functioned much as Curzon had predicted and was largely responsible for the tragedy in Mesopotamia in 1916 (see below pp. 477–80).

were at the top of the steps, but there was no sign of the Viceroy. The party retired to the drawing-room in a rather strained atmosphere which was not lightened by Curzon's entrance, a few minutes later, in slippers and a shooting jacket. He was very affable, however, and dined alone with Minto to discuss various issues. The following morning the Curzons drove down to the harbour with the full viceregal escort of two cavalry regiments and a battery of horse artillery, said goodbye to Lord Minto and departed.[97]

The new Viceroy, who originally believed his welcome was merely slipshod, later convinced himself that it had been an intended slight. Although Curzon had meant to be friendly, Minto surmised, his 'intense vanity overcame him, and . . . he could not miss the opportunity of minimising his successor's reception, whilst doing all in his power to glorify his own departure'. This theory, communicated to Brodrick, was accorded widespread currency, and very soon the King, the Prince of Wales and many others were able to share Minto's outrage. In fact Curzon was guilty of insensitivity rather than vanity or insult. The reception had been cancelled by Lamington, Minto's official host, who knew of Curzon's desire to spend time with his successor and seems to have tried to anticipate his wishes; on learning this, however, the Viceroy could and should have countermanded his orders. As for the meeting in slippers and shooting jacket, this too was an act of thoughtlessness. Nevertheless, Curzon should have realized that Minto, modest about his own talents and apprehensive of the great task facing him, would be particularly sensitive to any suggestion that he was being belittled. It is not difficult to imagine Curzon's reaction if he had been greeted in similar fashion by Elgin.[98]

On that sullen discord ended a viceroyalty often seen as both the apogee of the British empire and the beginning of its decline. Unquestionably it lacked an elementary dimension, a vision of what India might become or of what she might one day want to become. Curzon thought that what she needed was beneficent rule, a Roman proconsulship or an enlightened despotism, not sympathetic guiding towards constitutional development. He loved the people of India, as he claimed, but he did not love them as a parent who watches his children grow from dependant infants via stages of increasing independence to adulthood. He was like the headmaster of a school whose pupils are always the same age and whom he therefore treats in the same way from one year to the next. Such treatment, in India as elsewhere, may be good for certain people for a certain time, but it cannot last and it cannot become a permanent system. At best, as in Curzon's case, it may induce respect, but it brings neither affection nor gratitude.

No doubt Curzon will always be remembered in India for the partition of Bengal and for his failure to show sympathy for nationalist aspirations; he will continue to be criticized for his reluctance to appoint Indians to senior posts in the higher services. But as the years go by and the indignation subsides, the perspective alters, the magnitude of the aim becomes clearer and more impressive, the personal failings diminish in significance. Looking back in the late 1960s over a long and distinguished career, the pro-Congress journalist, Durga Das, was able to appreciate the merits of Curzon's rule. Three generations after the Viceroy's university reforms had been condemned as an insult to the Bengali nation, an Indian nationalist could accept that they had in fact borne 'the stamp of a courageous vision'. Once his myopia towards Congress was set aside, Curzon emerged, according to Das, as 'one of the principal architects of modern India', a statesman whose assertion of the Subcontinent's rights and autonomy made him 'the midwife of India's emergence on the world scene'. Like Gandhi, he had 'worked steadfastly to lift India to the status of Britain's greatest partner in the Empire'. But the true comparison, asserted Das, was with Nehru. 'Both were patrician intellectuals endowed with an abundance of gifts . . . two men of destiny' who devoted themselves to the wellbeing of India.[99]

If Curzon's attitude to nationalism showed that he was not the most far-sighted of rulers, he was surely the greatest of administrators. His viceroyalty had been great in many things, in the efficiency of government and the zeal for reform, in the pursuit of justice and of the welfare of the people, in the sympathy for India and the preservation of its monuments. It had been ambitious but honourable, egotistical but high-minded, proud but not vainglorious, resolute but never squalid nor underhand. Even Mr Gokhale, the nationalists' most eloquent spokesman, recognized that the Viceroy was a rare spirit who lived for lofty ends and made a religion of his work.[100] Later generations have seen the glitter but not the glory, have not known or cared about the achievement because the inhabitants of a small island almost without overseas possessions cannot share the ideals of a great empire, even one run by their grandfathers. But at the time, before the First World War changed everything, Curzon's work was admired by those who shared his view of imperial duty and even by some who did not. Speaking of the former Viceroy in 1909, John Morley, the embodiment of the highest tradition of Little England Liberalism, told the House of Lords that

you will never send to India, and you have never sent to India, a viceroy his superior, if, indeed, his equal, in force of mind, in unsparing and remorseless industry, in passionate and devoted interest in all that concerns the well-being of India, with an imagination fired by the grandeur of the political problem that India presents – you never sent a man with more of all these attributes than when you sent Lord Curzon.[101]

22

'Every Man's Hand'

T HE FALLEN VICEROY reached England on 3 December 1905. His elder sister, Sophy MacMichael, had met the family at Marseille and taken the children to Cap Martin, leaving their parents to return home alone. The first night was spent at the Lord Warden Hotel in Dover where two of his supporters, Younghusband and Barnes, travelled down to meet him. Curzon talked till midnight about Indian events, recalled Younghusband, and was 'exceedingly sore' at his treatment by the Government.[1] The following morning they reached Charing Cross Station, twenty-four hours before the terminus roof collapsed. 'How like St John', remarked Mary afterwards, 'to bring it off a day too late!'[2]

A crowd of friends and well-wishers were waiting on the platform to greet them. The saddest absentee was Clinton Dawkins, Curzon's old friend from Balliol and the Viceroy's Council, who had died two days earlier. Less excusable was the absence of friends in the Cabinet and among the Souls, several of whom were skulking guiltily at Stanway. The King had felt strongly that the Prime Minister and the Secretary of State should be at Charing Cross to welcome the returning Viceroy. But Brodrick had excused himself, citing precedents of other Viceroys who had not been given a 'reception' and relaying a report that Curzon would refuse to speak to him. He urged Balfour to decline also, remarking that he had arranged to be at some hours' distance from London on the 4th and hoping that his chief would find the date equally inconvenient for himself.[3] But the Prime Minister had no need to invent an excuse: he had decided to resign his office that very afternoon.

Lady Cowper had assured Mary that her husband's achievements would survive long after Brodrick's failures in public life had been forgotten.[4] But most of their mutual friends had been converted to Brodrick's point of view by assiduous propaganda conjoined with sorrowful assertions that Curzon's behaviour was the result of illness and near insanity. Alfred Lyttelton managed to believe that Kitchener had been greatly misrepresented, and Arnold-Forster, despite his admiration for Curzon and his own experience of Brodrick's intrigues at the War Office, came to a similar conclusion. From South Africa Lord Selborne advanced a less one-sided opinion. While accepting the view of his recent colleagues that Curzon was 'hopelessly in the wrong' and had become impossible to work with, he told Lady Salisbury that her hero Kitchener was 'absolutely unscrupulous' and declared that he was still convinced of Curzon's 'vast potentialities for good'.[5]

Brodrick was also largely responsible for the fact that Curzon, alone among Viceroys, returned home without an honour or any official recognition of his services to India and the empire. Undeceived by Brodrick's flow of epistolary misinformation, King Edward had been on the Viceroy's side during the controversy with Kitchener, a stance supported by his Private Secretary, Lord Knollys, and by the Keeper of the Privy Purse, Sir Dighton Probyn, a veteran soldier who had won the Victoria Cross in the Mutiny. The monarch wanted to telegraph Curzon an honour immediately after his resignation and at the beginning of September told Balfour that he should be offered an earldom at once. The Secretary of State objected, on the grounds that Curzon would soon be airing his grievances in public, and urged Balfour to oppose the idea. If an honour had to be given, he begged the Prime Minister to make it a viscountcy rather than an earldom.[6]

At Balmoral a few days later, the King questioned Sandars, Balfour's Private Secretary, about both Kitchener's behaviour and Brodrick's mismanagement of the crisis. After talking at length of the need to give the former Viceroy an honour, the monarch added, 'Poor Curzon, with all his faults a great man – a popular man – but more – very likely a dangerous man if he is allowed to come home with no laurels on his brow'.[7] Soon afterwards Brodrick took advantage of an audience to attempt to change the King's mind, but without success. His Majesty retained his 'strong opinion' about the honour and did not agree with Brodrick's view that the memories of the last few months could 'dwarf' Curzon's previous achievements. Indeed he held the opposite view that any recent shortcomings should not be allowed to obliterate the distinguished services of the previous five years. Brodrick's response was to send Knollys some articles from the *Pioneer*, a newspaper which had invariably criticized Curzon, and to argue that an honour for the former Viceroy would be misinterpreted by Bengalis.[8]

The Prime Minister's views were more subtle and his tactics more sophisticated. Sandars's advice to refuse the King's appeal on the grounds of Curzon's behaviour was rejected in favour of prevarication. Balfour decided to dispute not the merits of the honour but the timing, arguing that its award in the aftermath of the Viceroy's resignation would be regarded as a slight upon Brodrick and Kitchener. When the King suggested that the peerage should come from him personally rather than from the Government, the Prime Minister persuaded him that such a course would be unconstitutional. The monarch did not give in, however, and in October Balfour told Brodrick that only after 'a good deal of trouble' at Balmoral had their views on the issue prevailed. The King had already urged Curzon not to continue the controversy at home and suggested to Balfour that he should be given an honour on condition that he did not attack the Government. The Prime Minister replied that he could not offer a peerage as the price of silence, repeated his view that the award should not be made so soon after the dispute, and finally convinced his sovereign to postpone the issue until the New Year.[9]

Brodrick's further denunciations of Curzon seem to have had some influence on the views of the royal entourage. At the end of November Knollys admitted to the Secretary of State that the former Viceroy had 'certain defects' in his character which went far 'towards marring his really remarkable qualities'. Ten days later he told Brodrick the King had sent him on a mission – with 'no hope of success' – to call on Curzon soon after his arrival 'to try and prevent him making a fool of himself'.[10] According to the former Viceroy, the purpose of Knollys's visit was to discover whether he was anxious to proceed to the House of Lords in the near future. Seven years earlier Curzon had accepted an Irish peerage from Queen Victoria so that he could re-enter the House of Commons on his return. Now, in view of his poor health and the fluid political situation, he had not yet decided whether to accept one of half a dozen invitations from various constituencies to stand in the forthcoming general election. At an audience two days later, however, the King gave his opinion that an ex-Viceroy should not go into the House of Commons or at any rate fight a contested seat soon after his return from India. But he would not object if he stood for the City of

London or the University of Oxford, constituencies in a separate class which had both approached Curzon.[11] As it happened, neither of the expected vacancies in these seats occurred. Denied by royal wish the chance of fighting the January 1906 election, Curzon thus had no excuse for disobeying his doctor's orders to take Mary and himself to the Riviera to rejoin the children.

Three weeks of the December cold had had a disastrous effect on Mary's health. She coughed incessantly, and an infection of the lungs made it difficult for her to breathe properly. Walking upstairs was such an effort that she needed to rest for several minutes once she had reached the top. The French respite began inauspiciously. After a long train journey in a crowded compartment with screaming children who kept tripping over their feet, the Curzons reached Cap Martin to find the hotel expensive, the cooking poor and the rooms so cold that Mary's cough worsened. They moved to Cannes in search of warmth, but it was some time before she began to improve; even while dressing she nearly suffocated from breathlessness. A doctor diagnosed that her heart had not recovered from the strain of the previous year but assured her that, if she was careful, she had a good many years of life ahead of her.[12]

From Cannes Curzon wrote to commiserate with a friend who had also found himself unexpectedly unemployed. They must now, he declared, 'do nothing and do it devilish well'. 'We must build and decorate houses and buy pictures and entertain each other and lead a Renaissance life without the crime.'[13] Although Curzon did devote much of his future leisure to these and other Renaissance activities, hard work remained by far his most time-consuming activity until the end of his life. At Cannes he occupied his days preparing the third part of his Indian vindication. Immediately after his resignation he had compiled 'Indian Military Organisation 1902–1905', an essay with documents on his dispute with Kitchener which he had privately printed and circulated to a small group of friends such as Cromer, Lawrence and R.B. Haldane. Later he produced a short and restrained pamphlet on the issue which he planned to publish until friends persuaded him that the public was too engrossed in the political situation to interest itself further in the controversy. The third production, suggested by Sir Thomas Raleigh, his old colleague on the Viceroy's Council, was an edition of some of his speeches in India. Curzon was asked by the publisher Macmillan to supply the introduction, but he thought it wiser to distance himself from the work and left the task to Raleigh. Nevertheless, he took immense trouble over its production, spending Christmas and New Year going through his speeches and writing twenty-three letters to Macmillan between January and March on margins, page widths and other details of publication. In one he complained that the photograph selected for the frontispiece made him so dark that he might be taken for a Hottentot and asked to be relieved of this suspicion. The work was published in both Britain and India, but its appeal was limited: by 1918 it had sold less than 4,000 copies and had earned its author only £210, barely half of his advance. Macmillan blamed the disappointment on 'a prejudice in the mind of the ordinary reader against speeches as such'.[14]

The Unionist Government had limped through 1905, unconvincing both to itself and to the country. When it lost its seventh by-election of the year in October at Barkton Ash, a seat the party has never managed to lose at any other time, it became clear to Arnold-Forster that he and his Cabinet colleagues had outstayed their time and ought to go.[15] Balfour hung on until December, resigning on the day of Curzon's arrival, and two days later, when the former Viceroy went for his royal audience, he coincided with the Liberal leader, Sir Henry Campbell-Bannerman, who had just been asked to form a government. The divisions which had bedevilled the Liberal Party since Gladstone's retirement, and which had been exacerbated by the Boer War, were adroitly healed by this patient and imperturbable Scot, who proceeded to form the most talented single-party ministry of the twentieth century. His first exhibition of statesmanship was to thwart the 'Relugas compact' – an absurd and irresponsible attempt by the leading Liberal imperialists to force him into the House of Lords – and unite his party by rewarding the conspirators, Asquith, Grey and Haldane, with three of the most senior posts in the Cabinet. After sorting out his allies, Campbell-Bannerman dissolved Parliament and confronted the Unionists.

The 1906 general election provided the worst Unionist result of all time and the last occasion on which the Liberal Party gained an absolute majority. Such are the vagaries of the electoral system, however, that, although the Unionists lost 60 per cent of their seats and were reduced to 157 MPs, they won 43.4 per cent of the vote, a higher proportion than the party has sometimes gained in later 'landslide' victories. Among the new Liberal intake were several former members of the ICS who had conceived personal grudges against Curzon.* Among the defeated Tories were Balfour himself, who was easily beaten in East Manchester, Alfred Lyttelton, who was defeated at Leamington, and Brodrick, who was turned out at Guildford. Gerald Balfour went down at Leeds, and Lord Stanley, the Postmaster-General who had referred to Post Office workers as 'blood-sucking' blackmailers, suffered a humiliation in his Lancashire family fiefdom. 'With sober gaiety', Curzon wrote to Pearl Craigie from Cannes, 'we witness the disappearance of those who have treated us so ill.'[16] When Parliament reassembled, only three members of the late Cabinet were sitting on the Opposition benches.

The result has usually been seen as a defeat for Tariff Reform, whose adherents did well only in Birmingham, Liverpool and Sheffield. Balfour, however, preferred to ascribe the débâcle primarily to 'Chinese slavery', regarding Milner's decision to allow overseers to inflict corporal punishment on coolies in the South African mines as an 'amazing blunder' which violated 'every canon of international morality, of law, and of policy'.[17] Another factor must have been the electorate's boredom with a party that had been in power for the last ten years and had led it into a mismanaged war. Balfour, who was unprepared for the scale of the disaster or for the size of his own defeat in Manchester, was thought to be 'seriously upset'. But there was a masochistic streak in Balfour, and his reactions were not those of other politicians. To Lady Salisbury he confessed that he was 'horribly ashamed at feeling a kind of illegitimate exhilaration at the catastrophe' which had occurred. It had made him 'more violently and pleasurably interested in politics' than he had been since the Home Rule Bill.[18]

The new Secretary of State for India was that fastidious and umbrageous man of letters, John Morley, a former Chief Secretary for Ireland and a Victorian veteran as out of sympathy with Liberal imperialism as he was with the social reforming ambitions of Lloyd George. He had not wanted to go to the India Office and was uncertain whether the British Raj could or should survive. A believer in the Whig tenets of history and a champion of Gladstonian Liberalism, he knew that political ideas which may have been appropriate to Western Christian societies were not often applicable to India.[19] Liberal rule in the

---

*These included Donald Smeaton, whom he refused to make Lieutenant-Governor of Burma, Sir Henry Cotton, whom he did not appoint to the lieutenant-governorship of Bengal, and John Rees, whom, in spite of reiterated applications, he did not recommend for a knighthood.

Subcontinent, he believed, could not therefore be a mapped journey with a clear destination, but an illuminating trusteeship that removed grievances, granted certain freedoms and implanted, slowly and prudently, British ideas of justice and humanity.

Morley's first important task at the India Office was to decide whether to implement Brodrick's scheme of military administration; a telegram was therefore quickly sent to Minto informing him that the issue was to be reconsidered. Like most Liberals, Morley had instinctively supported Curzon in the dispute, and in a speech at Arbroath in October declared that the Viceroy had been chased out of power by the military with the sanction of the Secretary of State. 'If there is one principle more than any other', he added, 'that has been accepted in this country since the day when Charles I lost his head, it is this – that the civil power should be supreme over the military power.'[20] Among Morley's new Cabinet colleagues, the former Viceroys, Ripon and Elgin, had opposed Brodrick, and several others, notably Grey and Haldane, believed the whole question should be re-opened. The Prime Minister felt similarly on the matter. When General Brackenbury told him he hoped the 'awful blunder' in India would be reversed, Campbell-Bannerman replied that he fully sympathized with his views.[21]

One of Morley's earliest visitors at his new post was Curzon. He was 'powerful, eloquent and vehement,' the Secretary of State reported to Minto, and seemed impatient at the minister's determination to take time to review the case. Morley told the Viceroy that the importance of the issue had been exaggerated by both sides but admitted he thought Brodrick's scheme was a mistake. Before leaving for the South of France, Curzon sent him a copy of Kitchener's famous letter to General Stedman, which he himself had only just seen. Morley considered it 'outrageous, almost too ugly for belief', and said that it deepened and completed his impression of the C-in-C's methods.[22] Over Christmas and the New Year, several of the former Viceroy's supporters reinforced his case with Morley, including the last two Military Members, Collen and Elles, who submitted a compromise proposal. Godley reported to Minto that his new chief had been 'tremendously battered by Curzon, and by Curzonians great and small', and he was sure they had made an impression upon him. From Cannes Curzon admitted to Barrow that he felt hopeful though 'not absolutely confident' that Brodrick's policy would be reversed.[23]

Meanwhile a vigorous campaign was being waged from the opposite quarter. Kitchener suffered from the disadvantage of having fewer admirers in the Liberal hierarchy than among the Unionist leaders. His most eminent supporter there was Lord Rosebery, whom he had arranged for Colonel Hamilton to brief,[24] but the former Liberal premier had refused to become involved with the Government, and his influence was declining. Morley himself was no admirer of Kitchener. Apart from disapproving of his methods, he found him 'a most uninteresting type' and had been one of a small minority of MPs to vote against a grant for his services in the Sudan.[25] Kitchener's partisans felt it wise, therefore, for him to stay out of the conflict and leave matters to them. Lord Esher, the most influential of this group, advised him to keep quiet, be nice to Minto, and designate someone in London to look after his interests rather than leave them in 'the somewhat tactless hands of Mr Brodrick'.[26] As in the previous campaign, an important figure was Repington, who reported developments to Marker, now back on Kitchener's staff in India, from where he wrote aggressive letters to newspapers which held pro-Curzon opinions. Repington set about his task of helping Kitchener by 'readying' Morley for a meeting with Curzon and by 'spoon-feeding' him with flattery and propaganda. At the end of January he gave a lunch for the Secretary of State, sat him between two of the most intelligent generals (Smith-Dorrien and Ian Hamilton) 'with instructions to ply him hard', and completed the party with three civilian partisans, Buckle of *The Times*, Clarke of the Imperial Defence Committee, and Esher. 'Very fortunately,' he reported, 'Ian had a letter from Lord K in his pocket which said the nicest things about Morley.'[27] The Secretary of State, whose vanity was seldom satisfied that his talents were sufficiently appreciated, was so delighted that he took the letter away with him.

In a finely balanced contest, with Morley inclined to one side and Godley and the India Council on the other, the crucial factor was the attitude of the Viceroy. Minto had listened to Curzon's case at Bombay and, according to Morley, was *'thoroughly roused'* to the dangers of Brodrick's scheme.[28] But he had been subjected much more to the arguments of the other side, from the Unionist Government to which he owed his appointment when he was in Britain, and from Kitchener whom he had to live beside in India. In addition, his resentment at his reception in Bombay had rapidly transformed itself into a grievance of obsessive proportions. Curzon had belatedly realized his mistake, and a former member of his staff had written to Minto's secretary explaining that he had been eager to see the incoming Viceroy, that no slight had been intended, and that he had gone to a lot of trouble and stayed up late when he was ill, overworked and depressed to prepare notes for his use.[29] But by then it was too late. Minto had already described the episode to the King and had told the Prince of Wales in detail about Curzon's extremely casual greeting and the 'very hugger-mugger swearing in' on the following day.[30] Walter Lawrence, who had returned to India with the Prince of Wales's party, told his former chief that the incident may have helped push Minto into Kitchener's camp.[31] More damagingly for Curzon's future, it had greatly 'pained' the King and turned the Prince of Wales, a stickler for these things, into a lifelong enemy. From the vantage point of his shooting camp, where he had got 'a very good bag' of tigers and panthers, the future George V satisfied himself that Kitchener had been greatly misrepresented by his opponents and that Curzon had 'never done a single thing right so long as he was in India'. Even Godley, who loved to feed Minto gossip about his predecessor's misfortunes, thought the language and 'rather vigorous' tirades of this very dim prince were excessive.[32]

The Viceroy's prejudices were fortified by a series of sycophantic letters from Brodrick abusing Curzon and congratulating the Mintos on establishing a regime 'which maintains dignity without swagger, and which combines magnificence with simplicity'. The former Secretary of State naturally urged him to stand by the policy of his despatch of 31 May and, to assist his argument, made the thoroughly mendacious claim that 'every soldier on this side of the water who was consulted and every official was [sic] a party to the decision of last summer'. He also advised Minto to warn Morley that 'all the dogs of war' would break loose if Kitchener was overruled.[33] But Minto had little need of Brodrick's sophistry to help him make up his mind. Kitchener had taken Esher's advice to be friendly and co-operative, and this new phenomenon, combined with the memory of the Bombay reception, was enough for the Viceroy. A month after his landing Minto concluded that the C-in-C had been 'very much misjudged', and three weeks later he told Morley that the late Government's scheme of military administration was 'the most workable that can be proposed'.[34]

Kitchener was no longer in a minority of one on the Viceroy's Council. Apart from Minto, he had converted Baker, the Finance Member, to his side, and could count on the support of Scott who, as Curzon had foreseen, was a 'placid old dummy' willing to do what he was told. Although Ibbetson, Hewett and the other two members remained loyal to Curzon's viewpoint, the Council was now evenly divided on the issue. This was another obstacle for Morley. He had wanted to reconstruct the old Military Department and was not frightened of resignation threats from Kitchener; indeed he had let it be known that the C-in-C's resignation would be immediately accepted. But he did not want to be the second consecutive Secretary of State to overrule the Viceroy on the matter, especially when Minto was supported by half his Council in India, the India Council in London, and a public opinion in England which seemed to prefer a provisional and even unsatisfactory settlement to the prolongation of a dispute which few people understood. Morley thus accepted the principles of the previous Government's scheme while partially disarming the dissentient members of the Viceroy's Council by adopting their views on a subsidiary matter, the functions of the Secretary of the new Army Department.[35]

Curzon, however, was not in the least disarmed. In a move that did little good to himself or his cause, he wrote a long letter to *The Times* denouncing Brodrick's plans and his proceedings, and pointing out that Morley's concession on a small and relatively unimportant issue did not re-establish the principle of civilian control that had been impugned the previous year.[36] He was indignant because Morley had led him to believe that he would reverse the decision and had then climbed down under pressure while the former Viceroy was at Cannes. But it had not been, as Curzon believed, a case of mere pusillanimity, a decision taken simply in order to avoid a row after Morley's arrival at the India Office. Curzon's compromise of the previous June had complicated matters for the Secretary of State because it would clearly have been difficult to reverse a scheme that had been accepted in principle, however reluctantly and subjected to whatever modifications, by the Viceroy and his Council.[37]

The Liberals soon had another disappointment for Curzon. In the summer of 1904, when the Viceroy was still on good terms with his party leader, Balfour had suggested recommending him for a peerage in case the Government fell before his second return from India and its Liberal successor decided not to honour him. Curzon mentioned several precedents for cross-party elevations of a returning Viceroy but agreed to refer the matter to Lord Knollys, who said he would discuss it with the King. Accordingly, he received a letter from Knollys in September that year conveying the monarch's view that the office of Viceroy was above party politics and that the King would insist on him being offered an honour even if the Liberals were in power. Curzon regarded this, understandably, as a categoric pledge.[38]

A year and a half later, after accepting his sovereign's plea not to stand at the 1906 election, Curzon heard from Knollys that the King was anxious to give him an earldom and that Campbell-Bannerman and Morley had approved of the proposal. Curzon agreed to leave the decision to King Edward but was so surprised to hear nothing more that after three weeks he wrote to Knollys to find out what had happened. From Bath, where the King's Private Secretary had gone for a cure, he received an embarrassed reply communicating the monarch's profound regret that Campbell-Bannerman had decided after all not to recommend an honour. Enclosed was a copy of the Prime Minister's letter which argued that the Government could not be expected to offer a peerage which had ostentatiously been withheld by the former Viceroy's 'friends'. Had Curzon returned from India after the Liberals had come to power, Knollys said, the King would have been in a better position to insist on an honour. But in the circumstances there was nothing much that could be done.[39]

Curzon was extremely disheartened by the Prime Minister's 'petty and mean' letter. 'One wonders where the hail storm that rains upon us is to stop,' he wrote to Mary. 'We are nearly beaten to the ground.'[40] The injustice of the case almost overwhelmed him. Northbrook had been given an earldom by Disraeli although he was a Liberal appointed by Gladstone and had resigned as Viceroy after a disagreement with the Tory Government. Elgin had been given the Garter by Salisbury although he too had been appointed by Gladstone and was now a member of the Liberal Cabinet. Yet Curzon was denied recognition after seven years' service during which he had enjoyed the support of the Liberal Party on most issues and above all in the controversy over which he had resigned. He rejected Campbell-Bannerman's argument about his 'friends'. For Curzon, the only possible explanation for his exclusion was the Government's fear of being attacked on the military question in the House of Lords where the Liberals had no effective debaters on Indian affairs. Support for this view came from conversations with Knollys and later with Morley, and further evidence, which naturally he did not see, is contained in the correspondence between the India Office and Lord Minto. In May Godley suggested to the Secretary of State that, if the Liberals wanted to honour Curzon without giving him political status, they could promote him from his Irish barony to an Irish earldom, which would get him no nearer the House of Lords. 'J.M. laughed heartily,' he reported to Minto, 'and I really believe meant to mention it to C.B.'[41]

Excluded from the House of Commons by the wishes of the King and from the House of Lords by the decision of the Prime Minister, Curzon found himself suddenly, for the first time in his life, with no political prospects. As the Liberals had an overall majority of 130 in the Commons and were thus unlikely to be forced out of power before the end of their term, he seemed destined to spend at least the next six years without even the consolation of parliamentary opposition. In April 1906, on the advice of Knollys, he sent a rather desperate letter to the King summarizing the case, and shortly afterwards he was informed that the monarch had made it a 'point of honour' to press for a peerage on his official birthday in June. As the date approached without bringing any further information, Curzon went to see the Prime Minister to find out if his name would be included in the forthcoming list. According to Morley, Campbell-Bannerman was astonished and extremely displeased by his visitor's haughty air. According to Curzon, the Prime Minister hummed and hawed, repeated his argument against proposing an honour which had been withheld by Balfour, and said he wished to consult certain friends before giving a final decision. Once the former Viceroy was off the premises, it did not take Campbell-Bannerman long to make up his mind, and that same day he told Curzon by letter that he did 'not expect to find it' his duty to raise him to the British peerage. Unable to pursue the matter further with either the Liberals or the King, Curzon shortly afterwards went and harangued Balfour, whom he blamed for his inability to enter the House of Lords, his exclusion from public life while a Liberal ministry remained in power, and the refusal to grant him, alone among Viceroys, recognition of his services to India. Balfour replied that he could not have recommended an honour with the dispute still in progress and that, in any case, no one was bound to make an offer which he was confident would be refused.[42]

Few politicians have fallen further for political reasons. Even Prime Ministers ousted by their own colleagues retain their seats and a parliamentary following. Curzon was in despair, sometimes breaking down and describing his life as a failure and a mockery.[43] But if his career had reached its nadir, his life outside politics had some way still to drop.

Mary had looked so much better in the spring that her friends thought she had recovered. But she herself had doubts and in June told her brother she feared she would never be well. Soon she was an invalid again, unable to do anything more strenuous than accompany her husband on afternoon drives in Battersea Park. Suffering from what she called 'these devilish ills', she broke down one day in early July, made a scene and cried all night. The following evening she left a letter on Curzon's pillow apologizing for being such a burden just when he needed help, and promising to be brave, to keep her nerve and not to add to the shadows in his life. The letter sent her husband to bed in tears. In reply he praised her courage and temper and said he thought of nothing but making her better 'so that we may both lift our heads again and go ahead. Nothing else matters but to make my darling well again, and then if she is happy, my cup will brim over'.[44]

Over the next few days, however, she deteriorated, and on the 19th her strength gradually went. The doctors kept her alive through the day with oxygen, champagne and strychnine, but her breathing finally collapsed in the late afternoon and after a last struggle she died in her husband's arms. Like Curzon , she had had a horror of anyone seeing the dead, and no member of the family saw the body. That night she was placed in her coffin with his photograph in her hand and a flower he had chosen on her breast. To her mother he wrote that same evening:

> There has gone from me the truest, most devoted, most unselfish, most beautiful and brilliant wife that a man ever had, and I am left with three little motherless children and a broken life. Nothing, however, can take from me the memory of eleven happy and long years, and somewhere her spirit is watching over me and doing what good she can . . .'[45]

Mary Curzon was buried at Kedleston the following Monday to the strains of 'Abide with me' and Chopin's Funeral March; a similar service was held at the same time at St Margaret's, Westminster. Only members of the two families were invited to the funeral in Derbyshire, which was conducted by Welldon. Curzon was ill in bed on the morning of the ceremony, and in his misery inveighed to his old friend against those who had been his enemies in his Indian career.[46] He stayed at Kedleston for a week, visiting the grave each day, and in future years made a point of spending the anniversary of her death at his ancestral home. It was at Kedleston that he made his memorial for her, a lovely Gothic chapel built to the north side of the nave of the family church. It took him six years to collect everything he needed, the Aventurine quartz for the floor, the Serravezza marble for the tomb, the stained glass, the chapel furniture, the iron grilles he designed from the *rejas* of Spanish cathedrals. He thought much about the scenes to be depicted in the windows and accepted Sibell Grosvenor's idea that they should contain the St

Marys of the New Testament. Although he hesitated about including
Mary Magdalene, in the end he divided three windows between the nine
Marys of the Church and devoted the fourth to St George and the
Dragon. In the centre of the chapel he designed his Mary's tomb in
white marble and – in accordance with the promise he had made at
Walmer – arranged for her recumbent figure to be joined by his.[47] On
the north wall he placed a memorial tablet with the inscription:

MARY VICTORIA
LADY CURZON OF KEDLESTON
BORN MAY 27, 1870   DIED JULY 18, 1906
PERFECT IN LOVE AND LOVELINESS
BEAUTY WAS THE LEAST OF HER RARE GIFTS
GOD HAD ENDUED WITH LIKE GRACES
HER MIND AND SOUL
FROM ILLNESS ALL BUT UNTO DEATH
RESTORED ONLY TO DIE
SHE WAS MOURNED IN THREE CONTINENTS
AND BY HER DEAREST
WILL BE
FOR EVER UNFORGOTTEN

Curzon received more than eleven hundred letters and telegrams of
condolence, and to the vast majority he replied in his own hand. Later
he sorted through Mary's belongings, finding brooches and ornaments
and asking her friends to accept them 'in memory of the days that are
no more'. Without her he was broken, for she had given him unselfish
love and support throughout his troubles. Valentine Chirol reminded
him of a conversation in the Persian Gulf in 1903 when, speaking of the
loneliness and isolation of the Viceroy, Curzon had said, 'I hardly think
I could bear it if it were not for Mary by my side to share all my thoughts
and hopes and fears'. And some months before her death, while
showing the journalist various papers connected with his downfall, he
said with an outburst of emotion, 'I think if Mary had died two years
ago [*sic*] at Walmer, and I had not had her by my side to help me bear all
this, it would have killed me'.[48] Time did little healing, and in future
years he sometimes said he was not afraid of dying because it would
enable him to be with Mary in heaven.

After her death he went to Scotland to the house where they had
planned to entertain friends. One of them, Ian Malcolm, recorded how

he acted 'the genial host, the delightful *raconteur*, the keen sportsman' anxious for his guests to obtain as much enjoyment as possible from the hills. But beneath the pose he could see 'a broken-hearted misery and distraction' such as he hoped never to witness in anyone again. From his closest friends Curzon was unable to conceal his unhappiness. 'Every man's hand', he wrote to one, 'has long been against me, and now God's hand has turned against me too.'[49]

23

Picking up the Pieces

THERE WAS LITTLE chance of Curzon becoming a forgotten figure in the political wilderness. Few people accepted his own dismal view of his career or doubted that he would come back to play a prominent part in public life. Hoping to keep him out of national politics, Balfour urged him to accept the chairmanship of the London County Council. According to Margot Asquith, Lord Cromer wanted Curzon to join him in forming a new political party. Others, who shared Hugh Cecil's view that Curzon was the one Unionist politician whose reputation had not fallen in recent years, hoped he would bid for the leadership of his own party. In the autumn of 1906 Chirol noted that, with Balfour discredited and Chamberlain incapacitated by a stroke, the rank and file of the Unionists were beginning to look to Curzon or Milner as 'the only leaders who may pull the Party out of the wreckage'.[1]

Since King Edward had failed to deliver the promised peerage, Curzon again thought of standing for Parliament and was hoping to re-enter the Commons in the course of 1907. 'We have a safe and soft seat in London waiting for him', Lord Balcarres, a party whip, noted in his journal, 'if AJB can make up his mind to offer it.'[2] But Balfour, he added, was 'rather nervous', and clearly hoped Curzon would exclude himself from Parliament by going to the LCC. In spite of pressure on constituencies from defeated Unionists, the former Viceroy was offered a number of safe seats by sitting members willing to retire so that he could return to public life. Sometimes he asked friends for advice on a particular offer: Lord George Hamilton recommended the rejection of

Hornsey on the grounds that it was too suburban and its constituents would demand the 'genteel drudgery' of tiresome and exacting social gatherings.[3] In the end all were rejected, however rural and undemanding, on medical advice. By the end of 1907, when Morley saw him looking 'very bad' at Windsor, Curzon had reluctantly accepted that he would never be well enough for life in the Lower House.[4]

Single, celebrated and under-employed, Curzon was in much demand as a public speaker. Except during his period of mourning, he spoke frequently at the dinners of institutes and societies all over the country. Delivered from a few notes scrawled on envelopes, his orations asserted the imperial creed in sonorous and majestic tones. At the Birmingham and Midland Institute, of which he was President, he told his audience that 'the true imperialism' must have a moral basis: to the people of the mother state it must be 'a discipline, an inspiration, and a faith', and to the people of the circumference it must give a 'sense of partnership in a great idea, the consecrating influence of a lofty purpose'. At an Empire Day dinner in Milner's honour he declared that the British were unable to escape their imperial destiny. 'The voyage which our predecessors commenced we have to continue. We have to answer our helm, and it is an imperial helm, down all the tides of Time.' Wherever peoples were living in backwardness or barbarism, he told another audience, 'wherever ignorance or superstition is rampant, wherever enlightenment or progress [is] possible, wherever duty and self-sacrifice call – there is, as there has been for hundreds of years, the true summons of the Anglo-Saxon race'. Like Kipling, he did not hesitate to criticize his people's ignorance of imperial matters or to warn them of the consequences of losing their empire. Awarding the public school medal of the Royal Asiatic Society, he observed that for every Englishman who could correctly list the names and number of the Indian provinces, there were one hundred who could give all the Derby winners since the race was first run. If Britain lost India, he had once warned Balfour, she would straightaway become a third-rate power, and in Birmingham Town Hall he told his listeners that their nation without its empire, a country with 'no aspiration but a narrow and selfish materialism', would become merely 'a sort of glorified Belgium'.[5]

Curzon's speeches revealed the nostalgia he felt for his Indian years and youthful travels. On the fiftieth anniversary of the Mutiny he addressed surviving veterans in the Albert Hall in tones similar to those of Kipling who hailed them in verse as 'Keepers of the House of Old'. The 'call of the East' was particularly evident in his installation address as Rector of Glasgow University, a post he had won narrowly in a contest with Lloyd George in 1908. Entitled 'East and West', it contained magniloquent descriptions of the Orient, 'splendid and pathetic, sunlit and sombre, rich beyond dreams and poverty-stricken beyond conception, marvellous and commonplace, cultured and barbarous, the greatest of all contrasts and the most paradoxical of all contradictions'. The mysteries of the East, the recondite philosophies and powerful creeds 'commingled in bewildering juxtaposition with strange idolatries and savage superstitions', remained inscrutable. Asia was like 'some beautiful spirit whose heavy eyelids seem to be always half closed, and who nods, with a half smile on her face, in a land of everlasting dreams'.[6]

Not all his speeches dealt with Oriental enigmas or Britain's custody of them. He spoke on occasions as diverse as the 'Pop' centenary at Eton, a lecture on Tennyson at the Royal Academy and the opening of a working men's club in a Peak District village. Mourning prevented him from addressing the inaugural meeting of the Liverpool branch of the National Anti-Gambling League, but he sent a rather pompous message confessing his inability to see why sport, 'a very manly and noble thing', should be accompanied by gambling, which was neither, nor why spectators, not content with the excitement provided for them, should require 'the additional and unhealthy excitement of staking their money upon efforts over which they have no control'. The growing spirit of gambling, he added, 'must be bad for the race that encourages or practises it'.[7]

The most satisfying moment of Curzon's extra-political years was his election as Chancellor of Oxford University in March 1907. He had hoped to be chosen at the time of the previous vacancy in the autumn of 1903, but the Conservatives, divided behind several candidates, had eventually accepted Lord Goschen as a compromise. Three and a half years later, Curzon's supporters included Salisbury, Milner, Ampthill and Hugh Cecil, while Lansdowne acted as chairman of his London committee. In spite of this array, he expected to be beaten by Rosebery, whose cause was promoted through a vigorous campaign from Christ Church. But in the end the strength and solidity of Oxford conservatism prevailed, giving Curzon an easy victory with 1,001 votes to 440.

Over the previous century the Chancellor had become as insignificant as the Lord Warden of the Cinque Ports, a figurehead without power or even pomp whose installation was effected by a university deputation at his own home. Such a proceeding was not in the style either of Curzon or of the Vice-Chancellor, Herbert Warren, who hoped that a prominent and energetic Chancellor might defend the university from radical critics agitating for reforms. A search for precedents disclosed an account of a ceremony nearly two hundred years earlier which described the new Chancellor's procession to Wren's Sheldonian, his installation in the theatre by the Vice-Chancellor, and the enthusiasm and celebrations which attended it. To this rather vague outline Warren added a ritual, mostly invented by himself, which included an oath and various speeches in Latin.[8] The resulting pageant, highly eclectic and largely bogus, took place in May and was generally regarded as a great success. Two months later Curzon broke another recent tradition by presiding at Encaenia and choosing his own candidates for honorary degrees. They included Campbell-Bannerman and the Duke of Connaught (Curzon's guest at the Delhi Durbar), as well as the slightly more inspired choices of Saint-Saëns, Rodin, Kipling and Mark Twain. If the Prime Minister's selection was intended to disturb his conscience over the peerage issue, it had no discernible effect.

Curzon made it clear straightaway that he did not intend to emulate the passivity of past Chancellors. The university generally welcomed his energy, especially when it was directed towards fund-raising and certain reforms, but he generated less enthusiasm with his determination to supervise matters that had been of no concern to his predecessors. On a rare visit to Balliol, Cecil Spring Rice heard that Curzon was 'making himself objectionable and ruling Oxford like an Indian province'.[9] But as in India he was often objectionable about things that needed to be objected to. When asked to use his influence to gain a baronetcy for someone prepared to endow a Spanish professorship, he replied angrily that the purchase of honours was a scandal of which he wholly disapproved. He also objected to the frequent failure to inform him about honorary degrees, a subject on which he held strong views. The university was never slow to ask his assistance when necessary, he observed, but seemed to have a prejudice against consulting him at other times.[10]

Curzon realized his principal task was to persuade the university to reform itself in order to escape the attentions of a royal commission. Oxford's archaic teaching, antiquated administration and bias in favour of wealthy undergraduates was attracting pressure on the Liberal Government to set up a commission to look into the situation and force comprehensive reforms upon the university. The Chancellor therefore approached two of the ministers, Asquith and Lord Crewe, to ask for time so that he could try reform from the inside first. After securing the Government's agreement, he resided for a brief period in Oxford – at the Judge's Lodgings in St Giles – and characteristically threw himself into an intensive investigation of the University's affairs. Later, after long consultations with senior academic officials, a book appeared, written entirely by himself, about the reforms that were required.

Many of the proposals dealt with the running and organization of the university, its financial administration and improvements in facilities for advanced study and research. Others aimed at encouraging the admission of poor undergraduates and ending the anomaly by which women were allowed to attend lectures and to sit certain examinations without being able to take a degree. He also advocated the abolition of compulsory Greek for BA candidates because the existing law excluded many of the best pupils from secondary schools and was unfair on those coming to read mathematics or science. Greek would retain its influence, said Curzon, as long as learning existed, but it should not be compulsory for all.[11]

The Chancellor's proposals were generally welcomed in Oxford, where they were discussed by the Hebdomadal Council, the university's governing body. After twenty-three special sittings of the Council and one hundred and five meetings of Council sub-committees, a report largely based on Curzon's book was drawn up and published in August 1910. At the end of that year legislation began to make its way through Congregation, the dons' representative body. But its progress was slow. The attempt to abolish compulsory Greek was blocked, and only a modified statute, making the subject optional for undergraduates taking mathematics and natural science, was passed the following summer. Other reforms remained obstructed, and by May 1911 Curzon was in despair. 'I have given up the government of Oxford as beyond hope,' he remarked, adding that he was tempted to ask Asquith for a commission after all. The only consideration that dissuaded him from doing so was his belief that it would destroy the good as well as the bad and result in the disappearance of the Oxford he had known and loved. Much less had been achieved than he had hoped by the autumn of 1914, when academic legislation ceased, and at the end of the war the dreaded commission was at last appointed. The conclusions of the commissioners, however, differed remarkably little from those of the Chancellor, and the expected revolution did not take place.[12] Too radical for the Oxford of their day, Curzon's reforms were thus enacted under a later dispensation.

In the summer of 1908 Curzon was involved in a motor collision near Sunningdale station. His chauffeur was thrown unhurt into a ditch, but he himself was severely gashed across the forehead and knocked senseless. He was carried unconscious to the house of a local barber, Mr Corns, where by good fortune a doctor was delivering a baby of Mrs Corns, a piece of timing which prompted the barber to ask his visitor to be the child's godfather. The prostrate former Viceroy accepted with pleasure, and in due course the baby was christened George Nathaniel Curzon Corns.[13]

This felicitous event did not alas speed the victim's recovery. In poor physical shape already, the accident was a severe shock to his system. Six weeks later his forehead was still swollen and bandaged, and he remained weak and bedridden. Eventually his doctors persuaded him to go away on a long sea voyage. The owners of the other vehicle brought an action against Curzon – which they lost – and thus forced him to defend himself with a rather ambitious counter-claim. Although he could ask for substantial damages on the grounds that he had been ordered abroad for a rest, it would be difficult, his lawyer told him, to show that a tour of South Africa was a necessary part of the cure.* For the journey was not one that any doctor would have recommended but a typically Curzonian combination of long distances, intensive sightseeing and hard writing in spare moments. The composition of his Oxford book recalls the writing of his prize essay on Justinian in the Mediterranean a quarter of a century earlier. Never, he reported to Warren, had a 'Memo' been written in 'more diverse circumstances, in cabins, on decks, in hotels, in trains, at odd moments, 6,000 miles away from England and books'. Begun on the voyage to the Cape in December 1908, the book was completed on his return in February.[14]

Oxford absorbed only a part of Curzon's intellectual energy on the journey, which he made with his sister Blanche. In the Canary Islands, where they spent a fortnight, he read a manuscript history of the Canning Club and despatched a long letter to its author, the son of his friend Selborne, congratulating him on the work but advising him to alter the style, syntax and organization of the text. He also found time to write a thirty-six page letter to Balfour on the seditious state of India, which he blamed on Minto's weak Government, and to read a 'miniature library' about Napoleon's last years at St Helena, a subject he

---

*In December of the following year, after a strong summing-up in his favour, the jury awarded Curzon £155 for the repair of his car and £100 for general damages.

thought had been misinterpreted by historians and which he was tempted to write about himself. By the time they reached St Helena, he felt he was as familiar with the house at Longwood as if he had lived there himself. While he did not observe a minute's silence in the house of his hero's death – as Winston Churchill once did in the house of his birth[15] – he corrected the French Consul (who lived there) so authoritatively on a matter of detail that he was invited to act as guide to a house he had never previously seen. After identifying the room Napoleon had used for billiards at Longwood, he then managed to find his billiard table in an unused part of the Governor's residence.[16]

In South Africa Curzon was able to pursue both human and natural grandeur. A connoisseur of great waterfalls, he found the Victoria Falls of the Zambezi to be the most wonderful of all with 'those towers of descending foam, the shouting face of the cataract, the thunder of the watery phalanxes as they charge and reel and are shattered in the bottom of the abyss . . .'[17] He stayed in Cecil Rhodes's house at Cape Town and visited his grave in the Matopo Hills near Bulawayo. As he travelled through the wide solitudes of the veld, he reflected on the spirit of Rhodes and was heartened by what he saw of the efforts of British and Boers to forget the past and build the dead man's vision of unity. The South African journey was Curzon's closest attempt at a holiday for many years and did much to restore his spirits and improve his health. It also left an imperishable image in the memory of his host at Cape Town, Sir Walter Hely Hutchinson, who took him one day for a drive along the coast. Curzon was busy doffing his hat to people who cheered as they drove past, when a whale swam close to the shore and spouted. Delighted by this act of homage, the former proconsul stiffly raised his hat to the whale.[18] As a master of self-parody Curzon was unequalled.

His new interests and activities did not displace India as the central preoccupation of Curzon's life. Morley's settlement of the military issue neither reduced his attention to the Subcontinent's affairs nor led to improved relations between the former Viceroy and his successor. Curzon's tactlessness towards Minto on his arrival and on a couple of subsequent matters had bred such virulent resentment that the Viceroy could no longer refer to him politely. An unhealthy proportion of Minto's correspondence with the Secretary of State was devoted to denunciations of Curzon's policies and behaviour, exaggerated claims about his unpopularity, and references to his 'extraordinary tyranny and egotism'. Not understanding the depth of the grievance he had provoked, Curzon was hurt by Minto's refusal to write to him and annoyed by his repeated public pronouncements that he had come to India to bring peace and security to a distracted country. Minto's attitude towards his predecessor disturbed Ampthill, who told him that the failure to acknowledge Curzon's services to India was regarded by the former Viceroy as an unprecedented slight and a great unkindness. After trying to convince Minto that the Bombay muddle had been prompted by Curzon's eagerness to see him, Ampthill suggested that an appreciative reference in a public speech would go far to heal his soreness. The advice was disregarded.[19]

Minto's new grievances stemmed from the conviction that his predecessor was trying to retain influence in India at his expense. Suggestions made by Curzon to Morley, often at the Secretary of State's request, were treated in a disproportionate manner, magnified and depicted as gross examples of interference. Advice on an appointment to the Viceroy's Council, a matter on which it was normal for a former Viceroy to be consulted, was regarded by Minto as 'perfectly monstrous', an example of 'unbearable' and 'unpardonable' behaviour and of 'the utter bad taste' of Curzon's attempts to influence Indian affairs.[20] Early on in his viceroyalty, Minto managed to convince himself that his predecessor was manipulating the British press. One letter to his wife contained a twenty-two page postscript of denunciation, alleging among other things that Curzon had worked to discredit him through the newspapers. He even ascribed the attitude of *The Times* to Curzon's malign influence over the editor, who was in fact heavily influenced by Repington and was a strong supporter of Kitchener. It does not seem to have occurred to Minto that the paper might form a lukewarm view of his rule without being told to do so by Curzon. Chirol, the foreign editor, was indeed a friend of the former Viceroy, but he also had much knowledge and experience of India, wrote several books on the subject, and became a close confidant on Indian affairs of Minto's successor. He did not need pressure from Curzon to form the unfair opinion that the current viceroyalty was 'disastrous'.[21]

Like Brodrick's allegations of 1905, Minto's charges of press manipulation lacked any evidence, as indeed did his belief – again following Brodrick – in Curzon's madness. The Viceroy once reproduced Lady Caroline Lamb's other criticisms of Byron, calling his predecessor 'bad and dangerous' as well, though he generally contented himself with the more colloquial description of Curzon as 'a rank bad 'un'.[22] Unfortunately, Minto was unable to restrict his feelings to private hostility. The new regime, a senior ICS officer noted, exhibited an 'extraordinary animosity' towards Curzon even in the most trivial matters.[23] Minto's jealousy was particularly apparent in what Chirol called 'a petty proneness to reverse things' begun during the previous administration.[24] Work was stopped on the Victoria Memorial Hall, the Cadet Corps languished, a nursing scheme started by Mary Curzon was transformed and re-named Lady Minto's Indian Nursing Association. More serious was the refusal to promote ICS officers reckoned to be 'Curzonians'. 'All your men are damned', Lovat Fraser told Curzon, 'because they are your men, because you advanced them.' Two obvious candidates for the Viceroy's Council, Miller and Risley, were passed over principally because the first had succeeded Lawrence as Curzon's Private Secretary and the second had been associated with some of the former Viceroy's leading measures.[25] 'I hope you won't think I am becoming childish in my suspicion of Curzonian influence,' wrote Minto to Godley, 'but really I want no more of it here . . . I am altogether apprehensive of any Curzonian connection.'[26] He need not have been. While Morley encouraged him to reverse Curzon's projects, Godley incited the witch-hunt against 'Curzonians', distrusting those 'tarred with the Curzonian brush' and declaring his reservations about two candidates for the India Council because of their 'Curzonian attachments'.[27]

A legitimate if minor cause for complaint by Minto was his predecessor's mildly tiresome behaviour over the Clive Memorial Fund. In 1907, struck by the fact that the founder of the British empire in India possessed no public monument, Curzon decided to raise money for statues of Lord Clive to be erected in London and Calcutta. The cause should be supported, he joked to Morley, because it was due to Clive that the Secretary of State had a job; Morley replied that he would rather put up a monument to Garibaldi.[28] Fund-raising was one of Curzon's undisputed talents, and he soon managed to collect sufficient subscriptions from wealthy friends in Britain and India. The matter did not require the Viceroy's consent, but it would have been tactful to mention it to him, especially as he wanted Minto's Private Secretary, James Dunlop Smith, to organize the fund in India. The attempt to borrow his secretary without asking caused the Viceroy almost as much vexation as the cancelled reception at Bombay. Minto also objected, less reasonably, to Curzon's requests for contributions from native chiefs, and instructed Dunlop Smith to tell them he did not consider the scheme expedient for India at that moment. Clive's commemoration, he argued, would be needlessly provocative at a time of agitation and unrest in Bengal.[29]

Agreeing with the Viceroy, Morley observed that life would have been much less troublesome for the two of them if Clive had been defeated at Plassey. But Curzon dismissed the point about Bengali provocation because it was like saying 'we ought to refrain from doing honour to Wellington for fear of giving offence to our very good friends and allies the French' – although presumably he would not have thought it appropriate to appeal for French money to erect a statue of the Waterloo hero in France. Unveiling a mural tablet to Clive at Merchant Taylors' School, he argued that no moment could be unfavourable for 'retrieving a great neglect or paying a long-retarded tribute of honour'.[30] He thus continued on his course, embarrassing his friends among the chiefs and on the Viceroy's Council by his appeals, and after much exertion reached his goal. A bronze statue of Clive was eventually set up outside the India Office and a replica in white marble placed inside the Victoria Memorial Hall.

An almost simultaneous dispute erupted over the military record of Curzon's viceroyalty. It was the custom for the various departments to prepare confidential summaries of each administration which were kept as records by the retiring Viceroy, the Private Secretary's office at Simla, and the departments themselves. Before leaving India Curzon had read and passed the summary compiled by the Military Department and thought no more about it until in the summer of 1907 he received a letter from the new Army Department explaining that certain passages in the original were confidential and had therefore been suppressed on the Viceroy's orders. As the summaries were meant to be confidential anyway, Curzon was surprised by the letter, but he did not protest to Morley until he had received a copy of the publication. Morley relayed the subsequent complaint to Minto, who at first denied that any 'bowdlerising' had taken place, but then, on checking the papers, admitted that alterations had been made without his permission and apologized. A copy of the original summary was sent to Curzon who compared the two versions and realized that the principal object of the official edition had been to eliminate those passages which credited him or his administration with successful reforms. Complimentary references to Elles and Collen, as well as paragraphs on policy opposed by Kitchener, had been similarly deleted.[31]

When Curzon's indignant protest reached the Army Department in March 1908, Minto seems genuinely to have believed that Kitchener had not inspired the distortions.[32] Major-General Bayly, the Secretary of the Army Department, sent a blandly arrogant reply, not answering any of the charges but informing Curzon, on the Viceroy's authority, that the C-in-C had not intervened in the matter. At what stage Minto realized that this statement was false is not clear; at all events he never apologized for it. Four months later Dunlop Smith confessed to Curzon in London that the 'shameful' and 'disgraceful' performance had been authorized by Kitchener and that 'no one had been angrier about the matter than Lord Minto'. The actual instructions, he said, had been given by the C-in-C's amanuensis, Colonel Mullaly, who in 'a long and insulting' note had laid down the lines along which the summary was to be bowdlerized. After receiving Curzon's epistle, the Government of India tried to bury its guilt by destroying all copies of the expurgated version, but Curzon refused to surrender his. So did Ampthill, who regarded Kitchener's behaviour as a 'contemptible scandal' but hoped, 'for the sake of public decency', that no need to expose it would arise.[33] Curzon, honourably, never publicized the affair, an example of restraint that need not have been followed by Kitchener's biographers.

Among Curzon's critics of his post-Indian years, the behaviour of Morley is the most interesting. There is a predictability about the attitudes of Minto, Godley, Kitchener and Brodrick, obsessively and gleefully writing to each other about Curzon's vicissitudes. Anger is the most prominent feature of Minto's correspondence, *schadenfreude* the key to Godley's, exaggeration and tastelessness the hallmarks of Brodrick's: although Godley was very harsh about Mary after her death, only Brodrick could have told Kitchener that if the event had 'the result of making [Curzon] more sane as regards his relations to the world at last some good will come out of evil'.[34] Yet with Morley there was an ambivalence which bordered on the schizophrenic. As Chirol observed, he always spoke of Curzon 'in terms of the utmost admiration' and believed him to be 'the one viceroy who had shown a broad grasp and sympathetic insight with regard to Indian questions', yet whenever it came to action he always took the opposite view. Chirol ascribed his behaviour to the 'dualism of the politician and the thinker'.[35]

The Secretary of State often told Curzon that he was one of his greatest admirers and, as Chancellor of Manchester University, awarded him an honorary degree. He considered the former Viceroy's parliamentary eloquence the finest in either Chamber and in 1913 told the House of

Lords that Curzon was one of their 'two or three most accomplished men'.[36] Whenever they dined together, said Godley, Morley fell 'under the spell' and talked afterwards about Curzon's brilliant gifts. Somewhat tactlessly, he also expatiated on them to the Viceroy, extolling his oratory, his 'strenuous public spirit' and 'his very powerful qualities', yet at the same time being careful to mention his 'very weak and unlikeable ones'.[37] In November 1906 he told Minto that

> When I see his immense gifts – and they impress me more every time I see them – I cannot but be sorry that the gods poured some evil dose into the bowl and spoiled the whole brew. It is a loss to the country: for what we want now is a leading man or two with the quality of *Energy*. Balfour lacks it altogether.[38]

Yet the month after making this statement Morley was encouraging Minto, for whose intelligence he had little respect,[39] to destroy Curzon's work in India. 'Here the more you reverse Curzonian projects', he wrote, 'the more popular you will be, and I am ready to back you in Parliament to any extent.'[40]

Curzon himself was puzzled by Morley's attitude. He regarded the Secretary of State as a 'warm friend' who freely consulted him on various subjects, particularly appointments, although he was anxious that no one should know of this. Yet for someone who made such frequent protestations of friendship and admiration, his behaviour was sometimes inexplicable. Dining together shortly before the Indian budget debate in June 1907, Morley alluded to a remark of the Afghan Emir, who was reported to have said that, while he had refused to go to the Delhi Durbar, he had accepted an invitation to visit India from Minto because it had been phrased in 'such a proper form'. Curzon pointed out that the remark could not be true because the Emir had not been invited to the Durbar. Yet unable to resist an innuendo about the implied lack of courtesy, the Secretary of State went ahead and used it, forcing Curzon, who could not reply in Parliament, to make a statement of contradiction in *The Times*. When challenged privately by Ampthill, Morley agreed he should have restrained himself and admitted that Curzon had dealt with the matter in 'a singularly magnanimous way'.[41]

A characteristic example of Morley's ambivalence was his behaviour over the peerage controversy. This was a subject which caused an immense amount of pleasure to Curzon's enemies, particularly Godley and Brodrick, who sent inaccurate bulletins of its various stages to the

Mintos. In June 1906 Brodrick colourfully described to Lady Minto how Curzon had 'cajoled, threatened or implored everyone in Govt and Court to obtain' an earldom, and a month later he told her husband how both the current Government and its predecessor had been 'bombarded ad infinitum' and that even the King had been 'pestered'.[42] In fact the person who had done the most pestering was King Edward himself. Morley, who was fully acquainted with the truth, also spread this falsehood, telling Minto in May 1906 that Curzon had 'renewed (in a highly objectionable way) his pressure in high quarters for an honour'. While he was at Windsor the following month, the King asked his advice on whether, following Campbell-Bannerman's change of mind, the sovereign could take any further action over a peerage for Curzon. Morley replied that it was impossible, within the limits of constitutional practice, for His Majesty to press the question. 'Our constitution being what it is,' he added to Knollys, the Prime Minister's decision really ended the matter.[43]

In the summer of the following year, while they dined together at the Athenaeum, Morley asked Curzon when he was going to re-enter the House of Commons. On hearing that medical considerations ruled out any hope of a return to the Lower House, and that therefore Curzon was excluded from public life during the existence of the Liberal ministry, he expressed surprise and regret. He also evidently felt remorse at the role he had played at Windsor for he now decided to tackle Campbell-Bannerman and persuade him to lift his veto. The Prime Minister reacted favourably, reported Morley, although with 'no zeal exactly', and suggested the peerage should be announced on the King's birthday in November.[44] Having squared the Prime Minister, or so he thought, Morley wrote to explain his change of heart to the Viceroy, arguing that, as Curzon could not be silenced or suppressed, it would be better to have him in the Lords, where he would be responsible to Lansdowne, than in his present position of absolute irresponsibility outside.[45] Minto bristled angrily, refused to admit that his predecessor deserved any honour for his services to India, and believed that promotion to the Lords would only give him 'further opportunities for mischief'. A subsequent letter attempted to reinforce his case by listing 'the heritage of troubles' Curzon had allegedly left behind – especially in Bengal – and repeating yet again that he had 'behaved abominably' ever since Minto's arrival in India.[46]

The Viceroy need not have worried because, to Morley's 'extreme mortification', the Prime Minister had once again changed his mind. At a college banquet at Cambridge in June, Campbell-Bannerman had expressed the hope that Curzon's return to public life would not be delayed, yet in October he took a decision calculated to delay it at least until the country had a new Prime Minister. Having refused the peerage on constitutional grounds the year before, he told Morley the current reason was opposition inside the Liberal Party. Another factor, Curzon learnt from other sources, was the hostility of the King who, since the return of the Prince of Wales with his Indian gossip and pro-Kitchener views, had also been changing his attitude towards the former Viceroy.[47]

Curzon was tempted to take advantage of an official visit to Windsor as Chancellor of Oxford to lay his grievances before the King. But on the day he set off for the Castle he received a letter from Lansdowne, the Unionist leader in the Lords, suggesting that he might like to be elected to the Upper House as a representative Irish peer in place of the late Lord Kilmaine. Two of Ireland's most prestigious noblemen, the Duke of Abercorn and the Marquess of Londonderry, backed the plan and set about convincing the Irish peers that Curzon's election would greatly strengthen the Unionist position in the House of Lords. Brodrick, who had recently succeeded his father as Lord Midleton, claimed thirty years later in his memoirs to have been one of the prime movers in this campaign but, as with other reminiscences of Curzon, his memory seems to have failed him. Surviving letters at Bowood alleging that his old friend was not being 'overwise' on Indian issues, that he was 'intriguing in more than one direction' and that there was 'unquestionably a considerable amount of opposition' to his candidature were clearly designed to persuade Lansdowne to withdraw his support.[48]

Entry to the House of Lords as an elected Irish baron was obviously less attractive to Curzon than elevation to an English earldom in recognition of a brilliant viceroyalty. But he was feeling so desperate and isolated at the time the offer reached him that he welcomed it. Lansdowne had hoped and predicted that his election would be uncontested. Yet it was hardly unreasonable for Irish peers to demur at the thought of being represented by someone who, in spite of having travelled more extensively than any leading politician of any age, had never been to Ireland. Another drawback was the fact that vacancies in the representative peerage only occurred after a death and that therefore Curzon's eventual succession to the Scarsdale barony would deprive the Irishmen of a peer in Parliament. This argument, sedulously advanced by the Irish nationalist MP, J.G. Swift MacNeill – a foe of the island aristocracy on any other issue – lost some of its force when it was pointed out that sixty-two of the unrepresentative peers also had English peerages which entitled them to sit in the House of Lords. Other objections were raised by Irish lords in the columns of *The Times*, and a further difficulty cropped up when it was learnt that the writs had already been sent out and that some peers had therefore voted before they heard that Curzon was a candidate. When Lansdowne realized there would be a contest, he hesitated to press on because, as he told Londonderry, it was not 'fair to Curzon to expose him to what might seem to be a rebuff'. Told by a number of peers that they had voted or pledged themselves to vote before his nomination was known, Curzon himself expected to be beaten. Nevertheless, he decided not to withdraw and in January 1908, by a very narrow margin, defeated his two rivals. Claiming that Curzon was ineligible to stand because he had not qualified himself by voting in a previous contest, MacNeill denounced the election as 'a Parliamentary and constitutional scandal of the first magnitude'.[49]

Curzon's elevation disturbed Godley, worried Kitchener and incensed Minto, who claimed that, if people knew as much about him as he did, their 'hair would stand on end'. Godley was apprehensive at the thought of Curzon 'blazing away' on Indian subjects in the House of Lords without anyone effective to answer him, and suggested jokingly to Morley that he should go 'upstairs'. While recognizing the incongruity of his presence in a chamber of hereditary peers, the Secretary of State took Godley's point seriously. Of the two Liberal ex-Viceroys in the Lords, he pointed out that Ripon, 'though wonderfully stout of heart', was now 80, while Elgin was not of the 'slightest use in debate'. Deciding that it would be easier to answer Curzon direct than 'to undergo the toil of coaching somebody else', he therefore accepted a peerage and in May 1908 entered the Upper Chamber as Viscount Morley of Blackburn.[50]

Curzon had always liked the House of Lords although he had long been an advocate of its reform. As the eldest son of a peer, he had listened to debates from the steps of the throne as a boy, and he did not take long to acclimatize himself. Nor, after his two-year exclusion, did he waste time before raising debates on subjects that interested him. Since the previous autumn he had been chafing at his inability to debate the Anglo-Russian Convention, an agreement reached between Sir Edward Grey and the Russian Foreign Minister to limit rivalry between their two empires in Asia. On its ratification in September 1907, Curzon had criticized the Convention for surrendering so much of what Britain had for so many years been fighting for: 'the efforts of a century sacrificed', he moaned, 'and nothing or next to nothing in return'.[51] The following February, in his first major speech in the House of Lords, he embarked on a dissection of the agreement that lasted one and a quarter hours.

The speech demonstrated a variety of Curzon's strengths and failings. He combined the ability to find the doubtful points of a diplomatic deal with an inability to judge whether the deal as a whole might be better than nothing. He thus criticized details of the Anglo-Russian Convention, in many cases with justice, without considering the overall advantage of limiting Russia's territorial expansion and thus ending the 'Great Game' that had exercised imperialist imaginations on both sides for so long. The 'bargain', he told the House of Lords, was 'doubtful in respect of Afghanistan, bad in respect of Tibet, and worse in respect of Persia.' While he was mistaken over Afghanistan, which Russia had conceded was within Britain's sphere of influence, his points about Tibet and Persia were reasonable. It was a strange concession for the Government to agree to consult the Russians over withdrawal from Tibet's Chumbi Valley, which did not concern them. As for Persia, her division into three zones not only greatly upset the Persians but also gave Britain a much smaller and less important sphere of influence than Russia. Nevertheless, Britain's chief interest in Persia – as in Afghanistan – was strategic, and the security of India was on the whole improved by the agreement.

The composition and delivery of Curzon's speech also displayed characteristic qualities and defects. 'He marshalled the points', Morley reported, 'in singularly lucid order' and demonstrated that he was an 'excellent speaker'.[52] He was also moderate, attacking neither the policy nor the principle but only the nature of the bargain. This disarmed the new Lord Midleton (Brodrick), who had primed himself diligently at the India Office in expectation of an attack on his Tibetan policy. Yet for all its skill and presentation, Curzon's speech was too long, too detailed and too condescending. He was unlikely to win the affection of his audience with remarks such as 'your lordships may have heard of the Karun River' or 'you are doubtless familiar with the general facts as regards Tibet', before explaining that it was a country which stretched for many hundreds of miles alongside the northern frontier of India. Nor can their lordships have been flattered by the imputation of ignorance conveyed by the remark that he wished for a large map to demonstrate his argument or his subsequent admission that he had only

desisted from strewing copies of a small map over their benches for fear
that it would be considered impertinent.*

Curzon was not a perceptive judge of the mood of the House of
Lords and he soon miscalculated its limited appetite for debates on
India. Raising one in June 1908, he discussed the various causes of
unrest – eliminating the partition of Bengal from among them – and
urged the Government to take action against native newspapers inciting
sedition. 'A great deal of what he had to say', Morley told the Viceroy,
'was as true as gospel, and nobody now in Parliament could have said it
better.' The problem was that few peers, even on the Opposition
benches, wanted to hear it. Sensing this, Morley discarded his prepared
speech and made what he called 'a rough onslaught' on Curzon. In fact
it was a typical combination of flattery and provocative misinterpretation which forced Curzon to get up and deny his insinuations. As
Morley predicted, shots aimed at the Liberals were bound to hit
Curzon's own colleagues as well, and Midleton duly gave him 'ten
minutes of sound towelling' for suggesting that the publication of the
telegram of 16 August 1905 had provoked agitation in Bengal.**
Curzon was outraged by this 'most unwarrantable personal attack' but
was restrained by Lansdowne from replying.[54]

He had more success with his Indian speeches in the following year.
Morley described his performance on the Indian Councils Bill as that of
a 'first-rate parliamentary speaker' who took point after point 'without
acrimony but with the air of a grand drill-sergeant at the blundering
manoeuvres of new recruits'.[55] In June he initiated a two-day debate on
recent developments in Indian military administration. As he had predicted four years earlier, the Military Supply Member had not enough work
to justify his existence, and the Secretary of State had therefore decided
to dispense with him. Morley saw no reason to pay the salary of the C-
in-C's 'mumbling shadow' who merely duplicated the military vote in the
Council and, against the opposition of both Minto and Kitchener (who
approved of an MSM he could dominate), the post was abolished in
January 1909.[56] The centralization at Army Headquarters had thus been
further increased shortly before Kitchener, who had already served an
extension, was replaced by General O'Moore Creagh. Premonitions of
chaos quickly concentrated the minds of those who had acquiesced in

---

*Many years later Morley came to the conclusion that he and Grey had been wrong
about the Anglo-Russian Convention and that Curzon had been right.[53]
**See above p.324.

the change in 1905. Roberts told Lansdowne he hoped that the Military Member would be resuscitated on the Viceroy's Council. Lansdowne agreed. He could not believe that 'this gallant Irishman' (Creagh) was 'fit to discharge, by himself, the duties which in old days took the whole time of such men as Roberts plus Chesney or Brackenbury'.[57] His fears were justified. The new C-in-C did not distinguish himself in his post, which should have gone to Barrow: Sir Guy Fleetwood Wilson, who sat on the Viceroy's Council with him for four years, was not alone in finding Creagh an 'impossible old fool' and 'absolutely gaga'.[58]

Both sides were well prepared for the debate. Kitchener's staff sent 'ammunition' to Midleton and prepared a brief for Morley.[59] Curzon supplied Roberts with letters from Barrow, who had written from India to predict (correctly) that the present system would break down in war even if it managed to survive in peace.[60] Roberts had promised to take part in the debate but tried to pull out a week beforehand. The destruction of the Military Department, he told Curzon, had been a 'grievous mistake', but he was reluctant to attack Kitchener just as he was vacating his post, and suggested waiting for the system to break down before criticizing it. Curzon, who had postponed the debate in order to enable Roberts to speak, was dismayed and appealed successfully for a change of mind.[61] On 29 June he introduced his motion with the observations that the issue had not been debated in Parliament since August 1905 and that he had made no public statement on the matter for over three years. His speech, composed of traditional arguments and delivered, according to Morley, in a 'rather sincere and dignified sort of tone', somehow provoked an intemperate performance from the Secretary of State. On reading it later, Kitchener regretted that Morley had lost his temper and neglected the 'excellent brief' despatched from India by the Chief of Staff. Particularly childish was the reference to a remark Curzon had once made about the Viceroy's responsibility in the event of war, which Morley twisted to imply that he had been planning to take the field in person.[62]

The debate went in Curzon's favour, with Cromer, Lansdowne, Roberts and Ampthill all strongly taking his line. Midleton criticized the abolition of the Military Supply Member but otherwise, as Curzon remarked in his summing-up, indicated that he was still 'not thoroughly acquainted with the manner and method' of military administration in India.[63] The debate delighted its promoter, who considered it a 'wonderful vindication' of his position in 1905 because his own party was now condemning the Liberals for taking Brodrick's policy to its logical conclusion. He knew he could not force a change on the current Government, but believed he could do so when the Unionists were back in office.[64] Alas, that was too late for the Indian army.

One curious by-product of the debate was a letter from Midleton who, while listening to Curzon's speeches, had reflected on the mists and misunderstandings that had gathered around their quarrel. He had recently been thinking of old days, of the friendships between the two of them and Alfred Lyttelton – all of whom had lost their wives – and wondered whether anything justified 'life passing away in bitterness and neglect after 30 years of unstinted friendship'. Curzon did not know the lengths to which Midleton had gone to denigrate and malign him in recent years, but he knew he could not with sincerity resume his old friendship with 'the Brodder'. 'I would sooner', he replied, 'leave things as they are and not rake up the past. Too much is involved in it that touches the innermost springs of my being. I have been too deeply scarred to wish to reopen the wounds.'[65]

Curzon's return to public life coincided with a threat of assassination. In June 1908 he was informed that he and Morley were the intended targets of an Indian terrorist group, and later heard that Italian anarchists, unwilling to jeopardize their asylum in England, had refused a request to carry out the killings.[66] Curzon reported the matter to Scotland Yard but heard no more of it until the following summer when he received a warning from the Home Secretary, Herbert Gladstone. After Sir William Curzon Wyllie, who had been the Agent in Rajputana, was murdered in London by an Indian nationalist, photographs of the former Viceroy annotated with abusive epithets were found in the assassin's possession. On the assumption that these were intended to help identify the second victim, Curzon was assigned police protection in London and at the Hampshire country house he then leased; a detective was even ordered to accompany him on the grouse moors above Macclesfield.[67] Curzon himself took no safety precautions but arranged his will and papers 'in perfect order' and gave instructions to his brother Frank about what should be done in the event of his death. Still unable to see any reason for Indian enmity, he asked Barrow whether it was 'not a strange irony that I who sacrificed almost everything to my passionate love for India and the Indians . . . should be pursued by the native party as their bitterest enemy?' To his father he was uncharacteristically fatalist. 'I have given the best part of my life to India', he wrote, 'and have no objection to giving the remainder. Besides I should join Mary which would be worth anything.'[68]

24

The Conversion of a Diehard,
1909–1911

———————————◆———————————

A S THE EARL OF CRAWFORD once observed, George Curzon could not 'conceive life except as a governor of men'.[1] Opposition was particularly frustrating to someone who was not only primarily an administrator but who also lacked the aptitude and temperament for parliamentary manoeuvre. It was hard, he told an old Indian colleague in 1910, to have been 'on the shelf' for five years in the prime of his life, 'able to exercise only the most microscopic influence on public events', his speeches and articles exciting 'only the faintest and most transitory interest'.[2] Despite the Unionist recovery in the elections of that year, he thought his party would need the best part of a decade before it returned to power. In the meantime there was little for him to do on the Opposition benches. Lord Lansdowne, he acknowledged, was an able and tactful leader in the House of Lords but so conscientious in the discharge of his duties that he refused to delegate.[3]

For nearly four years after his return from India, Curzon found little to interest him in domestic politics. Of all the debates he initiated in the House of Lords in the years before the First World War, only one – a vote of censure on the Government's tactics on the Parliament Bill – was not about some region of Asia. On Tariff Reform, the issue which damaged and divided his party for twenty years, he remained an agnostic, unconvinced by the doctrines of either Joseph Chamberlain or his Free Trade adversaries. This stance is not explained by Harold Nicolson's much-quoted jibe that Curzon was 'not interested in economics, and his interest in finance was confined to his own income'[4] –

he had understood both the Indian economy and the finances of Oxford University – but by his belief that fiscal policy should be regulated not by 'crusted and immutable dogmas, but by considerations of expediency and self-interest'. As he once told Lord George Hamilton, he was a Free Trader in theory who thought protectionism should be embraced whenever circumstances required it.[5]

Curzon was attracted by a programme intended to bind the empire by economic interest as well as by ties of culture and sentiment. But he was unconvinced by the arguments of Selborne, who tried to convert him to Chamberlain's cause, that the empire could only compete with the growing power of Russia, Germany and the United States through tariffs and preferential trading terms for its components.[6] Examining the proposals from India, his Government had concluded that they were unlikely to benefit Britain's most important possession and might well expose her to considerable risks.[7] He retained that view after his return but realized that a compromise was needed to avoid splitting the party; addressing his first political meeting for ten years in April 1908, he told Unionists at Basingstoke that at least a part of Chamberlain's programme should be accepted. His enthusiasm for the cause increased a year later when Lloyd George's most radical budget convinced him that it was the only alternative to high taxation. At a speech at Leeds in October 1909 he argued that Tariff Reform would reduce unemployment and asked whether the British were 'the only wise people in the world, who go on worshipping free trade long after it has become a dilapidated image in an empty shrine? And are all the countries to be regarded as fools because they flourish by declining to follow our example?'[8]

Yet an awareness of the shortcomings of Free Trade did not turn him into an enthusiast for Tariff Reform. Realizing that food taxes, an inevitable ingredient of the programme, would be electorally disastrous, he supported Balfour's pledge during the second election of 1910 to submit them to a referendum if the Unionists came to power. When food taxes were restored to the party's programme and the referendum pledge was dropped in 1912, the most prominent dissenters in the Shadow Cabinet were Salisbury, Derby and Curzon, who at the beginning of the following year were able to force a return to a more lukewarm position. Near the end of his life, when the issue had once more proved a vote loser in the 1923 election, Curzon declared that he had never been a Tariff Reformer.[9]

For more than a year after his election to the House of Lords, Curzon had remained somewhat aloof from his Unionist colleagues, by whom he was regarded as rather a maverick, obsessed by Asian issues and still resentful of those who had opposed him in India. For his part, he looked on critically as the peers of his own party used their vast preponderance to block legislation which the Government, led by Asquith since Campbell-Bannerman's death in April 1908, had passed by enormous majorities in the House of Commons: he particularly disapproved of their treatment of the Old Age Pensions Bill and was dismayed by their rejection of the Licensing Bill. A crisis was needed to bring him back into the mainstream of the Unionist Party as an active member of the Shadow Cabinet, and in 1909 the man he referred to as the 'little Welsh bruiser' provided it. Lloyd George's budget and its repercussions placed Curzon once more in the forefront of national politics, where he remained until his death.

Lloyd George's decision as Chancellor of the Exchequer to raise taxes to pay for the Government's social reform programme as well as for a larger navy provoked the most appalling display of aristocratic indignation that the country has ever seen. One after the other, great territorial magnates, particularly dukes, declared that the increases in income tax and estate duty would force them to sack their labourers, cancel their subscriptions to football clubs and reduce their contributions to charity. These manifestations of upper-class selfishness were deeply embarrassing to much of the rest of the party: one MP publicly regretted that all the dukes had not been locked up for the duration of the budget debate.[10] Curzon reacted much less hysterically than the dukes, but his argument that the principles of the budget would lead to social demoralization was not one of his best. Lloyd George amused himself and his audiences up and down the country with his speeches on the ducal antics and his description of the House of Lords as 'five hundred men, ordinary men chosen accidentally from among the unemployed'. At an overflow meeting after his celebrated Limehouse speech at the end of July, he added Curzon, who had threatened to amend the budget in the Lords, to his targets. In a passage which infuriated the former Viceroy, the Chancellor declared that he did not 'mind Lord Curzon so long as he keeps to those bombastic commonplaces which have been his stock-in-trade through life; but if he is going to try here that arrogance which was too much even for the gentle Hindu, we will just tell him that we will have none of his Oriental manners'.[11]

In neither the eighteenth nor the nineteenth century had the House of Lords rejected a Finance Bill, and the decision of Balfour and

Lansdowne to let it happen in 1909 remains a puzzle today. In the short term rejection might please both the reactionaries enraged by 'confiscatory' legislation and the more progressive Tariff Reformers who were encouraged by Balfour's acknowledgement in September that their programme was the only alternative to the Government's policies. But it is not easy to understand how they imagined that an assertion of aristocratic privilege could have helped them win the general election that would inevitably follow a rejection. Nor is it clear why they were prepared to risk the loss of the Lords' veto on non-financial measures merely for the sake of delaying the budget for a few months. Only an unprecedented electoral tide, engulfing the Liberals and Labour and thus reducing the Irish to impotence, could have destroyed the Bill altogether.

In November, after the budget had passed its Third Reading in the House of Commons, Lansdowne moved that the Lords were not justified in giving consent to the Bill until it had been submitted to the judgement of the country. At the end of four days of debate Curzon defended the Opposition case in a speech Morley described as powerful but long and over-elaborate. However forceful his delivery may have sounded, the printed version suggests that he was not entirely convinced by his own arguments. Resenting Liberal imputations that his party was indifferent to social questions, he declared that social reform was (with defence) the most pressing issue of the day but claimed that at no time in history had poverty or its evils been mitigated by taxation or its products; how he proposed to alleviate poverty without spending money was not explained. In a further unconvincing passage, he argued that it was better to force a dissolution then than to suffer two more years of 'insufficient attention to the defences of the country, two more years of Socialistic experiments, two more years of tampering with the Church' and other unspecified national institutions.[12] From this list Curzon's only genuine anxiety was the weakness of the army.

Later that evening Lansdowne's motion was carried by an enormous majority, and two days afterwards Asquith announced the dissolution of Parliament. In the absence of Balfour, who was ill for most of December, the Unionist campaign was dominated by Curzon, who soon established himself as the ablest, most active and most unapologetic defender of the House of Lords. It was his first election since 1895, and he relished his speech-making tour of Lancashire and the inordinate amount of attention it received in the press: *The Times* regularly gave him four or five columns while relegating his colleagues in the

Commons to a couple of paragraphs. At the Empire Theatre in Oldham in mid-December he proudly proclaimed himself 'an out-and-out defender of the line that the House of Lords has taken'. After telling his audience that the hereditary constitution of the Upper Chamber should be reformed, he went on to defend its record, its role as a stabilizing factor in national life, and the achievements of its most illustrious dynasties such as the Cavendishes and the Cecils. Immune to 'great gusts of passion' that sometimes swept the country, he claimed that the House of Lords had long represented 'the permanent sentiment and temper of the British people', an argument which Asquith effectively ridiculed at Liverpool a few days later. In another passage, which understandably caused some disorder in the audience, Curzon quoted Ernest Renan's view that 'all civilisation [had] been the work of aristocracies' as well as Sir Henry Maine's opinion that, if Britain had had a large electorate over the previous four centuries, there would have been no Reformation, no change of dynasty, no toleration of dissent and no Industrial Revolution. The correspondent of *The Times* observed that these remarks were 'more courageous than politic', and the following day Lloyd George suggested that a carpenter's son from Nazareth may have had a greater impact on civilization than Renan's aristocracies.[13]

Appealing to an electorate from which the working classes were still largely excluded, the Unionists performed substantially better than in 1906. But although they destroyed the Liberals' overall majority, they were in no position to form a government themselves, and there seemed little chance of preventing Asquith from taking his revenge on the Unionist peers. Curzon, aware that his party had no hope of an outright victory, had thought the first priority after the election should be to produce comprehensive proposals for the reform of the House of Lords. If the Prime Minister persisted with his plans to abolish the peers' veto, he pointed out to his colleagues, the Unionists would at least have an alternative scheme when Asquith appealed to the country.[14] Until recently Curzon had been a member of a committee, set up under Rosebery's chairmanship, to study the reform of the House of Lords. But Balfour and Lansdowne had been unenthusiastic, the Government had shown little interest, and Rosebery himself had been an unsatisfactory chairman, his principal faults being, in Curzon's view, 'a tendency to treat grave matters frivolously, and his feminine sensitiveness to criticism'.[15] After the election Curzon managed to persuade some of his colleagues, notably Austen Chamberlain, to take a more urgent view of the matter, but the cause had made little progress by May when the political situation was transformed by the sudden death of King Edward.

Although Curzon had been trying to produce a plan to counter the Government's expected move against the House of Lords, Asquith had returned to Westminster apparently without a clear idea of what that move should be or of how the King could be expected to endorse it. After several weeks of hesitation, the Prime Minister finally announced resolutions that would prevent the Upper Chamber from vetoing money bills and allow it only a suspensory veto of two years to delay other legislation. Their lordships were to be denied the chance of redeeming themselves by passing the budget, which they did without a division in April, or by transforming their House into a more representative assembly.

Asquith hoped he could persuade the House of Lords to accept his resolutions in the shape of a Parliament Bill without having to obtain a Liberal majority by flooding it with new peers. Partly for that reason and partly from a desire not to embarrass the ill-trained and inexperienced new monarch, he tried to resolve the issue through an intimate constitutional conference between leading members of both parties. Only after it had broken down at the beginning of November did he finally decide to ask George V for private guarantees that, if the Liberals were returned to power at another general election, a sufficient number of peers would be created to ensure the passing of the Parliament Bill. The dissolution took place in late November, and in a brief campaign Asquith returned to his old form. The result, however, was another stalemate which left all the parties in much the same positions they had occupied beforehand.

The second Unionist campaign was dominated by Balfour who, by promising to submit food taxes to a referendum, averted a heavy defeat but at the same time weakened his position as leader. Curzon congratulated him on his performance but simultaneously warned him of widespread dissatisfaction with the party's organization and with its leaders' apparently *ad hoc* methods of making policy.[16] He also again urged his colleagues to agree to a scheme of House of Lords reform. Just before the election the party leaders had met at his country house in Hampshire to formulate a complicated series of resolutions whereby disputes between the two chambers could be resolved by means of joint sittings, a joint committee or on 'a matter of great gravity' a referendum. Early the following year he produced plans, based partly on the conclusions of Rosebery's committee, for a House of Lords chosen in various ratios by hereditary peers, the Prime Minister and an electoral college of local government officials.[17] The Unionist Chief Whip, Lord Balcarres, privately scoffed at these 'fanciful ideas', arguing that the involvement of mayors and councillors would merely introduce party politics into places where they were now absent; he also disparaged the former Viceroy's suggestion that a category of peers should be created from retired ambassadors and colonial governors.[18] Although Curzon's proposal for the composition of the electoral colleges did not prevail, his scheme formed the basis of a Bill introduced by Lansdowne in May. During the Second Reading a few days later, Curzon declared that its supporters wanted a second chamber in which different interests, classes, minorities and points of view were represented. Turning to the hereditary principle, he wondered why it should be accepted in the case of the Crown but regarded 'as absurd in its partial application to one branch of the legislature'. In any case, he pointed out, an hereditary peer would only become a member of the reformed House if he had performed 'some recognised service to the state' and was chosen by one of the categories of electors.[19]

Like every other scheme of House of Lords reform which Curzon supported over a span of forty years, this one collapsed. As usual it found little enthusiasm from peers unwilling to surrender their traditional roles, but this particular attempt was really destroyed by the attitude of the Government. Peers might have been induced to support the Bill if by doing so they had managed to avoid the chastisement of the Parliament Bill. But when Morley announced that the Government's measure would be passed whether the House of Lords was reformed or not, they lost interest. It was clearly pointless to volunteer a reduction in their numbers if they were to be forced in any case to submit to a reduction in their powers. Realizing this, Lansdowne and his colleagues allowed the Bill to drop and concentrated their attention on the Parliament Bill.

While the abortive reform scheme was receiving its Second Reading in the Upper House, the Parliament Bill was completing its passage through the Commons. But before reaching the committee stage in the Lords, where Lansdowne warned that it would be heavily amended, Parliament broke up for the Whitsun recess and the coronation of King George. At the ceremony in Westminster Abbey Curzon carried the standard of the Empire of India and, in one observer's description, 'processed as if the whole proceedings were in his honour: the aisle was just wide enough for him'. But the former Viceroy himself found the pomp humorous and thought 'most of the peers in their coronets looked exquisitely ridiculous'.[20] In the King's Coronation Honours Curzon was at last given an earldom for his services to the Indian empire as well as the intermediary titles of Baron Ravensdale and Viscount Scarsdale. But nothing concerning Curzon's titles ever lacked controversy, and the matter was not settled without a long dispute about the special remainders of his titles if he died without a male heir, and an unsuccessful protest to Asquith about the huge fees and stamp duty (totalling over £2,000) that he was required to pay.[21] 'Introduced' by Lord Roberts and Lord Cromer, he took his seat as Earl Curzon of Kedleston the following February.

When Parliament reassembled the Lords carried out Lansdowne's threat to mutilate the Parliament Bill in Committee. As the King's guarantee to Asquith was still a secret, many Unionist peers were inclined to believe that the Government's threat to create hundreds of new peers was a bluff. The previous year Curzon himself had scoffed at the idea that the House of Lords could be intimidated by it and even after the election he had unwisely advised an audience of MPs and candidates 'to fight in the last ditch' and to dare the Government to make peers.[22] Some Unionists remained deluded to the end that the threat was all bluster. Others were undeceived in early July by information which Balfour had acquired about the King's guarantee. Later in the month Asquith made the matter still more explicit through letters to the Opposition leaders explaining his intention of asking the Commons to reject the Lords' amendments and acquainting them with the King's agreement 'to exercise his Prerogative to secure the passing into law of the Bill in substantially the same form in which it left the House of Commons'.[23]

At what stage Curzon realized that Asquith was not bluffing is unclear, but he did not need the letters to be convinced. 'Many of the Lords are d---d fools,' he had told Violet Cecil three days earlier, but their numbers would 'dwindle daily as they are brought face to face with facts'.[24] Much as he disliked the Bill, he had concluded that it would be preferable to retain a House of Lords with a two-year veto rather than acquiesce in the virtual destruction of the assembly and the rapid enactment not only of the Parliament Bill but also of Home Rule, Welsh Disestablishment and other radical measures. Convinced now that dying in the last ditch was 'unpatriotic and unwise', damaging alike to the monarchy, the party and the House of Lords, he threw himself with characteristic energy into battle against the 'foolish and insensate' policy of those who had not undergone his conversion.[25]

Bringing the Unionists 'face to face with facts' did not persuade many of them to accept reality. At a meeting at Balfour's house on 21 July, the Shadow Cabinet split down the middle with the party leader mystifying his colleagues as to his own position. The divide was only partly ideological, for the 'no surrender' group – subsequently known as 'Diehards' or 'Ditchers' – included Austen Chamberlain and F.E. Smith as well as Selborne, Balcarres and such stalwarts of the party Right as Salisbury and Lord Halsbury. Among those, subsequently known as 'Hedgers', who agreed with Curzon that the only realistic course was to let the Bill pass when it returned stripped of its amendments from the Commons, were Derby, Midleton, Bonar Law and Walter Long. Neither in the Shadow Cabinet, nor at a meeting of two hundred Unionist peers immediately afterwards, did Lansdowne do anything more decisive than leave an impression that he favoured prudence.[26]

The meeting of the peers, at which Selborne spoke vigorously against surrender, convinced Curzon of the need to organize a campaign to save the Government, which could rarely muster more than seventy-five supporters in the Lords, from being defeated by the Diehards. He thus invited like-minded peers to yet another meeting at his own house where a committee was set up to promote the view of the Hedgers. This group, consisting principally of Curzon, Midleton and the Duke of Devonshire, wrote individually to each peer, asking for his intentions and, if doubtful, trying to persuade him to follow Lansdowne's decision to abstain. On Sunday, 23 July, Curzon managed to induce Lord Northcliffe to back his case and that evening wrote a long letter which appeared the following morning in *The Times*. Replying to the accusation that he was running away, a charge that dogged him for long afterwards, he said he was

> not aware that the Duke of Wellington, when he bent his head in similar circumstances in 1832, was ever taunted with cowardice ... Rather may it be said that the greater courage is that which is willing to be miscalled cowardice, to face estrangement, and to endure reproach sooner than advise a course which, when stripped of its superficial appearance of valour, is found to be indifferent to the permanent interests of the state.

The King, miserable at the prospect of having to honour his guarantee, sent a message of approval.[27]

Curzon's object was to persuade all but the irreconcilable Diehards to follow the lead of Balfour and Lansdowne. It was not always easy, however, to predict what at any moment Balfour's position might be. The former Prime Minister had so confused the Shadow Cabinet on the 21st that the next day he composed a memorandum to correct mistaken impressions. At his most whimsical, he suggested that comparisons between the Diehards and Leonidas at Thermopylae were for 'Music Hall consumption' before admitting that it did not matter playing up to the 'Music Hall attitude of mind' provided 'the performance [was] not too expensive' – that is, if it did not *swamp the House of Lords* – and finally declaring that for him the creation of fifty or a hundred new peers was 'a matter of indifference'. Realizing that this document would only encourage the Diehards, Curzon dissuaded Balfour from circulating it and two days later induced him to write a letter for publication associating himself with Lansdowne's advice on abstention.[28] As Balcarres bitterly recorded, this was a triumph for Curzon who had acquired a powerful influence over both Lansdowne and Balfour: 'without scruples in forcing himself upon those he wishes to influence', the former Viceroy was 'so determined and persevering that he makes his wishes prevail'.[29]

The publication of Balfour's letter was a great disappointment to the Diehards. The crisis had been visible for a year, a pained Austen Chamberlain told his party leader, but no lead had been given until now, when he repudiated his earlier opinion that the Bill was an issue each individual should decide for himself.[30] Balfour was upset by the Unionist split and unable to understand it. 'What funny people I have to deal with,' he exclaimed to Balcarres. 'I wonder why people are quarrelsome and so jealous of each other – I love them all, but at times they vex me with their naughtiness.'[31]

The first public display of the Diehards' feelings, exhibited in the House of Commons on Monday, 24 July, was a poor advertisement for their cause. Led by Lord Hugh Cecil, they screamed insults at the Prime Minister, refused to let him speak and, in the words of Asquith's daughter, 'behaved, and looked, like mad baboons'.[32] A somewhat more dignified event took place two days later when six hundred guests attended the 'Halsbury Banquet' at the Hotel Cecil. Named after the group's nominal leader, a former Lord Chancellor approaching ninety, the dinner was a lengthy Diehard rally, presided over by Selborne, and notable for its series of demagogic speeches and for Chamberlain's assertion that the Government's threat to create peers was a 'fraudulent bluff'. At the dinner Balfour's Private Secretary, J.S. Sandars, found much concern about 'the well-advertised fact' that Curzon and Midleton were encouraging peers not merely to abstain but to vote with the Government. Chamberlain told him that Lansdowne should express his disapproval of anyone voting in favour of the 'obnoxious measure', a view repeated to the Marquess two days later by Balfour, who was now veering back towards the Diehards. Lansdowne replied that he would not ask anyone to vote for the Government but he did not see why, if the Diehards took a line of their own in one direction, a few Unionists who disagreed with them should not take another.[33] George Wyndham told Sibell that this policy was 'an abdication of leadership', and Balcarres was in no doubt who was behind it. While Balfour, he noted in his diary, was showing increasing sympathy for the Diehards 'Lord Lansdowne would not budge. George Curzon won't let him; won't leave him.'[34]

By the end of July the Chief Whip thought the issue had become almost a personal contest between Selborne and Curzon, 'two determined and somewhat jealous statesmen'. The former he considered 'persistent, obstinate, and full of common sense', the latter 'brilliant, witty, paradoxical, and not wholly devoid of cunning'.[35] The day before the final debate, they went into the same lobby on Curzon's motion censuring the Government for the way it had obtained the King's pledge to create peers. Selborne declared his entire agreement with the motion but said he could not understand how anyone holding Curzon's views could help the Government carry the Parliament Bill. In an alarming indication of Liberal weakness, the motion was passed by 281 votes to 68.

The next day, 9 August, was the hottest ever recorded in Britain. The temperature in the shade almost touched 100°F and no doubt helped to inflame feelings during the two days of passionate speech-making. After brief opening comments from Morley, the Government allowed the debate to pursue its natural course as an argument within the Unionist Party, Diehard after Diehard following Lansdowne with slightly differing opinions on the seriousness of Asquith's threat. On the second day Midleton gave an exhibition of his perennial tactlessness by complaining that a few inexperienced peers recruited by the Diehards might be in a position to swing a vote in which the vast majority of Unionists would abstain. In the course of the debate the Duke of Norfolk emerged unexpectedly as a key figure. On the first day England's premier duke had asked Balfour how he should vote and had received predictably ambiguous advice.[36] The Diehards themselves were not sure whether they wanted him: Wyndham was anxious lest his adherence to their cause might provoke other peers to vote for the Bill. On the next day, however, they had to take the risk, because twenty-one Unionists (known in Diehard parlance as 'rats') as well as ten bishops had declared their support for the Government. According to Diehard calculations, that would result in a dead-heat. There was therefore 'only one move left', Wyndham told his wife. 'Norfolk will speak and vote with us [and] ought to carry a few with him.' Nevertheless, he added, Curzon and Midleton were working so passionately for the Government that they might still convert other abstainers into 'rats'.[37]

As the hours went by, the tension increased. Wyndham thought the Diehards might win or lose by a single vote, depending on whether Norfolk frightened two or four people into the Government lobby. But he was not making enough allowance for the last-minute decisions of the undecided. In the evening Midleton dined at Lord Cadogan's house and found to his amazement that none of his fellow diners – a former Prime Minister (Rosebery), a former Chancellor of the Exchequer (Hicks Beach, now Lord St Aldwyn), a former Viceroy of India (Minto) and a former Lord-Lieutenant of Ireland (Cadogan himself) – had made up their minds how to vote. Two weeks earlier Minto had been urged by the King's Private Secretary, Lord Stamfordham, to come down from Scotland and 'if necessary vote for the Parliament Bill; much as we all hate it, everyone ought to do all in their power to prevent the disastrous creation of peers'. But by the time Midleton had returned to hear the final speeches, neither Minto nor any of the others had resolved what to do. Only shortly before the division did Cadogan inform Midleton that he had persuaded Rosebery to speak for the Bill and that he himself and Minto would be voting for it.[38]

As the debate neared its climax, several peers competed for the last word. Curzon, who had not yet spoken, wound up for the moderates in a heat so intense, Midleton observed, that his usually immaculate collar gradually dissolved into a shapeless mass. In a temperate and well-judged speech he observed that Lord Halsbury and his friends could retard the Bill for a few days or even a few weeks but they could not prevent its ultimate passage: 'We have reached a point at which it must be admitted that the powers of effectual resistance have gone from us.' Addressing the Diehards, he asked what good their victory and the subsequent creation of peers would do for themselves, the party, the constitution or the country. No one, he continued, sat in that Chamber without acquiring 'some measure of inspiration, some idea that this House is the centre of a great history and of noble traditions – the idea that he is part of an Assembly that has wrought and is capable of doing in the future great and splendid service to this country'. Therefore he asked his fellow peers to pause before they did anything to precipitate a change in their House which could only have 'the effect of covering it with ridicule and of destroying its power for good in the future'. In conclusion he doubted whether a more momentous division had ever taken place in the House of Lords. As a result of the vote, four hundred new peers might be created, and if that was done, 'the Constitution is gone as we have known it. We start afresh to build a new Constitution. God knows how we shall do it. We may do it with success or failure . . .'

Lord Halsbury refused to let the House divide after such an appeal and angrily told Curzon that he and his followers had long been considering their duty to the country and had no need of exhortations to do so from him. Then Rosebery stood up and announced the decision, made at the end of Lord Cadogan's dinner, to fulfil his painful duty and vote for the Bill. Finally Selborne rose and in a short and passionate speech injected a note of Gothick heroism into the Diehards' stance.

> The House of Lords as we have known it, as we have worked in it, is going to pass away. We ourselves, as effective legislators, are doomed to destruction. The question is – Shall we perish in the dark by our own hand, or in the light, killed by our enemies? For us the choice is easy.

The suspense continued until the final minutes, and even during the division rumours credited both sides with victory. In the end they each received more votes than expected, but the Diehards' 114 were exceeded by a combination of Liberals, bishops and 'rats' that totalled 131. Apart from Government peers and Lansdowne's abstainers (whom Curzon as a member of the Shadow Cabinet felt obliged to join), only two categories of peer demonstrated group solidarity: thirteen bishops voted with the Government and only two against; eight dukes voted for the Diehards and none against. The crucial grouping, however, was that of the thirty-seven Unionist 'rats'. Without the work of Curzon, Midleton and (through Stamfordham) the King, there would not have been enough of them to win.

During his fifty-eight years in Parliament, Midleton later recalled, this was the only occasion that close friends cut off all relations with each other for a long period.[39] George Curzon's role, widely held to have been the decisive factor, earned him the gratitude of the King, a great many abusive letters and a good deal of personal vituperation. His 'desertion' was bitterly felt by Austen Chamberlain who said, in that overworked image of the time, that he would not go 'tiger-shooting' with him again. Much more vitriolic was the reaction of George Wyndham who ascribed his friend's behaviour not to realism or moderation but to mere snobbishness. 'He could not bear to have his Order contaminated with the new creations.'[40] Declaring just after the result that the House of Lords had voted for revolution, he told Sibell, 'Of course we can never meet George Curzon or St John Brodrick [*sic*] again, nor can we ever consent to act with Lansdowne or Balfour if they summon Curzon to their counsels.' These were not just the sentiments of the hour. A week later he repeated that he would never meet Curzon again in a Shadow Cabinet called by Balfour, and in December he told F.E. Smith he would retire from politics rather than submit to the leadership of Curzon and the 'renegade peers'.[41]

The accusation of snobbery was patently absurd because Curzon had long advocated a large reduction in the number of hereditary peers and their substitution by elected members. Even more unjust was the charge, made later by Lord Beaverbrook and like-minded historians, that he was a persistent 'rat' who, beginning with the Parliament Bill, frequently changed his mind for the sake of political advantage.[42] Any move less calculated to enhance a career than Curzon's on this issue is hard to imagine. Since his performance in the first election of 1910, he had been variously talked of as the next Foreign Secretary, the next leader of the party and even, as Wyndham told Blunt, the next Prime Minister.[43] His crusade against the Diehards made him so unpopular, however, that he was nearly excluded from the Coalition Cabinet of 1915. Long afterwards L.S. Amery declared that it 'undoubtedly contributed to the mistrust and personal unpopularity which was to cost him the Prime Ministership twelve years later'.[44]

While the Parliament Bill blighted Curzon's future career, it put an end to Balfour's current one as leader of the party. A.J.B. had never been very popular with Unionist backbenchers. Lloyd George's remark that he was 'not a man but a mannerism' may have been a political quip from someone who in fact admired him, but many Conservative supporters really did hold such a view. As Chief Whip in 1907, Sir Alexander Acland-Hood had reported to Sandars that 'from every shooting party and every smoking room in the country', he was hearing complaints

about Balfour's 'want of backbone' and his 'vacillating policy'.[45] Two
election defeats in 1910, the change of tack on food taxes and tortuous
indecisiveness over the Parliament Bill left him with still fewer admirers.
In the autumn of 1911, as pressure mounted on him to go, he decided
to resign. After leading the party in the House of Commons for twenty
years, he suggested that he needed a break while it needed a 'slower
brain' which did not 'see all the factors in a situation'.[46]

Conscious though he was of Balfour's defects, Curzon tried to dissuade him from resignation. Earlier in the year he had publicly
defended him against critics who 'disparaged services greater than
those which had been rendered by any other living statesman to the
Unionist Party and abilities which equalled . . . those of any parliamentary leader since the days of Pitt'.[47] In November he privately implored
him to stay, arguing that his departure would weaken the party both in
the Commons and the country and 'turn it into the hands of the
extreme Birmingham school' which would lead it to disaster.[48] But
Balfour refused to be persuaded and three days later he resigned.

It had generally been expected that if he went, Lansdowne would
also resign as leader of the Unionist peers. Asked who would succeed
them, Balfour replied that Chamberlain would be the leader in the
Commons and Curzon in the Lords. Yet both were divisive figures
whose succession would split the party in one chamber between Tariff
Reformers and Free Traders and in the other between Hedgers and
Diehards. Curzon was so clearly the dominant Unionist in the Lords
that it would have been difficult to pass him over; nevertheless, his
selection would have been deeply unpopular with those who regarded
Selborne as their natural leader. Strong and ultimately successful pressure was therefore put on Lansdowne, who was innocent of many of
the charges laid against Balfour, to stay on.

Similar fears of splitting the party in the Commons led to the selection of the outsider, Andrew Bonar Law. As Diehards and Tariff
Reformers lined up behind Austen Chamberlain, a broadly equivalent
number of Hedgers and Free Traders backed Walter Long, a former
Chief Secretary for Ireland usually regarded as the worthy representative of 'squirearchical' Toryism. While the aspirants prepared for a
close contest, Bonar Law, who was a Tariff Reformer but not a Diehard,
allowed his name to go forward as a compromise candidate.
Chamberlain was advised by Balcarres to stand down and wait for Long
to make a hash of the job before succeeding to the leadership unopposed, but he refused to take a step likely to damage the Unionist posi-

tion. Instead he wrote to Long with the suggestion, which his opponent accepted, that in the interests of party unity they should both withdraw in favour of Bonar Law. Chamberlain nevertheless resented the fact that the victor, who was a friend, had allowed himself to be put up as a candidate. F.E. Smith's later quip that Austen 'always played the game and he always lost' should not be interpreted to mean that he was a good loser.

25

Suffragists and Other Targets,
1911–1914

———————◆———————

ALTHOUGH GEORGE CURZON chafed at the idleness enforced by
opposition, he lived a more active life than any of his colleagues
and many of his opponents in the Cabinet, including the Prime
Minister. Some of his energy was consumed by his work in the House
of Lords and as Chancellor of Oxford, but a good deal of it remained to
be directed into numerous causes and trusteeships, mainly conserva-
tionist in nature, which were the things that approximated most closely
in his life to the *Who's Who* category of recreations. While Asquith
relaxed with bridge, Bonar Law with chess and Edward Grey with
ducks, Curzon's non-political hours were largely absorbed by the commemoration of history and the restoration of ancient buildings.
Representative images of this time would be the sight of an increasingly
portly figure scurrying along a station platform to catch a train seconds
before its departure, a glimpse of a railway carriage full of scattered
papers on the subject to be declaimed at his destination, and a view of
the speech in delivery, witty, orotund, probably a little too long. If it was
about a great man, the topic might be the birthplace of Shakespeare, the
trial of Warren Hastings, Livingstone's centenary or Captain Scott's
heroic failure in the Antarctic. The peroration would almost certainly be
accompanied by the demand for a monument or at the least a commemorative tablet. He liked to compose the inscriptions, as he did for a
memorial fountain to Ouida, and sometimes he planned and paid for
the commemoration himself. Simla's Christ Church contains his personal memorial to Sir Denzil Ibbetson, the most admired ICS officer of

his generation, who died in 1908 not long after his appointment as Lieutenant-Governor of the Punjab.

At home as in India, Curzon was obsessed by the preservation of ancient monuments, but in industrialized England he was also greatly preoccupied by threats to wildlife and the countryside. He joined or gave donations to bodies such as the Selborne Society, formed to protect wild animals and plants from 'needless destruction', and the Scapa Society for the Prevention of Disfigurement in Town and Country. He was an early enthusiast of the National Trust, urging it to buy scenic areas threatened by development, and a defender of the nearly hopeless cause of preserving English villages. It would be a 'national tragedy', he declared, if 'the picturesque and smiling cottage' was replaced by rows of monotonous houses resembling dog kennels.[1]

In India his Government had passed legislation to combat international traffic in rare birds, and in England he called for stricter laws for their protection. Presiding in 1913 over the annual meeting of the Royal Society for the Protection of Birds – of which he and Grey were vice-presidents – he suggested that in their attitude to birds human beings were 'not far removed from a barbarian age'. It was disgraceful, he said, that British society could tolerate boys stealing eggs, gamekeepers killing kingfishers because they were 'supposed to devour juvenile trout', and the pseudo-sportsman 'whose one ambition was to kill any rare bird that appeared in his vicinity so that he could stuff it and put it in a glass case'. As positive measures he urged the greater use of nesting-boxes and the creation of bird sanctuaries. Why did not each of the great landowners, he asked in words that might have come from Lloyd George, turn one of his woods into a sanctuary 'instead of filling it with wretched pheasants to be driven to the guns once or twice in the year?'

The worst example of barbaric behaviour, thought Curzon, was the traffic in plumage for women's hats, a trade that was not only cruel and wicked in itself, but one which would lead to the extinction of creatures unlucky enough to produce fashionable feathers. After giving statistics of the number of tropical birds sold annually for this purpose in London, he asked what difference it made for a woman to wear in 'her headpiece' a 'plume innocently or artificially produced' instead of 'an aigrette that had been torn from an egret in its nesting season?' Nothing, he concluded, would be more desirable than legislation to ban imports of exotic plumage and prohibit women from wearing it.[2]

Threats to historic buildings remained as always one of Curzon's chief concerns. Writing to *The Times* in 1912, he denounced the 'rapacious instincts' of 'vandal hands' which tore out the panelling and fireplaces of ancient buildings in order to sell them abroad.[3] He urged legislation to prevent such despoliation and, although he supported Government measures to protect monuments, he criticized them for being insufficiently radical. It was outrageous, he declared in the House of Lords, that Britain could permit such acts of vandalism as the removal of Temple Bar and its replacement by 'a ghastly griffin which glares at us every time we go down to St Paul's'.[4] Holding strong views about possible improvements and potential threats to the capital, he outlined his vision of its future at the inaugural meeting of the London Society in January 1913. While the finest areas of the city north of the river should be preserved, he thought, the 'gloomy tenements' and 'grimy wharves' on the other bank could be cleared and a new city erected in their place. Efforts should also be made to revive the life of the Thames and to prevent the erection of monstrous new buildings. It was almost incredible, he said, that in a 'cultured, civilised city such a horrible phantasmagoria as Queen Anne Mansions should ever have been allowed to rear its hideous head in the air'.[5] On only one issue affecting the city does he seem to have been unperceptive: asked at an inquiry whether traffic should be restricted to a speed of ten miles an hour in Berkeley Street, he answered, according to the correspondent of *The Times,* that he was 'entirely against the imposition of a speed limit anywhere in London, and did not consider it conduced to the public safety'.[6]

In 1913 Curzon remarked that he was so overwhelmed with work for leagues, societies and committees that he did not have enough time for politics and other business. The two institutions with which he was most closely involved, and which reflected two of his main intellectual interests, were the National Gallery and the Royal Geographical Society. He loved buying pictures and often dropped in to browse at Christie's, conveniently close to both Carlton House Terrace and his clubs: one observer commented, with that exaggeration typical of Curzonian stories, that he could not 'bid for a picture or a curio at Christie's, without seeming to patronise Cellini or Rembrandt as well as the auctioneer'.[7] After his appointment as a trustee of the National Gallery in 1911, Curzon set up a committee to investigate various matters concerning the national art collections and in particular the question of how important pictures could be retained in Britain. His own farsighted suggestion was to exempt owners from death duties on their houses and paintings if they undertook to keep their collections intact and opened them to the public. To the immense loss of the national heritage, such a proposal was not adopted for many years, and the committee's report concentrated on ways of raising more funds for the acquisition of pictures by the nation. Although the impact of the report, published in 1914, was blunted by the outbreak of war, many of its recommendations, such as those on the administration of the Tate Gallery, were later carried out.[8]

Curzon's description of himself in 1909 as an 'austere and venerable flâneur'[9] is less accurate than his prediction a few years earlier that he would have nothing to do after India but lead a Renaissance life without the crime. While it is difficult to envisage Curzon himself as a colleague of the Borgias, the scope and nature of his interests would certainly have been well suited to the period. If the first of his Renaissance roles was that of architectural restorer and the second that of historian and antiquarian,* then in third place came the connoisseur of art and in fourth the amateur geographer. Always more curious about the mysteries of the globe than about the enigmas of human nature, Curzon was engrossed by abstruse geographical phenomena: fascinated by the 'singing sands', he devoted many hours to their investigation and published an eighty-page essay on the topic in his book *Tales of Travel*. He once said that the gold medal of the Royal Geographical Society (RGS), which he received after his journey to the Oxus, gave him more pleasure than any other award, and he encouraged younger men also to explore. As Viceroy he had urged expeditions to Everest and Kanchenjunga, lamenting that the British, 'the mountaineers and pioneers par excellence of the universe', had made no sustained and scientific attempt to climb them.[10] In 1911 he became President of the RGS and tried, unsuccessfully, to persuade the Maharaja of Nepal to allow an expedition to Everest to be mounted from his country. His most useful achievement as President, however, was to raise an enormous sum of money for spacious new premises he found in South Kensington; typically, he also designed the building's railings, bought some of its furniture and supervised the hanging of its pictures. Another change he carried out was the admission of women to the society's membership, a proposal he had helped to defeat twenty years earlier. Aware that it might seem illogical to champion such a reform at a time when he was leading the fight against women's suffrage, he argued, not very persua-

---

*See below pp.417–18.

sively, that to give women 'a share in the Sovereignty of the country and the Empire' was a wholly different thing from giving them a voice in a society which existed for 'nothing more formidable or contentious than the advancement of a particular department of human knowledge'.[11]

Curzon's views on the emancipation of women had not changed over the years, but he no longer dismissed it as 'the fashionable tomfoolery of the day'. The growing violence of the suffragettes, the window-breaking, the arson and the assaults on politicians persuaded him to join and ultimately to lead a crusade against them. He supported the fusion of the two main anti-suffrage movements, a men's group led by Lord Cromer and a women's association headed by Lady Jersey, and he was the principal fundraiser for the new body that came to be known as the National League for Opposing Women's Suffrage. In July 1910 he and Cromer launched an appeal that collected £20,000 in three weeks. Cromer, who was President of the new society, soon found that the labour involved was bad for his health. 'I am physically incapable', he told Curzon, 'of doing eternal battle with all these rampaging women,' a reference not to the suffragettes but to the female members of his committee.[12] At the beginning of 1912 he resigned and was succeeded by his fellow former proconsul.

Later that year, at an anti-suffrage meeting in Glasgow, Curzon set out his views in what was arguably the most unattractive speech of his career. After reading out a message of support from Asquith, he remarked that the extensions of the franchise in his lifetime had added to the electorate 'a large element, which is necessarily, from the conditions of its life and labour, imperfectly acquainted with some aspects of politics'. He accepted it as a price worth paying for democratic institutions and pointed out that in any case men read newspapers, attended political meetings and were being educated in public affairs. But it would be dangerous, he argued, to add to this 'untrained electorate' millions of women who, on account of 'the conditions of their education, the physiological functions they have to perform [and] the duties of their lives', could not acquire sufficient training and experience in democratic ways. In an absurdly illogical comparison he declared that giving the vote to women, who formed a majority of the population, would be like the management of a Glasgow factory handing over the machinery to 'a body of untrained apprentices, who had never even had the advantage of previously entering the building'.

There was worse to come. Admitting that on some issues decisions by women might prove beneficial, he denied that this would be the case on the crucial questions of peace and war. 'An unwise decision . . . and still more an emotional decision on those ideas might lead to the disruption and even to the ruin of the Empire.' As a highly patronizing finale he paid homage to the role of women in the empire 'as mothers, as wives, as nurses, as teachers in a hundred benign and beautiful capacities for which God Almighty has fitted them'. He was not sure, he added, 'that women have not something more important to guard even than the Empire itself. They have to guard the womanhood of women with all its responsibilities, its ideals, its spiritual endowment.'[13]

Curzon's views on the subject were not inspired by the violence of the suffragettes, although he did wonder how anyone could favour 'entrusting political responsibilities to the women who go about smashing innocent people's windows'.[14] Nor obviously can they be ascribed to misogyny: his current mistress, the romantic novelist Elinor Glyn, perceived that he preferred the company of women to that of men and that they were the 'natural companions' of his leisure.[15] Nor did he hold his opinions out of a desire to exclude women from professional careers and keep them in the kitchen, the boudoir and the bedroom: opening some new buildings at Oxford's Lady Margaret Hall in 1910, he urged women to broaden their ambitions and to become not only teachers but also journalists, librarians, archaeologists, historians, organists, interior decorators and garden designers – a revealing list of professions all of which, with the exception of organ playing, Curzon practised in an amateur way himself.[16] The real reasons are to be found in his fundamental ignorance of women, whom he loved but could seldom understand, and in that same misplaced sense of chivalry which had led Gladstone to oppose their emancipation on the ground that it would 'trespass upon their delicacy, their purity, their refinement, the elevation of their whole nature'.[17] Politics, like war, were a man's game, appropriate for masculine intelligence and masculine brutality. It was not the duty of those charming creatures of the 'gentler sex' to worry their pretty little heads about them.

Writing at the end of 1910 to his old associate General Barrow, now in command in Madras, Curzon gave a depressed account of the state of British politics and admitted that 'a large slice' of his heart would be in India for ever.[18] He still kept closely in touch with the affairs of the Subcontinent, reading its newspapers each week, maintaining a wide correspondence and continuing to speak on Indian matters in

Parliament. Excluded from influence in viceregal circles by Minto's hostility, he hoped for better luck with his successor. There was an alarming moment when it looked as if the new Viceroy would be Kitchener, an appointment which was apparently King Edward's last wish and among the first of his son's.[19] Back in London, the former C-in-C was intriguing with members of the Cabinet, exaggerating the extent of agitation in India in an effort to persuade them to send out a strong man, while Margot Asquith intrigued from the other side, telling one of her husband's colleagues that Kitchener was a 'natural cad' and a 'remarkably clever . . . liar'.[20] Confident of receiving the post, the Field Marshal had already chosen his staff when Morley, whose low opinion of him had not altered, threatened to resign if he was appointed.

The new Viceroy was Sir Charles Hardinge, the former head of the Foreign Office and an old friend of Curzon, who gave him a barouche to take out with him to Calcutta in 1910. Shortly after the appointment Morley resigned anyway, although he remained in the Cabinet, and was replaced by another of Curzon's friends, Lord Crewe. The new Secretary of State soon received an ominous letter from the former Viceroy asking to be allowed 'occasionally' to write 'a thing or two' about a country to which he had given the best of his life.[21] Crewe was probably unaware that in Curzon's language 'occasionally' was a synonym for 'almost weekly'.

At the beginning, however, it was the Viceroy who received most of his predecessor's attention in the form of long letters consisting of reminiscences and suggestions. For a time Curzon shared vicariously Hardinge's early experiences of the Subcontinent. 'I can imagine you now,' he wrote to his successor soon after he had arrived, 'and indeed at every moment of the day. It all comes back with an emotion half of pleasure half of pain.'[22] He wrote about Naldera and the monsoons of Simla, about the site of the proposed town hall of Calcutta, about whether his old friend Scindia would marry the daughter of his old enemy Baroda.* But his principal concerns were those of his projects which Minto had ignored such as the Imperial Cadet Corps and the Victoria Memorial Hall. Hardinge reported that the latter had made no progress during his predecessor's time and that its foundations were barely above the ground. Encouraged by Morley to neglect the construction, Minto had subsequently claimed that the site had not been

---

*He didn't. She jilted him after buying her trousseau and married the brother of the Maharaja of Cooch Behar.

properly studied, and the works had been suspended on suspicions of subsidence.[23] When these were proved false, building began again, but it was not until 1921 that it was finally completed. The gardens of the hall were designed by Curzon himself and laid out at the same time.

Several months passed before Curzon realized that his advice was not always welcomed by Crewe and Hardinge. As he had almost single-handedly organized the Coronation Durbar of 1903, he was naturally in a good position to make suggestions for George V's Durbar, also to be held in Delhi, at the end of 1911. But he made them in so tact-less a way, and complained so openly about the proposed expenditure, that he managed to antagonize both of his old friends. Crewe marvelled at 'George Curzon's peculiar incapacity for understanding what is and what is not, the proper occasion for interfering in other people's affairs'.[24]

A more reasonable matter for interference was the future of the Directorate-General of Archaeology in India. After telling Hardinge on his arrival that the department sighed 'for a little revival of viceregal patronage', Curzon was horrified to learn a few months later that the Indian Government was proposing the abolition of its senior official and of various other posts established by himself, on grounds of economy. In October 1911 he sent Crewe a long memorandum attack-ing the proposal and published his case in *The Times*.[25] Surprising support came from Lord Minto, who stated in the same newspaper that he agreed 'with every word' of his predecessor's letter and added that it was 'impossible to over-estimate the magnificent work Lord Curzon' had done for Indian archaeology.[26] Replying to a debate on the matter a few weeks later, Crewe adopted Morley's method of treating Curzon with elaborate flattery. Not since 'the palmy days of Mr Gladstone', he told the House of Lords, had there been 'any public man who com-bined so wide a range of interest in many subjects, and such an easy grasp of their general features, with so close and laborious attention to detail and the power of working out that detail'.[27] He also defused Curzon's hostility by overruling Hardinge's Government on the ques-tion of the Director-General of Archaeology while permitting the abo-lition of less contentious posts.

That autumn Lovat Fraser, the former editor of *The Times of India* and then on the staff of *The Times* in London, published a highly adulatory account of Curzon's viceroyalty in his book *India under Curzon and after*. Reviewing it in *The Times* itself, Milner delivered an immense encomium of the book's protagonist, a tribute Curzon found 'so high and splendid' that he regarded it as 'the most gratifying incident' in his public life; he would rather be judged – and praised – by Milner, he told him, than by any other man.[28] Among the most 'constructive and permanent' achievements of Curzon's rule, Fraser gave first place to the partition of Bengal, a work of statesmanship which he believed had already brought enormous and tangible benefits to millions of people in the new eastern province. While the agitation had died down in the west, a new spirit and prosperity were visible in the east. Chirol and other observers agreed. Even the *Pioneer*, the most relentless critic of Curzon's rule, had changed its view. 'After six years of carping and cavil', Curzon told Hardinge, the newspaper had discovered that partition was an 'act of courage and statesmanship. These, my dear Charlie, are the experiences, shall I call them the solaces of Indian administration!'[29]

In December 1911, a few weeks after the publication of Fraser's book, the 'constructive and permanent' partition was revoked by George V at the Delhi Durbar: to the delight of the Hindus, eastern Bengal was to be reunited to Calcutta and the west, Assam was to revert to a chief commissionership, and a third new province was to be created by detaching the non-Bengali-speaking areas of Bihar and Orissa. Shortly beforehand Morley met Lansdowne and Curzon to prepare them for the announcement. The leader of the Unionist peers, Morley recounted, exhibited his customary calm, but Curzon was 'not only vehement but violent', denouncing the scheme and claiming as his right its immediate discussion in Parliament (which was about to be prorogued).[30] The former Viceroy was infuriated not only by the decision but also by the way in which it was taken, 'a deplorable surrender to clamour' made by 'a very disgraceful proceeding'. Crewe and Hardinge, he protested, 'embarked without consulting anybody, without personal knowledge and by means of an unprecedented and unjustifiable use of the royal prerogative'.[31]

Hardinge, who had privately opposed the scheme when it was first mooted, attempted to soothe Curzon's feelings by claiming that the original partition, 'a great administrative measure, both necessary and justified', had not been annulled but merely modified. There had not been a reversal of policy but 'only a readjustment of the administrative boundaries'.[32] This extraordinary definition can only be explained by the fact that Hardinge was a diplomat by training and a courtier by instinct. Curzon, in any case, was not fooled. While he could see that the new plan was not a reversion to the status quo ante, he knew very well that the essence of his own scheme, the division of the Bengali-speaking areas and the opening up of Assam, had been destroyed. Writing to Hardinge, who had hoped the disagreement would not mar their friendship, Curzon declared that partition

> had been no particular child of mine. But I had fought for it, suffered for it, borne the whole brunt for 6 long years, and then to have it lightly tossed on one side at the very moment when it had thoroughly vindicated itself and when the agitation against it was, as Minto said, stone-dead; and to have this done by a new viceroy before he had been more than a few months in the country and could not be [apprised] of the whole case, a viceroy who more-over happened to be a personal friend of my own – well, I should not have been human had I not felt it profoundly.[33]

The King's proclamation had contained the equally contentious decision to transfer the capital of India from Calcutta to Delhi, a move Curzon considered almost as great a blunder as the change in Bengal. Delhi was in his view a 'cemetery of dead monuments and forgotten dynasties', an inappropriate home for a government that would be isolated from public opinion and far from the protection of the British navy.* Besides, the advantages of having a capital in the centre of the country – one of the reasons given for the change – were not so obvious that Britain, France or the United States had ever felt the need to shift their governments to a central location.[34]

Warning Crewe that he would need to make a speech of 'inordinate length' to cover all the ground, Curzon attacked the Government's decisions in the House of Lords in February 1912. They were, he said, by far the most important taken since the Mutiny, yet they had been made by a Viceroy and a Secretary of State both new to their offices who had neither consulted any of the surviving Viceroys nor allowed the matter to be discussed in Parliament. After countering the geographical and other arguments in favour of building a new capital at Delhi, he attacked the decision to reunite Bengal at a time when the benefits of partition were at last being understood, and he told the Government it had 'yielded to a dying and . . . factitious agitation'. Finding nothing to say in favour of the plans, he then ridiculed the idea that Biharis would

---

*In 1911 Delhi was the seventh largest city in India with 232,837 inhabitants. Calcutta and its adjoining municipalities had a population of 1,222,313, Bombay 979,445 and Madras 518,660. The non-military British population of Calcutta was 12,080, of Bombay 10,131 and of Delhi 84.

welcome unification with Orissa because it would give them access to the sea. The Biharis already had two railway lines to Calcutta which they would continue to use, while they had no railway connection with Orissa, a region, moreover, which did not even have a seaport.[35]

Curzon sat down after an hour and thirty-five minutes and was followed by Crewe who accused him of combining the 'well-disciplined exaggeration of the practised advocate' with the tones of 'a prosecuting counsel'. To Hardinge the Secretary of State admitted it had been 'a very able speech' but would have been 'infinitely more effective if the censure had not been so unrelieved'. Crewe, who was a competent but very dull speaker himself, took nearly two hours to answer Curzon's points, and after that the House adjourned. On the following day Minto criticized the Government for giving in to agitation that had died out by the time he had left India, and a similar line was taken by Lansdowne. But several former provincial governors, including MacDonnell and Ampthill, welcomed the changes. Four months later an almost identical debate took place on the Government of India Bill, during which Curzon scoffed – with much justice as it turned out – at Hardinge's claim that the new city would cost only £4 million and take only three years to build. The line-up in the debate was much the same as on the previous occasion – Minto once again wanting 'very fully [to] associate' himself with all the remarks of his noble friend Lord Curzon – but this time, in addition to Lansdowne, he had the assistance of Midleton. He also enjoyed the moral support of Morley who, after deliberately absenting himself, confided to a friend that he had agreed with every word Curzon had said.[36]

As the changes had been announced publicly by the King, Curzon realized there was little chance of overturning them, at any rate in the near future. Although he hoped that the folly and expense of the move to Delhi would one day become apparent even to the Government, he was determined to be involved in the changes if they went ahead. He thus sought assurances from Crewe about the future of Government property in Calcutta such as Hastings House and the paintings and sculptures of the viceregal residence. He also sent an immensely long letter to *The Times* about the architectural style of New Delhi, which he thought should be Classical with an Indian flavour. Hardinge was sent the same advice and fortunately agreed with it. In a subsequent letter Curzon told the Viceroy he would write no more about the matter because it was no concern of his, but could not resist adding a postscript criticizing the preliminary drawings of Edwin Lutyens: the proposed buildings lacked grace, he thought, and had 'too much wall surface and too many straight lines'.[37]

In the spring of 1913 Hardinge asked Chirol, his closest confidant at home, to persuade Curzon to stop criticizing the Delhi transfer because it was a *fait accompli* which he should patriotically accept. Chirol, who had drifted apart from the former Viceroy partly because he supported the change of capital, tried and failed.[38] At the annual Calcutta Dinner in London Curzon admitted that the decision could not be changed but continued to condemn the abandonment of the seat of British rule in order 'to go hunting about for a new capital amid the graveyards that surround the deserted cities of forgotten kings'.[39] The speech, which also contained a passage on the shortcomings of the military administration, produced a despairing reaction from Chirol. Expressing the view, shared by others, that Curzon was more of a statesman than anyone else on the Opposition benches, he told Hardinge that the former Viceroy's knack of 'saying the wrong thing, or even, when he says the right thing, of saying it in the wrong way, is quite extraordinary. I can recall no instance of a man whose personal unpopularity has to the same extent neutralised his immense abilities and his power . . . of rendering great services.'[40]

Curzon's attitude eventually produced from Hardinge a similar reaction to that which he had provoked from Minto. It was curious, the Viceroy told Chirol in the spring of 1914, that someone claiming to be a friend should have done his utmost to embarrass him almost since the day of his arrival, especially when he had loyally pushed forward Curzon's schemes, including 'even that wretched Victoria Memorial'. His offence, he correctly surmised, was the change in Bengal, for which he had never been forgiven. In another letter of the same period, the Viceroy referred to the hatred felt for his predecessor among Indians. Despite his current differences with Curzon, Chirol could not let that pass. 'Please do not forget', he replied, 'that few things are more discreditable to Indians than the hatred they have indulged against him, for no one has ever challenged unpopularity among his own people so fearlessly as he did in his endeavours . . . to secure even justice for Indians against Europeans.'[41] Hardinge's relations with Curzon never recovered and some years later deteriorated further when they worked together at the Foreign Office. His memoirs, written after his critic's death, are little more than a catalogue of compliments received during his career, leavened and enlivened by malice towards Curzon.[42]

Until the end of his life Curzon remained unreconciled to the deci-

sion to leave Calcutta. In May 1914 he initiated a debate on the extravagance of Delhi which, according to Chirol, fell 'absolutely flat' because
nobody cared about anything just then except Ulster.[43] In 1916 he prepared a memorandum on the subject for his Cabinet colleagues which
made equally little impact. And at the end of his life, in the book he was
working on at the time of his death, he repeated his condemnation of
a transfer which was still being carried out 'at an inexcusable cost to
the finances of India, and without any resultant advantage to a single
public interest'.[44]

George Curzon was a restless and uneasy figure among the higher
councils of the Unionist Party. To his annoyance, Bonar Law tried to
avoid holding meetings of his Shadow Cabinet, which all former senior
ministers had a right to attend, except when vital issues such as food
taxes required a decision. Lord Balcarres, who succeeded his father as
Earl of Crawford in 1913, listed some of the defects of this unwieldy
body in a letter to Lady Wantage: George Curzon talked too much,
Harry Chaplin was stone deaf, some members such as Halsbury were
obtuse, others like Lansdowne were lazy, and few were 'as modest and
capable' as Law.[45] Crawford and his colleagues were impressed by
Curzon's powers of argument, but they seem to have taken a certain
pleasure in contesting them. In December 1912 Curzon opened one
Shadow Cabinet meeting with a fifteen-minute speech proposing that
detailed policies on various subjects should be worked out by newly
appointed subcommittees. Nobody was interested. Balfour doubted
laconically whether there was any point in preparing 'half-a-dozen
colossal bills' while the Unionists were in opposition, and was 'cordially
supported' by Law.[46]

In spite of their many disagreements, Curzon and Balfour had been
friends together in the 'Souls' and spoke the same kind of language. But
the former Viceroy had nothing in common with the melancholy teetotaller who now led the Unionists in the Commons, a man who cared
nothing for art or society or even country life, a widower who, in his
biographer's words, lacked 'both the cheerfulness of the pagan and the
consolations of the puritan'.[47] Curzon made an effort to get on with
Law, sent him a history of chess as a Christmas present, and even
acquired, according to the wife of Law's Private Secretary, a 'puzzled
affection' for him.[48] 'Puzzled' in fact sums up Curzon's attitude to his
party leader from beginning to end. He was puzzled how this gloomy

Glaswegian industrialist had managed to become the heir of Disraeli, Salisbury and Balfour, just as many years later he could not understand what Law had done to deserve burial in Westminster Abbey.[49]

The style and content of the two men's politics contrasted almost as much as their personalities. While Curzon had learnt his debating skills at the Oxford Union, Law had apparently acquired his from speaking at Glasgow bankruptcy meetings when his iron company was a creditor.[50] Whether this experience was responsible for the violence of his early speeches as leader is unclear, but repeatedly insulting the Liberals as corrupt gamblers and Gadarene swine was all very unlike Balfour. Curzon was appalled by Law's vehemence and his 'departure from the traditions of parliamentary form'.[51] He was also disheartened that Law's two political obsessions – Ulster and Tariff Reform – were causes with such little appeal to himself.

Since the Liberals had lost their overall majority in January 1910, Home Rule had returned to the political agenda. The issue itself had not changed greatly since Gladstone's last attempt to tackle it in 1893, although Irish grievances over land were now weaker while nationalist agitation, inspired by the example of the Boers, was much stronger. But the political rules were very different. While the House of Lords could still defeat a Home Rule Bill by enormous majorities, the Parliament Act gave the Government the power to bring the measure back in the following two sessions and to enact it over the heads of the peers at the end of that time. It was a laborious and time-wasting procedure, but it ensured that the Government could pass any bill it liked if it was still in power two years after first voting for it in the Commons.

The Third Home Rule Bill, very similar to its predecessor, began the first of its three journeys through Parliament in April 1912. Bonar Law, who had roots in Ulster as well as Scotland and Canada, fought it fiercely from the beginning and in his notorious Blenheim speech said he could 'imagine no length of resistance' in Ulster which he would not be prepared to support. Curzon again disapproved of his extremism and also of his failure to consult his colleagues on the matter. It might be right, he thought, 'to let Ulster play her game if she is so resolved', but it was surely wrong for the leaders of the Unionist Party 'to abet and encourage in advance defiance of the law'.[52]

Curzon once candidly confessed to Midleton that he had never understood Ireland and never would.[53] Certainly he made no effort to acquire first-hand knowledge of the problem. Like Cavour, who studied agrarian conditions far from Italy but never saw the need to investigate what was happening south of Pisa, Curzon was prepared to travel thousands of miles to examine rural life in Asia without ever taking the trouble to cross the Irish Sea. He opposed Home Rule for all of Ireland because he had little insight into nationalism and because he was convinced that, whatever the mistakes of the past, Westminster would provide better government than a parliament in Dublin. His sympathies were thus with the 'Old Guard' Unionists such as Lansdowne and Midleton, both of them landowners in southern Ireland, rather than with Bonar Law, who was an extremist on Ulster but prepared in the last resort to concede the south.

Although he felt no passionate attachment to Ulster, Curzon believed that the province could not be forced to accept Home Rule by a Government which depended on the votes of Irish MPs, who were in any case over-represented at Westminster, to force through a measure that had not been approved by the British electorate. Speaking in the House of Lords in January 1913, he asked why the Liberals, who had 'constituted themselves the international champions of the right of insurrection', refused to recognize the right of the people of Ulster merely to be left alone and to carry on as before. Lord Sheffield countered this rather simplistic point with the almost equally simplistic statement that Liberals championed rebellions of the oppressed, while Tories supported those of oppressors such as Carlists and Confederates. On the Second Reading Curzon returned to the point, asking why the Liberals wished 'to give back Crete to Greece, to carve out a new state in Albania, to divide Macedonia into a number of provinces – except for the very reason that justifies Ulster in demanding separate treatment in the present instance?' Warning the Government of the consequences of disobedience in Ulster, he said the people of Britain would be 'very loth to condemn those whose only disloyalty it will to be to have been excessive in their loyalty to the King' and whose only form of rebellion was to insist on remaining under the British Parliament. Finally he appealed to the Government to hold a general election before the Bill became law. If the Liberals won, they would 'deprive Ulster of the moral support of the Unionist Party' and 'escape the awful odium' of coercing Ulster and risking civil war with half the country against them. And if they lost, so much the better, for they would escape the consequences of 'a most appalling blunder'.[54]

Curzon's main aim throughout 1913 was to force a general election before Home Rule was passed. In March he had suggested to Cromer that a bill should be introduced in the Upper House with a single clause postponing the presentation of the Home Rule Bill for royal assent until after a general election. In September he went to Balmoral to make a suggestion to King George. After the monarch explained that the Government was telling him he had no option but to assent to the Bill, Curzon advised him to write a memorandum for the Cabinet about his position, repeating the argument that the matter should be referred to the electorate, pointing out the consequences and the possibility of civil war, and disclaiming any responsibility on his part for such an outcome. Curzon still disliked a settlement that merely saved Ulster from Home Rule and was critical of the extremism of Carson and F.E. Smith, the champions of such a solution. But by the autumn he believed there was no other way of preventing a civil war. The avoidance of conflict now became his principal concern. On New Year's Eve he warned the country that 1914 would be the most momentous year in modern politics because Britain would be confronted with her greatest catastrophe since the seventeenth century, the prospect of civil war.[55]

After completing two of its parliamentary circuits by the end of 1913, the Home Rule Bill was launched on its final tour at the beginning of 1914. Like other Unionists, Curzon repeated his demands for an election, but he was nervous of any action that bordered on the unconstitutional. He did not think the King should refuse his assent if the Bill passed a third time and he was alarmed by Bonar Law's proposal to amend the Army Act in the House of Lords and thereby prevent troops from being used to coerce Ulster. The Unionist leader had come to the conclusion that such a move was the only means left to save the north from Home Rule, and he was backed by Chamberlain, Selborne, the Cecils and Carson. Like Lansdowne, Curzon thought the proposal extremely hazardous and seems to have been partly responsible for its abandonment.[56] In any case the matter became largely academic in March when the possibility of deploying the army in Ulster was removed by the Curragh 'mutiny', an incident so mishandled by the Government that it gave Unionist politicians the chance to berate it for incompetence and to exalt the 'mutineer' officers for their sense of honour. The Bill meanwhile continued its tortuous and engrossing progress. For a week at the beginning of July, just after the assassination of the Archduke Franz Ferdinand, the House of Lords remained absorbed in the debate on its Second Reading.

26

Lord Curzon at Home

———◆———

G EORGE CURZON'S STYLE of living after his return from India soon became legendary. Until the age of 36 his adult life had been largely divided between rented rooms in London and the generally rough accommodation he found on his Asian travels. But marriage and then India had so altered his outlook that, by the time he had settled in England in his mid-forties, he required a stately mansion in London in addition to one, then two, and eventually three large houses in the country. Only in August, when he accompanied the children to his seaside villa at Broadstairs, did he reside in less than palatial surroundings. An existence bounded by such extensive dimensions was one he hoped his friends would be able to emulate. 'I will not disguise from you, my dear Lang,' he wrote inimitably to the new Archbishop of York, 'what pleasure it gives me, as the years advance, to see my friends inhabiting spacious places.'[1]

The splendour was acquired with Leiter money. George Curzon's personal income was much the same after India as it had been before his marriage. Once again he had no salary, and his own income was limited to the £1,000 annuity from his father and such amounts as he earned from his writing and a few investments. But in addition he received a third of the income from his marriage settlement trust, an act of generosity from Levi Leiter which assured him of at least £4,000 annually for the rest of his life. On her father's death Mary should have received a sum estimated to produce a further £25,000 a year, and she wrote several times to her mother and brother asking why she had not

413

received her share of the will. Joe Leiter prevaricated, refusing to distribute her portion until all debts had been paid on the estate, and by the time of his sister's death two years later he had still failed to hand over all the securities due to her, or transmit more than a portion of the income, or even inform her about the extent of her fortune.[2]

Mary had hoped she would be well enough to go to the United States to settle the problem in the summer of 1906. After her death Joe remained as uncooperative as ever, and Curzon resolved to pursue the matter himself. In November 1906 he therefore arrived in Chicago. He had not been there for nineteen years and found it a 'god-forsaken city' where everything was very expensive, especially his breakfast and his seat at a match of American football, a sport that struck him as barbarous. America was 'a very strange country', he thought, 'so vital, so prodigious, so blatant, so much on the nerves.'[3] It seems that he and the Leiter family were also pretty much on their nerves during his visit. What actually occurred is difficult to trace beyond the facts that there was a monumental row, that Mrs Leiter refused to speak to him afterwards, and that he did succeed in obtaining Mary's share of her father's estate for his children. His former mother-in-law was so incensed by his behaviour that she refused to let Daisy dine with him and ignored his warning that her attitude would lead to a severance of relations between her and her grandchildren. When she invited them to Paris a year and a half later, he insisted that before seeing his daughters she must end her quarrel with him.[4] This apparently was too much for her, and she seems to have disappeared from their lives, leaving her revenge to her will. When Mrs Leiter died in 1913, her enormous fortune of over £6 million was divided not between the families of her four children but between her son and her surviving daughters. The Curzon girls received small legacies totalling barely one per cent of her wealth instead of the twenty-five per cent their father had expected. He was 'deeply hurt', he told Lady Suffolk, by her mother's behaviour, but Daisy was unsympathetic. Mrs Leiter's wishes had to be accepted, she replied, adding primly that she would have made no complaint if her children had been similarly treated.[5]

Even without their grandmother's wealth, Curzon's daughters were very rich little girls. Besides their two-thirds share of the marriage settlement, the annual income from Levi Leiter's will which their father secured for them in Chicago came to £23,000 and by 1914 had risen to £41,000. It was this money which Curzon as their guardian was anxious to control and which was later to cause such problems between him and his elder daughters. To gain that control, he needed an order from the Court of Chancery permitting him to spend a certain amount of it for the benefit of the children. At the end of 1906, after Curzon told his lawyer, Mr Humbert, that he planned to buy pictures for Kedleston and build a memorial chapel for Mary, he was warned that the judge might feel that these were projects which would not greatly benefit the children. Curzon did not see the point either then or at a later date when he overspent their income on restoring country houses. But he allowed Humbert to modify his claims, which were subsequently regarded with surprising sympathy by the judges. As the children's income increased, so did the proportion he was permitted to spend: £15,000 of £23,000 in 1907 rising to £31,000 from £41,000 in 1914.[6] Added to his share of the marriage settlement, Mary's life insurance and income from other sources, he was thus able to spend on the eve of the First World War £40,000 a year,* the figure which Lord Durham had thought a man 'might jog on with' nearly a hundred years earlier.[7] Curzon could not be said to have jogged along at any stage or on any level, but the money was just about enough – until his daughters grew up.

No. 1 Carlton House Terrace remained Curzon's London residence until his death. It was an ideal place for him to live, the Foreign Office a short walk across St James's Park with Parliament beyond, the Athenaeum (his favourite club) just around the corner, and the Carlton nearby. The only drawback was the proximity of Big Ben, whose chimes kept him awake at night and which he tried, incredibly, to have silenced.[8] The house itself, built by Nash around 1830, was suitably magnificent, especially when seen from the park with its terrace and Corinthian columns rising above the Mall. The interior gave an impression of spaciousness and grandeur which Curzon highlighted by the extensive use of gold and reds. But he knew it was not a particularly well con-structed house and, like many of Nash's buildings, it lacked the solidity and attention to detail displayed in Edinburgh's mansions of the same period. A large drawing-room with four windows ran along the width of the house overlooking the park, and a dining-room of similar dimen-sions stretched across the north side. In the hall Curzon arranged his ivory furniture from India and upstairs he devoted an octagonal room to a collection of Napoleonic furniture which he left to Oxford University. Although he worked in a spacious study overlooking the

---

*Although such comparisons are always misleading, this sum would have been the equivalent of about £1½ million after tax in 1994.

Mall, he slept in a small bedroom on the second floor, simply furnished, according to Harold Nicolson, with a 'white washing-stand, a servant's chest of drawers, and a cheap brass bedstead'.[9] He liked what he called the 'simple squalor' of the room and was dismayed when his second wife redecorated it while he was absent, throwing out the bed and the shabby Edwardian wallpaper. He was particularly sad to lose his old mattress and complained that it had taken many years to get used to his shape.[10]

The question of a country residence had been considered while the Curzons were in India. In the first years of their marriage they had rented the Priory, a house near Reigate, but they wanted something rather larger on their return. Walmer Castle had briefly seemed to provide the answer while Lord Scarsdale was still alive and inhabiting Kedleston. But on returning to Calcutta after their disastrous experiences there, Curzon began making enquiries about Hackwood, an eighteenth-century Palladian house in Hampshire which its owner, Lord Bolton, wanted to let. The Duke of Wellington, a landowner nearby, told him the park would be excellent for pheasant shooting, but the thrifty Scarsdale, who inspected the property on his son's behalf, thought the rent too high and the house too expensive to maintain. A far more ambitious project, the leasing of Warwick Castle, was then contemplated, and arrangements had been almost completed by the time of Mary's final illness. Her husband subsequently abandoned the plan, returned briefly to the Priory and, on hearing that Lord Bolton's new tenant might be prepared – for a large premium – to assign him the lease, re-opened negotiations for Hackwood. Heedless of his father's renewed warnings, Curzon moved in during the spring of 1907 and immediately set about making such improvements as altering windows, adding bathrooms and putting radiators and electric bells in the bedrooms.

Like Carlton House Terrace, Hackwood was of too recent construction to require much archaeological attention, and he found more to occupy himself in its grounds where he employed sixteen gardeners and two boys. On taking possession, his daughter Irene recalled, he demonstrated to an astonished gardener, who had been there for many years, the correct method of keeping lawns free of plantains. His projects included restoration of an open-air cockpit, the rebuilding of the summerhouse, and the very expensive levelling of a mound which obscured the view from the south front, an operation requiring the removal of 15,000 cubic yards of earth. But his principal enterprise was the landscaping of a large area of wild garden. In her private unprinted memoir of Curzon, Elinor Glyn perceptively observed that wild nature did not move him unless, like mountains or waterfalls, it was on a magnificent or colossal scale. Otherwise it needed to be interpreted by poets or painters, or to form the background for a temple or a palace, before he really appreciated it. This love of nature harmonized by man made him admire and attempt to emulate the great landscape gardeners of the eighteenth century. At Hackwood he cleared a large garden amphitheatre of trees and undergrowth and restored it with slightly altered lines close to its original appearance. Being particularly proud of this achievement, he was very hurt when Lady Helen Vincent told him she preferred the old lines. Their friendship, she recalled long afterwards, instantly cooled and never fully recovered.[11]

George Curzon was almost incapable of owning or inhabiting a piece of property without attempting to write a book about it. A house, he once said, had 'a history as enthralling as that of an individual. If an old house it has a much longer existence, and it may be both beautiful and romantic, which an individual seldom is.'[12] For the last twenty years of his life he devoted an immense amount of time to researches into the histories of Walmer, Hackwood, Montacute, Bodiam, Tattershall, Kedleston and its church, and Government House, Calcutta. By his death the manuscripts of Bodiam and Government House had been finished, and were published posthumously. Pages, notes and a mass of accumulated material allowed scholars to complete the monographs on Walmer and Tattershall. Kedleston was never written (though a history of its church had been published in Curzon's lifetime), Montacute was not finished, and the manuscript of Hackwood remains among his unpublished papers. Although the book on Calcutta is delightful, one cannot help feeling that his reputation would have been better served if he had spent his spare time writing his memoirs instead of filling it with the rather pedestrian labours of local antiquarian research.

Curzon's restless quest for medieval records reinforces the view of those who thought he should have been a historian instead of a politician. Arthur Benson, who disliked him intensely, believed that without the advantages of birth and rank he would have been a rather unpopular professor at Oxford.[13] Curzon himself thought he could have made a living as an architect. But he would probably not have excelled in either of these professions, because his zeal was not matched by his imagination. As an architect, or as a Viceroy overseeing an architect, he was unable to envisage other than traditional forms, although this did not of course prevent him from restoring or helping to create very beautiful buildings. In history he combined the devotion of the archivist with a dramatic sense of stirring events while lacking a great historian's ability to understand and interpret an era. His talent in both fields was considerable but it was essentially that of a gifted amateur obsessed by his hobbies while pursuing what was for him a more appropriate profession.

An opportunity for exercising both these subordinate gifts was provided by Tattershall Castle in Lincolnshire. Between 1910 and 1911 this magnificent fortress-mansion from the fifteenth century changed hands several times before ending up in those of a syndicate of American speculators who removed the famous fireplaces which Pugin had used as his models in the Houses of Parliament. Learning that these were destined for the United States, and hearing that the ruined castle itself might be dismantled and shipped across the Atlantic, Curzon intervened. Informed that he had twenty-four hours in which to save the building, he rushed to Lincolnshire to see it and made an offer which enabled the Americans to sell at a profit. Tattershall was thus purchased with its surrounding land so that both the castle and the moat could be restored and opened to the public. Six months later Curzon discovered the mantelpieces packed ready for export to America and managed to raise enough money to buy them. For the rest of his life he supervised the restoration of the building and the enhancement of its surroundings; observing on an early visit that a red brick cottage spoilt the view from the castle, he called upon its owner and offered her an unlimited supply of ivy to cover up the eyesore.[14] In his will he bequeathed Tattershall to the nation with the explanation that 'beautiful and ancient buildings which recall the life and customs of the past are not only a historical document of supreme value but are a part of the spiritual and aesthetic heritage of a nation imbuing it with reverence and educating its taste'.

Ill health had ended the days of the 'youthful rover' and the traveller 'with a purpose'. Curzon now seldom went abroad unless his doctors advised it, and even then the man who had found the source of the Oxus was restricted to northern Italy and the South of France. Yet he retained the inquisitiveness of former years. Sent to convalesce in the Italian Alps in 1912, he stopped on the way to see Voltaire's house and the family home of Madame de Staël. Finding his destination enveloped in mist and snow, he descended to Lake Maggiore and in its 'divine surroundings' worked undisturbed and dreamed of buying one of the Borromean islands.[15]

Within Britain he travelled much more but usually only to make speeches or inspect buildings. A succession of weekend house parties at the end of 1913 was thus uncommon or, as he put it, 'an unexampled spasm of frivolity'.[16] Since King George was present on two of these occasions, Curzon's reasons for going cannot have been entirely frivolous. He arrived at Chatsworth in December to find his sovereign enraged by Lloyd George's classic pronouncement that the mangold-worzels of hard-working farmers were being devoured by landowners' pheasants. King George, he observed, was somewhat overexcited and, forgetting that 'Lady Crewe was the wife of an eminent Cabinet minister, he poured into her astonished ear terrific denunciations of Lloyd George on the subject of pheasants and mangold-worzels'.[17]

More agreeable than royal house parties were occasional motoring expeditions with female companions. Easter 1913 was spent in this fashion with Lady Dudley and Lady Essex: 'we motored about,' he recounted, 'and rang up unknown people in country houses and discussed the ethics of conjugal separation'.[18] Odder expeditions were undertaken in pursuit of ghosts. Curzon was a strong believer in phantoms and went to great lengths to try to see them. From Broadstairs he visited haunted houses in Kent and on one occasion was accompanied by Sir Arthur Conan Doyle. In 1913 he organized a vigil in a Somerset house with Elliott O'Donnell, the author of numerous books on the subject, and spent two nights watching with friends and a photographer. After failing to see or hear anything unusual, the party moved to another house on the third night but was equally unsuccessful there. According to O'Donnell, Curzon was a most genial and thoughtful companion on these jaunts, but he was disappointed by his inability to see ghosts. Even the 'white lady' of Hackwood, observed by others, remained invisible to him.[19]

Curzon enjoyed his moments of squirearchical existence in Hampshire, laying out his garden, reading the lesson in church, sending a brace of pheasants to friends and colleagues from India who did not have estates of their own. An associate from Oxford used to come across him cheerfully raking his gravel paths. But it was not a life he allowed himself more than brief periods to appreciate, for he was always on the move, always thinking of the next project, the next speech, the next committee meeting. As Walter Lawrence rightly observed, he 'never knew the meaning of rest and contentment'.[20] To Nancy Astor, he described his existence in 1909 as 'always at work, at Oxford one day, in town another, speaking, writing and generally energizing, with insignificant results'. Two years later he depicted his life as a 'country squire', his presence the week before at the servants' ball, 'self with arm entwined round the waist of portly housekeeper', and on the day of writing at a party of schoolchildren with a performance of Pierrots. In between, however, he had had an evening

> with my two leading Oxford dons to discuss academic politics – have attended a meeting to resist the enfranchisement of your delightful sex, have made a speech on the Chinese frontier, have assisted to found a women's hostel in London,* have bought a Louis XV set of furniture, written a biography of dear Lord Cowper for the Dictionary of National Biography, contributed some Eton reminiscences to a forthcoming work, laid out a new flower garden here, made a pergola at Broadstairs, written a letter to *The Times* about the administration of the National Gallery and ordered some stained glass windows for a church.[21]

Even Curzon's Hackwood routine was far from tranquil. One of the peculiarities of his character was that the running of little things caused him as many problems as the administration of great offices. Much of his time was spent quarrelling with Lord Bolton's agent and interviewing usually unsatisfactory applicants for the staffs of his various houses. The children's arrangements were equally time-consuming. At the beginning of each term he entered the schoolroom, arranged all the books and pictures, and drew up the timetable of lessons. He also organized the children's music lessons, inspected and bought their instruments, and corresponded personally with the piano tuner. He did not appear in the nursery himself but he went through the nursery accounts, questioning the children's nanny over the cost of his daughters' 'bloomers' from Gorringe's and wondering why they needed more than one new pair a year. Nanny Sibley, whose character and methods could hardly have been more different from those of Miss Paraman, was in fact the one member of the staff who never caused him trouble. Although engaged to an Englishman in India, she refused to leave the children after their mother's death and stayed with them until she herself died ten years later.[22]

Curzon was not an easy father either for small children or for teenagers. Bored as he was even by adult games, he could not bring

---

*The Mary Curzon Hostel for 'poor but respectable women' was founded by Curzon and the Duchess of Marlborough. The building near King's Cross Station was opened by Queen Alexandra in 1913.

himself to play with toys or do jigsaw puzzles with his daughters. If Baba toddled into his bedroom after breakfast, he might dab her face with shaving cream, but there were few other moments of light-heartedness. When she went to see him in the drawing-room after tea, he remained at his writing table, throwing her occasional remarks as she played around him, but keeping his mind on his work. Weekend lunches, if there was no house party, were more unbending occasions. He loved to give a graphic account of an historical incident, imitating the participants and then asking Baba what event he was describing. As her governesses all started their history lessons with the Romans and seldom stayed after they had reached the Norman Conquest, she could truthfully reply that she had not yet studied the period under description. Her father then turned to the terrified governess who, blushing all over, invariably lost her head and was also unable to guess the incident. After an embarrassing silence he would exclaim, 'Come Miss Fisher, surely you have heard of the Congress of Vienna!'[23]

Curzon's idea of a joint family activity was to persuade his daughters to help him carry out some tiresome task like weeding the garden – for which they were rewarded at the rate of a penny a plantain or sixpence a thistle – hanging pictures or dusting books, all of them undertaken because he believed gardeners could not weed, picture hangers could not hang pictures straight, and no housemaid could be trusted to dust books correctly. Irene remembered him wobbling at the top of a stepladder while the three girls held on to the base and with their free hands passed up the foot-ruler, nails, hammer and cord in the right order. Almost as little indulgence was shown to his children as he had received from his father. He did not allow his eldest daughters dogs because he believed they could never be properly house-trained and were bound to stain the carpets; when later he let Baba have a Pomeranian, the animal proved his point. Nor did he sympathize with Irene's love of fox-hunting, which he regarded as a 'shocking waste of time', although when he heard that she jumped five-bar gates, he was sufficiently impressed to appear 'on the keeper's nag dressed in his Indian jodhpurs to attend the lawn meet'.[24] He gave her a very grand coming-out ball at Carlton House Terrace with 500 guests, but as she had not been allowed to attend dances or meet young men beforehand, it is unlikely that she enjoyed herself. Nor can her dinner placement, between the Duke of Rutland and the Marquess of Lansdowne, have provided an exciting start to the evening. 'The Curzon daughter has none of her mother's looks', observed Asquith in her débutante year, and 'seemed quiet and a trifle gauche. I expect he is rather an over-whelming father.'[25]

The children did not enjoy visits to their relations at Kedleston, at that time an uncomfortable and inhospitable place. Their grandfather, who entered his eighties in 1911, was a remote and forbidding figure who forced the entire household to attend prayers before breakfast. Other inhabitants included Curzon's widowed and unmarried sisters who used to take the children in a cart to deliver milk puddings to the wives of estate workers. The property was run by Scarsdale's second son, Affie, a lazy and rather ill-humoured individual who lived nearby. His daughter recalled how the two households used to congregate at Kedleston after church on Sunday and denounce the absent members of the family; little Christian sense of charity, she observed, was derived from their religious attendance.[26]

Curzon's main pleasure in visiting his ancestral home was to inspect the work on his memorial chapel to Mary. In 1913 the beautiful shrine was finally completed, and the Queen, leaving her husband to grumble on about Lloyd George, motored over from Chatsworth to see it. Typically, Curzon had taken the opportunity provided by the chapel works to restore and embellish the whole church. Among other changes he reorganized and renovated the family monuments, added heating, electricity and stained glass, enlarged the west window and installed an electrically powered organ. But he found little else to occupy him at Kedleston. He itched to restore its dilapidated fabric, to put in heating and more bathrooms, but Lord Scarsdale was enraged even by the suggestion that his heir should make improvements with his own money. They also had disagreements over the running of the estate. Scarsdale handed over the detached farmland to his eldest son and afterwards regretted his generosity. Later, when he insisted on retaining an elderly agent, Curzon protested that his own interests and point of view were being unfairly neglected.[27]

A recurring headache for the whole family was the financial irre-sponsibility of Curzon's youngest brother Assheton, a trait charitably ascribed by Affie's daughter to Scarsdale's decision to economize on school fees by not sending him to Eton.[28] In 1901 Curzon received the news in India that Assheton required £15,000 to avoid the immediate bankruptcy of his business firm. Under pressure from the family, the Viceroy reluctantly agreed to guarantee, jointly with his brother Frank, a loan of that sum from their brother-in-law, Sir James Miller. In the event the money merely retarded bankruptcy for a few months and was then lost. Although Frank had assured his eldest brother that the loan was a nominal one, Miller's lawyers called it in after their client's death in 1906, and to his indignation Curzon was forced to pay his sister £7,500. Scarsdale reacted to the crisis by making Assheton sign a promise never to speculate again, and Frank insisted that the 'poor boy' would be tied up so tight that he could never make another business decision without consulting him. This did not prevent Assheton from spending money and by 1911 he was in debt again. Three years later a far worse crisis blew up when he was caught stealing securities from his office in order to speculate on the Stock Exchange. Frank delivered the 'very unpleasant news' to his father, declaring that the miscreant must leave the country. Once again George and Frank, the only members of the family who ever pursued a career, had to save their brother, although their father now also made a contribution. On this occasion, however, they provided cash to replace the missing securities and thus saved Assheton from criminal proceedings, but they declined to rescue him from bankruptcy.[29]

George Curzon never fully recovered from the trauma of his Indian resignation. Convinced of the righteousness of his case and embittered by the behaviour of his colleagues, the experience blighted his career and left a discernible mark on his personality. Since Eton he had aroused strong reactions, favourable on the whole when he was young, but after India the balance tilted as the faults became more noticeable, the charm more private, the querulousness more strident and sustained.

Many men, and even more women, saw behind the mask and found him 'extremely sensitive and sympathetic'.[30] But those who knew him less well encountered a man quickly wounded by criticism yet apparently insensitive to the hurt he often caused others. To them he seemed cold and intimidating, impatient of their opinions and exasperated by their mistakes. Always vulnerable to the charge of arrogance, he became increasingly ridiculed by people who disliked him. They mocked him not for his opinions or his intelligence but for his idiosyncrasies, his pride, his archaic diction, his accent – what Harold Nicolson called 'that eccentric amalgam of Derbyshire and Eton'[31] – that made glass rhyme with lass. Arthur Benson, who knew him slightly for fifty years, sneered at the short 'a's, but conceded that his voice was 'mobile, youthful, and beautiful in cadence and timbre'. Irritated by Curzon since their Eton days, he considered him a 'pompous, able, self-absorbed, unpleasant man . . . tho' with an undoubted strength'.[32] A more representative view of those not well acquainted with him comes from the diary of the MP, Arthur Lee, who had the happy experience of encountering Curzon at Madame Tussaud's in 1910, 'gazing with concentrated attention, but . . . a trace of disappointment, at his own effigy in wax'. This memory prompted Lee to recall later that 'with all his great talents and even flashes of greatness, [Curzon's] monumental egotism was as irrepressible as it was diverting'. He had a keen sense of humour, even about himself, but it was 'usually shrouded in an Olympian pomposity'.[33]

Elinor Glyn observed that the people who most irritated and thus most resented Curzon were club secretaries, petty officials, head tradesmen and unintelligent bureaucrats. But he could also be thrown into 'small transports of anger' by inanimate objects such as a jammed door or a window that would not open. The principal causes of this irritability were insomnia and acute physical pain, which plagued him more and more as he grew older. Both his spine and his leg regularly gave way and forced him to spend weeks at a time in bed. Even when well, he could not stand for long periods and was granted permission by the King to sit during ceremonial occasions. At the same time he became increasingly neurotic about his sleeplessness. Mrs Glyn, who had to suffer the consequences, thought he had hypnotized himself into the belief that he could only sleep in total darkness. To ensure that no chance ray of light disturbed him, he shut out all air, and the combination of airlessness and his neurotic state of mind naturally produced insomnia.[34]

Curzon's private papers do not give the impression of a man of insufferable haughtiness governed by ambition. They tend to show a melancholic and self-pitying figure who, despite his shortcomings as a father, felt 'indescribably lonely' when his children were away. For him the 'most tragic time' of year was autumn, 'sodden with disappointment and vocal with decay'.[35] He brooded constantly on the past, on his love for Mary and the success of their marriage. Elinor Glyn believed his melancholia was caused by self-depreciation: 'He has moods when he thinks so humbly of himself that he is sad.'[36] Although this view would have been derided by most people who knew him – and even more by those who did not – it contains a certain amount of truth. He longed to be great – and in many ways he was great – but behind the lofty façade was an empty feeling of failure, a desperate fear, which the fourth Lord Salisbury noticed, of being second-rate.[37] He admitted privately that he had industry, method, a certain type of courage and a willingness to lead. But he made no claims for his intellect or oratory and, a few years after his return from India, he managed to convince himself that he had virtually renounced ambition. An autobiographical note, written in 1910 and left among his papers, contains an emotional disclaimer.

As for ambition I am supposed to be consumed with this half-vice half-virtue, and to think that the world must go wrong unless I am there to control it. Ah me! Ambition I once had – an honourable ambition I think – to 'do noble deeds, nor dream them, all day long', to excell, to lead on to great enterprises, to guide the state . . .

But since I came back from India shattered in health – and since I lost my darling wife – what ambition have I had? None, absolutely none. A hundred times have I resolved to retire from public life – never to make another speech, never to challenge another attack . . . I am supposed to seek the footlights. Little do [my critics] know what a business it is to get me on to the stage. How many of them I wonder have any idea of the long hours spent in bed, of the aching back, of the ulcers and nerve pain in the leg, of the fearful steel cage in which I have to be encased when I undergo any strain in which standing up is involved. They think me strong and arrogant and self-sufficient. Little do they reck that it is an invalid addressing them, who has only been driven to the duty because it is a duty, who has to be mechanically supported in order to stand upright for an hour and who presently goes back to his bed to writhe in agony as expiation for his foolishness.[38]

Such sentiments, though no doubt genuinely felt, were surely self-deceptive. Far from curtailing his ambition, Curzon's physical handicaps in fact seemed to drive him on. Pearl Craigie once remarked to T.P. O'Connor, one of Curzon's more improbable friends, that his 'apparently arrogant self-assertion' was in reality 'assertion against himself'. It was a perceptive observation which the Irish MP expanded many years later in his obituary of Curzon.

Whenever he felt weakest in health, he flogged his spirit up to resistance, and the arrogant look, the chest thrown forward, sometimes even the arrogant language, were not his declaration of defiance to the world, but his vindication of the strength of his spirit against the frailty of the suffering and appealing body.[39]

In middle age George Curzon seldom made new friendships with members of his own sex. Two of the few were with his former fellow proconsuls, Milner and Cromer. He always enjoyed meeting Milner, 'so tranquilly aloof from petty perturbations', and their friendship deepened later through co-operation in the War Cabinet. Curzon's relation-

ship with Cromer flourished while working together in the less stimulating atmosphere of the anti-suffragist movement. During the long last
illness of her husband, Lady Cromer later remembered, Curzon called
every day to enquire about his health and often dined with her, discussing 'the high things that matter' and never referring to himself. 'No
one', she told the Dean of St Paul's, 'realises the depth of character and
loyalty in that man.'[40]

While Curzon could be a difficult and critical friend, he was also a
loyal and often generous one. He still wrote regularly to Oscar
Browning, who lived mostly in Italy, lent him money and cancelled the
debt when it had been only half repaid.[41] One of the melancholy duties
of his middle age was to act as *The Times*'s obituarist for those friends
who died young. Two of his finest and most moving pieces were written
on George Wyndham and Alfred Lyttelton, who died within a month of
each other in the summer of 1913. After reading them Lord Grey
observed that their deaths at least had had the merit of lifting the
curtain behind which Curzon hid his real and compassionate nature.[42]

Curzon's favourite method of seeing his friends was to have as many
as possible in his house at the same time. Even before his second marriage, he much preferred to be a host at Hackwood than a guest anywhere else. His entertaining was, as always, meticulously planned and
supervised. On arriving early one Saturday, Cynthia Charteris found
him putting out the soap and towels in her room; afterwards, during a
tour of the house, she was shown the menus, written in his own hand,
for the next fortnight's meals in both the dining-room and the servants'
hall.[43] Guests were divided into different categories: family parties of
his brothers and sisters, gatherings of old Indian colleagues such as
Barnes and Lawrence, and shooting weekends for those former ADCs
who used to amuse him with their poor marksmanship in India.
Sometimes he gave a dreaded 'dinner of neighbours'. But the grandest
occasions were the large house parties each Whitsun. Although he
described one of these to Rosebery as 'rather a pleasant little cluster', it
was in fact a festivity lasting ten days during which more than forty
guests each passed several nights in the house. Whitsun regulars
included the Asquiths, the Salisburys, the Elchos and Balfour. Diana
Manners, who went with her mother, later recalled those Hackwood
parties, 'made up of the "Souls" and Cabinet Ministers, with their wives
or the ladies they loved. They strolled, high-heeled, with parasols on the
lawns, through the aisles of beeches . . .' Her host, she remembered, was
always kind to her. Indeed, he usually seems to have been better with

other people's children than with his own. Julian Grenfell, the Desboroughs' son, thought him merry and indulgent and liked him the best of his parents' friends.[44]

Hackwood resurrected in a rather grand and elderly way some of the spirit of the Souls. Unlike most of his contemporaries, Curzon never saw the point of card games and tried to restrict after-dinner entertainment to conversation and word games. He remained a brilliant talker, various guests recalled, dominating the party yet knowing how to draw out the best from his companions. In good company he was a surprisingly willing listener. He did not deliver monologues, said Lord Spencer, because he was 'interested in the other fellow as well as himself'. As a 'host of wits', observed Elinor Glyn, he was incomparable, enjoying the conversation of others and encouraging them to perform. But with 'ordinary people' the mask was put on and he seemed to 'paralyse their ideas'. No one, she added, had 'a greater art of crushing with a polished sentence'.[45]

Mrs Glyn thought that Curzon had 'no insight at all about women' and accepted 'as an angel' anyone who amused him and satisfied 'his fastidious refinement'. He was 'the most loyal friend' to them even when they no longer attracted him, but he did not understand them. For their part, she thought, women failed to appreciate his character and, although many were 'frantically in love with him', their adoration was 'largely composed of sexual emotion'. Curzon was 'superbly virile, vital and voluptuous', a 'most passionate physical lover' and so 'physically attractive' that he aroused passion even in casual friendships. Yet he would never treat a woman as an equal partner in a relationship or allow her to influence his life; the most she could hope to be was 'a solace, a recreation, a physical joy, an intermittent but sympathetic companion'.[46]

Elinor Glyn's unpublished memoir of her lover is often gushing and occasionally absurd. Curzon is depicted for example, as 'the noblest ruler since Augustus Caesar', a statesman who stood 'above other men as St Paul's among village churches'. Her less laudatory judgements are also open to criticism. Since she did not of course observe his relationships with Mary or Sibell Grosvenor, she was unqualified to call him incapable of loving 'any woman with a supreme love'. Yet she was his mistress over a period of eight years, and her assessment of his attitudes and behaviour towards women rings fairly true. Whether so many of them really were 'frantically in love with him' is not known. There was speculation at the time about his possible mistresses and rumours that he had had a son from an affair with a married woman. One diarist noted that he had shared 'the tempestuous bed' of the American actress Maxine Elliott,[47] and Curzon himself told Nancy Astor of gossip linking him with three women simultaneously. But with his usual care he erased evidence of any liaisons from his papers.

One woman who resisted him was the beautiful young wife of Waldorf Astor. At the beginning of their friendship in 1909, Curzon disclaimed any dishonourable intentions towards Nancy and praised her 'irresistible combination' of 'virtue and gaiety'. He even asked, disingenuously, 'Why can't a man be fond of a woman without wanting to be her lover?' But it soon became obvious that he himself was unable to forsake the aspiration. The following year he tried his old ploy of giving her a copy of Rossetti's poems and asking her to read and re-read 'The Blessed Damozel'. He loved her letters which were 'like a Scotch burn, racing along and leaping over hidden rocks with a sound of eternal laughter', and in one reply declared that she had 'dropped an anchor deep' in his heart. 'My dear Nancy' became 'My dear little girl', 'My dearest', 'Darling Nancy' and at one stage 'My poppet', followed by the admission that he did not know what a poppet was, but it sounded close and affectionate. He confessed to a recurrent desire to kiss her neck and to dally with her in the 'exquisite glades' of a Borromean island. But eventually he realized that his wishes would not be granted and he accepted the situation so long as she did not grant those of any other suitor. 'No man', he told her, 'can chase with dignity after 50 or with success after 53' – his age at the time of writing. But he still loved to see her, at Hackwood or Cliveden, and looked forward to one meeting when she would 'leap like a fawn' into his 'chaste embrace'. He felt clever and rejuvenated in her company, he said, and not like a 'tired elderly curate'.[48]

No similar evidence exists about his feelings for Elinor Glyn because she burnt all his letters at the end of their relationship. Elinor was a strikingly handsome woman with red hair and green eyes, married to a country squire who was both a spendthrift and an alcoholic. Five years younger than Curzon, she was a popular romantic novelist who in 1907 had a *succès de scandale* with *Three Weeks*, a ludicrous tale about a young Englishman's affair with a Balkan queen which Puccini was tempted to turn into an opera. The novel, which enjoyed enormous commercial success, was attacked for allegedly glorifying adultery and, as tends to happen in these cases, many of the most outraged critics were people who had not read it. Edward Lyttelton banned it from Eton on the strength of its reputation, although he later read it with enjoyment (but did not rescind the ban). In an attempt to counter the allegation of immorality, Elinor decided to invite London socialites to a private theatrical version of the book in which she herself played the queen. Amazingly, Curzon attended the matinée in the summer of 1908 and afterwards wrote to congratulate her on the play, her acting and her courage in attempting such a bold vindication. A few weeks later they made a rendezvous at Heidelberg and their affair began then or soon afterwards.[49]

Her love for Curzon caused Elinor endless anguish, not because she felt guilty about her husband, who lived drunkenly off her money, but because it completely dominated her life. In her diary she wrote that he could do no wrong, that she worshipped him blindly and would subjugate every wish or even die for him. Sometimes she tried to pull herself together, to 'cease brooding for hours if his little finger' ached, to stop praying for his glory and happiness all through the day, to try not to be 'the miserable slave of an obsession'. But it was no use: she admitted that for her he would be 'the sun, moon and stars to the end of time'.[50]

Both Curzon's wives complained that he did not spend enough time with them, and with a mistress he was bound to spend even less. Elinor occasionally went to Hackwood with her daughters, but she was not included in the large Whitsun parties. Once she stayed with him at Crag Hall, a lodge Curzon rented for grouse shooting in Derbyshire. At mealtimes he played his historical inquisition game and in the evenings read Aristotle aloud. Sometimes she wished she could have loved Milner, who loved her and used to read her Plato; if for her Curzon reproduced 'the highest Roman spirit of the Augustan age', Milner was 'the reincarnation of Socrates'.[51] But unfortunately all her feelings were concentrated on Curzon, 'My Beloved Lord', whose attitude to her oscillated between passion and near indifference. Early in 1911 she ascribed his coldness to the fact that he had another mistress, but he denied it and said he loved her the same as ever.[52] Once he told her the affair must end because the servants were beginning to talk, and Elinor replied spiritedly that she was not accustomed to having her life determined by servants' gossip. In the event, after a short separation, Curzon resumed the affair.

In the summer of 1912 Elinor published *Halcyone*, the novel she considered to be her masterpiece. A copy was sent to Curzon who, she later claimed, merely acknowledged the book's arrival and pointed out two spelling mistakes in the covering letter. At the time, however, she told her mother that he had been very complimentary and had made her feel that he was 'really impressed' by her brains. But her claim that he considered the book 'masterly in its restraint' and in its 'superlative knowledge of human nature' seems incredible. Apart from the fact that both judgements are absurd, it is unlikely that he would have praised a book containing such an unflattering portrait of himself in the character of John Derringham. Not only did her anti-hero have a youthful career similar to her lover's – Captain of the Oppidans at Eton followed by Oxford, election to Parliament and appointment as Under-Secretary for Foreign Affairs – but Derringham's faults were an extreme caricature of his own. The fictional character is an ambitious individual with an '*insouciante* arrogance' and a 'sublime belief in himself', a man who thinks that women were 'meant to be feminine, dainty, exquisite creatures' and a politician who complains that, as a consequence of 'pandering to mediocrity', he has to use simple words so that 'uneducated clods can grasp his meaning'. In the end this unpleasant creature is converted to civilized values by Halcyone, an intended self-portrait of the author, whose head is full of 'true philosophy and profound knowledge of truth' and who displays 'a promise of all pure and tender things in her great soft eyes'. Derringham's transformation and his recognition that women do after all have souls are unlikely to have redeemed him in the eyes of his original.

How Curzon really reacted to *Halcyone*, why he continued the affair in spite of the servants' gossip, and indeed how strong his feelings were for Elinor can only be conjectured. He was generous to her, he lent her husband a large sum of money, and his presents included a tiger skin, a Della Robbia bust of Venus which he thought resembled her, several items of expensive jewellery, and a number of leather-bound books including, inevitably, Rossetti's poems. But of his love for her we know nothing except for the physical passion she described in her memoir. The enduring image from the diary is of a rather tragic woman tormented by her inability to see more of the man she repeatedly refers to as her Idol. In 1912 she took a house in London for her daughter's début but was disheartened that Curzon did not visit her as often as she had hoped. The following year she moved to Paris and installed a secret staircase in her house so that he could come and go discreetly. But he postponed his visit and, when finally it took place, it was not a great success. She took him to Versailles, her favourite building in the world, and led him with his eyes closed across the terrace. When she told him to open them, she expected him to dissolve into romantic raptures at the sight of the palace. Instead he said drily, 'Architecturally correct but monotonous'. Yet his bouts of indifference did nothing to shake her love or her hero worship. One of her most emotional experiences was to watch him address a public rally. 'Oh! My heart!' she confided to her diary,

> To see you there, master of those ten thousand people, calm, aloof, unmoved. To hear your noble voice, and listen to your masterly argument. To sit there, one of a rough crowd, gazing up at your splendid face and to know that in other moments that proud head can lie upon my breast even as a little child. Ah! me. There are moments in life worth living for.[53]

27

In Search of a Role,
1914–1915

———————————◆———————————

OPPOSITION NEVER APPEALED to George Curzon, and never less so than in August 1914. At the outbreak of the Great War he offered his services to Asquith for non-political work in any capacity, but no use was found for them. It was rather pitiful, he reflected, that 'a man who at 39 was thought good enough to rule 300 millions of people – and did rule them – is apparently useless at 55 when the existence of his country is at stake'.[1]

Later in the month he wrote to *The Times* offering to go anywhere in the country where recruiting was slow and on a cross-party platform explain the causes and circumstances of the war. Rapidly inundated with requests for meetings, he wrote to Churchill at the Admiralty to co-ordinate plans and compose responses.[2] Identifying the north as the region where recruiting was slackest, he then embarked on a ten-day speaking tour at the beginning of September. At Aberdeen he explained that Britain was fighting not for France or Belgium but for herself and her freedom, which could not be secure until the German military system had been dismantled. Two days later in Glasgow he spoke of the empire's expected contribution to victory, colourfully picturing the lances of the Bengal cavalry 'fluttering down the streets of Berlin' and 'the little dark-skinned Gurkha making himself at ease in the gardens of Potsdam'.[3] The thought of Nepalese soldiers lounging about in a Prussian palace offended German newspapers, but an Austrian journalist with a sense of humour retorted that the Central Powers would punish a defeated England by placing her under the administration of a viceroy like Curzon.[4]

George Curzon's personal response to the crisis was generous. He immediately gave 500 guineas to the National Relief Fund and donated substantial sums to other appeals, including the Serbian Relief Fund, of which he became Vice-President. He offered his house at Broadstairs to the Red Cross and the War Office, which both rejected it as a convalescent home, and then lent it to wounded Belgians. At Hackwood he had Belgian refugees in the stables and the Belgian royal family in the house, while at Carlton House Terrace the Belgian Relief Fund was installed in one part of the building and the Indian Soldiers Fund took over the dining-room. An early advocate of bringing Indian troops to Europe, Curzon went to great trouble to ensure that they were adequately provided with flannel shirts and other equipment. As a personal gift he gave each unit of Indian troops an enormous thirty-gallon water boiler for making tea. These contraptions, made in Hammersmith and inscribed in Hindustani, were much appreciated by the soldiers but their size and weight made them difficult to transport. Curzon's paternalist affection for the Indian people displayed itself again in his concern for the welfare of their fighting men. He was much saddened when some of them ran away and deeply upset to learn that the little Gurkhas, unable to see the advancing Germans from their trench, had been easily overwhelmed.[5]

Curzon's hospitality to the Belgian royal family lasted for the entire war. The German sweep westwards failed to capture a slice of Belgian territory around La Panne, where King Albert subsequently set up his headquarters. Not regarding it as a suitable place to bring up his children, however, he accepted Curzon's offer to have them at Hackwood. The Queen brought them over at the end of August and, although she returned after a week, the two princes and their sister remained at Hackwood for much of the war. After persuading the King to send his sons to Wixenford and Eton, Curzon personally supervised their progress by visits to the schools and correspondence with their tutors. Following the educational footsteps of the former Viceroy did not prove a complete success. The Belgian monarch thought the inadequate breakfasts and excessive football made his elder son too thin, while the opportunities presented by a prep school encouraged his younger boy to display an unattractive side of his character. As the headmaster explained to Wixenford's most distinguished old boy, Prince Charles was a bully who had been caught whacking a smaller boy with a cricket bat, a complaint which Curzon passed on to La Panne, adding that the same trait had been noticed at Hackwood, where the Prince was 'disposed to be rough and at times cruel'. From Belgium the King replied that he would send his son 'a warning not to recommence his brutal conduct towards his comrades'.[6]

Shortly after the outbreak of war, Kipling suggested to Curzon that Oxford University should be temporarily closed down and its under-graduates given military training.[7] Although the idea made little headway, Curzon himself was partly in sympathy because he thought the British people were not yet putting their backs into the war effort. There was too much unthinking optimism, he felt; the sporting and pleasure-loving world was still selfish, the middle classes were slack and the lower classes were indifferent.[8] Responding to a request from the editor of *The Times*, Geoffrey Robinson, Curzon wrote a letter to his paper denouncing the continuation of horse-racing at a time when 'the flower of our race' was dying so that 'we (and incidentally the English thoroughbred) may continue to live'. Referring to the Epsom and Ascot meetings, he asked whether the country was going to persevere with the 'two great yearly "beanfeasts" against a background of awful tragedy and a vale of tears?' What would the European allies think of such a spectacle? he wondered. Would 'they think it a sufficient justification that this is done to maintain the English thoroughbred for the benefit of mankind?'[9] Although the most ostentatious 'beanfeasts' – an unCurzonian word suggested by Robinson – were abandoned, racing continued at Newbury, Newmarket and a couple of smaller courses. Two years later Curzon appealed to Lloyd George, by then Prime Minister, not to close the Victoria and Albert Museum because thou-sands of wounded soldiers visited it. 'If our race courses are to be left open,' he added, 'why not at least one or two museums? At least they consume no oats.'[10]

Frustrated by his lack of a serious role, Curzon turned to his pen. He began translating the poems of the Belgian royalist, Emile Cammaerts, which were published in the *Observer* and in 1915 in a book, *War Poems and Other Translations*. Declaring that its proceeds, if there were any, would go to the Belgian Relief Fund, he also included some Classical translations together with the poem, masquerading as a 'Love Song from the Indian', he had written for Mary on her return to Calcutta in 1905. A volume of selected speeches was published in the same year with an introduction by Lord Cromer extolling the author as 'the most able, as he is certainly by far the most eloquent, exponent of that sane Imperialism to which our country is wedded as a necessity of its exis-tence'. On re-reading them, Curzon was rather pleased with his speeches, observing that they were in some cases prophetic and in general showed him to be independent of party considerations. Less edifying than their content was the usual lengthy wrangle with his publishers over some insignificant costs.[11]

A second, almost unremitting task for his pen was the composition of letters to the long list of friends, colleagues and ICS officers who had lost sons in the fighting. 'One is stunned', he wrote in November 1914, 'as day by day the horror goes on and one sees not so much the loss of individuals as the obliteration of a whole generation.'[12] For the first time in his life he must have been relieved that neither of his eldest children were boys. Many of his closest friends were bereaved: Sibell Grosvenor and Violet Cecil lost sons in the first weeks; Mary Elcho and Ettie Desborough each lost two; five of the late Lord Salisbury's ten grandsons were killed in the war. 'For one's friends' sake,' he wrote, 'one almost longs to hear that such and such a one is wounded.' He tried to reassure himself with the thought that dying for one's country on the battlefield was glorious, for did not the individual life go on in the life of the race and the slain acquire immortality in the spirit life of the nation?[13] Letters of condolence brought out the best in Curzon. 'You have the gift of touching the right note,' Lord Redesdale wrote after his son's death, 'a rare talent given to few men.'[14] As he showed in the obituaries of his friends, death enabled Curzon to reveal a sensitivity and human sympathy that was seldom otherwise exposed.

Like the other Unionist leaders, Curzon agreed to support the basic war aims of the Government and to abstain from raising controversial issues. And like Bonar Law in the Commons, he criticized Asquith for putting Irish Home Rule and Welsh Disestablishment on the Statute Book – while postponing their implementation until the end of the war – because the Prime Minister had pledged not to revive controversy; but he did not try to emulate Law by leading a protesting exodus from the Chamber. In the middle of November Lansdowne fell ill, leaving Curzon to deputize for him as the Unionist leader in the House of Lords. Some surprise was expressed that the role was not filled by Salisbury or his brother-in-law Selborne, both of them former cabinet ministers who appealed to the Diehard peers very much more than their friend. But in the crisis of 1914 it was felt that qualities of leadership were more important than personal popularity. In welcoming the appointment, the *Daily Mirror* described Curzon as 'the most picturesque personality and the finest orator' in the Unionist Party, while the *Daily Sketch* considered him 'the one orator now left among active politicians in the Upper House'.[15]

On a visit to Lansdowne at Bowood, Curzon himself fell ill but insisted on making a major speech when the House of Lords reassembled at the beginning of January. Robinson of *The Times* visited him at Carlton House Terrace beforehand and found him 'still almost speechless with his cold, but full of energy and oratory as ever!' When Midleton dropped in a few minutes later, Robinson witnessed 'a most comical shy meeting with Curzon, who treated him with a magnificent superiority and proceeded to practise his speech for the afternoon' on them both.[16] In the Lords Curzon referred to the problems of an Opposition which gave unstinting support to the Government without being informed of what was happening and which refrained from making speeches and criticisms 'where speech was tempting and criticism would have been easy'.[17] To his colleagues he protested on paper that their party was

> expected to give a mute and almost unquestioning support to anything done by the Government, to maintain a patriotic silence about the various blunders that have been committed in connection with the war . . . to dismantle our Party machinery, to forego all possibility of Party advantage, and to allow, without a protest, the most outrageously partisan of measures, such as the Plural Voting Bill, to be carried over our heads, or even with our consent. In other words the Government are to have all the advantages, while we have all the drawbacks of a coalition.[18]

His particular exasperation was concentrated on his old adversary Kitchener, whom Asquith had made in what he admitted to be a 'hazardous experiment' Secretary of State for War. Kitchener's enduring prestige with the British public was an asset that clearly needed to be exploited in wartime. After leaving the Subcontinent, the Field Marshal had been Consul-General in Egypt where he had enhanced his reputation partly by copying Curzon's Indian reforms for protecting the peasantry: one of his measures was almost a replica of the Punjab Land Alienation Act. At the beginning of the war he had grasped that it would be a long struggle requiring millions of soldiers, and his part in the creation of the new armies was the greatest achievement of his life. Yet he was no easier as a Cabinet colleague than he had been as a member of the Viceroy's Council. Installing himself in Carlton Gardens as a neighbour of Curzon – who was equally prophetic about the scale and duration of the war – Kitchener was entrusted with even more power than he had enjoyed in India: besides being a great recruiting poster, he was in charge of munitions, enlistment and military strategy. In none of these spheres, however, did he volunteer information either to the Opposition or even to the Cabinet. As Curzon continued in the complaint to his colleagues,

> The Secretary of State for War reads us [in the House of Lords] exiguous Memoranda of platitudes known to everybody, is acclaimed by the Liberal Press as having delivered an almost inspired oration and scored off his impertinent antagonists. He interpolates a curt affirmative or negative to the solitary speech to which he deigns to listen, and he then marches out and leaves the rest of the debate to colleagues who either affect to know nothing or screen their silence behind his authority.[19]

Long and Lansdowne supported Curzon's demands for more information and the right to make some criticisms when necessary, but they were opposed by the Unionist leader and his predecessor. Balfour, who for the next ten years was in almost regular disagreement with Curzon, could imagine nothing more inexpedient than debates on the Government's war blunders. 'Conceive the folly', he suggested to Law, 'of putting under the limelight of Parliamentary rhetoric all the things that have gone wrong, or that have not gone quite right'. Abroad, he added, the effect on both friends and enemies would be disastrous. Law agreed with him and told Curzon in less combative language that the only alternative to carrying on 'without responsibility and with a very limited amount of criticism' was a coalition which nobody wanted.[20]

Much as Curzon liked and admired Lansdowne, he was dismayed by the 'anaemic calm' which settled on the House of Lords after his return. It was incredible, he thought, that only a handful of peers should turn up to hear 'the greatest authorities in the Empire' speak at a time of national crisis: the only way to arouse interest, he told Cromer, was to organize debates, but Lansdowne refused to do so. The Earl of Crawford, that most acute and acerbic of diarists, despaired at the reappearance of Lansdowne and the 'relapse into the coma' from which the Lords had only recently been rescued by Curzon. Like many of their contemporaries, Crawford's view of Curzon fluctuated between extremes of admiration and censoriousness. In 1915 the judgement of Scotland's premier earl was that the former Viceroy should become the party leader in the Lords. He was 'wise and experienced' and, despite poor health, an indefatigable worker. Achievement, Crawford optimistically predicted, 'would soften asperities and mellow his temperament' as well as eradicate those 'little jealousies' which were often rather noticeable.[21]

In April 1915 Curzon took Princess Marie José with him to Belgium to celebrate her father's birthday. He liked King Albert and was impressed by his modest manner, although later in the war he was irked by the monarch's apparent desire to recover 'his country by warfare anywhere else but in or near to Belgium itself'.[22] On leaving La Panne he went on a tour of the Flanders front and met Sir John French, the British Commander-in-Chief, who complained at length about Kitchener's interference with his plans and dispositions. The Belgian troops struck him as short and pale, without 'the bloom or physique or virility of the English soldier', but he was impressed by the vigour and morale of his own countrymen whom he saw in the trenches and behind the lines at Armentières, where he was shown them splashing about in huge steaming wooden tubs and emerging 'clean and jolly, and noisy with delight'.[23] This was doubtless the spectacle which inspired one of the most celebrated Curzonisms – 'Dear me! I had no conception the lower classes had such white skins' – a story he himself much enjoyed but which even detractors admitted was apocryphal.[24] Before returning to England he heard some lurid stories about the German character. On the body of one officer a letter had been found from his wife exhorting him to rape every foreign woman he came across. 'There is a world of psychology in that tale,' Curzon noted in his diary. 'Conceive the low and perverted and almost bestial morality of such a people.'[25]

Curzon returned for the last few weeks of purely Liberal government in Britain. In May Asquith was beset by a series of crises: an army crisis created by Repington who in an article in *The Times* blamed recent military failures on a shortage of shells – and therefore by implication on his old master Kitchener; a naval crisis when Lord Fisher abandoned Churchill at the Admiralty and resigned as First Sea Lord; and a personal crisis after Venetia Stanley, the Prime Minister's confidante, disclosed her intention of marrying the Liberal MP Edwin Montagu. The combination of the first two, coming after the failure of the Dardanelles and the losses on the Western Front, made it impossible for Bonar Law to keep his party in a state of 'patriotic opposition'; and the revelation of the third, which greatly upset Asquith, may have helped to weaken the Prime Minister's powers of resistance. Persuaded by Lloyd George that there was no alternative to a coalition, he set about the 'most intolerable task' of welcoming into 'the intimacy of the political household, strange alien, hitherto hostile figures'.[26]

Most senior Unionists disliked the idea of joining the Liberals in government. In January Curzon had said he was 'entirely against' a coalition which would 'tie our hands and close our lips even more effectively than at present': only if the country was actually invaded did he think one would be necessary.[27] After Fisher's resignation he realized that the 'much dreaded coalition' was inevitable, but he himself was uncertain whether he would be invited to join it and, if so, whether he should accept. Pressure from a powerful quarter was exerted to relieve him of the need to face such a dilemma. On 17 May Chamberlain told Bonar Law that he and Carson would 'infinitely sooner' have Selborne as a colleague than Curzon, who was a '*mauvais coucheur*' with untrustworthy judgement. The former Viceroy, he thought, had little influence and would only be dangerous if Long was also excluded. Law was therefore exhorted by his monocled colleague, who had admired Curzon before the Parliament Bill and distrusted him since, to urge Asquith to find a place for Long.[28]

Whether Bonar Law was tempted to follow Chamberlain's advice is unknown. Lansdowne, who realized it was undesirable to omit the ablest figure in the Lords, argued against it and offered to stand down himself so that both Curzon and Selborne could be included.[29] In the end all three of them joined the Government, but only Selborne, as President of the Board of Agriculture, was given a department to run. The other two became ministers without portfolio, though Curzon's post was gilded with the title of Lord Privy Seal. In the negotiations for places between the two leaders, Bonar Law did poorly for his party and even worse for himself. He and Chamberlain, the leading Unionists in the Commons, received the Colonies and India, sideshows in an essentially European war. Only Balfour, who as a member of the War Council had been a sort of one-man coalition since November 1914, was given a crucial post. At the Admiralty he replaced Churchill, who was made to carry his share of the blame – as well as that of Asquith and Kitchener – for the failures at the Dardanelles.

Curzon was certainly happy to obtain, at the age of 56, a rank it had been confidently predicted he would reach in his thirties. Observers noticed how 'cabinet air' suited him, while Cromer watched 'with mingled admiration and amusement the graceful ease and elasticity' with which his friend had 'doffed the mantle of the critic and donned that of the responsible minister'.[30] But no one was less suited to be a minister without portfolio than Curzon. He longed to find something to do and on the day of his appointment even told Lloyd George, the new Minister for Munitions, that he hoped he might be found 'useful for any odd jobs'.[31] It has often been said that Curzon was the principal Unionist supporter of Asquith, who valued his advice and preferred to consult him rather than Bonar Law. While the Prime Minister certainly had little respect for the Unionist leader, his closest ally among his coalition partners was in fact Balfour. His esteem for the Lord Privy Seal's advice may have been real, but he was reluctant to give it much scope.

After two months with nothing to do, Curzon told Asquith he could not accept a salary for holding a nominal office and was therefore making arrangements to return the money he had already received to the Exchequer. He then asked whether he might have a place on the Imperial Defence Committee or even on one of its subcommittees. Having been at the Foreign Office and in India and in almost every country in Asia and Europe, he felt he could surely be of greater use than he was now. He was supposed to know something about administration, he added, but he had been placed in the one position where there was nothing to administer.[32] Asquith thanked him for the public-spirited renunciation of his salary and offered him an as yet non-existent job in charge of war trade problems. On learning that both the Foreign Office and the Board of Trade opposed the creation of such an office, Curzon advised him not to persevere with the idea.[33]

After nearly ten years without even a nominal position in government, the Lord Privy Seal was eager to please. Officials found none of the arrogance or aloofness which they expected, and observers were impressed by his willingness to do anything useful.[34] Colleagues too decided that they had misjudged him. After eighteen months in office Chamberlain told his brother Neville that he had come to appreciate Curzon's qualities after seeing him at work, and Selborne, who had disagreed with him on Tariff Reform, the Parliament Bill and women's suffrage, regained his earlier esteem after co-operation in the Cabinet. In the private 'reports' which Selborne wrote on his colleagues' performances in 1916, Curzon's 'great ability, courage, driving power and vision' won him top marks with Chamberlain. Judging people, as was often done, on whether they would be trustworthy out tiger-shooting, Selborne wished 'for no better company when after tigers; neither of them would ever leave a friend in the lurch'.[35] Crawford, who succeeded Selborne at the Board of Agriculture, also gave a most positive verdict. Curzon had greatly improved, he noted, since giving up 'princely entertainments' at the beginning of the war, and had become 'more of the private citizen and less of the Viceroy'. He was maturing in wisdom, he added, and now possessed the 'best judgment of any man in our party'.[36]

Soon after the formation of the Coalition, Curzon became a member of the Dardanelles Committee, set up to regulate the offensive in the eastern Mediterranean although in fact it oversaw other campaigns as well. In opposition he had had doubts about the expedition but, once troops had dug in on the Gallipoli Peninsula, he opposed all proposals of withdrawal. In June he suggested that an attack should be contemplated on the Asiatic shore of the Dardanelles, adding very typically that he was probably the only member of the committee who had travelled in that part of the world. The following month he was one of a group of ministers who persuaded Kitchener to send reinforcements to the Mediterranean, and in September he and his colleagues agreed that plans for a winter campaign at Gallipoli should be drawn up. But the recommendation of a committee of military experts that all efforts should be concentrated on the Western Front, followed by the fall of Belgrade and the entry of Bulgaria into the war on the enemy side, strengthened the view of those who believed the operation had no chance of success. As Carson asked the committee in mid-October, were the troops merely meant to hold on to the peninsula and prepare to resist the Turks, the Bulgarians and the Germans? Curzon questioned the wisdom of pouring all resources into the Western Front, where 50,000 men had just been sacrificed for a paltry territorial gain at the Battle of Loos. Turning to the Dardanelles, he complained that his idea of an operation on the Asiatic shore had been treated 'cavalierly', and suggested that if nothing could be achieved in the area it might be better to come to terms with the Turks. But evacuation from Gallipoli without an agreement would, he thought, have a disastrous effect on Britain's position in Asia.[37]

At the same meeting Asquith declared that withdrawal from Gallipoli was 'out of the question', while Kitchener maintained it would be 'the most disastrous event in the history of the empire'. But military opinion now favoured evacuation and, after a visit to the area and several changes of mind, Kitchener accepted it. The overcrowded Dardanelles Committee was disbanded and succeeded in November by the War Committee, a more compact body from which Curzon and Churchill, the most vociferous opponents of withdrawal, were excluded.

'Anxious and miserable' about the new trend in policy, Curzon wrote a long paper on the Dardanelles which he distributed to the Cabinet before a meeting on the 24th. Suggesting that military advice did not always have to be taken because it was itself so often changing, he observed that on 6 November Kitchener had been in favour of staying put at Gallipoli, on the 10th he had recommended sending the troops to Alexandretta, on the 15th he had decided to leave them where they were, and on the 22nd he had declared that they must be withdrawn because their position was untenable. Once again Curzon stressed the catastrophic effect withdrawal would have on the East, which had never before seen the British running away from an Asiatic enemy, and luridly envisioned the inferno of withdrawal, the shells 'falling and bullets ploughing their way into this mass of retreating humanity . . . the crowding into the boats of thousands of half-crazy men, the swamping of craft, the nocturnal panic, the agony of the wounded, the hecatombs of the slain'.[38]

This document, which received backing from Selborne and Lansdowne, was described by the Cabinet Secretary, Maurice Hankey, as 'one of the most able papers' he had ever read.[39] But the cause had already been lost, and a staged withdrawal began the following month. Although the retreat was unaccompanied by any of the horrors Curzon had predicted, he remained convinced that it was 'as great an error as any of the earlier blunders of the Dardanelles campaign'. Had the British at Gallipoli been reinforced by some of the troops at Salonika, he believed they could have mounted a successful offensive in the spring.[40]

Gallipoli led to the high point in the erratic thirty-year relationship between Curzon and Winston Churchill. Demoted from the Admiralty in May and excluded from the War Committee in November, Churchill resigned from the Government and went off to fight at the Front. After receiving a letter from Curzon describing the Cabinet struggle over Gallipoli, he was tempted to return and campaign against evacuation. But as he told his wife, 'a fresh uncompromised champion like Curzon', who had stated the case as well as he could have done, had a better chance of success. Eager to encourage the new friendship, Clementine Churchill passed on these compliments – slightly embellished – and invited Curzon to lunch at her house; she wished, she told her husband, that her guest would become War Secretary instead of 'that cowardly and base old K'. The following February Churchill took the Lord Privy Seal on a tour of the trenches while shells and bullets came, he reported, 'discreetly and tactfully in the places which we had left or in those we had not reached'. On his return Curzon invited Clementine to lunch to tell her about his visit and give her some bottles of brandy for her husband.[41]

In October 1915 Margot Asquith told Hankey it was as 'clear as day that LLG, Curzon and Winston are going to try and wreck the Gov'.[42] One of those rare people whose judgement is either very acute or else completely wrong, the Prime Minister's wife was on this occasion at her most perspicacious. The observant Chirol had noticed that relations between Curzon and Lloyd George were 'most cordial' and he believed that the two men constituted 'the real driving force in the Cabinet'. Liberal ministers might dislike Curzon but they felt compelled to admire him. He was 'the brazen pot', thought Sir John Simon, 'among the earthen vessels' of the Unionist Party and would become its leader.[43] In the autumn Curzon dined at least twice with Lloyd George and Churchill, and discussed plans almost as subversive as that envisaged by Mrs Asquith. According to Frances Stevenson, Lloyd George's secretary and mistress, Curzon said at the first dinner that the Unionists could not accept the present situation and would demand both the removal of Kitchener and the introduction of conscription. Lloyd George then declared that he too could not be 'a party any longer to the shameful mismanagement and slackness', and that he and Churchill would throw in their lot with Curzon and his followers.[44] While at the Front, Churchill believed that the salvation of his career depended largely on these two dining companions. In letters to his wife he told her to keep in touch with them and other politicians. The group he wanted to work with, he told her, were Lloyd George, F.E. Smith, Curzon, Carson and Bonar Law. 'Keep that steadily in mind. It is the alternative Government when "wait & see" [Asquith] is over'.[45]

This potential triumvirate of vigorous men emanated from a shared view of the defects of Asquith and Kitchener. But it was never likely to develop or even last in its current form. Acute differences of character, temperament and ideas separated two essentially intuitive politicians from a man with weak political antennae whose judgement rested on facts. Churchill, Curzon observed, 'is impetuous with or in spite of knowledge. Lloyd George is impetuous *without* it.'[46] Neither was a natural ally. Curzon's friendship with Churchill declined after he became President of the Air Board, a post the younger man wanted for himself, and only sporadically and less wholeheartedly was it afterwards revived.

Margot Asquith had identified conscription as the issue with which the triumvirs would try to destroy her husband's Government. Curzon's stand on the question was well-known. As Vice-President of the National Service League, he had argued in favour of universal military training since 1909. In a speech to the Primrose League made shortly before joining the Cabinet, he had observed that Britain had mustered 700,000 men for the Front from a population of 45 million, while France, with only 40 million, had put 2½ million soldiers into the field. On Saturday, he added, 'while our men were going through indescribable agonies in Flanders, there were at Manchester 30,000 looking on at 22 other men kicking a leathern ball about'.[47] Like Kitchener, he had realized from the beginning that the war would last several years and need armies of millions. But unlike the War Secretary, he believed that compulsory military service would be required to find them.

Pressure for conscription had been reduced by the early successes of voluntary recruitment, and at the formation of the Coalition Curzon claimed he was 'the only avowed compulsionist in the cabinet'.[48] He soon produced a memorandum for his colleagues arguing that married volunteers, who formed a third of the recruits, should be replaced as far as possible by single men. As he showed in his reaction to the slaughter at Loos, he opposed offensives which achieved little beyond comparable casualties on both sides, but he realized that the vast German army would not be defeated unless Britain increased her own forces and took adequate steps to replenish them. A National Register, he argued, should therefore be set in place from which to draw men if voluntary recruitment failed.[49]

As the enlistment figures dropped over the summer, Lloyd George, Churchill and the Unionist ministers came round to Curzon's point of view. After a National Registration Act was passed in July, Lord Crewe was appointed to head a War Policy Committee to examine the need for conscription. Curzon, Selborne and Chamberlain were named as its Unionist members, to the annoyance of their party leader who asked the Prime Minister why he had been excluded; Asquith failed to appease Law by explaining that, after consultation with Curzon, he had decided his original list was too long and had therefore left him out.[50] The committee examined ministers and civil servants with such divergent views on the issue that it was unable to come to a conclusion. A majority, however, consisting of the three Unionists and Churchill, produced their own memorandum stating that conscription was both viable and necessary.

As the compulsionists realized, their chief obstacle was not those Liberal ministers who opposed conscription on principle but Kitchener, who refused to accept that his voluntary system was no longer adequate. Campaigning assiduously during the late summer to convert people to the cause, Curzon found some compensation for his 'irksome and mortifying' inactivity in the Government. His policy seemed on the point of triumph in early October when Asquith produced the 'Derby scheme', an attempted compromise between the two factions whereby all men between the ages of 18 and 41 were invited to 'attest', that is to agree to 'volunteer' when their year was called up. Kitchener believed that the scheme, named after the bluff Lancashire magnate who was appointed to carry it out, would succeed in preserving the voluntary element in his system. Churchill and the Unionist members of Crewe's committee regarded it as a time-wasting exercise that was bound to fail, but they could not prevent the experiment from taking place. They demanded, however, that some form of compulsion should be introduced if the Derby scheme did not produce enough volunteers. The Prime Minister, who had hoped that a series of ambiguous pronouncements might prevent a split in the Government, reluctantly agreed and asked Curzon to help prepare a draft bill for the Cabinet's consideration.[51]

After Christmas Asquith proposed that Curzon should become a Knight of the Garter, the only honour the former Viceroy had said he wanted in India thirteen years earlier. But now he hesitated about accepting and asked for a delay before giving a definite reply. The 'Derby scheme' had plainly failed, but the Cabinet remained divided, the Prime Minister's ambiguousness had resurfaced, and the future of the Compulsory Service Bill seemed in doubt. Curzon felt he could not accept the Garter and then resign, which he was strongly inclined to do, if conscription was not introduced. On being reassured, however, of the eventual outcome, he accepted the offer and set about acquiring the diamond badge and star of the order. Garrards the jewellers offered him these accoutrements for the immense sum of £2,100, but Lord Derby told him he could buy fake ones for £92; in evening light, he added, one could not tell the difference. Curzon was not the sort of man who could happily wear a paste badge, and in the end he bought second-hand but authentic articles from Lord Cadogan.[52]

Kitchener's exploits in the battle for compulsion removed any remaining doubts his colleagues may have had about his unfitness to be War Secretary. Following his performances over the Dardanelles, munitions shortages and the Allied offensive in the West, they had come to realize how far he was from being 'Britain's answer to Hindenburg'. He was 'at his very worst in Cabinet', recorded Selborne. 'He seldom knew his case, his figures were usually wrong, his statements were muddled and confused, and it was impossible to trust them. His conception of truth was distinctly oriental.'[53] Even long-serving admirers of the Field Marshal such as Esher and Midleton now criticized him. In October 1915 Carson resigned as Attorney-General in protest at his incompetence, and Lloyd George and Bonar Law threatened to follow suit unless he was dismissed. It would have been unnatural for Curzon not to 'sit and smile' as he listened to the very complaints about Kitchener that he had made ten years earlier, especially when they now came from 'the very lips to whom he was then the Law and the Prophets'.[54]

The Prime Minister had considered getting rid of the War Secretary when he formed the Coalition but had been dissuaded by, among others, his wife, who had denounced Kitchener in the past but whose feelings towards him were now moving, characteristically, in the opposite direction to everybody else's. In the autumn Asquith managed to avoid further Cabinet resignations by sending Kitchener to the eastern Mediterranean and reducing his powers while he was away. Passing on to Curzon a paper recommending that some of the War Secretary's duties should be assigned to the Chief of the Imperial General Staff, the Prime Minister admitted that the real problem was Kitchener's standing with public opinion: while not regarded as 'a source of confidence or strength' by anyone who worked with him, he remained 'in the eyes of the world, a figure of great and as yet undimmed authority and therefore a national asset'.[55] Discussing various schemes to get Kitchener out of the way without diminishing his prestige, Curzon strongly deprecated the suggestion that he should be made Viceroy of India, a post for which he was not young enough, 'upright' enough or sufficiently competent to fill. 'You know now,' he told Asquith, 'and I found it in India, that he is no organiser, no administrator, no thinker out of big problems.'[56]

Kitchener returned from the Mediterranean before the end of 1915 to his desk at the War Office. On learning he was no longer to be in charge of military strategy, he threatened to resign but was persuaded to stay in his post as little more than a figurehead. Six months later, when he was drowned off the Orkneys after setting off on a mission to Russia, his prestige was still intact, although Churchill and General Hamilton, who had commanded the Gallipoli forces, were preparing an assault on it with evidence for the Dardanelles Commission. 'The fact that he should have vanished', wrote Hamilton, 'at the very moment Winston and I were making an unanswerable case against him was one of those *coups* with which his career was crowded –he was not going to answer!'[57] Churchill solemnly quoted Tacitus, 'Fortunate was he in the hour of his death', a tag that simultaneously occurred to several of Kitchener's former colleagues. Never, said Lansdowne, 'was the old saw *"felix opportunitate mortis"* more applicable'. In death as in life, sighed Curzon,

> the papers and the public have got hold of the wrong end of the stick about K. 'Genius for organisation', 'wonderful foresight' – alas, as we know only too well, the very things he had not got. His death came in a most fortunate hour for his reputation. For he will now always be a national hero.[58]

28

Air Board and War Cabinet,
1916

━━━━━━━━━━◆━━━━━━━━━━

A T THE BEGINNING of 1916 George Curzon received a good number of letters congratulating him on the Garter and expressing the hope that he would soon be Foreign Secretary and in due course Prime Minister. Doubtless it was gratifying to learn what people thought him capable of, and certainly he would have agreed with the correspondent who believed that, as head of the Government, he would 'bring efficiency into this welter of well-meaning jellyfish'.[1] But such opinions also exacerbated his frustration with his current position. Sometimes he wondered why he had been invited to join the Cabinet. As Lord Privy Seal he had neither a department to administer nor a role in the House of Lords. Furthermore, since the demise of the Dardanelles Committee he no longer had any deliberating work. He was not consulted by the Foreign Office, he grumbled, about countries on which he was supposed to be an expert, while he had been excluded from the War Committee which daily dealt with places and issues he had been studying for thirty years.[2]

Curzon had accepted Asquith's suggestion that he should represent the Ministry of Munitions in the House of Lords. But as he was not invited inside the ministry, nor apprised of any of its proceedings, nor sent a single item of information about its work, he severed the putative connection. After seven months on the sidelines, he told Crewe, the Leader of the House of Lords, that he saw no justification for remaining in a Government he was not permitted to serve. Twenty years earlier, he pointed out, Lord Salisbury had considered him worthy to represent the Foreign Office singlehandedly in the House of Commons, but now he was apparently unqualified to represent the Government in any debate in the Lords.[3] The most he was asked to do was to hold himself 'in reserve' in case Crewe or Lansdowne was ill, a somewhat humiliating position which entailed a good deal of reading-up followed by watching a perfectly healthy Crewe deliver a very dull speech on one of Curzon's pet subjects. 'I might surely have relieved you', he protested on one occasion, 'of stating the government case about Persia.' Crewe replied with an emollient letter comparing Curzon's position to a 'Rolls-Royce car, with a highly competent driver, kept to take an occasional parcel to the station'. But he was trying, he added, to find ways of utilizing Curzon's powers of speech, 'so infinitely superior' to his own.[4] He did not succeed.

From time to time Curzon's colleagues came up with inappropriate ideas for his employment. Following Asquith's proposal that he should be in charge of war trade problems, Balfour suggested, shortly after the Easter Rising, that he should become Lord Lieutenant of Ireland. The idea was regarded as most humorous by the Cabinet, above all by Curzon: it would have been a classic, even by British standards, to appoint the minister with unrivalled knowledge of the rest of the world to the one place he knew less about than his colleagues. A few months earlier, Curzon had accepted the unglamorous but useful post of Chairman of the Shipping Control Board, a committee which allocated shipping resources between the competing demands of the navy, the army and the merchant marine. By its members he was regarded as a chairman of exceptional ability and, more surprisingly, as a generous and considerate chief. The idea that Curzon paid no attention to his staff's interests, wrote the committee's secretary many years later, was 'entirely contrary' to their experience. 'To describe him as ungracious towards those who served under him, to say that he was unapproachable when he was in fact more accessible and much less grand than many Cabinet Ministers and City merchants, is untrue and unjust.'[5]

Curzon laboured dutifully with the problem of shipping tonnage but hankered after more demanding and imaginative work. At the end of March 1916 he wrote the Prime Minister a rather desperate letter, its tone perhaps influenced by the death of his father a few hours before, begging for something more substantial to do when he returned from Derbyshire after the funeral. The important work of the shipping committee had been completed, and he now felt 'utterly useless' in a Cabinet where he had nothing to do. He had greater administrative experience than most of his colleagues, he told Asquith, and thought he 'must still be good for something'. 'I feel quite ashamed at the position I occupy in the greatest crisis of our history when all my experience and knowledge, such as they are, are thrown away.'[6] Asquith answered much in the manner of Crewe, thanking Curzon for the 'patriotic spirit' of his letter and claiming to have spent 'the best part of the last year . . . trying to discover an ampler and worthier field for your great administrative talents and experience'. He doubted, however, whether his correspondent's specific proposal was viable.[7]

Curzon's aim was to persuade Asquith to set up an air ministry headed preferably by himself or, failing that, by another minister of Cabinet rank. He had long recognized the importance of air power in the war, and his first paper for the Cabinet had dealt with the problem of defending London from the threat of Zeppelins. On a visit to the Front he had persuaded Sir John French to let him go up in an aeroplane and had felt exhilaration but no sense of alarm as the machine swooped and lunged through the clouds, 'very much like a boat tossing in a heavy sea'.[8] But his admiration for the pilots was not extended to the organizations which controlled them. The aeroplanes were divided between the Royal Flying Corps and the Royal Naval Air Service, respectively under the War Office and the Admiralty, which jealously protected their own spheres of aerial activity. A Cabinet committee headed by Lord Derby was supposed to co-ordinate questions of supply and design for the two air services but it had neither the authority to make them co-operate nor the power to determine policy. As Curzon told Asquith, the committee merely sat and listened to its three naval representatives disagreeing with its three army officers while the chairman, who knew little about the subject, tried to keep the peace.[9] At the end of March Derby resigned, citing the impotence of the committee and the obstructiveness of the Admiralty as his reasons, and advocated the unification of the two services.

Curzon had identified the inherent defects of the committee at its inception and had argued in mid-February for the creation of an air ministry which would initiate policy itself as well as end the sparring between the War Office and the Admiralty. The proposal found little support in the Cabinet and in April, after Derby's resignation, Curzon issued a second paper with the less ambitious aim of establishing an air board along the lines of his shipping committee. As he had already told Asquith, air power was going to be a major factor in the war and needed the foresight and initiative which could not be generated by a committee absorbed in trying to prevent the Admiralty and the War Office from 'flying at each other's throats'. Above all a sense of urgency was required. 'When some great attack is made and Birmingham or some other place is laid in ashes, Co-ordinating Committees will be swept away in a blast of public wrath and the Government will very likely fall.'[10]

Asquith initially believed that the creation of an air ministry would increase friction between the two fighting departments, but by the end of April opinion within the Government had come to favour the less far-reaching of Curzon's proposals. The Army Council accepted it at the beginning of May, and on the 11th the War Committee recommended the establishment of an air board with a president and a parliamentary spokesman, positions subsequently filled by Curzon and Major J.L. Baird. Only the Admiralty under Balfour remained unconvinced. The First Lord was considered to lack drive and enterprise in his post – certainly in comparison with his predecessor Churchill – but he managed to display these qualities in his duel with Curzon over the Air Board. In a Cabinet paper of 6 May he agreed to accept the body if it was confined to a co-ordinating role between the army and the navy – that is, if it remained as powerless as Derby's committee – but not if it became 'a third fighting department controlling all aerial operations'.[11] Hankey observed that the Admiralty, having wrecked the Co-ordination Committee, was determined to be hostile to the Air Board but evidently did not appreciate that 'Curzon was a far more redoubtable antagonist than Derby'.[12] Although he was not disturbed by Balfour's fear that the Board might be too powerful, Curzon was greatly annoyed by Churchill's prediction that it would be too weak to achieve anything worthwhile. Proud of the Board, which he referred to as 'my own creation', the President overreacted to the criticism by publicly observing that Churchill's disappearance from the Government at least removed 'one chance of disturbance' from his new job.[13] Churchill, who was an aviation enthusiast longing to head an air ministry himself, thought the remark unkind and uncalled for, and pointed out that there had been nothing personal in his criticism.[14]

The Air Board immediately became both active and useful, meeting several times a week and relieving the War Committee of much of its work. Curzon's behaviour in his new post did not, however, enhance his popularity with his colleagues. Hankey, who admired the Board's work, found him 'an intolerable person to do business with – pompous, dictatorial and outrageously conceited', though 'an able, strong man with it all'. This outburst in the Cabinet Secretary's diary was provoked by constant telephone calls from Curzon asking him to help on various matters concerning the Board. 'Thank Goodness,' noted the overworked Hankey, 'I shall not have much to do with it.'[15]

Now that Curzon had got his own department to talk about, his Cabinet colleagues suffered from his verbosity. He was inclined, noted Crawford, to give discourses on aeroplane exploits and at one meeting described at length the destruction of a Zeppelin. No such criticism could be made of Balfour who, as Selborne observed, rarely spoke and 'when he did it was critically and destructively'. At the Cabinet meeting after Jutland, fought on the last day of May, the First Lord of the Admiralty decided not to say anything about the event. Curzon passed him a note suggesting it would be rather strange if the greatest naval battle since Trafalgar was not mentioned, to which Balfour replied that he knew no more about it than anyone else.[16] Nothing better illustrates the difference between the two men unless it is Balfour's surprise twenty-seven years before that Curzon should prefer to ride round Persia rather than spend a sporting vacation with his friends in Scotland. The puzzle is not why they opposed each other so consistently during this period but how they had been such close friends earlier. And yet even at their most antagonistic they retained the outward forms of friendship, writing to each other as 'my dear George' and 'my dear Arthur'. In December 1916, after their most extended bout of hostilities since India, Balfour assured Curzon he was one of his 'oldest and most devoted friends'.[17]

After five months at the Air Board, Curzon decided that the body could achieve none of the objectives for which it had been set up unless the Admiralty ceased its obstructiveness. Together with his civilian colleagues, Baird and Lord Sydenham, he composed a lengthy report which criticized the uncooperative attitude of the Admiralty, recommended the reorganization of its relations with its air service, and proposed the amalgamation of the existing supply departments, as far as aerial material was concerned, under the direction of the Air Board.[18] As Curzon admitted to Bonar Law, it was a very strong indictment of the Admiralty, whose administration of its air service was 'little short of a scandal', but he did not think it violent or impatient.[19] So convinced was he of the importance of his proposals, which envisaged the eventual creation of an air ministry, that he and his colleagues threatened to resign if they were rejected.

Military and public opinion were on Curzon's side, and on 24 October

The Times came out with a strong leading article in his support. But he was anxious about the attitude of the Cabinet. Advised by Churchill that the backing of Lloyd George was crucial, Curzon asked Bonar Law to intercede on his behalf because the Welsh MP was 'never very courteous' to him and he did not like to ask for favours. The Unionist leader was not helpful, stating inaccurately that he had 'no influence whatever' with Lloyd George and suggesting that Curzon should thrash the matter out with Balfour before it reached the Cabinet.[20]

Curzon duly sent an advance copy of the report to his old friend who, in thanking him, observed that 'as it seems to contain 30 solid pages of abuse of the Admiralty you will not expect me to agree with it'. Few of Balfour's dialectical exercises can have given him so much pleasure as the composition of his polished, feline and quite inadequate response to the criticism. Claiming that he had 'little time and no inclination' for controversy, he then devoted five pages of witty, deflating and insubstantial sarcasm to the pretensions of the Air Board and its 'consciousness of superior abilities', an ill-disguised crack at its President.[21] The performance entertained some of his colleagues and disgusted others. Derby, who had himself come to grief at the hands of the Admiralty, said he agreed 'absolutely' with Curzon, but he disliked him personally so much that he exulted at his discomfiture. 'Have you read Balfour's answer?' he asked Lloyd George, who was an unenthusiastic student of memoranda. 'If not *do* – it is not very convincing – but it is the most amusing production I have read for a long time. It will make George C furious.'[22] Crawford was more censorious. Never slow to criticize Curzon when necessary, he found that on this occasion the President of the Air Board had been 'staid in tone and weighty in substance' while Balfour's reply had been 'petulant, flippant and at times personal': had it been published, he thought, it would have caused so much indignation that the First Lord would have had to resign.[23] From outside the Cabinet, Churchill expressed the view that Balfour's was 'an astonishing performance' considering the loyalty Curzon had showed him and the times in which they all lived.[24]

Nearing the end of his long premiership, Asquith showed as much reluctance to adjudicate on this issue as he had on several others since the formation of the Coalition. In early November he put off discussions and a decision by the War Committee and then suggested the matter should be resolved on a day when he and Lloyd George would be absent.[25] Meanwhile Curzon responded to Balfour's paper with what Crawford described as a 'decorous' reply which reinforced the general view that the Air Board was in the right.[26] The duel consumed a lot of Cabinet time and might have continued indefinitely had not Asquith fallen and the antagonists been elevated in December. In 1918, when they had transferred their rivalry to other spheres, Curzon was vindicated by the establishment of an air ministry.

Long after his death Curzon was described by Lord Beaverbrook as 'the most active supporter of Asquith in the Tory ranks'[27] and therefore the most treacherous of those who joined Lloyd George in 1916. The view is entirely mistaken. Curzon and Asquith had long been friends and admired each other's intelligence; one of the Prime Minister's ways of combating boredom in Cabinet was to send Classical quotations down the table to Curzon with enquiries about their authors.[28] But they were never political allies. Asquith made negligible use of his friend's talents until he had been in the Cabinet for a year, while Curzon never respected the premier as a war leader. Not as outspoken as Churchill or Lloyd George, Curzon had nevertheless agreed with them over a year before Asquith's fall that radical changes had to be made in the running of the war. He was pleased at the decision to replace the Dardanelles Committee by a policy-making committee of three but dismayed by its proposed membership. It would be 'rather a curious outcome', he told Selborne at Cabinet in October 1915, 'if the result of our discussion is to install a triumvirate' consisting of Asquith, 'whose power of leadership and decision we all distrust', Kitchener, 'whose incompetence is proven', and Balfour, 'who does not err on the side of decision'.[29] In the end the committee was enlarged to five, and Kitchener was left out.

Curzon's dissatisfaction with Asquith's leadership increased during 1916. He was exasperated by the confusion of Cabinet meetings, complaining that there was no agenda, no order, no record of proceedings, that ministers often left the table without knowing what had been decided or even if a decision had been taken.[30] In the intimacy of their diaries and private papers, Unionist colleagues were more forthright. Selborne, who resigned over Irish negotiations in July, accused Asquith of lacking vision and initiative, while Crawford found the Prime Minister's 'somnolence . . . heart-rending'. Like Curzon they were appalled by his failure to exercise control at Cabinet meetings. Selborne thought him the worst chairman of any committee he had ever sat on, because 'the desire on all occasions to avoid a decision was an absolute disease with him'. Curzon, he added, 'hated the P.M.'s ways' as much as he did: 'we simply stumbled on from day to day, and I think it was purgatory to almost all of us'.[31]

Despite his view of Asquith's leadership, Curzon played only a late and minor role in the manoeuvres that led to his resignation. He knew nothing of the schemes to set up a small war council, consisting of Lloyd George, Bonar Law and Carson, designed in effect to run the war while Asquith remained in distant supervision as Prime Minister. Informed of these developments by their party leader on the last day of November, the Unionist members of the Cabinet gathered at Law's house to formulate a response on Sunday, 3 December.* They were annoyed by the secrecy of the intrigue and also by a newspaper report stating that Lloyd George was going to resign if his plan was not accepted. But they did not, as Beaverbrook alleged, decide to resign themselves in order to strengthen the Prime Minister's hand against Lloyd George. In fact the intentions of the Unionist ministers were completely different. As Crawford noted later that day, they decided to resign because they were convinced that the country needed 'a more businesslike system' which could not be achieved under Asquith, whom they regarded as 'discredited and unpopular thro' his invincible indecision'. Reconstruction of the present Government was impossible, they concluded, because 'the country and press don't want a reshuffling of the cards, they want a new pack'.[32] Many years later Chamberlain told Asquith's biographers that the Unionists realized they could not have held their party together if Bonar Law joined Carson and Lloyd George in opposition; and furthermore, they had 'all reluctantly come to the conclusion that Asquith was not the man to win the war'.[33] It was therefore decided that Bonar Law should see the Prime Minister that afternoon and deliver a resolution urging him to tender the resignation of the Government; if he refused to do so, the Unionist ministers would resign unilaterally. Later that day Curzon reported the concluding view of the meeting to Lansdowne.

Had one felt that reconstitution by and under the present Prime Minister was possible, we should all have preferred to try it. But we know that with him as Chairman, either of the Cabinet or War Committee, it is absolutely impossible to win the War, and it will be for himself and Lloyd George to determine

---

*Apart from Bonar Law the meeting consisted of Curzon, Chamberlain, Long, Smith, Crawford and Lord Robert Cecil. Balfour was ill and Lansdowne had remained in the country.

whether he goes out altogether or becomes Lord Chancellor or Chancellor of the Exchequer in a new Government, a nominal Premiership being a pro tem compromise* which, in our view, could have no endurance.[34]

The papers of Curzon, Crawford and Chamberlain make it clear that at the time they expected to see a Lloyd George administration. But this was not made obvious by the wording of the resolution, nor by Law's interview with Asquith, during which he failed to hand over the text, and certainly not by a short letter sent by Curzon to the Prime Minister on the following day. The author of this bewildering missive began by assuring Asquith that the Unionist resignations were 'far from having the sinister purport' which the premier had apparently ascribed to them. Yet rather than explain what that purport was – and if not sinister it was certainly detrimental to Asquith's prospects – he wished to 'strike a note of gaiety in a world of gloom' by quoting some lines of Matthew Arnold seeming to imply that resignations and their consequences were decreed by the Almighty.**[35] Historians, and Asquith's biographers in particular, have naturally been astonished by this document, especially when studied in conjunction with what Curzon had written the day before to Lansdowne. Yet perhaps they have read too much into it. Unattractive though it may be, the letter cannot really be construed as a message of support or as an assurance designed 'to lull the intended victim into a false security'.[36] At worst it was a message of friendship calculated to ingratiate its author with the Prime Minister if, against the odds, he pulled through.

On Sunday evening Asquith appeared to have solved the crisis by agreeing to 'reconstruct' the Government around a small war council under Lloyd George. But enraged by a leading article in *The Times*, which disparaged him while praising Lloyd George as 'the man best fitted to preside over a real War Council', Asquith began to back-track the following morning. The events of Monday have been confused by Beaverbrook's claim that Curzon, Cecil and Chamberlain (the 'Three Cs' as he called them) went to assure Asquith of their support and were

---

*Unfamiliar with Curzon's handwriting, Lansdowne's biographer, Lord Newton, transcribed these words as 'a Protean compromise', a phrase copied by all subsequent historians. Suitably Curzonian though it sounds, the term is meaningless in this context.
** We, in some unknown Power's employ,
  Move on a rigorous line:
  Can neither, when we will, enjoy;
  Nor, when we will, resign.

therefore responsible for the Prime Minister's change of mind.[37] In fact they did not see him until Tuesday when they delivered a very different message. On Monday afternoon they and other Unionist ministers met in Chamberlain's room at the India Office, but so ignorant were they of events that they sent out for an evening paper to see what was happening. Later on they met in Law's room, where they were told by Lansdowne, who had just seen the Prime Minister, that he thought Asquith would come to terms with Lloyd George.[38] By then, in fact, the premier had decided either to resign himself or to force the resignation of his rival by rejecting the scheme he had accepted the night before. After discussing the matter with his closest Liberal associates, he wrote to tell Lloyd George of his revised opinion that the proposed committee could not be made workable and effective unless the Prime Minister was its chairman. The following morning Lloyd George sent in his resignation.

Asquith clearly acted in the belief that he could count on the support of all the Unionist ministers with the exception of Bonar Law. For a man of such acute political judgement it was a mysterious miscalculation, based on no more tangible evidence than the confusing interview with Law on Sunday, the ambiguous letter from Curzon on Monday, and a brief conversation with Lansdowne, the minister most opposed to Lloyd George. He made no effort to discover the real state of Unionist opinion. He did not even consult Balfour, still the party's most prestigious figure, who, although ill in bed in Carlton Gardens, was capable of reading and writing a letter. And even if he had assured himself of the support of Balfour, the 'Three Cs' and the other ministers, it was surely a mistake to think he could carry on after Lloyd George and Bonar Law had joined forces with Carson in opposition.

Asquith's assumptions were blown away the next day by two letters from Balfour, who argued that Lloyd George should be allowed to run a war committee, and by a meeting at his request with the 'Three Cs'. At the Downing Street gathering the three explained the meaning of their Sunday resolution and told the Prime Minister that they could not continue their support for him without Lloyd George and Bonar Law in the Government. Asked about their attitude towards a Lloyd George administration, they said they would be prepared to support any government that seemed capable of conducting the war successfully. Cecil then suggested to Asquith that the 'finest and biggest thing' he could do would be to offer to serve under Lloyd George, but according to Chamberlain the idea was 'rejected with indignation and even with scorn'.[39]

Immediately after the meeting, the 'Three Cs' told their colleagues that Asquith had misunderstood their decision of Sunday and seemed 'flabbergasted' when its meaning was explained to him. Turning to their own predicament, Chamberlain said he was reluctant to join a Lloyd George government in any capacity. Curzon, supported by Cecil and Crawford, disagreed: if invited to serve, he believed they should do so as 'a public duty'. The group then sent Curzon back to Downing Street with a letter repeating their view that the Government should resign immediately. After asking Curzon some questions, Asquith told him in the presence of Liberal colleagues that he had decided to resign. Curzon replied that it was the right decision and reiterated the view that the Sunday resolution had not been an attack on the Prime Minister but an embodiment of the Unionist view that the Government could not carry on as it was. Asked whom Asquith should recommend as his successor, Curzon advised Lloyd George on the grounds that he had promoted the crisis and the public looked to him for a lead.[40] Shortly afterwards Asquith drove to Buckingham Palace to tender his resignation.

Curzon had nothing to do with the manoeuvres of the following day over whether Bonar Law or Lloyd George would become Prime Minister, whether Asquith would serve under either, or what would happen to Balfour, who in the event astonished the Liberal leader by accepting the Foreign Office. But a day later he was offered a place in the War Cabinet by Lloyd George, who regarded him as the inevitable Leader of the Lords.[41] Curzon has been criticized for agreeing to serve without consulting his colleagues. But since his present and previous leaders had already signed up, it is not clear why he should be blamed. In any case, when he advised the Unionist ministers on Monday that they should join, the one dissentient had been Chamberlain, who had told him three days before that he would only serve under a War Cabinet if Curzon was a member.[42]

On the afternoon of the 7th the 'Three Cs' and Long met Lloyd George to discuss the composition of his administration. In form and membership the War Cabinet emerged rather differently from what the new premier had envisaged. Chamberlain, backed by Curzon, argued that the committee charged with running the war should itself be the Cabinet and not a separate entity: the departmental ministers would therefore forfeit Cabinet status because they could not be responsible for decisions reached by the committee.[43] Chamberlain was not prepared to 'sit in a *Cabinet* with *no* power under a War Committee with *all* the power', but he was prepared to renounce his Cabinet rank and serve under the committee if its composition was right. Lloyd George had originally wanted a committee consisting of Bonar Law, Carson and himself. Chamberlain, who the previous year had tried to exclude Curzon from the Coalition, had since then 'learned to appreciate his qualities' and now insisted that he was added to the committee. He and Curzon also urged Lloyd George to appoint Milner in place of Carson. In the end the committee became very much what Chamberlain wanted, both Curzon and Milner joining Lloyd George and Law, with Arthur Henderson coming in as the Labour Party's representative. But in arranging the Government in such a form, Chamberlain left himself on the periphery as Secretary of State for India without a seat in the Cabinet. Curzon was very impressed by the dignity and unselfishness of his colleague's behaviour and said he hoped they would collaborate in future. Admitting that he did not like his position, Chamberlain told him 'it was clearly my duty to take it, and it is your presence in the small inner circle which alone made that possible'.[44]

In addition to his membership of the War Cabinet, regarded as a full-time post dealing with daily developments of the war, Curzon was given the job of Leader of the House of Lords with the title of Lord President of the Council. Denied useful work by a friend, he was now given excessive though welcome duties by a man whom he never got on with, who frequently mocked and mimicked him, and yet who kept him at his side in the highest posts for the duration of his premiership. Lloyd George never liked Curzon and had enjoyed baiting him in his election speeches six years earlier. But he had seen his drive in Cabinet and, even before the crisis, had thought of him as a member of a small war committee. Curzon was valuable, he told Lord Riddell on various occasions, because of the 'great knowledge' he had acquired from his travels and his reading, 'information of a sort which is uncommon amongst British politicians' and which made him 'useful in council'. His 'great defect', however, was that he always felt he was 'sitting on a golden throne and must speak accordingly'.[45]

Curzon's behaviour during the political crisis did not differ substantially from that of his Unionist colleagues. None of them noticed anything dishonourable in his actions. If there was something faintly distasteful and *faux bonhomme* about his letter to Asquith, the fastidious might also have reservations about Bonar Law's performance in his interview on the Sunday and the alacrity with which Balfour accepted the Foreign

Office. But Curzon has gone down in history as the 'deserter' and 'turn-coat' because of Beaverbrook's claim that on the Monday he had given Asquith 'an absolute pledge' not to take office under Lloyd George.[46] After Beaverbrook's account of the crisis was published in the early 1930s, Chamberlain questioned the author about the claim and corrected his assertion that the 'Three Cs' had met Asquith on Monday; to Cecil, Chamberlain declared that 'the tendency to suspect Curzon of ulterior motives' was 'quite unfounded'. When Beaverbrook repeated the claim without providing evidence, Chamberlain replied that such a promise would have been incompatible with the letter he had written Lansdowne on the Sunday.[47] But the newspaper tycoon paid no attention to the views of this most scrupulous of politicians and for the rest of his life maintained his line on the Monday meeting that took place on the Tuesday and the pledge to Asquith that was never given.

Beaverbrook's vendetta against Curzon's memory would have mattered less had it not been continued by later historians. It was to be expected that Leonard Mosley, commissioned by Beaverbrook to demolish Curzon's reputation in the late 1950s, should exalt the 'classic study' and 'masterly account' of his boss and even repeat his falsehood that Curzon gave the alleged assurance at the mythical Monday meeting.[48] But it is surprising to find real historians endorsing these views. A.J.P. Taylor, Beaverbrook's employee and biographer, admitted that his subject had been wrong about the Monday and revealed that he once told Arnold Bennett of an attack Curzon had made on him in the Lords which turned out to be pure invention. Yet awareness of his employer's unreliability did not deter Taylor from stating without additional evidence that Curzon 'promised to stand by Asquith and then abandoned him' or from accusing him of being 'one of nature's rats'.[49] It is not necessary to dwell on those other historians who have repeated and embellished Beaverbrook's remark, even in one case alleging that Curzon had said he 'would rather die than serve under Lloyd George'.[50] As Professor Fraser has pointed out in an essay on the 'fabrications' of Beaverbrook's history of the period, the tycoon's 'falsifications' have been 'sustained because later historians have chosen to waive the prime rules of historical verification under the magnetism of a great personality'.[51]

29

The Second Lady Curzon

THE OWNERS OF large country houses tended to restrict their scale of
living and their domestic commitments during the war. Lord
Curzon did not. Admittedly, he had committees, refugees, wounded soldiers and the Belgian royal family taking up parts of his houses. But he
was not inclined merely to retreat with a much-reduced staff to the
unoccupied rooms. In the middle of the First World War he acquired
three large and dilapidated properties on which he had to spend a great
deal of money and most of the time he could spare from his political
duties. It was not of course his fault that he inherited Kedleston on
Lord Scarsdale's death in 1916. But it was eccentric to take the lease of
Montacute a few months earlier, when he knew his father was dying,
and even odder to buy Bodiam Castle and its estate in 1917. Yet both
these acquisitions were made from excellent motives. He did not plan to
hold court and entertain extravagantly at either place. His objective was
simply to preserve and restore the buildings and in due course hand
them on. 'If you renovate a beautiful house,' he said once in reference
to Montacute, 'it does not matter that it will pass from your family. You
are preserving a lovely thing for the nation.'[1] Like Tattershall, which he
had also saved by purchase and restoration, he left Bodiam to the
National Trust in his will.

The renovation of Kedleston was a daunting task in itself. Scarsdale
had presided there for sixty years without throwing away a bill or the
most trivial of documents; even the paper relics of his predecessors had
been left undisturbed, many buried in dust, some white with mildew.

461

Curzon excavated every cupboard and drawer himself in case it contained records of the house's history, before destroying the things that
seemed worthless. He was determined to clear out the detritus of previous generations and establish an archive of valuable documents before
starting on the building's much-needed restoration. On his brief visits
to Kedleston he also had to supervise the running of the estate, a chore
attenuated by such squirearchical pleasures as wandering around the
park with a gun, which he had not done since before India, drinking a
glass of creamy milk at the home farm, and forbidding the new parson
to allow his 'primitive choir' to *sing* the psalms.[2]

Curzon consulted his eldest daughters about the Montacute lease,
thinking they might like to use the house after restoration, and 'trusting
to an interest on their part which very speedily evaporated'.[3] The choice
of Montacute throws an interesting light on Curzon's architectural
tastes. It is usually thought that he could conceive of no finer architecture – apart from the seventeenth-century Mogul – than the Classical
Adam style of Kedleston. But although he was something of a
Renaissance man in life, in taste he was a medievalist. He loved Italian
cities which had been fortunate enough to have 'no Popes or
Renaissance architects to wipe out the beauties of medievalism'. It was
terrible, he once told Oscar Browning, 'to see how Rome suffered in
their hands'.[4]

His taste in English country houses had a similar bias. He never
thought that the style of Kedleston, either in architecture or decoration,
was 'congenial to the English character, to English surroundings or to
English life'. Hatfield was to him the finest country house, representative of 'the one truly' British style that lasted from the second half
of Queen Elizabeth's reign to the death of James I. Although he had
only seen Montacute from photographs, he considered it to be the most
beautiful of the smaller stately homes of the period, and he was unable
to resist the opportunity to restore it when its lease came on the market.
After agreeing to the owner's condition not to alter the main fabric,
which he would have 'regarded as a crime to do', he embarked on a programme to 'eliminate the desperate mid-Victorian trappings' with
which he 'found the place disfigured and disguised', to preserve or
restore all traces of original work in wood or stone, and to collect suitable Elizabethan furniture from the Somerset towns nearby.[5]
Montacute is one of four great buildings now belonging to the National
Trust which were restored by Curzon. It is an unmatched record.

In May 1917, after work on both Kedleston and Montacute had

begun, he heard that Lord Ashcombe was selling Bodiam Castle in Sussex. On seeing the place some years earlier, he had fallen 'an immediate victim to its charm' and had tried unsuccessfully to buy it. Surrounded by its 'watery cincture', the castle was a jewel 'environed by parkland and . . . embowered by trees', a ruin so untouched by the modern world, he wrote, that

> it could hardly surprise anyone, were a train of richly clad knights, falcons on their wrists, and their ladies mounted on gaily caparisoned palfreys, suddenly to emerge from the Barbican Gate, for the enjoyment of the chase, or even were the flash of spearheads and the clatter of iron-shod hooves to indicate the exit of a party with more serious intent.[6]

News of the intended sale greatly excited him. 'I am only interested in the castle,' he told a friend, ' and if I bought it, should repair it and leave it to the nation.'[7] But later in the summer he instructed his agents to make an offer of £19,000 for the whole estate, including farmland and a manor house, to prevent the surroundings of the castle from being built over. After taking possession, he arranged for a team of twenty-five men to excavate the building, to drain and dredge the moat and to begin work on the restoration. On occasional free days he motored down from London with an architect to discuss plans to rebuild towers, drawbridges and the barbican.

Even Curzon must have realized that for once he was too busy to undertake the redecoration of all his acquisitions himself. Accordingly, he asked Elinor Glyn to do the job at Montacute. The novelist cannot have enjoyed the task, for she was much happier sitting in front of a fire with a book than standing on step-ladders in draughty Elizabethan rooms. But she agreed to go because she was still in love with Curzon and hoped, after her husband's death in the autumn of 1915, that he would marry her. She was at Montacute in August of the same year when she wrote her long memoir of his character. She was there decorating when he visited the house several times during the autumn of 1916. And she was there, alone, when she opened *The Times* of 11 December to see what position her lover had achieved in the new Government: there on page nine was the list of ministers, while opposite on page eight was the announcement of his engagement to Grace Duggan. Elinor reacted by burning Curzon's hundreds of letters and never spoke to him again. At some stage he followed his usual custom with adulterous correspondence and destroyed all of hers. Elinor's sister ranted about the 'waste of time and the bondage' of decorating Montacute, referred to Curzon as an 'ungrateful sneaking cad' and declared that she would never again have faith in *noblesse oblige*.[8]

No episode in Curzon's life is harder to explain than this one. There is no reference to it in his papers, and no evidence exists apart from that of Elinor and her family. That he behaved badly seems impossible to doubt. But that he behaved quite so badly – neither giving her a warning beforehand nor an explanation afterwards – is difficult to believe, because it would have been out of character. Curzon may have been harsh to men, but there is no evidence – with the exception of the Westbourne Terrace mistress in 1891 – that he ever was with women. Pearl Craigie had once described him as 'always kind to all women – young, or middle-aged or old', and Elinor herself had called him 'the most loyal friend to women even after they have ceased to attract him'.[9] Why he should have made an exception in this case, and done so with such apparent brutality, is incomprehensible.

In the month that Elinor wrote her memoir of Curzon, her hero began a passionate love affair with Grace Duggan, a handsome American lady of 38 loosely married to a wealthy Argentinian of Irish extraction who died, unmourned by his widow, a few months later. Tall, shapely and eighteen years younger than Curzon, her appearance inspired Lady Desborough's feline observation – 'What an odd doll-like look a middle-aged face gets when it is so well massaged as not to show a single line'.[10] For a decade she had been living in London, where her husband held the undemanding post of Honorary Attaché at the Argentine Legation, and where she devoted her life to society, fashion and discreet love affairs. Unencumbered by intellectual interests, she epitomized the type of frivolity Curzon most detested.

After meeting Grace at a lunch party given by the Duchess of Rutland, Curzon invited her to dine at the Royal Automobile Club, apparently because the location would excite less gossip than a rendezvous in a restaurant. Grace was somewhat alarmed by the intellect of her new admirer. Candidly admitting her stupidity, she told him she was proud of the way he talked to her and very 'anxious to understand'. Their affair began a month after the RAC dinner, transforming Grace in her own words from a 'miserable lonely' creature to a woman who now understood the meaning of true love. 'I have unlocked all the doors and shown you my soul,' she wrote. 'I want to be pure . . . teach me to please you in every way, not only in passion – my love for you makes that all too easy.'[11]

The logistics of the affair were complicated for a few months by Grace's marriage and for rather longer by Curzon's sense of propriety. Their assignations usually took place in London, but they also saw each other at Hackwood and at the various country houses she rented for her sons' school holidays. When he joined her at one of them for Christmas 1915, Grace observed that he looked worn out and worried, unable to eat, unwilling even to talk. But after a summons to the telephone, he returned to the dining-room, bright and beaming, and suddenly broke down. 'That was Arthur Balfour,' he said with tears streaming down his face. 'Gallipoli has been evacuated without a single casualty! . . . Without one single casualty . . . and we had feared the most terrible massacre . . . all those gallant men!'[12]

In the course of the following year he stayed for weekends with Grace at Trent, a house she rented in Hertfordshire. A fellow guest on one occasion was the novelist George Moore, whose jealousy had been aroused more than twenty years before by Pearl Craigie's love for Curzon. He may have had a similar problem at Trent. Moore was told to leave before breakfast on Sunday because, as Grace explained to Edward Marsh, he had blasphemed the sacrament in front of her sons (who were Catholics), he had abused Curzon to her face, and he had told her the previous evening that she was a 'dainty little morsel', surprisingly inappropriate adjectives for a novelist to choose. A week later Marsh again encountered Curzon at Trent and recorded the Lord Privy Seal's supervision of a séance at which it was predicted (inaccurately) that he would be one of Britain's representatives at the peace conference.[13]

Jealousy, both current and retrospective, was an almost instant ingredient of their love affair. During the first month Grace assured Curzon that she had ended her relationship with her previous lover, Lord Colum Crichton-Stuart, and put his photographs away. But since she was unable to explain her new status, it was difficult to dissuade Crichton-Stuart from coming to see her. Grace's jealousy was stronger and longer-lasting. She admitted at the beginning that she was excessively jealous of Elinor Glyn, and throughout their marriage she accused him of seeing her – or trying to see her – or of visiting other former mistresses.[14] But she never produced evidence that he went to see any of them.

One summer morning in 1916, Grace recounted in her memoirs, Curzon took her to Bodiam, where he described his plans for its restoration, and then to Winchelsea, where he led her to a pew of the lovely medieval church and in 'the most solemn manner possible' asked her to marry him. Accuracy is not a strong point of the memoirs – since he had not yet bought Bodiam nor knew whether it was coming up for sale, he is unlikely to have discussed his plans for restoring it – but the elaborate staging sounds authentic, the display of the fairy-tale castle, the pilgrimage to a favourite church, the immaculately formal proposal; had he been younger and fitter, he would no doubt have gone down on bended knee. Having botched his proposal to Mary, he wanted to do the thing properly next time round.

Grace asked for time to consider but she did not need long. At the end of July, twelve months after the start of the affair, she told him she no longer had any qualms, that she wanted to be 'worthy to mother your children' and that she would 'always keep the thought of your dear loved one before me'.[15] The effect of this dignified letter was marred by a renewed outburst of hysterical jealousy, but she quickly apologized. In September Curzon told Grace's mother, Mrs Monroe Hinds, of the engagement, which he wanted to keep secret until November, a year after her husband's death. In the meantime Grace sailed to the Argentine to sort out her affairs and to give the news to her former mother-in-law.

On 22 September Curzon escorted Grace to Southampton with a mass of books, fruit and flowers, which he proceeded to arrange in her cabin. He also left her a letter, to be opened after he had gone, promising love and fidelity. They had 'sifted and tested each other' for more than a year, he told her, 'and the gold [had] come forth purified from the fire'. While she was away, he assured her, she 'need have no fear' that he would have 'any thought, wish, fancy or hope for anyone' but her; his life would be one of 'willing solitude'. This epistle was followed by many others lamenting their separation, missing her 'fawn like tread', her kisses that had 'trembled' on his lips, and 'the floating webby hair of the Egyptian'.*[16]

The constant professions of love were no doubt genuine, but the aspirations to physical fidelity were probably less wholehearted. At any rate he went several times during her absence to Montacute, where Elinor Glyn was busy decorating. One cannot, of course, know what happened between them, but it would appear that Elinor still considered herself to be his mistress when she opened *The Times* on that December morning.

---

*The author has been unable to discover why Grace was called 'the Egyptian' or what is meant by 'webby hair'.

Curzon went to eccentric lengths to keep their affair concealed from both contemporaries and posterity. He made Grace return all his letters written before their engagement, presumably so that he could burn them.* And for her voyage he provided her with a stack of envelopes addressed to himself in his own hand, a tactic that must have caused comment in the servants' hall about the master's habit of writing letters to himself from Buenos Aires. The affair seems to have been a reasonably well-guarded secret for about a year because during 1916 rumours circulated that both of them were going to marry other people. Grace was apparently matched with Sir Edward Grey, a far more inappropriate spouse even than Curzon: it really would be difficult to find something which the voluptuous socialite had in common with that retiring and high-minded ornithologist, whose first wife had died in the same year as Mary Curzon. 'I think you are well out of that,' Grace was told by her fiancé, who considered Grey to be 'a most bloodless man'.[17] Gossip linked Curzon's name with another wealthy American widow, Ava Astor, who later married Lord Ribblesdale, the widower of his old love Charty. This rumour was reinforced by Curzon uncharacteristically muddling up his monumental correspondence: an envelope addressed to Lady Cunard, intended to convey an answer to an invitation, contained a letter to Ava Astor beginning, 'My beautiful white swan, I long to press you to my heart'.[18] London society was much amused by Lady Cunard's renditions of the story.

By the autumn the truth was becoming known, mainly because Grace was not good at keeping a secret, although her sister claimed to have guessed from the 'eloquence' of Curzon's eyes. Many people, Mrs Hinds was told by her future son-in-law, had tried to prevent the marriage, but he did not explain who they were or why they had done so. One of them seems to have been Nancy Astor, whom he told two days before the announcement that, in spite of her warnings, he had decided to take 'the fatal step'.[19] Announcing the news to his friends, recorded Lord Crawford, Curzon devoted an 'eloquent and very touching sentence or two to his undying affection for the late Lady Curzon', passed on to a 'very friendly appreciation of Mrs Duggan' and remarked that she had been maltreated by her husband. The congratulations of Sir Pertab Singh, an eccentric Rajput warrior who spoke the most pidgin of English, gave Curzon particular pleasure. Unconsciously replying in the

---

*An ineffective precaution, as it turned out, because Grace's letters have for some reason survived.

same idiom, the former Viceroy heard himself saying, 'Me very pleased, me like very handsome woman'.[20]

The suggestion that Curzon twice married for money has equally little foundation in both instances. Rumour credited Grace with enormous riches – Lord Cowdray believed she had an income of £60,000 – on account of her extravagant style of living. But much of her magnificence appears to have been run on credit, a concept she never fully understood, and she amassed formidable debts. Like everyone else, Curzon may have thought her richer than she was, but he made no attempt to ascertain the truth: their correspondence shows that they never discussed financial matters before their marriage nor even asked each other questions about their respective wealth.[21] The assumption that he used Grace's fortune to maintain his establishments and to restore his houses is simply false. Both operations remained funded almost entirely by Leiter money. Whatever expectations he may have had, Grace's reluctant and often tardy contribution to the upkeep of herself and her three children was £400 a month. Considering her natural extravagance, the sum was not vastly generous and represented about a tenth of Curzon's total expenditure.

The money factor may have been advanced in an attempt to explain Curzon's decision to marry someone apparently so unsuitable. Crawford found Grace 'handsome in her florid way', a woman of opulent charms and a tiresome simper, but 'a good-hearted creature, admirably groomed and an excellent foil' to Curzon.[22] Others were less charitable. Cynthia Asquith thought her conversation 'briskly banal' and predicted that she would be 'greatly in the way at his debating society parties at Hackwood'.[23] On many counts Elinor Glyn would have made a better wife. She was more intelligent, more loyal, more understanding and more interested in his career. But unfortunately she was too old to have more children and she lacked Grace's sensual attractiveness. These were the determining factors in Curzon's decision, his desire to produce an heir and his physical adoration of a woman of strong sexuality. He never loved Grace in the way that he had come to love Mary, but his second wife did represent his physical ideal of a woman. Embarrassed by her curvaceousness, Grace asked the painter Sir John Lavery to portray her with a slenderer figure than she possessed. But on seeing the result, Curzon angrily asked the artist, 'What have you done with her curves?' He subsequently refused to buy the picture because it showed none of that 'snowy amplitude' which he considered to be 'the greatest beauty of the female form'.[24]

The wedding, conducted by the Archbishop of York, took place at Lambeth Palace on 2 January 1917. Since marriage did not result in an early pregnancy, Curzon made some enquiries into gynaecological problems and persuaded Grace to have a small operation. Assuring her that it would be quick and painless, he observed that 'there would not even be any need for chloroform were it not that modesty requires it'. As a prelude to the operation, Grace quarrelled furiously with her husband, accusing him of appearing 'false and almost cruel' and of not fully reciprocating her love. Admitting afterwards that the row was not 'an over-good augury for our future', she promised to try to trust him a little better.[25] What Curzon had done to appear false is not explained in their letters, but the evidence of future scenes suggests that her jealousy was not well-founded.

The operation was a success so far as it went. Grace became pregnant soon afterwards but then suffered the first of a series of miscarriages. Over the next few years she conceived at intervals of four or five months only to miscarry after a few weeks. Curzon became desperate and miserable, asking why Providence plagued him with so many false alarms and misplaced hopes. Their marriage soon settled into a most unsatisfactory pattern. Grace underwent regular treatment, in England until the end of the war and afterwards on the Continent, then returned home, became pregnant and sat at Hackwood with nothing to do except smoulder with jealousy at the thought of how her husband might be spending his time in London. Taking one day in August 1917 as an example, he divided his morning between the War Cabinet and an Allied conference, prepared a speech over a quick and solitary lunch, returned to the Cabinet, looked in again at the conference, spent three hours at the House of Lords during which he delivered his speech, and ended up at a dinner for the French delegation at Downing Street.[26] At some stage in this schedule he found time to write a letter to his wife, as he always did on any day when they were apart.

Grace managed to convince herself that her husband found time during his fourteen-hour working days to see Elinor Glyn or another lover. Once, when she heard that Elinor was in London, she assumed that they had arranged to meet. Observing that she was incorrigible, Curzon assured her he had kept his word not to communicate with his discarded mistress since their marriage. Grace declined to believe him and pronounced, as usual without evidence, that he was neither honest nor true. At other times, however, she accepted his assurances, enabling them to spend a few tranquil days together, only to wind herself up for a fresh row when he came down for the following weekend. Exhausted by ill health and overwork, Curzon found this tactic particularly wearying. 'Do not let me come down', he once pleaded, 'only to quarrel with me and make me miserable.' On one occasion she accepted the plea, refusing to let him celebrate their second wedding anniversary in his own home. Her unpredictable moods, no doubt exacerbated by the miscarriages and the boredom of her Hackwood solitude, bewildered her husband, who could not understand why she insisted on bickering about the past. 'We can both be happy', he told her, 'if we are not always reverting to a past which has perished and gone.'[27]

One of the few things the couple had in common, a taste for stylish entertaining, was denied them by the war. In March 1917 they celebrated Irene's coming of age with a small party at Trent which the press transformed into a great ball in London reported under the headline 'Curzon dances while Europe burns'.[28] He was highly sensitive to the charge of his family ostentatiously enjoying themselves in wartime and angered his elder daughters, who had felt ignored by their father since his marriage, by criticizing Nancy Astor for inviting them to the theatre. But he thought it justified to provide less frivolous entertainments, such as hosting a concert of Belgian musicians performing voluntarily in recognition of his services to Belgium,* or giving a reception for American officers early in 1918. He also provided meals and guests for the visits of the Queen of the Belgians, and staged a memorable ceremony for her husband. Since it was impossible to hold Encaenia at Oxford, he organized the proceedings in Carlton House Terrace. Dressed in his Chancellor's robes and preceded by proctors, mace-bearers and other university dignitaries, he processed upstairs to his drawing-room, watched by a select audience, and solemnly awarded the Belgian King an honorary degree. As Crawford observed, few others could have carried the thing off with such verve, aplomb and self-satisfaction.[29]

Curzon's ability to maintain standards at his dinner table was also noted by Crawford. An 'immense luncheon' at Carlton House Terrace

---

*Curzon's services to that country were not restricted to entertaining her royal family and some of her wounded soldiers. In both the Cabinet and the Imperial War Cabinet he argued against the bombing of those German targets in occupied Belgium that was likely to cause casualties among civilians. He also submitted to his colleagues, though without endorsement, King Albert's claims to the strip of Dutch Flanders on the left bank of the Scheldt.

in November 1917 was served by a large staff and presided over by Grace, draped in her most fashionable clothes, while the other women, who included Lady Salisbury, were dressed 'like housekeepers'. A large dinner the following June was 'an immense and opulent spread' which Crawford thought must have consumed twelve months' rations of butter. It was a peculiar party, consisting of sixty men, most of them leading politicians, and a small number of selected women. The guests whose wives had not been invited were extremely annoyed by this apparent slight, especially Midleton whom Curzon had not invited to his house since pre-India days twenty years before. As Balfour remarked to Ettie Desborough, it appeared 'strange to take the trouble to have a dinner for sixty people in these difficult days in order to offend thirty of them'.[30] Curzon's talent for misjudging human reactions was not dimmed by age.

30

Eastern Questions, 1917

———————✦———————

GEORGE CURZON'S WORK in the War Cabinet was the most sustained, vital and concentrated he had been required to do since leaving India. In the intervening eleven years he had worked as hard as anyone, but his energies had been dispersed over a large number of different and often unconnected fields. Now again he was at the heart of things, one of the key members of the War Cabinet, meeting day after day with his colleagues to discuss and direct the main areas of the war effort. Although he complained, as always, of the quantity of work, he was delighted of course to be doing it.

Apart from Lloyd George, the crucial figures were Curzon and Milner. Henderson owed his position less to administrative ability than to the Prime Minister's need for Labour support, while Bonar Law's duties as Chancellor of the Exchequer and Leader of the House of Commons required frequent absences which Curzon did not much regret: the smell of Law's new and very rank cigars, he complained, was 'most offensive'. Observers such as L.S. Amery praised Curzon's industry, knowledge and power of draftsmanship, yet regarded Milner as more influential and 'the acknowledged mainstay' of the group. Hankey, who remained Cabinet Secretary under Lloyd George, appreciated Curzon's 'unique gift of setting out in proper perspective and with eloquence the facts of a complicated issue', but noted that he lacked resource in finding solutions to the problems he could state so well.[1] In subsequent years Churchill and others remarked on the same defect, which no one had accused him of in India and which was also absent when he served under Bonar Law and Baldwin. It seems to have been almost exclusively associated with his years under Lloyd George.

Curzon now became a committee man. Apart from attendance at the War Cabinet, which met seven to nine times a week on all days except Sunday, he was required to be the chairman or a member of a large number of subcommittees. Lloyd George tended to respond to a problem by setting up a committee under Curzon or Milner to investigate it and report back to the War Cabinet. Economic questions went to Milner, and almost everything else ended up with the Lord President. While he was the obvious choice for the chairmanship of committees on the Middle East, and even for one contemplating the exchange of Gibraltar for Ceuta, Curzon was on less congenial ground in charge of deliberations on timber, merchant shipping, import restrictions, the allocation of guns, and a settlement for Ireland; and he was particularly disconcerted to discover that as Lord President he automatically became head of the Department for Scientific and Industrial Research. Work on these and other committees tended to be frustrating as well as laborious. Much of Curzon's time was spent interviewing experts who disagreed with each other, before having, as a complete non-expert, to adjudicate. In April 1917 he was asked by the War Cabinet to decide whether the country should build 'mammoth' merchant ships that might or might not prove unsinkable. Confronted by Admiralty advice to go ahead and a warning from the Shipping Board to desist, he recommended that one should be built as an experiment.[2]

Curzon was undoubtedly vain about his contribution to this type of work. Perusing the minutes of one subcommittee and noting that his name seldom appeared, he asked Amery, its secretary, whether he had a 'personal down' on him. He was partially satisfied, according to Amery, by the assurance that he had been fulfilling his role as chairman by eliciting members' views and summing them up in his conclusion.[3] But he was not at all mollified by a very long explanation of a similar omission from Hankey. To Curzon's protest that his decisive contribution to a discussion about the War Museum had not been included in the Cabinet's minutes, Hankey replied that, if he had been speaking on India or some other subject on which he was an expert, his remarks would have been included as fully as possible. But on questions such as the War Museum, where he spoke 'rather as a member of the Cabinet than as a special expert', his comments had been incorporated anonymously in a résumé of the discussion. The suggestion that he was not an expert on cultural matters, recorded Hankey, provoked 'such a catalogue of Curzon's contributions to art galleries and museums and so forth, not only in this country but in India and elsewhere, as took my breath away. It was some time before my lapse was forgiven and forgotten!'[4]

At the end of March 1917 the members of the War Cabinet joined other ministers and representatives from the Dominions in the Imperial War Cabinet, a gathering reflecting the enhanced wartime status of the empire's components which sat three times a week until the beginning of May. Its principal work was entrusted to two subcommittees, inevitably headed by Curzon and Milner, appointed respectively to examine war aims and acceptable terms for peace. Curzon's group, which included Long, Chamberlain and Smuts, the South African Defence Minister, as well as the Prime Ministers of Canada and New Zealand, set to work and produced a rather hawkish report considered by the Imperial War Cabinet on 1 May. Curzon argued that German East Africa, which had been mainly conquered by Smuts, should never be handed back because of its potential use as a submarine base from which to attack Britain's sea communications. He also urged the retention of Palestine, which had not yet been captured, as well as Mesopotamia, but left open the question of German West Africa, which would be restored to the enemy in return for the surrender of Alsace-Lorraine. When Lloyd George observed that the subcommittee seemed rather greedy, recommending that Britain should acquire so much more than the French or the Russians, Chamberlain suggested that France might receive the German colonies in West Africa in addition to Alsace-Lorraine, while Russia would have Armenia.* In accepting the arguments of the report, the Prime Minister stressed that they should be regarded as recommendations rather than instructions to future delegates.[5]

The question of the captured German colonies continued to exercise Curzon for the rest of the war, and in the end his views largely prevailed over those of Lloyd George, Balfour and Henderson. He had never wanted to extend India's responsibilities in any direction, but Turkey's declaration of war had resulted in the occupation of Mesopotamia, an

---

*In 1916 the Governments of Britain, France and Russia had come to a secret understanding on sharing the Middle East between them after the war. Known as the Sykes-Picot Agreement (see below, p. 519), it was not discussed by the Imperial War Cabinet and remained a secret until November 1917 when the Bolsheviks published it soon after taking power.

area which could not be handed back now, he thought, without break-ing Britain's pledges to the local Arabs and giving renewed life to 'the shattered German ambition of a great Teutonised dominion' stretching through Europe and Asia Minor to the Gulf.[6] As for Africa, he believed that without Germany the continent had a chance of civilized develop-ment. But an Africa with a Teutonic presence would become 'a cockpit of sanguinary conflicts and pernicious ambitions'.[7]

Once the principle of an Africa without Germans had been accepted, Curzon had to contend with suggestions that it should be divided between other people. To a proposal that German East Africa should be handed over to Indian colonization, he countered that the soil belonged to the natives and warned against the planting of exotic customs and society in an alien continent.[8] And to a paper from Balfour, in which the Foreign Secretary suggested giving the captured territories to Britain's allies or submitting them to a condominium of European powers, he replied with a catalogue of objections to all conceivable candidates. Why, he asked, should German East Africa be given to France, which was already in possession of Togoland and the Cameroons (won partly by British troops), when she had 'neither inter-ests, rights, nor concern' in the region. And if France, the only other serious colonial power, was excluded, it surely could not be contem-plated increasing the possessions of Belgium, 'who already has more of Africa than she can conveniently and properly administer', or of Portugal, 'incurably incapable of ruling or keeping anything, except by virtue of her weakness', or of Italy, 'who has no connection whatever with this part of Africa, and has shown herself in other regions of that continent the most unaccommodating of allies and neighbours'.[9]

The three blocs of Germany's African territories were eventually divided, in roughly equal proportions, between Britain, France and the Union of South Africa. Curzon's reasons for excluding Germany and the minor Allied powers might sound jingoistic, but they were logical. If the Germans had been allowed to stay in Africa – as Churchill sug-gested in 1918 – the continent would have become far more than 'a cockpit of sanguinary conflicts' in 1940. Curzon's views were the product of strategic foresight and awareness of the colonial per-formances of Belgium, Italy and Portugal. The extension of British rule was not an aim in itself, for his view of empire, focused on Asia and the Dominions, had little room for Africa. He recognized the importance of the Cape and admired the vision of Rhodes, but he was unmoved by most of the continent. The colonization of East Africa was far from being his idea of imperial trusteeship. He would have hated – as he did in India – the racism of the planters, and he would have been disgusted by the society of Kenya's 'Happy Valley', so much more frivolous and debauched than Simla.

Five months of the Cabinet, the subcommittees and the Imperial War Cabinet practically knocked Curzon out. During the comparatively idle months under Asquith, his health had stood up well: apart from a brief convalescence after breaking his elbow in the spring of 1916, he had barely missed a meeting of the Cabinet or the Dardanelles Committee until severe backaches laid him out in October. But by the end of May 1917 he was on the verge of a breakdown, his private secretary told Hankey, and needed a holiday. The Cabinet Secretary informed Lloyd George, who said he had heard Curzon was 'so done' that he sometimes burst into tears.[10] Yet since the next few weeks were expected to determine the country's strategy for the rest of the war, no opportunity for a holiday arose. That summer yielded, however, a personal vindication that did him as much good as any holiday.

Curzon had not been averse to campaigning against Turkey in Syria: he would have liked to send an expeditionary force to cut the Hejaz railway in 1914, and the following year he supported the proposal to land troops at Alexandretta. But he was wary of more entanglements and consequently more commitments in the Middle East. Sceptical of proposals for an Arab caliphate and a tribal revolt in Arabia, he deprecated the idea of promising the Arabs an enormous state on former Ottoman territory. Britain would be in a very unfortunate position, he told Cromer in April 1915, if she gave them pledges which she failed to redeem.[11] But once they had erroneously been made, he saw no option but to honour them. Britain 'must be very careful', he told his Cabinet colleagues in October 1917, 'that any peace programme did not work to the detriment of the Arabs and the promises' made to them.[12] He thus opposed commitments made to other peoples in the Sykes-Picot Agreement and the Balfour Declaration.

Curzon was equally cautious about extending Britain's commitments in Arab lands further east. He agreed with the occupation of Basra, which protected Britain's position in the Gulf and her oil interests in Persia, but he thought it would be foolhardy to advance up the Tigris to Baghdad. Such an operation, he observed in March 1915, would involve defending an enormous area of Mesopotamia, taking over part of Persia's neutral zone to protect it, and in the process acquiring a coterminous frontier with Russia which would have to be held with Indian troops.[13] On joining the Government, he argued against the proposed advance later in the year. It would lead to the dispersal and weakening of British forces, he told the Dardanelles Committee, leaving them exposed to a German swoop through Mosul or a Turkish flank attack on Basra; moreover, a small British army at Baghdad, at the end of long and difficult communications, would be in a precarious position, liable to be cut off and surrounded.

Kitchener suggested that the British might raid Baghdad, destroy everything of military value and then withdraw, an action that would hardly have endeared them to the Arabs or added to Britain's prestige in the area. But the strongest advocates of an advance on the ancient Abbasid capital were Grey, who was still Foreign Secretary, and Balfour, neither of whom had been near the place and who were quite ignorant of local conditions. Baghdad's capture, pronounced Grey, would have a great effect on the Arabs and bring them over to the British side. Balfour agreed with the Foreign Secretary, declaring that the offensive was a gamble worth taking.[14] As Curzon later reported to General Townshend, the officer entrusted with the advance, the Cabinet then opted for 'a splashy and momentary triumph at the cost, or at least the risk of subsequent reverse and disaster'.[15] The wrong decision was taken against the advice of the best informed minister, an occurrence with which Curzon was by now familiar. As he told his former foe Repington, who like Chirol thought the expedition was folly, 'anyone who knows any particular subject connected with the war is sure to be overruled when the subject is discussed'.[16]

British troops finally entered Baghdad in March 1917, seventeen months and several disasters after the Cabinet's decision to go there. Advancing up the Tigris in November 1915, Townshend's 14,000 men had been defeated by a larger Turkish force at the Battle of Ctesiphon. Losing a third of their strength in that encounter, they had then retreated down river to Kut el-Amara where the rest of the force was lost during the subsequent siege and surrender. In the meantime thousands of other troops had perished in attempts to relieve them from Basra. It was a humiliation to rival Yorktown and Kabul, an almost unique combination of strategic blunders, tactical mistakes and organizational incompetence. Medical facilities on the Tigris were scandalous, worse than anything experienced by a British army since the Crimea.

The campaign was conducted under the orders of the Commander-in-Chief in India, General Sir Beauchamp Duff, a desk officer who had never commanded so much as a regiment and who owed his appointment to his service as Kitchener's Chief of Staff. Having to combine the duties of C-in-C with the advisory role of the former Military Member, Duff remained at the Viceroy's side at Simla during the campaign. He did not go to the operational headquarters at Basra; he did not even visit Bombay, where the troops embarked and whence the wounded returned, nor did he station any member of his staff there to find out what was going on. He seldom left his office and yet refused to let anything be decided outside his office. When Sir George Buchanan, sent from Burma to advise the military authorities in Basra, gave Duff a report, the Commander-in-Chief 'assured him it disclosed a state of affairs of which he had not the remotest conception'.[17]

From Bombay Valentine Chirol was in a good position to appreciate the absurdity of the military system set up by Kitchener and Brodrick ten years earlier. 'No man', he reported, 'ever could be both head of a great military administration and at the same time C-in-C – least of all in war time.'[18] A good many people were coming to agree with him. There were even grudging admissions from its perpetrators that the scheme which had brought down the Viceroy in 1905 might have been mistaken. So far as the failures in Mesopotamia were due to his reforms, Midleton told Curzon at the end of 1916, 'I am ready to take my share [of the blame] if any is due to me'; he believed, however, that no system could have made up for the failings of the men fighting the campaign.[19] A more candid and revealing admission came from Kitchener even before the disasters had occurred. Talking in the summer of 1915 to General Barrow, who was now Military Secretary at the India Office, the War Secretary 'expressed himself very forcibly about the shortcomings of Duff' and his staff at Army Headquarters. After Barrow protested that 'they were his own nominees and the system his own making, Kitchener retorted, "We shall have to revive the Military Department to keep them all in order and impose a little sense into them".' When Barrow replied, 'That was always my view,' the former C-in-C 'smiled grimly'.[20]

Kitchener witnessed the Mesopotamian débâcle from afar but did not live to read the official report that damned his system. Nor did several of the staff officers who had helped him set it up: Maxwell and Hamilton were killed on the Western Front in October 1914; Marker died of wounds a year later. Voluntary incarceration at Simla spared Duff, however, and enabled him to study the Royal Commission's verdict on his performance, his inability to fulfil the duties entrusted to him, and the 'astounding system' which had 'only to be described to be condemned'. Trying to manage the expedition from Simla, he read, was like using Thurso or Wick as headquarters for the Western Front.[21] Asked to analyse the report for the benefit of the War Cabinet, Curzon remarked on Duff's unsuitability as C-in-C, his responsibility for the system that had broken down, and his 'degree of culpability which [had] seldom been exceeded in modern times'. He was also highly critical of Surgeon-General Hathaway, whose ignorance and negligence merited dismissal from the service, and General Nixon, who had first urged the capture of Baghdad and who 'had made every consideration of prudence and foresight bend to the requirements of this over-mastering desire'.[22]

The report was widely seen as a vindication of Curzon's struggle twelve years earlier. The current Viceroy, Lord Chelmsford, observed that it was 'not often that a man in his lifetime has his prophecies fulfilled', but in this case Curzon had been thoroughly justified. Milner wrote with a similar message and said the report had confirmed his opinion that 'we never had a better man in India than yourself'.[23] Gratified though he was by the plaudits, Curzon remained bitter about the attitude of the last Unionist Cabinet. 'Of one thing I am certain,' he told Grace: 'not one of my then colleagues from Balfour downwards will say one word to me in acknowledgement of their error or regret for the great wrong that they did me at that critical moment of my career.'[24] The grievance was somewhat exaggerated. At least two of them, Lansdowne and Chamberlain, admitted he had been right, and three others who might have done so – Lyttelton, Wyndham and Arnold-Forster – were dead. Unrepentance seems to have been restricted to Balfour, Midleton, Salisbury and Derby.

In the House of Lords debate on the report, Lansdowne blamed the Mesopotamian fiasco on the changes that had turned the Commander-in-Chief into a bureaucrat. Had there been a Military Member or even a Military Supply Member to advise the Viceroy, Duff could have gone to the Front or at any rate to Bombay. Later, after the Under-Secretary for India, Lord Islington, had cited over-centralization as the cause of the breakdown, Midleton rose to defend his abolition of the Military Department and to claim that the fault was Morley's for getting rid of the MSM. But although he was unable to admit publicly his recent doubts on the matter, he did pay a gratuitous tribute to Curzon. In a passage combining a swipe at Hardinge with an oblique attempt at atonement, Midleton asserted that Curzon as Viceroy would never have stayed at Simla nor allowed the C-in-C to remain there throughout the operations. The following afternoon, after Curzon had ridiculed the idea that the MSM could have averted the disaster, Midleton passed him a note along the benches: 'May I say how fine I thought your speech, though you will not expect me to endorse every paragraph? It was like old times. St. J.B.'[25]

In his speech Curzon defended General Barrow, whose role at the India Office had been criticized unfairly by the report, and Chamberlain who, as Secretary of State, felt he had to do 'the right thing and resign'. Curzon congratulated his colleague for his 'punctilious and honourable chivalry' and wrote of the 'absurd illogicality' which condemned him 'while leaving others untouched'.[26] The last phrase was presumably a reference to Hardinge. The soldiers criticized most severely in the report never held an official post again, but Hardinge had returned from India to resume his old job as head of the Foreign Office. Plainly more culpable for the débâcle than Chamberlain, his position appeared untenable after the publication of the Commission's findings. Hardinge had vigorously urged Duff's appointment as C-in-C and had later insisted on keeping him at Simla; he had also been an ardent promoter of the advance on Baghdad during which he had sent Chamberlain Panglossian reports on the military and medical situations. Believing that the interests of the Government and the Foreign Office required his resignation, the members of the War Cabinet deputed Curzon to tell him their views. In his memoirs, which reinforce Crawford's view of their author as a 'monument of vanity and fussiness', Hardinge gives an improbable account of their interview at which he claims to have argued so powerfully that Curzon 'slunk' from his room 'like a whipped hound'.[27] In fact he owed his survival to his chief, Balfour, who seldom otherwise got heated about anyone's career, even his own. In the Commons the Foreign Secretary defended Hardinge in a petulant speech, recorded Crawford, which showed A.J.B. 'really at his worst, resembling an angry schoolgirl' and reminding his colleague of his 'deplorable controversy' over the Air Board.[28]

In the autumn of 1917 it dawned on Curzon that the British were about to make another blunder in the Middle East. Almost submerged by the problems of his subcommittees, he had paid little attention to the Government's negotiations with the Zionist movement. Indeed, he seems to have been scarcely aware of those strange combinations of romanticism and strategic reasoning, zealotry and altruism, pro-Jewish sympathy and professed anti-Semitism that were converting so many leading politicians – Balfour, Lloyd George and Milner above all – into champions of the idea of a Jewish homeland in Palestine.* He did not intervene until reading a paper circulated at the end of August by Edwin Montagu, the only Jewish member of Lloyd George's Government, who denounced Zionism as 'a mischievous political creed' that would promote anti-Semitism and jeopardize the status of Jews living outside Palestine. It was in any case a futile aspiration, argued Montagu, because the land could not hold more than a third of the world's Jews even if all its other inhabitants were driven out.[30]

Curzon agreed with Montagu's arguments. Having ridden over the country, he thought it unsuitable for large-scale Jewish immigration from Europe. 'I cannot conceive a worse bondage', he told Montagu, 'to which to relegate an advanced and intellectual community than to exile in Palestine.' He also saw there was room for only a small portion of the Jewish people. One could not 'expel the present Moslem population', he believed, nor 'turn all the various sects, religions and denominations out of Jerusalem'.[31]

Balfour and Montagu came to the War Cabinet to argue their cases on 4 October. The Foreign Secretary believed that a pro-Zionist declaration was necessary to pre-empt a similar announcement from Germany and to gain the support of American Jews, who might provide financial aid to the Allies, and Russian Jews who, despite the turmoil of their country, might help persuade their Government to stay in the war. Montagu stuck to the issue of British Jewry, arguing that its homeland was Britain rather than Palestine, and pointing out that most English-born Jews were opposed to Zionism. Concentrating the discussion on Palestine and its inhabitants, Curzon asked his colleagues how it was 'proposed to get rid of the existing majority of Mussulman inhabitants and to introduce the Jews in their place?' Afterwards he returned to the point in a paper for the Cabinet. 'What is to become of the people of the country?' They had been there for 1,500 years, they owned and worked the soil, and they would not be content 'either to be expropriated for Jewish immigrants, or to act merely as hewers of wood and drawers of water' for the Zionists. Besides, Jerusalem was a city in which too many peoples and too many religions had 'a passionate and permanent interest' for it to become a future Jewish capital.[32]

---

*These contradictions are at their most blatant with Balfour, who had restricted Jewish immigration to Britain with the Aliens Act when Prime Minister, had told Chaim Weizmann, the Zionist leader, that he shared Cosima Wagner's 'anti-semitic postulates',[29] and yet believed the Jews were the 'most gifted race' in the world and that Arab interests should be ignored so that they could live in Palestine.

Curzon's intervention was too late to affect an issue on which he was almost unanimously opposed by his colleagues. At a meeting of the War Cabinet on 31 October, he once again stated his misgivings but admitted the force of Balfour's diplomatic arguments in favour of a pro-Zionist declaration. He warned, however, against raising false expectations and urged the use of guarded language.[33] The Balfour Declaration, embodied in a letter to Lord Rothschild on 2 November, was certainly a more cautious document than its author had originally intended. The Foreign Secretary's assertion of 'the principle that Palestine should be reconstituted as the national home of the Jewish people' was replaced by Milner's milder statement that 'His Majesty's Government view with favour the establishment in Palestine of a national home for the Jewish people'.[34] The final version of the letter deferred to the anxieties of both Curzon and Montagu by declaring that nothing would be done which might 'prejudice the civil and religious rights of the existing non-Jewish communities in Palestine, or the rights and political status enjoyed by Jews in other countries'.

'One of Curzon's characteristic weaknesses', wrote Churchill after his death, 'was that he thought too much about stating his case, and too little about getting things done.'[35] At first sight this criticism might seem justified by his behaviour over the Balfour Declaration, for he acquiesced in a policy which he knew to be mistaken and which proved to be disastrous both for British interests in the Middle East and for the indigenous people of Palestine. Yet it is difficult to see what Curzon could have done apart from resigning over a minor issue concerning a small area still under Turkish rule at a time when the Bolsheviks were seizing power in Russia and British soldiers were dying in their thousands at Passchendaele. He had no hope of converting Balfour or the War Cabinet to his point of view. The Foreign Secretary was committed to Zionism – one of his officials thought he never cared passionately about anything else[36] – and could not be influenced by anxieties over the fate of Palestine's current inhabitants. As he later told Curzon, 'Zionism, be it right or wrong, good or bad, is rooted in age-long traditions, in present needs, in future hopes, of far profounder import than the desires and prejudices of the 700,000 Arabs who now inhabit that ancient land'.[37]

The debate over the Balfour Declaration was one of a series between 1905 and 1923 in which Curzon won the argument and Balfour won the battle. As with India and Mesopotamia, Curzon was familiar with the area and its inhabitants, and his experience made him doubt that they could absorb a Jewish influx from Europe: indeed he predicted, accurately as it happened, that Zionism could not be established without the removal of many of the native Arabs. Balfour, by contrast, knew and cared nothing about Palestine's Arab inhabitants. He was a Zionist because he admired Weizmann and Jewish culture and because he hoped to see in Palestine a sort of modern equivalent of Classical Athens. No doubt he believed in the pro-Zionist diplomatic arguments he expounded, although in the event these turned out to be illusory: his Declaration had no effect, for example, on the actions of Trotsky and other Bolshevik Jews. But his real impulse was romantic, intellectual and politically frivolous. As Chief Secretary of Ireland he had experienced the problem of sectarianism and had striven to contain it. Yet in Palestine he promoted a more spectacular and intransigent antagonism without making any attempt to understand or reassure one of the parties involved. Three-quarters of a century of conflict have been the result.

One area of the world Curzon still watched closely, although he had no official connection with it, was the Subcontinent. Crawford once observed that Curzon did not like people talking about India unless they had 'qualified by a five year residence, preferably seven'.[38] It was an unkind jibe coming from Crawford, whom Curzon had tried to have appointed Viceroy after Hardinge, but it was not entirely unfair. Curzon was liberal with advice to successive Viceroys and Secretaries of State, putting forward names, recommending policies, trying to resuscitate favourite schemes like the Cadet Corps or commissions for Indians in the army. Chamberlain had been amenable – in favour of Crawford's candidacy, sympathetic on the question of military administration, and sceptical about transferring the capital to Delhi. But his successor, Edwin Montagu, was less congenial to the former Viceroy. Although he and Curzon had been equally critical of the Balfour Declaration, they agreed on little else. An ambitious and highly intelligent politician, Montagu was a fractious and abrasive colleague, quick to take umbrage and excelling even Curzon in his determination to pursue a grievance or an argument until the last point had been cleared up. As Under-Secretary with Crewe he had derided Curzon's views on India, and he had later urged Asquith to sack both Curzon and Churchill for their stance on Gallipoli. In 1917 he was reluctant to become Secretary of State for fear of being blocked by Curzon and manacled by the Council of India whenever he tried to intitiate reforms. Curzon did not want him in the post either, because he thought Montagu's programme of 'Federal Home Rule for India' would excite 'prodigious expectations' which could not be realized. He was 'rather a strong partisan of Montagu', he told Lloyd George, but warned that as Indian Secretary he would try to drag the Government 'into a policy where some would find it impossible to follow'.[39]

The new Viceroy, Lord Chelmsford, had convinced Chamberlain that the circumstances of the war required some public statement on Britain's eventual goal in India. In the past Conservative statesmen had believed there was no goal beyond the maintenance of ever higher standards of British rule, while Liberals had tried not to think about an ultimate aim but to concentrate rather on a slow and piecemeal extension of Indian liberties. The Minto-Morley reforms of 1909 had put Indians on the executive councils and increased the size and representative element of the legislative councils. Eight years later Montagu was eager to go beyond this modest advance and encourage the development of Indian institutions, a process he hoped would eventually culminate in self-government within the empire.

Curzon realized that such a step could not be avoided. The wartime atmosphere, stirred by the Russian Revolution, the growing demands of Congress since the death of its moderate leader Gokhale, and above all 'the free talk about liberty, democracy, nationality, and self-government which had become the common shibboleths of the Allies', meant that substantial concessions would have to be made. It was plainly anomalous, for example, to have three Indians accredited to the Imperial War Cabinet in London while their countrymen enjoyed negligible political power in India and were still unable to hold commissions in the army. Curzon admitted that he was more interested in granting the commissions, a proposal he had urged eighteen years before, and in setting up an advisory Council of Princes than in 'the dissemination of parliamentary institutions'. But he did not 'dissent from the broad view' that it was desirable to state that 'self-government within the British Empire is the goal at which we aim' so long as it was made clear that it was 'under British guidance that this end must be pursued, and can alone be achieved', and that the essential safeguards of British justice and British power would not be weakened. Britain must guide the process steadily, he told his colleagues, gradually increasing Indian participation in government, carefully nurturing the new representative institutions, and waiting until India could manage both her defences and her domestic concerns before allowing her 'to claim the rights of a self-governing nation'.[40]

The wording of the statement of aim was discussed at meetings of the War Cabinet attended by other senior ministers in August 1917. Montagu had proposed a simple sentence, stating that the Governments of Britain and India had 'in view the gradual development of free institutions in India with a view to ultimate self-government within the Empire'. But in a note regarded by Curzon as 'very stubborn and rather reactionary', Balfour objected to the use of the word 'self-government'. 'East is East and West is West', A.J.B. told his colleagues, and even in the West parliamentary institutions had 'rarely been a great success, except amongst the English-speaking peoples'.[41]

Curzon thought 'self-government' was a misleading phrase which, 'as understood and desired by the extremists, would simply mean setting up a narrow oligarchy of clever lawyers'. He therefore suggested that Montagu amend his phrase to read 'the gradual development of self-governing institutions with a view to the fuller realization of responsible government in India under the aegis of the Crown'. This formula, accompanied by a declaration favouring 'the increasing association of Indians in every branch of the Administration', was approved by the War Cabinet on 14 August with the word 'fuller' substituted at Montagu's behest by 'progressive' – an important change because 'fuller' does not imply that something will become full, whereas 'progressive' indicates a continuous progress until, in this case, responsible government is realized. Informing Chamberlain afterwards that the meeting had gone 'as merrily as a wedding feast', Curzon told him that he and Montagu had defeated Derby, Carson and others on the issue of Indian commissions, that they had agreed on the wording of the pronouncement, and that he had successfully supported Montagu's request to visit India to investigate how the statement could be embodied in a constitutional form. Yet although it appeared that the Victorian proconsul himself had embraced 'the common shibboleths of the Allies', the declaration was still open to misinterpretation. For Curzon it did not mean a handover of power within the foreseeable future but a developing process, he told the Cabinet, which might extend for hundreds of years.[42]

After a winter tour of India, Montagu came back with a scheme whereby native ministers, chosen by elected members of enlarged provincial legislatures, would run various 'transferred subjects' such as health, education and agriculture, while the local governor would retain control over finance, the police and other 'reserved' matters. The proposed form of government, later known as the dyarchy, appalled Curzon, who believed it would lead to federalism and a parliamentary system. Asked to comment on Montagu's report for the Cabinet, he alleged that the scheme would create a revolution in the governing relations between Britain and India, 'a revolution all the more incalculable' because parts of the plan were clearly a transitory expedient that would provoke early agitation for further concessions.[43]

Astonished by this note, Montagu claimed that his proposals were based on the principles of the declaration they had jointly composed the previous August. As he rightly saw, dyarchy was a step towards 'the progressive realization of responsible Government in India'; and as Curzon rightly feared, it was a step towards the dismantling of the empire. The former Viceroy wanted the 'progressive realization' to be an extremely slow process and was horrified that Montagu should have returned from India with radical proposals which he wanted to have rapidly enacted. Chamberlain tried to persuade the Secretary of State to be more tactful and less impatient. 'We ought to be particularly conciliatory and forbearing', he told him in July 1918 because, in accepting the reforms, Curzon was having to relinquish the ideas of a lifetime.[44] But Montagu was neither tactful nor patient by nature. When Curzon reluctantly agreed to the setting up of two committees to examine the functioning of the dyarchy, the Secretary of State suggested the appointment of a third to investigate future changes in relations between the British and Indian Governments. Coming simultaneously with a proposal to nominate extra Indian ICS officers, the idea exasperated Curzon. 'In many respects I have gone very far,' he told Montagu, 'but the sense of being perpetually pushed does not heighten one's zest in going further.'

> Why is it necessary to proceed at breakneck speed in a case that constitutes a revolution of which not one person in a thousand in this country realizes the magnitude, and which will probably lead by stages of increasing speed to the ultimate disruption of the Empire?[45]

After reading this letter with 'intense dismay', Montagu drafted an angry reply which his predecessor advised him not to send. Curzon was 'uneasy, nervous and in consequence a little irritable', Chamberlain said, and the draft would not be 'the best salve for a person in his condition'.[46] The Secretary of State reluctantly took the advice. Although his tongue as well as his pen frequently ran away with him, Montagu knew he needed Curzon's support if his reforms were to be accepted by a House of Lords in which many Unionists with Indian experience were likely to be hostile. He therefore tried to associate him with the measure at each stage of its development. In October 1918 Curzon co-operated with suggestions for a Cabinet note by Montagu and with a speech in the Lords defending the Government's procedure over the Report. But he was too disenchanted with the proposals themselves to serve on the Cabinet committee appointed to prepare legislation. When the Bill came up for its Second Reading in December 1919, Curzon told the Lords it was a 'daring experiment' which was unlikely to lead to better government. But he accepted it as necessary because in that age of nationalism and self-determination people attached 'much more importance to being governed, even though not so well governed, by themselves, than they do to being even superbly governed by another race.'[47] It was a phenomenon he had recognized in Persia thirty years before, but one which he had hoped would never arise in India.

31

Lord President

A S LORD PRIVY SEAL, George Curzon's role in Cabinet had been almost as ornamental as his title. He rarely spoke in the House of Lords and, until the creation of the Air Board, had almost nothing to administer. But with the equally venerable title of Lord President of the Council, he not only had a key role in the running of the war but also the laborious task of explaining and defending Government policy in the Lords. In December 1916 he initiated his new work with a much-admired speech describing the structure of the new Government and the policy it intended to pursue.

The War Cabinet had been conceived as an antidote to the long, meandering, indecisive gatherings of Asquith's ministers. Executive power was now concentrated in a small group of people unencumbered, except for Bonar Law, by departmental duties. Decision-making was thus very greatly improved. But the drawbacks of the small Cabinet soon became apparent, at any rate to those ministers who were not in it. Crawford, the new Lord Privy Seal, told Curzon that there should be some form of ministerial conference to take the place of the old Cabinet; otherwise the secretaries of state would have no idea what was going on outside their departments. Curzon suggested, presumably only half seriously, that dinner parties at Carlton House Terrace with its new hostess might be a congenial substitute.[1] In the event the system remained in place and unaltered. Apart from Derby and Balfour, who as Secretaries for War and Foreign Affairs frequently attended the Cabinet, the departmental ministers did feel isolated. They seldom conferred or exchanged notes about their departments, and general papers were not circulated. Out of touch with the most recent political developments, they could feel little sense of collective responsibility.[2]

Much as he hated delegating, Curzon realized he needed some assistance. If he was going to spend most of the day with the War Cabinet and its subcommittees, he told Bonar Law, he required 'one or two lieutenants to help to do the work' in the House of Lords. Three potential 'lieutenants' he suggested were old friends and, in different degrees, more recent enemies: Salisbury, Selborne and Midleton. When Lansdowne suggested that Salisbury would be the most effective of this trio, Curzon made a strong appeal for his appointment as Lord Privy Seal, arguing that the Government would thereby 'disarm a rather formidable critic'.[3] On learning that the post had already been given to Crawford, Curzon went straight to the Scottish earl and asked him to stand down in favour of Salisbury, who was in any case unwilling to take the job. Marvel though he did at Curzon's ability to make the request 'without confusion or apology', Crawford felt unable and doubtless unwilling to withdraw.[4]

Curzon was happy to be in charge of the House of Lords but distressed by Lloyd George's failure to treat his Chamber with sufficient consideration. Frustrated in his initial efforts to recruit 'lieutenants', Curzon also resented the Prime Minister's refusal to reward his later staff officers. Outside the War Cabinet, he pointed out in the summer of 1918, there were forty-four ministers in the Commons and only five in the Lords. The departments in the Upper House were thus voluntarily represented by unpaid peers with virtually no prospects of promotion. Had Lord Peel been an MP, he told Lloyd George, he would have been a minister long ago. But because he was a peer he was expected to represent two ministries and conduct bills through the House 'simply as an act of patriotism and good will'.[5] Curzon was eventually successful with the advancement of Peel, who became Under-Secretary at the War Office and in 1922 succeeded Montagu as Indian Secretary, but otherwise his 'team' received inadequate recognition.

Curzon was generally regarded as a fine Leader of the Lords. Carefully prepared and powerfully delivered, his speeches usually managed to see off persistent and concerted attacks on the Coalition by those would-have-been lieutenants, Salisbury and Midleton. Crawford noted that they sounded better than they read, leading people to feel they had heard a 'great and historic oration' even when the content was ordinary.[6] One Liberal peer considered that Curzon's first nine months

as Leader had been 'uniformly successful' because, on top of his knowledge and oratory, he had added courtesy and 'kindly greetings' to his
colleagues. Crawford also seems to have discovered a new side to
Curzon, describing him as a 'wondrous patient' taskmaster whom he
'rejoiced' to work under.[7] The partnership between the Lord President
and his deputy was not an easy one because Curzon's membership of
the War Cabinet frequently prevented him from attending the Upper
House. Crawford thus often found himself answering delicate questions about Cabinet policy which he had no part in deciding and which
he often knew little about. Able though he was, he could not always
cope with the situation, and Milner was reluctantly forced to intervene
to set matters straight.[8]

Curzon had become 'quite undeservedly' unpopular, thought
Selborne, as a minister in Asquith's Cabinet. Since he never made any
effort to increase his popularity, matters did not improve under Lloyd
George. He was a friend of Milner and to a lesser extent of
Chamberlain, Crawford and Robert Cecil. But even by those colleagues
who liked him, he was regarded with alternate bursts of admiration and
exasperation. Hankey often told him he was a good friend and then told
his diary he was impossible to deal with. Less ambivalent was the attitude of Lord Derby who, as his biographer Randolph Churchill pointed
out, never missed an opportunity of thwarting or embarrassing Curzon.
In the spring of 1917 he sent Bonar Law an appalling letter, alleging
among other things that Curzon was abusing the privilege of his official
car by allowing Grace and their guests to travel in it. The following
winter he wrote 'as an old friend' to Curzon himself about the matter,
but was forced to admit that his correspondent's explanation was 'so
excellent' that the incident was 'absolutely closed'.[9] Derby had little
further opportunity to investigate the Lord President's consumption of
petrol because in April he was forced to relinquish the War Office.
Hearty, blunt and unintellectual – qualities which endeared him to the
British public – Derby had proved a most malleable minister who did
what the generals told him. Lloyd George therefore despatched him to
the Paris embassy where it would not be 'obvious that his bluffness was
only bluff',[10] and where he appealed to the French as a fine specimen of
a *milord*. As Crawford recorded in his diary, 'he dines out with people
whose faces he doesn't know, whose names he can't remember and
whose language he is unable to talk, but with his own cheerful counte-
nance and bonhomie he sails through all kinds of difficulties and
embarrassments with complete success'.[11]

Curzon had a more complicated relationship with the Prime Minister. In character and personality he and Lloyd George could hardly have been more dissimilar: their ways of thinking and working, their values and assumptions, their manners and temperaments, all seemed designed as opposites. 'Our natures', recalled Curzon with laconic understatement, 'were not naturally harmonious.'[12] Yet he was the only man who stayed in Lloyd George's Cabinet from beginning to end. Their views were not in fact so different as their personalities, and they had a reluctant mutual respect for each other's ability. Lloyd George recognized that Curzon was 'not very accessible to new ideas' but thought him 'very able, very just' and 'a great public servant' who had 'never had sufficient credit for his Indian administration'.[13] He also found him useful, as a chairman of committees, as a source of knowledge on distant places, even as a companion on his famous mission to the Admiralty in April 1917 to insist on the use of convoys.

Yet they never 'got on' personally. They were regarded as good company by other people but not by each other. Each exaggerated the other's idiosyncrasies and at the same time drew attention to his own. Curzon liked to think of Lloyd George as 'a bit of a Bolshevik at heart' who found Trotsky 'the one congenial spirit on the international stage'.[14] Lloyd George liked to regard Curzon as a patrician of incomparable hauteur and imagined himself leading a medieval revolt of oppressed Kedleston peasantry. According to Hankey, the Prime Minister loved to hear funny stories about Curzon, whose 'little peculiarities – his pompous manner, ignorance (partly a pose) of democracy, and so forth – were a source of inexhaustible amusement' to him.[15] Yet Curzon in the flesh often grated, particularly when he was being long-winded, and sometimes Lloyd George was unable to resist a snub. On these occasions Curzon protested, not with angry rejoinders or threats of resignation, but with wounded stateliness. It had been a 'very trying' and 'unmerited experience', he wrote in January 1918, to be pulled up by his chief at a Cabinet meeting attended by outsiders and to be cut short in a manner that left 'a painful impression on all who heard it'. Lloyd George apologized for his rudeness but maintained he had been right to protest because two trustees of the British Museum had been invited to a Cabinet meeting at which Curzon behaved not like a minister but as an advocate opposing the plan to install the Air Board in the museum. The Prime Minister's constitutional punctiliousness may have been correct, but one cannot help thinking that the proposal, which Curzon foiled, was a peculiarly bad one.[16]

Until the end of 1916, Curzon had been unable to influence the strategy of the war. His constructive work, on the Shipping Committee and the Air Board, had been organizational; his strategic advice, wrong on the evacuation of Gallipoli, right on the advance to Baghdad, had been ignored. But on joining Lloyd George's War Cabinet he became part of that small body set up to direct the running of the war after the slaughter on the Somme. And in the following June he and Milner successfully urged the formation of a War Policy Committee consisting of themselves, Lloyd George and Smuts, with the invaluable Hankey as secretary, to consider future strategy.* Starting on 11 June, the committee met three or four times a week to examine the options until the middle of July. As chairman, Milner told Amery, the Prime Minister tended to babble away 'with every sort of wild notion', and it was better when 'Curzon took the chair, and they really got through a lot of business'.[17]

One might have expected Curzon, with his admiration for Napoleon and Wellington, to have enjoyed the role of military strategist. But he admired them as much for their administrative genius as for their fighting ability. Unlike Churchill, he did not thrill to the sound of bugles; he did not imagine himself at Napoleon's camp fire, conjuring with divisions, plotting an encirclement of the Austrians, designing a manoeuvre around the left flank of the Prussian army. Despite his experience in India and the evidence of the Somme, he was averse to overruling current military advice. Curzon and other Unionists had insisted on the retention of General Sir Douglas Haig as Commander-in-Chief on the Western Front. And although the Cabinet's decision to place him under France's General Nivelle during the spring of 1917 indicated limited confidence in his ability, the Unionists still preferred his plodding professionalism to the intuition and imagination of Lloyd George.

Haig came over in June to justify his proposals for a new offensive on the Western Front. Backed by General Sir William Robertson, the Chief of the Imperial General Staff, he urged the War Policy Committee to sanction an attack in Flanders intended to capture the German submarine bases on the Belgian coast and relieve the pressure on a demoralized French army. After Haig claimed his offensive had 'a reasonable chance of success', Curzon asked him whether this meant he

---

*Although he was not officially a member, Bonar Law often attended the committee's meetings.

merely expected to capture his initial objectives. The C-in-C replied that he expected the entire operation to be successful.[18] It might even, thought the generals, win the war. On that night, 20 June, the committee dined at Carlton House Terrace and tried to come to a decision. After several glasses of champagne, Curzon told his wife, the Prime Minister became 'quite hilarious',[19] but the party broke up in the small hours without having come to a conclusion. Smuts, the only soldier among them, backed the generals, Curzon and Bonar Law were undecided, while Lloyd George and Milner wanted to delay an attack until American troops arrived in 1918.

During a further session with Haig and Robertson the next day, Curzon supported Lloyd George's proposal for an Italian offensive, assisted by French and British forces, to capture Trieste and knock the Austrians out of the war. Such a scenario was not much less illusory than clearing the well-entrenched Germans from the Belgian coast, but it would have avoided the hecatomb of Passchendaele. The generals, however, were unmoved. When Lloyd George later asked them to reconsider their plans, they restated their confidence in their strategy. Curzon became increasingly impressed by the unanimity of military opinion, backed as it was by Smuts and the Admiralty, and agreed with Bonar Law that the Cabinet could hardly ignore the recommendations of all its military advisers. Realizing that he was the civilian minister most sympathetic to their viewpoint, Robertson appealed to Curzon to help thwart other schemes such as an attack on Alexandretta or sending reinforcements for a further advance on the Salonika Front: 'attacking an enemy from two different directions', he told the Lord President, had always failed except at Waterloo and one or two other places. When Lloyd George pressed for the Salonika plan, the CIGS asked Curzon to explain the nature of the Balkan country to the Prime Minister, who seemed 'quite unable to envisage it', and to point out that it was a mountainous and easily defensible region where 'a small army would be murdered and a large army would starve'; only in the unlikely event of a Bulgarian collapse or a strong Russian attack from the north would there be any reasonable prospect of a military success. Convinced by the argument, Curzon obliged Robertson by telling the committee what would happen to a small or large army stranded in the Balkan interior.[20]

Curzon's late and reluctant support for Haig's disastrous offensive was influenced by an Eastern anxiety. Germany, he believed, needed to be defeated decisively in the West in order to prevent her causing chaos in the East. The Russian convulsions of 1917 opened up for Curzon a nightmare scenario whereby the the Germans could relinquish their gains in Western Europe and yet still emerge successfully from the war by compensating themselves in the opposite direction. They might offer to evacuate Belgium and give back Alsace-Lorraine to France on condition that their colonies were returned and they were given a free hand in the East. The French and Belgians would be unable to resist the deal, and the only loser, apart from Russia, would be Britain, who would gain nothing except a new and very dangerous threat to her Asian empire. An undefeated Germany, having exchanged small areas in Europe for large territories in the East, would, thought Curzon, cause a fresh war within twenty years.[21]

In September the Germans did make a vague peace approach along these lines. Yet although the British army was by then floundering once more through the quagmires of Flanders, the Cabinet rejected the idea of a negotiated peace. While that decision may have been understandable, it is difficult to see by what logic Haig was allowed to go on with his offensive until the village of Passchendaele was captured in November. 'We *laid it down* expressly', Milner reminded Curzon later, 'that we should *call it off* if the results seemed incommensurate' with the sacrifices. Yet four months after the great breakthrough had failed to materialize, the British attack was still churning away a few miles outside Ypres. Regretting that he had ever agreed to it, Milner urged Lloyd George to call a halt in September. But the Prime Minister, who had never believed in the offensive anyway, refused to do so, probably because he feared that a showdown with Haig would lead to the break-up of his Government. Afterwards Milner told Curzon that he very much doubted if the policy of 'Hammer, Hammer, Hammer on the Western Front' would ever succeed.[22]

After Passchendaele Curzon's opinion of Haig began to drop. During the autumn he received a series of percipient letters from the journalist Lovat Fraser, who criticized the C-in-C for flinging division after division at hopeless targets, for never knowing 'when not to fight', and for making silly plans about pouring cavalry 'through the gap' and capturing towns 'at the point of the sabre'. Unlike the Germans, he told Curzon, the British had failed to learn the lessons of Verdun. 'We are being beaten', he declared, 'in brain power'.[23] Curzon began to see that Fraser might have a point, at any rate with regard to the cavalry, whose manoeuvres Haig was still supervising as late as September 1918 in anticipation of pouring them through a gap in the Hindenburg Line.[24]

When in January of that year Haig told the War Cabinet that 'the value and importance of cavalry would be very great not only in offensive but also defensive operations', Curzon politely suggested that 'the character of warfare during the ensuing few months would [seem to] present few opportunities for the use of cavalry'.[25]

Curzon never wavered in his belief that the war must continue until Germany was defeated. He refused to accept the pessimism of Lansdowne, Smuts and Milner, all of whom recommended a compromise peace during the last two years of the war. Smuts wanted a settlement before Britain exhausted herself and ended up as a second-rate power compared to the United States and Japan. He and Milner advocated the kind of peace that Curzon particularly feared, an agreement that required German withdrawal from the West in return for eastern spoils such as the Ukraine. Smuts thought that only by such concessions to Germany could 'a great tide of invasion rolling' towards the Indian empire be prevented. Curzon believed that such an arrangement now would only encourage the 'great tide' to roll later on. In his view it was 'essential to go on hammering till Germany was beaten and brought to a different frame of mind'. Then Britain could 'secure a peace which Germany would keep and not have the strength to break'.[26]

At the Imperial War Cabinet, which congregated again in London in June 1918, Curzon once more stressed the danger of German ambitions in the East. In his role as Chairman of the Eastern Committee, a recent amalgamation of various Foreign Office and Cabinet subcommittees, he surveyed the situation in the Middle East and pointed out that the Russian-German Treaty of Brest-Litovsk now gave their enemies the choice of an Asian invasion through the Caucasus and Turkestan or by a southern route via Mesopotamia and Persia. In his contributions he also emphasized the importance of Britain's co-operation with the Arabs, both now and in the post-war Middle East settlement. He saw Britain as a sort of godfather to Arab aspirations, not only in Mesopotamia but also in the other Arab lands conquered from the Turks. He was well aware of the obstacles that had been placed in the way of Anglo-Arab co-operation by contradictory British promises: the 'embarrassing' pledges to Sharif Hussein,* the Sykes-Picot Agreement

---

*These were contained in the ambiguous correspondence between Sir Henry McMahon, the British High Commissioner in Egypt, and Hussein, the Sharif of Mecca, in 1915 and 1916. Curzon was referring to McMahon's pledge of British support for Arab independence in territories conquered from the Turks except in those 'portions of Syria lying

('a millstone round our necks') and above all the Balfour Declaration. Yet he believed that most of these and other contradictions could in due course be resolved. Only in Palestine did he foresee that it would be impossible, and for that reason he hoped that the area might be handed over to American trusteeship.[28]

When the end of the war loomed unexpectedly in the autumn, Curzon argued that the Allies must not be robbed of their legitimate rewards simply because victory had been a result of voluntary capitulation rather than disaster on the battlefield. The armistice, he told the War Cabinet, must 'contain the evidence, both to Germany and to the world', that the Germans had been defeated. Its conditions should therefore include compensation to Belgium, reparations for the invaded countries, and indemnities to the Allies for 'the colossal expenditure enforced upon them'. He also wanted to see the establishment of an International Tribunal to which 'certain specified and notorious German malefactors' should be surrendered for trial.[29] Expatiating on this last idea in November, he told Lloyd George that 'the supreme and colossal nature' of the Kaiser's crime called for 'supreme and unprecedented condemnation'. He did not think that execution or imprisonment would be necessary but recommended 'an inglorious and ignoble exile under the weight of such a sentence as has never been given in the history of mankind'.[30] A few days later, after discussing the matter with the French premier Clemenceau, he urged the Cabinet to decide whether to try the Kaiser while he could be regarded as a prisoner-of-war. Lloyd George disagreed with Curzon's view of the appropriate sentence and said the Kaiser should be hanged for a crime against humanity that had caused the deaths of several million people. To Chamberlain, who had suggested that the process would be like trying Napoleon, the Prime Minister replied that it was not at all the same thing. Napoleon had not only shown great talent and power but had also fought with his troops, while the Kaiser was merely a coward without strength of character.*[31]

(*cont.*) to the west of the districts of Damascus, Homs, Hama and Aleppo'. Although Britain later claimed that these were intended to include Palestine, the Arabs have disputed the point because the Holy Land in fact lies to the south-south-west of Damascus, the southernmost town. Curzon agreed with the Arabs. He had never been able to satisfy himself, he said long afterwards, that McMahon 'really had excluded Palestine when talking about the areas to the west of the towns'.[27]

*The debate turned out to be academic. Kaiser Wilhelm fled to Holland, which had remained neutral in the war and which refused to hand him over to the Allies afterwards.

The conclusion of the Armistice gave Curzon the opportunity, in the form of a congratulatory Address to the King, to make an eloquent and moving appraisal of Britain's role in the war. As Churchill showed a generation later, anachronisms of speech, which might provoke sniggers in periods of normality, can strike emotional chords in times of crisis that speakers more attuned to their age cannot achieve. So it was with Curzon on 18 November when he rose in the House of Lords to deliver a speech which, in Lord Harcourt's words, 'not only expressed what we all wanted to have said' but was 'the most perfect piece of English eloquence and literature' he had ever listened to.[32]

Among the many miscalculations of the enemy was the profound conviction, not only that we had a contemptible little army, but that we were a doomed and decadent nation. The trident was to be struck from our palsied grasp; the Empire was to crumble at the first shock; a nation dedicated, as we used to be told, to pleasure-taking and the pursuit of wealth, was to be deprived of the place to which it had ceased to have any right, and was to be reduced to the level of a second-class, or perhaps even a third-class Power. It is not for us in the hour of victory to boast that these predictions have been falsified; but at least we may say this – that the British flag never flew over a more powerful or a more united Empire than now; Britons never had better cause to look the world in the face; never did our voice count for more in the councils of the nations, or in determining the future destinies of mankind.

Later he turned to the future, prayed for continued Allied unity in the building of the peace and quoted Shelley. 'A little more than one hundred years ago, the great romantic poet of our land, looking on the birth of a new Hellas, wrote these prophetic words:

> The world's great age begins anew,
> The golden years return,
> The earth doth like a snake renew
> Her winter weeds outworn;
> Heaven smiles, and faiths and empires gleam
> Like wrecks of a dissolving dream.

'A similar vision', he added, 'now rises above a far wider horizon. May we see it, under the guidance of Providence, assume form and substance before our eyes.'

A few weeks later the country went to the polls for the first time in eight years. Although Curzon had opposed suggestions for a merger between the Unionists and Lloyd George's Liberals, he believed the two groups should seek a fresh mandate as a coalition and then jointly undertake the labours of a peace conference.[33] He himself played little part in the massive Coalition victory that reduced Asquith's Liberals to a parliamentary strength of under 30 and saw the emergence of Labour, with twice as many MPs, as the principal Opposition party. In fact his main contribution to the election had taken place nearly a year earlier when one of his most controversial speeches was influential in adding over eight million people to the franchise.

Curzon was still President of the anti-suffragists' National League when the Representation of the People Bill came before the House of Lords in Committee at the beginning of 1918. The Bill included one clause introducing universal suffrage for men aged 21 or over and another giving the vote to women who had reached the age of 30. Although the House of Commons had passed the clause on the enfranchisement of women by an enormous majority, Curzon recommended resistance to it in the Lords. As Leader of the House he did not think he himself could vote for an amendment that would kill the clause, but he agreed to support it in his speech and he encouraged the League to send a circular letter which might persuade 'a good many' peers to attend the debate and to vote for it. On 10 January he spoke solemnly of the 'vast, incalculable and almost catastrophic change' the clause would bring, and told the Lords that by passing it they would be 'opening the flood gates to a stream which for good or evil [would] submerge many landmarks' they had known. He then paused, admitted that he should logically support the amendment but suddenly changed tack, pointed out that the clause had been overwhelmingly passed in the Commons and warned his fellow peers against provoking a conflict with the Lower Chamber.

The effect was palpable. While the League's bewildered supporters stared dumbfounded at each other, waverers rallied to the suffrage side and helped defeat the amendment. Afterwards Lansdowne told Curzon that his speech stampeded many peers who had intended to vote against the clause but were 'deterred by [his] emphatic statement of the consequences'.[34] Members of the League naturally wondered why they had been advised to encourage peers to vote one way only to hear their President encouraging them to vote the other. Curzon complained of the abusive letters he received afterwards but gave no convincing explanation for his change of mind. In fact he seems to have been swayed by the course of the debate, particularly by a speech from

Selborne. The ability to persuade – and be persuaded – is of course what democracy is all about, but the committee members of the League may be forgiven for not appreciating the point on this occasion. Indeed, their 'regret that he did not sever' his connection with their organization before making his speech was a far milder censure than he deserved.[35]

Curzon's experience of ceremonies made him a natural choice as an organizer of events and memorials to celebrate victory and commemorate the dead. His most tedious duty was to act as chairman of a committee to set up a House of Lords memorial for the two hundred peers or sons of peers who had been killed in the war. What should have been a straightforward task was complicated by divisions among the surviving peers over whether the structure should go in the Princes' Chamber or the Royal Gallery, and whether it merited the displacement of a statue of Queen Victoria. A month before his death Curzon was still wrestling with the problems of the memorial. For nearly six years, he complained to Lansdowne, he had 'borne the whole burden of this wretched affair, trying to carry out the wishes and instructions of the House without help from anybody'.[36]

More rewarding was his chairmanship of a committee set up by the Cabinet to organize peace celebrations in the summer of 1919. After these had passed off successfully, he was asked to supervise the erection of a permanent cenotaph in Whitehall and to make arrangements for its unveiling. At the head of a second committee he then designed a restrained and moving ritual centred on a two minutes' silence and the haunting lament of the 'Last Post'. Determined that the ceremony should be one of poignant simplicity rather than high-ranking grandeur, he insisted that widows and ex-servicemen should be given priority on the occasion. After it had been decided that the unveiling of the Cenotaph should be accompanied by the burial of an unknown soldier in Westminster Abbey, Curzon again planned the ceremony and again stipulated that places should be given 'not to society ladies or the wives of dignitaries, but to the selected widows and mothers of those who had fallen, especially in the humbler ranks'. Conducted in an atmosphere of emotional intensity seldom matched in Britain, the events aroused such strong feelings that popular opinion demanded an annual service at the site of the Cenotaph. One final ceremony was thus given to Curzon to devise, and it has lasted as long as anything he ever did. The Remembrance Day service, still performed three-quarters of a century later, is his creation.[37]

Curzon gave himself no public role in these ceremonies and, apart from a mention in the *Pall Mall Gazette*, received no credit for them. Yet they owed their success to his ability as an organizer and to the sensitivity with which he created events in which everyone could participate and share a common grief. Curzon was a man of almost unparalleled contrasts, but none is so remarkable as the fact that the director who staged the Delhi Durbar also produced Remembrance Day, a ritual that can move to tears even people born after the Second World War. It is typical of Curzon's fate that he has been remembered for the wrong ceremony.

32

The Foreign Office at Last

THE FIRST SIXTY years of George Curzon's life might logically be seen as a sustained preparation for the role of Foreign Secretary. The great Asian expeditions of his youth and the volumes that followed, the years as Lord Salisbury's deputy and the Indian experience afterwards, the immense correspondence at all times with British officials all over the world – the combination produced the most travelled and most knowledgeable Foreign Secretary of any period. From an early age the post had been earmarked for him by his friends, and he himself had long regarded it as the penultimate destination of his career.

His position as Lansdowne's natural successor had been lost through resignation in India and the decade of Liberal power that followed. On joining the Coalition he did not think of supplanting Grey, whose political life had been almost entirely absorbed by foreign affairs. But he was puzzled when Lloyd George awarded his predestined post to Balfour, whose appetite for distant travels had been more than satisfied by a round-the-world voyage in 1875. Early in 1918, exasperated by the Foreign Secretary's indolence and ignorance of issues, he complained to Hankey of the inefficiency of the regime at the Foreign Office. When the Cabinet Secretary remarked that the Prime Minister and all their colleagues shared his view of Balfour, Curzon asked why Lloyd George did not make a change. Hankey mentioned the difficulty of finding a successor without taking someone out of the War Cabinet, whereupon Curzon declared himself willing to sacrifice his position, adding that Lord Salisbury had trained him for the job and had designated him as his successor. Hankey reported the conversation to the Prime Minister, who said, 'Wonder what sort of Foreign Secretary he would make?' Until then he had refused to consider Curzon for the post.[1]

Following the electoral triumph of December 1918, Lloyd George decided to retain the system of the War Cabinet, at any rate while he was pursuing a peace treaty in Paris. In the New Year he asked Curzon to take charge of the Foreign Office although Balfour, who was also going to France, would remain Foreign Secretary. Curzon readily agreed. It was hardly an enticing proposition, but it did not entail giving up his seat in the War Cabinet, and it did establish him as Balfour's most likely successor.

Curzon's arrival at the Foreign Office in January 1919 marked the start of a crescendo of stories about his eccentricities which did not diminish until after his death. The first concerned his entry into his new domain. Advancing to the writing-table he looked distastefully at an object on its surface and asked an official what it was. On being told it was his inkstand, he expressed astonishment and ordered its removal. At the Privy Council Office he had been 'furnished with an inkstand of crystal and silver. This contraption', he observed, ' was merely brăss and glăss'.[2]

News of the appointment induced one official, Mr J.D. Gregory, to apply immediately for a foreign posting. Learning of this on his arrival, Curzon summoned him to his office, sat him down, chatted away and told him amiably that he could not go abroad. Soon, the astonished diplomat recorded, 'we were cracking jokes as though we were old boon companions who had suddenly come together after years of separation.' This happy impression was rather dissipated a few minutes later when he witnessed Curzon angrily instructing his secretaries how to pull down a window blind. And over the following days Gregory had the chance to observe his new chief's level of tolerance regarding his officials' enthusiasm for golf, their custom of eating at a most 'barbarous' hour – 'Whoever heard of anyone lunching at one?' – and their departure for 'some unfathomable reason' early in the evening.[3]

The divisions of labour and responsibility between the Foreign Secretary in Paris and the Lord President in London were seldom clear. In fact most important decisions were made by neither of them, Lloyd George dealing with matters that interested him and Curzon administering most of the others. During this period Balfour behaved more like a deputy Prime Minister than a Foreign Secretary. He asked the Lord President to make the ambassadorial appointments and showed a similarly abdicating spirit regarding parliamentary posts. Curzon was astonished to learn from the newspapers that Lloyd George had appointed an Under-Secretary for Foreign Affairs without consulting or even notifying the minister in charge of the Foreign Office.[4]

Even more frustrating for Curzon was Balfour's failure to keep him acquainted with what was happening behind the scenes at the Paris Peace Conference. On his visits to France during the year, the Lord President witnessed the gradual supersession of the Foreign Office and the assumption of many of its responsibilities by Lloyd George. In conversation, Curzon later recorded, 'Balfour freely admitted it, and in his half cynical half nonchalant way expressed his ignorance and astonishment as to what the little man was doing'. The Foreign Secretary played lawn tennis, went to concerts and charmed everyone with his exquisite manners, but foreign policy in its essentials was conducted by the Prime Minister.[5]

Curzon always recognized Balfour's great ability and lauded his success at the Washington Conference of 1921–2 as a 'masterpiece of tact and intellectual superiority'. But he also regarded him as 'the worst and most dangerous' Foreign Secretary he had ever come across.

> His charm of manner, his extraordinary intellectual distinction, his seeming indifference to petty matters, his power of dialectic, his long and honourable career of public service, blinded all but those who knew from the inside to the lamentable ignorance, indifference, and levity of his regime. He never studied his papers; he never knew the facts; at the Cabinet he had seldom read the morning's FO telegrams; he never got up a case; he never looked ahead. He trusted to his unequalled power of improvisation to take him through any trouble and enable him to leap lightly from one crisis to another.[6]

The acerbity of this judgement, made in 1922, doubtless owes much to the resentment of a man who attributed his own problems at the Foreign Office to the ascendancy Lloyd George had been able to attain in 1919. But the essence of Curzon's judgement is not contradicted by a survey of Balfour's career as Foreign Secretary or by the views of less hostile colleagues. At a lunch party in August 1918, A.J.B. himself disarmingly described one of the reasons for his indecisiveness. His officials would come to him with an issue, he related, set out the position and recommend a course of action before leaving him to write a minute or prepare a speech. 'But what I always forget', he admitted, 'is the decision come to. I can remember every argument, repeat all the pros and cons, and even make quite a good speech on the subject. But the conclusion, the decision, is a perfect blank in my mind.' Crawford, one of his listeners, wondered whether he had been 'suffering from this odd mental defect for the last fifteen years'.[7]

In August 1919 Curzon was asked by the Cabinet to deal with the Turkish and Middle Eastern questions in Paris while Balfour had a holiday. But although he had deplored the delays in discussing these issues, he felt unable to go immediately without risking a breakdown of his health. Since the beginning of the year his work at the FO and the House of Lords had been unremitting. Night after night he sat up, working his way through barricades of red boxes until two in the morning, his only respite an occasional day off spent searching through muniments at Kedleston, inspecting the moat at Bodiam, or trying to mend one of Grace's monthly quarrels at Hackwood. Informing the Cabinet he could go to France in September, he insisted on taking his pre-arranged holiday at Kedleston beforehand.

Unfortunately, the vacation was not a great success. As always, the prospects of Kedleston pleased him – but almost everything human annoyed. The chef's meals were so awful that he sent them back uneaten: 'Had I the spirit for a row', he told Grace, 'I would have sacked him on the spot.' Then the sermons in the church were too long, the parson repeating 'with his own idiotic comments' what Curzon had just read in the First Lesson. And furthermore the footmen had become impossible, spending their time seducing girls, rowing on the lake and handing in their notice in impertinent letters written on Grace's coroneted paper. 'Really,' he grumbled, 'the modern footman is a puzzler.'[8]

Nor was his family much less irksome. He recognized that Grace was doing the 'dutiful thing' by visiting her sick brother in St Moritz. But he was disappointed that she wrote so seldom and chose to linger in Paris on the way back rather than spend a few days with him at Kedleston. Meanwhile he looked after her sons, Alfred and Hubert, took them out shooting and showed them how to fish. Their little sister Marcella, whom Curzon adored, recalled her step-father's 'angelic patience' with her brothers, who broke his fishing rods and brought out some old cannons which they loaded on the lawn. He was less patient with his own children. Irene was 'careering about somewhere', he moaned, without even leaving him an address; in recent years she had seldom been able to see her father without quarrelling over her inheritance, and they rarely saw each other. Cimmie and Baba went to Kedleston with their father but hardly spoke and managed to give the impression they were doing him a great favour simply by being there. 'They do nothing', Curzon complained to Grace, 'but read novels and occasionally knit, and when I hint that life contains things more serious they get very angry and Cim says she reads Plato's *Republic* upstairs! Oh dear, I am not a great success with my children.' After they had gone, he admitted he had no idea how to deal with the 'modern girl'.[9] She seemed as much of a puzzler as the modern footman.

During his disappointing holiday, Curzon had plenty of time to reflect on the 'unsatisfactory and almost humiliating' situation in which he found himself at the Foreign Office. 'I am heartily sick', he told Grace, 'of this indeterminate position possessing full powers in one set of things but powerless in others, pursuing a definite policy here which may be thrown over any day in Paris.'[10] Fortunately, however, Balfour was now tired of being Foreign Secretary. Talking to one of Lloyd George's aides in July, he had suggested he might become Lord President and Curzon Foreign Secretary.[11] But it was an exchange of titles rather than a reciprocal trading of roles which Balfour envisaged: eager though he was to relinquish his work to Curzon, he had no desire to be encumbered by the Lord President's duties. On the eve of his seventy-first birthday, fourteen years after holding office as Prime Minister, A.J.B. aspired, quite appropriately, to the role of elder statesman.

In early September Curzon broke his holiday at Kedleston to meet Balfour on his way up to Scotland. At Victoria Station he found the Foreign Secretary looking 'very white in the head, clad in the most dilapidated of suits, but in tremendous spirits, calling everyone "old man" and beaming all round'. Taken off to dinner by Curzon, Balfour declared over a bottle of champagne that he would not return to the Foreign Office and wanted to resign before the Turkish treaty was negotiated.[12] Curzon's elation at the news evaporated, however, when the resignation was delayed at the request of the Prime Minister. A month later, after agonizing back pains had sent him to bed for a fortnight, he wrote to Balfour about his 'very delicate and ambiguous' position that was open to 'natural misinterpretation' by the public. As an incentive to resignation, he naïvely offered his old friend the leadership of the Lords, admitting that the burden of combining this position – 'with Jim Salisbury and Co incessantly on the war path' – and the Foreign Office in the conditions of 1919 was beyond the strength of a single man. Balfour found the bait unappealing. 'I cannot imagine', he replied fastidiously, 'a position less congenial to my tastes'.[13] But later in

October Lloyd George formed a new and much larger Cabinet in which the posts – though not the labour – were finally exchanged.

Curzon's succession was widely welcomed. 'Oh Lord how long it has taken,' sighed Sir Henry Wilson, who had succeeded Robertson as Chief of the Imperial General Staff.[14] Inside the Foreign Office the appointment was almost universally applauded except by Hardinge, its head, who never forgave Curzon for criticizing his viceroyalty. Crawford, whose brother was a senior diplomat, noted that its officials could not 'speak too highly of his tremendous industry and his scrupulous attention to every branch of the work'.[15] They knew they would have a more difficult time: in place of Balfour's 'slim nonchalance', wrote Robert Vansittart, a future head of the Office, 'a weighty figure sat like impatience on a monument, ready to pounce on our frailties'.[16] But they were prepared to tolerate extra work and criticism from a minister who could take decisions and control foreign policy. Nobody then realized that the cause of Foreign Office independence from Lloyd George was almost irretrievable, nor that the new Foreign Secretary, for the only time in his life, was serving someone he could seldom stand up to.

Curzon's five years at the Foreign Office left a bewildering range of impressions upon his officials. Gregory, who wrote a most perceptive portrait of his chief, did not attempt to explain the contradictions. Curzon was 'universally called pompous', he wrote, yet possessed 'the most intense sense of humour'. He suffered 'from absurd megalomania in regard to his knowledge of art, his worldly possessions and his social position', yet also displayed a 'humility about people and things which was almost pathetic'.

> I have seen him so hysterical that I have felt that he must go clean off his head at any moment; and I have seen him so sane and so balanced under the greatest provocation that I have felt that no one could compete with him in sanity and clarity of vision. I have seen him simple and unassuming in his manner, as jolly as a schoolboy and entirely unaffected; and I have seen him so theatrical that I have wondered whether he had not mistaken his vocation . . .[17]

Gregory realized that the Foreign Secretary's irritability – which surpassed anything he had 'ever experienced in the male sex' – was caused by pain and overwork. Lloyd George once remarked that Curzon's notes to him were always headed 'Carlton House Terrace 1 a.m.' and added, 'I never believe him of course.'[18] He was quite wrong; other correspondents received letters written as late as 2.45. For his part, Curzon was astonished by the working habits of a Prime Minister who seldom answered his letters, who spent his mornings either in meetings or 'closeted with cronies such as Churchill', and who had time for an afternoon sleep.[19] His own day was divided between Cabinet and committees in the mornings, interviews with foreign ambassadors in the afternoons, attendance at the House of Lords later on, occasional speeches at dinners after that, and then letters and 'the ceaseless stream of boxes, each pregnant with a crisis till 3 a.m.'[20]

Curzon resented the fact that his subordinates worked shorter hours than their chief, and complained when a junior official enjoyed a lot of 'social relaxation' while he was meant to be 'performing his duties'.[21] He also grumbled about their lack of initiative. Forgetting what he used to say about the ICS, he told Grace it was all very different from India where he had been 'magnificently served'.[22] On one occasion he decided not to answer a telegram from Washington with the 'rather malevolent object' of seeing how long it would take for the department to draft an official reply; after two days had elapsed without a sign, he did so himself.[23] At night the shortcomings of his officials seemed particularly glaring, and at his desk in Carlton House Terrace his blue pencil raced over their drafts, spraying the margins with comments such as 'I am not aware of it' or 'This is news to me'.

Curzon's unpredictability was notorious. 'He abused us like pickpockets one day', said Gregory, 'and wrote us ecstatic letters of appreciation the next.'[24] Sir Clement Jones, who worked in the Cabinet secretariat, recalled that he never knew which Curzon he was going to meet, the 'exacting boss' or the 'kind master who thought about the home life and holidays of his secretaries'.[25] One Private Secretary learnt to recognize his master's moods by his form of address, 'Mr Nicolson' increasing in geniality through 'Nicolson' to 'my dear Harold'.[26] Tongue-tied lesser staff tried to avoid direct communication and fled one day when the Foreign Secretary, imperiously commandeering the primitive lift, ended up in the Foreign Office basement. Yet he gave the messengers a party to celebrate his birthday at the Cheshire Cheese in the Strand, and he 'sat back and rocked with laughter' when a typist told him that a dictated sentence 'wasn't grammar'.[27] When Nicolson dared to say that the staff were frightened of him, he was genuinely distressed by the information.[28]

Despite Curzon's formidable defects as a chief, several subordinates admitted in their memoirs that they 'enjoyed' his regime and even 'got on very well with him'.[29] He might grumble about their leisurely ways but he interested himself in their lives outside the Office. Although not an habitual reader of novels, he read those of Nicolson's wife, Vita Sackville-West, and enthused about them. *Grey Wethers* was 'a magnificent book', he told her husband. 'The descriptions of the downs are as fine as any in the language. Such power! Such power! Not a pleasant book of course! But what English!'[30] Another Private Secretary, Vansittart, was very grateful to Curzon for the sensitivity shown towards the problems of his private life; he was given extra leave during his future wife's divorce proceedings against her first husband and during her frequent bouts of ill health later. 'Nobody was more delightful when he wished,' recalled Vansittart; 'he could charm birds from the bough, though he more often scared them into the air.'[31]

Curzon's strictures on his subordinates were exaggerated. He was one of those people who complain when anyone – a friend, a daughter, a valet, an under-secretary – behaves not quite as he thinks that he himself would have done. Duff Cooper and other junior officials might have led elaborate social lives, but they were clever men with distinguished careers ahead of them. And their seniors, as he well knew, were of proven calibre. He might scold Sir Eyre Crowe, Hardinge's successor as Permanent Under-Secretary, and make his life a misery with nocturnal telephone calls, but he strongly defended his performance against the criticisms of Lloyd George.[32]

In a similar category were the principal ambassadors, several of them appointed by Curzon despite their personal or political hostility to himself. He offered the Washington embassy both to Salisbury, his main antagonist in the Lords, and to Crewe, the leader of Asquith's Liberals in the Upper Chamber. Crewe later accepted the embassy in Paris, where he succeeded Hardinge, whose resentment of Curzon had not been quenched by his appointment. With these and other ambassadors Curzon worked extremely well. He did not much like Hardinge or his predecessor Derby, but he thought them capable diplomats with whom he was generally in agreement. Only at a personal level, when the Foreign Secretary was a guest at the Paris embassy, did problems arise. Derby was a 'very testy fellow', thought Curzon, and showed little pleasure in his company, while Hardinge protested at his late arrival at meals. Hardinge's main complaint, however, was Curzon's habit of summoning him for advice just after he had arrived in Monte Carlo for a holiday. He was not the only diplomat whose vacation plans proved inconvenient to his chief. 'Whenever a crisis occurs,' Curzon once grumbled, 'our Ambassadors always seem to be shooting or holidaying.'[33]

While the Foreign Secretary spent most of his life trying to sort out the post-war problems of the globe, he was not spared trivial but time-consuming duties as well. As Lord President he had had to handle such questions as whether peers should wear robes for the opening of Parliament in wartime. And as Leader of the Lords (which he remained throughout his years at the Foreign Office) he was required to compose – at a time when he was ill and in the middle of a diplomatic crisis over Greece – an immense memorandum on the order of precedence between the Lord Steward of the Household and the Lord Chamberlain, a tedious task made irritating by the King's failure to thank him for his labours.[34] From the Foreign Office Curzon had to handle such inter-monarchical matters as the King of Spain's grievance that he had not been invited to shoot grouse at Balmoral.[35] And from a sense of duty he told his sovereign the 'filthy' tale of the King of Siam who, 'addicted to unnatural vice', intended to procure an heir by 'conniving at immoral relations between his betrothed and one of his favourites'. King George, who thought exposed homosexuals ought to shoot themselves, was appalled. 'What a disgusting story!' he replied. 'How could any decent person talk to him again?'[36]

The Foreign Secretary no longer dominated the Government side in the Lords. On the Woolsack the Coalition now had another powerful orator in Lord Birkenhead (the former F.E. Smith), whom Curzon admired as a politician but did not like as a man. Together they confronted the official Liberal Opposition, mildly led by Crewe and Buckmaster, and the unofficial Diehard group, vehemently marshalled by Salisbury and Midleton, who criticized the Coalition at almost every opportunity. In July 1920 the Diehards attacked the Government for its treatment of General Dyer, the officer responsible for the massacre of more than 300 Indians at Amritsar the year before. Worried about the deplorable effect of a pro-Dyer vote on India, Curzon urged Crewe to persuade Liberal peers to vote for the Government; but although he, Milner and Birkenhead all made powerful speeches, the Diehards won by a comfortable margin. The following year an impassioned assault was made on the Government's Irish Treaty during which Carson made venomous attacks on both Curzon and Birkenhead in a speech regarded by the Foreign Secretary as 'an outrage on every convention of the House and on decency, the speech of a prosecuting counsel at the Old Bailey'.[37] After a fine rejoinder by Birkenhead, however, the Government was victorious.

Although the Lord Chancellor came to be loathed by the Diehards for his role in negotiating the Irish Treaty, he had been a more popular figure in the House than Curzon. The peers liked his speeches, observed Crawford, because they combined learning with banter, while the Foreign Secretary was too didactic and expository.[38] Curzon's orations were always forceful and well-argued, but they were too long and too lofty and they helped earn him the nickname 'the All-Highest'. Another contributory factor to a title that cannot be regarded as entirely unmerited was his graciousness with people he did not know well. Once, when trying to persuade a junior colleague to accept an appointment, he had flattered him while at the same time managing 'to give the impression that he was considering the engagement of a second footman'.[39] Although some people could laugh this sort of thing off as being 'Curzonish', others resented it. After inviting the Duke of Abercorn and Lord Gorell to propose and second the Address from the throne, Curzon summoned them to Carlton House Terrace and lectured them as if they were a public meeting. 'He assumed', recalled Gorell, 'that neither of us had ever read a paper in our lives and were, in consequence, completely ignorant of everything that then constituted public affairs.' He took them through the King's speech paragraph by paragraph, telling them how Abercorn was to commend such and such a section and his companion the next. Gorell thought the performance extremely funny, but the Duke was furious. 'He talked to us', he expostulated afterwards, 'as though we were a couple of schoolboys.'[40]

Similar characteristics irritated his colleagues in the Cabinet. He tended to quote recondite precedents, recorded Nicolson, who heard it from the Liberal minister H.A.L. Fisher, 'and summarise with astonishing mastery the elements as well as the antecedents of the problem before him'. But when asked what action should be taken, he would sometimes lean back in his chair, 'petulantly disconcerted, and gaze with injured indignation at the realist who had dared to advance so material an enquiry'.[41] When talking about some part of Asia, he had an annoying way of observing that he was probably the only minister who had ever been there; once, during a discussion on Persia, he cleared his throat and began, 'You may not be aware . . .' only to be interrupted by Balfour who said, 'It's all right George, we all know you have written a monumental work on Persia.'[42] Another irritating habit was his unpunctuality. Impatient ministers were waiting for him before one Cabinet meeting when a servant entered with the green baize footstool that now accompanied him everywhere. 'Lord Curzon has not yet arrived,' remarked Derby, who returned to the Government in 1922, 'but we see premonitory symptoms.' And he rose and bowed to the footstool.[43]

Such traits, and the resentment they caused, help to explain one puzzled entry in Lord Crawford's diary which in its turn illuminates the crucial human defects in this extraordinary politician.

The more I see of GC the more am I amazed at his versatility and his self-confidence. As a brain I put him as high as any living politician of my acquaintance – above Balfour, Ll G, Asquith – but somehow he doesn't 'cut ice' as the Americans say. His influence is far smaller than his profound knowledge and experience could justify. It is partly a question of manner – somewhat professorial and challenging, partly also because of his assurance which seems to provoke opposition. Why it should do so I can't surmise for his decision and resource are quite palpable in whatever clothing they may be clad.[44]

33

Middle Eastern Scrambles, 1919–1922

———◆———

THE NATURE AND conduct of foreign affairs have never changed more drastically than in the aftermath of the First World War. In any age George Curzon would have laboured at their problems until far into the night, writing to ambassadors, ploughing through his boxes, correcting the drafts of officials. But in 1919 even a fourteen-hour day was insufficient to deal more than cursorily with dozens of different problems. A quarter of a century earlier, when representing the Foreign Office in the House of Commons, he had had the leisure to work on several schemes for the abolition of slavery in Zanzibar. Now he barely had time even to consider matters of much greater urgency.

Post-war diplomacy was not merely a case of making peace treaties with the defeated powers. Most borders of Europe and many in Asia and Africa had to be redrawn; the disintegration of four great empires had to be overseen; and in the new nations the principle of self-determination was supposed, as far as possible, to be upheld. In the Middle East Britain had to try to reconcile competing promises to the French, the Arabs and the Zionists; in the old Tsarist domains she had to decide her position on the Bolshevik regime and the new independent republics of the Caucasus. Yet other issues could not be ignored while these matters were debated because, as Curzon pointed out, 'every place is a storm-centre, and our representative there a pivot'.[1] Old methods of business, suitable for a more confident imperial age, were no longer adequate for a crisis. Britain's rebuff to a delegation of Egyptian nationalists, who did not seem to be a priority in the weeks after the end of the war, led immediately to a political crisis in Cairo, rioting in the rest of Egypt, and the murder of several British soldiers. Accustomed by training and temperament to making decisions after exhaustive deliberation, Curzon hated having to improvise policies for situations that changed daily. Brought up under the patient and unostentatious regime of Lord Salisbury, he also deprecated the parade of showy conferences at which Lloyd George and other European leaders liked to exhibit themselves.

The divisions of labour, geographical and otherwise, between a Foreign Secretary with great Asian experience and a Prime Minister who had achieved the status of international statesman were not as unsatisfactory as is often supposed. In the post-war years there were too many issues for any Foreign Secretary to handle, even if he ignored vast areas of the planet such as South America, whose countries Curzon found 'undistinguished and undistinguishable, even in their vices'.[2] Furthermore, the major foreign problems of 1919 and 1920 could not be solved simply by diplomatic negotiation; they were the crucial issues of the time and required the close involvement of national leaders. It was logical that a Prime Minister who had waged the greatest war in history should also make the peace. In the first half of 1919, before Curzon became Foreign Secretary, Lloyd George had negotiated the Treaty of Versailles which imposed various conditions of territorial surrender and financial reparation on a defeated Germany. Afterwards Europe remained naturally in the Prime Minister's orbit, as indeed did Russia, for the Government's policy towards the Bolshevik regime was not a mere question for the Foreign Office. Had he restricted his interests to these areas and allowed Curzon to deal with the rest, Lloyd George might have established a better working relationship with his Foreign Secretary. But although he let him pursue his own policies in parts of the Near and Middle East, the Prime Minister insisted on retaining control of the region's most crucial issue, the peace settlement with Turkey. It was a mistake which ultimately cost him his office.

The war so upset patterns of diplomatic thinking that at its end British ministers found themselves in hopeless disagreement over areas where it had never been thought necessary to have a policy before. One such region was the Caucasus, visited by Curzon in 1888 and 1889 but of limited interest to his colleagues. Russia's defeat had resulted in the creation of three republics there – Georgia, Armenia and Azerbaijan – all of them vulnerable to the eastern ambitions of both Turkey and Germany. In the summer of 1918 Britain sent a small force to Baku on the Caspian to train its inhabitants to resist outside threats, but their unwillingness to defend themselves soon led to its withdrawal. The defeat of Turkey and Germany subsequently created a vacuum which Curzon was eager to fill with British troops. Arguing in October 1918 that they should be sent to protect the republics, he was surprised and disgusted to find that none of the Cabinet 'cared a damn' about the Caucasus; Lloyd George in particular, he later complained, seemed to have a 'peculiar grudge' against the area.[3] Curzon was exasperated by the Cabinet's failure to perceive what to him seemed obvious – that it was in British Indian interests to help build a buffer of friendly states before Russia, in whatever form, revived.

Some of his colleagues regarded Curzon's Caucasian interest as a product of his vanity, an excuse to demonstrate his knowledge of the area and to show them how to pronounce its names. More seriously, Balfour argued that 'the gateways of India' were always 'getting further and further from India' and that Britain should not take on fresh responsibilities in so distant a region. Dismissing Curzon's view that a Great Power should give the Caucasians 'a chance of standing on their own feet', he suggested they should be allowed to misgovern themselves and, if they wished, to cut each other's throats.[4] Although some troops did return at the end of the war to hold the Baku-Batoum railway from the Caspian to the Black Sea, almost every minister except Curzon wanted them withdrawn as soon as possible.

Curzon's most powerful opponent over the Caucasus was Churchill, who took charge of the War Office in January 1919. The new Secretary of State set out to reduce Britain's military expenditure everywhere except Russia, where he was prepared to spend whatever might be necessary to destroy the Bolshevik regime. If troops and money were available, he believed they should be used not to protect Persia or the Caucasus but to oppose 'the most horrible tyranny and brutality the world had ever seen'.[5] Curzon disagreed. His hatred for the Bolsheviks was almost as great as Churchill's, but his affection for the White Russians was very much less. He was not eager to spend millions to help General Anton Denikin overthrow the Bolsheviks when he suspected that, if triumphant, Denikin would simply return south, gobble up the Caucasian republics and renew the perennial Russian threat against the Indian empire. In June 1919, however, he was overruled by a Cabinet decision to withdraw the troops from the Caucasus and to increase aid to Denikin.

Curzon's Caucasian views were an adjunct of his policy on Persia, where Britain was now spending some £30 million annually to prevent the disintegration of a country over which motley forces from Turkey, Russia, Britain and Germany had recently been fighting. At the end of the war only the British remained, divided between two small units in the north and north-east, a few garrisons of Indian troops in the Gulf, and a native force under British officers called the South Persia Rifles. In these conditions Curzon saw the chance of making an Anglo-Persian treaty which would lead to the regeneration, under British tutelage, of a country he had long regarded as one of his special preserves. An Anglophile Prime Minister, Vossugh-ed-Dowleh,* governed in Tehran, where Sir Percy Cox, the former Viceroy's protégé from Muscat, was now head of the Legation. Curzon was confident that negotiations between the two of them, directed by himself from London, would lead to a diplomatic triumph so long as the Cabinet did not interfere and British troops remained in position.

The goodwill of the young Persian ruler, Ahmad Shah, had been bought the year before with a monthly subsidy of 15,000 tomans,** conditional on the appointment of Vossugh and subsequent support for him. His backing for an agreement, Cox reported in April 1919, would be only slightly more expensive. But it was a costlier operation to secure the services of the three key ministers, Vossugh himself and two Qajar princes, Firouz Mirza and Akbar Mirza. This group, known to the British as 'the triumvirate', demanded the immense sum of 500,000 tomans 'paid down and no questions asked' so they could 'square' the rest of the Cabinet, the newspapers and the Persian national assembly, the Majliss.[6] They also insisted on guarantees of asylum and assurances that they would not suffer financially if events turned out badly and forced them into exile. Curzon, who had offered the triumvirate £20,000 from Secret Service funds, thought the demands not 'merely exorbitant' but 'corrupt'. Yet he was so eager for an agreement that, in spite of his 'intense dislike for this phase of the transaction', he told Cox to secure a deal. Eventually the ministers accepted 400,000 tomans, a figure which Curzon stressed should be regarded as an advance on the official £2 million loan to be offered to the Government in Tehran.[7]

In the Anglo-Persian Agreement, signed on 9 August 1919, Britain

---

*Nowadays he is referred to as Wot̲ūq-al-Dawla. But as transliterative fashions in Persian and Arabic change fairly often, the English spellings of the time have generally been used here.

**£1 was worth just over 2½ tomans.

undertook to respect the integrity and independence of Persia, and to supply, apart from the loan, military equipment, assistance in railway construction, and advisers for the Government and the armed forces. The Agreement, Curzon told his colleagues, was in the interests of both countries. Persia had not been left 'to rot into picturesque decay' because Britain could not permit, on her Indian frontiers, the existence of a 'hotbed of misrule, enemy intrigue, financial chaos and political disorder'; such a situation would have led inevitably to Bolshevik intervention and a threat to the oil fields on which the Royal Navy depended. As for Persia, she had been freed from 'the reign of foreign intrigue' and, 'if she plays the game', had her best chance of recuperation for a century.[8]

The foreign press, particularly in France, protested that Persia's independence was now merely nominal; and even the *Manchester Guardian* admitted that, had the treaty been made by any other power, the paper would have said it 'amounted to a veiled protectorate'.[9] Curzon denied that it amounted to anything of the kind: Persia, he insisted, would lose no liberties, and Britain would gain no obligations. The Aga Khan, he told a sceptical Grey, regarded the Agreement as 'a model of what such a treaty should be, and as marking a definite stage in the resuscitation of Moslem influence in Central Asia'.[10] To Grace he crowed that it was 'a great triumph' which he had achieved 'all alone'. The newspapers, he added, had given the treaty 'a very good reception', but none, unfortunately, had mentioned his name or seemed to have 'the dimmest perception' that without him at the FO, it would never have been made.[11]

Believing that British policy was almost invariably beneficial to backward peoples, Curzon was astonished whenever the British turned out to be unpopular. He did not understand that the advisers might be resented by Persian nationalists or that the British could conceivably be regarded as more of a threat than the Bolsheviks. The Persians may be the most credulous of conspiracy theorists, but Britain – then and since – has provided them with much evidence for their beliefs. An agreement negotiated secretly with three pro-British ministers was bound to be unpopular, especially when it was rumoured, widely and correctly, that they had received 'baksheesh' through the British-run Imperial Bank of Persia.* Exaggerated though it was, the view that Britain was trying to colonize Persia 'under the guise of magnanimity' was not entirely unreasonable.[13]

---

*In February 1920 Prince Akbar Mirza tried to persuade the chief manager to make false entries in the Bank's books to disguise the bribes.[12]

Curzon did not understand how Persia had changed in the thirty years since he had ridden round the country, and he failed to sense the strong currents of nationalism. But he did realize that the Persians were unlikely to back a treaty if they could see Britain withdrawing her forces from the region. The Agreement had been negotiated at a time when British troops were still in the Caucasus and northern Persia, when a British flotilla patrolled the Caspian, and when Denikin seemed about to overthrow the Bolshevik regime. But the situation in central Asia was transformed by Denikin's collapse at the end of 1919. Unlike Churchill, Curzon did not believe that this development destroyed Britain's position in the area and in May of the following year he persuaded the Cabinet to delay withdrawal from Batoum in the Caucasus and from the Persian port of Enzeli on the Caspian. It was an unfortunate decision; two weeks later a Bolshevik force surprised the small British garrison at Enzeli and captured it.

In spite of this setback, Curzon continued to urge the retention of British forces in northern Persia. But the Cabinet now sided with Churchill who, disgusted that he had not received sufficient support for his pro-Denikin policy, had little sympathy with the failure of Curzon's schemes for the Caucasus and Persia. On 21 May the Cabinet decided to withdraw British troops from both Batoum and northern Persia, a decision which, according to Sir Percy Loraine, Minister in Tehran from 1921, 'shattered the Persians' belief in the will and the power of England to protect' them.[14] Curzon anticipated the disastrous effect this move would have on his Agreement and blamed Lloyd George and Churchill for being 'utterly indifferent to Persia' and for 'destroying the work of a century'. British troops were successively withdrawn from Tabriz, Khorasan and areas further south, until only 'a few necessary sepoys' were left at Bushire. 'No policy', he told Loraine, 'could have withstood the shock of such continuous withdrawals.'[15]

Apart from reproaching his colleagues, Curzon also blamed Herman Norman, who took over from Cox in June 1920 and spent sixteen unhappy months in charge of the Legation. Unable to perceive the change of mood in Tehran, Curzon could not see why a pro-British Government did not summon the Majliss to ratify the Agreement. Although Norman warned that Britain, Vossugh and the Agreement were all equally unpopular, he tried to persuade successive ministries, the composition of which he himself largely determined, to proceed with ratification. Early in 1921 he gave up, telling Curzon that even Britain's friends were unanimous in urging the repudiation of the

Agreement; a large group of well-disposed deputies, he added, now opposed it in order to rebut allegations that their original support had been bought.

Curzon refused to co-operate. Believing that Norman had managed 'utterly to misconceive the whole position', he decided to write him 'a much franker and more explicit' reply than the one suggested by his officials. His Majesty's Government, he declared, had not 'the slightest intention of denouncing the agreement and of accepting thereby the responsibility for a proceeding the blame for which must rest exclusively upon Persian shoulders'. If Persia rejected the means of her 'salvation', it must be her deed not Britain's, and she must extricate herself in her own way. Personally, he added in a bitter minute the following day, he would 'never propose another agreement with the Persians. Not unless they came on their knees would I consider any application from them, and probably not then.' In future Britain would look after her own interests in Persia, not those of the natives.[16]

A *coup d'état* in Tehran, carried out in February 1921 by an army officer, Reza Khan, brought to power a Government which quickly denounced the Agreement. Although the coup was carried out with the approval of British officers in Persia, and although the new Prime Minister was himself pro-British, Curzon rejected Norman's appeals for assistance to the new regime. 'I have not the slightest feeling', he said, 'for a Government which simultaneously denounces and fawns.'[17] Britain's position in Persia, he later wrote, was 'one of peculiar humiliation'. But he felt the humiliation more for himself than for his country. He had, he colourfully claimed, 'devoted more years of labour in the last 35 years to the cause of Persian integrity and freedom than most other people have devoted days or hours'. And the sole result of his labour was the 'complete collapse of British prestige and influence' in Persia.[18]

In May 1922, laid out by his bad back at Hackwood, Curzon wrote to Loraine about his defeat in Persia. Laboriously he catalogued the reasons, the incompetence of Norman, the indifference of the British Cabinet, the influence of Bolshevik propaganda. One can picture him in bed, scribbling away with increasing anger as he lists the failings of the Persians, the hostility of the Majliss, 'the desperate and colossal incapacity of the Shah', the 'incomparable, incurable and inconceivable rottenness of Persian politicians'.[19] There may have been truth in these charges, yet the list remains incomplete. Persian nationalism, for example, is omitted because he did not understand a phenomenon he had not come across in the bazaars of Isfahan or the pages of *Hajji*

Baba. But the crucial point was his miscalculation of British strength. The Russian and Turkish empires might have gone, but Britain had neither the power nor the wealth to dominate all the areas they had left. Caucasian escapades were all very well for *Greenmantle* and those obscure heroes of the Great Game, but they were not a realistic policy for an island whose new imperial responsibilities were already too great for its resources.

Curzon's personal and almost unfettered diplomacy was confined to Persia. In the rest of the Middle East Britain's post-war policy was shaped by several people, including Lloyd George and Balfour at the Paris Conference, Montagu at the India Office (which was responsible for Mesopotamia) and Churchill at the War Office, which controlled large numbers of British troops occupying former areas of the Ottoman Empire. It would have been difficult under any conditions to formulate a coherent policy from such diverse sources; it became impossible when the contradictions of Britain's wartime pledges had to be faced at the same time.

Curzon, who had opposed the giving of all pledges, was particularly scornful of the Sykes-Picot Agreement intended to divide the Arab territories north of Arabia into extensive spheres of French and British influence and smaller zones of direct imperial control. At the Eastern Committee in December 1918 he described it as 'a sort of fancy sketch to suit a situation that had not then arisen': that, he assumed, must be 'the principal explanation of the gross ignorance' with which the boundaries had been drawn, divisions so 'fantastic and incredible' that they would lead to incessant friction between the French, the British and the Arabs. Balfour replied that the Agreement was a signed commitment which could not be broken, a view in tune with a secret deal made a few days earlier between Lloyd George and Clemenceau. Far from wishing to scrap it, the British premier was keen to extend the Sykes-Picot Agreement by adding to the areas allotted to Britain: in particular he wanted Mosul, which had been placed in the French sphere of influence, and Palestine, most of which had been designated as an international zone. In exchange he told his Paris counterpart that Britain would not oppose a French administration either along the Syrian littoral or in the interior, an area which the McMahon letters had reserved for an Arab state.[20]

The schemes of Lloyd George and Clemenceau were threatened by

President Wilson's plan to send out an international commission to consult the inhabitants before their territories were distributed between the two powers. Curzon was one of the few European statesmen who saw any merit in the plan, for he thought a commission might extricate Britain from Palestine where her position, he believed, would soon become untenable. But he knew the proposal would be unacceptable because France was so unpopular (except in Mount Lebanon) that no commission could recommend a French mandate over Syria without ignoring all evidence presented to it.[21] In the event an American commission went out by itself, found that the feeling of the Arabs was 'particularly strong against the French' and recommended that the unity of Greater Syria should be preserved: sectarian differences would be intensified, it correctly predicted, by the creation of separate states in Palestine and Lebanon.[22] To the relief of the Governments of Britain and France, the commission's report was not made public for three years.

In the course of 1919 Britain's leaders realized they would have to take sides over Syria. Against Curzon's advice, Lloyd George and Balfour preferred to quarrel with the Arabs rather than with France, and they did not insist that the Emir Feisal, Britain's candidate selected by T.E. Lawrence, should be King of an independent Syria. Withdrawing its troops in November 1919, the Government left the contestants to sort it out, and in the conflict between French colonialism and Arab nationalism the conciliatory Feisal was an inevitable loser. The British were deeply embarrassed by his fate, especially Balfour who felt personally responsible,[23] but they did find some means of compensation. In 1921 Feisal was offered the throne of Iraq (Mesopotamia), a country which, after a rebellion in 1920, turned out to be one of Britain's more successful Middle Eastern ventures.

Disheartened by events in Syria, Curzon was even more dismayed by developments in Palestine, which since General Allenby's conquest in 1918 had been under British military administration. Encouraged by the Balfour Declaration, Zionist leaders were now calling for a 'Jewish commonwealth', an ambition Curzon felt sure would lead to clashes with the Arabs. In January 1919 he communicated these anxieties to Balfour who replied that Weizmann had never asked for a 'Jewish *Government* in Palestine' and that he himself would regard such a claim as 'inadmissible'. Turning to his dictionaries, Curzon decided that the then Foreign Secretary was quibbling over the difference between 'commonwealth' and 'government'.

I feel tolerably sure . . . that while Weizmann may say one thing to you, or while you may mean one thing by a national home, he is out for something quite different. He contemplates a Jewish state, a Jewish nation, a subordinate population of Arabs etc. ruled by Jews; the Jews in possession of the fat of the land, and directing the Administration.

He is trying to effect this behind the screen and under the shelter of British trusteeship.[24]

While Curzon was aware that Weizmann said one thing to his friends but sang to 'a different tune in public', he did not know that the Foreign Secretary was pursuing a similar tactic with himself. Although Balfour told him then that a Jewish government was inadmissible, he had confessed to a Zionist sympathizer the year before that he hoped for a Jewish state and, at a meeting with Churchill and Weizmann in 1922, he and Lloyd George admitted that the Balfour Declaration 'had always meant a Jewish State'.[25] Convinced by long acquaintance that Balfour did not really care about anything, Curzon never appreciated the strength of his attachment to Zionism. He believed that the driving force behind this particular policy was the Prime Minister who, he thought, 'clings to Palestine for its sentimental and traditional value, and talks about Jerusalem with almost the same enthusiasm as about his native hills'.[26]

The future of the Middle East was ordained at the San Remo Conference in April 1920. Until a few days beforehand Curzon was laid out with back aches, but he recovered in time to be present at the opening. An Italian diplomat, Daniele Varè, went to pick him up at the station, but he insisted on walking to the hotel, 'proceeding at a snail's pace in the middle of the road', attracting a large crowd and causing much perturbation among the police who had not expected to supervise what seemed like a procession of the Corpus Domini.[27] Curzon was depressed by the conference and by the town, which he compared to 'a second class English watering place'. He was also exasperated by Grace, who from England showed no interest in what he was doing except to suspect him of having an affair with Lady Beatty, whom he saw once in a crowded dining-room.[28] But the newspaper proprietor Lord Riddell thought he was in good form and found him 'a most complicated and interesting personality – vain but witty, amusing and extremely well-informed'. Curzon was working so hard, he observed, that he had 'nearly killed his secretaries by robbing them of their sleep'.[29]

The French delegation, Curzon told his uninterested wife, were gloomy and sulky and took little part, while the Italians contributed nothing except 'smiles and amiable but often ignorant generalisations'. The conference was dominated by Lloyd George, whose 'fits of impetuosity' took him alternately in right and wrong directions; he was at times 'conciliatory and genial' and at others 'excited, windy [and] ignorant'. The most trying occasions were the official dinners where everyone talked French except Lloyd George who spoke through an interpreter. At least one participant wished Curzon had also stuck to English. The trilingual Varè could translate from French into English or vice versa, but he found it difficult to translate Curzon's French into French.[30]

Several matters were discussed at San Remo, including the question of German reparations. But the crucial questions decided were the settlement with Turkey (which will be discussed in the next chapter) and the future of the liberated Arab territories. After scenes described by President Wilson as 'the whole disgusting scramble' for the Middle East,[31] France and Britain awarded themselves – through the agency of the new League of Nations – the mandates of Syria, Palestine and Mesopotamia. It was not an edifying moment in the history of either imperial power. In discussing populations under a foreign mandate, the Covenant of the League of Nations had declared that 'the well-being and development of such peoples form a sacred trust for civilization'. But the fact that the most advanced peoples of the region were placed under foreign domination while the primitive tribal areas of Arabia were given independence exposes the pretence that the mandates were designed to benefit the inhabitants rather than the powers that administered them. Greed was the predominant impulse and, if altruism was another motive, it did not attenuate the disastrous consequences. Britain's mandate in Palestine led, as Curzon predicted, to Arab-Jewish conflict, while France, in seeking to establish a Christian, pro-French state by separating Lebanon from Syria, created the essential condition for one of the longest and most brutal civil wars of all time.

As Foreign Secretary, Curzon told Allenby, he intended to carry out the Government's policy on Palestine in line with 'the narrower and more prudent rather than the wider interpretation' of the Balfour Declaration.[32] He continued to worry about the rights of the Palestinian Arabs and complained when they, who formed the overwhelming majority of the population, were described in the draft Mandate as a 'non-Jewish community'. He also objected to attempts to go beyond the aspirations of the Declaration in the wording of the Mandate by referring to 'the historical connection of the Jewish people with Palestine and the claim which this gives them to reconstitute Palestine as their National Home'. Although he managed to substitute a much blander phrase about the Jews 'reconstituting their National Home in that country', Curzon remained distrustful of Zionist ambitions and pessimistic about the future of Palestine. He always regarded the Balfour Declaration as 'the worst' of Britain's Middle East commitments and 'a striking contradiction of our publicly declared principles'.[33]

In the immediate aftermath of the war Egypt looked set to become the site of Britain's greatest Middle East disaster. Although Cromer and later Kitchener had been the effective rulers of the country, Egypt was never technically a part of the empire: in theory her Khedive had been the hereditary viceroy of the Ottoman Sultan until December 1914 when a protectorate was declared and he was given the title of Sultan. Yet in the following years Egypt had proved herself a vital element of the imperial system, a country which controlled the lifeline to India and from which Middle Eastern operations could be conducted. No one who believed in the future of the empire wished to abandon control.

Nationalist feeling, demonstrated by the riots of March 1919, was enjoying a powerful revival in Egypt. As the High Commissioner, Sir Reginald Wingate, explained to Curzon, its 'dormant embers' had been fanned by the war and by the much discussed idea of self-determination.[34] Wingate recommended conciliation and, for being too perceptive too soon, duly forfeited his post and was replaced by Allenby. But although Curzon was slow to understand the strength of Egyptian nationalism, he was quicker than most of his colleagues. The Egyptians, he later observed, considered themselves in 'the very front files of civilization' and were naturally unwilling to remain under the Protectorate when their 'more backward brothers' in Arabia were achieving self-government.[35]

At the end of 1919 Lord Milner, the Colonial Secretary, led a mission of enquiry to Egypt and in a subsequent report recommended that the Protectorate should be abolished and replaced by a bilateral treaty between Britain and Egypt. During negotiations in London the following summer, he came to an agreement with Zaghlul Pasha, the leading nationalist politician, which conceded most of the Egyptian case: while Britain's 'special interests' would be safeguarded, notably by a force to protect 'imperial communications', the Protectorate would be scrapped and Egypt recognized as an independent constitutional monarchy. This private agreement went well beyond Milner's instructions, but Curzon did not think it could be repudiated, especially as its terms had already appeared in the Egyptian press. His advice to accept it, however, was rejected by a Cabinet persuaded by Churchill that the Government was not bound by the recommendations of Milner's report.

The Cabinet's decision came in the middle of a lengthy dispute between Curzon and Churchill over control of Britain's Middle East policy. In Curzon's view the area should have had its own department with a secretary of state and an administrative service of its own. But if this solution was ruled out on grounds of expense, he thought it preferable to run the Middle East from the Foreign Office rather than, as Churchill suggested, from a department in the Colonial Office. The War Secretary, he told the Cabinet in June 1920, 'must be very imperfectly acquainted' with the views and interests of the area if he thought his proposal would be popular. 'A lethal blow would be dealt at the pride of Egypt' if the transfer took place, while 'the mandated territories would utter a cry of rage' at the thought of being treated like British colonies. Besides, it would be impossible to formulate coherent policies when adjoining countries (Mesopotamia, Persia and Afghanistan) would be under the respective control of the Colonial Office, the Foreign Office and a combination of the India Office and the FO.[36]

Curzon was backed by the foreign affairs heavyweights, Milner, Chamberlain and Montagu, who deplored any step that might look like the annexation of mandated territory. But they were outvoted in the Cabinet, and at the beginning of 1921 Palestine and Mesopotamia (but not Egypt) were transferred to the Colonial Office, just in time to be administered by the new Secretary of State – W.S.Churchill. Glad to be relieved of the responsibility for implementing the Balfour Declaration, Curzon was nevertheless anxious about the future. Churchill was 'a most dangerous man', he thought, who wanted to grab everything for his new department and become 'a sort of Asiatic foreign secretary'.[37]

In February 1921 Milner urged Curzon to make a settlement with the moderate Egyptian nationalists on the basis of his report. The Foreign Secretary brought the matter up at the Cabinet shortly afterwards and, with the support of Montagu, managed to persuade Lloyd George and his other colleagues to accept in principle the abolition of the Protectorate and a treaty between the two countries. Throughout the year, however, Churchill fought against concessions and irritated Curzon by insisting on holding a Middle East conference in Cairo and by 'stepping boldly' on Foreign Office ground during an indiscreet interview with the Egyptian Sultan. Personal relations improved after the Churchills stayed at Hackwood for the Whitsun recess. Asking afterwards if they could revert to the suspended superscriptions of 'My dear George' and 'My dear Winston', Churchill wrote that the visit 'recalled to my mind memories of the pre-war and even pre-Joe epochs'.[38] But although the private cordiality continued, particularly during the last illness and death of Churchill's mother, their political animosity deepened. At a meeting on Egypt in the autumn, Curzon told Grace, Churchill had been 'difficult and insolent' and was heard muttering that the Foreign Secretary's policy was always wrong.[39]

In June Curzon tackled the Colonial Secretary on his constant unauthorized pronouncements on foreign affairs. Singling out a reference to Egypt, he told Churchill he had caused great annoyance to the nationalists by implying that Egypt was an incorporated part of the British empire. But claiming the right to speak on Egypt in accordance with the Cabinet's views of the previous year, Churchill replied that he was not prepared to sit mutely watching 'the loss of this great and splendid monument of British administrative skill and energy'. Lloyd George thought Curzon was 'undoubtedly right' and told him it was 'most improper and dangerous' for a minister to make pronouncements on questions of foreign policy without consulting the Foreign Secretary. Sending a copy of this letter to Churchill, Curzon added that he could not make an exception in the case of Egypt simply because his correspondent held strong views on the subject. But the Colonial Secretary refused to give in and asked his colleague to remember how 'formidably' affairs in the rest of the Middle East would be affected by the belief that 'we are going to let ourselves be turned out of Egypt'.[40]

At the Imperial Conference in London the following month, Churchill again sounded off on foreign policy, this time denouncing a renewal of the Anglo-Japanese alliance. Curzon appealed by note to the Prime Minister, who sympathized and said he had done his best 'to stopper his fizzing'. Chamberlain agreed with the Foreign Secretary, telling him he was right to show his resentment at Churchill's 'constant and persistent interference'; it went far beyond anything he had ever experienced in a Cabinet. Curzon then sent the miscreant a note asking what he would say if the Foreign Secretary suddenly made a speech on a colonial question. The irrepressible Churchill replied that there was no comparison between vital matters affecting the whole future of the world and the mere departmental topics with which the Colonial Office was concerned. 'In these great matters', he added, 'we must be allowed to have opinions.'[41]

A few days later Curzon embarked on lengthy talks with Adly Pasha, a moderate Egyptian nationalist who was in the uncomfortable position of being Prime Minister under a High Commissioner administering martial law. The problem, as Curzon soon realized, was that Adly could not make concessions without being denounced by the extreme Zaghlul, while he himself could not go far to meet him without upsetting the Cabinet. He was 'trying hard to patch up something with Adly and Co,' he told Hardinge in late October. 'But the Jingoes in the Cabinet, of whom the strongest are the PM and Winston, want to concede nothing and to stamp out rebellion in Egypt by fire and sword.'[42] On the same day he predicted to Grace that the negotiations would lead to nothing. 'The Cabinet are much stiffer than I am in the matter and I am sure we will have an absolute rupture – with another Ireland in Egypt.'[43] Compelled to make conditions which he knew Adly could not accept, Curzon was not surprised that the negotiations merely led to the Egyptian's resignation when he returned home in November.

On an issue where two Tory imperialists, Curzon and Milner, took more liberal positions than the most prominent Liberals, Lloyd George and Churchill, the former proconsuls received the crucial support of Lord Allenby. Convinced that the Milner report offered the only logical solution, the High Commissioner decided to force the issue. While deporting Zaghlul and his associates for inciting further violence, he urged the British Government to give a new ministry a chance of survival by unilaterally declaring the Protectorate at an end and recognizing Egypt as an independent sovereign state. Lloyd George and his Cabinet majority held out until Allenby returned to London and threatened to resign. Then they gave in, the declaration was made – with some reservations about British interests – and in March 1922 Egypt was recognized as an independent monarchy under her Sultan, henceforth known as King Fuad I. The process was watched bitterly by Churchill, who blamed Curzon. 'It leaves me absolutely baffled', he told the Foreign Secretary, 'to comprehend why you should be on this side, or why you should have insisted on keeping Egyptian affairs in your hands only to lead to this melancholy conclusion.'[44]

Curzon knew that it was not a final settlement. Matters concerning the Sudan, the defence of Egypt, the protection of foreign interests and the security of imperial communications – all needed in due course to be solved, and took several decades in the solving. But it did at least unravel one of the most difficult of British entanglements. After misjudging nationalist strength in the spring of 1919, Curzon had soon realized what was and was not possible in Egypt. Had he had his own way, he would have made a settlement based on Milner's report in 1920. But he seldom did get his own way with Lloyd George. In the end this weakness was merely unfortunate for the Egyptians, but for the Greeks it proved disastrous.

34

Lloyd George and the Turks, 1919–1922

THE EXPERIENCE OF San Remo did not increase Curzon's appetite for conferences. He conceded that private chats over cups of tea between sessions could be useful. But they did not compensate for the tedium and the waste of time, the endless exhibitionist speech-making, the disruption of routines of work and of domestic existence. Moreover, he was always the number two, listening while Lloyd George took the stage, agreeing with him in most European discussions, silently deploring his views on Asian matters. They were an incongruous duo, aptly described as 'Impudence and Dignity' when they appeared together at the Spa Conference in 1920.[1] Two years later, after Lloyd George had failed to achieve anything at the Genoa Conference, Curzon hoped that there would be no more of 'these fantastic gatherings which are really only designed as a stage on which he is to perform'.[2]

The Foreign Secretary was not exactly bored by European issues. Nor did the question of German 'reparations' really fill him, as Harold Nicolson alleged, with 'bewildered distress'.[3] But he realized he had no special knowledge of Continental problems and that his views on them did not differ greatly from those of his chief. On the central questions of Europe's future, he was sensitive to France's security needs and a believer in the Entente; yet convinced that the health of Europe depended on the recovery of Germany, he opposed France's 'policy of revenge' against their late enemy. These admirable principles were somewhat dented, however, by the experience of dealing with the two countries. The Germans, he thought, were the stupidest and clumsiest of diplomats, and one could never tell whether they were being 'perfidious or merely perverse' nor whether they were 'actually dishonest or merely dull'. He was also astonished by their hostility towards Britain, which he believed had shown them more consideration than any victorious power had ever done to a vanquished one.[4]

Even if reasonable arrangements could be made between France and Germany, Curzon was pessimistic about the future relationship between the two countries. As early as 1921 he predicted that Germany would recover quicker than the victorious states and create a new problem. 'I suppose one day,' he sighed to his wife, though 'not in our life time – the whole trouble will begin again.'[5] Much younger and healthier than her husband, Grace long outlived the replay.

The Foreign Secretary's difficulties with Germany were minor compared to the trials of dealing on a daily basis with the French. Although he liked and admired Briand, who returned as Prime Minister for a year from January 1921, it often seemed that most other French politicians were trying to do down Britain and himself in particular by leaking confidential documents, negotiating behind his back and inciting the Paris press to abuse him. On going to the Foreign Office in 1919, Curzon believed he had been as keen on the Entente as anyone; two years later he thought it would be 'difficult to find anyone more disgusted'.[6] It was impossible to conduct Allied diplomacy if, whenever the British communicated a suggestion on Greece or Silesia or wherever, the proposal appeared in the *Echo de Paris* the following morning. The French Government, he told Hardinge, did 'not know what reticence or discretion or honour means'. Its ministers were 'simply the slaves and mouthpiece of the Press whom they are bound to feed in order to secure their support'.[7] When Poincaré, a former and future premier, visited London in 1921, Curzon refused to give a dinner in his honour because he could not make a speech eulogizing a man who had constantly maligned him and who had neither explained nor apologized for the publication of confidential British documents.[8]

Curzon's views on a formal Anglo-French alliance were coloured by his experiences with Poincaré. Dismissing Derby's espousal of the cause as a gesture for the nice things said about him in Paris, he thought the disadvantages of the proposal were too great. An alliance, he told the Cabinet, might guarantee peace in Europe for a generation, but France's chauvinistic diplomacy would create additional problems for the empire and the rest of the world. Yet his real objection, he confessed to Hardinge, was that the French could not be trusted. They were 'always after some gain of their own, sometimes political éclat, sometimes financial gain'. The only test of their diplomacy was the advantage to France, 'regardless of loyalty or sincerity or candour'. It was 'inherent in the mentality of the people'.[9]

Most of Curzon's problems with France stemmed from the settlements of the Middle and Near East. Purely European questions were mainly handled, usually without objection from the Foreign Secretary, by Lloyd George himself. Curzon did not mind playing little part in a matter such as Upper Silesia, which 'the little man' was very possessive about and regarded as 'his own pet child'.[10] But he was worried and resentful when his advice was ignored on the Greek-Turkish question.

Wartime pacts between the Allies had arranged the dismemberment not only of the Ottoman empire but also of Turkey herself. From the Sykes-Picot Agreement France was to receive Cilicia and most of eastern Anatolia, while Russia was given the Armenian provinces and a part of Kurdistan; by other secret treaties the Tsarists were also to gain Constantinople and the Straits, and Smyrna and south-western Anatolia were allotted to Italy. Curzon thought these schemes were neither fair nor feasible. It was right, he believed, for the non-Turkish areas to be detached and placed under foreign mandates before eventually achieving independence. And it was also reasonable to take Constantinople, where the Turkish population was a minority, and turn it under international administration into the 'cosmopolis' of the Eastern world; he even hoped that 'Justinian's great Byzantine fane of St Sophia, which was for 900 years a Christian church, and [had] only been for little more than half that period a Mohammedan mosque, would naturally revert to its original dedication'.[11] But to divide the Turkish heartland itself struck him as a crazy plan that would not only be unacceptable to its inhabitants but would also give a dangerous and unnecessary stimulus to 'Moslem passions' throughout the Eastern world.

These points were argued in three memoranda circulated by Curzon to the Cabinet early in 1919. The first dealt with the question of Constantinople, the second warned that delays would make a settlement impossible, and the third inveighed passionately against landing European troops in Asian Turkey. He was particularly scornful of a new suggestion to install the Greeks in Smyrna. While recognizing that for ethnic and historical reasons they had a much better claim than the Italians, he knew they were too weak for the assignment. If the Greeks were unable to keep order five miles outside Salonika, he wondered how they could be expected to rule a large province of Anatolia. But

Curzon's anguish in London made little impact on Balfour and Lloyd George in Paris. Motivated by loathing for the Turks, partisanship for Greece (especially her Prime Minister Venizelos) and, in Lord D'Abernon's words, his 'invincible devotion to what he conceived to be the oppressed',[12] the Prime Minister encouraged the occupation of Smyrna. Landing in the middle of May, Greek forces accomplished the first stage of the new Hellenization with notable brutality.

During the remainder of 1919 Curzon worked hard to overturn this policy. Greece should be rewarded in Thrace, he argued, not Anatolia; Turkey should be punished in Europe not Asia. Before the end of the year he and Philippe Berthelot, a senior French diplomat, devised a scheme along these lines that would retain Turkish sovereignty over Anatolia but not over Constantinople. Clemenceau was convinced by the plan, and so, surprisingly, were Lloyd George and Balfour. But determined opposition to parts of the scheme came from Montagu, who for months had been begging the Prime Minister to leave the Turks in Constantinople. For 500 years, he claimed in June, Sunni Muslims had been praying daily for the health of the Caliph in Constantinople:* if their spiritual leader was now turned out of his city, the Muslims of India would be estranged, probably permanently, from British rule. Three months later, in September, he told Lloyd George that the only ministers who opposed this view were Balfour, who 'cares nothing and knows nothing about the East and loves to be in a minority', and Curzon, who was 'making the mistake, which has haunted him throughout his career, of forming his policy on what people ought to think, not on what they do think'.[13]

While there may have been some justice in Montagu's criticism of his colleagues, he probably exaggerated the extent of Islamic feeling for Constantinople. The city was not Mecca, and India's Muslims were not greatly roused when the Caliphate was abolished by the Turks themselves in 1924. But his views prevailed in the Cabinet where the Curzon-Berthelot scheme was supported only by Balfour, Lloyd George and its author, an unusual trinity of vanquished. In his 'earnest and emphatic dissent' from the decision reached, the Foreign Secretary warned his colleagues that a Turkey largely occupied by foreign powers would

---

*In fact the Ottoman Sultans had only claimed the title of Caliph – Successor to the Messenger of God (i.e. to Muhammad) – from the end of the eighteenth century. Their supposed succession to the Abbasid Caliphate was a myth invented for political reasons at the same time.

cause them 'some surprise'. As Harold Nicolson observed, the surprise took 'the highly inconvenient form' of the Turkish nationalist movement.[14]

Curzon did not give up. Before San Remo he circulated to his colleagues a despatch from the High Commissioner in Constantinople warning that the Greek occupation of Smyrna would drive the Turks into the arms of the Bolsheviks, set the Middle East and central Asia aflame, and lead to generations of bloodshed.[15] When Lloyd George was sailing to San Remo – his sick Foreign Secretary joined him later by rail – Curzon asked him to 'think seriously' about Anatolia and the Greeks. While being 'the last man to wish to do a good turn to the Turks', Curzon said he wanted to achieve 'something like peace' in Asia Minor – an impossible objective if the Greeks were marching about inside it.[16]

His appeals were of no avail. Among other things, the settlement decided at San Remo – and later embodied in the Treaty of Sèvres – turned the Straits into a neutral zone and gave Greece Eastern Thrace, various islands in the Aegean, and control of the Smyrna area for five years, after which the local population would decide its future. As Curzon had predicted, this solution proved completely unacceptable to Turkish public opinion, which abandoned the Sultan in Constantinople and coalesced behind the rebellion of one of the nation's war heroes, Mustapha Kemal, the future Atatürk.

During the following year Curzon tried to prevent the impending conflict by persuading the Greeks that the occupation of Smyrna had been a 'lamentable blunder' and that a new settlement must be made. He found himself in the uncomfortable position of being accused by Montagu of being pro-Greek, by Lloyd George of being pro-Turk, and of being 'freely belaboured by both parties'.[17] But Montagu's criticisms, irritating and untrue though they were, did not matter. The problem was Lloyd George and his excitement over the success of a Greek offensive in the spring and summer of 1921. While Curzon was trying to persuade him that the Greeks could not win and that Britain should mediate between the belligerents, Lloyd George was exulting over the march on Ankara and secretly urging the Greeks to carry on.[18]

Curzon's attempts at a compromise were undermined by a Franco-Turkish agreement in the autumn of 1921. After military defeats inflicted by the nationalists in Cilicia, the French had decided to withdraw from their Turkish venture and recognize the nationalist regime of Mustapha Kemal. The resulting treaty, known after the diplomat who negotiated it as the Franklin-Bouillon Agreement, weakened the position of the Greeks and raised doubts about the future of the Allied forces in the neutral zone around Constantinople. Curzon was incensed that France should make a pact with an enemy without consulting her allies, especially as Briand had assured him that Franklin-Bouillon had not gone to Turkey to negotiate a treaty. But the worst feature of the deal was its disruption of his negotiations with the Greeks who, since their defeat in September at the Battle of Sakarya, had shown more willingness to compromise. Having persuaded them to agree to a withdrawal from Smyrna and accept an autonomous region under Turkish sovereignty, he found the balance of forces altered and the Allied position shattered by 'an act of great treachery'.[19]

A day or two after learning of the treaty, the Foreign Secretary reluctantly attended a dinner in Poincaré's honour at the French embassy. When Crawford asked him the next day how he had enjoyed the evening, Curzon replied that the food had been bad and the wine indifferent, but his main grievance was that for the first twenty-six minutes of the banquet he had been unable to utter a single remark. His hostess had been talking to the guest of honour, while on his left Madame Poincaré had been rivetted by the attentions of the Spanish ambassador, a man, Curzon drily observed, who thought himself 'capable of every gallantry'. The chagrin had been immense. To think, Crawford noted even more drily in his diary, of 'twenty-six minutes of silence inflicted on so bold and so eloquent a conversationist!'[20]

The year 1921 was a demoralizing one for Curzon who in the course of it achieved nothing much more substantial than a marquessate from Lloyd George. His Persian policy collapsed, his Egyptian negotiations went nowhere, his attempts to reach a compromise between Greece and Turkey were unsuccessful; and all the time relations with France and Germany were deteriorating. Although these developments were not really his fault, he was widely blamed for them, particularly by the press, and above all by *The Times*, which attacked him so vehemently for his 'business incapacity' in July that one of its journalists resigned in protest and another went on strike.[21] In April of the following year Crawford noted that the Foreign Secretary seemed 'generally looked upon as a failure'.[22]

Curzon himself was puzzled by his treatment. Apologizing for his 'vain reflections', he wrote a plaintive letter to Grace in September 1921.

I never seem to get any credit for anything nowadays. No one accuses me of any definite errors or blunders of statesmanship. But there seems to be a general tendency to run me down, or completely to ignore what I am doing or have done.

If we look at the record of this in any book of reference it is very substantial, as varied and in a way as successful as that of any statesman of my age living. And yet it does not seem to count for much, and I am treated as rather a back number.

Well perhaps I am. I suppose one gets what one deserves and I daresay the fault lies somewhere in me. Yet, girlie, how I have worked and toiled and never spared myself, while I see others treating work as a jest and life as a holiday.[23]

He was also dispirited by the behaviour of his colleagues, especially Churchill, who disagreed with him on almost every issue, and Montagu, who wrote unpleasant letters even when he was in broad agreement with the Foreign Secretary. Upon receiving one such missive from Montagu about Egyptian nationalism, Curzon replied that he could not write a despatch or draft a telegram without expecting him to find some cause for complaint. On several occasions he asked him how he could reconcile his repeated requests for Curzon's advice on India with 'great asperity of tone and pronounced hostility in Cabinet'. His correspondent sometimes admitted the justice of the grievance, apologized for his loss of temper and shortly afterwards repeated the offence. Montagu's letters, Curzon told their author at New Year 1922, always gave him the impression that everything he did was wrong in his eyes, and he felt 'considerably disheartened' in consequence.[24]

Yet the colleague who caused Curzon most trouble was the Prime Minister. During Balfour's time at the FO, Lloyd George had become accustomed to running his own foreign policies in his own way. Although a statesman and a patriot, he remained at heart an adventurer, fond of intrigue and surreptitious methods, who conducted his diplomacy through a secretariat of clever young men working under his supervision from temporary huts in the garden at Downing Street. Disparaging the Foreign Office and its conventional ways, he tried, as far as possible, to ignore it. Sometimes this was done blatantly, for instance by announcing to the Cabinet, without consulting the Foreign Secretary, that he proposed to send an ambassador to Poland.[25] More often he used intermediaries to negotiate with foreign ambassadors and their governments behind the back of the Foreign Office. Curzon discovered this was going on from intercepted telegrams, from information

Poincaré gave the British ambassador in Paris, and even from one of Lloyd George's own aides. But when challenged on a particular incident, the Prime Minister would simply deny that it had taken place and dismiss whoever suggested otherwise as a notorious liar.[26]

Although pleasant to Curzon in private, Lloyd George was frequently offensive to him in Cabinet. The Foreign Secretary was not the only target – Churchill was a fellow sufferer – but he was the most conspicuous and regular. Chamberlain found these attacks shocking and painful to witness and much admired Curzon's self-control under provocation; had he himself been the victim, he told Law, he would have marched out of the room.[27] Wounded and humiliated by these incidents, Curzon occasionally expostulated by letter and received a friendly apology in reply. But the Prime Minister's contrition was generally short-lived. In April 1921 Curzon told Grace that he was 'getting very tired of working or trying to work with that man': Lloyd George wanted his Foreign Secretary to be a valet or a drudge and had 'no regard for the convenances or civilities of official life'.[28]

Dining alone with Curzon some weeks earlier, Chamberlain had found his companion very depressed, doubtful of his usefulness and influence, and wondering whether there was any point in remaining in the Government. Chamberlain ascribed some of the depression to the impending retirement of Milner, Curzon's closest friend in the Cabinet, but more to the behaviour of Lloyd George, who treated him rudely, criticized his department and paid little attention to his opinions even on foreign affairs. Believing that the Coalition could not survive the resignation of Curzon, Law or himself, Chamberlain tried to combat the depression by assuring the Foreign Secretary of the respect of his colleagues and by telling him it was his duty to stay in office. Chamberlain then sent a report of the dinner to Bonar Law, asking him to show it to the Prime Minister and 'put things right'.[29] The success of this initiative was minimal.

Many people shared Lansdowne's view that there should be 'rather more FO and rather less PM in the salad'.[30] They wanted to see those areas of foreign policy which had been run in recent years from Downing Street removed and restored to their rightful place in the Foreign Office. In March 1921 Vansittart had the temerity to urge his chief to end a state of affairs whereby diplomacy was spasmodically conducted behind the back (as with Greece) or over the head (as with Russia) of the Foreign Office. Yet Curzon failed not only to assert the position of the FO but even to make a serious attempt to do so. The man who could display the most vehement indignation over trivial matters to almost everybody else, only recorded what he termed 'a gentle protest' when Lloyd George made a major announcement about the diplomatic corps without consulting the Foreign Secretary.[31] No doubt many strong characters come up against someone some time to whom they have to defer, but Curzon's subordination to Lloyd George – unparalleled in his relations with every other Prime Minister from Balfour to Baldwin – is bewildering.

Observers wondered why, after failing to assert himself, the Foreign Secretary did not resign. On several occasions, he later claimed, he was on the verge of doing so but desisted after appeals for him to stay. It is true that various people, including Balfour and Chamberlain, urged him to continue, and that the latter indicated that he too would resign if Curzon departed.[32] And it is true that ambassadors and Foreign Office officials also wanted him to remain in order to prevent Lloyd George from gaining further influence over foreign affairs. Moreover, he had no desire to see future policy conducted by either of his likely successors, Churchill or Birkenhead, both of whom he distrusted profoundly. Humiliating though his position may have been, he believed that, in those areas where the Prime Minister's 'peculiar passions' and 'devious methods were not involved', he could still do useful work and recover some of the authority of the Foreign Office.[33] As it happened he did, but not until Lloyd George's time was nearly up.

Yet there was a third factor which Curzon did not admit to anyone: he *knew* that resignation would be the end of him. A long time ago he had resigned with such catastrophic results that his career had never fully recovered. After sacrificing his position as Balfour's natural successor, he had just scraped in ten years later to a minor place in Asquith's Coalition. And now, in 1921, he was a far less popular figure than he had been in 1905. Had he resigned, neither press nor public opinion would have demanded his reinstatement. Chamberlain might have gone too and broken the Coalition, but there was no guarantee that the Foreign Secretary would ever get back into government.

Vansittart thought Curzon's fatal mistake was to have once threatened resignation without carrying it out,[34] an omission which enabled the Prime Minister to persecute him afterwards in the belief that he would never go voluntarily. Of course it would have been more admirable to behave like Milner who, when provoked, threatened to resign and would have done so had Lloyd George not climbed down. But Milner was a Cincinnatus, happy to serve his country when she needed him but equally happy to renounce or refuse office in less urgent times. Whatever his other qualities, Curzon was no Cincinnatus.

In the autumn of 1921 the Foreign Secretary found some solace at Kedleston, where he spent a short holiday and a few subsequent weekends. That year enjoyed an Indian summer, producing 'the most wonderfully pearly air and mellow sunlight – nature resting in a still trance and parading her exquisite beauties before she sinks into decay'. It was lovely to walk around the estate in this weather, stopping to chat with farmers and cottagers, and to drink a cup of fresh milk. Certain human irritations had disappeared since his previous sojourns. A kitchen maid provided far better meals than his expensive London chef, who 'almost drowned' him in 'elaborate and costly slushes with incomprehensible names'. And he was spared his daughters' silence, knitting and novel-reading, although Cimmie assailed him with 'extraordinarily offensive' letters about money.[35]

But there was little change in the deficiencies of most of his employees. Inside the house he avoided 'ructions' with the servants by doing many things himself, including shutting windows and drawing curtains; it meant one was 'a servant to one's servants', but at least there were no rows. Outside he tried to solve another problem by giving the parson a list of 150 good hymns to 'prevent him choosing the hideous ones he habitually' selected. Forceful intervention was also required to bring the park keeper into line. As he would not take the weed off the lake, nor keep the boat-house clean, nor cut the grass in front of it, Curzon drove into Derby to buy him a scythe, a broom, a rake and a pair of clippers.

The problem with the gardener, however, was not one of idleness but of misdirected fervour. On arrival Curzon was appalled to find the herbaceous borders filled 'exclusively with the most monstrous asters', one square of colour after another, 'thousands of blooms of the most hideous flower in creation'. Forestry was another activity that could not be left safely to his employees: the Foreign Secretary felt compelled to supervise to ensure that the right trees were cut down. And one exercise in altruism proved a melancholy failure. Some unemployed men from Derby, who were given work on the estate, turned out to be 'perfectly useless' and provided him with evidence that the 'so-called working classes [were] rotting at the core': the 'older generation of working men', he thought, 'alone set the tone'.[36]

As usual when he was at Kedleston, Grace was absent, undergoing a cure on the Continent followed by a lengthy holiday in Paris. Her husband sent her the best Muscat grapes from his greenhouses and hoped she would return to spend a few days of his leave in Derbyshire. Unhappy that she showed no interest in the improvements he was making, he became even more upset when she began making excuses for delaying her return. He had agreed that she should take things easy in Paris after her cure – 'dress trying on is most exhausting' – but, when she had done so, complained that it was time his 'sweet wife came back' and relieved him of his 'eternal solitude'. Pleading illness, however, Grace managed to extend her absence from three to nine weeks.[37]

On his return to London Curzon was again immersed in the Greek-Turkish imbroglio, from which he did not escape, except during an illness, for the next year and a half. His objective was to bring about an armistice between the two sides, followed by a Greek withdrawal from Anatolia and a revision of the Sèvres Treaty which had been made redundant by events. In December he opposed the holding of Near East discussions at the forthcoming conference at Cannes because he feared Lloyd George would 'barge in with disastrous results for he [was] still as mad for Greece as ever'.[38] But his hopes for a conference on the question soon afterwards were ruined by the resignation of Briand, who was replaced by the intractable Poincaré, and by the fall of Bonomi's Government in Rome. A date was finally arranged for the end of March 1922.

At the beginning of that month Montagu received a telegram from Lord Reading, the Viceroy in India, stating that the Delhi Government regarded as essential requirements of a Near East peace a Greek withdrawal from Smyrna, an Allied evacuation of Constantinople, and the restoration of Adrianople and the rest of Eastern Thrace to Turkey. As Reading was about to make himself unpopular by arresting Gandhi, he thought such a statement might appease India's Muslims and asked permission to publish it. On Friday, 3 March, Montagu circulated the telegram to his colleagues and over the weekend, without consulting them, cabled permission. He did not bring the matter up at a Cabinet meeting on Monday, but Curzon said privately that he supposed Montagu would not authorize publication of the telegram without the consent of his colleagues. When the Indian Secretary replied that he had already done so, two days earlier, Curzon returned dumbfounded to the table.

Astonishment soon turned to indignation, and later that day the Foreign Secretary sent Montagu a letter of protest. It was intolerable, he said, that shortly before a crucial conference 'a subordinate branch of the British Government 6,000 miles away' should dictate what line he ought to pursue on Thrace.[39] In bed with a painful attack of phlebitis, Curzon soon became even angrier, complaining to Chamberlain on the 9th that this 'really outrageous' incident had doomed his mission to 'certain and inevitable failure'. If he tried to argue with Poincaré or the Turks about Adrianople or the Straits, they would merely 'brandish . . . this fatal and suicidal declaration'. In the circumstances he had 'no desire to go to Paris at all'.[40]

Curzon also complained to the Prime Minister, who had missed the Cabinet meeting on the 6th because of illness. As he subsequently informed Hardinge, Curzon told Lloyd George that 'unless Montagu were publicly repudiated in both Houses of Parliament, I should decline to go to Paris and some other For. Sec. had better take my place'.[41] That such an unusually firm note had the effect, as Curzon believed, of forcing Montagu's resignation seems unlikely. Lloyd George appears to have jumped at the opportunity to get rid of a colleague so critical of his Greek policy and so unpopular with the Conservatives. He therefore assumed an extremely tough stance on the incident, lectured the Indian Secretary on his irresponsibility, and told him they could no longer 'usefully co-operate in the same Cabinet'. On the day of Montagu's resignation Curzon observed, unkindly and unfairly, that it was 'a fortunate riddance for he [had] pretty well ruined India'. If Reading followed, he added, no one would regret it, for 'a more lamentably weak and irresolute' man had never sat upon the viceregal throne.[42]

On the following Saturday the fallen minister attacked Lloyd George and Curzon in a speech in his Cambridge constituency. During a rehearsal the day before in front of a journalist from the *Evening Standard*, he was reported to have drunk a great deal of whisky.[43] Possibly he was under a similar influence on the platform when he abused Curzon for sending him after the Monday Cabinet meeting 'one of those plaintive, hectoring, bullying, complaining letters which are so familiar to his colleagues and his friends'.[44] As he had not kept a copy of the letter, Curzon asked Montagu to return it. To Chamberlain he deplored the fact that a former colleague should cite a private letter on a public platform 'with the manifest desire to injure' and 'thereby compel its publication'.[45]

Instead of returning the missive, Montagu would have been wise to pretend he had thrown it away. Curzon was quite capable of writing letters of the type described – as indeed was his correspondent – but this was not one of them. The gods must have driven Montagu mad,

Chamberlain told Lloyd George, before he so misquoted a letter that could be produced. On 14 March Curzon made a statement on the whole episode to the House of Lords. Peers crowded the benches, and many MPs deserted a Commons debate to watch from the steps of the throne. The House was on 'the qui vive for trouble', reported one of Lloyd George's aides, and listened in complete silence before coming down unanimously on Curzon's side. It was an impressive speech, commented the *Scotsman*, 'like a passage of Burke read by a master of oratory'. After hearing the text of the letter, Crawford noted that it was one of the best and most moderate epistles Curzon had ever written; its author could not be criticized for it, 'whatever his exploits in other envelopes'. Chamberlain thought the Foreign Secretary's statement was 'so complete and crushing' that afterwards there 'was not another word to be said, but Crewe said it at considerable length!'[46] The next day Montagu made a meandering and unconvincing attempt to defend himself in the Commons; but the career of one of the most abrasive, vigorous and talented politicians of the period was over.

In spite of his illness, Curzon went to Paris the following week for the conference. Before leaving, the Cabinet discussed its prospects 'in terms of unrelieved despondency', and the Foreign Secretary himself regarded his mission as hopeless.[47] Yet he managed to secure the agreement of France and Italy to a plan which included both the evacuation of Smyrna and the reversion of Constantinople to Turkey. The Greek Government of Demetrios Gounaris, financially stretched and tardily aware of its military weakness, accepted the terms for an armistice. But Kemal's Turkish nationalists, confident of their growing strength and fortified by French weaponry, refused to accept a solution which fell short of their demands for total independence in Turkey and Eastern Thrace.

Ill health prevented Curzon from further active involvement in the problem until August. In great pain from his leg and suffering from a combination of phlebitis, thrombosis and lymphangitis, in April he was taken on a stretcher to recuperate for a few days at his house at Broadstairs. Lying there in bed and looking out of the window, he remarked in a letter to Lloyd George that in bad times the sea was as great a consoler as mountains. And in his depressed and exhausted mood, he reflected on the iniquities of foreign politicians, especially Poincaré and 'those pestilential ruffians from Moscow'. 'My dear Charlie,' he sighed to Hardinge, 'I often think that the world of international diplomacy is the dirtiest thing alive and that a statesman is a synonym for a knave.'[48]

Returning to London for treatment, he was afflicted, in addition to his other ailments, with insomnia and backache. After a fortnight's sleeplessness, he summoned a hypnotist who informed him about 'the conscious self, the sub-conscious self and Heaven knows what', and then stood at the end of the bed, chattering on about having a tranquil night and a restful sleep and allowing the subconscious to fulfil itself. Told that he could not open his eyes and would soon be asleep, Curzon lay still with 'his eyes closed, thought of nothing, gave full chance to the sub-conscious self, and after one and a half hours was as wide awake as at noonday – nay more so'. Two nights later he tried another remedy requiring him to puff into a mouthpiece attached to some bag. It was equally unsuccessful. Even drugs, which he disliked taking, seldom gave him more than a couple of hours' light sleep.[49]

During this miserable period Curzon received little consolation from his wife who, in spite of his illness, decided to extend her current Continental jaunt. His 'sole joy', he told Grace, were the visits of his step-daughter Marcella, whom he thought delightful in every way. Almost no one else came to see him except 'two old peers' who called to enquire after he had been ill for ten days. He 'must be entirely forgotten', he reflected pathetically, 'or have no friends left'. Not one of the people he used to entertain year after year at Hackwood had written a line or even left a card. 'Well, such is the world. It does not wait even till you are dead to forget you.'[50]

The one compensation for his illness was the excuse it gave him not to accompany Lloyd George to the Genoa Conference in April. Churchill was furious because he had banked on Curzon's presence to block any chance of the Prime Minister recognizing the Bolshevik regime. Although he was in dispute with Churchill on most other issues, Curzon agreed with him on this one and feared that an unescorted premier might impulsively make a deal. But in the event the conference was a failure for Lloyd George, its principal outcome being an unexpected and unwelcome treaty between Russia and Germany.

Curzon's illness gave him no immunity from newspaper attacks. He often wondered why Balfour, who stood in for him at the Foreign Office, had such a good press in spite of his lack of achievement. It seemed strange and unfair that a man of such 'moderate genius' was so popular while he had to suffer the 'relentless persecution' of the *Daily Mirror*, the 'ceaseless vendetta' of *The Times* and the *Daily Mail*, and a persistent clamour from the *Daily Express* for his resignation.[51]

But he realized that it was not only the newspapers which wanted him to resign. Press statements about his forthcoming retirement prompted him to complain to Downing Street which, he suspected rightly, had inspired them. It was a 'distressing and even humiliating' experience, he told Lloyd George's Private Secretary, to read them 'constantly and categorically repeated even in an unfriendly press'.[52] Later he received information which convinced him there had been 'a deep-laid plot' to get rid of him during his illness. He was unable to identify his potential supplanter but thought the most likely candidates were Churchill, who had 'suddenly evinced the most affectionate interest' in his welfare, and Birkenhead. Later Derby told Grace he had been offered the Foreign Office several times during the summer – a remarkable revelation, if true, for Lloyd George had removed him from the War Office in 1918 and had told Curzon that he was quite unfitted for the post. The Foreign Secretary probably did not know that Hardinge was also angling for the job or that Bonar Law – who had left the Government for health reasons in May 1921 – had apparently been offered it on more than one occasion.[53]

The interesting point about these manoeuvres is not the existence of 'a deep-laid plot' but the failure to carry it out. Why didn't Lloyd George simply dismiss his Foreign Secretary instead of intriguing against him? It is not difficult to get rid of a minister who is out of action for four months – even one still conducting the business of his department from his bed. The Prime Minister cannot have feared that the disappearance of an ill and unpopular minister would have jeopardized the survival of his Government. Even Chamberlain, who had succeeded Law as leader of the party, would not have felt obliged to resign if a sick colleague had been persuaded to surrender his office.

The ambivalence of Lloyd George's attitude towards his Foreign Secretary perhaps provides a partial explanation. Although he was rude to him in Cabinet and enjoyed mimicking him to friends, he appreciated Curzon's knowledge and ability. In January 1922 he had even told C.P. Scott, the editor of the *Manchester Guardian*, that if the Coalition broke up, the three Tory ministers he would like to take with him were Chamberlain, Birkenhead 'and even Curzon – yes even old Curzon who has been quite decent of late'.[54] Neither this remark nor his later support over the Montagu affair help explain Lloyd George's intrigues over the following summer. But they do suggest that the Prime Minister was not consistently determined to remove a Foreign Secretary who after all posed no threat to himself.

In July doctors persuaded Curzon to go to France for a three-week course of treatment. The sojourn produced a characteristic crop of complaints. His destination, Orléans, was 'a most damnable place' – 'much more pretentious than Derby but not one whit better' – where sleep was impossible because a tram line passed outside his hotel window, someone clumped about in the room above, and after these nuisances ceased, he had to get up and hunt for a mouse scratching away behind the cupboard.[55] In spite of these disturbances, however, his phlebitis was temporarily cured.

Curzon returned in August just in time for the long-predicted débâcle in Asia Minor. At the end of the month the Turkish nationalists overwhelmed the Greek army and a fortnight later sacked Smyrna. After despatching the Greeks, they moved northwards to threaten Allied forces occupying Chanak in the neutral zone on the Asiatic shore of the Straits. At a meeting of the Cabinet on Friday, 15 September, Curzon warned against trying to stop the Turkish advance by military means. But Lloyd George and Churchill convinced the other ministers that the Straits must be defended and the Turks kept out of Europe; troops from Serbia, Greece and Romania, they argued, and later from the Dominions as well, could reinforce the Allied troops and help halt the Turks. The following day they drafted a press communiqué about the 'deadly consequences' if the 'violent and hostile Turkish aggression' succeeded in seizing control of the Straits. Curzon, who had gone to Hackwood, was furious to read what he called this 'flamboyant manifesto' in the newspapers. Churchill maintained, however, that a statesman who went to his country seat in a crisis should not complain if he was not consulted.[56]

Impulsive and bellicose, the communiqué had a disastrous effect: Australia and Canada refused to send troops, while France and Italy announced the withdrawal of theirs from the threatened areas of the neutral zone. The following week Curzon decided to go to Paris in an effort to repair the damage with Poincaré and restore a united Allied position. The Prime Minister tried to persuade him to take Birkenhead, who was as belligerent as Churchill and himself, and then arraigned the Foreign Secretary for his refusal in front of the Cabinet. Later Curzon heard that Lloyd George greatly regretted his failure to force the issue, because Birkenhead had been primed to obstruct an agreement with France and thus pave the way for war with Turkey and a victory for the Coalition in a khaki election.[57]

Yet the Foreign Secretary himself hardly behaved in Paris as if he was on a delicate diplomatic mission. On the 20th, at a meeting with

Poincaré and the Italian ambassador, Count Sforza, he catalogued French acts of disloyalty to Britain over the previous two years and complained several times that France had just abandoned her ally at Chanak. After one of these provocations, recorded Hardinge, the French premier suddenly 'lost his temper and shouted and screamed at Curzon, really in the most insulting manner, pouring out torrents of abuse and making the wildest statements . . .' Instead of replying in kind, Curzon trembled, muttered something about an adjournment, and hobbled out. A few minutes later Hardinge found him 'extended in another room, with tears pouring down his face and a brandy bottle by his side, speaking in maudlin tones' about going home unless 'that horrid little man' apologized.[58]

The British ambassador told Curzon he would only get an apology if he withdrew his statement that France had 'abandoned' her ally at Chanak. At first the Foreign Secretary refused, claiming it was an exact description of what had happened, but eventually he consented. Hardinge then returned to Poincaré who, after a lengthy bluster, agreed to apologize if the accusation of abandonment was withdrawn in the presence of Sforza. The squat French lawyer then went in search of the outstretched English magnifico – it must have looked like an encounter between Chauvelin and Sir Percy Blakeney – to make his apologies. Curzon said he understood there was some objection to the word 'abandon', but he personally attached no importance to the verb and was quite willing to substitute 'retreat'. After a delay of ten minutes, partly to show his displeasure and partly to regain his composure, the Foreign Secretary returned to the conference chamber.[59] Writing a few days later to the King's Private Secretary, he said it was 'hard to deal with a man who [was] always a lawyer and sometimes also a lunatic'.[60]

An hour after this embarrassing incident, the two combatants and Sforza somehow managed to agree on terms to offer Kemal. In a joint Note the Allies now 'viewed with favour' Turkey's claim to Eastern Thrace and agreed to remove their troops from Constantinople after a peace settlement; they also asked the Turks to respect the neutral zone, a request which the Turks, who recognized neither the zone nor the treaty which created it, subsequently ignored. On his return Curzon received the cordial congratulations of the Cabinet which had feared that the defections of France and Italy would result in even worse terms for Greece.

The Foreign Secretary's success was ephemeral. News of a revolution in Greece, which made Lloyd George's favourite Greek, Venizelos,

once more an influential figure, revived the spirits of the Cabinet's phil-
hellenes, outraged by Kemal's refusal to respect the neutral zone. The
Prime Minister was particularly annoyed by the insolence of the Turkish
troops at Chanak, who 'walked up to the wire entanglements of the
British forces and made grimaces'.[61] Since the Turks were violating the
neutral zone, Churchill and Lloyd George did not feel bound to renew
the offer of Eastern Thrace. Should Kemal invade Europe, they
believed he could be stopped by the revolutionaries of Venizelos and
cut off by British troops at Chanak.[62] Curzon was 'very much alarmed'
by the prospect of renewing the 'worthless alliance' with the Greeks,
destroying the Allied unity he had just rebuilt, and in all probability
ending up fighting the Turks with Greece alone on Britain's side.[63]

At a conference of ministers on the morning of 29 September, the
anti-Turk group was in an uncompromising temper. Churchill and
Birkenhead, the Foreign Secretary wrote afterwards, 'excelled themselves in Jingo extravagance' and gained the support of milder colleagues. On the advice of the three Service chiefs, they decided to
instruct General Sir Charles Harington, who commanded British forces
in Turkey, to deliver an ultimatum to the Turks. Although Curzon
managed to water down the instructions, he much regretted the 'violent
and incendiary' plan to threaten Kemal that Harington would open fire
with all the forces at his disposal unless the Turks left the neutral zone.[64]

The Foreign Secretary saw the nationalists' London representative
that afternoon and urged him to avoid a collision by persuading Kemal
to withdraw. He then requested another gathering of senior ministers
late that night at Carlton House Terrace to try to induce them to cancel
or at any rate to delay the ultimatum sent earlier in the day. Before
going to the country that afternoon Lloyd George had told
Chamberlain, the chairman of the meeting, that he was against any
delay. So was everybody else except its proponent. Birkenhead professed to be 'deeply desirous of averting war' but believed that during a
delay of twenty-four hours 'the spirit of the troops might . . . be affected
by the insolence of the Turks'. Churchill agreed that it was 'not physically possible to defer action without the gravest risk' and claimed that
the ultimatum would actually lead to a peaceful settlement.[65] Lord Lee,
Lord Cavan (the CIGS), Sir Robert Horne and Chamberlain himself
concurred with them.

Most of the next day, Saturday 30th, was consumed by full Cabinet
discussions. At the afternoon session Curzon told his colleagues that
the tension at Chanak appeared to have been reduced and said he hoped

fighting had not broken out. Lloyd George, however, was in a truculent mood, annoyed by Harington's failure to reply to the Cabinet's instructions and complaining that the general was so concerned with the political aspect – which was not his responsibility – that he was ignoring the military situation. Before the last meeting he dined with Churchill and Birkenhead. F.E. arrived at the Cabinet 'very much flushed and excited', recorded Crawford, while Churchill was in a 'nervous condition'. In belligerent tones all three criticized Harington. Lloyd George protested that Britain stretched every point in favour of the Turks, Churchill suggested cancelling a proposed conference with them at Mudania, and Birkenhead tried to censure the British general: 'in an angry tirade', recounted Crawford, the Lord Chancellor said he 'could not conceal his indignation at the conduct of soldiers who act as statesmen'.[66] Harington should have been defended by the War Secretary, Sir Laming Worthington-Evans, but since he maintained what Curzon called a 'discreet but inglorious silence', the Foreign Secretary assumed the task, expatiating on the advantages of caution and extolling the discretion of the man on the spot. As he told Hardinge the following day, after Harington's telegram had finally arrived, the general had shown 'far superior judgement and discretion' than had the warmongers in the Cabinet; realizing that the situation was not so dangerous as to require 'hysterics', Harington had simply and sensibly ignored the ultimatum and delayed his reply.[67]

Giving Crawford a lift home in the small hours, Curzon told him that all the trouble stemmed from the Prime Minister's hatred of the Turks and infatuation with the Greeks. He was 'terribly worried', recorded Crawford, and believed the trio of boisterous diners would drive him to resignation. The Scottish earl told him it was nonsense even to think of resigning in such a crisis. 'Ill and suffering' though he was, noted Crawford, the Foreign Secretary had 'invaluable qualities of coolness shared by few if any of his colleagues'.[68]

The following day the Cabinet met to discuss Harington's failure to carry out its instructions. On learning, however, that the situation had improved and that Kemal had agreed to meet the general, it decided that the ultimatum need not be delivered. In a break between meetings Curzon wrote to Grace of his 'Homeric encounter' with 'the fire eaters and war mongers' the night before, while to Hardinge he recounted how he had 'fought alone against this Ephesian band' that reeked of gunpowder.[69] Duff Cooper may have been right in observing that Curzon was 'a master of the art of modestly giving himself the *beau rôle* in conversations'.[70] But during that weekend there can be little doubt that he had earned it. On Saturday afternoon Crawford informed him that other ministers, including Lee (the First Lord of the Admiralty) and Worthington-Evans, were equally anxious to avoid war.[71] But since Lee backed the militants on Friday and Worthington-Evans failed to defend Harington on Saturday evening, their taciturn anxiety was not very useful. All the evidence suggests that Churchill, Birkenhead and Lloyd George, backed by other ministers, were really hoping that Kemal would attack Chanak and begin hostilities. That they were stopped from provoking a wholly unnecessary war over the weekend was primarily due to the good sense of Harington and the vigour of the Foreign Secretary.

Once the 'Homeric encounter' was over, Curzon did receive assurances of support. The popular press, which had regarded him as *passé* in the summer, now hailed his revival as a victory for the 'old diplomacy'; the *Sunday Express* even thought the notorious rhyme should be amended and that 'affable' was a more appropriate adjective than 'superior'.[72] From Paris Hardinge backed his position and described the hardliners in the Cabinet as 'lunatics who ought to be shut up'.[73] And from the quieter end of the Cabinet table he learnt that Lord Peel, Sir Arthur Griffith-Boscawen and Stanley Baldwin (who had been in France until the Sunday) also agreed with him. They asked to meet one evening that week at Carlton House Terrace in order to monitor the situation and discuss how it should be handled. Curzon later regarded that evening as the beginning of the end for the Coalition: 'When a group of Cabinet Ministers begins to meet separately and to discuss independent action, the death-tick is audible in the rafters'.[74]

For a couple of days it seemed that the crisis had passed. The Mudania negotiations opened successfully, the Turkish forces withdrew at Chanak, and Kemal's commander, Ismet Pasha, accepted the Paris Note of 23 September. But on 5 October a new crisis blew up, inspired this time not by the bellicosity of British ministers but by new demands from the Turks and another French 'abandonment' of her allies. Among other things the nationalists now insisted on occupying Eastern Thrace immediately, in advance of a peace treaty and without guarantees for the minorities. As far as France was concerned, they were at liberty to do so, and her commander on the spot announced that he was not going to interfere. Curzon was as determined as ever to avoid fighting a war on behalf of the Greeks, but he thought that both Turkish demands and French concessions went beyond the limit. Although ill and depressed, he therefore agreed to cross the Channel on the afternoon of the 6th and spend the weekend with that most 'repugnant' of imaginable companions, Raymond Poincaré.

Their first meeting began at 11 p.m. and continued until nearly three in the morning. After stating that the 'preposterous' Turkish demands were wholly inconsistent with the Paris Note, the agreed basis of Allied policy, Curzon asked Poincaré to be good enough to explain why the French commander in the zone had been ordered to accede to them. Replying that General Charpy had 'no orders but only latitude to avoid war', the premier said French troops would do nothing to halt a Turkish advance and would never under any circumstances fire a shot in the East. When Curzon observed that this seemed 'a most humiliating position' for a Great Power to adopt, Poincaré answered heatedly that it was not a question of humiliation. According to the notes of a British diplomat present, he said he 'needed no lessons from anyone and would take none. He represented France, and France required no lessons. He wished to make it clear once and for all that he would tolerate no criticism of any word or action of his . . .' Nor would he tolerate amusement. When Curzon smiled incredulously at the claim that there had been no inconsistency in the conduct of French policy, Poincaré screamed at him, '*Vous me riez au nez, je ne le permets pas*'.[75]

Once again, however, the antagonists reached agreement, and once more Allied unity was restored largely on the basis of the British formula. Curzon returned to a second round of unaccustomed plaudits, and the negotiations at Mudania recommenced. On the 11th the Turks signed the Mudania Convention by which they agreed to withdraw from the neutral zone until after a peace treaty, and accepted the proposal that Eastern Thrace should be administered by the Allies for a month before the Turks returned. Most people recognized that, between them, Curzon, Harington and Sir Horace Rumbold, the High Commissioner in Constantinople, had averted war. It now remained for the Foreign Secretary to negotiate a peace.

35

Resurgence: Lausanne,
1922–1923

COALITION GOVERNMENT HAD been a wartime expedient, accepted by the two main parties with great reluctance. Yet by the time of the Chanak crisis it had lasted for nearly four years of peace, a longer period than it had required to win the war. The Coalition survived despite its unpopularity with the party that had dominated it since 1916, an unpopularity that grew as the domination increased. By October 1922 there was widespread feeling inside the Conservative Party* that the Coalition had outlived its purpose, that Conservative electors were being prevented from voting for Conservative policies, and that a great political party had become the accomplice to such evils as the 'Honours Scandal' and the Irish treaty. These views were not confined to the party branches, the Diehard peers and the squires of the backbenches. They had permeated the junior ranks of the Government and had reached a couple of ministers who backed Curzon over Chanak.

The Coalition survived largely because some of its Conservative leaders had come to see themselves as figures above party politics. Birkenhead thought the country simply required an oligarchy consisting of the two most charismatic Liberals, Churchill and Lloyd George, allied to Chamberlain, Balfour and himself; anyone who disagreed he abused or lectured for lack of loyalty. A similar, though much less typical, arrogance was displayed by Chamberlain, who deluded himself

---

*After the Irish treaty of 1921 Unionists tended once more to call themselves Conservatives.

549

into thinking that the party needed its leaders more than they needed the party. The Conservatives were thus divided horizontally over the future of one man. The party wanted to shed Lloyd George; its leaders – with the exception of Curzon and the retired Bonar Law – were determined to keep him.

Realizing that the Coalition would be strongly criticized at the November meeting of the National Union – the precursor of the Conservative Party conference – the Cabinet planned to pre-empt the problem by holding a general election beforehand. The operation was delayed by the Chanak crisis, but on 10 October Chamberlain summoned the Conservative ministers to a meeting to reaffirm their decision to campaign under Lloyd George's leadership. After Balfour had backed an early election as a means of thwarting an adverse vote from the National Union, Curzon declared that such a transparent trick would have perilous consequences. But his principal reason for opposing the move was the dislocation of foreign policy it would entail on the eve of a crucial conference planned to settle the outstanding questions of the Near East. Griffith-Boscawen was also hostile to an election, but the strongest line was taken by Baldwin, the President of the Board of Trade, who considered Lloyd George an albatross around the party's neck and said that he would not serve under him again. At a further meeting two days later, Baldwin told his wife, Griffith-Boscawen supported him while Curzon was 'sympathetic'. But as the others were determined to follow Lloyd George, he thought he had no option but to 'drop out of politics altogether', to spend the winter abroad, and give up his seat at the next election.[1] The possibility that he might be Prime Minister within a few months must have seemed as remote to him as to everyone else.

Curzon, by contrast, had no thought of dropping out of politics and merely wished to be allowed to carry on with his job. As with the last days of Asquith in December 1916, his role in the manoeuvres that ended with the displacement of Lloyd George has been viewed with a cynicism sharpened by a confusion of dates. The main charge against him – that he told Churchill at a dinner in the middle of the crisis that he would support the Coalition's decision to fight an early election – is untrue.* And even if he did make the remark earlier on, it hardly turns

---

*Even though Churchill himself admitted that the dinner took place 'some weeks' earlier – that is, before the Chanak crisis – it is widely supposed to have been held at Churchill's house on 11 October, a week before the Coalition fell. As Curzon attacked the plan to hold an early election at meetings with his colleagues on both the 10th and the 12th, he is unlikely to have agreed to it on the 11th. No mention of the dinner, moreover, is made

him into the intriguer and turncoat depicted by the Beaverbrook histo-rians.* Curzon had been a member of the Coalition for nearly six years without showing the slightest conspiratorial tendencies. Frustration with the Prime Minister's meddling in foreign affairs had sometimes led him to contemplate his own resignation. It had never led him to plot for the overthrow of Lloyd George.

Yet his subservience to the Prime Minister, which had long surprised others, became in the course of 1922 increasingly unacceptable to himself. Outraged by the alleged plot during his illness, he returned to his desk in August to find Lloyd George's interference in foreign policy more objectionable than ever. Not only had the Prime Minister become more outspoken in public – as he demonstrated in an anti-Turkish speech in the Commons at the beginning of August – but his attempts to conduct diplomacy behind the FO's back had become still more blatant.

Encouraged perhaps by his 'Homeric encounters' over Chanak, Curzon decided to confront Lloyd George. After complaining on 2 October of confidential talks between the Prime Minister and the Romanian envoy, he drafted a further protest three days later about a series of secret meetings with the Greek representative. The second letter also criticized the whole system of dual diplomacy and contained a strong hint that he would resign unless he received a 'definite assurance' that the constitutional relations between his department and Downing Street would be re-established, thereby allowing the Foreign Office to 'resume its proper functions in the State'.[3] The letter was made redundant by developments. Before sending it, Curzon had planned to discuss the contents with both Chamberlain and Balfour. But he was delayed by his second visit to Poincaré and, by the time Chamberlain had seen it, the Coalition crisis was in full swing.

During his last days in power the Prime Minister declined to alter his ways. In the second week of October his Private Secretary, Sir Edward Grigg, was instructed to discuss secret Italian proposals for the forth-coming conference with an emissary, Signor Giannini. This proved to be too much even for a loyal Private Secretary. Realizing that no coher-

---

in the biographies of the other senior ministers who are alleged to have been present, while Churchill's official biographer records his subject spending the normal dining hours of the 11th sending telegrams to the Dominions.[2]
*See above, p.xii.

ent policy could emerge from such deceptions, Grigg sent his notes of the meeting to the Foreign Office with a request not to make them official.[4]

On 14 October, the day Curzon learnt of the intrigue with Giannini, the Prime Minister made a violent speech in Manchester denouncing the barbarity of the Turks and the treachery of the French. At a casual meeting with colleagues on the previous day, he had given a brief outline of what he intended to say. When he mentioned Turkish massacres, Curzon asked him to avoid the subject because since the Great War the Greeks had behaved as badly as the Turks.[5] The request was not heeded. On the morning of the 15th, a few weeks before Curzon was expected to conjure a peace treaty with the French and the Turks, the world learned of the Prime Minister's opinions of these peoples from the newspapers.

That evening Churchill gave a dinner for most of the Coalition ministers. A few days before he had called on Curzon at the Foreign Office to tell him that Lloyd George had virtually decided on an immediate election, that this had been accepted by himself, Balfour and various colleagues, and that the date and other details would be decided at the dinner. In an attempt to overcome Curzon's doubts about an election, Churchill told him it would be over before the start of the peace conference.[6]

During the five days before the dinner the Foreign Secretary had been upset both by Lloyd George's fresh incursions into foreign affairs and by his colleagues' attempt to ignore the views of the National Union. The combination induced him to refuse Churchill's invitation. Believing that an election would be disastrous both for the Conservatives and for the peace conference, he decided to appeal to his party leader. Accordingly, he telephoned Chamberlain at his country home and asked him to drop in at Carlton House Terrace before going on to Churchill's dinner. During a two-hour talk Curzon asked him to explain his absence to the assembled diners and declared that he would resign if the Cabinet insisted on an immediate election. Later that evening, in an anxious but defiant mood, he reported the conversation to Crawford. In case Churchill and his guests decided on a dissolution, he also drafted a letter of resignation stating that his principal reasons for going were the Prime Minister's constant interference in foreign policy and his own opposition to an election before the peace conference.[7]

Curzon's absence from the Churchill dinner gave rise to gossip the next day about him sitting on the fence until he could see which side was going to win.[8] As one of his friends later told D'Abernon, 'George wobbled up to the last minute'.[9] In fact there was no wobbling. Curzon did not take an intransigent position like Baldwin; for someone who had spent so many years in the Coalition it would have been ridiculous to do so. But he made it perfectly clear to his colleagues what he thought of the proposed election. He was obsessed by the forthcoming conference and believed, with reason as it turned out, that he was the man to direct it. Had the Coalition carried on as before – before the election talk, before the Chanak hysteria, before Manchester, before Giannini – the Foreign Secretary would have dutifully attended the conference on behalf of the Coalition Government. It was not Curzon who changed the rules; he had had no anterior intention of deserting his colleagues.

On the morning after Churchill's dinner Curzon called in at 11 Downing Street to find out from Chamberlain what had happened. The diners, it turned out, had not been unanimous about an election. After strong opposition to a dissolution from Sir Leslie Wilson, the Chief Whip, the Tory leader had offered to compromise by leaving the decision to a meeting of Conservative MPs and ministers at the Carlton Club on 19 October. While Curzon was talking to Chamberlain, Lloyd George telephoned to ask him to drop in next door when he had finished. Doubtless feeling unprepared for so critical an interview, Curzon suggested they meet in the afternoon. The Prime Minister wanted to go to the country, however, and arranged an appointment for noon on the following day. In the meantime Curzon attended a further gathering of Conservative ministers at which they all repeated their views, and went on to a meeting with the party's under-secretaries where Balfour expressed his 'philosophic inability to understand what it was [they] were all disputing about'.[10] According to Curzon, Chamberlain's remarks at the second meeting were 'needlessly stiff and uncompromising' – adjectives which with the addition of 'wooden' and 'unbending' were universally used to describe the Tory leader at this crisis in his career and which go far to explain his wholly unnecessary eclipse.

At midday on the 17th Curzon had 'one of the most curious' conversations of his life. For an hour and twenty minutes the Prime Minister tried to defend himself with charm and ingenuity against the Foreign Secretary's litany of grievances. To every charge of interference he had an explanation. Secret talks were depicted as unplanned encounters, a dinner party where so-and-so was an unexpected guest, Giannini dropping in for a casual chat with his old friend Grigg. If confronted with evidence of intrigue between foreign emissaries and his secretaries, he declared that the former must have invented it because his secretaries were men of honour. When presented with telegrams of March 1921, which showed he had advised the Greeks in private to reject the terms he had publicly offered them in conference, he 'expressed horror at this crowning demonstration of Greek mendacity'.[11]

Denials were followed by an apology for any injustice he may have committed against the Foreign Office and an appeal to sentiment. In a voice 'charged with emotion', recalled Curzon, Lloyd George asked him not to forget the great scenes in which they had participated and the common comradeship of the war. He also thanked the Foreign Secretary for his consistent loyalty. Curzon did not question the sincerity of these remarks and thereby enabled them to part on friendly terms. Before leaving he said his resignation was in the Prime Minister's hands and that he left it for him to act upon when he chose. Lloyd George replied that the matter could be left until Thursday, the 19th, when he himself would probably be resigning.[12]

The fate of the Coalition depended largely on one of its former leaders. A year and a half after his retirement, Bonar Law had re-emerged during the Chanak crisis to warn the British that they could not 'alone act as the policemen of the world'. Now the anti-coalitionists of his party urged him to return to front-line politics and overthrow Lloyd George. On the morning of the 18th, however, Law told Curzon he had neither the inclination nor the moral resilience for the task. Although he knew he could defeat Chamberlain at the Carlton Club meeting, he did not want to form a Government and was thinking of resigning his seat and retiring from public life. But constant appeals during the day persuaded him to change his mind, and Curzon found him in a very different mood that evening. After announcing what he intended to say next day at the Carlton Club, Law asked him to stay at the Foreign Office if he formed a government. Curzon said that he would not address or even attend the meeting out of loyalty to Chamberlain, although in public he described his absence as a protest against the exclusion of Tory peers who were not ministers.

A further display of rigidity by Chamberlain ensured his overwhelming defeat at the Carlton. More than two-thirds of the MPs present followed the lead of Law and Baldwin and voted to fight the next election as an independent party. Lloyd George resigned that afternoon, but Law refused to take office until he had formally been chosen as Conservative leader. Proposed by Curzon and seconded by Baldwin, he was unanimously elected at a party meeting on the 23rd. On the following day Law announced his Cabinet which, besides Curzon and Baldwin, consisted largely of landed magnates and promoted under-secretaries. Parliament was dissolved on the 26th and an election called for 15 November.

The sulky giants of the Coalition flung derisive epithets at Law's grey and modest-looking team, dismissing as 'second-class brains' and a 'Government of the second eleven' a Cabinet most of whose members had far higher academic qualifications than themselves.* But the chief source of bitterness and the main object of scorn was the least 'grey' of all their new opponents. Outraged though he was by Curzon's lack of solidarity, Birkenhead desisted from attacking him in the campaign and waited until the Foreign Secretary was at Lausanne – embroiled in the peace conference and unable to answer – before attempting his revenge. Churchill, however, went straight on to the offensive against the man who had become his 'pet aversion'. After telling Lloyd George he was going to 'let Curzon have it', he wrote to the *Morning Post* criticizing him over the Chanak crisis and disparaging his 'sudden and nimble' change over the Coalition.[13]

Curzon replied that the Chanak statement was characterized by 'copious inaccuracy and no small malevolence', and that his change had been neither sudden nor nimble 'but slow and perhaps even belated'.[14] He refused to admit that he had deserted the Coalition. 'Good Lord!' he exclaimed on reading in the press about his alleged disloyalty to Lloyd George, 'I have been too loyal to him to my own detriment for over three years.'[15]

On 15 November the Conservatives won a comfortable overall majority, Labour nearly doubled its representation and emerged as the second party, and Lloyd George's following was halved; in the new Parliament the 117 Liberal MPs were divided almost equally between those who supported the recent Prime Minister and those who were loyal to his predecessor Asquith. Two days after the poll the Foreign Secretary arrived at Victoria Station *en route* for the Continent. He was accompanied by a distinguished team from the Foreign Office, including Sir William Tyrrell, Harold Nicolson and Allen Leeper, and by a very drunk and incompetent valet called Tivendale.

---

*Three of them had fellowships of All Souls, six had first-class (or double first) degrees, and Amery had both. Among the leading Coalitionists only Birkenhead had a comparable record.

The Near East was the area of the world where the Allies had been least successful in obtaining a post-war settlement. San Remo and Sèvres had comprehensively failed to find solutions, and most of the disputes with Turkey, especially those concerning her borders and the future of the Straits, remained unresolved. A conference to redeem the earlier failure and procure a settlement of the outstanding differences had long been Curzon's principal diplomatic objective. And one of his chief personal objectives had been his own participation. Yet he knew the odds were piled against success, far more heavily now than when he had first suggested a feasible solution four years before. Gone was the chance to make a peace with a beaten foe; instead he had to deal with a resurgent country, buoyed by success, confident in its nationalism and now bolstered by the friendship of three of its former enemies, Russia, France and Italy. 'Hitherto we have dictated our peace treaties,' Curzon told D'Abernon, the British ambassador in Berlin. 'Now we are negotiating one with the enemy who has an army in being while we have none, an unheard of position.'[16]

The Foreign Secretary realized that the essential precondition of success was a common front with Italy and France. He therefore refused Poincaré's request to proceed to Lausanne without previous conversations or an understanding between the Allies. Such a plan, he believed, was designed to put him in a position where, 'deserted as usual by France and Italy', he would be 'beaten on every point and forced either to conclude a humiliating peace or to break up the conference'.[17] Only after receiving the promise of a 'warm and enthusiastic accord' with France did he agree to leave England.

His visit to Paris was certainly more agreeable than either of his previous forays. He enjoyed a pleasant interview with President Millerand at the Elysée and an official lunch at the Quai d'Orsay where he sat next to 'dear old Marshal Foch', with whom he was always able to 'colloque on terms of warm friendship and regard'. When the delegates went through the programme afterwards, however, 'old Foch's contributions were quite irrelevant' and showed he did not understand the Eastern Question at all. Fortunately, Poincaré was by his standards amiable and co-operative, and agreement on the agenda was reached. But later Curzon admitted he felt worn down by the 'eternal necessity of humouring, conciliating and consulting the two allies who neither fought nor won the war against Turkey'.[18]

Early the next morning the delegations assembled at the Gare de Lyon to catch a special train to Lausanne, a saloon for the British delegation at the front, another for the French at the back, and between them a 'drawing-room carriage' and dining car where nearly everybody except the two principals congregated. Curzon spent the journey writing letters in his saloon until he was interrupted in the evening by an irritating demand from the new Italian Prime Minister. Eager to demonstrate his importance and wishing to give the impression that the Allies were coming to see him rather than the other way round, Benito Mussolini had sent a message insisting that their leaders should continue their journey beyond Lausanne to Territet, where he would give them dinner. Curzon and Poincaré reluctantly agreed and after more than twelve hours in the train finally met the Italian leader, surrounded by blackshirts and a band playing the Fascist Party's anthem '*Giovinezza*'.

At Territet Mussolini said he would not go to the conference unless the Allied leaders made a public declaration of Italy's equality with Britain and France regarding interests, rights and duties in the East. Mussolini turned out to be the only person in the world capable of uniting Curzon and Poincaré. They refused the demand on the grounds that the equality did not exist and that in any case a declaration of common interests should follow rather than precede agreement on policy. After failing to carry out his threat, the Italian accompanied the Allied statesmen to Lausanne. There in the small hours Curzon reached the Hôtel Beau Rivage and installed himself in a comfortable suite overlooking the lake. It was to be his home for the next eleven weeks.

Although he was staying in the same hotel, Mussolini made another little demonstration the next morning by deliberately arriving late for an Allied meeting in Curzon's sitting-room. He was 'a very stagey sort of person', noted the Foreign Secretary that same day, doing everything simply for effect. Yet he was also plainly ill at ease, rolling his eyes and saying little more than '*Je suis d'accord*'. It was soon obvious, Curzon reported to the Cabinet, that he 'knew next to nothing of the subjects and his agreement was procured with little difficulty to all' the points in the Anglo-French programme. In the afternoon the conference was formally opened at the town's Casino, and on the following day Mussolini left Lausanne. He had done virtually nothing at the conference except strut around with his blackshirts and make eleven statements to the press. Yet Italian newspapers managed to describe this performance as their country's first diplomatic victory since 1860.[19]

Poincaré's departure on the same day left Curzon in a position to dominate the conference. The heads of the French and Italian delegations were diplomats, M. Barrère, whom he respected, and the

Marchese Garroni, whom he did not. The Greeks were represented by Venizelos and the Turks by Ismet Pasha who, under the name Iñönü, succeeded Atatürk as President in 1938 and remained active in politics until 1972. Delegations from Russia and the Balkans were also present.

Displaying an authority unseen since viceregal days, the Foreign Secretary seized control of the proceedings. Claiming to be the senior Allied representative, he took the chair at the plenary session which determined procedure, appointed himself chairman of the most important committee (on territorial matters), and arranged the agenda. Aware that the success of the conference depended on preserving the isolation of the Turks and the unity of the Allies, Curzon organized a timetable which invited the Turks to isolate themselves. They duly did so. Asked for his demands on Thrace, Ismet claimed not only the eastern half but also the western portion, most of which had been ceded to Bulgaria before the Great War and was now earmarked for Greece. Over four days Ismet and Curzon debated the subject in public, with the result that by the end of the first week not a single country was on Turkey's side, the Allied position had been consolidated, and the senior British delegate* had established a personal ascendancy over the conference.

Curzon treated the Turks with a mixture of courtesy and firmness. Although he managed to establish some private rapport with Ismet, he found him irritating and obstinate in public sessions. After two days he was pessimistic. The chances against success were so great, he told Grace, that he would never become Prime Minister; in any case, he added, he was not fitted for the post. But over the following days his mood lightened, encouraged by tributes to his skilful handling of the proceedings, a talent he ascribed to the fact that he knew his case and had 'the art of getting on with Orientals'. He was particularly heartened by the 'absolute novelty' of praise from the press.[21] As he remarked to Grace,

> I have suddenly been discovered at the age of 63. I was discovered when I was Viceroy of India from 39 to 46. Then I was forgotten, traduced, buried, ignored. Now I have been dug up and people seem to find life and even merit in the corpse.[22]

---

*Britain's second plenipotentiary was Sir Horace Rumbold, the High Commissioner in Constantinople. Recommending him for the post in 1920, Curzon had remarked for the King's benefit that 'behind a somewhat bovine and unimpressive exterior' there lay 'ability, sound sense, courage and discretion'.[20]

For a brief period the focus of his exasperation shifted from the Turks to Tivendale, the valet later immortalized as Arketall by Harold Nicolson in *Some People*. In India Curzon had been amused by the effrontery of a valet 'uncertain about his aspirates' and, although the breed annoyed him above all others, he had an unexpected tolerance for those who dared to answer back. According to Nicolson, he had a soft spot for Tivendale and was reluctant to dismiss him at Lausanne even though he was habitually drunk. No glimmer of affection is discernible, however, in Curzon's letters to his wife. The man was 'perfectly useless', he complained, forgot everything and was unable to pack; on the fourth night of the conference he was found reeling round the dance floor and was sent home the next day. After he had gone, it was discovered that all Curzon's trousers had disappeared. Panic spread among the Foreign Office staff until they were found hidden under the valet's bed beside a large pile of empty bottles. Tivendale had procured the drink, Curzon learnt, by convincing the hotel management that his master, frightened of being poisoned, had ordered him to taste every bottle before serving it.[23]

In spite of Turkish obstructiveness, the conference continued to go well in early December. Curzon persuaded the Turks to accept a Straits Convention, which simultaneously secured the freedom of the Straits, prevented the Russians from turning the Black Sea into a private lake, and ended any chance of a Russian-Turkish alliance. Later, after a long and painful discussion on minorities, Curzon lectured the Turks on their attitude in an indignant extempore speech. The result was a 'great triumph', he told Grace, for the next day they climbed down and agreed to join the League of Nations, an organization at which they had hitherto scoffed.[24]

One worry, however, was the residual temptation of France and Italy to curry favour with the Turks. While Barrère was loyal to the Allied cause, current differences between Bonar Law and Poincaré over Germany resulted in a less cordial atmosphere at Lausanne; they also led, to Curzon's disgust, to a resumption of the French trick of leaking documents to the press.[25] Although the Foreign Secretary did not blame this on Barrère, who was out of sympathy with Poincaré's policy and resigned his post in January, he was appalled by the way his partners fawned on Ismet. Left to himself, Curzon believed he could handle the Turk. But it was impossible while Barrère and Garroni toadied to him during their meetings, calling him '*Excellence*' every other sentence and behaving like 'old roués courting some youthful courtesan'. Servility, he had long since learnt, was 'the last way to approach an Oriental'.[26]

However irritated Curzon was by the French, he always treated France as a serious country and an important ally. Italy in his view was neither. A tiresome and unreliable nation at all times, her faults became even more noticeable under the new regime. After two weeks of watching Garroni obeying Mussolini's orders, Curzon realized that the Italian premier was not merely the ridiculous figure he had seemed at Lausanne but a 'thoroughly unscrupulous and dangerous demagogue, plausible in manner, but without scruple in truth or conduct'. From Rome the Fascist leader threatened almost daily ruptures of the alliance, and on 4 December his terrified delegates were forced to tell Curzon they would withdraw from the conference unless promised a slice of the mandated territories of the Middle East. According to Nicolson, the Foreign Secretary completely lost his composure, delivered a look of hatred and disdain towards Garroni, and stalked majestically out of the room. After a fit of violent trembling in the corridor, 'restoratives were applied', and he returned to inform the Italians that he would not submit to blackmail of any kind. They could withdraw from the conference if they liked, he said, pointing out that Orlando had done so at Paris without disturbing the progress of the conference there.[27]

Two days later Mussolini stopped at Lausanne on his way to a conference on reparations in London. Grace was staying at the time and sat next to him at a lunch in his honour given by her husband. Before and after, the Italian leader sent her enormous baskets of flowers and in between displayed a vanity and conceit 'beyond belief'. No more was said of the Italian threat to leave the conference. But Curzon retained his view that Mussolini's attitude to Eastern questions was a 'combination of the sturdy beggar and the ferocious bandit'.[28]

At the beginning of December Lord Birkenhead launched an attack which, had it been successful, would have forced Curzon's resignation and possibly wrecked the conference. After Gounaris, the former Greek Prime Minister, had been executed by the new regime in Athens at the end of November, Birkenhead published a letter that the unfortunate statesman had sent Curzon in February appealing for arms and money to resist the Turks. In the Lords on 7 December he read out the letter with Curzon's reply, declared that the Cabinet had never seen the correspondence and blamed the entire Greek calamity on the Foreign Secretary. On hearing of the planned assault, former members of the Coalition were gleeful. Chamberlain, Lloyd George, Horne and others were equally certain they had never been shown the pathetic appeal and

Curzon's advice to 'hold on'. Had they done so, they claimed, a different policy would have been adopted, the Greeks would have been saved, and the threat to Chanak would have been avoided.

The affair was in Lord Ronaldshay's words 'a truly remarkable case of collective amnesia'.[29] Curzon may have been wrong to urge the Greeks to hold on in Anatolia, although he had done so in the belief that an orderly evacuation after an agreement with the Turks offered them a better chance of escape than a retreat that might easily have become a rout. But in any case it had been Cabinet policy rather than personal diplomacy, as was quickly demonstrated when copies of the letters were unearthed in various departments signed or initialled by the former ministers, including Birkenhead himself.[30] As Vansittart observed to his chief, the manoeuvre was 'a beautifully complete boomerang'.[31] On 11 December Birkenhead apologized rather lamely in the Lords, and a week later Grace took great pleasure in cutting him at a ball. But 'I am afraid', she remarked to her husband, 'he was too drunk to notice.'[32]

Curzon's daily routine changed little during his eleven Swiss weeks. Meetings and discussions followed one another monotonously until the late evening when he settled down to his papers and his correspondence. He seldom went out except for an occasional afternoon drive with Tyrrell or a brief stroll along the front shadowed by a gloomy detective with a pipe. The main departure from previous practice was his conversations with journalists, whom he invited regularly to lunch; such 'encounters', he naïvely told Grace, did nothing but good. How tragic that a politician should reach the age of 63 before recognizing the importance of good press relations.

Although his health stood up relatively well during the conference, Curzon suffered a good deal from his back. Nicolson once heard cries of pain when his chief removed his 'steel cage' and allowed his muscles to resume their natural shape. But the main problem at Lausanne was the cage itself, which broke, leaving sharp fragments of steel to cut into him and tear his vests; uncomfortable though this was, he preferred to wear it rather than go without any support until Grace sent his old one out from England.

Christmas was a dismal festival for the Foreign Secretary, spent alone with a bad cold in Lausanne while the rest of the delegation went tobogganing. He was also depressed about the chances of a treaty and suspected that the Turks really wanted a rupture. Yet despondency and self-pity were for once minority moods. Curzon was happier with himself than he had been for a long time, relishing the ample stage, enjoying the general esteem, convinced of the historic importance of his task. He was happier, too, in his relationship with Grace, who visited him twice. She told him she did not 'deserve so wonderful a husband' and said that the 'little disturbances' in their marriage, which had been 'all mostly [her] fault', were over for good. Deeply touched by these sentiments – which alas did not prove enduring – Curzon said he was happy to look back upon their six years together and feel that he would do it a hundred times again.[33]

A further indication of contentment was his relatively harmonious relationship with his officials. While they did not pretend he was easy to work with, they liked him and enjoyed his company. 'Poor old man,' Nicolson noted in his diary, 'it is extraordinary how with all his petulance and difficulty one gets *really* fond of him.'[34] Their chief was sometimes depressed and frequently indignant, but he was often in excellent form, sitting with a brandy and soda at night and reliving the day's events with his assistants. He surprised them with a gift for mimicry, rising from his chair to do an imitation of Garroni addressing Ismet Pasha, 'fondling him, stroking him, cooing endearments as loud as he could'. During the performance, recorded Nicolson, Curzon was half laughing at the memory and half crying at the thought that he would soon have to witness the real act again.[35] One day he was persuaded to give his impersonation of Tennyson reciting 'Tears, idle tears', which Nicolson thought the most effective imitation he had ever heard. But afterwards a wave of depression descended upon the performer. Remembering the meeting with the poet so many years before in the company of Laura Tennant, he sighed.

> All that was years ago, when I was young and could still laugh at my elders. But all young men are remorseless. You will go upstairs this evening and chaff me behind my back. You will give imitations in after life of the old buffer imitating Tennyson. And so it continues.[36]

On the last day of 1922 Curzon was summoned to Paris to meet Bonar Law, who had arrived with a compromise scheme on German reparations which Poincaré did not accept and which quickly led to a rupture with France. Curzon was unimpressed by the Prime Minister's unsubtle approach to diplomacy and even more so by his views on the Near East conference. Depressed by the impending break with the French, Law wanted to avoid any chance of a conflict with Turkey. He was in a 'great funk', Curzon wrote home, 'longing to clear out of

Mosul, the Straits and Constantinople, wishing to give up anything or everything sooner than have a row'. 'Staggered at his flabbiness and want of grip', the Foreign Secretary 'endeavoured to give him some spirit and courage'.[37] Unsuccessful in the attempt, Curzon returned disheartened to Lausanne on 2 January. 'The feet of the Prime Minister', he told Nicolson, 'were glacial. Positively glacial.'[38]

Law believed that the achievement of a Near East settlement was being obstructed by the question of Mosul, the mainly Kurdish area of northern Iraq which had been under Ottoman rule and now formed part of the British mandate. He therefore wrote to his Foreign Secretary a week after their meeting to restate his view that Britain could not go to war over the area. Curzon was infuriated. He had no intention of provoking a conflict on the issue. But he was equally determined, in spite of strong press support for Law's views in England, not to allow Turkey to regain a region which had very few Turkish inhabitants and for which Britain had received a League of Nations mandate to administer. Fed up with successive exhortations from the Prime Minister, Curzon grumbled to Grace of his constant warnings on matters of which he was 'wholly ignorant'. Unfortunately he did not confine this grievance to his wife. In a letter which cannot have improved his career prospects, he told Law he was 'a little hurt' not to have received 'a word of encouragement' for his labours, while being constantly warned to beware of situations of which he was 'just as conscious as anyone at home and . . . perhaps able to appraise more accurately'.[39]

It would have been cruel to deny Curzon his dialectical triumph over Mosul, a performance which Harold Nicolson described as 'perhaps the most brilliant, the most erudite, the most lucid exposition which even he had ever achieved'.[40] Yet he had first tried to solve the question through direct negotiations between the British and Turkish delegations. It was only when these had failed that on 23 January, in full conference, he asked Ismet Pasha to explain his Government's reasons for placing the Vilayet of Mosul within the borders of the Turkish state. The Pasha did so, stating a bad case badly, and making the mistake of asking what Lord Curzon could know about the populations of Sulimanyeh and of southern Kurdistan. He soon found out.

Curzon began by explaining that Britain could not surrender Mosul without breaking her pledges to the inhabitants, to King Feisal and to the League of Nations. Then he turned to Ismet's ethnic arguments and demonstrated that they were not only absurd in themselves but also based on inaccurate statistics. Just one-twelfth of the population, he pointed out, were Turks, and even these were not Ottoman Turks but descendants of an earlier Turanian invasion who spoke a dialect of their own. Only by counting the Kurds, who formed 60 per cent of the inhabitants, could a case be based on population statistics. 'It was reserved for the Turkish delegation', remarked Curzon, 'to discover for the first time in history that the Kurds were Turks.' More expert authorities believed that they were people of an Iranian race speaking an Iranian language. He himself had stayed with Kurds in Kurdistan and, although he did not pretend to be an authority, he could 'pick out a Kurd from a Turk any day of the week'.[41] In any case, as he observed later on, the Kurds did not want to be part of Turkey.

Further arguments were piled up. Curzon did not see by what logic Mosul itself, an Arab city built by Arabs, should be handed back to Turkey. And if it was, the Arab kingdom of Iraq would become 'well-nigh impossible' because a Turkish army in Mosul would have Baghdad at its mercy. Finally, having demolished Ismet's case, Curzon said that Britain was prepared to submit the question to the arbitration of the League of Nations. The Turks protested but their position was destroyed; they could no longer threaten to disrupt the conference over an issue which had effectively been removed from the agenda.*

The day after his triumph Curzon summoned his French and Italian colleagues to discuss the ending of the conference. A treaty, he suggested, should be presented in a week's time to the Turks, who would then be given four days to decide whether to accept it; whatever they did, he himself would leave Lausanne at the end of that period, on the night of 4 February. Garroni and M. Bompard, who had succeeded Barrère, were disconcerted by the schedule. Curzon's committee had gained nearly all its aims on territorial matters – with which the British were most concerned – but theirs, dealing mainly with judicial and economic questions of particular interest to themselves, had not achieved very much. Bompard's reports on the current position prompted the French Government to try to sabotage the outcome by stating publicly on 30 January that the treaty to be given to the Turks on the following day was not a final document but 'a basis of future discussion'. Realizing that this intervention would merely encourage Turkey to make a separate treaty with Britain, Bompard hastily per-

---

*The Turks continued to dispute the issue for another three years before accepting the verdict of the League of Nations in 1926. The League's case was based, as they had feared, on Curzon's arguments, and Mosul remained part of Iraq.

suaded Poincaré to declare that the statement had been unauthorized.

Infuriated by this display of French 'perfidy', Curzon nevertheless refused to abandon the Allies and make a deal with Ismet on the basis of the decisions reached in the territorial committee. The next day he duly presented the entire treaty to the Turks and denied their request, which was backed by Bompard and Garroni, for eight days in which to consider it. Whatever happened, he was leaving in four days' time. Although he himself remained uncertain of the outcome, there was euphoria in the British delegation. Britannia had won, Nicolson told his wife, 'against the Turks, against treacherous allies, against a weak-kneed cabinet, against a rotten public opinion'. And it had been entirely due to Curzon: 'I am so proud of him. So *awfully* proud. He is a great man and one day England will know it.'[42]

During the final days the French asked Curzon to make concessions on points he had already won in order to induce Ismet to compromise on the economic and other questions. He duly obliged by agreeing to defer his appeal to the League of Nations on Mosul. Turkey's official reply to the draft treaty, delivered on the last day, accepted political and territorial questions such as the Straits Convention and the Thracian border and offered to sign a treaty on these issues while leaving economic and legal matters open for future negotiations. The way was thus clear for a separate peace. Asked by a Turkish delegate why Britain did not make one, Nicolson found himself assailed by the 'public school spirit' and replied that the empire did not do that sort of thing.[43] Nor did Lord Curzon. Tempting though it must have been to abandon them, he stood by his ungrateful allies. Many years later, Sforza admitted he had been 'very loyal'.[44]

In the course of the last afternoon the negotiations became more frantic. After finalizing their points, the Allied delegates summoned Ismet, who appeared looking unhappy and nervous for what Nicolson described as an 'emotional and confused' scene. In his biography of Atatürk, Lord Kinross criticized Curzon for thinking 'in terms of the old Ottoman Turk', believing that 'Ismet was holding out until the last moment, bargaining like a carpet merchant to get the best deal he could, but would yield in the end'.[45] Yet neither Nicolson's account nor the Foreign Office minutes suggest that Curzon took such a view. Instead he appealed to Ismet's sense of statesmanship and to feelings of sentiment. The world was looking to them for a solution, he told him, and they must find one before they left the room.

While the talking went on, suitcases and packing cases were accumulating in the corridors. After retiring for a few moments to reflect, the Turkish delegates resolved to accept the British conditions but not the economic paragraphs. Garroni and Bompard begged Ismet to reconsider and told him his 'responsibility was great and terrible'. Then Curzon made his final appeal for peace. According to the minutes, he observed that 'this might be the last time he would ever meet Ismet Pasha. He wished to carry back to London a memory of friendship and he would like to sign a common pact of peace and friendship with Ismet Pasha before he left'.[46] Mopping his forehead and dabbing his lips, Ismet longed to sign; yet although he was empowered to do so without reference to Ankara, he dared not take the responsibility. The British delayed the Orient Express for half an hour at Lausanne Station in case he changed his mind. Then they steamed towards Paris.

The failure to sign a treaty blinded only the popular press to the fact that Lausanne had been a great triumph. Political opinion in Europe as well as at home recognized that a settlement was now inevitable and that Britain had regained her prestige in the Near East. Ismet returned to Ankara and persuaded the National Assembly to vote for the draft treaty with minor modifications. In late March these were examined by Curzon during a London reunion with Bompard and Garroni, and a month later Rumbold represented Britain in a second and less contentious conference at Lausanne. The subsequent agreement contained some economic concessions to Turkey but did not dent Curzon's political settlement of the previous winter. The Treaty of Lausanne secured the freedom of the Straits, achieved a relatively high level of regional stability and, by restoring Turkish sovereignty to the Turkish heartland, enabled the new country to make the transition from enfeebled empire to nation state. It was the most successful and the most lasting of all the post-war treaties.

As Remembrance Day disturbs the traditional view of Curzon as a master of ceremonies, so Lausanne shows him in an altered light as a diplomatist. Amery, normally a hostile critic, believed that 'by sheer force of knowledge, debating ability and personality he secured a far better peace than could have been expected'.[47] Yet even these well-known qualities would not have been sufficient without the tact and patience which the almost incredulous FO officials observed.[48] As the Archbishop of Canterbury remarked, it was the 'combination of dignity and conciliatoriness, of firmness and resource' which had earned Curzon 'the plaudits of a grateful people'.[49]

But the greatest tributes, which Curzon never heard, came from the

Turks. Not only did Ismet convince his countrymen to accept Curzon's treaty; he also spoke to many of the 'very highest admiration and respect' he felt for the Englishman and his conduct at Lausanne. The respect outlived even Ismet. On the seventieth anniversary of the conference the Turkish Government invited Curzon's grandson, Lord Ravensdale, to a commemorative celebration at which, together with Ismet's son, he laid a wreath on Atatürk's grave.[50]

36

Family Sagas

IN JUNE 1920 the British ambassador in Washington told Lloyd George that a 'simply splendid photograph' of Curzon in coronet and robes had appeared in the American press. Several people had mentioned it, he reported, and apparently regarded them 'as his normal costume and as an exact repetition in concrete form of his inner mind'.[1] While the British were aware that their Foreign Secretary did not habitually walk about in a coronet, many at that time would have agreed with the second part of the remark. Public perceptions of Curzon changed after Chanak and Lausanne, and his public behaviour changed with them. Popular esteem made him more relaxed and less defensive, less inclined to think he was invariably surrounded by hostility. Journalists had found him human at Lausanne, and a little later the public shared the discovery.

'I made one of what are called my new class of speeches', he told Grace after a function in 1923, 'and had them all in roars of laughter for $\frac{1}{4}$ hour.'[2] He made another at the seventy-fifth birthday dinner of T.P. O'Connor, the veteran Irish MP, a performance of charm and humour which several listeners regarded as the best after-dinner speech they had ever heard. Broadcast on the wireless, it had an unexpected impact. Everyone 'marvelled', declared the *Daily Graphic*, 'at the revelation of a side of his character hitherto veiled'.[3]

It was of course no revelation to his diminishing band of friends. In private, away from the Cabinet table and the House of Lords, he was still affectionate, amusing, usually ready to laugh at himself. Lord

Riddell, who had got to know Curzon since the war, thought him 'first-rate company' and 'never' found him pompous.[4] Oliver Lyttelton, the son of his old friend Alfred, considered that 'in form' – 'and in form might perhaps be written when not in much pain' – Curzon was the 'best company' in the world. His stories were a memorable combination of 'rolling and majestic' passages illuminated by spontaneous bursts of wit. 'If only tape recorders had been invented, the replay would have given to posterity a very different view and a more endearing memory' of the speaker.[5]

Yet there was now little opportunity for intimate dinners with friends. As Foreign Secretary Curzon's life was divided, as it had been in India, between excessive work and a formal social life. Carlton House Terrace came almost to rival Buckingham Palace as a setting for magnificent entertainment, its tables graced by the statesmen and surviving royal families of Europe. The banquets were not immune to mishaps: the Queen of Portugal had her eyebrows singed by the butler's cigarette lighter, the Shah of Persia tripped up and rolled down the staircase, and the Queen of Spain arrived to find Grace wearing an identical dress made by Worth in Paris. Yet the furnishings were always perfect for the occasion – the banks of flowers from Hackwood, the platoons of footmen, Cassano's orchestra playing discreetly in a neighbouring room during dinner.

Curzon also entertained at Hackwood, though less often and on a smaller scale than before the war. The weekends still revolved around vast formal meals, walks in the park and gardens, and plenty of conversation. As always Curzon was a charming and attentive host, closely supervising the details of his guests' entertainment; before one weekend he substituted all the books Grace had placed in the spare bedrooms on the grounds that she 'had not correctly assessed the literary tastes' of their guests.[6] An unwelcome innovation started by his wife was a house party for Ascot, a very grand affair whose members included the Aga Khan and Prince Paul of Serbia. The racing took place in the week, which elicited a grumble from Curzon that 'much locomotion and fatigue' were required to combine the role of sporting host with the duties of Foreign Secretary. He himself never saw the point of racing and only once visited the course. But he took the trouble to have his family's old racing colours verified for Grace to use when she embarked on her ultimately ruinous career as a racehorse owner.

Yet behind the glitter of this life and the late success of his foreign policy, Curzon's last years were increasingly lonely and at times almost pathetic. As Vansittart recognized, there was an 'essential helplessness' about him, an enduring naïvety towards a world full of gadgets and novelties and things he did not like or understand: even the telephone remained an enemy never quite assimilated. He reacted to change by attempting, as far as possible, to ignore it. His tastes, like his ideas, belonged to the late Victorian era. He decorated his houses with damask and tablecloths and red carpets with large patterns on them. He wore frock coats after they had been abandoned by other men. And at home he insisted on keeping the Victorian hours of luncheon at two and dinner at nine.

Few people were more conservative about what they ate and drank than George Curzon. Preserving his enthusiasm for nursery food – especially cakes, puddings (except tapioca) and plenty of jam – he much preferred simple English dishes to 'greasy French cooking', by which he meant something with a sauce. Predictably, the modern world of cocktails was beyond him. He drank ginger beer for lunch, an occasional brandy and soda in the evening, and champagne for dinner. Accompanied by a box of Rumpelmayer's chocolates, champagne also sustained him as he worked through his Foreign Office boxes. But he never drank much. There is no recorded instance of him being drunk in his entire life.

It was a lonely existence, in spite of the house parties and the diplomatic entertaining. Friends died or quarrelled or fell away; his family found him querulous, intolerant and difficult to live with. The pursuits of his 'leisure' were perforce solitary rather than sociable: ill health denied him the pleasures of golf and other sport; lack of interest precluded enjoyment of music and the theatre. But solace continued to be provided by the restoration of old buildings and the chronicling of their past. Odd days were seized to inspect the works at Bodiam and Tattershall, odd moments taken to investigate their history. Sometimes he found a few hours to work on a volume of travel reminiscences or his long-delayed book on Calcutta. Most of his manuscripts were unfinished, but *Tales of Travel* appeared in 1923 – the year of his 'new class of speeches' – and revealed to an astonished readership that its author had a sense of humour.

Curzon's principal private project was the restoration and refurbishment of Kedleston, a task in which he received no assistance or interest from his wife. Grace might have liked the house, she admitted, if it had been built at Genoa or Naples, but she thought it gloomy and cheerless in Derbyshire and almost invariably found an excuse not to go there.

Trusting, however, to change her mind by making it comfortable, her husband worked to have the house modernized by 1925 when he planned to transfer his family from Hackwood. Ordering repairs to furniture and the re-framing of pictures, he also oversaw plans to extend electricity all over the house and install fifteen new bathrooms. When out of office in 1924, he spent much time supervising the laying-out of gardens in readiness for the move.

As he grew older, Curzon came no nearer to solving the problem that had marred both his life and his career – the problem of human relations, of how to get on with other people. Many would have agreed with Crawford, who attributed the failure to a 'mean personality' and a deficiency of 'heart' which ultimately prevented him from acquiring greatness.[7] But those who knew him better realized that this was not the explanation. Each stage of Curzon's career can produce witnesses of almost daily acts of kindness: he had enough heart to remember little things, to send his car round to take his nieces to the zoo, to stay up late during the Lausanne Conference to write a long and enthusiastic reference for an old servant.[8] No one who reads his letters of condolence could accuse him of lack of compassion; no one who peruses the list of charitable donations could think he was ungenerous.

And yet there *was* a certain meanness of character, exacerbated by pain. The characteristic was not dominant and it was not always visible, but it was there. He could be generous on a grand scale and mean on a petty one. He gave £500 for the restoration of St George's Chapel and sent 70 crates of champagne plus 1,000 books as a present to the British officers in Mesopotamia. Yet his tips were sometimes so parsimonious that Grace had to supplement them surreptitiously.[9] This type of contradiction pervaded other areas of his life. If he was kind and indulgent with one servant, he was more than likely to be odious and unreasonable with the next. Rarely capable of self-criticism, he was conscious, however, of this particular defect. Every morning, he told Nicolson, he prayed to God that he would not be rude or unkind during the course of the day, and every night he looked back and found that his prayer had been 'seldom vouchsafed'.[10]

Curzon longed to be the revered centre of a happy family circle. He was sentimental about family matters and wept at the christening of his first grandchild. But he was not a good family man. He was on reasonable terms with his brothers and sisters partly because he seldom saw any of them except Frank. Yet in his immediate family the only person with whom he always got on well in his last years was his young step-daughter. Making a point of seeing Marcella every day, in London or at Hackwood, he regarded their conversations as one of the best moments of his day. In recognition of this tender and untroubled relationship, she was left his house at Broadstairs in his will.

Curzon's own daughters, who in 1923 were aged 27, 25 and 19, were more of a problem. He wanted them to be like Mary, feminine, yielding, serious-minded, talented in a domestic way, and devoted to their father. He gave them what he imagined to be a perfect upbringing: a lovely country home, governesses and schools, a period of study abroad (except for Cimmie who was prevented from going by the war), and a grand coming-out ball. After that he hoped they would marry well, settle down and become loyal wives, good mothers and responsible citizens. Hoping even to have some influence in the selection of their husbands, he promoted both Lord Spencer and Oliver Lyttelton as potential candidates. 'It is my dearest wish,' he told Lyttelton at a ball at Carlton House Terrace, 'as I know it would have been of your dear father, that you should become affianced to one of my daughters.'[11]

Irene and Cimmie, recalled Lyttelton, were 'enchanted with this old-world wish, and the Trollopian terms in which it had been expressed'. But they had no intention of allowing their father to recommend husbands or to determine any aspect of their lives after they reached the age of 21. All three girls were stronger characters than Mary; they were after all Curzons, brought up beyond the influence of their mother's family. Moreover, they reached adulthood during a universal upheaval that devastated the society their father had grown up in. During the war, in which she lost many of her friends, Cimmie had worked on a farm as a landgirl and as a clerk in the War Office. After such experiences she became, as her husband later wrote, 'resistant to the exaggerated magnificence in which she had been brought up'.[12]

No man was less capable than Curzon of understanding the Twenties. An unindulgent parent by nature, he was bewildered by the combination of frivolity and independence, by what he regarded in his daughters' case as the failure to realize there were 'things in life beyond madcap enjoyment'. Censorious of rowdiness and modern dancing – mercifully, he did not quite live to see the Charleston imported to Britain – he was appalled when told they had returned from a nightclub with the Prince of Wales and two of his brothers for an impromptu party at Carlton House Terrace – though he might have been less angry if Prince Henry had not sat on the dining-room table and broken a table leg.[13]

When Irene protested that he was always telling her she was a failure, Curzon denied that he had ever said such a thing. But he felt it, partly perhaps because of an injudicious wartime engagement which she broke off, but more importantly because her only major interest was fox-hunting. Unsuccessful in establishing close relations with his daughters when they were young, he expected them to appreciate his lectures on the seriousness of life when they were older. It was a hopeless approach. After preventing Baba from going to America without a proper chaperon at the age of 19, he 'implored her not to live for pleasure and excitement only but to do or attempt something serious'. Not surprisingly, she 'raved and cried, and swore she would leave' the house.[14] Getting on badly with all three of his daughters made him realize that he must be at least partly to blame. But he never had any idea why. His letters to Grace contain numerous references to his failure as a parent and his inability to understand what he had done wrong.

The two main areas of conflict were men and money. Despite his own amorous career, Curzon refused to tolerate a hint of impropriety in his daughters' behaviour. He would not even let them have tea alone with a man at Carlton House Terrace. On one occasion Grace managed to prevent him throwing a friend of Baba's out of the house by agreeing to chaperon the couple as they munched through cucumber sandwiches; he nevertheless appeared in his daughter's bedroom the following morning to upbraid her for her behaviour.[15] On another equally innocent occasion Curzon noticed a hat and gloves in the hall, learnt that they belonged to Major Metcalfe (whom Baba later married) and after her visitor's departure told his daughter he 'would not allow any young man to call and have tea with her and that unless she promised not to do it again', he would refuse to let her go on a planned trip abroad.[16]

Potential suitors were regarded with suspicion not only because they might seduce his daughters but also because they might be after their money. From Lausanne the Foreign Secretary asked Lady Desborough to find out about Lord Westmorland, who was 'believed to be running after' Baba; convinced he had not 'a bob in the world', Curzon added that his 'antecedents' did not fill him with enthusiasm .[17] Earlier, when Cimmie told her father she wanted to marry a young Conservative MP called Oswald Mosley, he immediately asked if he was marrying her for love or thinking of her money. The girl naturally replied that the second idea had never crossed her fiancé's mind. Secretly relieved that 'her choice appeared on the surface' to be such a good one, Curzon felt obliged to lecture her on the responsibilities of married life and the need to renounce her frivolous existence of rushing about wherever she pleased.[18] After receiving good reports of Mosley from Lady Salisbury and a party whip, he met his aspiring son-in-law, asked various questions about devotion and fidelity, and gave his consent. Curzon's favourable impressions did not last long, partly because of Mosley's political behaviour and partly because it soon became apparent that he did indeed have designs on Cimmie's money. At a Cabinet meeting at the end of his life Curzon was heard referring to 'my sinister son-in-law'.[19]

He was not of course in a strong position to complain about men with strong libidos who married rich women. But he was naturally distressed that his daughters' coming-of-age had the effect of depleting the income he required to finance his style of living. In letters to Grace written after Cimmie's marriage, he frequently told her they must reduce their expenditure, that he must cut down on the garden at Hackwood, that he would have to sell both his Romney and his house at Broadstairs. Designed to induce Grace to make a larger contribution to their expenditure, the expression of anxieties had little effect. Indeed, his wife was often late with her monthly payments and on two occasions in the summer of 1920 she even stopped her cheques.

Curzon's financial quarrels with his eldest daughters form a melancholy saga. Accused by them of expropriating their income for his own projects, he retorted that his expenditure had been regulated by the Court of Chancery and that his sole extravagance had been the building of the memorial chapel for their mother and the restoration of the church at Kedleston; nearly everything else, including the house at Broadstairs and the lease of Montacute, had been purchased for his daughters' use. Their money also went, however, towards the upkeep of the 'family homes', Hackwood and Carlton House Terrace, places they decreasingly used as they grew older. At the age of 23 Irene decided to remove her fortune from her father's hands, whereupon he took advantage of a clause in his marriage settlement to redistribute a portion of its income to her sisters, whose money he still controlled. It was a legitimate manoeuvre but one which occasioned much ill feeling with the trustees, his brother Frank and his brother-in-law Hardress Waller, whom he criticized for rightly refusing to make the redistribution before they were sure it was legal.

When Cimmie married at the age of 21, lawyers acting for her and her father agreed that she would have all the money from her mother's will, producing an income of some £10,000, while leaving Curzon with her portion of her parents' marriage settlement, which came to an annual sum of around £3,000. About a year after their marriage, however, Mosley lost money on a provincial newspaper and persuaded her to insist on her entire inheritance. Cimmie then informed her father she was going to end his 'allowance' – a somewhat humiliating way of putting it – and followed his protests with a series of insulting letters. Unable to stand what he called 'the perpetual torrent of threats and abuse and insinuation', Curzon told her to take it all. 'My daughters seem to go mad', he wrote to Grace, 'when a question of money is concerned'. From now on he wanted no more financial transactions with them. 'They will squeeze the uttermost farthing, and generosity and kindness are thrown away upon them.' His relations with Irene and Cimmie never recovered.[20]

Although Grace unkindly observed that fatherhood was not Curzon's 'strong quality', she did her best to provide him with another child. For five years she continued her depressing cycle of cure, conception and miscarriage. In the autumn of 1921 she underwent a course of mudbaths in the Rhineland for what she called her 'last great effort'. For a time it seemed that finally she would be rewarded: she was 'feeling so well,' she told her husband the following March, 'and still full of hope – and so much love waiting for the future Earl of Kedleston as well as for his beloved Daddy'.[21] Disillusion, alas, quickly followed. Yet although Grace was by now in her mid-forties, Curzon did not quite abandon hope. His longing for a son was further increased by his dislike of his current heir, Richard (the son of Affy, who died in 1920), and his wife. Complaining at the end of 1923 that his nephew drove about in a Rolls-Royce but never did any work, he sighed, 'Oh if only we could still knock them out'.[22]

Curzon's affection for his wife is indisputable. He wrote to her every day when they were apart, he missed her during her absences and, unless he was actually making a speech, he was waiting for her on the station platform when she came back. He was grateful for her attempts to produce a child and for the way she fulfilled her duties as hostess at Hackwood and Carlton House Terrace. In addition, he was so proud of her appearance that he had her painted several times and longed for a portrait worthy to hang in the State Room at Kedleston. Much though he wanted Grace to be admired, however, he was anxious that she should expose her charms to no one but himself. When in Paris after the war, she was exhorted not to return with dresses showing 'too much either of the whitest of backs or the most beautiful of legs'. He could 'concede much to modern fashion,' he claimed, 'but not that'.[23]

There is not a great deal more that can be said for the marriage. Grace was proud of her husband's intellect and his achievements, but she took little interest in what he was doing. Excellent no doubt as a lover, a hostess, an adornment, an aspirant childbearer, she was never a companion like Mary. Her ignorance was colossal – when referring by letter to an historical figure such as Akbar, he felt obliged to put 'Mogul emperor' in brackets afterwards – and she made little effort to reduce it. Foreign affairs bored her as much as the restoration of Kedleston, and she had no qualms about letting her husband know. Once, after taking his usual trouble to describe the political situation, he was terribly hurt to be told his letters were 'so dull'. He felt 'very much disheartened', he said on another occasion, that she did not take 'the faintest interest' in anything he said or did.

It would not be fair to blame Grace, whose tastes were formed long before her second marriage, for the fact that she and her husband had so little in common. Their essential incompatibility, obscured by physical attraction, became apparent soon after their wedding. She was naturally drawn to the pleasures he most deplored, to horse-racing, to cards, to fashion, to dancing in nightclubs. He had no right to object, of course, because he had had plenty of opportunity to find out what she was like before they married. Nor could he have complained – and there is no evidence that he did – if she found married life rather dull. He worked so hard that he had virtually no social life apart from official entertainment and occasional weekends at Hackwood. During the first four months after Lausanne he only once went out to dinner. Almost every other night was spent working into the small hours, a regime which compelled him, as Lord D'Abernon exquisitely put it, 'to relegate to the morning hour the lighter amenities of conjugal life'.[24]

The marriage might have gone better if they had spent more holidays together. Had they gone, for example, to Venice, Curzon would have spent his days in the churches and the Accademia, and Grace would have gone to the Lido; yet at least they would have dined together and found something new to talk about. But whenever he had a short break, Curzon wanted to go to Kedleston. Grace joined him for parts of the conferences of Cannes and Lausanne, and they visited the French resort for a short holiday in 1920. But he did not enjoy the place and felt 'rather like a Bishop in Regent Circus at midnight'; Grace, he told her brother, liked 'the casino and dancing and polo and Cannes social life much better' than he did.[25] Perhaps that failure deterred him from future forays. Four years later, when out of office, he cancelled a planned holiday to Spain because of new planting he wanted to do at Kedleston.

In the circumstances it would have been surprising if Grace had not taken a lover more suited to her style of life. Her choice was Sir Matthew 'Scatters' Wilson, an archetypal bounder whose principal interests were horses, cards and rich women. The dates of this liaison, which continued long after her husband's death and resulted in the loss of most of her fortune, are unclear. The belief that it had started by the beginning of 1919, reproduced in a number of books, is based on a case of mistaken identity and is clearly wrong.* The affair probably began towards the end of Curzon's life and flourished during Grace's visits to Paris. It has been said that her husband knew about it and was upset, but no reference to the matter survives in their correspondence.[26]

Whatever the state of her own fidelity, Grace remained a jealous and suspicious wife. Her monthly quarrels with her husband continued, often provoked by the most trivial incidents. When he talked to Diana Cooper after a dinner party, she declined to speak to him. When she heard that he had met two old friends, Lady Desborough and Lady Essex, during a conference, she threw a tantrum, wrote a furious letter and made the incident an excuse not to go to Kedleston with him. Such behaviour left Curzon in despair. 'Surely,' he reasoned, 'after $3\frac{1}{2}$ years of married life you might learn to be a little more trustful, a little less jealous, a little more kind.'[27]

Other incidents inspired rows and a succession of 'My dear George ... yours ever Grace' letters. Curzon went to a great deal of trouble over the alcoholism of her son Alfred, talking to him, consulting specialists, planning for him to go on archaeological or geographical expeditions where he would find nothing to drink. But during one conversation in 1923 he told the boy something about his father's defects, a revelation which infuriated Grace and gave her the opportunity to let her husband know her current views on their marriage. 'I am only your wife in name,' she told him, adding that the last six years had been a disappointment to herself and her boys. 'When I get away and look at our life, forgive me if I don't feel very enthusiastic.' Three days later she declared that 'the

---

*A letter from Duff Cooper to his wife in January 1919 mentions 'Scatters' Marchesa', a reference which has been interpreted to mean Grace. But as she did not become a Marchioness until 1921, he must have been writing about someone else, presumably an Italian.

only possible thing is that we should lead our separate lives as much as possible'.[28]

Yet these bleak sentiments do not form the whole picture. Although it gave him none of the serenity of his first marriage, this most mercurial of relationships had high points as well as low. After a violent row and a period of coldness, Grace would come back to him as if nothing had happened, and Curzon would convince himself that their marriage was really a great success, that they were now 'growing ever happier and happier, and free from the storms that sometimes used to ruffle the surface'.[29] They did not quarrel anymore, he told her, and they would never do so in future. The cycle would begin again shortly afterwards, Grace would tell him she was his wife only in name, non-speaking terms would be reimposed, and in due course everything would be all right once more. On the last New Year's Eve of his life he was able to refer to 'our happy married life, the one and only source of happiness to me'.[30]

37

Ultimate Disappointments,
1923–1925

N ONE OF THE Cabinet, remarked Lloyd George in March 1923,
appeared to be doing much with the exception of Curzon, who
went on 'burnishing his own halo'.[1] Through the cynicism the former
premier was echoing a general view that, in a Government of apparently
grey men, the one outstanding figure was the Foreign Secretary. At the
Cabinet's formation Curzon had been pre-eminent among Law's ministers, and since Lausanne his position had been enhanced. When he
went to France for another treatment for phlebitis at the end of March,
his position as the number two in the Government hierarchy seemed
unassailable.

Bonar Law had left the Exchequer for health reasons in 1921, and he
was not expected to serve a long term as premier. If the expectation was
correct, Curzon seemed to be the only possible candidate to succeed
him. Chamberlain of course was also a potential leader, but by now he
and Law were distanced by a mutual lack of respect, and he refused to
set himself up as ally and heir to a man he thought had twice robbed
him of the leadership.

While he was in France, a seemingly incredible rumour reached
Curzon that a rival had emerged in the shape of Stanley Baldwin. Apart
from his moment at the Carlton Club, Baldwin still had few achievements to his name. He had reached the Cabinet only in 1921 after
spending four years as a competent but not distinguished Financial
Secretary to the Treasury. After promotion to the presidency of the
Board of Trade, he had impressed neither the Prime Minister nor the

two men he had served under at the Exchequer. Finding him 'always . . . disappointing', Lloyd George thought he did nothing to restore business confidence and wanted to move him. Equally disappointed, Chamberlain successfully resisted the idea that he should succeed Montagu at the India Office: Peel would be 'much better', he argued, than the indecisive Baldwin.[2] In October 1922 Law considered him too inexperienced to become Chancellor of the Exchequer and only made the appointment after his first choice, Mckenna, refused the post. Since then he had almost forced the Prime Minister's resignation after a disastrous visit to Washington in pursuit of an American debt settlement. No wonder he seemed an implausible threat to the Foreign Secretary.

On hearing the rumour that Law was about to retire and would be succeeded by Baldwin, Curzon reacted in the worst possible manner. In a pompous and indignant letter he reminded the Prime Minister of his claims to succeed him, his record and reputation, his years of service and his experience of high office. If the succession to Law had to be considered – which he 'devoutly' hoped would not be the case – he could not surrender those claims or consent to serve under any of his present colleagues; on this point he was 'quite clear'. The Prime Minister drily replied that the rumour was without foundation and that, although he had not been well recently, he had no intention of resigning.[3]

Curzon was not an astute tactician in the field of human relations. But even he should have realized that an unceasing barrage of complaint was unlikely to persuade an ailing Prime Minister to want him as his successor. Familiar protests from Tours about ministers making unauthorized speeches on foreign affairs were followed later in April by a furious reaction to the fact that Lord Winchester had consulted Downing Street rather than the Foreign Office about forming a syndicate to develop Turkey. Asked by the Prime Minister if he had any objection to the scheme, Curzon replied in a tone he would never have used with Lloyd George. After criticizing Law's Private Secretary for failing to send the applicant straight to the FO, Curzon denounced Winchester's morals (both private and financial) and added, 'When these persons go to No. 10 instead of here, they are really reproducing one of the least admirable features of the LG regime.'[4] The Prime Minister, who had done nothing to deserve the reprimand, was deeply hurt. According to Lord Blake, the episode was crucial in forming Law's decision not to recommend Curzon as his successor.[5]

Sick and in pain, the Prime Minister embarked on a Mediterranean cruise on the first day of May. Before leaving, he appointed the Foreign Secretary to act as Deputy Prime Minister, an arrangement which seemed to indicate the nature of his successor. In the same period Curzon's confidence was bolstered by press speculation and by the support of Sir George Younger, the Chairman of the Conservative Party. Lunching together on 9 May, Younger assured Curzon that his succession was inevitable because Baldwin lacked both experience and authority.[6]

From France Law wrote on the 11th to tell Curzon he was feeling much better. But as everyone else thought he looked iller than ever, his physician was summoned from England to examine him. Cancer of the throat was diagnosed on the 17th and, although Law himself was not told immediately, his friend Beaverbrook gave up trying to dissuade him from resigning. For two days the Prime Minister remained in Paris, gloomily contemplating the defects of his two possible successors. But he was greatly relieved to be told by the ambassador, Lord Crewe, that a Prime Minister was not obliged to give a recommendation to the King. After his conversations with Law, Crewe came to the conclusion that no successor but the Foreign Secretary was being considered and could thus tell Curzon a few days later that he had 'of course . . . anticipated' his selection.[7] Indeed Law seems to have regarded Curzon's succession as inevitable but did not want the responsibility of either recommending or rejecting him. This attitude is reflected in the letter in which he announced his resignation to his deputy.

> I understand that it is not customary for the King to ask the Prime Minister to recommend his successor in circumstances like the present and I presume that he will not do so; but if, as I hope, he accepts my resignation at once, he will have to take immediate steps about my successor.[8]

Unless he expected that successor to be Curzon, the second half of the sentence would have been both pointless and misleading.

Bonar Law would have been astonished to learn that the uncertain feelings of a dying man would excite so much interest among historians. The chief source of this interest is the behaviour of his Private Secretary, Ronald Waterhouse, who delivered the resignation to the King at Aldershot on the 20th and at the same time handed over a memorandum to the royal Private Secretary, Lord Stamfordham. Written by John Davidson, the Prime Minister's Parliamentary Private Secretary, the memorandum eulogized Baldwin and, after acknowledging Curzon's talents and past services, disparaged the Foreign Secretary's claims by alleging that 'temperamentally' he did 'not inspire complete confidence in his colleagues, either as to his judgement or as to his ultimate strength of purpose in a crisis'. The document also asserted that his methods were 'inappropriate to harmony', that he was regarded as 'representing that section of privileged conservatism' which could not 'in this democratic age . . . be too assiduously exploited', and that most MPs believed that a Prime Minister could no longer be in the House of Lords. Davidson later claimed that Stamfordham had asked for the memorandum as an expression of the views of 'an ordinary backbencher' – an extraordinary request if true, because he was not a neutral MP at all but a friend and former Parliamentary Private Secretary to Baldwin. In the event the document was handed over by Waterhouse with the statement that it 'practically expressed the views of Mr Bonar Law'.[9]

Several people claimed to have heard the Prime Minister state his personal preference for Baldwin, evidence which seems to suggest that Waterhouse did not misrepresent his views. But the fact that Law may have preferred Baldwin does not imply that he thought he should succeed him or that he wanted his preference to be known. Indeed the evidence suggests that he felt, in spite of Curzon's defects and the problem of having a Prime Minister in the Lords, that the Foreign Secretary should succeed him. After telling Baldwin on the morning of his resignation that Curzon was the automatic choice, he gave Salisbury the impression the following day that in 'this very grave and complex situation he would on the whole be disinclined to pass over Curzon'.[10] Salisbury passed this opinion on to Stamfordham, adding that he would 'strongly recommend' the appointment of Curzon, whose faults were 'improving' and who, from his point of view, was 'the only acceptable Prime Minister'.[11]. But such conflicting views on Law's real feelings understandably confused Stamfordham and seem to have reduced the impact of Salisbury's advice.

As Bonar Law resigned on Whitsunday, the King's Private Secretary found immediate consultation difficult. Although two pro-Baldwin ministers, Amery and Bridgeman, were anxious to give him their advice, Stamfordham knew what they wanted to say and saw no point in hearing it. They were able to convey their views, however, during a walk in St James's Park, an encounter which deluded Amery into believing for the rest of his life that he had been responsible for Curzon's defeat.[12] But the opinions Stamfordham most wanted – apart from Salisbury's –

were those of Balfour, who was summoned from a house party on the Norfolk coast. The King's Private Secretary agreed with Salisbury, but his master sympathized with Balfour.

At his two interviews with Stamfordham on the 21st, Balfour did not discuss the merits of the candidates but concentrated on the difficulties presented by having the Prime Minister in the House of Lords. The Upper Chamber, he pointed out, already had a high proportion of Cabinet ministers, and the addition of the premier would thus be resented by MPs; another problem, he felt, was the fact that the Labour Party, now the main opposition in the Commons, was unrepresented in the Lords.[13] George V welcomed advice which elucidated and reinforced his own feelings: no one, his biographer has pointed out, 'played a more decisive part than Balfour in clarifying the King's mind'.[14] It would appear, therefore, that the matter was decided entirely on the constitutional issue by a very responsible monarch and a much revered elder statesman.

Yet decisions rarely come from a single source, and few people are entirely immune to personal considerations when a choice has to be made. No doubt the King acted from the best of motives, grateful that hostile feelings and political arguments both militated against the same candidate.* But there is cause to question the role of Balfour who, during their long and complicated relationship, had sometimes appeared to oppose Curzon because he was Curzon rather than because he disagreed with him. Like others in the party, he seems to have thought the Foreign Secretary's chief drawback was not his peerage but his temperament, although he recognized that this was not a reason that could be advanced in public. According to Amery, he therefore suggested that the House of Lords issue should be the 'official' explanation for the preferment of Baldwin.[16] Convinced that his intervention had been decisive, he returned to his friends in Norfolk. 'And will dear George be chosen?' asked one of the ladies. 'No,' he replied placidly, 'dear George will not.' When she feared he would be 'terribly disappointed', Balfour answered, 'I don't know. After all, even if he has lost the hope of Glory, he still has the means of Grace.'[17] Tackled later over his behaviour by Grace herself, he claimed to have done her husband a

---

*King George took little trouble to disguise his antipathy for Curzon. After Herman Norman's return from Tehran in 1921, the diplomat found his sovereign 'a little indiscreet in his comments on Curzon's policy in Persia and character generally; he evidently dislikes him extremely'.[15]

good turn in saving him from 'such a detestable office', which he was unable to understand why anyone should want.[18]

Curzon was at Montacute on Whit Monday when he received Bonar Law's letter informing him of his resignation. As he had refused to install that 'disastrous invention' (the telephone) in the Elizabethan mansion, he could not ring anyone to find out what was happening. Nor could he hurry back to London in case his action was 'misinterpreted'. He therefore paced restlessly about the garden until the evening when the village policeman bicycled round with a telegram from Stamfordham asking to see him the following day in London. Curzon wired back that he would be at Carlton House Terrace at 1.20.

In the train the next morning he found that the bulk of the press supported his claims; the *Daily Telegraph* was particularly strong in his favour, though *The Times* dwelt on the problems of having a peer as a premier. For the rest of the journey he made plans, talked to Grace about ecclesiastical appointments and decided he would continue to live at Carlton House Terrace, using Downing Street for official purposes only; he was already resolved to combine the premiership with the Foreign Office, at least for a while. Confident of his destiny, he smiled for the press photographers at Paddington and outside his home. On learning that Stamfordham would not arrive until 2.30, he 'scented danger', but Grace assured him that, if the King was going to pass him over, he would not send his secretary to apologize.[19]

While he waited, Curzon received backing from an unexpected quarter. One of Chamberlain's followers, Oliver Locker-Lampson MP, called to tell him that the coalitionist faction would support him if he could unite the party. Chamberlain himself, who was in France, had not authorized the approach, but a number of his supporters had agreed to it. According to Worthington-Evans, they cast Curzon in 'the role of peacemaker and uniter of the Party', and sent Locker-Lampson to inform him that Chamberlain and the other ex-ministers 'would serve under him if thereby unity could be obtained'.[20] They were not prepared, however, to serve under Baldwin.

Lord Stamfordham arrived soon afterwards, and a distressing interview ensued. According to Curzon's account, the King's Private Secretary explained 'with obvious embarrassment and in halting language' that, while the monarch recognized the superiority of his claims to those of any other candidate, he had convinced himself that the Prime Minister must be in the House of Commons to answer the Labour leader and for that reason he had decided to appoint Baldwin.

Curzon was devastated by the announcement. He told Stamfordham that the decision amounted to a permanent exclusion of peers from the premiership; he said it was a slur on his long career that would force his retirement from public life; and he argued, after describing the encounter with Locker-Lampson, that he alone could reunite the party. As his visitor was leaving, Curzon asked him to put these considerations to the King.

Stamfordham's embarrassment was such that he could not bring himself to admit that it was too late for appeals. On discovering afterwards that Baldwin had already been summoned to the Palace, Curzon was extremely hurt. It seemed to him incredible that the decision could have been taken without even consulting the man who was the acting premier, the senior Cabinet minister and the Leader of the House of Lords. Such, he reflected bitterly, was his reward for those decades of public service. 'Such was the manner in which it was intimated to me that the cup of honourable ambition had been dashed from my lips and that I could never aspire to fill the highest office in the service of the Crown.'[21] His bitterness was understandable, for the disappointment had been accompanied by humiliation, the stigma of supersession by a man of inferior claims, the mortification, when he looked back, of that smile before the cameras.

Knowing the state of Curzon's feelings, Baldwin felt unable to face his disappointed rival and so sent a note asking him to continue as Foreign Secretary.[22] Curzon's first reaction, as he told Stamfordham, was to decline, but he allowed himself to be dissuaded by appeals from friends and admirers: Salisbury urged him to stay on, Lovat Fraser begged him not to resign and 'repeat the mistake of 18 years ago'.[23] On the following day, the 23rd, Curzon congratulated Baldwin on his appointment and told him of his desire to retire. But, he added, 'as there are certain things which in the public interest I ought, perhaps, endeavour to carry through, and as my retirement at this moment might be thought to involve distrust in your administration, which would be a quite unfounded suspicion, I will for the present continue at the Foreign Office'.[24] Five days later, in a speech of much charm and eloquence, he proposed Baldwin's election as leader of the Conservatives. Even his opponents inside the party admitted that towards both themselves and the new Prime Minister he behaved with singular magnanimity.

History – or rather hindsight – proclaims that the King made the right choice. It contrasts Baldwin's later achievements with the accepted view of Curzon, that compound figure of anecdotal absurdities and Beaverbrook's malevolent imagination. It ignores the fact that Baldwin gained the post with fewer credentials than any other Conservative leader; it disregards both Curzon's Indian record and his emergence since Lloyd George's fall as a Foreign Secretary whom people compared with Castlereagh. Baldwin's selection has thus acquired an aura of inevitability: the MPs, the associations, the country itself all wanted him. But Bonar Law thought the party wanted Curzon, who did indeed manage to attract the backing both of leading Diehards and of leading coalitionists. Claims of the inevitability of Baldwin and the impossibility of Curzon really belong to a later retrospect. No outcry had greeted Curzon's appointment as acting premier, and it is difficult to see what damage he might have done as Prime Minister. He would have rapidly reunited the Conservatives; he would have spared them (and the country) two wholly unnecessary elections; and his foreign policy would have continued along that route which ultimately found solutions to the problems of reparations and European security. Had he died twenty-two months later – as he did – he would probably have been succeeded by Austen Chamberlain.

Yet, leaving their credentials aside, Baldwin represented the post-war national mood very much better than Curzon. A generation earlier, in the confident world of late Victorian Britain, the outcome would have been different, whatever doubts might have existed about the Foreign Secretary's character. In politics and speech, observed T.P. O'Connor, Curzon personified those imperial feelings which Kipling had expressed in poetry and prose.[25] But neither the statesman nor the poet was comfortable in the Britain of 1923, a nation uneasy with its greatness, tired of empire and its responsibilities, wanting to turn inwards and concentrate on its social and economic ills. The country was glad, as it later demonstrated, to have a man well-attuned to the temper of the age, a rather ordinary, pipe-smoking Englishman with an ear for the concerns of ordinary people and a sympathetic approach to the Labour movement. It is ironic that he happened to be Kipling's first cousin.

The new Prime Minister allowed Curzon considerable freedom to carry out those unspecified tasks he had alluded to in his letter of congratulation. One of these was to wrap up the Turkish settlement, which was finally done in the Treaty of Lausanne signed in July. Another was to confront the Russians over certain outrages against British subjects and to demand the curtailment of their anti-British propaganda in various parts of Asia. Two years earlier he had rebuked the Bolsheviks for intrigues that were 'more than usually repugnant to normal international law and comity'. But as this had made no difference to their behaviour, he now threatened to denounce the Anglo-Russian Trade Agreement of 1921 unless satisfaction for the outrages was given and the agents were 'disowned and recalled from the scene of their maleficent labours'. Uncharacteristically, the Soviet Government returned a conciliatory reply and duly transferred its agents from Kabul, Tehran and elsewhere.[26]

The most critical problems remained the questions of French security and the reparation payments the Allies had imposed on Germany four years earlier in the Treaty of Versailles. During the Coalition Curzon had been happy to leave these matters largely in the hands of Lloyd George, who had handled them at the Paris Peace Conference, and since its fall he had been preoccupied with Turkey. By the time he took charge in the spring of 1923, the French had occupied the Ruhr and were attempting to collect by force the reparations which Germany had failed to deliver. Britain had taken up a position of neutrality which was morally respectable but politically ineffectual. Had she taken one side, the other would have been forced to back down.

Critical of both countries, Curzon was more sympathetic to the Germans. He did not consider that the 'passive resistance' to the occupation which they financed was a violation of the Treaty of Versailles. Indeed he thought it was the occupation itself, economically counter-productive for everybody, which the Treaty did not sanction. But he was not prepared to break the Entente on the issue, because he still believed, in spite of so many confrontations, that the Anglo-French partnership was crucial for the future of Europe. His policy was thus to prod the countries towards each other. While he exhorted the Germans to make a realistic offer of what they were prepared to pay, he urged the French to accept a moratorium on reparations while Germany reorganized her ruined currency, and to agree to an impartial inquiry into her financial capacity. As usual, the chief obstacle was Poincaré who, Curzon suspected, was not 'capable of a generous gesture or a genial thought'.[27] The French premier stuck to his intransigent demands on German payments and refused to admit that an inquiry was necessary. Curzon experienced his familiar feelings of exasperation when dealing with the French; if he spoke in favour of the Entente, he moaned, they reproached him with hypocrisy for not supporting them in the Ruhr, yet if he was critical of anything they did, they accused him of 'affronting their dignity' or siding with Germany.[28]

During the summer and autumn of 1923 a series of exchanges, dialectically brilliant but diplomatically sterile, sped between London and Paris. President Millerand complained privately that Curzon and Poincaré 'would do nothing but stand like Homeric heroes each in his country and fling denunciations at each other'.[29] In September the French hero appeared to have won. To Curzon's disgust, he managed to induce Baldwin, who had been holidaying in France, to issue a joint communiqué implying that Britain was no longer neutral between France and Germany but was once more on the French side. In the end, however, Poincaré's two main schemes to weaken Germany were defeated. Attempts to set up separatist states in the Rhineland and the Palatinate – subsidized by France and supported by French troops – were destroyed, largely thanks to Curzon's resolute opposition. 'The firmness of his attitude', noted the British ambassador in Berlin, 'was indeed fatal to the conspiracy of the separatists.'[30]

At the end of 1923 Poincaré was also forced to acknowledge that his position on reparations was untenable. Since June Curzon had been urging the appointment of a committee, in which America would participate, to enquire into the whole reparations question. The proposal was finally adopted in the autumn, a committee began its work in the winter, and in April 1924 it produced the Dawes Plan, a comprehensive attempt to reorganize German finances and to settle both the extent of reparations and the rate of payment. Although Curzon had nothing to do with the plan itself, he might justly be regarded in Harold Nicolson's words as its 'spiritual begetter'.[31]

In August 1923, after despatching a strong and highly critical Note to the French Government, Curzon went to France for medical treatment – to the derision of Lloyd George who thought it 'most fatuous' of him to threaten Poincaré and then spend his 'holiday' in the country he was 'trying to bully'.[32] But the Foreign Secretary's mind had left the Ruhr and was now back in Calcutta, recalling the city's buildings and directing his pen as it travelled over the foolscap pages of his final book. The hotel at Bagnolles provided the usual nocturnal comedy, Curzon rattling doors and banging on walls in unsuccessful attempts to disrupt the 'trumpeting' of snorers on all sides. But he retained enough humour to draw Marcella a diagram showing the location of the offenders, including an elderly Greek whose snores reverberated through the ceiling above.

While he was at Bagnolles, Mussolini inaugurated a policy that Smuts was to describe as 'running about biting everybody'.[33] When an Italian general working for an international boundary commission was mysteriously killed on Greek soil, Mussolini delivered an impossible ultimatum to Athens – 'much worse', thought Curzon, than Austria's to Serbia after Sarajevo – and then bombarded and occupied the island of Corfu. The British Foreign Secretary was appalled by the behaviour of this 'old fashioned buccaneer without scruple or remorse',[34] and supported Greece's demand that the matter should be dealt with by the League of Nations. Mussolini, however, insisted that it be referred to the Conference of Ambassadors, which represented the Great Powers in Paris, and for which the murdered general had been working. Infuriated by Britain's support for the Greek position, he accused her of defying 'every principle of international morality', ordered his admirals to prepare for war against the Royal Navy, and threatened to destroy the League of Nations if it tried to intervene.[35] According to the ambassador in Rome, the Italian leader attributed Britain's hostility to Curzon's personal dislike of himself.[36] Unlike many Conservatives, the British Foreign Secretary had no vestige of admiration for Mussolini or his regime, but there was nothing personal in his criticism of the bombardment of an undefended harbour and the killing of a number of innocent people.

The ideal solution would have been to defy Mussolini and have him slapped down by the League of Nations. But Curzon doubted whether such an outcome was feasible. He had little support from British public opinion and much opposition from the newspapers, above all the Rothermere press, which ridiculed the League of Nations, refused to condemn Mussolini and accused Curzon of 'war-mongering'. Furthermore, the French, in need of Italian support over the Ruhr, were playing a double game, secretly assuring the Italians of their sympathy while warning the British that humiliation for Mussolini would lead to his fall and an outbreak of communism in Italy. Further warnings came from the Italian ambassador to London and the British embassy in Rome, which believed Mussolini would be replaced by a military dictatorship. Persuaded that a condemnation from Geneva would merely result in Mussolini storming out of the League while leaving him in Corfu, Curzon reluctantly accepted the arbitration of the Conference of Ambassadors. As far as Corfu was concerned, he was probably right, for Mussolini clearly wanted to annex the island and had already issued postage stamps bearing its name. Yet it did nothing for the prestige of the League. And although the Italians were persuaded to evacuate, the Conference, under pressure from the Franco-Italian axis, pronounced what Curzon considered the 'unjust and in reality indefensible verdict' of forcing Greece to pay an indemnity of 50 million lire. 'Those wretched Ambassadors', he complained, 'had been utterly bamboozled by the Italian' and had given the aggressor a large bribe to go away. He sighed: 'To such a pitch of immorality have we sunk.'[37]

Although Curzon remained loyal to the concept of the Entente, his persistent opposition to French policy induced politicians on both sides of the Channel to try to get rid of him. In October 1923 he was shown an intercepted telegram from Poincaré to the Comte de Saint-Aulaire, the French ambassador to London, telling him to call on the Prime Minister and explain that France could no longer tolerate Curzon as Foreign Secretary. He also saw a telegram from Saint-Aulaire informing the French premier that Baldwin himself wanted to remove Curzon, and from further documents he learnt that H.A. Gwynne, the journalist who had schemed with Kitchener over the Military Member in India, was a party to the intrigue. Curzon sent the documents to Baldwin, who denied that, as far as he was concerned, there was any foundation for their insinuations. A month later, when confronted with another batch of evidence, the Prime Minister replied that 'Poincaré has got you on the brain and is always looking out for occasion of offence in all that you do or say'. To Lord Crewe in Paris Curzon described the operation as Poincaré's 'sinister attempt to hound me out of office in the mistaken belief that he would then get a pliant Baldwin with a complaisant Eddie Derby'.[38]

A simultaneous and possibly connected plot in England foundered on the inflexible integrity of Austen Chamberlain. At the end of October the former Conservative leader was approached with the suggestion that he should return to the Government and replace Curzon as Foreign Secretary. According to a go-between, the substitution would be welcomed by Baldwin, the Cabinet and the party, and would produce a 'more wholesome atmosphere' in Britain's foreign relations. Chamberlain answered acerbically that, although he was under no obligation to Curzon, he would not enter into any secret agreement against him, nor would he return to office 'in conditions which amount to an intrigue'.[39] How much Baldwin knew of either of these conspiracies is uncertain. Curzon heard rumours of the second but found no difficulty in dismissing them. 'You need attach no importance', he told Grace in December, 'to the silly stories of my being jettisoned. After all, where would Baldwin be without me? And that he knows full well.'[40]

In the Governments of Bonar Law and Baldwin, Curzon strove to maintain personal control of foreign policy and the House of Lords. In neither sphere was he prepared to delegate. When Salisbury, the Deputy Leader of the Lords, suggested taking over certain duties on the grounds that his superior could not be in the Chamber often enough to carry them out, he was imperiously rebuffed. Such an arrangement, Curzon told him, would mean his abdication of 'the main functions of leadership', an action which he had 'never contemplated', and for which he saw 'no present necessity'.[41] In similar style he attempted to enforce his view that foreign affairs should be the preserve of himself, his Parliamentary Under-Secretary (Ronald McNeill) and, up to a point, the Prime Minister. He deplored the way foreign policy was conducted in Cabinet where any minister, he complained to Baldwin, could make any suggestion and take the discussions off into 'hopeless irrelevancies'.[42] He also resented attempts to influence his policy, particularly from Derby who persistently tried to impose a strong pro-French line on the Cabinet and whose 'mission in life', grumbled Curzon, was 'to vary attendance at Parisian race meetings with attempts to correct the blunders of the British ambassador and Foreign Secretary'.[43]

Curzon's most difficult colleague was his friend Lord Robert Cecil, the newly appointed minister with special responsibility for the League of Nations. Cecil's position almost guaranteed conflict for, although the League's affairs came under the Foreign Office, Curzon refused to let him work in the building for fear that he would encroach on areas not directly connected with Geneva. The delimitation of spheres of responsibility for their intertwining roles would have taxed the most accommodating of politicians; it was well beyond the temperaments of Cecil and Curzon. Throughout the summer of 1923 they reproached each other for lack of co-operation, and the Foreign Secretary accused his colleague of aspiring to be an Assistant Secretary of State. They also disagreed on policy itself. Cecil was 'a terrible nuisance to me in Cabinet,' Curzon once remarked to Grace, 'talking interminably and always wrong about foreign affairs'.[44] On hearing that he had discussed Anglo-French relations with President Millerand without informing the Foreign Office, Curzon threatened to resign unless he could be assured that such incidents would not recur.[45] Yet another old friendship fell away.

There was little reason to complain of interference from the Prime Minister. Indeed the state of affairs had changed so completely since

Lloyd George's time that Curzon could claim he now not only ran his own foreign policy but also determined Baldwin's pronouncements on the subject as well. During his first month in office, he told Crewe, the Prime Minister had done nothing but read out in the Commons answers that Curzon had prepared for him, while in the Cabinet he said not a word except to endorse his Foreign Secretary's policy.[46] The situation had barely altered by November. Nothing exceeded Baldwin's 'cheerfulness, good temper and courtesy', Curzon told his wife, 'except his impotence. At the Imperial Conference he never opens his mouth and leaves the entire lead to me.'[47] The only unsatisfactory feature of this arrangement was the newspapers' habit of praising the Prime Minister for successes achieved by the Foreign Secretary. After winning a 'very considerable victory' over Poincaré in November, he was rather nettled to see it 'attributed in every paper to the courage and sagacity of Baldwin, who had no more to do with the thing than our butler . . .'[48]

The Imperial Conference of 1923, at which Curzon elaborately surveyed the problems of the planet, was his last triumph on an ample stage. The plaudits he received afterwards from the Dominion Prime Ministers were very gratifying in themselves but aroused some painful reflections. According to Smuts, all of them had been surprised by Baldwin's feebleness and regarded Curzon as the only effective figure in the Government. Mackenzie King, the Canadian premier, admitted he had come to the conference with a violent prejudice against the Foreign Secretary based on the press image of the 'superior person', but had been profoundly impressed by his knowledge, eloquence and affability. Curzon was almost overcome by emotion. 'Oh!' he groaned to Grace. 'How these cursed papers have killed me for half a lifetime. I can never recover now.' He was right, of course. The memory of Lausanne had evaporated from the mind of the popular press, and he was now again regularly assailed in the Beaverbrook and Rothermere papers. When Lord Riddell told him he was the 'most misjudged of men', Curzon replied bitterly that if journalists had taken the trouble to find out about him, they would have been 'spared the parrot-like repetition of a silly old tag' and might have helped his career instead of 'hindering it by every means in their power'.[49]

At the beginning of November the Cabinet considered whether it should appeal to the electorate for a mandate to introduce tariffs as a means of combating unemployment. Curzon led the opposition to the scheme, arguing that another election so soon after the last one would savour of trickery, lead very likely to electoral disaster and once again disrupt the conduct of foreign policy during a critical period. Like many people then and since, he could not understand why Baldwin should not go tranquilly on until 1927 rather than take a 'huge gamble' for little purpose. On hearing the election announcement on the 13th, he was for once tempted to agree with Derby who exclaimed that Europe was dominated by madmen, Mussolini and Poincaré, while England was ruled by a 'damned idiot'.[50]

Curzon's pessimism about the election was justified by the result. The Conservatives were reduced from 345 seats to 258, their lowest figure between the disasters of 1906 and 1945, while between them the Liberals and the Labour Party amassed 350. It was the price, Curzon observed to his wife, 'that we all have to pay for the utter incompetence of Baldwin and the madness of his selection by the King'.[51]

Since the Conservatives had lost their majority but remained the largest party, the political situation was confused. Curzon's immediate reaction was that Baldwin, as the architect of 'an act of blind folly', ought to resign: the King might then send for Asquith or MacDonald but, should he decide to invite another Conservative to form a government, he should 'logically' send for the Foreign Secretary. Curzon did not expect to be chosen, however, partly because of his peerage and partly because the *Daily Mail* (which complained about his lack of sympathy for Mussolini) had convinced many people that he was an enemy of the Entente and that his foreign policy was a failure.[52] In fact, even outside the readership of the *Daily Mail,* Curzon does not seem to have been mentioned as a possible successor. There were moves to promote Derby or Austen Chamberlain, but these soon collapsed, leaving Baldwin in office until January when a successful Labour amendment to the King's Speech brought about his resignation. On the 22nd of that month Ramsay MacDonald was summoned to the Palace and asked to form the first Labour Government.

Curzon had begun to say his farewells before the inevitable parliamentary defeat. He gave a party for junior Foreign Office staff at a Fleet Street pub and a dinner for senior officials at Carlton House Terrace. The second occasion, noted Nicolson, was an awkward affair, Curzon being genial and showing his Napoleonic collection, but everyone else feeling shy and embarrassed. On his last day at the Foreign Office Nicolson found him 'rather pathetic sitting there in his big room eating raspberry jam and knowing that he will be out of office in a few hours'.[53] Curzon had not got used to the idea of a Labour Foreign Secretary sitting in his place, and he was appalled to be told that MacDonald, who had decided to combine the office with the premiership, would refuse to read papers or see ambassadors. 'All I can say', he wrote to Crewe, 'is a) Good God! b) he will soon learn wisdom . . .'[54]

Shortly before MacDonald's arrival, he apologized to his secretaries for being a 'hard task-master' and vacated his office. He did not regard it, however, as a final farewell. Since the Labour Party had less than a third of the seats in the House of Commons, the Government could not last long, and he expected to return to the FO on its demise. But it was not to be. Curzon's tenure, which including those first nine months under Balfour had lasted for five years, was over for good.

The performance of a Foreign Secretary is perhaps more difficult to assess than that of other ministers because the success of a policy, however sound in theory and in application, depends on at least one extra dimension, the behaviour of other countries. Another difficulty, which tends to restrict the appreciation of contemporaries, is the long gestation period usually required for diplomatic success; foreign ministers are therefore often out of office before their achievements can be seen in perspective. This was particularly true in the case of Curzon.

A common criticism of the time, articulated by Amery in 1923, was that Curzon drafted magnificent despatches but pursued a 'purely static and argumentative' policy which did 'not attempt to deal with the development of live forces'.[55] This tendency, which others had noted earlier, undoubtedly existed. But in the post-Lloyd George era it did not manage to prevent a series of diplomatic successes. In the period Amery was writing about, Britain's 'static' foreign policy somehow helped to get the French out of the Ruhr and the Italians off Corfu, forced the Russians to behave more reasonably, prevented the disintegration of Germany and defused the reparations issue; above all, it almost singlehandedly solved the Turkish question.

In earlier years, working uncomfortably beside Lloyd George, there had been fewer achievements; Persia had been a failure, Egypt was only a modest success. Had Curzon been ousted during his illness of 1922, the balance sheet would have looked bleak. He would have been judged as a Foreign Secretary who lacked vision and purpose, a minister who could explain a problem without being able to solve it. Yet even in that period he was frequently more far-sighted than his colleagues. He did not share Balfour's vision of Zionism, Montagu's vision of the dyarchy, or Lloyd George's vision of an Hellenic revival in Asia Minor, because he foresaw that they would lead to Arab-Jewish conflict, Indian independence and a Greek-Turkish tragedy. The prophet and the visionary were on opposite sides, and the prophet was usually right. As with his later European policies, he did not of course receive praise for prophecies fulfilled while he was out of office or after his death. But they should be placed to the credit of a statesman too often assumed to have been gazing perpetually into the past. Curzon may not have liked or understood the modern age, but his knowledge and comprehension of the outside world remained unrivalled.

After nearly nine years of continuous service in the Cabinet, Curzon left his bench in the House of Lords and took up his new duties as leader of the Opposition peers. But in 1924 there was room for other things than politics. In January he became a member of the Fine Arts Commission and in the same month succeeded Lansdowne as Chairman of the Trustees of the National Gallery. A few weeks later he made a speech at an exhibition of British architecture and lamented the destruction of Nash's Regent Street. Kedleston took up much of his time, especially the spring planting, and so did his writing. Elated by the reviews and sales of *Tales of Travel,* he settled down to complete his long book on Calcutta and the Viceroys, which was published posthumously under the confusing title *British Government in India.* Yet he lingered over the writing in a way he had never done before, so that his publisher believed he could not bear to let go of it. In fact he merely wished to perfect a delightful work which he regarded as his literary monument and which he hoped would be read for 200 years after his death.[56]

A parliamentary defeat for the Government in October led to the third general election in just under two years. The Conservatives were expected to win, which they did with an enormous majority, and Curzon assumed he would go back to his old job. On hearing a rumour that he might be superseded, he wrote incredulously to Baldwin two days after the poll.

> I cannot believe that you would propose to put such a terrible slur upon my administration of [the Foreign Office] which was conducted amid extreme difficulties but not without success in the closest and pleasantest co-operation with yourself and your predecessor, and as I have always been led to think, with your just approval. It would be too much to expect me to accept such a situation.[57]

Baldwin, however, thought that a change was desirable and had already decided to replace him with Austen Chamberlain. The decision was generally welcomed. Putting Curzon back in the Foreign Office, declared the *Daily Chronicle,* would have been like returning the Quai d'Orsay to Poincaré, who had fallen from power the previous summer: 'memories of Anglo-French friction' would have been revived on both sides of the Channel.[58] At a painful interview on 5 November, Baldwin acknowledged Curzon's past achievements, told him foreign policy needed 'a fresh start' and, learning his lesson from the King, declared that 'in the present condition of public affairs' it was 'of the first importance' to have the Foreign Secretary in the Commons.[59] He hoped very much, however, that Curzon would accept the positions of Lord President of the Council, Leader of the House of Lords and Chairman of the Committee of Imperial Defence.

Earlier in the day Curzon had told Walter Lawrence that he would accept nothing but his old office. It was therefore rather difficult to explain why he had changed his mind, especially as he could not give the real reason, which was that he had been bullied by his wife. Grace was less discreet about the episode. Sitting next to Crawford at a dinner party a fortnight later, she told him her husband had sworn never to accept so subordinate a position. But she pressed him, Crawford recounted in his diary, 'said it was his duty to the state, but also his duty to her, as he would be intolerable at home if he was at the same time out of office and no longer Leader of the Opposition. So, like a sensible fellow, he allowed himself to be overborne.'[60]

Curzon's reluctance to participate in the new Government increased when he saw the list of ministers. It was 'impossible to imagine', he told Grace, 'a stranger collection of round pegs in square holes'. The Cabinet did indeed contain some bizarre appointments, notably Churchill, who went to the Exchequer although finance was one of the few things he did not claim to know about, and Birkenhead, who became Secretary of State for India although he had never been there and was not interested in the Subcontinent. The placing of Austen Chamberlain at the Foreign Office was in fact one of the more sensible decisions.

As Lord President, Curzon had to preside over the ceremony at which the new ministers were sworn in. It was 'rather a tragic moment' for him, he confessed, for he was reverting to the role he had filled eight years earlier when 'all was new and promising'. And there was another repetition of circumstances. Twenty years earlier, when he had come home from India the first time for a holiday, he had felt 'terribly stranded and rather miserable' without his work. Now, after years of cursing the red boxes which kept him up night after night until two in the morning, he experienced a similar desolation. 'I feel rather stranded,' he confessed to Grace, 'a new government formed and I with no boxes coming in and nothing to do.'[61] Had he been a ploughman he would have sighed when the last furrow was ploughed; had he been a navigator he would have grieved to see his home port. His life was a journey of labour, and however much he grumbled along the way, he never wanted the fireside at the end of it.

In January 1925 George Curzon had a holiday. He went to the South of France and stayed in a villa near Eze, where his old friend Consuelo Vanderbilt, the former Duchess of Marlborough, now lived with her second husband Jacques Balsan. He loved their house, the views of the sea, the walks on the hillsides, and even contemplated buying some property nearby. The enviable climate made him contrast the delights of working in a warm Provençal garden with the discomfort of splashing about in the cold mud of Derbyshire. Consuelo took him for drives along the coast in the afternoons, and one evening they dined at Monte Carlo's 'opera bouffe court'. The only dull moment in an idyllic stay came afterwards when they watched a Russian ballet from the royal box. Curzon was 'bored to tears' and made his bad leg an excuse for leaving before the end.

Of course it was not a complete holiday. Warned beforehand that he planned to edit his book on India, Consuelo had put a writing table in his bedroom and double-lined the curtains to help him sleep. Hoping he was not being 'an inordinate bore', Curzon remained working in his room in the mornings and in the late afternoon. Surveying the work he was engaged in, his hostess once asked him why he did not employ a secretary. His answer was true to form: 'Do you think that anyone but myself could master the intricacies of my Indian administration or the spelling of those Indian names?'[62]

Although he was in good spirits, he seems to have sensed that his end was not far off. One afternoon he surprised Consuelo by saying, 'I know that Mary will be the first to greet me in heaven', a remark which illustrates what Archbishop Lang called the 'amazing simplicity of his religious faith'.[63] Yet Lang was probably not aware that here, as in so many other areas of his friend's life, there was an apparently inexplicable paradox. Curzon said his prayers every day and retained his childhood view of heaven, but he was not an orthodox Christian. Spiritual contemplation rarely interrupted his life, and when it did it seems to have induced in him a vague deism, a belief in a Creator whose secrets had not been revealed to mankind through the prophets of any religion.[64]

In February he was back in London, berating his colleagues for their failure to sit through debates in the House of Lords. The Chamber's proceedings, he reminded them, were not 'as a rule prolonged, and the strain of attendance [was] very slight'.[65] Among the new members of the House, the most distinguished was Asquith who, since losing his seat in the recent election, had been ennobled as the Earl of Oxford and Asquith. In welcoming him, Curzon predicted that the elderly Liberal statesman would soon be seduced by the charms of the Upper House. But although they had worked on some improbable recruits in the past, they failed with Asquith. After six weeks in the Lords, he claimed to have heard only one good speech, 'poor Curzon's last' on 4 March.[66]

On the following day Curzon went to Cambridge to speak to the university's Conservative association. While dressing for dinner at Christ's College, he suffered a haemorrhage of the bladder and lost quantities of blood. A doctor arrived, made him lie down and refused, in spite of his protestations, to let him get up to deliver his talk. 'This is the end,' Curzon murmured later to his host, the Master of the College. 'I have worked overtime for forty years, and I have no resistance left in me. I know this is the end.'[67]

Grace arrived before breakfast the next morning to bring him home for treatment in London. 'I know I have not been a good man,' she recalled him saying in the motor car, 'but on the other hand, looking back, I don't think I have been a very bad one.' Later he said, 'If anyone asks you if I believe in a future life, you can tell them that I most certainly do.'[68]

On examining him that evening, Curzon's physicians decided to operate after leaving him for three days to recover some strength. He spent the interval in bed, tiring himself out by writing letters and making additions to his will with the help of his brother Frank. The night before the operation he wrote to his publisher at Cassell enclosing detailed instructions for his Indian book 'if anything goes wrong'. He also wrote to thank the King for his enquiries. Although 'not in the least alarmed at the prospect' of an operation, he admitted it was 'a bore being cut open' at his age.[69]

The operation, performed on the 9th, seemed briefly to have been successful. It was followed by a series of optimistic bulletins which, as the Lord Chancellor later revealed in the Lords, disguised the gravity of the situation in case the patient demanded to see a newspaper. Another precaution taken for the same purpose was to prevent Irene from entering the house. Had his estranged daughter appeared at his bedside, thought Grace, Curzon would have known he was dying. Of his immediate family, Grace and Baba were with him nearly all the time, as was Frank; Marcella, whom he would have loved to see, was on a journey to the Middle East which he had arranged for her.

Curzon was a difficult patient, restless and inquisitive, always wanting to know what the doctors had *really* said. At his funeral one of them told Vansittart, 'he did his best to teach us our business', and afterwards his former secretary added the appropriate coda – 'as he did most of us'.[70] The sick man's condition worsened a few days after the operation; there was further bleeding and congestion in one of the lungs; the suffering and overburdened frame was at last giving up. On the 18th he wrote his last letter, a pathetic and almost illegible document professing his loyalty to the King. 'I have been through the valley of the shadow of death,' he said, 'and have experienced the tortures of the damned.' But knowing that His Majesty was about to set off on a Mediterranean cruise, he wanted to wish him all success on the journey. The letter was signed, 'your faithful servant, Curzon'.[71]

That day the doctors told Grace he was dying. On asking what she should tell him, Sir Thomas Horder replied that her husband was a 'great man, and it would be wrong to deceive him any longer'; the truth should be revealed so that he could 'prepare his mind in his own way'.[72] When she told him, Curzon closed his eyes and repeated the Lord's Prayer several times. They were the last words he spoke. The next day, the 19th, he lost consciousness, and early on the following morning, with Grace and Baba at his side, he died. He was 66.

Five days later the first part of the funeral service took place in London. The coffin, made from the same tree at Kedleston that had encased Mary, was brought by motor-hearse from Carlton House Terrace along Whitehall to Westminster Abbey. The Archbishop of Canterbury officiated; Salisbury, Asquith, Baldwin and Churchill were among the pall-bearers. The music that had moved him all his life resounded through the Abbey: the hymns 'Abide with me' and 'Nearer, my God, to Thee', the psalm 'I will lift up mine eyes unto the hills', the thundering majesty of the 'Dead March' from *Saul*, the more restrained solemnity of Chopin's Funeral March.* Afterwards the coffin was taken

---

*Later a memorial tablet was placed in the Abbey in a small passage near the Chapel of Henry VII. A few feet away is the plaque which Curzon himself unveiled for Cromer, and close by another tablet commemorates Milner. No other nation would hide its proconsuls in such a place.

by train to St Pancras and placed on a special train for Derby. Accompanying it in other carriages were members of the family and a small group of selected mourners.

The coffin was taken in pouring rain to Kedleston and placed on a bier in the Marble Hall. The Archbishop of York conducted a simple and unaffected service the following morning, and the body was taken to the church next door and interred beside Mary in the family vault. At the end of the ceremony the congregation sang the hymn, 'Now the labourer's task is o'er'. The choice could not have been more appropriate.

Differences in tone separated the obituaries; a pedestrian and inadequate piece in *The Times* contrasted poorly with T.P. O'Connor's long, moving but not uncritical memoir in the *Daily Telegraph*. But the message in most cases was very similar: Curzon had been a great public servant, a man of brilliant intellect, unparalleled industry, anachronistic tastes and strange flaws of character. Shafts of insincerity only occasionally shone through. No one who knew him could have been impressed by Lord Hardinge's claims of long friendship, his eulogy of the 'greatest' of modern Viceroys and his concluding words, 'Peace! Let his critics be still!' – a command he himself notoriously failed to obey when writing his memoirs.[73]

Heartfelt tributes came from unexpected places both in Britain and abroad. Curzon would have wept had he been able to read the message of condolence from Ismet Pasha, the words of the trade union leader Ben Tillett describing him as 'one of the most humane men' he had ever met, and the opinion of *The Times of India*, which asserted that he was 'in his prime the greatest Englishman of his time; to India he gave his superb best'.[74] Surveying the acclaim a fortnight after Curzon's death, Harold Nicolson saw it as evidence of 'a sense of national loss manifested in an almost unexpected outburst of national homage'. It was a 'tragic satisfaction', he added, 'to record this posthumous understanding of a man who imagined always that he was misunderstood'. And in searching for the sources of Curzon's inspiration, he composed an appropriate epitaph: 'the magnitude of England, the integrity of beauty, the glory of work; such were the ideals by which he achieved his victory, by which he triumphed over pain and tragedy and disappointment'.[75]

Among the parliamentary tributes Baldwin and Asquith exhibited their high standards of oratory. After speaking of the façade which had concealed 'an intense and exquisite sensitiveness', the Prime Minister spoke movingly of those two events in which he had caused Curzon such disappointment: his winning of the premiership and his decision not to reappoint him as Foreign Secretary. In his reactions to both these occasions, Baldwin assured the Commons, Curzon had displayed 'a vein of the purest gold'.[76] Making his maiden speech in the Lords on the same day, Asquith encapsulated essential truths about his old friend when he described him as 'a great and unselfish servant of the state ... always ready in that service to scorn delights and live laborious days – a man who pursued high ambitions by none but worthy means ...'

The most charming and spontaneous of the parliamentary tributes was the last and the shortest. After the party spokesmen in the Commons had sat down, O'Connor rose to say that an Irish voice should be added to the other contributions. Ireland had 'some quaint prophecies', he remarked, which had 'an uncanny method of being realized'. And recently he had learnt that

an old Irish prophetess [had] prophesied that one day an Irishman would be found weeping over an Englishman's grave. Today I, as an Irishman, weep over a great Englishman's grave.[77]

Chronology

1859	Birth of Curzon on 11 January	
1869–72	Wixenford School	
1872–8	Eton College	
1875	Death of Lady Scarsdale	
1878–82	Balliol College, Oxford	
1882–3	Travels in the Near East	
1883	Fellow of All Souls College, Oxford	
1885	Conservative candidate for South Derbyshire	
1886	Elected MP for Southport	Salisbury forms his 2nd Government in August
1887–8	Journey round the world	
1888	Travels in Central Asia	
1889	Publication of *Russia in Central Asia in 1889*	
1889–90	Travels in Persia	
1891–2	Parliamentary Under-Secretary for India	
1892	Publication of *Persia and the Persian Question*	Conservatives defeated in July. Gladstone forms his 4th Government
	Sets off on 2nd journey round the world	

1893	Secret engagement to Mary Leiter	
1894	Publication of *Problems of the Far East*	
	Visits the Pamirs and Afghanistan	
1895	Marriage to Mary Leiter in Washington	Salisbury forms 3rd Government in June prior to winning July election
	Appointed Parliamentary Under-Secretary for Foreign Affairs and Privy Councillor	
1898	Appointed Viceroy of India and created Baron Curzon of Kedleston in the peerage of Ireland	
1899–1904	1st term as Viceroy and Governor-General of India	
1902		Balfour succeeds Salisbury as Prime Minister
1904	Lord Warden of the Cinque Ports	
	2nd term as Viceroy and Governor-General of India begins	
1905	Resignation as Viceroy	Balfour resigns as Prime Minister in December. Campbell-Bannerman takes over and leads Liberals to electoral victory in January 1906
1906	Death of Mary	
1907	Chancellor of Oxford University	
1908	Elected as Representative Irish Peer with a seat in the House of Lords	Asquith succeeds Campbell-Bannerman as Prime Minister
1910		Narrow Liberal victories in 2 general elections

1911	Created Earl Curzon of Kedleston	Parliament Bill
	President of Royal Geographical Society	Bonar Law succeeds Balfour as Unionist leader in the House of Commons
1915–16	Lord Privy Seal in Asquith's Coalition Government	
1916	Knight of the Garter Chairman of the Air Board Death of Lord Scarsdale	
1916–19	Lord President of the Council, Leader of the House of Lords and member of Lloyd George's War Cabinet	
1917	Marriage to Mrs Grace Duggan	
1919–24	Foreign Secretary	
1921	Created Marquess Curzon of Kedleston	
1922–3	At Lausanne Conference	Bonar Law replaces Lloyd George as Prime Minister in October 1922 and is succeeded by Baldwin in May 1923
1923	Publication of *Tales of Travel*	
1924	Leaves Foreign Office after Conservative defeat in election of December 1923	
	Appointed Chairman of the Trustees of the National Gallery	
	Lord President of the Council and Leader of the House of Lords in Baldwin's 2nd Government, November	
1925	Dies on 20 March	

Notes

Abbreviations: AMP=Lady Alexandra Metcalfe Papers
               C=Curzon
               CP=Curzon Papers
               IMO=Indian Military Organization 1902–1905 (Private correspondence relating to)

PREFACE

1. Lawrence to C, C to Lawrence, 27 June 1924, Lawrence Papers 143/33.
2. Beaverbrook, *The Decline and Fall of Lloyd George*, p. 46; *Men and Power, 1917–1918*, p. xv; *Politicians and the War*, p. 256.
3. Taylor, *English History*, pp. 204, 195.
4. Gollin, *Proconsul in Politics*, p. 382.
5. A copy of the agreement is in CP 112/772.

CHAPTER 1: ANCESTRAL SILENCE

1. C to Charles Pearson, 31 Aug. 1893, Pearson Papers.
2. H. Nicolson, *Curzon*, p. 10.
3. O'Byrne, *A Naval Biographical Dictionary*, pp. 254–5.
4. Bindoff, *The House of Commons 1509–1588*, p. 742; Sedgwick, *The House of Commons 1715–1754*, pp. 223, 269.
5. Sedgwick, ibid., pp. 598–9.
6. Thorne, *The House of Commons 1790–1820*, p. 554.
7. Harris, *Robert Adam and Kedleston*, p. 9; Sedgwick, op.cit., p. 599.
8. Namier and Brooke, *The House of Commons 1754–1790*, pp. 287–8; Thorne, op.cit. p. 553.
9. Harris, op.cit., pp. 9, 74.
10. Ibid., pp. 11–12, 22–4; C to Mary, 12 Nov. and 11 Dec. 1893, AMP.
11. Bray, *Sketch of a Tour*, p. 112.
12. Ibid., p. 111.
13. Boswell, *Life of Johnson*, Vol. 2, p. 354.
14. Rose, *Curzon*, pp. 15–16; National Trust, *Kedleston Hall*, pp. 64–5.

15. Sir Roger Cary to the author.
16. Riddell, *Intimate Diary of the Peace Conference*, p. 184.
17. Scarsdale to Mary, 26 Feb. 1895, Mary to C, 5 July 1901, AMP; N. Nicolson, *Mary Curzon*, p. 86.
18. Scarsdale and Lady Scarsdale to C, 2 Dec. 1874, CP 112/339.
19. Lady Aldington to the author.
20. C to Mary, 13 April 1904, AMP.
21. C to Mary, 25 Feb. 1895, AMP.
22. Frank Curzon to Scarsdale, 30 July 1914, C to Scarsdale, 24 Aug. 1914, CP 112/775.
23. Ravensdale, *In Many Rhythms*, p. 32.
24. CP 112/363.
25. Mrs Noreen Wright to the author.
26. David Yates Mason to the author.
27. C to Sophy Curzon, 26 April and 16 May 1869, Lady Aldington Papers.
28. David Yates Mason to the author.
29. See note 27.
30. CP 112/363; C to Brett, 20 Sept. 1878, Esher Papers 10/1.
31. Cowley Powles to Scarsdale, 30 July 1869, CP 112/755; Cowley Powles to Lady Scarsdale, 7 Oct. 1869, CP 112/782.
32. CP 112/363.
33. Ronaldshay, *Curzon*, Vol. 1, p. 20.
34. Mosley, *Curzon*, p. 10.
35. Riddell, op.cit.

CHAPTER 2: 'PASSIONATE RESOLVES': ETON, 1872–1878
1. Lyttelton, *Memories and Hopes*, p. 29.
2. J. Chandos, *Boys Together*, p. 245.
3. D. Cecil, *The Cecils*, pp. 219–20.
4. Welldon, *Recollections and Reflections*, p. 29.
5. Lyttelton, op.cit., p. 32; Welldon, ibid., p. 88.
6. Chandos, op.cit., pp. 335–7, 344; Honey, *Tom Brown's Universe*, p. 115.
7. CP 112/362.
8. Lyttelton, op.cit., pp. 29–30.
9. Chandos, op.cit., pp. 163–4, 316.
10. Browning, *Memories*, pp. 84–5; Wortham, *Victorian Eton and Cambridge*, pp. 299–300.
11. Benson, *Memories and Friends*, pp. 100–1; Anstruther, *Oscar Browning*, p. 9.
12. CP 112/362.
13. Ibid.
14. Ibid.
15. C to Browning, 10 Sept. 1876, CP 112/327, and 25 July 1878, Browning Papers.
16. C to Lady Scarsdale, 17 March 1873 and 16 March 1875, CP 112/786–7; Wolley Dod to Scarsdale, 10 Dec. 1872, 13 March and 27 July 1875, and June 1877, CP 112/774–5; C to Browning, 9 July 1877, Browning Papers.
17. *Pall Mall Magazine*, Oct. 1904.
18. Anstruther, op.cit., p. 63; Wortham, op.cit., pp. 99–100.
19. Scarsdale to Browning, 14 July 1874, CP 112/327.
20. Rose, *Curzon*, p. 31.
21. Anstruther, op.cit., p. 106.
22. C to Browning, 20 July and 23 Aug. 1874, CP 112/327.
23. Rose, op.cit., pp. 37–8; Mrs Noreen Wright to the author.
24. Scarsdale to C, 12 May 1875, CP 112/339.
25. Anstruther, op.cit., p. 79.

26. Browning, op.cit., p. 270.
27. A.C. Benson's unpublished diary, 22 March 1925, Vol. 179, p. 22.
28. Wortham, op.cit., p. 100.
29. A. Lyttelton to C, Whitsunday 1899, CP 111/121; Midleton, *Records and Reactions*, p. 26.
30. C to Brett, 4 March 1878, Esher Papers 2/10.
31. *Spectator*, 11 Aug. 1877; *Athenaeum*, 15 Sept. 1877.
32. *Out of School at Eton*, 1877.
33. CP 112/362.
34. Campbell, *F.E.*, p. 39; Mrs Noreen Wright to the author.
35. C to Lady Scarsdale, 5 Feb. 1874, CP 112/775.
36. C to Gladstone, 24 April 1878, Gladstone Papers Add.mss.44456, note by C in CP 112/344.
37. Report of the Captain of the Oppidans 1877–8, Magnus Papers.
38. Ibid.
39. *Daily News*, 5 June 1877 and 5 June 1878; C scrapbook, CP 112/344; Scarsdale to C, 4 June 1878, CP 112/339.
40. Enclosed with a letter from C to Brett, 25 Aug. 1878, Esher Papers 10/1.
41. CP 122/344.

CHAPTER 3: 'LAYING THE FOUNDATIONS': OXFORD, 1878–1883
1. Knatchbull-Hugessen to Scarsdale, 3 July 1876, CP 112/774; C to Browning, 10 Sept. 1876, CP 112/327; C's diary, Aug. 1887, CP 111/104; C to Browning, 6 Oct. 1878, Browning Papers.
2. C to Sophy Curzon, 5 Jan. and 28 Aug. 1878, CP 112/811; C to Browning, 25 July 1878, E. Lyttelton to Browning, 4 Sept. 1878, Browning Papers.
3. C to Brett, 9 Oct. 1878, Esher Papers 10/1; C to Browning, 6 and 24 Oct. 1878, Browning Papers.
4. Browning, *Memories*, p. 276.
5. C to Brett, 21 March 1879, Esher Papers 10/1; A. Lyttelton to C, 25 Dec. 1879, CP 112/333.
6. Lees–Milne, *The Enigmatic Edwardian*, p. 48.
7. Brett to C, 23 Aug. 1878, CP 112/328; Brodrick to C, 24 Sept. 1878, CP 111/9; A. Lyttelton to C, Aug. 1878, CP 112/333.
8. J. Jones, *Balliol College*, pp. 213ff.; Rodd, *Social and Diplomatic Memories 1884–1893*, pp. 6–8; Gwynn, *Letters and Friendships*, Vol. 1, p. 288; Faber, *Jowett*, pp. 244, 352.
9. Koss, *Asquith*, p. 5.
10. M. Asquith, *More Memories*, p. 187.
11. Robbins, *Sir Edward Grey*, pp. 16–17.
12. O'Brien, *Milner*, p. 132.
13. Ibid., p. 177.
14. Koss, op.cit., p. 8.
15. Brodrick to C, 29 May 1878, CP 111/9.
16. *Pall Mall Magazine*, Oct. 1904.
17. C to Brett, 20 Sept. 1878, Esher Papers 10/1.
18. Johnson to C, 6 Sept. 1884, CP 111/1.
19. Sumner to Ronaldshay, 28 Nov. 1925, Balliol mss.421.
20. Canning Club notes and minutes book, CP 112/354 and 356.
21. C to Browning, 28 Nov. 1878, Browning Papers.
22. C to Browning, 21 March 1879, Browning Papers.
23. D'Abernon, *An Ambassador*, Vol. 1, p. 51.
24. Ellmann, *Oscar Wilde*, pp. 139–40; Wilde to C, Nov. 1881, CP 112/325.

25. Lyttelton to C, 7 June 1882, CP 111/7–8; *Land and Water*, 24 May 1879; Sumner to Ronaldshay, op.cit.
26. Jowett to C, 15 July 1882 and 13 Sept. 1889, CP 112/331.
27. Sumner to Ronaldshay, op.cit.
28. Ibid.; Bliss to Ronaldshay, 26 Dec. 1925, Balliol mss.421.
29. Wilde to C, Nov. 1881 and 30 July 1885, CP 112/325.
30. Rodd to C, 26 Feb. 1891, CP 112/338.
31. Ronaldshay, *Curzon*, Vol. 1, p. 62.
32. C to Farrar, 17 Oct. 1880, CP 112/330.
33. Elinor Glyn memoir, AMP.
34. CP 112/362.
35. C to Browning, 27 June and 24 Oct. 1879, Browning Papers.
36. C to Farrar, 23 July 1882, CP 112/330.
37. Rodd, op.cit., p. 14.
38. C to Farrar, 23 July 1882, CP 112/330; C to Browning, 20 July 1882, Browning Papers; Raper to C, 3 July 1882, CP 112/359; Marriot to C, 5 July 1882, CP 112/359; A. and E. Lyttelton to C, 4 July 1882, CP 112/333 and 334; Jowett to C, 15 July 1882, CP 112/331.
39. C to Farrar, 23 July 1882, CP 112/330; Ronaldshay, op.cit., p. 5.
40. C to Farrar, 27 May 1883, CP 112/330.
41. Ibid., 2 Dec. 1882.
42. C diary, 1882–3, CP 111/101; C to Wolmer, 26 Dec. 1882, Selborne Papers.
43. Lyttelton, *Memories and Hopes*, p. 145.
44. C diary, op.cit.; C to Brodrick, 1 Jan. 1883, Midleton Papers Add.mss.50073.
45. C diary, op. cit.
46. C to Wolmer, 3 April 1883, Selborne Papers.
47. Rodd to C, 6 Feb. 1883, CP 112/338.
48. C to Farrar, 24 March 1883, CP 112/330; C diary, op.cit.
49. C diary, ibid.
50. C to Wolmer, 3 March 1883, Selborne Papers; C diary, 1883, CP 111/102.
51. C to Brodrick, 5 May 1883, Midleton Papers Add.mss.50073; C diary, 1883, ibid.
52. C to Brodrick, ibid.
53. C diary, 1883, op.cit.
54. Ibid; C to Brodrick, 5 and 19 May 1883, Midleton Papers Add.mss.50073.
55. Wilde to C, 16 July 1883, CP 112/325.
56. CP 112/362; Rose, *Curzon*, p. 100.

CHAPTER 4: TWIN PASSIONS: 'WOMEN AND WORK', 1882–1885

1. Brodrick to C, March n.d. and 5 Nov. 1881, CP 111/9.
2. C, *Modern Parliamentary Eloquence*, pp. 11–13, 23–9, 70.
3. C diary, 1886, CP 112/371.
4. M. Asquith, *Autobiography*, Vol. 1, p. 175; M. Tennant to C, 1 Sept. 1885, CP 111/12.
5. C. Ribblesdale to C, 3 Feb. 1883, CP 111/11.
6. CP 112/739.
7. M. Asquith, op.cit., p. 175.
8. C to Mary, 17 July 1893, AMP; CP 112/362.
9. Ibid.
10. *Daily Telegraph*, 19 June 1895.
11. Brodrick to C, 14 Dec. 1898, CP 111/10.
12. M. Asquith, op.cit., p. 184.
13. A. Lyttelton to C, 5 Aug. 1900, CP 111/121.
14. Brodrick to C, 30 Oct. 1883 and 7 Feb. 1884, CP 111/9.

15. C. Ribblesdale to C, 5 Dec. 1882, CP 111/11.
16. Brodrick to C, 17 Nov. 1879, CP 111/9.
17. Rose, *Curzon*, p. 74; H. Wentworth to C, 2 Dec. 1880, CP 112/32.
18. CP 112/737.
19. C's engagement book, CP 112/739; Brodrick to C, 25 Sept. 1882, CP 111/9; C. Ribblesdale to C, 4 Aug. 1884, CP 111/11.
20. C to Brodrick, Nov.–Dec. 1882, Midleton Papers Add.mss.50073.
21. A. Lyttelton to C, 1 April 1883, CP 112/333.
22. C to Brodrick, 9 May 1883, Midleton Papers Add.mss.50073.
23. C to Brodrick, 15 Aug. 1883, Midleton Papers Add.mss.50073.
24. C to S. Grosvenor, 4 Oct. 1883, Grosvenor Papers.
25. Brodrick to C, 21 Oct. 1883, CP 111/9.
26. CP 112/737.
27. C to S. Grosvenor, 31 Aug. 1883, Grosvenor Papers.
28. C to S. Grosvenor, 22, 24 and 27 Dec. 1883 and 2 Jan. 1884, Grosvenor Papers; Egremont, *The Cousins*, pp. 78–81.
29. Brodrick to C, 30 Sept. 1885, CP 111/9.
30. C. Ribblesdale to C, 6 June 1885, CP 111/11.
31. C. Ribblesdale to C, 12 Sept. 1885, CP 111/11.
32. L. Tennant to C, 28 Sept. 1884, CP 111/12.
33. C, *Subjects of the Day*, p. 223.
34. L. Tennant to C, 5 Feb. 1886, CP 111/12.
35. C to L. Tennant, 27 Jan. 1885, Chandos Papers 2/4.
36. C to Brodrick, 12 Nov. 1882, Midleton Papers Add.mss.50073.
37. C, *Tales of Travel*, pp. 213–14.
38. CP 111/24; C, *Subjects of the Day*, p. 241.
39. *Oxford Review*, 28 Jan. 1885.
40. C diary, 1885, CP 111/103.
41. Ibid.
42. Ibid.
43. C, *Tales of Travel*, pp. 254–7.

CHAPTER 5: THE JOURNEY TO WESTMINSTER, 1885–1887
1. C to Brodrick, 17 Oct. 1885, Midleton Papers Add.mss.50073. The electoral address is in CP 112/370.
2. C to Brodrick, 12 Nov. 1885, Midleton Papers Add.mss.50073.
3. Grace Curzon, *Reminiscences*, p. 148.
4. C, *Modern Parliamentary Eloquence*, pp. 34–6; C diary, 1886, CP 112/371.
5. Unsigned, unsent, undated (but probably 1890) letter, C to Churchill, CP 112/604.
6. C diary, op.cit.
7. Mackay, *Balfour*, pp. 6–8; Curtis, *Coercion and Conciliation*, p. 175.
8. C, *Modern Parliamentary Eloquence*, p. 44.
9. Marsh, *The Discipline of Popular Government*, pp. 85–9.
10. C diary, op.cit.
11. Magnus, *Gladstone*, p. 342.
12. Marsh, ibid., pp. 90–5; Feuchtwanger, *Democracy and Empire*, pp. 184–9; Foster, *Lord Randolph Churchill*, pp. 258–67.
13. Chairman of Southport Association to C, 25 May and 8 June 1886, CP 111/13; C to Brodrick, 15 Sept. 1886, Midleton Papers Add.mss.50073.
14. C to Brodrick, June 1886, Midleton Papers, Add.mss.50073.
15. *Southport Guardian*, 3 and 7 July 1886.
16. C to A. Lyttelton, 30 April 1886, Chandos Papers 2/4.

17. A. Lyttelton to C, 5 May 1886, CP 112/333.
18. Egremont, *The Cousins*, p. 178.
19. C to S. Grosvenor, 3 and 19 Sept. 1886, Wyndham to S. Grosvenor, 18 Oct. 1886, Grosvenor Papers; Egremont, ibid., p. 85.
20. C to S. Grosvenor, 19 Dec. 1886, Grosvenor Papers.
21. C to Brodrick, 24 Dec. 1886, Midleton Papers Add.mss.50073.
22. Wyndham to S. Grosvenor, 22 Dec. 1886, Grosvenor Papers.
23. C to S. Grosvenor, 24 Dec. 1886, Grosvenor Papers.
24. C to Brodrick, 24 Dec. 1886, Midleton Papers Add.mss.50073.
25. Foster, op.cit., p. 307.
26. C to Brodrick, 24 Dec. 1886, Midleton Papers Add.mss.50073.
27. C to Brodrick, 23 Jan. 1887, Midleton Papers Add.mss.50073.
28. Balfour to C, 17 Jan. 1887, CP 111/1.
29. 31 Jan. 1887.
30. *The Times* and *St James' Gazette*, 1 Feb. 1887.
31. *Observer*, 13 Feb. 1887.
32. R. Churchill, *Winston S. Churchill*, Vol. 2, pp. 16–17.
33. 25 March 1887.
34. *Daily News*, 26 March 1887; *Whitehall Review*, 31 March 1887.
35. Robbins, *Sir Edward Grey*, p. 40.
36. C, *Modern Parliamentary Eloquence*, p. 60.

CHAPTER 6: 'TRAVEL WITH A PURPOSE', 1887–1890
1. C, *Persia*, Vol. 1, p. 13.
2. C to Brodrick, 10 Sept. 1887, Midleton Papers Add.mss.50073.
3. Ibid.
4. C diary, 1887–8, CP 111/104.
5. C to Mary, 15 March 1899, AMP.
6. C diary, op.cit.; C to S. Grosvenor, 26 Sept. 1887, Grosvenor Papers.
7. Ibid.
8. C to Brodrick, 14 Nov. 1887, Midleton Papers Add.mss.50073; C diary, op.cit.
9. C diary, op.cit.
10. Ibid.
11. Ibid.
12. C to Brodrick, 1 Jan. 1888, Midleton Papers Add.mss.50073.
13. Speech at Agra, 11 Nov. 1905, CP 111/620.
14. Ronaldshay, *Curzon*, Vol. 1, p. 134.
15. *Scotsman*, 29 March 1888; *Observer*, 11 March 1888.
16. *National Review*, March and April 1888.
17. CP 111/25.
18. C, *Russia*, pp. 20–1, 26.
19. Ibid., pp. 56, 228.
20. Ibid., pp. 153–231 *passim*, pp. 383–413 *passim*.
21. Ibid., p. 45.
22. Ibid., p. 356.
23. Hopkirk, *The Great Game*, pp. 396–401.
24. *National Review*, March 1889; C to Dilke, 14 Feb. 1889, Dilke Papers Add.mss.43893.
25. *The Times*, 10 Oct. 1889; *Star*, 30 Nov. 1889.
26. Johnston to C, 9 May 1887, CP 111/7–8.
27. Letter in *Southport Guardian*, 30 March 1889.
28. 17 May 1889.
29. C to Gladstone, 20 June 1889, Viscount Gladstone Papers Add.mss.46067.

30. *Political World,* 22 June 1889.
31. Jowett to C, 13 Sept 1889, CP 112/331.
32. C to Vincent, 21 Dec. 1890, D'Abernon Papers Add.mss.48923; C to Brodrick, 3 and 11 June 1890, 27 Dec. 1891, Midleton Papers Add.mss.50073 ; Rose, *Curzon,* pp. 192, 232–4; C to Hamilton, 24 July 1901, CP 111/160.
33. Balfour to C, undated, CP 111/58.
34. Reported in *Southport Guardian,* 12 Oct. 1889.
35. C, *Persia,* Vol. 1, pp. 165, 263.
36. C to Selborne, 18 Feb. 1890, Selborne Papers; C to S. Grosvenor, 13 Nov. 1889, Grosvenor Papers.
37. C, *Persia,* Vol. 2, pp. 497–8, 523, and Vol. 1, p. 275.
38. Salisbury to C, 27 and 30 Nov. 1891, C to Salisbury, 28 Nov. 1891, Salisbury Papers and CP 111/1.
39. C, *Persia,* Vol. 1, p. 399.
40. Ibid., pp. 401–49 *passim,* and Vol. 2, pp. 627–8.
41. Ibid., Vol. 2, p. 630.
42. C to Mrs Bishop, 15 Oct. 1891, NLS 7179 (misc.); Longman to C, 17 Feb. 1891, CP 112/615.
43. C, *Persia,* Vol. 1, p. 587.

CHAPTER 7: 'THE COMING MAN', 1890–1895
1. 21 March 1890.
2. CP 111/25.
3. C to Mary, 13 Oct. 1890, AMP.
4. Ibid., 31 Jan. 1891.
5. C to Brodrick, 26 March 1891, Midleton Papers Add.mss.50073; C to Mary, 3 Feb. 1891, AMP; C to Cranborne, 21 Feb. 1891, Salisbury Papers.
6. C to Gladstone, 18 and 23 May 1890, Gladstone Papers Add.mss.44510; *Fortnightly Review,* 4 April 1891.
7. C to Mary, 6 Sept. 1891, AMP.
8. Salisbury to C, 10 Nov. 1891, CP 111/1.
9. C to Salisbury, 1 Jan. 1892, Salisbury Papers.
10. Longman to C, 27 Jan. 1892, and note by C, CP 112/615.
11. *Sunday Sun,* 5 June 1892; *The Times,* 19 May 1892; *Standard,* 21 May 1892; Ronaldshay, *Curzon,* Vol. 1, p. 155.
12. C to Mary, 14 Jan. 1893, AMP.
13. C to Brodrick, 1 Jan. 1888, Midleton Papers Add.mss.50073.
14. CP 112/604. See note 5, Chapter 5.
15. Ridley and Percy, *Letters,* p. 73.
16. C to Spring Rice, 26 Aug. n.d., Spring Rice Papers.
17. Harcourt Williams, *Salisbury–Balfour Correspondence,* p. 353.
18. C to Mary, 10 Oct. 1891, AMP.
19. A. Lyttelton to C, 17 Oct. 1891, CP 112/333.
20. C to Mary, 29 Nov. 1891, AMP.
21. Younghusband, *The Light of Experience,* pp. 62–3.
22. Kilbracken, *Reminiscences,* p. 188.
23. *St James' Gazette,* 13 Feb. 1892.
24. Rose, *Curzon,* p. 245.
25. 12 Feb. 1892.
26. Rose, op.cit., p. 237; Harris to C, 20 Nov. 1891, CP 111/1.
27. Harris to C, 8 Aug. 1892, CP 111/1.
28. Cross to C, 19 May 1902, C to Cross, 20 June 1902, CP 111/182.

29. *The Speaker*, 22 Aug. 1891 and 2 April 1892.
30. *Evening News*, 29 March 1892.
31. *Truth*, 19 Nov. 1891.
32. Harcourt Williams, op.cit., pp. 347, 423–4.
33. Bishop of London to C, 8 Nov. 1893, CP 111/1.
34. Longford, *Victoria*, pp. 518–21, 524; Magnus, *Gladstone*, pp. 395–8.
35. C to Mary, 22 March and 22 Aug. 1892, AMP.
36. Balfour to C, 2 Jan. 1893, copy in Balfour Papers Add.mss.49732.
37. E. Kirkwood to C, 2 March 1893, Spring Rice to C, 6 Sept. and 7 Oct. 1893, CP 112/617; C to Spring Rice, 13 Aug. 1893, Spring Rice Papers.
38. C, *Problems of the Far East*, pp. 128, 168, 394–6.
39. Gwynn, *Letters and Friendships*, Vol. 1, pp. 128–35.
40. C, *Problems of the Far East*, pp. 237–8, 245–53, 305–34 *passim*, 399.
41. C to Spring Rice, 18 Nov. 1892, Spring Rice Papers.
42. Gwynn, op.cit., pp. 136–7; Spring Rice to Farrar, 2 Dec. 1892, Spring Rice Papers.
43. C, *Problems of the Far East*, pp. 10, 56.
44. C diary, 1892–3, CP 111/105; C to Spring Rice, 28 Feb. 1893, Spring Rice Papers; C, *Leaves*, p. 344; C to Selborne, 12 April 1899, Selborne Papers.
45. Longman to C, 21 Feb. 1894, C to Colles, 14 April 1896, Colles to C, 26 May 1904, CP 112/619 and 628.
46. *Evening Post and Nation*, 10 June 1894.
47. Ronaldshay, *Curzon*, Vol. 1, p. 193.
48. C to Mary, 3 Aug. 1893, AMP; C to Spring Rice, 13 Aug. 1893, Spring Rice Papers.
49. 22 March 1895.
50. CP 111/131.
51. Wilson, *CB*, p. 163.
52. C to Mary, 19 Aug. 1893 and 10 July 1894, AMP.
53. C, *Tales*, p. 42.
54. Rose, op.cit., p. 256; Lawrence, *The India We Served*, p. 226.
55. C diary, 1894–5, CP 111/99.
56. C, *Leaves*, p. 176.
57. Ibid., pp. 346–7; C to Spring Rice, 13 Aug. 1893, Spring Rice Papers.
58. C, *Leaves*, p. 130.
59. Younghusband, op.cit., pp. 285–6.
60. Khan, *Abdur Rahman*, p. 141.
61. Bence-Jones, *Viceroys*, p. 139; C, *Tales*, pp. 9, 48–54.
62. C, ibid., pp. 60–4.

CHAPTER 8: HEARTS AND SOULS
1. Rodd, *Social and Diplomatic Memories*, Vol. 1, p. 250.
2. F. Warwick, *Afterthoughts*, pp. 128–9.
3. M. Asquith, *Autobiography*, Vol. 1, pp. 146, 175.
4. Ibid., p. 139.
5. *The Queen*, 14 April 1894.
6. Edel, *Bloomsbury*, p. 262.
7. Quoted in *England*, 19 Nov. 1892.
8. Ibid.
9. Asquith, op.cit., p. 87.
10. C to Mary, 8 Oct. 1893, AMP.
11. J. Wilson, *CB*, p. 248.
12. Egremont, *The Cousins*, p. 156.
13. C diary, 1894–5, CP 111/99.

14. Longford, *Pilgrimage of Passion*, pp. 289–90.
15. Harris, *Oscar Wilde*, p. 306; Longford, ibid., pp. 291–3.
16. Blunt, *My Diaries*, Vol. 1, p. 138.
17. 'Crabbet Club Poetry', CP 112/408.
18. C to Spring Rice, 17 May 1893, Spring Rice Papers.
19. Chandos, *From Peace to War*, p. 37.
20. C to E. Balfour, several undated letters, Chandos Papers.
21. Chandos, op.cit., p. 64.
22. Maison, *John Oliver Hobbes*, pp. 4–10; Craigie to Brown, 25 July 1906 and 18 Oct. 1904, Craigie Papers; C to Richards, 3 letters Nov. –Dec. 1915, CP 112/115.
23. P. Craigie to Brown, 13 Jan. 1900, 6 Sept. 1903, 7 Aug. and 8 Oct. 1904, Craigie Papers.
24. P. Craigie to Brown, 21 July and 10 Aug. 1906, 26 June 1904, Craigie Papers.
25. C to S. Grosvenor, 6 Aug. 1891, Grosvenor Papers.
26. C to Mary, 25 Feb. 1895, AMP.
27. C to Brodrick, 10 April 1895, Midleton Papers Add.mss.50073.
28. Craigie to Brown, undated and 26 June 1904, Craigie Papers.
29. Ellmann, *Oscar Wilde*, pp. 428, 434.
30. C to Wyndham, 13 April, 27 and 28 Nov. 1891, Grosvenor Papers; Egremont, op.cit., pp. 89–90.
31. P. Craigie to Brown, 27 July 1905, Craigie Papers.
32. C to Brodrick, 20 Oct. 1891, Midleton Papers Add.mss.50073.
33. Pollock to C, 27 Oct. and 1 and 4 Nov. 1920, CP 112/218; Rose, *Curzon*, pp. 174–5.
34. Darling, *Apprentice to Power*, p. 33.
35. N. Nicolson, *Mary Curzon*, pp. 1–2.
36. Butt, *Taft and Roosevelt*, Vol. 1, p. 123.
37. N. Nicolson, op.cit., pp. 12–30 *passim*.
38. Ibid., pp. 37–40; Mary to C and vice versa, 1 Aug. 1890, AMP.
39. Mary to C, 13 Oct. and 5 Nov. 1890, 7 Jan. 1891, C to Mary, 8 Aug., 13 Oct. and 22 Nov. 1890, and 3 Feb. 1891, AMP.
40. C to Mary, 27 May 1891, Mary to C, Thanksgiving Day 1893, AMP; N. Nicolson, op.cit., pp. 47–52.
41. C to E. Grenfell, 13 Aug. 1892, Desborough Papers.
42. C diary, 1892–3, CP 111/105.
43. C to Spring Rice, 28 Feb. 1893, Spring Rice Papers.
44. Note by C on his engagement, AMP.
45. Mary to C, 4 March 1894, AMP.
46. N. Nicolson, op.cit., pp. 56–61.
47. C to Mary, 3, 15 and 23 Sept. and 19 Nov. 1893, 4 Feb. and 22 April 1894, Mary to C, 22–23 Aug. 1894, AMP.
48. C to Mary, 23 Jan., 11 March, 22 April, 15 June and 4 Aug. 1894, AMP.
49. Mary to C, 25 March 1893 and 4 July 1894, C to Mary, 10 and 17 July 1894, AMP.
50. Mary to C, 1 and 6 Oct. and 15 Dec. 1894, 1 Jan. 1895, C to Mary, 2 Feb. 1895, AMP.
51. N. Mosley, *Julian Grenfell*, p. 52.
52. C diary, 1894–5, CP 111/99.
53. C to Mary, 5 Feb. 1895, AMP.
54. Pembroke to C, undated (1895), AMP.
55. C, *Tales*, pp. 67–8.
56. Brodrick to C, 7 April 1895, CP 111/10.
57. C to Brodrick, 10 April 1895, Midleton Papers Add.mss.50073.
58. C to Macmillan, 12 March 1895, Macmillan Archive Add.mss.55245.

59. Leiter to C, 18 March 1895, C to Scarsdale, undated and 26 Feb. 1895, Scarsdale's Indenture, 9 April 1895, CP 112/677.
60. Spring Rice to C, 6 March 1895, Mary to C, 4, 5 and 12 March 1895, AMP.
61. Mary to C, 12 March 1895, C to Mary, 20 and 23 March, 4 April 1895, AMP; C to Spring Rice, 3 April 1895, Spring Rice Papers.

CHAPTER 9: NUMBER TWO AT THE FO

1. C to Spring Rice, undated (1893), Spring Rice Papers.
2. *New Review*, April 1895; Garvin, *Joseph Chamberlain*, Vol. 2, p. 629, Marsh, *Joseph Chamberlain*, p. 363.
3. W. Churchill, *Great Contemporaries*, pp. 275–6.
4. C to Brodrick, 6 May 1895, Midleton Papers Add.mss.50073.
5. Salisbury to C, 27 June 1895, CP 112/1.
6. W. Churchill, *My Early Life*, p. 86; Manchester, *The Last Lion*, pp. 178–9.
7. Letter to C, 3 June 1895, AMP; N. Nicolson, *Mary Curzon*, p. 85.
8. *Pall Mall Gazette*, 12 July 1895, *Glasgow Evening News*, 17 July 1895, and *Tablet*, 20 July 1895.
9. Ronaldshay, *Curzon*, Vol. 1, p. 236.
10. Iremonger, *The Fiery Chariot*, p. 133.
11. Penson, *Foreign Affairs*, p. 16.
12. Salisbury to C, 14 March 1896 and 2 Nov. 1897, CP 112/1.
13. Note by C, 29 Jan. 1897, CP 112/1.
14. C to Spring Rice, 28 Nov. 1895, Spring Rice Papers; C to Salisbury, 24 March and 18 June 1896, Salisbury Papers.
15. C to Hamilton, 9 April 1901, CP 111/160.
16. C to Selborne, 3 Feb. 1898, Selborne Papers.
17. See *Daily Chronicle*, 11 Oct. 1898.
18. C to Dilke, 30 June and 1 July 1897, Dilke Papers Add.mss.43893; C to Harcourt, 28 July 1896, Harcourt Papers.
19. 5 June 1896.
20. Lucy, *Diary*, p. 133.
21. 12 June 1896.
22. *Weekly Sun*, 9 May 1897.
23. *Morning Advertiser* and *Daily Chronicle*, 11 Oct. 1898.
24. Labouchere to C, 16 Feb. 1898, Grey to C, 15 Feb. 1898, CP 111/116.
25. Stanley to C, 28 June 1899, CP 111/121.
26. C to Spring Rice, 28 Nov. 1895, Spring Rice Papers; C to Brodrick, 19 July 1900, Midleton Papers Add.mss.50074.
27. Lansdowne to C, 16 Feb. 1902, CP 111/161.
28. Salisbury to C, 15 April 1898 and 4 Dec. 1897, CP 112/1.
29. C to Selborne, 4 April and 12 June 1900, Selborne Papers; C to Lansdowne, 16 March 1902, CP 111/161; C to Hamilton, 10 April 1900, CP 111/159.
30. C to Brodrick, 16 Nov. 1899, Midleton Papers Add.mss.50073.
31. CP 111/160.
32. *The Times*, 7 Dec. 1894, 28 March and 4 April 1895.
33. Ibid., 7 Dec. 1897.
34. Hopkirk, *The Great Game*, p. 500.
35. C memo, 14 March 1898, CP 112/368; Salisbury to C, 15 April 1898, CP 112/1.
36. N. Nicolson, op.cit., pp. 82–6.
37. C to Mary, 17 July 1893, AMP.
38. C to Mary, 22 March 1892, 4 Nov. and 12 Dec. 1893, AMP.
39. N. Nicolson, op.cit., p. 90.

40. Will dated 16 Jan. 1896, AMP.
41. C to Spring Rice, 28 Nov. 1895, Spring Rice Papers.
42. N. Nicolson, op.cit., p. 99.
43. Ibid., p. 98; Ronaldshay, op.cit., p. 249.

CHAPTER 10: SAILING TO BOMBAY
1. V. Granby to C, 21 Aug. 1898, CP 111/218.
2. *Lord Curzon in India*, p. 4.
3. Brodrick to Mary, 8 Aug. 1898, AMP.
4. *Lord Curzon in India*, p. 6.
5. Chamberlain to C, 3 May 1895, CP 111/98; Grey to C, 19 July 1898, CP 111/218.
6. C to Salisbury, 18 April 1897 and 19 April 1898, Salisbury Papers; Salisbury to C, 26 April 1897, CP 112/1; Rose, *Curzon*, pp. 323–6; Dilks, *Curzon in India*, Vol. 1, p. 64.
7. Dilks, ibid., pp. 64–5.
8. Enclosed in C to Salisbury, 20 June 1898, Salisbury Papers.
9. Queen Victoria to Salisbury, 25 May 1898, CP 112/1.
10. Rodd, *Social and Diplomatic Memories*, Vol. 3, p. 203; Gwynn, *Letters and Friendships*, Vol. 1, pp. 257–9.
11. O'Connor to C, 10 Aug. 1898, and Grey to C, 12 Aug. 1898, CP 111/218.
12. Blunt to C, 11 Aug. 1898, CP 111/218.
13. Undated report, Aug. 1898, CP 112/326.
14. Cromer to C, 20 Aug. 1898, CP 111/218.
15. CP 112/775.
16. Midleton, *Records and Reactions*, p. 9.
17. CP 111/24.
18. Brodrick to C, 14 Dec. 1898, CP 111/10.
19. Lawrence, *The India We Served*, p. 220.
20. C to Hamilton, 5 Jan. 1859, Hamilton Papers 510/1.
21. C, *British Government in India*, Vol. 1, pp. 40–3, 97.
22. Mary to Leiter, 9 Feb. 1899, AMP.
23. C to Brodrick, 19 Jan. and 12 April 1899, Midleton Papers Add.mss.50073; C to Selborne, 12 Jan. 1899, Selborne Papers; C to Godley, 12 Jan. 1899, CP 111/158; introduction to Lawrence's diary, Lawrence Papers 143/26.
24. C to Queen Victoria, 23 March 1899, CP 111/135.
25. Welldon, *Recollections and Reflections*, p. 234.
26. C to Mary, 8 March 1899, AMP.
27. R. Churchill, *Winston S. Churchill*, Vol. 1, pp. 315, 436.
28. *Lord Curzon in India*, Vol. 1, p. 295.
29. C, *British Government in India*, Vol. 1, pp. 86–7.
30. Kanwar, *Imperial Simla*, p. 45.
31. Ibid., p. 1.
32. Ibid., p. 54.
33. Mary to C, 6 March 1899, AMP.

CHAPTER 11: THE GOVERNANCE OF INDIA
1. C to Hamilton, 18 June 1901, CP 111/160.
2. C to Brodrick, 2 Oct. 1903, CP 111/162.
3. Lawrence, *The India We Served*, p. 268.
4. Godley to C, 3 March 1904, CP 111/163.
5. Lawrence, op.cit., p. 267.
6. Godley to C, 22 Nov. 1900, CP 111/159, and 11 March 1904, CP 111/163; Kaminsky, *India Office*, pp. 105–6, 139–41.

7. C to Brodrick, 3 March 1899, Midleton Papers Add.mss.50073.
8. Gopal, *British Policy*, p. 298.
9. C to Brodrick, 5 April 1899, Midleton Papers Add.mss.50073; C to Hamilton, 10 May 1899, Hamilton Papers 510/1.
10. C to Godley, 26 Jan. 1899, CP 111/158.
11. C to Cunningham, 23 Jan. 1899, CP 111/199.
12. C to Ibbetson, 23 Dec. 1901, CP 111/204.
13. C to Hamilton, 2 Feb. 1899, CP 111/158.
14. C to Brodrick, 24 March 1904, CP 111/163.
15. Lawrence diary, 10 Oct. 1902, Lawrence Papers 143/27.
16. Fraser, *India under Curzon*, p. 214.
17. C to P. Craigie, 17 April 1899, AMP.
18. Ibid., 1 July 1899.
19. Hill, *India*, pp. 135–6.
20. C to Hamilton, 9 April 1901, CP 111/160.
21. Ibid., and 11 June 1901, CP 111/160.
22. Hamilton to C, 23 Jan. 1901, C to Hamilton, 13 Feb. 1902, CP 111/160–1.
23. C to Brodrick, 20 Sept. 1899, Midleton Papers Add. mss.50073.
24. Collen to C, 16 April 1909, CP 111/408.
25. C to Hamilton, 11 March 1900, CP 111/159.
26. C to Godley, 27 Nov. 1899, CP 111/158.
27. C to Arundel, 29 April 1901, CP 111/203.
28. C to Hamilton, 24 Nov. and 4 Dec. 1902, CP 111/161.
29. Wolpert, *Morley and India*, p. 36.
30. C to Brodrick, 17 April 1900, Midleton Papers Add.mss.50073.
31. C to Hamilton, 23 April 1900, Hamilton Papers 510/5.
32. C to Queen Victoria, 18 July 1900, CP 111/135.
33. C to Hamilton, 18 July 1900, Hamilton Papers 510/5, and 22 April 1901, CP 111/160.
34. Hamilton to C, 16 June 1899, CP 111/158; Lawrence diary, Lawrence Papers 143/26.
35. C to Hamilton, 7 June 1899, CP 111/158.
36. C to Sandhurst, 26 May 1899, CP 111/199.
37. C to Hamilton, 16 Nov. 1899, CP 111/158.
38. Ibid., 14 June 1899.
39. Ibid., 20 Dec. 1900, CP 111/159.
40. Ibid., 15 Aug. 1900; Havelock to C, 21 Aug. 1900, CP 111/202.
41. Hamilton to C, Aug. 1900 (undated), CP 111/159.
42. C to Selborne, 29 May 1901, Selborne Papers; C to Godley, 12 July 1899, CP 111/158.
43. Hamilton to C, 5 Sept. 1900, Hamilton Papers 126/2.
44. C to Hamilton, 4 and 10 June 1903, CP 111/162.
45. Ibid., 26 Aug. 1903.
46. Hamilton to C, 27 July and 20 Oct. 1899, CP 111/158.
47. Ibid., 5 April 1900, Hamilton Papers 126/2.
48. C to Hamilton, 21 May 1902, CP 111/161.
49. Lawrence diary, 23 June 1901, Lawrence Papers 143/26.
50. Younghusband, *The Light of Experience*, pp. 166, 286.
51. Hamilton to C, 15 Sept. 1903, CP 111/162.
52. C to Brodrick, 20 Sept. 1899, Midleton Papers Add.mss.50073.
53. See, for example, Crosthwaite to Thirkell White, 2 Feb. 1902, Thirkell White Papers 254/1b.

54. For C's account, see his letter to Latouche, 16 Aug. 1903, CP 111/208.
55. Introduction to Lawrence's 1901 diary, Lawrence Papers 143/26.
56. Maconochie, *Life in the Indian Civil Service*, p. 118.
57. Ibid.
58. Younghusband, op.cit., p. 150.
59. Lawrence diary, 1 April 1902, Lawrence Papers 143/27; Lawrence, *The India We Served*, p. 251.
60. Hamilton to Godley, 30 Aug. 1901, Kilbracken Papers 102/6b.
61. Winstone, *Gertrude Bell*, p. 180.
62. Cox to C, 2 Nov. 1916, CP 112/163.
63. Maconochie, op.cit., p. 122.
64. Feiling, *Neville Chamberlain*, p. 45.

CHAPTER 12: 'LET INDIA BE MY JUDGE'
1. H. Nicolson, *Diaries*, p. 155.
2. Lawrence, *The India We Served*, p. 250.
3. C to Mary, 17 Feb. 1904, AMP.
4. Ibid., 18 April 1903; C, *British Government in India*, Vol. 2, p. 220.
5. C, ibid., pp. 173–5, 217–20.
6. C to Morley, 17 June 1900, CP 111/181.
7. Gopal, *British Policy*, p. 121.
8. See note 6.
9. *Lord Curzon in India*, Vol. 1, p. 308.
10. Gandhi, *An Autobiography*, p. 287.
11. *Lord Curzon in India*, pp. 488–9.
12. Gopal, op.cit., p. 110.
13. C to Godley, 17 Dec. 1903, CP 111/163.
14. C to Cranborne, 18 Nov. 1901, Salisbury Papers.
15. Koss, *John Morley*, p. 141.
16. Gopal, op.cit., p. 120.
17. 20 March 1896.
18. Lawrence, op.cit., pp. 233–4.
19. C to Godley, 9 April 1901, CP 111/160.
20. C to Balfour, 31 March 1901, Balfour Papers Add.mss.49732.
21. C to Wedderburn, 17 April 1900, CP 111/181.
22. C to Hamilton, 11 Jan. 1900, CP 111/159.
23. Gopal, op.cit., p. 117.
24. Woodruff, *The Guardians*, p. 166; Mudford, *Birds of a Different Plumage*, p. 201.
25. Gopal, op.cit., p. 189.
26. C's note on conversation with the Gaekwar, 4 July 1899, CP 111/256.
27. C to Ampthill, 5 June 1903, CP 111/207.
28. C to Mary, 3 Jan. 1905, AMP.
29. *Lord Curzon in India*, p. 491.
30. C to Ampthill, 17 Sept. 1900, CP 111/181.
31. Banerjea, *A Nation in Making*, p.145.
32. Speech at Ajmer, 18 Nov. 1902, CP 111/620.
33. *Lord Curzon in India*, p. 477.
34. C to Hamilton, 30 Jan. 1902, CP 111/161.
35. Welldon, *Recollections and Reflections*, p. 291.
36. C to Welldon, 17 Nov. 1901, CP 111/182.
37. C to Hamilton, 1 April 1901, CP 111/160.
38. C to Godley, 9 April 1901, CP 111/160.

39. C to P.Craigie, 1 July 1899, AMP.
40. C to Lyttelton, 29 Aug. 1900, Chandos Papers 2/4.
41. C to Brodrick, 2 Oct. 1903, CP 111/162.
42. Godley to C, 13 Sept. 1900, CP 111/159.
43. Cromer to C, 18 Dec. 1898, CP 111/218.
44. C to Hamilton, 24 July 1901, CP 111/160, and to Northbrook, 15 May 1901, CP 111/181.
45. C to Hamilton, 23 Sept. 1903, CP 111/162.
46. C to Brodrick, 2 July 1903, Midleton Papers Add.mss.50074.
47. C to Hamilton, 9 Sept. 1903, CP 111/162.
48. C to Ampthill, 10 Nov. 1902, CP 111/206.
49. C to Queen Victoria, 12 Nov. 1899, CP 111/135.
50. Introduction to Lawrence diary, Lawrence Papers 143/26.
51. C to Hamilton, 8 Aug. 1900, Hamilton Papers 510/5.
52. O'Dwyer, *India as I Knew it*, p.39.
53. *New India*, 15 July 1905, quoted in Moon, *The British Conquest*, p. 941.
54. C to Mary, 21 Aug. 1901, AMP.
55. Ibid., 4 Sept. 1901.
56. C to Hamilton, 13 June 1900, Hamilton Papers 510/5.
57. C to Fryer, 9 July 1899, CP 111/200.
58. C to Mary, 9 Nov. 1903, AMP.
59. C to Hamilton, 5 March 1903, CP 111/162.
60. C's minutes in CP 111/279.
61. C to Ampthill, 15 June 1903, CP 111/207; C to MacDonnell, 17 Dec. 1899, CP 111/200; C to Woodburn, 19 Feb. 1901, CP 111/203.
62. Junagadh to C, 8 Aug. 1901, CP 111/204.
63. C to Bourdillon, 2 March 1904, CP 111/209.
64. Speech at Brindaban, 5 Dec. 1899, CP 111/620.
65. Speech at Agra, 5 Dec. 1899, CP 111/620.
66. C to Ampthill, 20 June 1902, CP 111/205.
67. *Lord Curzon in India*, Vol. 1, pp. 200–1.
68. Hamilton to C, 29 Nov. 1901, CP 111/620.
69. Note by C in CP 111/620.
70. C to Barnes, 11 June 1903, CP 111/620; Lawrence, op.cit., p. 236.
71. Note by C in CP 111/620.
72. C to Young, 25 April 1899, CP 111/199; C to Rivaz, 1 May 1902, CP 111/620.
73. Speech in Legislative Council, 18 March 1904, CP 111/620.
74. Ibid.
75. Rose, *Curzon*, p. 239.

CHAPTER 13: PARTNERS AND COLLEAGUES: THE PROBLEM OF THE PRINCES
1. C to Hamilton, 9 Nov. 1900, CP 111/159.
2. Gopal, *British Policy*, p. 14.
3. Hamilton to C, 9 Aug. 1899, CP 111/158.
4. C to Edward VII, 19 June 1901, CP 111/136.
5. Durand, *Alfred Lyall*, pp. 190–1.
6. Lawrence, *The India We Served*, p. 111.
7. C to Hamilton, 28 Nov. 1900, CP 111/159.
8. Ibid., and 12 July 1899, CP 111/158.
9. C to Hamilton, 27 Aug. 1902, CP 111/161.
10. C to Hamilton, 18 July 1900, Hamilton Papers 510/5; Hamilton to Godley, 30 Oct. 1900, Kilbracken Papers 102/6b.

11. C to Queen Victoria, 17 May and 27 Sept. 1899, 3 Aug., 12 Sept., 3 Oct., 9 and 28 Nov. 1900, CP 111/135.
12. C to Hamilton, 26 Nov. 1899, CP 111/158.
13. *Lord Curzon in India*, Vol. 1, pp. 237–8.
14. C to Hamilton, 25 July 1900, Hamilton Papers 510/5.
15. See C's note, 30 Dec. 1899, CP 111/256; C to Hamilton, 28 Dec. 1899, CP 111/158.
16. Lawrence, op.cit., p. 73.
17. Woodruff, *The Guardians*, p. 68.
18. Wyllie to C, 4 July 1900, CP 111/202.
19. Cooch Behar to Woodburn, 30 June 1901, CP 111/204.
20. Hamilton to C, 2 April 1901, CP 111/160.
21. Ibid., 24 Jan. 1901.
22. Ampthill to C, 28 May 1903, CP 111/207; C to Hamilton, 20 Dec. 1900, CP 111/159.
23. C to Hamilton, 18 July 1900, Hamilton Papers 510/5, and 9 April and 20 Aug. 1902, CP 111/161.
24. Ashton, *British Policy*, pp. 23, 34–6.
25. C to Lamington, 4 Jan. 1904, CP 111/209.
26. C to Hamilton, 24 July 1901, CP 111/160, and 29 Aug. 1900, Hamilton Papers 510/5.
27. Hamilton to Godley, 23 Sept. 1900, Kilbracken Papers 102/6b.
28. Kapurthala to Lawrence, 18 Jan. 1903, CP 111/207.
29. C to Hamilton, 1 April 1901, CP 111/160, and 4 June 1902, CP 111/16.
30. Hamilton to C, 29 May 1902, CP 111/161.
31. C to Ampthill, 25 Jan. 1905, CP 111/210; C to Scarsdale, 11 Nov. 1903, CP 112/775.
32. Maconochie to Nathan, 19 Jan. 1905, Mysore to C, 2 Feb. 1905, and Ampthill to C, 3 Feb. 1905, CP 111/210; C to Mary, 19 Jan. 1905, AMP.
33. C to Hamilton, 3 Dec. 1902, CP 111/161.
34. Ibid.
35. Hamilton to C, 7 Aug. 1902, CP 111/161.

CHAPTER 14: GUARDING THE FRONTIERS
1. C to Selborne, 4 April 1900 and 19 May 1901, Selborne Papers.
2. Salisbury to C, 23 Sept. 1901, CP 111/223.
3. C to Selborne, 9 Aug. 1901 and 21 Dec. 1903, Selborne Papers.
4. C to Hamilton, 17 Sept. 1899, CP 111/158.
5. C to Hamilton, 15 Feb. 1900, CP 111/159; C to P. Craigie, 8 Jan. 1900, AMP; C to Brodrick, 8 Jan. 1900, Midleton Papers Add. mss.50073.
6. C to Hamilton, 29 March 1900, CP 111/159, and 17 Sept. 1902, CP 111/160.
7. C to Hamilton, 21 Nov. 1901, CP 111/160.
8. Dilks, *Curzon in India*, Vol. 1, p. 215.
9. C to Brodrick, 3 March 1904, CP 111/163.
10. Hyam, *Empire and Sexuality*, pp. 126–7.
11. Kitchener's memo, Oct. 1905, Kitchener Papers PRO 30/57.
12. Palmer to C, 26 Nov. 1902, CP 111/206.
13. C to Hamilton, 13 June 1900, Hamilton Papers 510/5.
14. Gopal, *British Policy*, p. 263.
15. Ampthill to Godley, 27 July 1904, Ampthill Papers 233/37.
16. C's minute of 4 May 1900, CP 111/240.
17. C to Hamilton, 18 July 1900, Hamilton Papers 510/5.
18. C to Brodrick, 17 April 1900, Midleton Papers Add.mss.50073.
19. C to Hamilton, 2 Feb. 1899, CP 111/158.
20. C to Chamberlain, 28 June 1902, CP 111/182.
21. C's minute of 27 Aug. 1900, CP 111/132.

22. Swinson, *North-West Frontier*, p. 260.
23. Young to C, 20 and 26 Sept. 1900, CP 111/202.
24. C to Young, 23 and 30 Sept. 1900, CP 111/202.
25. Ronaldshay, *Curzon*, Vol. 2, p. 140.
26. C to Hamilton, 25 June 1902, CP 111/161, and 1 Oct. 1901, CP 111/160.
27. Caroe, *The Pathans*, p. 418; Swinson, op.cit., pp. 261–2.
28. Harcourt to C, 13 Aug. 1898, CP 111/218.
29. *The Times*, 17 July 1900.
30. Ibid., 3 Oct. 1911.
31. C to Hamilton, 4 Jan. 1900, CP 111/159.
32. Godley to C, 6 Jan. 1899, CP 111/158.
33. C to Hamilton, 2 May 1900, Hamilton Papers 510/5.
34. C to Hamilton, 15 Feb. 1900, CP 111/159, and 3 July 1901, CP 111/160.
35. C to Brodrick, 3 March 1899, Midleton Papers Add. mss.50073.
36. C to Salisbury, 18 Sept. 1900, Salisbury Papers.
37. C to Selborne, 29 May 1901, Selborne Papers; C to Lansdowne, 16 March 1902, CP 111/161.
38. C to Hamilton, 19 March 1903, CP 111/162; C to Percy, 30 April 1903, CP 111/232.
39. C to Godley, 12 April 1899, CP 111/158.
40. C to Lyall, 23 Aug. 1899, CP 111/181; C to Lansdowne, 5 April 1901, CP 111/160.
41. C to Selborne, 29 May 1901, Selborne Papers.
42. Salisbury to C, Aug. 1900, CP 111/159, and 23 Sept. 1901, CP 111/223.
43. C to Hamilton, 12 March 1903, CP 111/162.
44. Grenville, *Lord Salisbury*, p. 425.
45. C to Hardinge, 22 Feb. 1902, CP 111/205.
46. Marriott, *The English in India*, p. 259.

CHAPTER 15: THE VICEROY'S ROUTINE

1. C to Dawkins, 2 July 1902, CP 111/182.
2. Welldon, *Recollections and Reflections*, p. 219.
3. Dawkins to C, 25 July 1902, CP 111/182.
4. Lawrence, *The India We Served*, pp. 80–2: introduction to Lawrence diaries, Lawrence Papers 143/26.
5. C to H. Brodrick, 30 May 1900, Midleton Papers Add.mss.50073.
6. C to Mary, 31 July 1901, AMP.
7. Lawrence, op.cit., p. 249.
8. C to MacDonnell, 2 June 1901, MacDonnell Papers.
9. C to Mary, 17 June 1901, AMP.
10. C to Brodrick, 30 April 1903, 18 June 1900 and 25 June 1903, Midleton Papers Add.mss.50074; C to V. Cecil, 30 April 1903, Violet Milner Papers 251/3; Lawrence diaries, 9 Aug. 1901, Lawrence Papers 143/26.
11. Introduction to Lawrence diaries, Lawrence Papers 143/26.
12. Welldon, op.cit., pp. 263, 265.
13. Havelock to C, 31 March 1900, CP 111/201; C to Hamilton, 15 Feb. 1900, CP 111/159.
14. Lawrence diaries, 3 Feb. 1902, Lawrence Papers 143/27.
15. Butt, *Taft and Roosevelt*, pp. 188, 810.
16. C to Brodrick, 18 June 1900, Midleton Papers Add.mss.50074.
17. Ibid.
18. C to Godley, 17 Sept. 1902, CP 111/161.
19. C, *British Government in India*, Vol. 2, p. 45; Lawrence diaries, 10 March 1901, 2 and 11 Feb. 1902, Lawrence Papers 143/26 and 27.

20. C to Mary, 23 July 1901, AMP.
21. Hart-Davis, *End of an Era*, p. 286.
22. C to Hamilton, 24 July 1901, Hamilton Papers 510/8.
23. Dilks, *Curzon in India*, Vol. 1, p. 84.
24. Benson diary, 1 March 1903, Vol. 25, p. 45, Benson Papers.
25. C to Godley, 30 June 1902, CP 111/161.
26. Lawrence diaries, 11 Nov. 1902, Lawrence Papers 143/27.
27. Lawrence, op.cit., p. 236.
28. C to Hamilton, 28 Nov. 1900, CP 111/159.
29. C, *Tales*, pp. 160–4.
30. Bradley, *Lady Curzon's India*, pp. 62–6; C, *Leaves*, pp. 5–7; introduction to Lawrence diaries, Lawrence Papers 143/26.
31. C to Mary, 3 March 1904, AMP.
32. C to Scarsdale, 14 March 1903, CP 111/775.
33. C to Mary, 13 April 1904, AMP.
34. Ibid., various letters April–Oct 1903.
35. C to Ampthill, 10 April 1901, CP 111/203.
36. Lawrence, op.cit., p. 227; introduction to Lawrence diaries, Lawrence Papers 143/26.
37. C to Mary, 5 April 1903, AMP.
38. Lawrence diary, 6 March 1902, Lawrence Papers 143/27.
39. Ibid., 15 March.
40. C to Hamilton, 13 Jan. 1903, CP 111/162.
41. C to Selborne, 12 April and 1 July 1899 and 12 June 1900, Selborne Papers.
42. C to Maxwell, 12 June 1900, C to Cust, 15 Jan. 1900, Cust to C, 13 Feb. 1900, CP 111/181.
43. C to Knollys, 10 June 1901, AMP; see also CP 112/418.
44. C to P. Craigie, 18 March 1901, AMP.
45. C to Mary, 23 Sept. 1901, AMP.
46. Chirol, *Fifty Years*, p. 230.
47. C to Milner, 6 April 1905, Milner Papers dep. 32.
48. Mary to Leiter, 19 July 1900, AMP.
49. Welldon, op.cit., p. 208.
50. C to Mary, Oct. 1901, AMP.
51. Letters between C and Mary, Oct. 1901, AMP.
52. C to Mary, 21 April 1903, AMP.
53. Mary to C, 19 Dec. 1903, AMP.
54. Godley to Minto, 27 July 1906, Minto Papers 12736.
55. C. Vanderbilt Balsan, *The Glitter and the Gold*, p. 137.
56. P. Craigie to Brown, 10 Aug. 1906, Craigie Papers.
57. Mary to C, 11 Jan. 1903, AMP; N. Nicolson, *Mary Curzon*, p. 170.
58. Mary to C, 30 March 1901, AMP.
59. Ibid., 18 May 1901, AMP.
60. Buck, *Simla*, p. 57.
61. P. Craigie to Brown, 24 Jan. and 12 Oct. 1903, 21 July 1906, Craigie Papers.
62. Lawrence diary, 11 Feb. and 10 March 1902, Lawrence Papers 143/27.
63. Mary to C, 14 July 1910, AMP.
64. C to Mary, 10 June 1901, Mary to C, 28 June 1901, AMP.
65. Mary to C, 27 July 1901, AMP.
66. Ibid., 18 May.
67. Ibid., 5 July.
68. C to Mary, 3 and 8 July 1901, C to P. Craigie, 14 May 1903, AMP.

69. C to Selborne, 9 Aug. 1901, Selborne Papers.
70. C to Dawkins, 22 Nov. 1901, CP 111/182.
71. C to Lyttelton, 26 June 1901, Chandos Papers 2/4.
72. Mary to C, Sept. 1901, AMP.
73. Ibid., and 6 Aug. 1901, AMP.
74. Lyttelton to C, 5 Aug. 1900, CP 111/121; Mary to C, 5 July 1901, AMP.
75. J. Wilson, *CB*, p. 144.
76. C to Mary, 18 March 1903 and 21 Aug. 1901, AMP.
77. P. Craigie to Brown, 19 May 1904, Craigie Papers.
78. N. Mosley, *Julian Grenfell*, p. 76.

CHAPTER 16: 1902: PROCONSULAR ZENITH
1. C to Balfour, 31 March 1901, Balfour Papers Add.mss.49732.
2. C to Brodrick, 8 Jan. 1900, Midleton Papers Add.mss.50073.
3. C to Hamilton, 18 June 1901, CP 111/160.
4. C to Scarsdale, 26 Feb. 1903, CP 112/775.
5. Ibbetson to C, 22 June 1905, CP 111/210.
6. Esher to C, 2 Dec. 1901, CP 111/182.
7. Brett, *Journals*, Vol. 1, p. 321.
8. Hamilton to Godley, 22 April 1900, 4 April 1901, 29 June 1902, Kilbracken Papers 102/6b; Godley to Ampthill, 19 and 31 May 1904, Ampthill Papers 233/4.
9. Northcote to Salisbury, 4 Oct. 1900, Salisbury Papers.
10. Hamilton to Godley, 2 June 1903, Kilbracken Papers 102/6b.
11. C memo on Berar, 25 Sept. 1901, CP 111/246.
12. C to Elles, 23 Sept. 1901, CP 111/245.
13. Hamilton to C, 25 March 1902, CP 111/161.
14. See Ritchie to C, 11 Feb. 1902, CP 111/161.
15. Mary's journal, AMP.
16. C to Hamilton, 2 April 1902, CP 111/161; C to Montagu, 31 May 1921, FO 800/149.
17. Lawrence diaries, 1 April 1902, Lawrence Papers 143/27.
18. C to Godley, 18 June 1902, CP 111/161.
19. Dilks, *Curzon in India*, Vol. 1, p. 212.
20. Blood, *Four Score Years*, p. 346.
21. C to Godley, 30 July 1902, CP 111/161.
22. C to Mary, 14 Dec. 1902, AMP.
23. Roberts to C, 23 Jan. 1903, CP 111/182.
24. Ritchie to C, 12 July 1901, CP 111/160.
25. Crosthwaite to Thirkell White, 2 Feb. 1902, Thirkell White Papers 251/1b.
26. C to Hamilton, 28 May and 4 June 1902, CP 111/161.
27. C to Godley, 18 June 1902, CP 111/161.
28. Hamilton to Godley, 16 June 1902, Kilbracken Papers 102/6b; Hamilton to C, 19 June 1902, CP 111/161; Hamilton to Mary, June 1902, AMP.
29. Salisbury to C, 9 Aug. 1902, CP 111/224.
30. Ridley and Percy, *Letters*, p. 186.
31. C to Hamilton, 16 July 1902, CP 111/161.
32. Arnold-Forster diary, 29 June 1904, 27 Feb. and 5 April 1905, Arnold-Forster Papers Add. mss.50339.
33. Asquith to C, 13 Jan. 1901, CP 111/223.
34. CP 111/25.
35. Egremont, *Balfour*, p. 147.
36. Amery, *Joseph Chamberlain*, Vol. 5, pp. 75–6.
37. Egremont, *Balfour*, p. 167.

38. Brodrick to C, 6 Nov. 1903, CP 111/162.
39. C to Brodrick, 9 Feb. 1905, CP 111/164.
40. C to Hamilton, 24 Jan. 1901, CP 111/160.
41. Welldon, *Recollections and Reflections*, p. 263; Lawrence, *The India We Served*, p. 241.
42. Queen Victoria to C, 4 Sept. 1899, C to Queen Victoria, 4 Oct. 1899, CP 111/135.
43. *Lord Curzon in India*, p. 534.
44. C to Esher, 12 April and 12 June 1901, CP 111/181; C, *British Government in India*, Vol. 1, pp. 188–9.
45. C to Hamilton, 25 June 1902, CP 111/161.
46. Knollys to C, 1 March 1901, C to Knollys, 30 May 1901, CP 111/136.
47. C to Hamilton, 21 Aug. 1901, CP 111/160.
48. Lawrence to Pudukotta, 17 Dec. 1901, CP 111/204.
49. C to Hamilton, 20 March 1902, CP 111/161.
50. C to Hamilton, 17 April 1902 and 11 Nov. 1901, CP 111/160–1.
51. C to Bikanir, 24 May 1902, CP 111/205; Bikanir to C, 24 June 1902, CP 111/182.
52. Hamilton to C, 29 May and 12 June 1902, CP 111/161.
53. C to Hamilton, 3 Aug. 1902, CP 111/161; Lawrence, op.cit., p. 215.
54. C to Hamilton and Balfour, both 16 July 1902, CP 111/161.
55. C to Hamilton, 30 July 1902, CP 111/161.
56. Godley to C, 1 Aug. 1902, CP 111/161.
57. C to Mary, 9 and 27 Aug. 1902, AMP.
58. C to Hamilton, 8 May 1901, CP 111/160.
59. *Lord Curzon in India*, p. 308.
60. C to Hamilton, 28 May 1903, CP 111/162.
61. Kipling to C, 16 Sept. 1902, CP 111/224.
62. C to Hamilton, 16 Dec. 1901, CP 111/160, and 3 Sept. 1902, CP 111/161.
63. Hamilton to C, 16 Nov. 1902, C to Hamilton, 13 Nov. 1902, CP 111/161; Lawrence diary, 11 Dec. 1902, Lawrence Papers 143/27; Dilks, *Curzon in India*, Vol. 1, pp. 255–8.
64. Brodrick to C, 19 Nov. 1902, CP 111/172.
65. C to Balfour, 20 Nov. 1902, and to Hamilton, 23 Nov. 1902, and Balfour to C, 12 Dec. 1902, CP 111/161.
66. C to Mary, 9 Dec. 1902, AMP; C to Brodrick, 26 Feb. 1902, Midleton Papers Add.mss.50074.
67. Brodrick to C, 15 March 1903, C to Brodrick, 9 April 1903, Midleton Papers Add.mss.50074; Mary to C, 12 Dec. 1902, AMP.
68. Lawrence diary, 11 Dec. 1902, Lawrence Papers 143/27; C to Hamilton, 28 Dec. 1902, CP 111/162.
69. A. Wilson, *Letters from India*, p. 273.
70. Mrs Thompson's diary, Thompson Papers 137/3.
71. *Lord Curzon in India*, Vol. 1, p. 227.
72. Mrs Thompson's diary, op. cit.
73. C to Hamilton, 8 Jan. 1903, CP 111/162.
74. C to Mary, 12 Jan. 1903, AMP.
75. Mary to C, 11 Jan. 1903, AMP.
76. C to Brodrick, 24 Dec. 1903, CP 111/163.
77. A. Wilson, op.cit., p. 272.
78. C to Mary, 5 April 1902, AMP.
79. Winstone, *Gertrude Bell*, p. 86.
80. Ridley and Percy, op.cit., p. 197.
81. Selborne to C, 4 Jan. 1903, CP 111/229.

CHAPTER 17: FATAL APPOINTMENTS, 1902–1903
1. Repington, *Vestigia*, p. 160.
2. I. Hamilton, *The Commander*, pp. 99–100.
3. T. Pakenham, *The Boer War*, pp. 312, 318–19.
4. Roberts to Kitchener, 27 March 1903, Kitchener Papers PRO 30/57; C to Hamilton, 25 March 1903, CP 111/162.
5. Gopal, *British Policy*, p. 276.
6. Lansdowne to C, 20 April 1900, CP 111/121.
7. Northbrook to C, 15 Nov. 1900, CP 111/181.
8. C to Hamilton, 9 Feb. 1900, Hamilton Papers 510/5.
9. Dilks, *Curzon in India*, Vol. 1, p. 204; Gopal, op.cit., p. 277.
10. Brodrick to C, 20 March 1899, CP 111/10; Mary to C, September 1901, AMP.
11. Mary to Kitchener, 9 Dec. 1902, Kitchener Papers PRO 30/57.
12. C to V. Cecil, 30 April 1903, Violet Milner Papers 251/3.
13. Magnus, *Kitchener*, p. 200.
14. Kitchener to A. Cranborne, 19 March 1903, Salisbury Papers.
15. Royle, *The Kitchener Enigma*, pp. 144, 218; Richardson, *Mars without Venus*, p. 124; Mary to Mrs Leiter, 8 March 1905, AMP.
16. Kitchener to A. Cranborne, 25 Jan. and 16 July 1903, Salisbury Papers.
17. Note by C after Mary's death, AMP.
18. Dawkins to C, 25 July 1902, CP 111/182.
19. V. Cecil to C, 8 April 1903, CP 111/225.
20. Smith–Dorrien, *Memoirs*, pp. 313–14; Reed, *The India I Knew*, p. 50.
21. C to Hamilton, 3 Dec. 1902, CP 111/161; IMO, p. 1, CP 111/412.
22. Dawkins to C, 10 Nov. 1905, CP 112/183.
23. Kitchener to Rosebery, 12 Sept. 1903, Rosebery Papers.
24. Roberts to Kitchener, 19 March 1903, Kitchener Papers, PRO 30/57.
25. C to Hamilton, 26 Feb. 1903, CP 111/162.
26. IMO, op.cit., pp. 4–5.
27. Kitchener to C, 21 and 25 May 1903, CP 111/207; Kitchener to A. Cranborne, 21 May 1903, Salisbury Papers.
28. C to Scarsdale, 28 May 1903, CP 112/775.
29. C to Brodrick, 2 July 1903, Midleton Papers Add.mss.50074.
30. Kitchener to A. Cranborne, 6 Aug. 1903, Salisbury Papers.
31. Cromer to C, 14 Aug. 1898, CP 111/218.
32. C to Scarsdale, 2 April 1901, CP 112/775.
33. C to Brodrick, 30 June 1902, Midleton Papers Add.mss.50074.
34. Mary to C, 2 and 17 Feb. and April 1903, AMP.
35. C to Mary, 16 and 21 April 1903, AMP.
36. Dawkins to C, 11 Feb., and C to Dawkins, 9 March 1904, CP 111/182.
37. McDonnell to C, 29 April, 4 Oct. and 29 Dec. 1903, CP 111/114.
38. C to Balfour, 5 Feb. 1903, CP 111/162.
39. Ibid., 30 April; C to Brodrick, 30 April 1903, Midleton Papers Add.mss.50074; C to Mary, 9 April 1903, AMP; C to Scarsdale, 7 May 1903, CP 112/775.
40. Malcolm to C, 12 June 1903, CP 111/225.
41. Minto, *India, Minto and Morley*, p. 115.
42. Hamilton to C, 27 March 1903, CP 111/162.
43. C to P. Craigie, 14 May 1903, AMP.
44. Lawrence diary, 22 June 1902, Lawrence Papers 143/27; Lawrence to C, 25 Nov. 1903, CP 112/417.
45. Lawrence, *The India We Served*, pp. 249–50.
46. Hamilton to C, 23 July, C to Hamilton, 22 and 29 July, 19 and 26 Aug. 1903,

CP 111/162.
47. Wyndham to C, 26 May 1899, CP 111/121.
48. Hamilton to C, 16 March 1899, CP 111/158.
49. A. Lyttelton to C, 29 May 1901, CP 111/223.
50. Egremont, *Balfour*, p. 143.
51. R. Churchill, *Winston S. Churchill*, Vol. 2, p. 20.
52. Egremont, op.cit., p. 154.
53. C to Godley, 13 March, Godley to C, 14 Feb. 1902, CP 111/161.
54. Hamilton to C, 16 Aug. 1903, CP 111/162; Dilks, op.cit., Vol. 2, pp. 37–8.
55. Brodrick to C, 19 Aug., C to Brodrick, 10 Sept. 1903, Midleton Papers Add.mss.50074.
56. McDonnell to C, 29 March 1903, CP 111/114.
57. Hamilton to C, 13 and 27 Feb. 1903, CP 111/162.
58. Ibid., 28 Jan.
59. Ridley and Percy, *Letters*, p. 198.
60. W. Churchill, *Great Contemporaries*, p. 242.
61. Arnold-Forster diary, 27 July 1904, Arnold-Forster Papers Add.mss.50339.
62. Selborne to C, 4 Jan. 1903, CP 111/229; Selborne to Balfour, 9 June 1904, Sandars Papers Eng. Hist. c748.
63. C to Hamilton, 19 and 26 Feb. 1903, CP 111/162; Dawkins to C, 20 Feb. 1903, CP 111/182.
64. Hamilton to C, 27 March 1903, CP 111/162.
65. Crosthwaite to Thirkell White, 6 Oct. 1903, Thirkell White Papers, 254/1b; Kitchener to Mary, 25 Sept. 1903, AMP.
66. Opinions quoted in the *Daily Mail*, 22 and 26 Sept., and 6 Oct. 1903.
67. C to Brodrick, 2 Oct. 1903, CP 111/162.
68. Godley to C, 1 Jan., C to Godley, 27 Jan. 1904, CP 111/162.
69. Sent on 6 and 11 Nov. 1903; C to Mary, 12 Nov. 1903, AMP.
70. C to Brodrick, 15 Nov. and 1 Dec. 1903, CP 111/162; C to Gell, 22 July 1900, Milner Papers dep. 5.
71. Mary to C, 6 March 1904, AMP.
72. C to Mary, 6 April and 21 Jan. 1904, AMP.
73. Brodrick to Mary, 16 Feb. 1904, AMP; Brodrick to Scarsdale, 21 March 1904, CP 112/777.
74. C to Mary, 22 Feb. 1904, AMP; Brodrick to C, 12 Feb. 1904, CP 111/163.
75. C to Minto, 25 Nov. 1905, Minto Papers 12774.
76. Brodrick to C, 14 Dec. 1898, CP 111/10.

CHAPTER 18: THE GULF, BENGAL AND TIBET
1. C to Hardinge, 21 Nov. 1903, CP 111/182.
2. Ronaldshay, *Curzon*, Vol. 2, p. 316.
3. Bradley, *Lady Curzon's India*, p. 153.
4. Brodrick to C, 17 Dec. 1903, CP 111/162.
5. C to Mary, 24 March 1904, AMP.
6. Ibid., 18 Dec. 1903.
7. *Lord Curzon in India*, Vol. 1, p. xxxii.
8. Fraser, *India under Curzon*, pp. 194–5.
9. Ray, *Social Conflict*, pp. 142, 147; C to Brodrick, 5 April 1904, CP 111/163.
10. Banerjea, *A Nation in Making*, p. 161.
11. Fraser, op.cit., pp. 376–80.
12. C to Hamilton, 30 April 1902, CP 111/161.
13. Fraser to C, 28 Nov. 1902, CP 111/206; Bourdillon to C, 22 May 1903, CP 111/207.

14. See note 12.
15. Goradia, *Lord Curzon*, p. 214.
16. Zaidi, 'The Partition of Bengal', pp. 87–8.
17. C to Brodrick, 31 Dec. 1903, CP 111/162.
18. Banerjea, op.cit., p. 279.
19. Zaidi, op.cit., pp. 69–72, 98; C to Brodrick, 17 Feb. 1904, CP 111/163; Sarkar, *Modern India*, p. 107; C to Brodrick, 2 Feb. 1905, CP 111/164.
20. C to Hamilton, 28 May 1902, CP 111/161; Gopal, *British Policy*, pp. 236–7.
21. C to Mary, 30 Jan. 1904, AMP.
22. C to Hamilton, 13 Feb. 1903, CP 111/162.
23. C to Hamilton, 13 April and 7 May 1903, CP 111/162; C to Barnes, 16 June 1903, CP 111/207.
24. Fleming, *Bayonets to Lhasa*, pp. 89–90.
25. Balfour to Brodrick, 18 Oct. 1903, Add.mss.50072; Fleming, op.cit., pp. 93–5; Younghusband to C, 1 Jan. 1904, CP 111/209.
26. C to Younghusband, 23 Jan. 1904, CP 111/209.
27. C to Mary, 6 April 1904, AMP.
28. C to Hamilton, 16 Oct. 1901, CP 111/160, and 5 Feb., 19 March and 23 July 1903, CP 111/162.
29. C's annotation of C to Hamilton, 22 July 1903, CP 111/162; Ampthill to Brodrick, 5 and 19 May, Ampthill to Godley, 5 May, Godley to Ampthill, 19 May 1904, Ampthill Papers 233/37.

CHAPTER 19: 'AN INFINITUDE OF TROUBLE': ENGLAND, 1904
1. Mary to C, 12 Feb., C to Mary, 12 March and 8 May 1904, AMP.
2. Mary to C, 24 and 27 Jan., C to Mary, 28 Jan. and 11 Feb. 1904, AMP.
3. Maxwell to A. Salisbury, 9 March 1904, Salisbury Papers; King, *The Viceroy's Fall*, pp. 100–1.
4. Maxwell, ibid.
5. C to Mary, 12 March 1904, AMP.
6. C to Mary, 24 March and 6 April, Charlotte Knollys to Mary, 20 March 1904, AMP; Lady Alexandra Metcalfe to the author.
7. C to Scarsdale, 24 March 1904, CP 112/775.
8. Mary to Leiter, 8 May 1904, AMP.
9. C to Mary, 12 and 24 March 1904, AMP.
10. Mary to Mr and Mrs Leiter, 8 and 9 May 1904, AMP.
11. C to Mary, 8 May 1904, AMP.
12. Ibid., 17 Feb.
13. C to P. Craigie, 18 May 1904, AMP.
14. Mary to Leiter, 17 May 1904, AMP.
15. C to Ampthill, 23 June, 19 July and 7 Sept. 1904, CP 112/413.
16. C to Salisbury, 25 and 28 June, 16 July, 22 Aug. and 6 Sept. 1904, Salisbury to C, 5 Sept. 1904, Salisbury Papers.
17. Cannadine, *Aspects of Aristocracy*, pp. 94–5.
18. Godley to C, 21 July 1904, CP 112/413.
19. C to Selborne, 23 Jan. 1900, Selborne Papers; C to Younghusband, 19 Sept. 1901, CP 111/182.
20. *Lord Curzon in India*, Vol. 1, pp. 34–51.
21. Selborne to C, 22 July, Arnold-Forster to C, 31 July 1904, CP 112/413; Grey to Ampthill, 30 Oct. 1904, Ampthill Papers 233/40.
22. Gopal, *British Policy*, p. 294.
23. C to Ampthill, June 1904, CP 112/413.

24. *Daily Mail*, 16 April 1904.
25. See Arnold-Forster diary, numerous entries 1904, Arnold–Forster Papers Add.mss.50337– 9
26. C to Mary, 10 March 1904, AMP.
27. Younghusband to C, 18 June 1904, CP 112/413; Fleming, *Bayonets to Lhasa*, pp. 195–7.
28. C to Ampthill, 8 July, Godley to Ampthill, 8 Sept. 1904, Ampthill Papers 233/37.
29. Brodrick to Ampthill, 1 July 1904, Ampthill Papers 133/37; Fleming, op.cit., p. 211; Dilks, *Curzon in India*, Vol. 2, pp. 90–1.
30. Fleming, ibid., pp. 211–15; Dilks, ibid.
31. Fleming, ibid., pp. 237–9, 241.
32. Ibid., pp. 251–61.
33. Ibid., p. 274; Dilks, op.cit., pp. 96–7.
34. Balfour to A. Salisbury, 4 Oct. 1904, Salisbury Papers; Fleming, ibid., p. 273.
35. Dilks, op.cit., pp. 99–100.
36. Younghusband to Mary, 14 Dec., C to Mary, 26 Nov. 1904, AMP.
37. Gilbert, *Servant of India*, p. 20.
38. C to Mary, 4 Sept. 1904, AMP.
39. Brodrick to C, 31 Oct. 1904, CP 112/413.
40. Brodrick to Ampthill, 4 Nov. 1904, Ampthill Papers 233/37.
41. Mary to Barlow, 28 May 1904, Barlow Papers.
42. Notes by C in AMP; see N. Nicolson, *Mary Curzon*, pp. 176–80.
43. C to Mary, 23, 25 and 26 Nov. 1904, AMP.
44. Mary to C, various letters Nov. 1904, AMP.
45. C to Mary, 9 Dec. 1904, AMP.
46. Lamington to Mary, 10 Dec. 1904, AMP.
47. Dilks, op.cit., pp. 148–9.

CHAPTER 20: KITCHENER'S CONSPIRACY

1. Kitchener to Mary, 12 May 1904, AMP.
2. Kitchener to Marker, 15 Feb. 1905, Kitchener-Marker Papers Add.mss.52276a; Kitchener to A. Salisbury, 16 Feb. 1905, Salisbury Papers; IMO, C's annotation p. 32, CP 111/412.
3. Kitchener to Marker, 30 Jan. 1905, Salisbury Papers.
4. H. Hamilton to Marker, 31 Oct. 1904, Kitchener-Marker Papers, Add.mss.52277a.
5. Repington to Marker, 25 Aug., 11 and 23 Oct. 1904, and 15 Dec. 1905, Kitchener-Marker Papers Add.mss.52277b.
6. Balfour to A. Salisbury, 16 Oct. 1904, A. Salisbury to Balfour, 17 Oct. 1904, Salisbury Papers; A. Salisbury's drafts to Kitchener are in an unsorted box at Hatfield.
7. Kitchener to A. Salisbury, 25 Jan., 29 July and 6 Aug. 1903, 28 March and 27 Oct. 1904, Salisbury Papers.
8. H. Hamilton to A. Salisbury, 11 Aug. 1904, Salisbury Papers.
9. Ibid., 2 Nov. 1905; see also note 35.
10. Stedman to Kitchener, 23 Nov. 1905, Kitchener Papers PRO 30/57.
11. Brodrick to Kitchener, 29 April and 9 June 1904, Midleton Papers PRO 30/67.
12. Kitchener to Roberts, 27 Nov. 1904, Kitchener Papers PRO 30/57.
13. Kitchener to Roberts, 9 June 1904 and 26 Jan. 1905, Roberts to Kitchener, 28 July and 28 Dec. 1904, Kitchener Papers PRO 30/57; Kitchener to White, 5 Jan. 1905, Duff to White, 25 May 1905, White Papers 108/87.
14. Mackay, *Balfour*, p. 124.
15. Balfour to A. Salisbury, 4 Oct. 1904, Salisbury Papers.

16. Brett, *Journals*, Vol. 2, pp. 55–6.
17. C to Ampthill, 4 Aug. 1904, CP 112/413.
18. From the departmental notes quoted in IMO, op.cit., p. 11.
19. Roberts to Kitchener, 18 Aug. 1904, Kitchener Papers PRO 30/57.
20. Ampthill to Brodrick, 9 June 1904, Ampthill Papers 233/37.
21. Ibid., 7 July.
22. Ampthill to C, 3 Aug. 1904, CP 112/413; Ampthill to Brodrick, 21 Sept. 1904, Ampthill Papers 233/37.
23. Ampthill to Brodrick, ibid.
24. Ibid., 28 Sept. 1904.
25. Kitchener to Ampthill, 23 and 24 Sept., Ampthill to Kitchener, 23 and 25 Sept., Ampthill to Brodrick, 27 Sept. 1904, Birdwood Papers 686/14, 16 and 20.
26. Godley to Ampthill, 13 Oct. 1904, Ampthill Papers 233/37; Dilks, *Curzon in India*, Vol. 2, p. 123.
27. Brodrick to C, 1 Nov. 1904, CP 111/413.
28. C note, 2 Nov. 1904, in IMO, op.cit., pp. 69–72, CP 111/412; Dilks, op.cit., p. 124.
29. Balfour to C, 4 Nov. 1904, IMO, ibid., pp. 12–13.
30. Balfour to Brodrick, 10 Nov. 1904, Midleton Papers Add.mss.50072.
31. Brodrick to C, 12 Jan. 1905, CP 111/164; Brodrick to Balfour, 18 and 20 Jan. 1904, Balfour Papers Add.mss.49271; IMO, op.cit., pp. 17–20.
32. C to Brodrick, 9 Feb. 1905, CP 111/164; Kitchener to Marker, 30 Jan., Salisbury Papers, and 15 Feb. 1905, Kitchener-Marker Papers Add.mss.52276a.
33. A. Wilson, *Letters from India*, pp. 305–7.
34. C to Mary, 2 Feb. 1905, AMP.
35. Kitchener to Birdwood, 18 Jan. 1905, Birdwood Papers 686/58. The remark is repeated with slight variations to A. Salisbury, 19 Jan. 1905, Salisbury Papers, and to Marker, 19 Jan. 1905, Kitchener-Marker Papers Add.mss.52276a.
36. Dawkins to C, 1 June 1905, CP 111/183.
37. Repington to Marker, 2 Jan. 1906, Kitchener-Marker Papers Add.mss.52277b.
38. C to Kitchener, 31 Jan. and 1 Feb., Kitchener to C, 1 and 2 Feb. 1905, CP 111/210.
39. Kitchener to A. Salisbury, Feb. 1905, Salisbury Papers.
40. Ibid., 5 Jan. 1905; Kitchener to Marker, 4 Jan. 1905, Kitchener-Marker Papers, Add.mss.52276a.
41. Members' notes in CP 111/400; Kitchener to Birdwood, 3 May 1905, Birdwood Papers 686/58.
42. C to Brodrick, 16 March 1905, CP 111/164.
43. Kitchener to A. Salisbury, 14 March 1905, Salisbury Papers.
44. Kitchener to C, 12 March 1905, CP 111/210.
45. 1 Aug. 1905.
46. Kitchener to Stedman, 8 March 1905, copy in CP 111/400; Dilks, op.cit., p. 193.
47. Esher to Kitchener, 1 April, Clarke to Kitchener, 13 April 1905, Kitchener Papers PRO 30/57; C's annotated copy of IMO, op.cit., p. 28.
48. IMO, ibid., p. 32; Dilks. op.cit., p. 189.
49. Amery, *My Political Life*, Vol. 1, pp. 207–8.
50. Kitchener to Marker, 15 Feb. 1905, Kitchener-Marker Papers Add.mss.52276a; King, *The Viceroy's Fall*, p. 147.
51. Chirol, *Fifty Years*, p. 228.
52. *The Times*, 29 May 1905.
53. C to Kitchener, 31 May and 1 June, Kitchener to C (2 letters), 1 June 1905, CP 111/210.
54. Hamilton, *Parliamentary Reminiscences*, p. 305.

55. Barrow to C, 5 Aug. 1905, CP 111/183.
56. Roberts to C, 2 March 1905, CP 111/183.
57. IMO, op.cit., p. 31.
58. C to Godley, 16 March 1905, CP 111/164.
59. Balfour to A. Salisbury, 4 Oct. 1904, Salisbury Papers; Gopal, *British Policy*, p. 283.
60. Ampthill to Brodrick, 2 and 16 May 1905, Ampthill Papers 233/7.
61. Ibid., 2 and 19 April.
62. Privately printed pamphlet by C in CP 111/416.
63. Kitchener to Marker, 25 May 1905, Kitchener-Marker Papers Add.mss.52276a.
64. Brodrick to C, 18 June 1905, CP 111/164; Brodrick to Cromer, 12 May 1905, Cromer Papers FO 633/7.
65. Ampthill to Brodrick, 23 May 1905, Ampthill Papers 233/7.
66. Godley to C, 26 May 1905, CP 111/164, Godley to A. Salisbury, 24, 25, 26 and 31 May 1905, Salisbury Papers.
67. Lansdowne to C, 26 May 1905, CP 111/164.
68. Dilks, op.cit., p. 210.
69. Brodrick to Cromer, 12 May 1905, Cromer Papers FO 633/7.
70. Midleton, 'Relations of Lord C as Viceroy with the British Government 1902–5', privately printed at the FO in 1926, Midleton Papers PRO 30/67.
71. Cromer memo, 21 May 1905, Cromer Papers FO 633/7.
72. Godley to Minto, 9 March 1906, Minto Papers 12729.
73. Godley to A. Salisbury, 24 May 1905, Salisbury Papers.
74. Hamilton to C, 7 Feb. 1906, CP 111/407.
75. Hamilton, op.cit., p. 303.

CHAPTER 21: THE BREAKING OF THE VICEROY

1. C to Mary, 13 Dec. 1904, AMP.
2. Arthur, *A Septuagenarian's Scrapbook*, p. 107.
3. C to Mary, 18 Jan. and 2 Feb. 1905, AMP.
4. Mary to Mrs Leiter, 21 and 26 Feb. and 15 March 1905, AMP.
5. Note by C, 1909, in AMP.
6. Nathan to Rivaz, 30 March 1905, CP 111/620; C to Mary, 2 April 1905, AMP.
7. C to Mary, 4 April 1905, AMP.
8. Ibid., 29 Dec. 1904 and 3 Jan. 1905.
9. Ibid., 2 and 9 Feb. 1905.
10. Dilks, *Curzon in India*, Vol. 2, p. 173.
11. C to Rodd, 9 April 1905, Rennell Papers; C to Brodrick, 21 Feb. 1905, CP 111/164; Dilks, ibid., pp. 173–6; Fleming, *Bayonets to Lhasa*, pp. 286–7.
12. Das, *India under Morley and Minto*, p. 14.
13. Zaidi, 'The Partition of Bengal', pp. 151–2; C to Ampthill, 8 June 1905, CP 111/210.
14. Zaidi, ibid., pp. 179–83.
15. Das, op.cit., pp. 18–19.
16. Lydgate, 'Curzon, Kitchener . . .', p. 397; Godley to C, 26 May and 7 June 1905, CP 111/164.
17. Lydgate, ibid.
18. Brodrick telegram, 16 Aug. 1905; Zaidi, op.cit., p. 162.
19. Kitchener to Marker. 17 May and 1 June 1905, Kitchener-Marker Papers Add.mss.52276a; Kitchener to Birdwood, 21 May 1905, Birdwood Papers 686/58; Kitchener to A. Salisbury, 25 May and 1 June 1905, Salisbury Papers.
20. C to Scarsdale, 16 March 1905; CP 111/405; C to Elles, 14 June 1905, CP 111/136.
21. Knollys to Brodrick, 31 May 1905, Midleton Papers PRO 30/67.

22. Edward VII to C, 2 June 1905, CP 111/136; Godley to C, 30 May 1905, CP 111/164.
23. 2 June 1905, IMO, p. 38, CP 111/412.
24. C to Dawkins, 21 June 1905, CP 111/183.
25. Roberts to C, 2 June 1905, CP 111/183.
26. Despatch of 31 May, CP 111/400. For C's views on it, see his privately printed pamphlet on military administration, pp. 31–4, CP 111/416.
27. Ibid., pp. 25–6; C's notes, CP 111/400.
28. C to Lyttelton, 13 July 1905, Chandos Papers 2/4.
29. C to Edward VII, 6 July 1905, CP 111/136.
30. Brodrick to C, 1 Aug. 1905, IMO, op.cit., p. 40.
31. 1 Aug. 1905.
32. See, for example, Sandhurst to Elgin, 27 June 1905, Elgin Papers.
33. *The Times*, 29 June 1905; H. Hamilton to A. Salisbury, 5 July 1905, Salisbury Papers; Stedman to Kitchener, 28 July 1905, Kitchener Papers PRO 30/57; Minto to Morley, 10 Jan. 1906, Minto Papers 12735.
34. C to Mary, June 1905, Mary to C, 21 June 1905, AMP.
35. C to Ampthill, 23 July 1905, CP 111/211; IMO, op.cit., p. 44.
36. C to Balfour, 26 June 1905, IMO, ibid., pp. 73–4.
37. IMO, ibid., pp. 45–6.
38. Kitchener to Stedman, undated, Kitchener Papers PRO 30/57; Kitchener to A. Salisbury, 6 July 1905, Salisbury Papers; Kitchener to Marker, 6 July 1905, Kitchener-Marker Papers Add.mss. 52276a; King, *The Viceroy's Fall*, pp. 180–1; C and Kitchener to Balfour, 30 June 1905, IMO, ibid., p. 75.
39. Balfour to Salisbury, 11 July 1905, Salisbury Papers.
40. IMO, op.cit., pp. 75–7; C to Kitchener, 5 July 1905, Kitchener Papers PRO 30/57 .
41. IMO, ibid., pp. 78–9.
42. Ibid., pp. 80, 83.
43. Ibid., pp. 105–8.
44. Dilks, op.cit., p. 222.
45. IMO, op.cit., pp. 85–6.
46. 4 July 1905.
47. C to Ampthill, 23 July 1905, CP 111/211.
48. Ampthill to C, 17 Aug. 1905, CP 111/211.
49. C to Crewe, 2 Nov. 1905, Crewe Papers C/11; C to Ampthill, 23 July 1905, CP 111/211.
50. C to Mary, June 1905, AMP.
51. Brodrick to C, 18 July 1905, IMO, op.cit., pp. 82–3.
52. Mary to C, 5 Feb. and 28 March 1905, AMP; N. Nicolson, *Mary Curzon*, p.169.
53. Kitchener to A. Salisbury, 23 March 1905, Salisbury Papers.
54. King, op.cit., p. 172.
55. Mary to A. Salisbury, 4 and 13 July 1905, Salisbury Papers.
56. Mary to Mrs Leiter, 27 July 1905, AMP.
57. Barrow diary, 8 July 1905, Barrow Papers 420/30; Barrow to Lawrence, 29 Aug. 1905, CP 112/417; Barrow to C, 29 Oct. 1905, CP 111/407; IMO, op.cit., pp. 55–6.
58. Blunt, *My Diaries*, Vol. 2, p. 286.
59. IMO, op.cit., C's annotation, p. 59.
60. IMO, ibid., p. 56; Dilks, op.cit., p. 285, footnote 9; Kitchener to Marker, 3 Aug. 1905, Kitchener-Marker Papers Add.mss.52276a.
61. IMO, ibid., pp. 59–61, 88–90; C to Ampthill, 12 Aug. 1905, CP 111/211; King, op.cit., pp. 200–1; C to Crewe, 2 Nov. 1905, Crewe Papers C/11.

62. C to Dawkins, 3 Aug. 1905, Lawrence Papers 143/36.
63. IMO, op.cit., pp. 62, 90–3; Godley to Brodrick, 7 Aug. 1905, Midleton Papers Add.mss.50072; Young, *Balfour*, p. 242.
64. Benson diary, Vol. 56, p. 67, Benson Papers.
65. House of Lords, 1 Aug. 1905.
66. IMO, op.cit., p. 92.
67. IMO, ibid., pp. 93–7; Mary to P. Craigie, 16 Aug. 1905, AMP; Balfour to Brodrick, 14 Aug. 1905, Midleton Papers Add.mss.50072.
68. C to Ouida, 27 Sept. 1905, CP 111/235; C to Beresford, 24 Oct. 1905, Eton College.
69. C to Ampthill, 12 Aug. 1905, CP 111/235.
70. See, for example, Moon, *The British Conquest*, p. 941, Cassar, *Kitchener*, p. 153, and Lawrence, *The India We Served*, p. 248.
71. Magnus, *Kitchener*, p. 222.
72. Ibbetson to C, 20 Aug. 1905, CP 111/421.
73. Younghusband to Mary, 11 Oct. 1905, AMP.
74. Ampthill to Lamington, 24 Aug. 1905, Lamington Papers.
75. Lamington to C, 22 Aug. 1905, CP 111/421.
76. Quoted in King, op.cit., pp. 209–10.
77. Brodrick to Knollys, 12 Sept. 1905, RA/W4/30.
78. Lawrence to C, 12 Sept. 1905, CP 111/183.
79. Sandars to Balfour, 15 Aug. 1905, Brodrick to Balfour, 16 Aug. 1905, Balfour Papers Add.mss.49763 and 49721; Kaminsky, *India Office*, p. 178.
80. Brodrick to Salisbury, 8 Aug. 1905, Balfour to A. Salisbury, 17 Aug. 1905, Salisbury Papers.
81. Brodrick to Salisbury, ibid.; Brodrick to Scarsdale, 19 Aug. 1905, CP 112/777.
82. Brodrick to Cromer, 10 Nov. and 20 Dec. 1905, Cromer Papers FO 633/7.
83. IMO, op.cit., pp. 64–7, 97–122 *passim*; Kitchener to A. Salisbury, 30 Aug. 1905, Salisbury Papers.
84. *The Times*, 28 Aug. 1905; IMO, ibid., pp. 102–4; Ripon to Sandhurst, 30 Aug. 1905, Ripon Papers Add.mss.43639.
85. Brodrick to Balfour, 22 Sept. 1904, 13 and 16 Aug. 1905, Balfour Papers Add.mss.49721; Balfour to Brodrick, 15 Aug. 1905, Midleton Papers PRO 30/67; Balfour to A. Salisbury, 17 Aug. 1905, Salisbury Papers; Knollys to Sandars, 9 Sept. 1905, Balfour Papers Add.mss.49685; Churchill to C, 22 Aug. 1905, CP 111/183; R. Churchill, *Winston S. Churchill*, Vol. 2, p. 95.
86. Minto, *India, Minto and Morley*, p. 48.
87. C to Minto, 15 Sept. 1898, 5 Dec. 1904 and 23 Aug. 1905, Minto Papers 12379 and 12747; C to Salisbury, 2 June 1898, Salisbury Papers; Minto to C, 21 Aug. 1905, CP 111/183.
88. Brodrick to C, 19 Aug. 1905, IMO, op.cit., p. 101.
89. C to Prince of Wales, 23 Aug. 1905, CP 111/217.
90. Minto to Brodrick, 18 Sept. 1905, Minto Papers 12787; Minto diary, 4 Oct. 1905, Minto Papers 12501.
91. Mary to Mrs Leiter, 18 Oct. 1905, AMP.
92. Fraser to Mary, 7 Nov. 1905, AMP.
93. King, op.cit., p. 217.
94. Chirol, *Fifty Years*, p. 230.
95. *Lord Curzon in India*, pp. 589–90.
96. *The Times* and *Westminster Gazette*, 21 Sept. 1909; Lydgate, op.cit., pp. 464–5.
97. Minto to Edward VII, 26 Nov. 1905, Minto to Brodrick, 21 Nov. 1905, Minto Papers 12735; Gilbert, *Servant of India*, pp. 28–9; Minto, op.cit., pp. 10–11.

98. Minto to Brodrick, ibid.; Minto, ibid.; Bigge to M. Minto, 13 Feb. 1906, Minto Papers 12445.
99. Das, *India from Curzon to Nehru*, pp. 45–9.
100. Ronaldshay, *Curzon*, Vol. 2, p. 390.
101. 23 Feb. 1909.

CHAPTER 22: 'EVERY MAN'S HAND'
1. Younghusband, *The Light of Experience*, p. 166.
2. Godley to Minto, 15 Dec. 1905, Minto Papers 12729.
3. Brodrick to Knollys, 2 Dec. 1905, Midleton Papers PRO 3/67; Brodrick to Balfour, 29 Nov. 1905, Balfour Papers Add.mss.49721.
4. Lady Cowper to Mary, 20 Sept. 1905, AMP.
5. Selborne to A. Salisbury, 21 Aug. 1905, Salisbury Papers.
6. Brodrick to Knollys, 4 Sept. 1905, Midleton Papers Add.mss.50072; Brodrick to Balfour, 4 Sept. 1905, Balfour Papers Add.mss.49721.
7. Sandars to Balfour, 11 Sept. 1905, Balfour Papers Add.mss.49763; Sandars to Brodrick, 10 Sept. 1905, Midleton Papers Add.mss.50072.
8. Knollys to Brodrick, 19 Sept. 1905, Brodrick to Knollys, 22 Sept. 1905, Midleton Papers Add.mss.50072.
9. Balfour to Brodrick, 15 Oct. 1905, Balfour to Knollys, 7 Oct. 1905, Midleton Papers Add.mss.50072.
10. Knollys to Brodrick, 24 Nov. and 3 Dec. 1905, Midleton Papers PRO 30/67.
11. C memo, 1 July 1906, CP 112/526.
12. Mary to Mrs Leiter, 9 Jan. 1906, AMP.
13. C to Vincent, 20 Jan. 1906, D'Abernon Papers Add.mss.48923.
14. C to Macmillan, 27 Feb. 1906 *et seq.*, Macmillan Archive Add.mss.55245; Macmillan to C, 14 May 1906, CP 111/632.
15. Arnold-Forster diary, 14 Oct. 1905, Arnold-Forster Papers Add.mss.50351.
16. C to P. Craigie, 28 Jan. 1906, AMP.
17. Balfour to Selborne, 21 Sept. 1905, Balfour Papers Add.mss.49708.
18. Balfour to A. Salisbury, 17 Jan. 1906, Salisbury Papers.
19. Koss, *John Morley*, pp. 130, 135–6.
20. Ronaldshay, *Curzon*, Vol. 3, p. 36.
21. Chirol to Barrow, 8 Jan. 1906, Barrow Papers 420/20; Brackenbury to C, 31 Jan. 1906, CP 111/407.
22. Morley to Minto, 22 Dec. 1905, Minto Papers 12729; Morley to C, 25 Dec. 1905, CP 111/407.
23. Godley to Minto, 29 Dec. 1905, Minto Papers 12729; C to Barrow, 17 Jan. 1906, Barrow Papers 420/20.
24. Kitchener to Rosebery, 21 Dec. 1905, Rosebery Papers.
25. Brett, *Journals*, Vol. 2, p. 275; Koss, op.cit., p. 117.
26. Esher to Kitchener, 21 Dec. 1905, Kitchener Papers PRO 30/57.
27. Repington to Marker, 2 and 26 Jan. 1906, Kitchener-Marker Papers Add. mss.52277b.
28. Morley to C, 26 Dec. 1905, CP 111/407.
29. Nathan to Dunlop Smith, 22 Dec. 1905, Minto Papers 12774.
30. Minto to Edward VII, 26 Nov. 1905, RA/W4/54; Lawrence to C, 22 Feb. 1906, CP 112/417.
31. Lawrence to C, ibid.
32. Bigge to M. Minto, 13 Feb. 1906, Minto Papers 12445; Prince of Wales to Minto, 6 Feb. and 21 March 1906, Minto Papers 12779; Godley to Minto, 11 and 23 May 1906, Minto Papers 12729.

33. Brodrick to M. Minto, 9 Feb. 1906, Minto Papers 12445; Brodrick to Minto, 19 Dec. 1905, Minto Papers 12729.
34. Minto diary, 8 Dec. 1905, Minto Papers 12502; Minto to Morley, 10 Jan. 1906, Minto Papers 12735.
35. Morley to C, 7 Feb. 1906, CP 111/407; Chirol to Barrow, 31 May 1906, Barrow Papers 420/20; Morley to Minto, despatch of 9 Feb. 1906, Morley Papers 573/39.
36. 1 March 1906.
37. Chirol to Barrow, 2 March 1906, Barrow Papers 420/20.
38. Knollys to C, 21 Sept. 1904, CP 112/526.
39. Ibid., 20 March 1906, CP 112/526.
40. C to Mary, 21 March 1906, AMP.
41. C to Malcolm, undated, quoted in *Quarterly Review*, July 1925; Godley to Minto, 18 May 1906, Minto Papers 12729.
42. C to Edward VII, 2 April 1906, Knollys to C, 18 April and 8 May 1906, Campbell-Bannerman to C, 9 June 1906, Balfour to C, 2 July 1906, CP 112/526; Morley to Minto, 15 June 1906, Minto Papers 12729.
43. P. Craigie to Brown, 7 July 1906, Craigie Papers.
44. Mary to C, 7 July 1906, AMP; N. Nicolson, *Mary Curzon*, pp. 208–9.
45. C to Mrs Leiter, 19 July 1906, AMP.
46. Welldon to Midleton, 14 Jan. 1933, Midleton Papers PRO 30/67.
47. C to S. Grosvenor, 15 March 1908, Grosvenor Papers; Ronaldshay, *Curzon*, Vol. 3, pp. 371–3; C, *Kedleston Church*, pp. 82–7.
48. Chirol to C, 14 Aug. 1906, CP 112/13; Chirol to Barrow, 2 Oct. 1906, Barrow Papers 420/20.
49. Malcolm in the *Quarterly Review*, op.cit.; Dilks, *Curzon in India*, Vol. 2, p. 249.

CHAPTER 23: PICKING UP THE PIECES

1. Balfour to C, 4 March 1907, Cecil to C, 2 Aug. 1907, CP 112/14; Chirol to Barrow, 2 Feb. 1906, Barrow Papers 420/20.
2. Vincent, *The Crawford Papers*, p. 100.
3. Hamilton to C, 6 March 1907, CP 112/14.
4. Morley to Minto, 26 Dec. 1907, Minto Papers 12731; C to Selborne, 9 Aug. 1907, Selborne Papers.
5. From speeches reported in *The Times*, 12 Dec. 1907 and 22 May 1909; others reproduced in C, *Subjects of the Day*, pp. 5, 33–4.
6. Speech at Glasgow, Jan. 1911, CP 112/31.
7. *The Times*, 29 Nov. 1906.
8. Cannadine, *Aspects of Aristocracy*, pp. 97–8.
9. Gwynn, *Letters and Friendships*, Vol. 2, p. 119.
10. C to Warren, 1 March 1913 and 2 July 1911, Bodleian MS DON C150.
11. C, *Principles and Methods of University Reform*.
12. See Warren's chapter in Ronaldshay, *Curzon*, Vol. 3, pp. 104–10.
13. Duke of Portland to Kenneth Rose, Rose Papers.
14. Ronaldshay, op.cit., p. 102; C note in CP 112/26.
15. Hassall, *Edward Marsh*, p. 224.
16. C, *Tales of Travel*, pp. 164–9.
17. Ibid.
18. Magnus Papers.
19. Minto to Morley, 9 April 1906, Minto Papers 12735; C to Lawrence, 2 Feb. 1906, Lawrence Papers 143/33.
20. Minto to Morley, 29 March 1906, Minto Papers 12735.

21. Minto to M. Minto, 5 May 1907, Minto Papers 12416; Chirol to C, 8 June 1915, CP 112/106.

22. E.g. Minto to M. Minto, 5 May 1907, 19 March, 9 and 15 April 1908, Minto Papers 12416–7.

23. Risley to C, 9 May 1906, CP 112/13.

24. Chirol to C, 31 Aug. 1906, CP 112/13.

25. Fraser to C, 9 Feb. 1907, CP 112/14; Risley to C, op.cit.

26. Minto to Godley, 3 April 1906, Minto Papers 12735.

27. Godley to Minto, 23 March 1906 and 22 March 1907, Minto Papers 12729 and 12731.

28. Morley to C, 12 April 1907, CP 111/149.

29. Minto to Morley, 16 May 1907, Minto Papers 12737, Minto to M. Minto, 5 May 1907 and 19 March 1908, Minto Papers 12416–7; Gilbert, *Servant of India*, p. 94.

30. 13 Dec. 1907, CP 112/534.

31. Minto to Morley, 9 and 28 Oct. 1907, CP 112/421; C to Bayly, 5 March 1908, CP 112/421.

32. Minto to M. Minto, 25 March 1908, Minto Papers 12417.

33. Bayly to C, 10 April 1908, C memos, 25 July 1908 and 30 Aug. 1916, Ampthill to C, 12 May 1908, CP 112/421; Dunlop Smith to Hirtzel, 6 May 1908, Morley Papers 573/43; King, *The Viceroy's Fall*, pp. 261–4.

34. Brodrick to Kitchener, 30 Aug. 1906, Kitchener Papers PRO 30/57.

35. Chirol to Barrow, 2 Oct. 1906, Barrow Papers 420/20.

36. Fitzroy, *Memoirs*, Vol. 2, p. 525; House of Lords debate, 15 July 1913.

37. Godley to Minto, 2 Nov. 1906, Minto Papers 12736; Morley to Minto, 23 Aug. 1907, Minto Papers 12731.

38. Morley to Minto, 2 Nov. 1906, Minto Papers 12736.

39. Koss, *John Morley*, p. 81.

40. Morley to Minto, 27 Dec. 1906, Minto Papers 12736.

41. *The Times*, 15 June 1907; C to Ampthill and Ampthill to C, 19 June 1907, CP 112/14.

42. Brodrick to M. Minto, 21 June, Brodrick to Minto, 31 July 1906, Minto Papers 12446 and 12787.

43. Morley to Minto, 3 May 1906, Minto Papers 12729; Morley to Knollys, 10 June 1906, CP 112/526.

44. Morley to C, 30 July 1907, CP 112/526.

45. Morley to Minto, 23 Aug. and 8 Oct. 1907, Minto Papers 12731.

46. Minto to Morley, 12 Sept. and 9 Oct. 1907, Minto Papers 12737.

47. Morley to C, 15 Oct., C to Morley, 18 Oct. 1907, CP 112/526; C memo, 18 Feb. 1909, CP 112/526.

48. Midleton, *Records and Reactions*, p. 210; Midleton to Lansdowne, 27 Nov. and 7 Dec. 1907, Lansdowne Papers.

49. Lansdowne to Londonderry, 23 Nov. 1907, Lansdowne Papers; C to Balfour, 18 Jan. 1908, Balfour Papers Add.mss.49733; *The Times*, 2 and 28 Jan. 1908.

50. Minto to Godley, 23 Jan., Godley to Minto, 3 Jan. 1908, Minto Papers 12738; Morley to Minto, 24 April and 15 May 1908, Minto Papers 12738.

51. Ronaldshay, *Curzon*, Vol. 3, p. 38.

52. Morley to Minto, 6 Feb. 1908, Minto Papers 12738.

53. Morley to C, 10 Sept. 1919, CP 112/313.

54. *Hansard*, 30 June 1908; Morley to Minto, 15 May and 2 July 1908, Minto Papers 12738; C to Lansdowne, 13 May 1909, Lansdowne Papers.

55. Morley to Minto, 25 Feb. 1909, Minto Papers 12739.

56. Morley to Minto, 28 June 1907, Morley Papers 573/39; Lydgate, 'Curzon, Kitchener', p. 446.

57. Roberts to Lansdowne, 18 March, Lansdowne to C, 6 April 1909, CP 111/408.
58. Goold, 'Lord Hardinge', p. 920.
59. Kitchener to Morley, 28 Jan. 1909, Kitchener-Marker Papers 52276b.
60. Barrow to C, 29 Dec. 1908, CP 111/408.
61. Roberts to C, 21 June, C to Roberts, 22 June 1909, CP 111/408.
62. Morley to Minto, 2 July 1909, Minto Papers 12739; Kitchener to Marker, 1 July 1909, Kitchener-Marker Papers 52276b.
63. 29 June 1909.
64. C to Barrow, 2 July 1909, Barrow Papers 420/22.
65. Brodrick to C, 2 July, C to Brodrick, 4 July 1909, CP 111/408.
66. Information sent from address in Forest Hill, 10 June and 14 Aug. 1908 (correspondent's name illegible), Rose Papers.
67. C to Gladstone, 3 July 1909, Viscount Gladstone Papers, Add.mss.46067; C to Barrow, 2 July and 8 Sept. 1909, Barrow Papers 420/22.
68. C to Barrow, ibid.; C to Scarsdale, 4 July 1909, CP 112/775.

CHAPTER 24: THE CONVERSION OF A DIEHARD, 1909–1911
1. Vincent, *Crawford Papers*, p. 469.
2. C to Barrow, 29 Dec. 1910, Barrow Papers 420/20.
3. C to Hardinge, 28 May 1911, Hardinge Papers.
4. H. Nicolson, *Curzon*, p. 235.
5. Ronaldshay, *Curzon*, Vol. 3, p. 24; C to Hamilton, 10 Jan. 1901, CP 111/160.
6. Selborne to C, 21 Oct. 1903, CP 111/229.
7. *Hansard*, 21 May 1908.
8. *The Times*, 16 Oct. 1909.
9. Vincent, op.cit., pp. 492–3.
10. Jenkins, *Mr Balfour's Poodle*, pp. 88–9.
11. Grigg, *The People's Champion*, p. 208.
12. 30 Nov. 1909.
13. Blewett, *The Peers*, pp. 115–22; *The Times*, 15, 16, 17 and 21 Dec. 1909.
14. C to Selborne, 27 Jan. 1910, Selborne Papers; C to Balfour, 1 Feb. 1910, Balfour Papers Add.mss.49733.
15. C to Milner, 27 Jan. 1910, Milner Papers dep. 36; Brett, *Journals*, Vol. 2, p. 329.
16. C to Balfour, 23 Dec. 1910, Sandars Papers, Eng. Hist. c762.
17. C memo, 29 March 1911, Balfour Papers Add.mss.49733.
18. Vincent, op.cit., p. 179.
19. 17 May 1911.
20. Rose, *King George V*, p. 104; C to Hardinge, 26 June 1911, Hardinge Papers.
21. Correspondence between C, Knollys and Asquith, July–Oct. 1911, CP 112/526.
22. Ronaldshay, op.cit., pp. 55–6.
23. Jenkins, *Asquith*, pp. 226–7.
24. C to V. Cecil, 17 July 1911, Violet Milner Papers.
25. C note, CP 112/89.
26. Newton, *Lord Lansdowne*, pp. 421–3.
27. C to Stamfordham, 24 July 1911, RA/GV K1552(2)/3.
28. Newton, op.cit., pp. 425–6; Jenkins, op.cit., pp. 225–8.
29. Vincent, op.cit., p. 201.
30. Chamberlain to Balfour, 26 July 1911, Chamberlain Papers AC 9/2/1.
31. Vincent, op.cit., p. 207.
32. Bonham Carter, *Winston Churchill*, p. 207.
33. Sandars diary, 12 Aug. 1911, Balfour Papers Add. mss.49767.
34. Vincent, op.cit., p. 213.

35. Ibid., p. 206.
36. Egremont, *Balfour*, p. 237.
37. Wyndham to S. Grosvenor, 9 and 10 Aug. 1911, Grosvenor Papers.
38. Midleton, *Records and Reactions*, pp. 274–5; Stamfordham to Minto, 25 July 1911, Minto Papers 12787.
39. Midleton, ibid.
40. Blunt, *Diaries*, Vol. 2, p. 377.
41. Wyndham to S. Grosvenor, 10 and 17 Aug. 1911; Egremont, *The Cousins*, pp. 278–82.
42. See notes 2, 3 and 4 of Preface.
43. Blunt, op.cit., p. 372.
44. Amery, *My Political Life*, Vol. 1, p. 381.
45. Egremont, *Balfour*, p. 212.
46. Mackay, *Balfour*, p. 238.
47. *Daily Mail*, 11 Feb. 1911.
48. C to Balfour, 4 Nov. 1911, Balfour Papers Add.mss.49733.

CHAPTER 25: SUFFRAGISTS AND OTHER TARGETS, 1911–1914
 1. Letter to *Country Life*, 18 Oct. 1913; Ronaldshay, *Curzon*, Vol. 3, p. 79.
 2. Speech of 6 March 1913, CP 112/534.
 3. *The Times*, 1 Aug. 1912.
 4. 30 April 1912.
 5. C, *Subjects of the Day*, p. 99.
 6. *The Times*, 6 Feb. 1913.
 7. *Everyman*, 30 June 1918.
 8. See CP 112/56 and 63.
 9. C to N. Astor, 27 July 1909, Astor Papers.
10. C to Freshfield, 24 Feb. 1905, Minto Papers 12774.
11. Ronaldshay, op.cit., p. 65.
12. Cromer to C, 15 Dec. 1911, CP 112/32–3.
13. Speech of 1 Nov. 1912, CP 112/38.
14. C to Bonar Law, 3 March 1911, Bonar Law Papers 18/7.
15. E. Glyn memoir, AMP.
16. C, *Subjects of the Day*, p. 151.
17. Quoted in Grigg, *The People's Champion*, p. 165.
18. C to Barrow, 29 Dec. 1910, Barrow Papers 420/20.
19. Lees-Milne, *The Enigmatic Edwardian*, pp. 214–15.
20. Lydgate, 'Curzon, Kitchener', pp. 466–7; Jenkins, *Asquith*, p. 343.
21. C to Crewe, 6 Nov. 1910, Crewe Papers C/11.
22. C to Hardinge, 28 Dec. 1910, Hardinge Papers.
23. Minto to M. Minto, 5 May 1907, Minto Papers 12416.
24. Pope–Hennessy, *Lord Crewe*, pp. 101–2.
25. *The Times*, 7 Oct. 1911.
26. 10 Oct. 1911.
27. 2 Nov. 1911.
28. *The Times*, 3 Oct. 1911; C to Milner, 5 Oct. 1911, Milner Papers dep. 38.
29. Fraser, *India Under Curzon*, pp. 18–19, 392–3: C to Hardinge, 21 April 1911, Hardinge Papers Vol. 69.
30. Fitzroy, *Memoirs*, Vol. 2, p. 473.
31. C to Scarsdale, 15 Dec. 1911, CP 112/775; C to Balfour, 4 Nov. 1914, Balfour Papers Add.mss.49733.
32. Hardinge to C, 21 April 1912, CP 112/19.

33. C to Hardinge, 24 July 1912, Hardinge Papers Vol. 70.
34. Speech in the House of Lords, 21 Feb. 1912.
35. C to Crewe, 11 Oct. 1911, Crewe Papers C/11; ibid.
36. House of Lords, 21–22 Feb. 1912; Pope-Hennessy, op.cit., p. 101; Fitzroy, op.cit., p. 488.
37. *The Times*, 7 Sept. 1912; Hardinge to C, 30 Oct., C to Hardinge, 24 Nov. 1912, Hardinge Papers Vols. 70 and 93.
38. Hardinge to Chirol, 9 April, Chirol to Hardinge, 1 May 1913, Hardinge Papers Vol. 93.
39. C, *Subjects of the Day*, p. 71.
40. Chirol to Hardinge, 12 June and 11 Sept. 1913, Hardinge Papers Vol. 93.
41. Hardinge to Chirol, 29 April 1914 and 14 April 1915, Hardinge Papers Vol. 93; Chirol to Hardinge, 12 May 1915, Hardinge Papers Vol. 94.
42. Hardinge, *Old Diplomacy*.
43. Chirol to Hardinge, 15 May 1914, Hardinge Papers Vol. 93.
44. C, *British Government in India*, Vol. 1, p. 181.
45. Vincent, *Crawford Papers*, p. 320.
46. Ibid., p. 290.
47. Blake, *The Unknown Prime Minister*, p. 61.
48. N. Waterhouse, *Private and Official*, p. 199.
49. Grace Curzon, *Reminiscences*, p. 180.
50. Blake, op.cit., p. 37.
51. C to Hardinge, 14 Nov. 1912, Hardinge Papers Vol. 70.
52. C to Lansdowne, 10 Sept. 1912, Lansdowne Papers.
53. Midleton, *Records and Reactions*, p. 243.
54. 30 Jan. 1913 and 15 July 1913.
55. Memo of conversation with George V, 16 Sept. 1913, CP 112/95; Robinson note on conversation with C, 3 Oct. 1913, Dawson Papers; *The Times*, 31 Dec. 1913.
56. Gollin, *Proconsul in Politics*, p. 205.

CHAPTER 26: LORD CURZON AT HOME

1. Lockhart, *Cosmo Gordon Lang*, p. 218.
2. Leiter to Mary, 2 Feb. and 8 April 1905, Ravensdale Papers; Mary to Mrs Leiter, 5 July, C to Mrs Leiter, 28 July 1905, AMP.
3. C to Barrow, 30 Nov. 1906, Barrow Papers 420/20.
4. C to Mrs Leiter, 31 Aug. 1908, AMP.
5. *Washington Post*, 19 March 1913; C to D. Suffolk, 20 April, D. Suffolk to C, 22 April 1913, Ravensdale Papers.
6. Letters between C and Humbert, 1906–8, Ravensdale Papers.
7. Gore, *Creevy*, p. 219.
8. Vincent, *Crawford Papers*, p. 400.
9. H. Nicolson, *Some People*, p. 189.
10. Mrs Marcella Rice to the author.
11. Pryce–Jones, *Little Innocents*, p. 29; E. Glyn memoir, AMP; Lady D'Abernon to K. Rose, Rose Papers.
12. Ronaldshay, *Curzon*, Vol. 3, p. 73.
13. Benson diary Vol. 141, Oct. 1913, Benson Papers.
14. CP 112/76; Holmes, *Self and Partners*, p. 296.
15. C to V. Cecil, 22 Aug. 1912, Violet Milner Papers; C to N. Astor, 31 Aug. 1912, Astor Papers.
16. C to N. Astor, 23 Dec. 1913, Astor Papers.
17. Rose, *King George V*, p. 151.

18. C to N. Astor, 28 March 1913, Astor Papers.
19. Lady Alexandra Metcalfe to the author; O'Donnell to K. Rose, Rose Papers.
20. Lawrence, *The India We Served*, p. 252.
21. C to N. Astor, 2 Nov. 1909 and 18 Jan. 1912, Astor Papers.
22. Lady Alexandra Metcalfe to the author.
23. Ibid.
24. Pryce–Jones, op.cit., p. 29; I. Ravensdale, *In Many Rhythms*, pp. 27, 30.
25. Asquith, *Letters to Venetia Stanley*, p. 221.
26. Lady Alexandra Metcalfe and Sir Roger Cary to the author.
27. C, *Kedleston Church*, pp. 25–8; C to Scarsdale, 3 Aug. 1913 and 2 Dec. 1914, CP 112/775.
28. Sir Roger Cary to the author.
29. Notes and correspondence in CP 112/680; F. Curzon to Scarsdale, 30 July, C to Scarsdale, 24 Aug. 1914, CP 112/775.
30. N. Waterhouse, *Private and Official*, p. 199.
31. H. Nicolson, *Curzon*, p. 2.
32. Benson diary Vol. 160, June 1916, Benson Papers.
33. Clark, '*A Good Innings*', p. 111.
34. E. Glyn memoir, AMP.
35. C to Browning, 23 Sept. 1907, Browning Papers; C to N. Astor, 7 Oct. 1912, Astor Papers.
36. E. Glyn memoir, AMP.
37. Egremont, *Balfour*, p. 327.
38. C note, CP 112/531.
39. *Daily Telegraph*, 21 March 1925.
40. Inge, *Diary of a Dean*, p. 59.
41. C to Browning, 19 July 1910 and 3 July 1911, Browning Papers.
42. Grey to C, 9 July 1913, CP 112/19.
43. C. Asquith, *Remember and Be Glad*, p. 183.
44. C to Rosebery, 9 May 1909, Rosebery Papers 10121; D. Cooper, *The Rainbow Comes and Goes*, p. 81; N. Mosley, *Julian Grenfell*, p. 38.
45. C. Balsan, *The Glitter and the Gold*, p. 160; interview with Spencer in Magnus Papers; E. Glyn memoir, AMP.
46. Glyn, ibid.,
47. James, *Chips*, pp. 234–5.
48. Letters from C to N. Astor, 1909–14, Astor Papers.
49. Glyn, *Elinor Glyn*, pp. 127, 168–71; Etherington–Smith and Pilcher, *The 'It' Girls*, pp. 119–22.
50. Glyn, ibid., pp. 171, 193, 228.
51. Marlowe, *Milner*, p. 149.
52. Etherington-Smith and Pilcher, op.cit., p. 143.
53. Ibid., p. 140.

CHAPTER 27: IN SEARCH OF A ROLE, 1914–1915

1. C to V. Cecil, 22 Aug. 1914, Violet Milner Papers.
2. *The Times*, 28 Aug. 1914.
3. Ibid.
4. Chirol to C, 19 Sept. 1914, and article by Hauptmann in the *Neue Freie Presse*, CP 111/472.
5. C to Lansdowne, 20 Nov. 1914, Lansdowne Papers.
6. See C's correspondence with Belgian royal family in CP 112/580–2.
7. Kipling to C, 24 Aug. 1914, CP 112/105.

8. Ronaldshay, *Curzon*, Vol. 3, p. 122.
9. Robinson to C, 9 and 12 March 1915, CP 112/97; *The Times*, 13 March 1915.
10. C to Lloyd George, 1 June 1917, Lloyd George Papers F/11/8.
11. *Subjects of the Day*, p. xv; C to Cromer, May 1915, Cromer Papers FO 633/24; Unwin, *The Truth*, pp. 144–5.
12. C to V. Cecil, 13 Nov. 1914, Violet Milner Papers.
13. C to N. Astor, 20 Sept. n.d., Astor Papers.
14. Redesdale to C, 25 May 1915, CP 112/108.
15. *Daily Mirror*, 12 Nov. 1914, and *Daily Sketch*, 8 Jan. 1915.
16. Notes by Robinson, 6 Jan. 1915, Dawson Papers.
17. 6 Jan. 1915.
18. C to Selborne, Jan. 1915, Selborne Papers: also distributed to other colleagues.
19. Ibid.
20. Long to Bonar Law, 4 Jan. 1915, Bonar Law Papers 36/1; Balfour to Bonar Law, 30 Jan. 1915, Bonar Law Papers 117/1; Bonar Law to C (copy), 29 Jan. 1915, Balfour Papers Add.mss.49693.
21. C to Cromer, 9 May 1915, Cromer Papers FO 633/24; Vincent, *Crawford Papers*, p. 347.
22. CP 112/179.
23. C diary, April 1915, AMP.
24. H. Nicolson, *Curzon*, p. 48; Repington, *First World War*, Vol. 2, p. 252.
25. C diary, op.cit.
26. Jenkins, *Asquith*, p. 360.
27. C to Selborne etc., Jan. 1915, Selborne Papers.
28. Chamberlain to Bonar Law, 17 May 1915, Bonar Law Papers 37/2.
29. Lansdowne to Bonar Law, 21 May 1915, Bonar Law Papers 117/1.
30. Cromer to C, 24 June 1915, CP 112/114.
31. C to Lloyd George, 26 May 1915, Lloyd George Papers D/16/10.
32. C to Asquith, 5 Aug. 1915, Asquith Papers.
33. Asquith to C, 5 Aug. 1915, CP 112/114; C to Asquith, 10 Aug. 1915, Asquith Papers.
34. Addison, *Four and a Half Years*, Vol. 1, p. 85; Chirol to Hardinge, 1 June 1915, Hardinge Papers Vol. 94.
35. Selborne notes 1916, Selborne Papers ms. 80.
36. Crawford diary, 14 Aug. 1916, Balcarres Papers.
37. Meeting on 11 Oct. 1915, Minutes of Dardanelles Committee, CP 112/161.
38. Cabinet Paper of 25 Nov. 1915, CP 112/125.
39. Hankey, *Supreme Command*, pp. 460–1.
40. See C's paper for the Dardanelles Commission, 10 March 1917, CP 112/619.
41. Gilbert, *Churchill*, Vol. 3, pp. 601–4; M. Soames, *Clementine Churchill*, pp. 143, 166–7.
42. Roskill, *Hankey*, p. 228.
43. Chirol to Hardinge, 16 Sept. 1915, Hardinge Papers Vol. 94; Wilson, *C.P. Scott*, pp. 133–4.
44. Taylor, *Lloyd George*, p. 59.
45. Gilbert, op.cit., pp. 688, 697.
46. C to Lansdowne, 7 June 1916, Lansdowne Papers.
47. *The Times*, 1 May 1915.
48. Ronaldshay, op.cit., p. 137.
49. Cabinet Paper of 21 June 1915, CP 112/167.
50. Blake, *The Unknown Prime Minister*, pp. 262–3.
51. C, Selborne and Chamberlain to Asquith, 3 Nov. 1915, Asquith Papers; Asquith's reply to Chamberlain, 7 Nov. 1915, CP 112/165.

52. See papers in CP 112/537.
53. Selborne notes 1916, Selborne Papers ms.80.
54. C to Lansdowne, 6 Jan. 1915, Lansdowne Papers.
55. Asquith to C, 8 Dec. 1915, CP 112/114.
56. C to Asquith, 8 Dec. 1915, Asquith Papers.
57. Hamilton, *Listening to the Drums*, p. 254
58. Lansdowne to C, 11 June 1916, CP 112/117; C to Lansdowne, 7 June 1916, Lansdowne Papers.

CHAPTER 28: AIR BOARD AND WAR CABINET

1. Lawrence to C, 24 Dec. 1915, CP 112/110.
2. C to Crewe, 6 Jan. 1916, Crewe Papers 6/12.
3. Ibid.
4. Ibid; Crewe to C, 7 Jan. 1916, CP 112/116.
5. Jones, 'Lord Curzon', *International Affairs*, July 1961.
6. C to Asquith, 23 March 1916, Asquith Papers.
7. Asquith to C, 25 March 1916, CP 112/116.
8. C diary, CP 112/541.
9. C to Asquith, 23 March 1916, Asquith Papers.
10. Ibid.
11. 6 May 1916, CP 112/171.
12. Roskill, *Hankey*, p. 271.
13. Churchill in House of Commons, 17 May 1916; C in House of Lords, 24 May 1916.
14. Churchill to C, 26 May 1916, CP 111/170.
15. Roskill, op.cit., pp. 271–2.
16. Notes between C and Balfour, 16 June 1916, CP 112/116.
17. Balfour to C, 12 Dec. 1916, CP 112/538.
18. Cabinet Paper of 23 Oct. 1916, CP 112/224.
19. C to Bonar Law, 22 Oct. 1916, Bonar Law Papers 53/4.
20. Ibid.; Bonar Law to C, 23 and 24 Oct. 1916, CP 112/170.
21. Balfour to C, 26 Oct. 1918, CP 112/170; Balfour's Cabinet Paper of 6 Nov. 1916, CP 112/125.
22. Derby to C, 1 Nov. 1916, CP 112/170; Derby to Lloyd George, 12 Nov. 1916, Lloyd George Papers E/1/1.
23. Crawford notes, 19 Nov. 1916, Crawford Papers 97/4.
24. Churchill to C, 22 Nov. 1916, CP 112/170.
25. C to Bonar Law, 14 Nov. 1916, Bonar Law Papers 53/4.
26. Crawford notes, op.cit.
27. Beaverbrook, *Politicians and the War*, p. 482.
28. CP 112/114.
29. Notes of 22 Oct. 1915, CP 112/115.
30. Hankey, *Supreme Command*, pp. 176–7.
31. Selborne notes of 1916, Selborne Papers ms. 80; Crawford diary, Nov. 1916, Balcarres Papers.
32. Beaverbrook, *Politicians and the War*, Vol. 2, p. 211; Crawford notes, op. cit., 3 Dec. 1916.
33. Chamberlain to Spender, 23 June 1931, Chamberlain Papers AC 15/3.
34. Curzon to Lansdowne, 3 Dec. 1916, Lansdowne Papers.
35. C to Asquith, 4 Dec. 1916, Asquith Papers.
36. Spender and Asquith, *Asquith*, p. 260.
37. Beaverbrook, *Men and Power*, p. 312, and *Politicians and the War*, Vol. 2, p. 256.

38. Crawford notes, op. cit., 4 Dec. 1916.
39. Chamberlain, *Down the Years*, p. 124.
40. Crawford notes, op. cit., 5 Dec. 1916.
41. Wilson, *C.P. Scott*, p. 306.
42. Beaverbrook, *Politicians and the War*, p. 516; Crawford notes, op cit, 4 Dec. 1916; Chamberlain. op.cit., p. 129.
43. Chamberlain, ibid.; C to Lloyd George, 9 Dec. 1916, Lloyd George Papers F/11/8.
44. Chamberlain, ibid., pp. 128–9; C to Chamberlain, 8 Dec. 1916, Chamberlain Papers AC/15/3; Chamberlain to C, 8 Dec. 1916, CP 112/116.
45. Riddell, *War Diary*, pp. 213, 229–30.
46. Beaverbrook, *Politicians and the War*, Vol. 2, p. 256.
47. Chamberlain to Beaverbrook, 29 June 1931 and 17 June 1932, Chamberlain to Cecil, 10 July 1931, Beaverbrook to Chamberlain, 16 June 1932, Chamberlain Papers AC 15/3.
48. Mosley, *Curzon*, pp. 158–61.
49. Taylor, *Beaverbrook*, pp. 118, 141–2; Taylor, *English History*, p. 204.
50. Young, *Balfour*, p. 371.
51. Fraser, 'Lord Beaverbrook', p. 166.

CHAPTER 29: THE SECOND LADY CURZON
1. Riddell, *Intimate Diary*, p. 185.
2. C to Grace, 23 Sept. 1916 and Whitsunday 1918, CP 112/790 and 792.
3. C note, 26 June 1922, Ravensdale Papers.
4. C to Browning, 17 Dec. 1912, Browning Papers.
5. Notes in CP 112/730.
6. C, *Bodiam Castle*, p. xii.
7. C to V. Cecil, 13 May 1917, Violet Milner Papers.
8. Etherington-Smith and Pilcher, *The 'It' Girls*, p. 187.
9. P. Craigie to Brown, undated 1903, Craigie Papers; E. Glyn memoir, AMP.
10. R. Churchill, *Derby*, p. 373.
11. Grace to C, 4 and 30 Sept. 1915, CP 112/689.
12. Grace Curzon, *Reminiscences*, p. 52.
13. Hassall, *Edward Marsh*, p. 396.
14. Grace to C, 25 Aug. and 30 Sept. 1915 and 20 April 1916, CP 112/689–90.
15. Ibid., 30 July 1916, CP 112/690.
16. C to Grace, 22 and 27 Sept. and 25 Oct. 1916, CP 112/790.
17. C to Grace, 11 Oct. 1916, CP 112/790.
18. C. Asquith, *Diaries*, p. 176.
19. C to Mrs Hinds, 25 Sept. 1916, CP 112/790; C to N. Astor, 9 Dec. 1916, Astor Papers.
20. Crawford diaries, 5 Dec. 1916 and 22 March 1917, Balcarres Papers.
21. C to Grace, 22 Oct. 1916, CP 112/790.
22. Crawford diaries, 22 April 1917 and 17 Feb. 1919, Balcarres Papers.
23. C. Asquith, op.cit., p. 412.
24. Grace Curzon, op.cit., p. 88; Barnes and Nicolson, *Leo Amery Diaries*, p. 422.
25. C to Grace, 25 June 1917, CP 112/791; Grace to C, 10 July 1917, CP 112/691.
26. C to Grace, 7 Aug. 1917, CP 112/791.
27. C to Grace, 16 May and 3 Jan. 1919, CP 112/799 and 793, and 31 Dec. 1917, CP 112/791.
28. See press cuttings for March 1917 in CP 111/473.
29. Crawford diaries, 12 July 1919, Balcarres Papers.
30. Ibid., 22 Nov. 1917 and 26 June 1918; R. Churchill, op.cit., pp. 372–3.

CHAPTER 30: EASTERN QUESTIONS, 1917

1. Amery, *My Political Life*, Vol. 2, p. 98; Hankey, *Supreme Command*, p. 578.
2. Cabinet memo, 30 April 1917, CP 112/125.
3. Barnes and Nicholson, *Leo Amery Diaries*, p. 150.
4. Hankey to C (copy), 4 Sept. 1917, Magnus Papers; Hankey, op.cit., pp. 587–8.
5. Minutes of Imperial War Cabinet, CP 112/137.
6. C memo, 21 Sept. 1917, CP 112/125.
7. C memo, Dec. 1917, CP 112/124.
8. C memo, Oct. 1918, CP 112/183.
9. C memo, 25 July 1918, CP 112/183.
10. Roskill, *Hankey*, p. 393.
11. C to Cromer, 22 April 1915, Cromer Papers FO 633/24.
12. Minutes of War Policy Com., 3 Oct. 1917, CP 112/136.
13. C to Cromer, 19 March 1915, Cromer Papers FO 633/24.
14. Minutes of Dardanelles Com., 14 and 21 Oct. 1915, CP 112/161.
15. C to Townshend (copy), 8 Jan. 1916, Magnus Papers.
16. Repington, *First World War*, p. 90.
17. Chirol to C, 10 March 1916, CP 112/163.
18. Ibid., 15 April 1916.
19. Midleton to C, 19 July 1916, CP 112/117.
20. Barrow to C, 11 July 1915, CP 112/114.
21. Copy of the report in CP 112/164.
22. C memo, 4 June 1917, CP 112/164.
23. Chelmsford to C, 17 Nov. 1917, CP 111/438; King, *The Viceroy's Fall*, p. 250.
24. C to Grace, 27 June 1917, CP 112/791.
25. Debate on 12–13 July 1917; Midleton to C, 13 July 1917, CP 111/408.
26. Chamberlain to C, 15 July 1917, CP 112/112; C to Chamberlain, 12 July 1917, Chamberlain Papers AC 13/3.
27. Crawford diaries, 4–9 April 1919, Balcarres Papers; Hardinge, *Old Diplomacy*, p. 216.
28. Crawford, ibid., 18 July 1917.
29. Egremont, *Balfour*, p. 263.
30. Montagu memo, 23 Aug. 1917, CP 112/267.
31. C to Montagu, 8 Sept. 1917, Montagu Papers AS 3/2/9.
32. PRO CAB 23/4; C memo, 26 Oct. 1917, CP 112/266.
33. PRO CAB 23/4.
34. Drafts in CP 112/266.
35. Churchill, *Great Contemporaries*, p. 281.
36. Vansittart, *The Mist Procession*, p. 232.
37. Balfour memo to C, 11 Aug. 1919, PRO FO 371/4183.
38. Crawford diaries, 6 Aug. 1918, Balcarres Papers.
39. C to Lloyd George, undated, Lloyd George Papers F/11/8.
40. C memos to Imperial War Cabinet, 17 June 1917, and War Cabinet, 2 July 1917, CP 112/164.
41. PRO CAB 23/3
42. Ibid.; C to Montagu, 13 Aug. 1917, Montagu Papers AS 3/2/15; C to Chamberlain, 25 Aug. 1917, Chamberlain Papers AC 14/1.
43. C note for Cabinet, 3 June 1918, CP 111/124.
44. Chamberlain to Montagu, 12 July 1918, Chamberlain Papers AC 8/6/2.
45. C to Montagu, 25 July 1918, Montagu Papers AS 3/2/15.
46. Montagu to Chamberlain, 27 July 1918, Chamberlain to Montagu, 29 July 1918, Chamberlain Papers AC 8/6/2 and 21/5/57.
47. *Hansard*, 12 Dec. 1919.

CHAPTER 31: LORD PRESIDENT

1. Crawford diaries, 15 Dec. 1916, Balcarres Papers.
2. Ibid., 19 June 1918.
3. C to Law, 8 Dec. 1916, Bonar Law Papers 81/1.
4. Crawford diaries, op.cit., 12 Dec. 1916.
5. C to Lloyd George, 1 Aug. 1918, Lloyd George Papers F/11/9.
6. Crawford diaries, op.cit., 17 April 1917.
7. Sandhurst to C, 28 Aug. 1917, CP 112/120; Crawford to C, 8 Aug. 1918, CP 112/121.
8. Milner to C, 7 June 1917, CP 112/113.
9. R. Churchill, *Lord Derby*, pp. 260–4.
10. Ibid., p. 336
11. Crawford diaries, op.cit., 23 May 1918.
12. C memo, Nov. 1924, CP 112/319.
13. Wilson, *C.P. Scott*, p. 325.
14. C to Balfour, 10 Feb. 1918, Balfour Papers Add.mss.49733.
15. Hankey, *Supreme Command*, p. 578.
16. C to Lloyd George, Jan. 1918, Lloyd George Papers F/11/9.
17. Barnes and Nicholson, *Leo Amery Diaries*, p. 161.
18. Minutes of War Policy Com., 20 June 1917, CP 112/136.
19. C to Grace, 21 June 1917, CP 112/791.
20. Robertson to C, 6 and 4 July 1917, CP 112/119; minutes of War Policy Com., 6 July 1917, CP 112/136.
21. Woodward, *Lloyd George and the Generals*, p. 167; Crawford diaries, op.cit., 18 June 1918.
22. Milner to C at Cabinet, June 1918, CP 112/122; Milner to C, 17 Oct. 1917, CP 112/113.
23. Fraser to C, 25 Oct., 18 and 23 Nov. and 10 Dec. 1917, CP 112/536.
24. Winter, *Haig's Command*, p. 158.
25. Unpublished minutes of War Cabinet, 7 Jan. 1918, CP 112/137.
26. Minutes of Imperial War Cabinet, 15 Aug. 1918, CP 112/137.
27. Minutes of Cabinet Com., 5 July 1923, CP 112/266.
28. Minutes of Imperial War Cabinet, 25 June and 15 Aug. 1918, CP 112/124; Busch, *Britain, India and the Arabs*, p. 277.
29. Cabinet note, 15 Oct. 1918, CP 112/124.
30. C to Lloyd George, 13 Nov. 1918, Lloyd George Papers F/11/9.
31. Cabinet minutes, 20 Nov. 1918, CP 112/137.
32. Ronaldshay, *Curzon*, Vol. 3, p. 200.
33. C to Law, 25 Feb. 1918, Bonar Law Papers 82/9; ibid., p. 196.
34. Lansdowne to C, 15 Jan. 1918, CP 112/122.
35. C's papers on women's suffrage are in CP 112/37.
36. CP 112/192; C to Lansdowne, 22 Feb. 1925, Lansdowne Papers.
37. Cannadine, *Aspects of Aristocracy*, pp. 102–7.

CHAPTER 32: THE FOREIGN OFFICE AT LAST

1. Roskill, *Hankey*, p. 506.
2. Nicolson, *Curzon*, p. 45.
3. Gregory, *On the Edge*, pp. 245–9.
4. Balfour to C, 1 July 1919, Balfour Papers Add.mss.49733; C to Law, 10 July 1919, Bonar Law Papers.
5. C note, Nov. 1922, CP 112/319.
6. Ibid.

7. Crawford diary, 3 Aug. 1918, Balcarres Papers.
8. Letters from C to Grace, Aug.–Sept. 1919, CP 112/793.
9. Ibid.; Marcella Rice to the author.
10. C to Grace, 9 Sept. 1919, CP 112/793.
11. Kerr to Lloyd George, 18 July 1919, Lloyd George Papers F/89/3/6.
12. C to Grace, 11 Sept. 1919, CP 112/793.
13. C to Balfour, 13 Oct. 1919, Balfour Papers Add.mss.49733; Balfour to C, 16 Oct. 1919, CP 112/208.
14. Wilson to C, 24 Oct. 1919, CP 112/214.
15. Crawford diary, 24 Oct. 1919, Balcarres Papers.
16. Vansittart, *Mist Procession*, p. 232.
17. Gregory, op.cit., pp. 251, 254.
18. Vansittart, op.cit., p. 244.
19. C note, op.cit.
20. C to Hardinge, 27 May and 5 June 1921, Hardinge Papers 44.
21. Cooper, *Old Men Forget*, p. 115.
22. C to Grace, 26 Sept. 1921, CP 112/795.
23. C minute, 6 Oct. 1919, PRO FO 371/3864.
24. Gregory, op.cit., p. 254.
25. Jones, 'Lord C', *International Affairs*, July 1961.
26. Information from Nicolson to K. Rose, Rose Papers.
27. Holmes, *Self and Partners*, p. 324.
28. Lees-Milne, *Prophesying Peace*, p. 33.
29. See, for example, Gregory, op.cit., p. 251, and Young, *The Independent Arab*, p. 284.
30. Nicolson, *Vita and Harold*, p. 123.
31. Rose, *Vansittart*, p. 55; Vansittart, op.cit., p. 254.
32. C to Lloyd George, 9 Dec. 1919, Lloyd George Papers F/12/2/10.
33. Hardinge, *Old Diplomacy*, pp. 262, 269; Medlicott and Dakin, *Documents*, p. 980.
34. C to Wigram, 12 March 1922, RA/GV/01390/26.
35. Howard to C, 26 Feb. 1921, CP 112/220.
36. C to Stamfordham, 10 July 1921, with minute by George V, CP 112/221.
37. Birkenhead, *F.E.*, p. 388.
38. Vincent, *Crawford Papers*, p. 414.
39. Clark, *A Good Innings*, p. 151.
40. Gorell, *One Man*, p. 221.
41. Nicolson, *Curzon*, p. 193.
42. Information from Amery to K. Rose, Rose Papers.
43. Information from Samuel to K. Rose, Rose Papers.
44. Vincent, op.cit., p. 400.

CHAPTER 33: MIDDLE EASTERN SCRAMBLES, 1919–1922
1. C to de Robeck, 19 Sept. 1920, FO 800/157.
2. Information from Swinton to K. Rose, Rose Papers.
3. C to Montagu, 25 and 28 Oct. 1918, Montagu Papers AS 3/2/100–1; C to Hardinge, 26 Feb. 1919, FO 800/153.
4. Beaverbrook, *Politicians and the War*, p. 167; Mackay, *Balfour*, pp. 321–2.
5. Gilbert, *World in Torment*, p. 318.
6. Cox to C, 11 April 1919, PRO FO 371/3860.
7. Ibid.; C minute, 27 July 1919, PRO FO 371/3862; see also Wright, 'Curzon', *Encyclopaedia Iranica*, p. 468, and *The Persians*, pp. 193–4.
8. C memo, Aug. 1919, CP 112/253.
9. 16 Aug. 1919.

10. C to Grey, 18 Nov. 1919, CP 112/211.
11. C to Grace, 17 Aug. 1919, CP 112/793.
12. Jones, *Banking and Empire*, p. 191.
13. Loraine quoted in Waterfield, *Professional Diplomat*, p. 64.
14. Ibid.
15. C to Hardinge, 17 Jan. 1921, Hardinge Papers 44; Waterfield, op.cit., p. 62.
16. Norman to C, 11 Feb. 1921, C to Norman, 16 Feb. 1921, and C minutes, 15 and 17 Feb. 1921, PRO FO 371/6401.
17. C minute, 1 March 1921, PRO FO 371/6401.
18. C minute, 26 Oct. 1922, PRO FO 371/7810; Waterfield, op.cit., p. 62.
19. Ibid., pp. 62–3.
20. Wilson, *Lawrence of Arabia*, pp. 589–91.
21. C to Balfour, 25 March 1919, CP 112/208.
22. The report is reproduced in Antonius, *The Arab Awakening*, pp. 443–58.
23. Meinertzhagen, *Middle East Diary*, p. 26.
24. Balfour to C, 20 Jan. 1919, C to Balfour, 26 Jan. 1919, PRO FO 800/215.
25. Meinertzhagen, op.cit., p. 9; Gilbert, op.cit., p. 621.
26. C to Balfour, 20 Aug. 1919, CP 112/208.
27. Varè, *Laughing Diplomat*, pp. 163–4.
28. C to Grace, 25 April 1920, CP 112/799.
29. Riddell, *Intimate Diary*, p. 183.
30. C to Grace, 20, 24 and 25 April 1920, CP 112/794; Varè, op. cit., pp. 163–4.
31. Monroe, *Britain's Moment*, p. 66.
32. C to Allenby, 16 July 1920, CP 112/215.
33. Ingrams, *Palestine Papers*, pp. 94–104; Wilson, *C.P. Scott*, p. 376; C to Law, 14 Dec. 1922, Bonar Law Papers 111/12/46.
34. Wingate to C, 25 March 1919, CP 112/259.
35. C statement to Imperial Conference, 6 July 1921, CP 112/307.
36. C memo to Cabinet, June 1920, CP 112/281.
37. C to Hardinge, 24 April 1921, Hardinge Papers 44; C to Grace, 14 Feb. 1921, CP 112/795.
38. Churchill to C, 20 May 1921, CP 112/219.
39. C to Grace, 24 Oct. 1921, CP 112/795.
40. C to Churchill, 13 June 1921, CP 112/232; Churchill to C, 13 June 1921, CP 112/219; Lloyd George to C, 14 June 1921, CP 112/220; Churchill to C, 16 June 1921, CP 112/219.
41. These notes are in CP 112/317.
42. C to Hardinge, 21 Oct. 1921, Hardinge Papers 44.
43. C to Grace, 21 Oct. 1921, CP 112/795.
44. Churchill to C at Cabinet, 26 Jan. 1922, CP 112/317.

CHAPTER 34: LLOYD GEORGE AND THE TURKS, 1919–1922
1. D'Abernon, *An Ambassador*, Vol. 1, p. 50.
2. C to Grace, 16 May 1922, CP 112/796.
3. Nicolson, *Curzon*, p. 58.
4. C speech at Imperial Conference, 5 Oct. 1923, CP 112/307; C to D'Abernon, 29 Oct. 1921, D'Abernon Papers Add.mss.48924a.
5. C to Grace, 3 Sept. 1921, CP 112/795.
6. C to Hardinge, 30 Dec. 1920, Hardinge Papers 44.
7. Ibid., 19 Dec. 1920.
8. Ibid., 21 Oct. 1921.
9. Ibid., 28 Dec. 1921.

10. C to D'Abernon, 22 April 1921, D'Abernon Papers Add.mss.48924a.
11. Cabinet memo, Jan. 1919, CP 112/124.
12. D'Abernon, op.cit., p. 38.
13. PRO CAB 23/37; Montagu to Lloyd George, 22 June and 8 Sept. 1919, Lloyd George Papers F/40/2/55 and 60.
14. Nicolson, op.cit., pp. 113–15.
15. Kinross, *Atatürk*, p. 231.
16. C to Lloyd George, 9 April 1920, Lloyd George Papers F/12/3/24.
17. C to Montagu, 26 April 1921, Montagu Papers AS 3/3/143.
18. C to Lloyd George, 20 April 1921, Lloyd George Papers F/13/2/15; C note, Oct. 1922, CP 112/319.
19. C to Stamfordham, 15 Nov. 1921, RA GV M1731/7; C to Hardinge, 2 Nov. 1921, Hardinge Papers 33.
20. Crawford diary, 3 Nov. 1921, Balcarres Papers.
21. *The Times*, 13 July 1921; Fraser to C, 24 July 1921, CP 112/219.
22. Vincent, *Crawford Papers*, p. 420.
23. C to Grace, 10 Sept. 1921, CP 112/799.
24. C to Montagu, 1 April and 21 Nov. 1921, and 2 Jan. 1922, Montagu Papers AS 1/12/21, 125 and 72.
25. C to Lloyd George, 20 July 1920, Lloyd George Papers F/13/1/1.
26. Hardinge to C, 21 Feb. 1922, CP 112/200; C note, Nov. 1922, CP 112/319.
27. Chamberlain to Law, 6 Jan. 1921, Bonar Law Papers 100/1/8.
28. C to Grace, 22 April 1921, CP 112/795.
29. See note 27.
30. Lansdowne to C, 14 Aug. 1920, CP 112/217.
31. Vansittart to C, 30 March 1921, CP 112/221; C to Lloyd George, 20 July 1920, Lloyd George Papers F/13/1/1.
32. See note 27.
33. C memo, Nov. 1924, CP 112/319.
34. Vansittart, *The Mist Procession*, p. 244.
35. Letters from C to Grace, Sept. –Nov. 1921, CP 112/795.
36. Ibid.
37. Ibid.
38. C to Hardinge, 24 Dec. 1921, Hardinge Papers 44.
39. C to Montagu, 6 March 1922, Montagu Papers AS 1/12/101.
40. C to Chamberlain, 9 March 1922, Chamberlain Papers 23/7.
41. C to Hardinge, 9 March 1922, Hardinge Papers 45.
42. Ibid.
43. McCurdy to Lloyd George, undated but 14 March 1922, Lloyd George Papers F/35/1/33.
44. *The Times*, 13 March 1922.
45. C to Chamberlain, 13 March 1922, Chamberlain Papers.
46. Chamberlain to Lloyd George, 15 March 1922, Lloyd George Papers F/7/5/8; Grigg to Lloyd George, 14 March 1922, LIoyd George Papers F/86/1/24; *Scotsman*, 16 March 1922; Crawford diary, 15 March 1922, Balcarres Papers.
47. Grigg to Lloyd George, 20 March 1922, Lloyd George Papers F/86/1/31.
48. C to Lloyd George, 8 May 1922, Lloyd George Papers F/13/3/22; C to Hardinge, 2 May 1922, Hardinge Papers 45.
49. C to Grace, 18 and 20 May 1922, CP 112/796.
50. Ibid., 22 May 1922.
51. Vincent, op.cit., pp. 414, 426; C to Grace, 17 May, 4 and 19 July, CP 112/796.
52. C to Grigg, 6 July 1922, Grigg Papers.

53. C note, Nov. 1922, CP 112/319; Hardinge to Lloyd George, 12 May 1922, Lloyd George Papers F/53/1/67; Blake, *Unknown Prime Minister*, p. 437; Beaverbrook, *Decline and Fall*, pp. 132, 172.
54. Wilson, *C.P. Scott*, p. 416.
55. Letters from C to Grace, July 1922, CP 112/796.
56. *Morning Post*, 10 Nov. 1922.
57. Tyrell to C, 27 Oct. 1922, CP 112/227.
58. Hardinge, *Old Diplomacy*, p. 272; Busch, *Hardinge*, pp. 307–8; Nicolson, op.cit, p. 274.
59. Hardinge, op.cit., p. 273; Vincent, op.cit., p. 437.
60. C to Stamfordham, 29 Sept. 1922, RA GV M1811/55.
61. Lloyd George at Cabinet, 30 Sept. 1922, CAB 23/31.
62. Gilbert, *World in Torment*, p. 841.
63. Ronaldshay, *Curzon*, Vol. 3, p. 305.
64. C note, Nov. 1922, CP 112/319.
65. Conference of ministers, 29 Sept. 1922, CAB 23/31.
66. Vincent, op.cit., p. 439.
67. C to Hardinge, 1 Oct. 1922, Hardinge Papers 45.
68. Vincent, op.cit., p. 439.
69. C to Grace, 1 Oct. 1922, CP 112/796; C to Hardinge, 1 Oct. 1922, Hardinge Papers 45.
70. Cooper, *Old Men Forget*, p. 114.
71. Vincent, op.cit., p. 439.
72. 1 Oct. 1922.
73. Hardinge to C, 2 Oct. 1922, CP 112/200.
74. C note, Nov. 1922, CP 112/319.
75. Minutes and telegrams of meetings are in CP 112/292 and CAB 23/31; Hardinge, op.cit., p. 274.

CHAPTER 35: RESURGENCE: LAUSANNE, 1922–1923
1. Vincent, *Crawford Papers*, p. 449; Mrs Baldwin's diary account, Baldwin Papers 42.
2. For discussions of the dinner, see W. Churchill, *Great Contemporaries*, p. 282, Ronaldshay, *Curzon*, Vol. 3, pp. 312–13, and Nicolson, *Curzon*, pp. 277–9.
3. Draft letter, 5 Oct. 1922, CP 112/224.
4. The notes are in CP 112/319.
5. C note, Oct. 1922, CP 112/319.
6. Ibid.
7. Ibid.; Vincent, op.cit., pp. 450–1; draft letter in CP 112/319.
8. Clark, '*A Good Innings*', pp. 230–1.
9. D'Abernon, *Ambassador of Peace*, Vol. 2, p. 145.
10. C note, op.cit.
11. Ibid.
12. Ibid.
13. Gilbert, *World in Torment*, p. 868; *Morning Post*, 10 Nov. 1922.
14. *Morning Post*, 10 Nov. 1922.
15. C to Hardinge, 24 Oct. 1922, Hardinge Papers 45.
16. C to D'Abernon, 20 Dec. 1922, D'Abernon Papers Add.mss.489 24a.
17. C to Stamfordham, 9 Nov. 1922, RA GV M1811/107.
18. C to Grace, 19 Nov. 1922, CP 112/796.
19. Ibid., 20 Nov. 1922; C telegram to FO, 20 Nov. 1922, CP 112/231; Nicolson, op cit., pp. 289–90; Mack Smith, *Mussolini*, pp. 59–60.
20. C to Stamfordham, 5 Oct. 1920, RA GV M1632/7.

21. C to Grace, 22 and 23 Nov. 1922, CP 112/796.
22. C to Grace, 28 Nov. 1922, CP 112/796.
23. Ibid.
24. Ibid., 14 Dec. 1922.
25. C to Barrère, 21 Jan. 1923, CP 112/283.
26. Nicolson, op.cit., p. 319; C to Grace, 21 Dec. 1922, CP 112/796.
27. C to Law, 4 Dec. 1922, Bonar Law Papers 111/12/39; Nicolson, op.cit., pp. 303–4.
28. C to Law, 14 Dec. 1922, Bonar Law Papers 112/12/46.
29. Ronaldshay, op. cit., p. 330.
30. C to Law, 9 Dec. 1922, Bonar Law Papers 111/12/43; Campbell, *F.E.*, pp. 621–2; the Gounaris-Curzon letters are in CP 112/246.
31. Vansittart to C, 8 Dec. 1922, CP 112/228.
32. Grace to C, 20 Dec. 1922, CP 112/693.
33. Grace to C, 22 Dec. 1922, CP 112/693, and 1 Jan. 1923, quoted in Grace Curzon, *Reminiscences*, pp. 172–3; C to Grace, 1 Jan. 1923, CP 112/797.
34. Lees-Milne, *Harold Nicolson*, Vol. 1, p. 190.
35. Nicolson, op.cit., p. 319.
36. Lees–Milne, op.cit., p. 190; Nicolson, *Some People*, p. 213.
37. C to Grace, 1 Jan. 1923, CP 112/797.
38. Nicolson, *Curzon*, p. 324.
39. C to Grace, 1 Feb. 1923, CP 112/797; C to Law, 1 Feb. 1923, Bonar Law Papers 111/12/62.
40. Nicolson, op.cit., p. 334.
41. Ibid., p. 336; Ronaldshay, op.cit., pp. 333–7.
42. Nicolson, *Harold and Vita*, p. 120.
43. Nicolson, *Curzon*, p. 346.
44. Information from Sforza to K. Rose, Rose Papers.
45. Kinross, *Atatürk*, p. 359.
46. The British secretary's minutes are in CP 112/293.
47. Amery, *My Political Life*, Vol. 2, p. 248.
48. Fitzroy, *Memoirs*, Vol. 2, p. 795.
49. Archbishop to C, 4 Feb. 1923, CP 112/284.
50. Information from Lord Ravensdale to the author.

CHAPTER 36: FAMILY SAGAS
1. Geddes to Lloyd George, 4 June 1920, Lloyd George Papers F/60/4/1.
2. C to Grace, 9 Nov. 1923, CP 112/797.
3. For press comments on speech see CP 112/587.
4. Riddell, *Intimate Diary*, p. 310.
5. Chandos, *From Peace to War*, p. 64.
6. Balsan, *The Glitter and the Gold*, p. 138.
7. Vincent, *Crawford Papers*, pp. 507, 414.
8. Evidence of E.A. Stone, 20 Oct. 1960, Rose Papers.
9. Marcella Rice to the author.
10. Nicolson, *Curzon*, pp. 322–3.
11. Chandos, op.cit.
12. Mosley, *My Life*, p. 113.
13. Lady Alexandra Metcalfe to the author.
14. C to Grace, 20 Nov. 1923, CP 112/797.
15. Lady Alexandra Metcalfe to the author.
16. C to Grace, 10 Nov. 1923, CP 112/794.
17. C to E. Desborough, 17 Jan. 1923, Lady Desborough Papers.

18. C to Grace, 21 March 1920, CP 112/794.
19. Information from Halifax to K. Rose, Rose Papers.
20. Most of the documents on the dispute are in the Ravensdale Papers. But see CP 112/696 and letters from C to Grace, Sept. –Oct. 1921, CP 112/795.
21. Grace to C, 23 March 1922, CP 112/693.
22. C to Grace, 17 Dec. 1923, CP 112/797.
23. C to Grace, 10 and 16 May 1919, CP 112/793 and 799.
24. D'Abernon, *Ambassador of Peace*, Vol. 2, p. 222.
25. Grace Curzon, *Reminiscences*, p. 97.
26. Cooper, *A Durable Fire*, p. 132; Lady Alexandra Metcalfe to the author.
27. Grace to C, 15 Aug. 1920, CP 112/691; C to Grace, 14 Aug. 1920, CP 112/794.
28. Grace to C, 30 Sept. and 3 Oct. 1923, CP 112/695.
29. C to Grace, 3 Jan. 1923, CP 112/796.
30. C to Grace, 31 Dec. 1924, CP 112/798.

CHAPTER 37: ULTIMATE DISAPPOINTMENTS, 1923–1925

1. D'Abernon, *Ambassador of Peace*, Vol. 2, p. 185.
2. Lloyd George to Chamberlain, 16 March 1922, Chamberlain to Lloyd George, 16 and 17 March 1922, Lloyd George Papers F/7/5.
3. C to Law, 2 April 1923, CP 112/320; Law to C, 5 April 1923, CP 112/230.
4. C to Law, 25 April 1923, Bonar Law Papers 112/15.
5. Blake, *Unknown Prime Minister*, p. 511.
6. C to Grace, 9 May 1923, CP 112/797.
7. Ronaldshay, *Curzon*, Vol. 3, p. 351.
8. Law to C, 20 May 1923, CP 112/230.
9. Blake, op.cit., pp. 520–1; James, *Memoirs of a Conservative*, p. 151.
10. Middlemas and Barnes, *Baldwin*, p. 162; Blake, op.cit., p. 519.
11. Middlemas and Barnes, ibid., p. 165.
12. Barnes and Nicholson, *Leo Amery Diaries*, p. 329.
13. Egremont, *Balfour*, pp. 326–7.
14. Rose, *King George V*, p. 269.
15. Waterfield, *Professional Diplomat*, p. 56.
16. Information from Amery to K. Rose, Rose Papers; Amery, *My Political Life*, Vol. 2, p. 260.
17. Blake, *The Conservative Party*, p. 213.
18. Note by C, CP 112/319.
19. Ibid.
20. Worthington-Evans to Chamberlain, 22 May 1923, Chamberlain Papers AC 35/2.
21. Note by C, op.cit.
22. Note by Chamberlain, 27 May 1923, Chamberlain Papers AC 35/2.
23. CP 112/320.
24. C to Baldwin, 23 May 1923, Baldwin Papers 42.
25. *Daily Telegraph*, 21 March 1925.
26. Hopkirk, *Setting the East Ablaze*, pp. 141–2, 171–5; Nicolson, *Curzon*, pp. 359–60.
27. C to Crewe, 28 April 1923, Crewe Papers C/12.
28. Ibid., 11 May 1923.
29. Cecil, *All the Way*, p. 178.
30. D'Abernon, op.cit., p. 8.
31. Nicolson, *Curzon*, p. 378.
32. Lloyd George to Rothermere, 15 Aug. 1923, Lloyd George Papers G/17/1/4.
33. Mack Smith, *Mussolini*, p. 94.
34. C to Grace, 8 Sept. 1923, CP 112/797; Medlicott and Dakin, *Documents*, p. 944.

35. Mack Smith, op.cit., p. 72.
36. C to Graham, 9 Oct. 1923, CP 112/232.
37. C to Crewe, 16 and 17 Sept. 1923, Crewe Papers C/12; C to Cecil, 27 Sept. 1923, Cecil of Chelwood Papers; Medlicott and Dakin, op. cit., pp. 974–80 *passim*, p. 996.
38. C to Crewe, 13 Oct., 12 Nov. and 11 Dec. 1923, Crewe Papers C/12; Baldwin to C, 12 Nov. 1923, CP 112/320.
39. Hannon to Chamberlain and Chamberlain to Hannon, 31 Oct. 1923, Chamberlain Papers AG 35/3.
40. Grace Curzon, *Reminiscences*, p. 201.
41. C to Salisbury, 19 Feb. 1923, Salisbury Papers.
42. Middlemas and Barnes, op.cit., p. 179.
43. C to Law, 8 Dec. 1922, Law Papers 111/12.
44. C to Grace, 18 Nov. 1923, CP 112/797.
45. C to Baldwin, 8 Aug. 1923. CP 112/229.
46. C to Crewe, 20 June 1923, Crewe Papers C/12.
47. C to Grace, 5 Nov. 1923, CP 112/797.
48. Ibid., 24 Nov. 1923.
49. Ibid., 10, 18 and 13 Nov. 1923.
50. Ibid., 18 Nov. 1923.
51. Ibid., 1 Jan. 1924, CP 112/798.
52. Ibid., 6 Dec. 1923, CP 112/797.
53. Lees-Milne, *Harold Nicolson*, Vol. 1, p. 214.
54. C to Crewe, 25 Jan. 1924, Crewe Papers C/12.
55. Barnes and Nicholson, op.cit., pp. 353, 563.
56. *Sunday Times*, 23 March 1925.
57. C to Baldwin, 31 Oct. 1924, Baldwin Papers 42.
58. 7 Nov. 1924.
59. Baldwin to C, 5 Nov. 1924, CP 112/319.
60. Vincent, *Crawford Papers*, p. 501.
61. C to Grace, 6, 7 and 10 Nov. 1924, CP 112/798.
62. C. Balsan, *The Glitter and the Gold*, pp. 210–11.
63. Ibid., p. 213; *Daily Telegraph*, 27 March 1925.
64. See Ronaldshay, op.cit., pp. 393–4.
65. A copy of this memo is in the Salisbury Papers.
66. Jenkins, *Asquith*, p. 509.
67. *United Methodist*, 16 April 1925.
68. Grace Curzon, op.cit., p. 227.
69. C to Stamfordham, 7 March 1925, RA GV O1979/1.
70. Vansittart, *The Mist Procession*, p. 308.
71. C to George V, 18 March 1925, RA GV AA49/82.
72. Grace Curzon, op.cit., p. 228.
73. *Sunday Times*, 22 March 1925.
74. Ibid., *The Times of India*, 21 March 1925.
75. *Spectator*, 4 April 1925.
76. 23 March 1925.
77. Ibid.

Sources and Bibliography

---

1. MANUSCRIPT COLLECTIONS

D'Abernon, Lord, British Library
Ampthill, Lord, India Office Library
Arnold-Forster, H.O., British Library
Asquith, H.H., Bodleian Library
Astor, Lady, Reading University Library
Baldwin, Stanley, Cambridge University Library
Balfour, A.J., British Library
Barlow, Sir Thomas, Wellcome Institute for the History of Medicine
Barnes, Sir Hugh, Bodleian Library
Barrow, Sir Edmund, India Office Library
Benson, A.C., Magdalene College, Cambridge
Birdwood, Sir William, India Office Library
Brodrick, St John, *see* Midleton
Browning, Oscar, King's College, Cambridge
Burns, J.A., British Library
Campbell-Bannerman, Henry, British Library
Cecil of Chelwood, Lord, British Library
Chamberlain, Austen, Birmingham University Library
Craigie, Pearl, Reading University Library
Crawford, Earl of, Balcarres and National Library of Scotland
Crewe, Marquess of, Cambridge University Library
Cromer, Earl of, Public Record Office
Curzon, Lord, India Office Library

Curzon, Lady (Mary), private collection
Davidson, J.C.C., House of Lords Record Office
Desborough, Lady, Hertfordshire County Council Record Office
Dilke, Sir Charles, British Library
Elgin, Earl of, India Office Library
Esher, Lord, Churchill College, Cambridge
Foster, Sir William, India Office Library
Gladstone, Mary (Mrs Drew), British Library
Gladstone, Lord, British Library
Gladstone, W.E., British Library
Godley, Sir Arthur (Kilbracken Papers), India Office Library
Grosvenor, Countess of, Eaton Estate Office
Haldane, R.B., National Library of Scotland
Hamilton, Lord George, India Office Library
Harcourt, Lord, Bodleian Library
Harcourt, Sir William, Bodleian Library
Hardinge, Lord, Cambridge University Library
Kitchener, Lord, Public Record Office and British Library
Lamington, Lord, India Office Library
Lansdowne, Marquess of, Bowood
Law, Andrew Bonar, House of Lords Record Office
Lawrence, Sir Walter, India Office Library
Lloyd George, David, House of Lords Record Office
Long, Walter, Wiltshire County Council Record Office
Lyttelton, Alfred (Chandos Papers), Churchill College, Cambridge
MacDonnell, Sir Antony, Bodleian Library
Macmillan Archive, British Library
Magnus, Sir Philip, private collection
Marker, Raymond (Kitchener-Marker Papers), British Library
Midleton, Earl of, British Library and Public Record Office
Milner, Lady, Bodleian Library
Milner, Lord, Bodleian Library
Minto, Earl of, National Library of Scotland
Montagu, Edwin, Trinity College, Cambridge
Morley, John, India Office Library
Murray, Gilbert, Bodleian Library
Pearson, Charles, Bodleian Library
Ravensdale, Lord, private collection
Richards, H. Erle, India Office Library
Ripon, Marquess of, British Library

Robinson, Geoffrey (Dawson Papers), Bodleian Library
Rodd, Sir Rennell (Rennell Papers), Bodleian Library
Rosebery, Earl of, National Library of Scotland
Salisbury, 3rd Marquess of, Hatfield
Salisbury, 4th Marquess of, Hatfield
Salisbury, Marchioness of, Hatfield
Sandars, J.S., British Library
Selborne, Earl of, Bodleian Library
Spender, J.A., British Library
Spring Rice, Cecil, Churchill College, Cambridge
Thomson, Mrs J., India Office Library
White, Sir George, India Office Library
White, Thirkell, India Office Library
Wyndham, George (Grosvenor Papers), Eaton Estate Office

Public Record Office: Cabinet and Foreign Office Papers. (Where copies of these exist in the Curzon Papers, they have been studied, for the sake of convenience, at the India Office Library.)

Royal Archives: Letters from Curzon to King George V and Lord Stamfordham. (Copies of the viceregal correspondence with Queen Victoria and King Edward VII are in the India Office Library.)

I have also consulted Curzon papers in the possession of Lady Aldington, Mr John Grigg, Lady Alexandra Metcalfe, Mr Nigel Nicolson, Lord Ravensdale, Mr Kenneth Rose, Eton College and Balliol College, Oxford.

2. PUBLISHED SOURCES

(The editions listed are not necessarily the earliest but those which have been consulted. The place of publication is London unless otherwise stated.)

Abdy, Jane, and Gere, Charlotte, *The Souls*, Sidgwick & Jackson, 1984.
Adams, R.J.Q., and Poirier, Philip P., *The Conscription Controversy in Great Britain, 1900–18*, Macmillan, 1987.
Addison, Christopher, *Four and a Half Years*, Vol. 1, Hutchinson, 1934.
Allen, Charles, *Lives of the Indian Princes*, Arrow, 1984.
—— *Plain Tales from the Raj*, André Deutsch, 1975.
Amery, J., *The Life of Joseph Chamberlain*, 3 vols., Macmillan, 1951–69.
Amery, L.S., *My Political Life*, 2 vols., Hutchinson, 1953.

Anstruther, Ian, *Oscar Browning*, John Murray, 1983.

Antonius, George, *The Arab Awakening*, Hamish Hamilton, 1945.

Arthur, George, *A Septuagenarian's Scrap Book*, Butterworth, 1933.

Ashton, S.R., *British Policy towards the Indian States, 1905–1939*, Curzon Press, 1982.

Asquith, Cynthia, *Diaries*, Hutchinson, 1968.

—— *Remember and Be Glad*, Barrie, 1952.

Asquith, H.H., *Letters to Venetia Stanley*, Oxford University Press, 1982.

Asquith, Margot, *Autobiography*, 2 vols., Thornton Butterworth, 1920.

—— *More Memories*, Cassell, 1933.

Baldwin, Stanley, *On England*, Philip Allan, 1926.

Ballhatchet, Kenneth, *Race, Sex and Class under the Raj*, Weidenfeld & Nicolson, 1980.

Balsan, Consuelo Vanderbilt, *The Glitter and the Gold*, Heinemann, 1953.

Banerjea, Surendranath, *A Nation in Making*, Oxford University Press, Calcutta, 1925.

Barnes, John, and Nicholson, David (eds.), *Leo Amery Diaries*, Hutchinson, 1981.

Beaverbrook, Lord, *The Decline and Fall of Lloyd George*, Collins, 1963.

—— *Men and Power*, Hutchinson, 1956.

—— *Politicians and the War*, The Lane Publications, 1932, and Oldbourne, 1959.

Bence-Jones, Mark, *The Viceroys of India*, Constable, 1982.

Benson, A.C., *Memories and Friends*, John Murray, 1924.

Bindoff, S.T., *The House of Commons, 1509–1558*, Secker & Warburg, 1982.

Birkenhead, (1st) Earl of, *Contemporary Personalities*, Cassell, 1924.

Birkenhead, (2nd) Earl of, *F.E.*, Eyre & Spottiswoode, 1959.

Blake, Robert, *The Conservative Party from Peel to Thatcher*, Methuen, 1985.

—— *The Decline of Power, 1915–1964*, Granada, 1985.

—— *The Unknown Prime Minister*, Eyre & Spottiswoode, 1955.

Blewett, Neal, *The Peers, the Parties and the People*, Macmillan, 1972.

Blood, Bindon, *Four Score Years and Ten*, G. Bell, 1933.

Blunt, Edward, *The ICS*, Faber, 1937.

Blunt, Wilfrid Scawen, *My Diaries*, 2 vols., Martin Secker, 1920.

Bonham Carter, Violet, *Winston Churchill as I Knew Him*, Eyre & Spottiswoode and Collins, 1965.

Boswell, James, *The Life of Samuel Johnson*, 3 vols., Macmillan, 1900.

Bradley, John, *Lady Curzon's India*, Weidenfeld & Nicolson, 1985.

Bray, William, *Sketch of a Tour into Derbyshire and Yorkshire*, n.p., 1783.

Brett, Maurice V. (ed.), *Journals and Letters of Reginald, Viscount Esher*, 2 vols., Ivor Nicholson and Watson, 1934.

Browning, Oscar, *The Memories of Sixty Years*, Bodley Head, 1910.

Buck, Edward J., *Simla Past and Present*, The Times Press, Bombay, 1925.

Busch, B.C., *Britain, India and the Arabs, 1914–1921*, University of California Press, Berkeley, 1971.

—— *Hardinge of Penshurst*, Archon, Conn., 1980.

Butt, Archie, *Taft and Roosevelt: The Intimate Letters of Archie Butt*, Kennikat Press, Port Washington, 1970.

Campbell, John, *F.E. Smith*, Pimlico, 1991.

Cannadine, David, *Aspects of Aristocracy*, Yale University Press, 1994.

Caroe, Olaf, *The Pathans*, Macmillan, 1958.

Cecil, David, *The Cecils of Hatfield House*, Cardinal, 1975.

Cassar, George H., *Kitchener, Architect of Victory*, Kimber, 1977.

Cecil of Chelwood, Lord, *All the Way*, Hodder & Stoughton, 1949.

Chamberlain, Austen, *Down the Years*, Cassell, 1935.

Chandos, John, *Boys Together*, Oxford University Press, 1985.

Chandos, Lord, *From Peace to War, 1857–1918*, Bodley Head, 1968.

Chirol, Valentine, *Fifty Years in a Changing World*, Jonathan Cape, 1927.

—— *India*, Ernest Benn, 1926.

—— *Indian Unrest*, Macmillan, 1910.

—— *India Old and New*, Macmillan 1921.

Churchill, Randolph, *Lord Derby*, Heinemann, 1959.

—— *Winston S. Churchill: Youth, 1874–1900*, Heinemann, 1966.

—— *Winston S. Churchill: Young Statesman, 1901–1914*, Heinemann, 1967.

Churchill, Winston S., *Great Contemporaries*, Thornton Butterworth, 1937.

—— *My Early Life*, Thornton Butterworth, 1930.

Clark, Alan (ed.). *'A Good Innings': The Private Papers of Viscount Lee of Fareham*, John Murray, 1974.

Coleridge, Gilbert, *Eton in the Seventies*, Smith, Elder & Co, 1912.

Connell, John, *The Office*, Allan Wingate, 1958.

Cooper, Artemis (ed.), *A Durable Fire*, Collins, 1983.

Cooper, Diana, *The Rainbow Comes and Goes*, Hart-Davis, 1958.

Cooper, Duff, *Old Men Forget*, Hart-Davis, 1953.

Copland, Ian, *The British Raj and the Indian Princes*, Sangman, 1982.

Curtis, L.P. Jr, *Coercion and Conciliation in Ireland*, Princeton, 1963.

Curzon, George N., *Bodiam Castle*, Jonathan Cape, 1926.

—— *British Government in India*, 2 vols., Cassell, 1925.

—— *Kedleston Church*, privately printed at the Chiswick Press, 1922.

—— *Leaves from a Viceroy's Notebook*, Macmillan, 1926.

—— *Modern Parliamentary Eloquence*, Macmillan, 1913.

—— *The Pamirs and the Source of the Oxus*, Royal Geographical Society, n.d.

—— *Persia and the Persian Question*, 2 vols., Frank Cass, 1966.

—— *Problems of the Far East*, Longman, 1894.

—— *Russia in Central Asia in 1889*, Frank Cass, 1967.

—— *Subjects of the Day*, George Allen & Unwin, 1915.

—— *Tales of Travel*, Hodder & Stoughton, 1923.

—— *Walmer Castle and its Lords Warden*, Macmillan, 1927.

—— *War Poems and Other Translations*, Bodley Head, 1915.

Curzon, Grace, *Reminiscences*, Hutchinson, 1955.

D'Abernon, Lord, *An Ambassador of Peace*, 2 vols., Hodder & Stoughton, 1929.

Darling, Malcolm, *Apprentice to Power*, Hogarth Press, 1966.

Das, Durga, *India from Curzon to Nehru and after*, Collins, 1969.

Das, M.N., *India under Morley and Minto*, George Allen & Unwin, 1964.

Dilks, David, *Curzon in India*, 2 vols., Hart-Davis, 1969 and 1970.

Dodwell, H.H., *The Indian Empire, 1858–1918*, Cambridge University Press, 1932.

Durand, Mortimer, *Sir Alfred Comyn Lyall*, Blackwood, Edinburgh, 1913.

Dutton, David, *Austen Chamberlain*, Ross Anderson, Bolton, 1985.

Edel, Leon, *Bloomsbury*, Hogarth Press, 1969.

Edwardes, Michael, *High Noon of Empire*, Eyre & Spottiswoode, 1965.

Egremont, *Balfour*, Collins, 1980.

—— *The Cousins*, Collins, 1977.

Ellmann, Richard, *Oscar Wilde*, Hamish Hamilton, 1987.

Etherington-Smith, Meredith, and Pilcher, Jeremy, *The 'It' Girls*, Harcourt Brace, San Diego, 1986.

Faber, Geoffrey, *Jowett*, Faber, 1957.

Feiling, Keith, *The Life of Neville Chamberlain*, Macmillan, 1946.

Feuchtwanger, E.J., *Democracy and Empire: Britain, 1865–1914*, Edward Arnold, 1990.

Fitzroy, Almeric, *Memoirs*, Vol. 2, Hutchinson, n.d.

Fleming, Peter, *Bayonets to Lhasa*, Hart-Davis, 1962.

Foster, R.F., *Lord Randolph Churchill*, Oxford University Press, 1988.

—— *Modern Ireland*, Penguin, 1989.

Fraser, Lovat, *India under Curzon and after*, Heinemann, 1911.

Fraser, Peter, 'Lord Beaverbrook's fabrications in *Politicians and the War, 1914–1916*', *Historical Journal*, Vol. 25, No. 1, 1982.

—— *Lord Esher*, Hart-Davis, MacGibbon, 1973.

Fromkin, David, *A Peace to End All Peace: Creating the Modern Middle East, 1914–1922*, Penguin, 1991.

Gandhi, M.K., *An Autobiography*, Penguin, 1982.

Garvin, J.L., *The Life of Joseph Chamberlain*, Vol. 2, Macmillan, 1933.

Ghani, Cyrus, *Iran and the West*, Kegan Paul, 1987.

Gilbert, Martin, *Servant of India: A Study of Imperial Rule from 1905 to 1910*, Longman, 1966.

—— *Sir Horace Rumbold*, Heinemann, London, 1973.

—— *Winston S. Churchill, 1914–1916*, Heinemann, 1971.

—— *World in Torment*, Minerva, 1990.

Gilmour, Ian, *The Body Politic*, Hutchinson, 1969.

—— *Inside Right: A Study of Conservatism*, Hutchinson, 1977.

Glyn, Anthony, *Elinor Glyn*, Hutchinson, 1968.

Glyn, Elinor, *Halcyone*, Duckworth, 1912.

—— *Three Weeks*, Duckworth, 1907.

Gollin, A.M., *Proconsul in Politics*, Anthony Blond, 1964.

Goold, Douglas, 'Lord Hardinge and the Mesopotamia Expedition and Inquiry, 1914–1917', *Historical Journal*, Vol. 19, No. 4, 1976.

Gopal, S., *British Policy in India, 1858–1905*, Cambridge University Press, 1965.

Goradia, Nayana, *Lord Curzon*, Oxford University Press, Delhi, 1993.

Gore, John (ed.), *Creevey*, John Murray, 1948.

Gorell, Lord, *One Man . . . Many Parts*, Odhams, 1956.

Gregory, J.D., *On the Edge of Diplomacy*, Hutchinson, 1929.

Grenville, J.A.S., *Lord Salisbury and Foreign Policy*, Athlone Press, 1964.

Grigg, John, *Lloyd George: From Peace to War, 1912–1916*, Methuen, 1985.

—— *Lloyd George: The People's Champion, 1902–1911*, Eyre Methuen, 1978.

Gwynn, Stephen (ed.), *The Letters and Friendships of Sir Cecil Spring Rice*, 2 vols., Constable, 1929.

Hamer, W.S., *The British Army: Civil-Military Relations, 1885–1905*, Oxford University Press, 1970.

Hamilton, Lord George, *Parliamentary Reminiscences and Reflections, 1886–1906*, John Murray, 1922.

Hamilton, Ian, *The Commander*, Hollis & Carter, 1957.

—— *Listening for the Drums*, Faber, 1944.

Hankey, Lord, *The Supreme Command, 1914–1918*, 2 vols., George Allen & Unwin, 1961.

Harcourt Williams, Robin (ed.), *Salisbury-Balfour Correspondence*, Hertfordshire Record Society, 1988.

Hardinge of Penshurst, Lord, *Old Diplomacy*, John Murray, 1947.

Harris, Frank, *Oscar Wilde*, Constable, 1938.

Harris, Leslie, *Robert Adam and Kedleston*, National Trust, 1987.

Hart-Davis, Duff (ed.), *End of an Era: Letters and Journals of Sir Alan Lascelles, 1887–1920*, Hamish Hamilton, 1986.

Hassall, Christopher, *Edward Marsh*, Longman, 1959.

Hill, Claude H., *India – Stepmother*, Blackwood, Edinburgh, 1929.

Holmes, C.J., *Self & Partners*, Constable, 1936.

Honey, J.R. de S., *Tom Brown's Universe*, Millington, 1977.

Hopkirk, Peter, *The Great Game*, John Murray, 1990.

——— *Setting the East Ablaze*, John Murray, 1984.

Hyam, Ronald, *Empire and Sexuality: The British Experience*, Manchester University Press, 1991.

'Indian Mahomedan, An', *British India from Queen Elizabeth to Lord Reading*, Pitman, 1926.

Inge, W.R., *Diary of a Dean*, Hutchinson, 1950.

Ingrams, Doreen (ed.), *Palestine Papers, 1917–1922*, John Murray, 1972.

Iremonger, Lucille, *The Fiery Chariot*, Secker & Warburg, 1970.

James, Lawrence, *Imperial Warrior: The Life and Times of Field Marshal Viscount Allenby*, Weidenfeld & Nicolson, 1993.

James, Robert Rhodes (ed.), *Chips: The Diaries of Sir Henry Channon*, Weidenfeld & Nicolson, 1967.

———*Memoirs of a Conservative*, Weidenfeld & Nicolson, 1969.

Jenkins, Roy, *Asquith*, Collins, 1988.

——— *Mr Balfour's Poodle*, Collins, 1989.

——— *Sir Charles Dilke*, Collins, 1958.

Jones, Clement, 'Lord Curzon of Kedleston', *International Affairs*, July 1961.

Jones, Geoffrey, *Banking and Empire in Iran*, Vol. 1, Cambridge University Press, 1986.

Jones, John, *Balliol College: A History, 1263–1939*, Oxford University Press, 1988.

Jones, Thomas, *Lloyd George*, Oxford University Press, 1951.

Kaminsky, Arnold P., *The India Office, 1880–1910*, Mansell, 1986.

Kanwar, Pamela, *Imperial Simla*, Oxford University Press, Delhi, 1990.

Kedleston Hall, National Trust, 1988.

Keith, A.B., *A Constitutional History of India, 1600–1935*, Methuen, 1936.

Khan, S.M. (ed.), *The Life of Abdur Rahman*, John Murray, 1900.

Kilbracken, Lord, *Reminiscences*, Macmillan, 1931.

King, Peter, *The Viceroy's Fall*, Sidgwick & Jackson, 1986.

Kinross, Lord, *Atatürk: The Rebirth of a Nation*, Weidenfeld & Nicolson, 1964.

Koss, Stephen, *Asquith*, Hamish Hamilton, 1985.

——— *John Morley at the India Office, 1905–1910*, Yale University Press, 1969.

———*The Rise and Fall of the Political Press in Britain*, Vol. 2, Hamish Hamilton, 1984.

Lamb, Richard, *The Drift to War, 1922–1939*, W.H. Allen, 1989.

Lambert, Angela, *Unquiet Souls*, Macmillan, 1984.

Lawrence, Walter, *The India We Served*, Cassell, 1928.

Lees-Milne, James, *The Enigmatic Edwardian: The Life of Reginald 2nd Viscount Esher*, Sidgwick & Jackson, 1988.

—— *Harold Nicolson*, Vol. 1, Chatto & Windus, 1980.

—— *Prophesying Peace*, Chatto & Windus, 1977.

Levine, Naomi, *Politics, Religion and Love*, New York University Press, 1991.

Lloyd George, David, *War Memoirs*, Vol. 1, Odhams, 1938.

Lockhart, J.G., *Cosmo Gordon Lang*, Hodder & Stoughton, 1949.

Longford, Elizabeth, *A Pilgrimage of Passion: The Life of Wilfrid Scawen Blunt*, Weidenfeld & Nicolson, 1979.

—— *Victoria R.I.*, Weidenfeld & Nicolson, 1964.

Lord Curzon in India (issued simultaneously in a single volume and a two-volume edition), Macmillan, 1906.

Lowe, C.J., and Dockrill, M.L., *The Mirage of Power*, Vol. 2, Routledge & Kegan Paul, 1972.

Lucy, Henry W., *A Diary of the Unionist Parliament, 1895–1900*, Arrowsmith, Bristol, 1901.

Lydgate, John, 'Curzon, Kitchener and the Problem of Indian Army administration, 1899–1909', University of London doctoral thesis, 1965.

Lyttelton, Edward, *Memories and Hopes*, John Murray, 1925.

Mack Smith, Denis, *Mussolini*, Weidenfeld & Nicolson, 1981.

—— *Mussolini's Roman Empire*, Longman, 1976.

Mackay, Ruddock, *Balfour: Intellectual Statesman*, Oxford University Press, 1985.

Maconochie, Evan, *Life in the Indian Civil Service*, Chapman & Hall, 1926.

Magnus, Philip, *Gladstone*, John Murray, 1954.

——*Kitchener*, John Murray, 1958.

Maison, Margaret, *John Oliver Hobbes*, Eighteen Nineties Society, 1976.

Manchester, William, *The Last Lion*, Cardinal, 1990.

Mann, Mary, *The Memories of Ronald Love*, Methuen, 1907.

Mansfield, Peter, *The British in Egypt*, Weidenfeld & Nicolson, 1971.

Marks, Sally, *The Illusion of Peace*, Macmillan, 1989.

Marlowe, John, *Milner: Apostle of Empire*, Hamish Hamilton, 1976.

Marriott, J., *The English in India*, Oxford University Press, 1932.

Marsh, Peter, *The Discipline of Popular Government: Lord Salisbury's Domestic Statecraft, 1881–1902*, Harvester Press, Sussex, 1978.

—— *Joseph Chamberlain: Entrepreneur in Politics*, Yale University Press, 1994.

Mason, Philip, *A Matter of Honour*, Papermac, 1974.

Medlicott, W.N., and Dakin, Douglas, *Documents on British Foreign Policy*, 1st series, Vol. 24, HMSO, 1983.

Meinertzhagen, Richard, *Middle East Diary, 1917–1956*, Cresset Press, 1959.

Mersey-Thompson, E.C., *India of Today*, Smith, Elder, 1913.

Middlemas, Keith, and Barnes, John, *Baldwin*, Weidenfeld & Nicolson, 1969.

Midleton, Earl of, *Records and Reactions, 1856–1939*, John Murray, 1939.

—— 'Relations of Lord Curzon as Viceroy with the British Government, 1902–5', privately printed at the FO in 1926 (PRO 30/67).

Minto, Countess of, *India, Minto and Morley, 1905–1910*, Macmillan, 1934.

Monroe, Elizabeth, *Britain's Moment in the Middle East, 1914–1956*, Chatto & Windus, 1963.

Moon, Penderel, *The British Conquest and Dominion of India*, Duckworth, 1989.

Moorhouse, Geoffrey, *Calcutta*, Penguin, 1988.

—— *India Britannica*, Harvill, 1988.

Morgan, Ted, *Churchill, 1874–1915*, Jonathan Cape, 1983.

Morley, John, *Recollections*, 2 vols., Macmillan, 1917.

Morris, J., *Pax Britannica*, Penguin, 1979.

—— *Stones of Empire*, Oxford University Press, 1987.

Mosley, Leonard, *Curzon: The End of an Epoch*, Longman, 1960.

Mosley, Nicholas, *Julian Grenfell*, Weidenfeld & Nicolson, 1976.

—— *Rules of the Game*, Secker & Warburg, 1982.

Mosley, Oswald, *My Life*, Nelson, 1968.

Mudford, Peter, *Birds of a Different Plumage*, Collins, 1974.

Nanda, B.R., *Gokhale, Gandhi and the Nations*, Allen & Unwin, 1974.

Newton, Lord, *Lord Lansdowne*, Macmillan, 1929.

Nicolson, Harold, *Curzon: The Last Phase*, Constable, 1934.

—— *Diaries and Letters, 1930–1939*, Collins, 1967.

—— *King George V*, Constable, 1952.

—— *Some People*, Constable, 1927.

Nicolson, Nigel, *Mary Curzon*, Weidenfeld & Nicolson, 1977.

—— *Vita and Harold*, Weidenfeld & Nicolson, 1992.

O'Brien, Terence, *Milner*, Constable, 1979.

O'Byrne, William R., *A Naval Biographical Dictionary*, John Murray, 1849.

O'Dwyer, Michael, *India as I Knew it, 1885–1925*, Constable, 1925.

Pakenham, Thomas, *The Boer War*, Weidenfeld & Nicolson, 1979.

Penson, Lilian, *Foreign Affairs under the Third Marquess of Salisbury*, Athlone Press, 1962.

Pope-Hennessy, James, *Lord Crewe*, Constable, 1955.

Pryce-Jones, Alan (ed.), *Little Innocents*, Cobden-Sanderson, 1932.

Ramm, Agatha, *Europe in the Twentieth Century*, Longman, 1984.

—— *William Ewart Gladstone*, GPC, Cardiff, 1989.

Ravensdale, Baroness, *In Many Rhythms*, Weidenfeld & Nicolson, 1953.

Rawlinson, H.G., *The British Achievement in India*, William Hodge, 1948.

Ray, Rajat Kanta, *Social Conflict and Political Unrest in Bengal*, Oxford University Press, Delhi, 1984.

Reed, Stanley, *The India I Knew*, Odhams, 1952.

Repington, C. À Court, *The First World War, 1914–1918*, 2 vols., Constable, 1920.

—— *Vestigia*, Constable, 1919.

Richardson, Frank M., *Mars without Venus*, Blackwood, Edinburgh, 1981.

Riddell, Lord, *Intimate Diary of the Peace Conference and after, 1918–1923*, Gollancz, 1933.

—— *War Diary*, Ivor Nicholson, 1933.

Ridley, Jane, and Percy, Clayre (eds.), *The Letters of Arthur Balfour & Lady Elcho*, Hamish Hamilton, 1992.

Robb, Peter, and Taylor, David (eds.), *Rule, Protest, Identity*, Curzon Press, 1978.

Robbins, Keith, *The Eclipse of a Great Power*, Longman, 1983.

—— *Sir Edward Grey*, Cassell, 1971.

Roberts, Lord, *Forty-one Years in India*, 2 vols., Richard Bentley, 1897.

Rodd, J. Rennell, *Social and Diplomatic Memories, 1884–1893*, Edward Arnold, 1922.

Ronaldshay, Earl of, *The Life of Lord Curzon*, 3 vols., Ernest Benn, 1928.

Rose, Kenneth, *Curzon: A Most Superior Person*, Weidenfeld & Nicolson, 1969.

—— *King George V*, Weidenfeld & Nicolson, 1983.

—— *The Later Cecils*, Harper & Row, 1975.

Rose, Norman, *Vansittart*, Heinemann, 1978.

Roskill, Stephen, *Hankey: Man of Secrets*, Collins, 1970.

Rowland, Peter, *Lloyd George*, Barrie & Jenkins, 1975.

Royle, Trevor, *The Kitchener Enigma*, Michael Joseph, 1985.

Sarkar, S., *Modern India, 1885–1947*, Macmillan, 1989.

Sedgwick, Romney, *The House of Commons, 1715–1754*, HMSO, 1970.

Smith-Dorrien, Horace, *Memories of Forty-eight Years' Service*, John Murray, 1925.

Soames, Mary, *Clementine Churchill*, Cassell, 1979.

Spear, Percival, *A History of India*, Vol. 2, Penguin, 1990.

Spender, J.A., and Asquith, Cyril, *Life of Herbert Henry Asquith*, Vol. 2, Hutchinson, 1932.

Stein, Leonard, *The Balfour Declaration*, Valentine-Mitchell, 1961.

Swinson, Arthur, *North-West Frontier*, Hutchinson, 1967.

Sykes, Christopher, *Nancy: The Life of Lady Astor*, Collins, 1972.

Taylor, A.J.P., *Beaverbrook*, Hamish Hamilton, 1972.

—— (ed.), *Lloyd George: A Diary by Frances Stevenson*, Hutchinson, 1971.

—— *English History, 1914–1945*, Oxford University Press, 1981.

Tidrick, Kathryn, *Empire & the English Character*, I.B.Tauris, 1992.

Trevelyan, G.M., *Grey of Fallodon*, Longman, 1937.

Unwin, Stanley, *The Truth about a Publisher*, Allen & Unwin, 1960.

Vansittart, Lord, *The Mist Procession*, Hutchinson, 1958.

Varè, Daniele, *Laughing Diplomat*, John Murray, 1938.

Vincent, John (ed.), *The Crawford Papers*, Manchester University Press, 1984.

Waley, S.D., *Edwin Montagu*, Asia Publishing House, London, 1964.

Warwick, Countess of, *Afterthoughts*, Cassell, 1931.

Waterfield, Gordon, *Professional Diplomat: Sir Percy Loraine*, John Murray, 1973.

Waterhouse, Nourah, *Private and Official*, Jonathan Cape, 1942.

Welldon, J.E.C., *Recollections and Reflections*, Cassell, 1915.

Wilson, Jeremy, *Lawrence of Arabia*, Heinemann, 1989.

Wilson, John, *CP: A Life of Sir Henry Campbell-Bannerman*, Constable, 1973.

Wilson, Lady, *Letters from India*, Century, 1984.

Wilson, Trevor (ed.), *The Political Diaries of C.P. Scott, 1911–1928*, Collins, 1970.

Wingate, Ronald, *Wingate of the Sudan*, John Murray, 1955.

Winstone, H.V., *Gertrude Bell*, Jonathan Cape, 1978.

Winter, Denis, *Haig's Command*, Penguin, 1992.

Wolpert, Stanley A., *Morley and India, 1906–1910*, University of California Press, 1967.

Woodruff, Philip, *The Founders*, Jonathan Cape, 1963.

—— *The Guardians*, Jonathan Cape, 1963.

Woodward, David R., *Lloyd George and the Generals*, Associated University Presses, East Brunswick, 1983.

Wortham, H.E., *Victorian Eton and Cambridge*, Arthur Barker, 1956.

Wright, Denis, *The Persians amongst the English*, Tauris, 1985.

Young, Hubert, *The Independent Arab*, John Murray, 1933.

Young, Kenneth, *Arthur James Balfour*, G. Bell, 1963.

Younghusband, Francis, *The Light of Experience*, Constable, 1927.

Zaidi, Syed Zawwar Husain, 'The Partition of Bengal and its Annulment – a Survey of the Schemes of Territorial Redistribution of Bengal 1902–1911', doctoral thesis, University of London, 1964.

Acknowledgements

I WOULD LIKE TO thank the following individuals for permission to quote from papers in their possession: Lady Aldington (Lord Curzon and Mrs Sophy MacMichael), the Earl of Crawford and Balcarres (27th Earl of Crawford), Mr John Grigg (Sir Edward Grigg), Mr Murray Lawrence (Sir Walter Lawrence), Lady Alexandra Metcalfe (Lord and Lady Curzon), Lord Ravensdale, Mr Kenneth Rose, Mr Charles Sebag-Montefiore (Sir Philip Magnus), the Marquess of Salisbury (3rd Marquess and 4th Marquess and Marchioness), the Earl of Selborne (2nd Earl of Selborne) and the Duke of Westminster (Countess of Grosvenor and George Wyndham).

I am also grateful to the following for permission to quote material from their archives: the Master and Fellows of Balliol College, Oxford, the Bodleian Library (H.H. Asquith, Lady Milner and 2nd Earl of Selborne), the University of Birmingham (Austen Chamberlain), the Trustees of the Bowood Manuscripts Collection (5th Marquess of Lansdowne), the British Library Board (H.O. Arnold-Foster, A.J. Balfour and 1st Earl of Midleton), the Syndics of Cambridge University Library (Stanley Baldwin, 1st Marquess of Crewe and 1st Lord Hardinge of Penshurst), the Master and Fellows of Churchill College, Cambridge (Alfred Lyttelton and Cecil Spring Rice), the Clerk of the Records of the House of Lords Record Office (Andrew Bonar Law and David Lloyd George), the Kedleston Trustees (Lord Curzon), the Provost and Fellows of King's College, Cambridge (Oscar Browning), the Master and Fellows of Magdalene College, Cambridge (A.C. Benson), the Trustees of the National Library of Scotland (27th Earl of Crawford and 4th Earl of Minto), the Librarian of the Oriental and India Office Collections of the British Library (Lord Ampthill, Sir Edmund Barrow, Sir William Birdwood, Lord Curzon, Lord Kilbracken, Lord George Hamilton, Sir Walter Lawrence and John Morley), the University of Reading (Lady Astor and Mrs Pearl Craigie), and the Master and Fellows of Trinity College, Cambridge (Edwin Montagu).

Material from the Royal Archives at Windsor Castle is reproduced with the gracious permission of Her Majesty the Queen.

Quotations from Crown Copyright documents in the British Library, the Oriental and India Office Collections of the British Library, the National Library of Scotland and the Public Record Office appear by permission of the Controller of HMSO.

Index